HISTORY OF HALIFAX, VERMONT

BORN IN CONTROVERSY
HISTORY OF HALIFAX, VERMONT

Chartered 1750

Researched, written, and compiled by the

History Committee
for the
Halifax Historical Society, Inc.

Forward by Howard Coffin
Illustrations ©2007 ⟨signature⟩ Mariette Sanders
Photo restoration Carrie Perna and Mariette Sanders
Layout & design Constance Lancaster, Carrie Perna and Mariette Sanders

Library of Congress Control Number: 2008925592

ISBN 978-1-60585-869-2

Published by
Itty-bitty Publishing
Halifax, VT 05358

Printed and bound by
Acme Bookbinding
Charlestown, MA, USA

Dedicated to

The town clerks of Halifax, whose diligence in recording

and preserving records have made this history possible

and to the children of Halifax.

May they carry on this legacy.

Acknowledgments

We would like to thank all those who have had a part in this work. We are indebted to the Halifax Historical Society for collecting and preserving artifacts, documents and historical materials, which provided the genesis of this endeavor. And to those who have had an interest in Halifax and shared with us their stories, letters, diaries, and photographs. We would especially like to thank the family of Porter Thayer for granting permission to use his photographs of Halifax.

We thank the following individuals for their written contributions: Clara Crosier Barnard, Norris Johnson, Rev. Don Perna, and Bertell (B. B.) Woods. We wish to thank Ray Henry for his written contribution, his valuable guidance and financial support; also to Muriel Russell for her interest, and considerable time and research. A special thank you to our editor, Hilly van Loon who has gone far beyond her initial job description, to become our mentor, our friend, our inspiration.

We appreciate the generous assistance provided by our town clerk, Laura Sumner. We are indebted to Ruby Bruffee Austin whose legacy lives on through the careful lists she compiled from her research of the Halifax town records. We are thankful for the staff and resources at the following institutions: Vermont Historical Society, Windham County Historical Society, Vermont State Archives, New Hampshire State Archives, New York State Archives, New England Historic Genealogical Society, State of Vermont Probate Court District of Marlboro, Windham County Courthouse in Newfane, Brooks Memorial Library in Brattleboro, Bennington Museum Library, Historic Deerfield and Potumtuck Valley Memorial Association Libraries, and the town clerks of Colrain, Massachusetts, and Whitingham, Vermont.

We thank the Windham Foundation and the Crosby Foundation for their significant financial contributions to the publication of this history, as well as the many individuals and businesses who donated funds. We also thank the Town of Halifax for its support.

Most important in our efforts has been the unfailing support, sacrifice, patience, and forbearance of our families. Words cannot convey our gratitude!

Bernice Barnett, Elaine Fairbanks, Constance Lancaster, Carrie Perna,
Susan Rusten, Mariette Sanders, Stephen Sanders, and Molly Stone

PREFACE

As the result of many years of diligent preparation, this history grew and grew until it became necessary to divide it in two. Howard Coffin's foreword, included in the first volume was written before the reality of the two volumes. Thus there are references made to material contained in both.

In the first, we are led through the controversies that were the prelude to statehood. It describes the growing pains, taking us through the political process negotiated among the governments of New Hampshire, New York, Massachusetts, Great Britain, and the United States, with the state of Vermont the victor. It documents the birth of Halifax as the second town chartered by Benning Wentworth in 1750 under the New Hampshire Grants to those first Massachusetts proprietors, or land speculators, who never called Halifax home. It includes many of those very first families who purchased land so cheaply and who carved farms and villages out of the wilderness. It profiles Halifax men most instrumental in the state political process, along with those involved in town affairs. In spite of the absence of early town records, persistent research turned up ancient maps, important political and historical information, documents, and land records located among New Hampshire, Massachusetts, New York and Vermont state papers, as well as account books, diaries, family photographs, Bibles and letters that confirm colonial life and migration activities.

With such modern marvels as the computer and scanner, those original documents have been copied into the text. The reader will note that the odd-looking "ſ" is not a misspelling, but is the style of calligraphy used in all forms of communication of that time, both handwritten and printed matter. The "ſ" should be read as the s̲ sound.

Documented are military records that reveal the extensive contributions made by Halifax residents in support of various wars. Whole companies of Halifax men were involved in major Civil War battles of the Peninsular Campaign where so many Halifax men so valiantly fought and died.

The first volume has a section called Community Life that includes meeting houses, churches, schools, and the health of citizens. The latter documents physicians who practiced in Halifax. Other sections talk about farm life and industries. In the Appendix are several important early maps and documents, including lists of elected town officers and several petitions.

After a stroll down Main Street in Halifax Center and West Halifax, the second volume concentrates on people and social activities like dances and celebrations. It includes historic neighborhoods, early families and houses, and organizations such as the Grange and the Historical Society. This volume introduces a number of natives who became prominent far beyond the borders of Halifax. You will meet Elisha Otis of elevator fame. The next time you step on an elevator, look down. You will see "Otis." You will be surprised to learn the founder of Redlands, California, was Russell Waters, and Dr. Edward Samuel Niles is to be thanked the next time you have a tooth filled. He pioneered the amalgam filling. Halifax has also produced a fair share of lawyers, physicians, teachers, ministers, missionaries, writers, poets, and politicos. The ambiance of Halifax has attracted dignitaries from all walks of life, including writer Saul Bellow, artist Kyra Markham, as well as numerous doctors, lawyers, high ranking military men, among others.

These two volumes, very well researched and written, will continue to be a work in progress as new information is discovered and history continues to be made. This compilation of historical documents raises questions for which answers are not available at this time, but there comes a point that we must call for an ending. It is time to publish this history! Here is the charge for the next generation: get excited about Halifax history and never stop looking for "the rest of the story."

~ *Molly Stone*

FOREWORD

by

HOWARD COFFIN

On a soft upland evening late in the last millennium I walked into an old hall in Halifax to speak of the Civil War and found a crowd filling the place. I wasn't surprised because history, particularly that of the Rebellion, is alive and thriving in Vermont's small towns. Certainly Halifax cared a lot about history and thus I readily agreed to write a forward when the phone call came from Elaine Fairbanks about the new town history. Now the book is about completed and having read it, I can say it's a first-rate job.

But first, back to that evening in Halifax. I was talking about Vermont's Civil War and had begun a description of the 1864 Battle of Cedar Creek when an elderly gentleman rose from his chair in the second row and asked if he could say something. Speakers like to get a rhythm going in their talks and I recall that I was just hitting my stride when the interruption came, but I said, "All right, what would you like to say?"

The man said he'd had a grandfather in the Eighth Vermont Regiment who had fought at Cedar Creek, indeed had been seriously wounded there. He proceeded to put on an old round hat and then removed it to poke a finger through a hole just above the narrow brim. "That's where the bullet went through that hit him in the head," said the man. I said, "You can interrupt any talk of mine any time you want to."

Ernest Kelly was the man's name, and I found out that he had very deep Vermont roots, in Randolph in fact. Ernest Kelly at the time was edging into his tenth decade. He has since passed from the earth. But because of him and a lot of people who showed me that evening they cared deeply about history, that Windham County evening stands out among the far more than one hundred and a quarter I have spent talking Civil War Vermont.

Few things do I enjoy more than talking history in some Green Mountain hill town and one of them is sitting down with a good book of history. I wasn't disappointed when I took the unbound Halifax book to my favorite chair one below-zero Montpelier winter night. Halifax is one of Vermont's oldest towns, and I learned there's even the grave there of an Eleanor Pennell that's dated 1770. Having been settled in the time of the French and Indian War when the danger of raids from the north was ever present, being too far from Fort Dummer and the Massachusetts forts to take up residence in Halifax was a dangerous undertaking. Yet Woodwards, Reads, Pattisons, Crosiers, Pratts, Clarks and many more came up the river valleys to chop farms out of the steep hillside and winding valley forests. Eventually, they would live under six flags, the last being red, white and blue. I learned that some of those early people had been citizen warriors, like James Clark who responded to the alarm from Lexington and Concord, and then later marched to the Hudson Valley to confront Burgoyne's formidable British army in 1777.

Early on I read with delight the account written in 1866 for a Fish family golden wedding anniversary. Henry Clay Fish's son said, " . . . home was of the simplest of farm houses—a mere nest, sheltered by friendly orchards; enlivened by running brooks; encircled by the grand old hills; smiled upon, we are certain, from heaven." The words speak to an almost disappeared Vermont way of life that has become the stuff of legends. Yet the epitaph of Rebecah Pattison, carved in 1822, reminds us that the supposedly idyllic farm life could be anything but:

> This lovely bud so young and fair
> Call'd hence by early doom
> Just came to show how sweet a flower
> In Paradise would bloom

The early people lived always with danger. It took courage to populate backcountry Vermont: "Mrs. P. had no means of obtaining fire but from her neighbors. She took her two children, one in her arms, leading the other, and started for Captain Pannel's through a dense forest guided by marked trees. When she had gone a little distance from her home she roused a bear who ran up a tree. With self-possession she took her apron and tied it around the tree, and hanging her bonnet upon a stake she placed it against the tree and passed on. Captain Pannel returned with her and shot the bear, which had been kept upon the tree by the bonnet and apron."

This is a town history that, while deeply researched and well noted, is readable for the telling of so many good stories. There's also much of the Vermont essence in these pages, such as the tale of the history seekers who found warning signs blocking their way: " . . . some descendants of Peter [Worden] were poking around after visiting the Stafford cemetery, but stopped when NO TRESPASSING signs were observed. Later, Jerry Freeman met one of the current-day Wordens while doing business in a local bank, and asked him and his sister to visit him so he could learn about the early settlers on his land. During the conversation, the signs were mentioned and he said, "Oh, don't pay any attention. That sign's not for people that SHOULD be there, but for others."

There's a wealth of information on Halifax families, old and new. Halifax industries are documented, including sawmills, tanneries, a boot shop, blacksmith shops, stores, a slate quarry, taverns, and the Halifax Electric Co-op. Apparently telephones came to some homes before electricity: "1880: Isaac Stetson and Clifford Haager sent away for two phones and strung a wire between farmhouses to talk with each other."

Also, I read of taverns and a local ski tow, and some brave efforts to found a town library. The Guiding Star Grange did get up and running. I even found information on local murders, and the sighting of an unidentified flying object. One who saw strange lights outside her house was a Mrs. Bickle, who happened to have a pacemaker implant. She told investigators she guessed the aliens must have been looking " . . . for an old lady with a pacemaker to study."

The military history was well researched and I took a particular interest in Halifax and the Civil War. The town sent a respectable number of men, 109, to the Union forces, and nineteen died in the service. Halifax lads were in most of the major battles, particularly in the east. Thirty-two served in the gallant Fourth Vermont Regiment of the Old Brigade and thus saw action at Lee's Mill, Antietam, Salem Church, Petersburg, Spotsylvania Court House, Cold Harbor, and many other bloody fields. Five Halifax lads were shot amid the horror of the Wilderness: James Crosier was fatally wounded at Third Winchester, Isaac Stowe and John Whitney were wounded at First Fredericksburg.

I applaud the information on Halifax in World War II. Edwin Whitehorne's eyewitness account of a naval engagement with the Japanese in Surigao Strait was deeply touching. He wrote home of facing battle: "I went up by myself to the flying bridge, by the G. O. station, and there in the darkness I talked to God. I thought of all of you so hard that I almost had you there with me. I could plainly hear that peculiar little laugh that is typical of Dorothy, and I remember how I grinned to myself as I imagined I could hear it. I thought of the kid, and prayed hard to get home with all you once again, then I said my Rosary and felt a lot better. I make my peace as best I could." Came the battle: "We see a Jap ship blow up, her ammunition going over the sky. The sky is torn apart by the full boom of the big guns, and explosions send great red gouts of fire up into the darkness. . ."

There is so much in this book, but my favorite passages had to do with the life of a small Vermont farming community remembered by those Halifax people who, like myself, are getting a bit senior now. The memories are vivid of a time when Vermont was a farming state, when the small towns were the center of agricultural communities. It is a Vermont that has almost disappeared, and for that I am sad. Thus, this history of Halifax has come along just in time. It has caught a disappearing Vermont in its words and will hold it, I trust, for a very long time.

I grew up in a small Vermont town that was in the midst of many farms. My grandfather Jillson farmed acres from which his father went off to the Civil War. The Vermont that is going away is the Vermont of my heart. Thus, I loved the Hubbard Hill section: "On up the 'steep pitch,' as it was called, past the sugar maples, the former Learnard property begins. . . . As we pass the Learnard property, we are reminded of the old home, which could be seen from the road, and the big black bear rug on the floor of the bedroom off the parlor. The kitchen was graced with a low ceiling, a black iron sink and a large round table in the corner of the room. Outside, by the driveway, were several old rose bushes, no doubt planted many years ago."

Many fond personal memories were triggered by the remembrance of dances at the Community Hall in the fifties and sixties: "Both young and old kicked up their heels to lively square dances and polkas as well as the more sedate waltzes. As children we ran and slid across the sawdust covered floor while the older folks danced around us. The bands . . . usually consisted of a piano, guitar, and sometimes a fiddle, and sometimes an accordion, as well as a caller."

The description of old schools reminded me of tales my mother told of her childhood: "The wind whipped across Dean's Flat as we pushed our way to school along the wind swept road. . . . I remember the head scarf wrapped around my face and tied in at the back of my neck and trying to breathe through the air hole. As we rounded the top of the hill beyond Niles Cemetery, we could see the school in the distance. The white building blended with the snow and seemed farther away than it was."

And, "The front lawn at the school was large and we made snow forts and had lots of snowball fights in the winter. We played games, such as Prisoners Base, Fox and Geese, Softball, Hide and Seek. . . . There was a swing, which hung from an old oak tree. There were shade trees on one side of the building, which helped in the summer, but inside there were no fans to cool us when it was hot. The area around us was open, farms were nearby and a lumber mill was across the road from the school. The Stone family operated this mill, and the mill whistle blew every day at noon." "Hayed Until the Stars Shone", the title of one of the book's sections, alone spoke volumes about farming Vermont. Also: "I spent a lot of summer vacations in the hayfield helping my grandparents. By myself, I hitched the horse, Old Dan, to the Whipple tree and took the hay wagon down into the field where my grandfather was tumbling hay with his hand rake."

The section on baseball brought back fond recollections of Sunday afternoons with my father at the Vail Field in Woodstock, watching the town team: "How the crowd used to cheer when a batter hit the ball into the bushes, as this was usually a home run. One field that had a brook and one good hitter was noted for batting the ball time after time into the brook. Finally, a rule was made that any ball that went into the brook was considered a double base hit instead of a home run. About halfway through the game, someone would pass the hat through the crowd and people would toss in loose change that would be given to the home team to pay for balls and bats."

This new town history is many things, certainly a resource for the future generations searching out the history of one particular town, Halifax, but also for anyone curious about all of long-ago Vermont and America. Also, it is a wonderful reminiscence of a Vermont that is vanishing. Why we Americans seem to let slip away the things we say we love the most is, to me, one of this nation's greatest mysteries and disappointments. The frontiers are gone; the land is all within our grasp. We must now choose the kind of America we want for ourselves, and create, or recreate it. I hope that before all the old farmlands are filled with condominiums and pre-made homes, the Vermonters of the new millennium will decide to bring the farms back. But buildings are the last crop and that crop is growing, spreading fast. One need only to look in this Halifax history to know that what we are letting die had a value almost beyond imagining. It was the stuff of which dreams are made, and fine history, too.

Contents

ABBREVIATIONS
for
FREQUENTLY USED SOURCES

Beers   Beers, F. W. *Atlas of Windham Co. Vermont.* New York: F. W. Beers, A. D. Ellis, & G. G. Soule, 1869. Reprinted as a portfolio box of color reproduced maps. Brattleboro, VT: The Book Cellar, 1969. Halifax Map.

Child   Child, Hamilton, ed. *Gazetteer and Business Directory of Windham County, Vt.* 1724–1884. Syracuse, NY: Journal Office, 1884.

Hall   Hall, Benjamin H. *History of Eastern Vermont from its Earliest Settlement to the Close of the Eighteenth Century.* New York: D. Appleton, 1858.

Hemenway   Hemenway, Abby Maria, ed. *The Vermont Historical Gazetteer: A Magazine, Embracing a History of Each Town, Civil, Ecclesiastical, Biographical, and Military.* Vol. 5. Brandon, VT: Mrs. Carrie E. H. Page, 1891.

HHS   Halifax Historical Society Museum, West Halifax, VT. Letters, photographs, postcards, scrapbooks, taped interviews and *Halifacts* (the newsletter of the Historical Society). [HHS] *Notebooks of Halifax Houses,* compiled and edited by Pat Johnson [HHS: Johnson]; *Halifax* a book of news clippings compiled by Charles Addison Niles, from newspapers that he did not reference, including *The Vermont Phoenix, The Athens Gleaner,* and others, 1881–1887 [HHS: Niles].

HLR   Halifax Land Records in the office of the town clerk, West Halifax, VT. Begins with Volume 1A, 1778. Cited within the text. [HLR 1A: 15]

HTC   Halifax Town Clerk, West Halifax, VT. Census Records– [HTC: CR], Grand List–[HTC: GL]; Loose Papers–[HTC: LP]; Safe–[HTC: S]; Selectmen's Records–[HTC: SR], Town Reports–[HTC: TR], Vital Records– [HTC: VR].

McClellan   Chace, J., Jr. *McClellan's Map of Windham, County, Vermont.* Philadelphia: C. McClellan, 1856. Reprint in atlas format, West Chesterfield, NH: Old Maps, 1984. Halifax Map.

NARA   U. S. National Archives and Records Administration, northeast region, Pittsfield, MA.

NEHGS   New England Historic Genealogical Society, 101 Newbury St., Boston, MA.

Patrie   Patrie, Lois McClellan. *A History of Colrain Massachusetts, with Genealogies of Early Families.* Troy, NY: published by author, 1974. Endnotes reflect two sections: History and Genealogy. Example: Patrie, p. 1-H. or Patrie, p. 100-G.

Phoenix   *Vermont Phoenix.* Published weekly in Brattleboro, VT from September 12, 1834 to March 1, 1913.

PVMA   Pocumtuck Valley Memorial Association, Deerfield, MA.

Reformer   Published weekly in Brattleboro, VT, from August 1876 to March 1913, originally called *Windham County Reformer*, which became the *Brattleboro Reformer*, published daily since 1913 in Brattleboro, VT. Excerpts and/or quotations used with permission.

Stone   Stone, Arthur F. *The Vermont of Today: With Its Historic Background, Attractions and People.* New York: Lewis Historical Publishing, 1929.

Thompson   Thompson, Zadock. *History of Vermont, Natural, Civil, and Statistical.* Burlington, VT: Chauncey Goodrich, 1842.

UVM   Special Collections, Bailey/ Howe Library, University of Vermont, Burlington, VT.

VHS   Vermont Historical Society, Barre, VT.

VSS   Vermont State Archives, Office of the Secretary of State, Montpelier, VT. Manuscript Vermont State Papers, MsVtSP.

* * *

In order to guide the reader, related subject matter is marked within the text with arrows followed by the page number.
Example: [↶ 1] Looks back to page 1 and [↷ 50] look forward to page 50.

INTRODUCTION

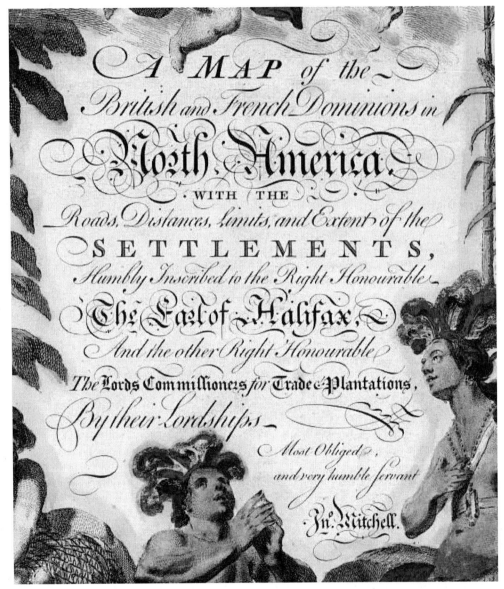

A MAP of the British and French Dominions in North America WITH THE Roads, Distances, Limits, and Extent of the SETTLEMENTS, Humbly Inscribed to the Right Honourable The Earl of Halifax, And the other Right Honourable The Lords Commissioners for Trade & Plantations, By their Lordships Most Obliged, and very humble servant Jn.º Mitchell.

John Mitchell's map, Library of Congress Geography and Map Division, Washington, DC: Andrew Miller, London, 1755. Accessed July 28, 2006. http://memory.loc.gov/ammem/index.html

Detail from the cartouche of what is considered the most comprehensive map of eastern North America during the colonial era. John Mitchell began work on the map in 1750, the year Halifax was chartered. His friendship with George Dunk, Second Earl of Halifax, the man after whom Halifax was named, proved invaluable. The Earl provided the mapmaker access to volumes of material collected by the British Board of Trade and the British Admiralty. Mitchell, to show his appreciation, dedicated his completed map, first published in 1755, to the Earl of Halifax.

TOPOGRAPHY, GEOGRAPHY, AND NATURAL HISTORY

Halifax, Vermont lies in the southern part of Windham County at 42° 47' and longitude 4° 20' and is bounded north by Marlboro, east by Guilford, west by Whitingham, and south by Colrain, Massachusetts.

Halifax was the second Vermont township to be granted by Benning Wentworth, the first in Windham County, and has its original charter dated May 11, 1750. According to the first plat plan, the town's 23,040 acres were divided into sixty-four equal shares. The lot of each owner was marked at the corners with "stake and stones." In the center of the town was a large space in the shape of a hexagon taken from surrounding lots for public uses [↪504].

"The surface of the town is very rough and uneven, though there are no elevations of sufficient altitude to warrant their being designated as mountains."[2] Several elevations such as Ballou Mountain, Stowe Mountain, Stark Mountain, French Hill, Pennell Hill, and Clark Hill are named after local families. The names Jolly Mountain and Prospect Hill are exceptions. Origins of those names are not certain. Ballou Mountain lies in the north central part of Halifax, Jolly Hill in the central part, Stowe Mountain in the south central part, and Stark Mountain in the southeasterly part.

The town is named for the English nobleman and politician who has often been called the Father of the Colonies. George Montagu-Dunk (1716–71) was the second Earl of Halifax. He had succeeded his father in 1739 and added Dunk to his surname when he married the heiress to Sir Thomas Dunk's enormous fortune. The Earl of Halifax is considered to have been one of the most prominent English officials in colonial administration. From 1748 to 1761 he was president of the board of trade and plantations, and in that role he was instrumental in founding Nova Scotia, where the city of Halifax is named in his honor.[1]

Esther Munroe Swift

Although much of the land in Halifax is not suited for large-scale commercial farming, there were many fine farms, and a large amount of land possessing rich, arable soil. This soil was well adapted to the growing of grass, making Halifax land a great grazing territory, which contributed nicely to the raising of sheep. The timber is mostly beech, birch, maple, ash, hemlock, and spruce,[3] providing the early settlers not only with substantial homes but industry as well.

Two main rivers flow through Halifax: North River, which begins in the town of Whitingham, flows through the southwest part of Halifax, eventually reaching the Deerfield River in Shelburne Falls, Massachusetts. On this river is a famous gorge. Its deep, cool, waters became a favorite spot for a swim in the hot summertime.

GORGE, HALIFAX, VERMONT

Postcard C. Lancaster

"On the margin of North river is a curious cavern, called *Woodard's cave or Dun's Den*. . . . The sides and the top are of solid rock. This is also a place of resort for the curious." Thompson, p. 85.

CASCADE BETWEEN THE UPPER AND LOWER POOLS   Photo Porter Thayer HHS

The Green River starts in Marlboro and flows through the easterly part of Halifax, emptying into the Deerfield River in Greenfield, Massachusetts. While Halifax has only two rivers, it has an abundance of smaller brooks: The main brooks are Branch, Sperry, and Roaring Brook. These rivers and brooks provided waterpower for the mill industry in Halifax. Branch Brook begins in a swamp in the northeastern part of Halifax and flows southerly through the village of West Halifax until it reaches the North River at the intersection of Branch Road and Route 112. Sperry Brook, named for A. O. Sperry, who purchased the mill property in 1863, begins in Halifax Center on Tucker Road near the original Joseph Tucker home and flows southerly until it reaches Branch Brook, approximately one half mile north of Route 112.

A pond in the Deer Park section of Halifax is the headwaters for Roaring Brook, which flows southeasterly until it reaches the Green River near the Halifax/Guilford line, on the Jacksonville Stage Road.

The township of Halifax has plenty of rocks. Geologically speaking, these rocks are gneiss, talcose schist, and calciferous mica schist. The gneiss is found in the northern part, the talcose in the western part, and mica in the eastern part. Iron pyrite (fool's gold) has been seen in some areas.[4] Though Halifax has miles and miles of gravel roads, gravel in Halifax is in limited supply, making it necessary to get good quality gravel from banks in surrounding towns.

~ Bernice Barnett and Elaine Fairbanks

LOWER POOL   Photo Porter Thayer HHS

ENDNOTES
1. Esther Munroe Swift, *Vermont Place-Names – Footprints of History* (Brattleboro, VT: Stephen Green Press, 1977).
2. Child, p. 216.
3. Ibid.
4. Ibid.

Photo Lewis R. Brown. HHS

View of the former Academy School located on the common at Halifax Center, where Rev. Thomas H. Wood, first Halifax historian, taught Greek and Latin to young men preparing for college. The first Congregational Meeting House, where Rev. Wood preached for thirty-six years, was located in the grassy area where the gravestones and stonewall are pictured. The stonewall that served to enlarge the cemetery was built after the meeting house was taken down circa 1865. Rev. Wood and his family are buried in the original part of the old meeting house cemetery located adjacent to and behind what is shown in this photograph.

HALIFAX HISTORIANS

In the 250 years since it's founding, Halifax, Vermont has never been the subject of a full-length history. Over the years, those seeking historical accounts of the town have parsed the pages of the gazetteer triumvirate: Thompson, Child, and Hemenway. Zadock Thompson's *Gazetteer of the State of Vermont* was originally published in 1824, with updates printed in 1833, 1842, and 1853. Hamilton Child's *Windham County Gazetteer* appeared in 1884; and Abby Hemenway's *Vermont Historical Gazetteer, Vol. V, The Towns of Windham County*, was published, posthumously, in 1891. This trio of nineteenth-century gazetteer editors relied on advance subscriptions to pay for the printing of their volumes and engaged writers, gratis, to supply the content. Many of their writers were clergymen. For each assigned town, the author would provide a compendium of civil, natural, ecclesiastical, military, and political history flavored with bits of biography, genealogy, and colorful tales. The stories published about the earliest settlers were gleaned from the memories of a handful of older residents. In the absence of written records, oral tradition prevailed. Few, if any, sources were documented in these accounts to the great disappointment of the modern researcher. However, the existence of shaky oral tradition is probably more desirable than no early settlement stories at all. Undeniably, such stories are fun to read, and endure as local legends.

Today's Halifax historians, like their predecessors, are unpaid volunteers, whose efforts are motivated by enthusiasm for the subject. There are, however, real differences. The current writers have endeavored to consult primary sources and to document their research. Not one member of the current Town History Committee is clergy, and mighty few are men.

FIRST GAZETTEER

The title "First Historian of Halifax" properly belongs to Rev. Thomas Hough Wood (1772–1842), who appears to have earned that honor by default. He stepped in when it seemed likely that Zadock Thompson's ambitious first gazetteer for the State of Vermont might go to press without any Halifax information other than statistics such as longitude and latitude, census figures, and location. In October of 1823, Thompson sent out copies of his prospectus and a query form to hundreds of towns in the state "asking local postmasters to pass them on to a citizen who would be willing to write and return a descriptive account of the town"[1] The questions in Thompson's form directed citizens throughout the state to collect and record information about their towns while those few folks who had memory of the earliest period of settlement were still alive. Land, church, and census records were useful. However, without Thompson's effort, and the efforts of subsequent gazetteer editors who followed his lead, many of the diverse details packed into those volumes might have been forever lost. Thompson mailed the following letter and questionnaire:

Sir, —

If you will take the trouble to furnish an article, describing your town, in answer to the following queries, together with such other particulars as you may deem proper for a complete Gazetteer of Vermont; and will also make some exertions to procure subscribers for the work, you will oblige

Yours Respectfully,
ZADOCK THOMPSON

QUERIES. —When was the charter of the town given, and who was the principal proprietor? When was the first settlement commenced, and by whom? What is there remarkable respecting the first settlement and subsequent history of the town? Whence did the first settlers emigrate? When was the town organized, and who was the first town clerk representative, etc. What are the religious denominations, and number of the several churches? — names of the clergymen? —when settled, and dismissed? Have there been any remarkable revivals of religion? — instances of longevity? — remarkable seasons of mortality? —personages? What are the names of the physicians and attorneys? What are its streams, ponds, mill privileges, mountains, soil, timber, minerals, springs, caverns, and curiosities? What are its public buildings? — when erected? What is the number of school districts and school houses, grist, saw, and oil mills, cotton and woollen factories, stores, taverns, distilleries, tanneries, forges, furnaces, potteries, etc. If there be a village, or villages, a particular and separate description is requested. A particular description of any river, or rivers, would be acceptable. N. B. Communications may be forwarded to me, at Woodstock, accompanied by a statement of the number of subscribers procured, any time between this and the first of April next.

October 1823[2]

The questionnaire for Halifax should have been delivered to postmaster Thomas H. Wood at Joseph Henry's store, which probably served as the post office in 1823.[3] Whether it was the 1822 town representative, George Boardman; the 1823 representative, James L. Stark; or the town clerk, Darius Bullock, whoever received the query, did not reply. In 1824, as publication time drew near, Thompson again contacted those towns from which he had no response. Late in August, he finally received the completed Halifax questionnaire from Rev. Thomas H. Wood, Congregational minister, postmaster, and teacher at the brick Academy School in Halifax Center. The three-page letter penned in black ink on parchment, in which Rev. Wood systematically answered the questions, remains in excellent condition in the Special Collections of Bailey/Howe Library at the University of Vermont.[4]

History and Description of Halifax Vt.

First settled by Abner Rice from nr.   1761
Worcester Massachusetts ——————

The next settlers from Colerain & Pel-   1763 &
ham, Ms.

     First town Clerk, of which we have
any account, Samuel Wood and It is not
known when the town was organized,
probably about ——————————   1770

The first representatives, of which we have
any account, were Hubbel Wells and
Edward Harris.

Religious Denominations, Congrega-   organized
tional and Bap. — Cong. Ch. 120 members   1778
Bap. Ch. —————————————   208

Clergymen, Tho. H. Wood, Cong. Samuel
Fish, Bap. First settled Cong. minister,
~~Joel Goodall~~ David Goodall, ~~ordained~~   1781
16 years was ordained —————   1796
Goodall dismissed
Jesse Edson ordained ———————   1805
     Died
Tho. H. Wood ordained, Sept. 14 ———   1806

— Special revivals, ———————   1849
                                 1800
Longevity. Mr — Rice, commonly call'd   1817
Dr Rice, died about the year 1812 aged
112 years. —————

Mortality — seasons ———————   1806
                                     and
Physicians. Henry Niles, Henry Will-   1812
iams   and 13

Lawyers. Jedidiah Stark, James L.
Stark.

Streams. North River, a large, good
mill stream, on the West and South; &
Green River, the same bigness as
the North. — very commodious streams
for mills.

Continued

Mill-privileges good, on 9 different streams
in the town
Mountains, none worthy of notice
There is a chain of cascades, in a branch of
the North river on the farm of Henry
Niles, 100 rods or more in extent, where
the water falls, from many of them 15
and from some of them 20 feet They are
overlooked on the right, as one ascends the
stream, by projecting rocks, rising to the
height of 15 and 20 feet. It is visited by the
curious, —

On the margin of the
North river is a curious cave, called Wood
ands Cave, in Deer Den It is about 5
feet in length, 5 in breadth, and
the same in height. The two sides are solid
rock, and the covering a large flat stone
This is a resort for people, fond of exploring the works of nature — The soil strong
and good. Timber, beech, maple, birch, hemlock, spruce and white & black ash. Dows
4 miles square — noted for dances, cheese &
cotton. — Inhabitants industrious, & wealthy.
Public buildings. Cong meet-house,
built, 1732, Bap. meet. h. built, 1804
Tauerns, 3. Stores 2. — School-houses 14,
On the centre of the town, is an elegant
brick School-h. 42 by 24 feet, in which
a school is kept, during the most of the
year, by a well qualified instructer, and
the higher branches of literature, are often

Continued

In 1824, it was customary for the name of the addressee to appear at the end of a letter; i.e., Zadock Thompson, Esq.

Courtesy UVM

The Halifax description published in the first edition of Thompson's gazetteer ends with the date August 24, 1824 and the initials T. H. W. When editing Rev. Wood's response, Thompson made almost no changes. The words of the now very familiar opening portion of that historical account have been repeated, verbatim, in nearly every published description of Halifax for more than one hundred and fifty years.

The settlement was commenced in 1761, by Abner Rice from
Worcester county, Mass. He was joined by others from Colerain
and Pelham, Mass. in 1763. The time the town was organized is
not precisely known, but was about the year 1770. The first town
clerk, of whom any information has been obtained, was Samuel
Woodard, and the first representatives, Hubbell Wells, and
Edward Harris.[5]

Who was Thomas Hough Wood? A letter from Miss Ella Wood of
Hamden, Connecticut, responding to Susan McBride's letter about Halifax in the
July 1967 issue of *Yankee Magazine* provides the following biographical details:

My great-grandfather was Thomas Hough Wood, who was born
in Bozrah, Connecticut, the son of Zebedee Wood, one of the
first settlers of Hawley, Massachusetts. He was graduated from
Williams College in 1799 and became a minister. He preached in
Hawley, and was ordained in Halifax where he married for his
second wife Millicent Swain, daughter of Joseph Swain and
Millicent Barrett of Concord, Massachusetts. . . . It is my understanding that Thomas Hough Wood resided in Halifax when
his son, William Lyman, was born, and died there. He was the
minister, farmed, taught boys for college, and was known as
"Priest" Wood.[6]

Miss Wood mentions that she visited Halifax several years ago and
wonders if the grave she saw behind the little schoolhouse and marked with a
patriot's Revolutionary marker, is that of Meliscent Barrett Swain or Meliscent
Swain Wood. "As each springtime approaches" she wishes to make the trip again
to Hawley and Halifax, but finds it difficult to do so; therefore, she would
appreciate any other word about her Swain and Wood ancestors. She notes that
she "has not been successful in finding any books with much information about
Halifax."[7] Evidently, Ella Wood had no inkling that whatever information she had
found was due, largely, to the efforts of her great-grandfather and that he was, in
fact, the first historian of the town.

Thomas Wood was born into a pioneer settler family. His father, Zebedee
Wood, "came [from Bozrah, Connecticut] to spy out the land in Hawley,
Massachusetts," a journey of twenty-three days covering two hundred and forty
three miles.[8] He brought his family to live in Hawley in 1775 when Thomas was
three years old. Mr. Wood was a farmer, tanner, shoemaker, and town clerk for
several years, and a minuteman at the Battle of Bennington. Thomas Wood's
mother, Esther Hough, was a "tailoress" and, for several years, the only person in
town who acted the role of physician. In Hawley, Thomas married, Olive,
daughter of Col. Edmund and Alice Longley. The Woods moved to Halifax in
1806 where he assumed the pastorate left vacant by the death of Rev. Jesse
Edson.

The Thomas Wood family resided in Lot 29 north of Halifax Center, on the east side of Old County Road, south of the intersection of "the road leading to Arthur Crosier and Jonathan Kellogg" [HLR 2:145], now called Deer Park Road. Olive Wood, who bore four children, died March 13, 1817 at the age of thirty-five. Rev. Wood married Meliscent Swain in August 1817. To them were born two sons and a daughter. In the fall of 1823, their son, Andrew, died at age three years. Thomas Wood and his family are buried in the Halifax Center Cemetery, adjacent to the sites of the Academy School where he taught and the Congregational Church where he was pastor for thirty-six years.

SECOND GAZETTEER

Sixty years after Thompson's publication, the enterprising Hamilton Child of Syracuse, New York, who had published gazetteers for most of the counties of New York State and a few for Pennsylvania, turned his attention to the counties of Vermont. His *Windham County Gazetteer and Business Directory,* published in 1884, included a seven-page narrative of Halifax full of historical and biographical detail, plus a meticulous listing of every property owner in town with location reference, acreage, occupation, and property holdings, such as trees and livestock. In his introduction, Child thanked the "editors and managers of the county papers for furnishing material for the work."[9] County papers in 1883 were: the *Vermont Phoenix* and *The Windham County Reformer.* Also Child commented, "We have found valuable aid in works by Thompson, Hiland Hall, B. H. Hall, Deming and the *Documentary History of New York* as well as Beers, Ellis and Soule's atlas. . . . Our thanks also to the clergy throughout the county."[10]

While Child does name some of the local authors and contributors, he acknowledges no specific source for the Halifax write-up. Hamilton Child published in Syracuse, New York, and unless there is an archive of his correspondence and prepublication papers, it is unlikely that we will ever know for certain the identity of the Halifax contact person for this gazetteer. Analysis of the article, however, suggests a likely candidate, Baptist clergyman, Horace Fowler. There are numerous clues. At the time Child was amassing material for his *Windham County Gazetteer,* Fowler was the only settled pastor in Halifax. Every family included in the early settler descriptions belonged to the Baptist Church. Nearly every family mentioned came from Stonington, Connecticut and/or had ties to the Niles family. Horace Fowler resided with Samuel Niles and was married to his daughter, Lucy. It is reasonable to assume that Fowler, having been asked by Child for information, would have interviewed those folks with whom he had the most contact. A disproportionate amount of space in the article is devoted to the family and life of Elder Samuel Fish, longtime Baptist clergyman and Halifax resident. Fish died in January 1883, the year of this gazetteer's preparation, thus his biography would have been recently written and readily available from the local newspaper. It may be worth noting that the Halifax description published in Child's volume does not mention Rev. Thomas Wood or the previous existence of a local Congregational Church. The article ends, "The churches of Halifax are a Baptist Church at Halifax Village, with no regular pastor; a Baptist Church at West Halifax with Rev. Horace Fowler, pastor; and the Universalist Church at West Halifax, with no stated supply."[11]

In contrast, the business directory portion of *The Windham County Gazetteer* appears to include everyone in town. Child states the "information was obtained by actual canvass. Each agent is furnished with a map of the town he is expected to canvass, and he is required to pass over every road, and to call at every dwelling and place of business in the town, in order to obtain the facts from the individuals concerned wherever possible."[12] The map published with the gazetteer has numbered roads so that the reader can identify the locations of the town's inhabitants. This detailed business directory continues to be a vital source of reliable information about Halifax families, industries, and neighborhoods [↪ 392].

THIRD GAZETTEER

Halifax is indebted to yet another gazetteer historian, Abby Maria Hemenway, who passionately pursued her dream of rescuing the stories of early Vermont settlement for all localities in the state. She struggled with physical and monetary hardships, and a fire that destroyed a major portion of what had been completed of volume five of her historical gazetteer. After the 1886 fire, she gathered up her notes and spent hours every day in her Chicago apartment typesetting the 857 pages of Windham County. She died in 1890 with the work still in progress. After her death, her sister, Carrie Page, edited and completed volume five, which she published in Abby's memory in 1891.

Unlike Child, Hemenway named the authors she engaged to write about each town. Rev. Hubbard Eastman, author of the Halifax chapter, was a Methodist minister residing in Jacksonville at the time he compiled material for Abby Hemenway. The account as published, is rambling, redundant, choppy, and disorganized but so packed with detail that one finds something new in every reading. Perhaps Eastman submitted a file full of topical writing, notes, statistics, news clippings, obituaries, parts of sermons, and, either because of the fire or Hemenway's unexpected death, his material never received proper or coherent editing. For someone who never lived in the town, Eastman managed to rescue a substantial amount of local Halifax history. He states,

> It might be supposed that in an age of so much reading as ours,
> and where there is no end to the demand for the making of books,
> that the history of separate communities would be carefully
> preserved, so that the people might be well informed in the
> history of their own immediate neighborhood. But in this respect
> we are sadly deficient. The records of this town throw but little
> light upon its early history, and the generation that was conversant
> with the first settling of the town has passed away, with the
> exception of a single individual, [Jane Gault Crosier] now upwards
> of 105 years of age, so that the sources of information are not very
> abundant. Such information, however, in relation to the history of
> the town as I have been able to glean from different sources I
> shall present.[13]

In addition to collecting family stories and other bits of oral history, Eastman included specific provisions of the town charter and details of early political incidents. He included news reports and lists of office holders and material taken from Thompson's gazetteer. In speaking about her recently published biography, *The Passion of Abby Hemenway*, Deborah Pickman Clifford said, "For a while my working title for the book was *One more Bear Story, and that will do!*"[14] Rev. Eastman obtained more than one Halifax bear story for Hemenway's publication and for posterity. The bear, according to Clifford, was probably the most pervasive symbol of settler hardships.

Who was Hubbard H. Eastman? Born on a farm in Grafton, Vermont in 1809, Hubbard Eastman later lived in nearby Athens with his first wife and preached in Putney where he clashed with John Humphrey Noyes, the founder of the Oneida Community. In 1849, he published in Brattleboro, the work *Noyesism Unveiled History of the Sect Self-styled Perfectionists*. By 1865, he was farming and preaching in Guilford, Vermont. The news from the town's section of the *Vermont Phoenix* on October 6, 1865, reports, "Rev. Hubbard Eastman of Guilford raised this year four squashes from one seed whose weight was 309 ½ lbs, the largest weighing 120 lbs." After the death of his second wife in 1866, Eastman moved to Jacksonville where he remarried. Child's 1884 business directory lists "Hubbard Eastman, Jacksonville Center. Minister of the M. E. church in the Vt. Conference, sec'y of conference 4 years, presiding elder 4 years, (now retired) correspondent for newspapers."[15] It is not known how Hemenway met and recruited this man who had never lived in Halifax, to write the town's history for her Windham County volume. Rev. Eastman died in May 1891, six months before publication of the gazetteer. He is buried in Jacksonville Cemetery. Neither he nor Abby Hemenway lived to read the published version of their history of Halifax. Another fire, this one in 1911, destroyed trunks full of Hemenway's notes and correspondence, both for Windsor and Windham counties, including, in all probability, all remnants of Hubbard Eastman's Halifax contribution.

THE MAKING OF THE TOWN HISTORY

Other short Halifax histories have appeared over the years. The Halifax Town Report for 1941 included a Historical Outline of Halifax introduced as follows: "In commemoration of the Sesquicentennial Celebration of the State of Vermont's entrance to the Union the Selectmen of the town are incorporating into the town report a brief history of Halifax for the general information of the Townspeople." It would be nice to be able to acknowledge the author of this well-written account of early Halifax history, but no name is given in the town report. The 1941 selectmen were Fred May, Scott E. Courser, and Z. A. Learnard. The town clerk was Harry E. Goodnough. One of those four men must have been the author. Twenty years later, Mrs. Emory B. (Maude) Hebard prepared and circulated an eleven-page typescript called *History of the Town of Halifax, Vermont 1750–1761.* She said she used prior published sources as well as "information from former and present residents of Halifax."[16] Since the formation of the Halifax Historical Society in 1972, a number of articles of historical interest have been published in the newsletter known as *Halifacts.* In addition, the book, *Epitaphs from Halifax Vermont,* published in 1973 by Elaine Claire Fairbanks and Regina Carr Hardgrove, includes, between visits to cemeteries, about a dozen pages of lively historical narrative. Also, during the last twenty-five years or so, Bernice Barnett has published several books and many newspaper articles about the history of her Green Mountain hometown.

In 1991, a committee formed to write an in-depth, official history of the town. The initiative began at an informal gathering in August when a group of folks decided it was about time Halifax had a full-length history. Elaine Fairbanks remembers those present were Lucie Sumner, Ray Ouelette, Bernice Barnett, Regina Hardgrove, and herself. The first book committee meeting was held at the Grange Hall September 16, 1991. Joining the group were Steve and Mariette Sanders, Arlene Fairbanks, Malcolm Evans, Susan Rusten, Henry and Marie Taylor, and Annie Putnam. Tom O'Brien joined in an advisory role. Sue and Tom offered to research the militia; Mariette volunteered to do illustrations. A news release encouraging new members to join caught the attention of Connie Lancaster, who attended the meeting on October 21, 1991. Carrie Perna joined in November 1998 and Molly Stone joined August 1999. Sadly, a number of the original participants have passed away.

From the beginning the committee met regularly and volunteered many hours of time. Research for the project has involved long trips to libraries and archives, as well as countless hours researching records at the town clerk's office. It also has meant travel to other states because Halifax, at times, belonged to New Hampshire and New York. Anyone who wonders why it has taken more than a decade to complete this project might imagine trying to work full-time, care for a family, send out fund-raising letters, prepare grant proposals, learn all one can learn about Halifax past and present, write text, correct edits, take pictures, select and scan photographs, organize, design and publish the book, and negotiate with printing companies, all while working as a committee!

If the object of a town history is to enable the reader to imagine the town and the people as they were in the past, then the benefit of having many authors is that they look at different times and different people and tell the stories in different voices. A grant from the Windham Foundation enabled the committee to engage an editor. Besides copyediting, Hilly van Loon has helped organize the material and coordinate the different voices. She has been an inspired guide. Halifax is fortunate to have a full set of legible town records dating from 1778. Pre-1778 records that have survived can be found in New Hampshire, New York, Massachusetts and Newfane, Vermont. Some of the earliest deeds were transcribed into the town books after 1778 and bear dates from the original transactions. It would take many years to read the entire set of books, but this group has made a significant start. In the beginning, it was difficult for the committee to know what information was available beyond the local records and to know where and what to look for. In the late 1990s, came the proliferation of historical and genealogical postings on the Internet. It became possible to search archives and library catalogues and to read books online. It has enabled the committee to locate and share information with descendants of many of the earliest settlers. One of the rewards of historical research is knowing the pursuit is endless. New Halifax information, legends and lore will be discovered from many sources for years to come. We hope our work inspires interest in the history of the town and enthusiasm for continuing the search.

©2008 *Constance Lancaster*

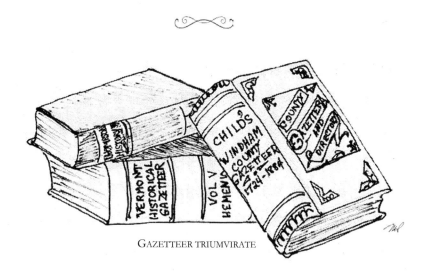

GAZETTEER TRIUMVIRATE

ENDNOTES

1. J. Kevin Graffagnino, "Zadock Thompson: Nineteenth Century Vermont Historian," (master's thesis, University of Vermont, February 1978) p. 12.
2. VHS, MS Box 72, folder 4.
3. NARA, Record Group 028 Postmasters, M1131 Roll 2, 1812–1824. The first postmaster appointed in Halifax was Thomas H. Wood on December 2, 1816. Joseph Henry, owner of the store in Halifax Center, pledged a surety of $700 on behalf of Wood, and may have received mail deliveries at the store.
4. UVM, Zadock Thompson Papers, (1813–1977), Box 2, Folder 7.
5. Zadock Thompson, A. B., *A Gazetteer of the State of Vermont.* (Montpelier, VT: E. P. Walton, 1824) p. 149.
6. HHS, Family files, *Letter from Ella Wood,* 1967.
7. Ibid.
8. William Giles Atkins, *History of the Town of Hawley, Franklin County, Massachusetts,* 1887, p. 100.
9. Child, p. 3.
10. Ibid., p. 3.
11. Ibid., p. 222.
12. Ibid., p. 4.
13. Hemenway, p. 409.
14. Deborah Clifford Pickman presentation at the Vermont History Expo, Tunbridge, VT, June 22, 2002.
15. Child, p. 523.
16. Mrs. Emory B. Hebard, *Halifax, Vermont 1750–1961* (Halifax, VT, 1961) p. 1.

SECTION ONE

EARLY SETTLEMENT

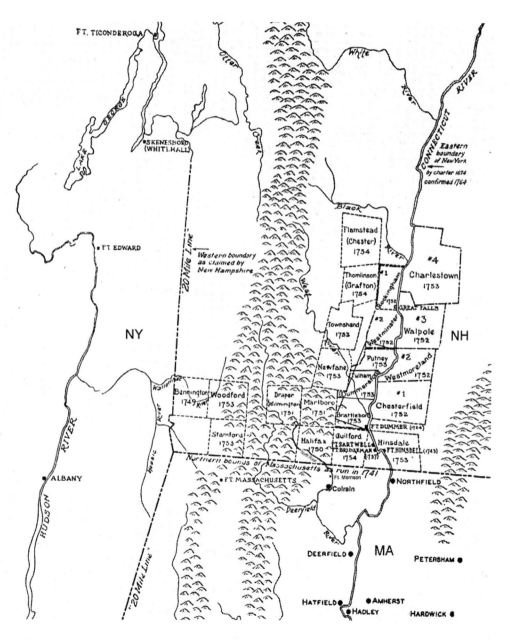

Adapted from *The Vermont Story, A History of the People of the Green Mountain State, 1749–1949* (Burlington, VT: Lane Press) Frontier Map, p. 52.

EARLY MAP OF NORTHERN NEW ENGLAND

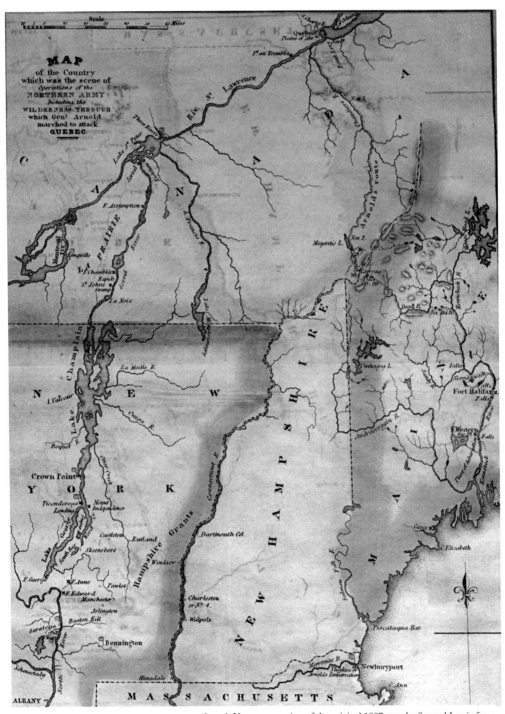

Joseph Yeager engraving of the original 1807 map by Samuel Lewis for
the *Atlas to Marshall's Life of Washington.* (Philadelphia: J. Crissy, 1832).

BACKGROUND PRIOR TO 1761
A BRIEF NARRATIVE

Events leading to the founding of Halifax, Vermont (claimed by New Hampshire, New York, and finally, Vermont) extend as far back as the seventeenth century, when France and England first struggled for the supremacy of North America. The resulting wars continued intermittently until 1760. During this period of conflict, what is now Vermont, strategically located between two waterways, the Connecticut River and Lake Champlain, was a corridor for French and Indian raiding parties harassing English settlements to the south, making it dangerous for settlement. The governors of New York and New Hampshire both claimed title to this land. New York's claim was based on the 1664 grant to the Duke of York, specifying the Connecticut River as New York's eastern boundary with New Hampshire, and New Hampshire's claim was based on the premise that the New Hampshire border logically extended as far west as the Massachusetts and Connecticut borders. Furthermore, New Hampshire had been maintaining Fort Dummer, which happened to be on the west side of the Connecticut River, north of the Massachusetts border. Boundaries between provinces, established by British officials who had never set foot in America, could be confusing and conflicting in this period. By the middle of the eighteenth century, King George's War between England and France was under way and was to continue through 1748, followed by a short period of peace.

Perhaps Governor Benning Wentworth of New Hampshire thought this would be a favorable time to create the first two towns under the New Hampshire Grants—Bennington in 1749 and Halifax in 1750[1]—and see what New York's reaction would be. Predictably, Governor Clinton of New York objected and informed Governor Wentworth that he was trespassing.[2] Since the two governors could come to no agreement, the dispute was referred to King George II, but it was not until 1764 that King George III finally ruled in favor of New York that the boundary between the two provinces was to be the west bank of the Connecticut River. Meanwhile, Governor Wentworth made an astonishing 131 grants between 1749 and 1764, when the ruling forced him to desist.[3] This was the opening phase of the New Hampshire Land Grants disputes, which were to continue, with changing adversaries, until Vermont entered the Union in 1791.[4] King George II made the six-miles square[*] grants of land in furtherance of the Crown's policy of promoting settlement (as compared to the French who were more interested in trade, i.e., furs).

Population pressure was building in southern New England, and younger sons were looking northward to "the wilderness" for inexpensive land to farm and to raise families. Perhaps they could purchase one of the undeveloped lots of 360 acres each, or portion thereof, held by the original 1750 grantees (proprietors) of Halifax, most of whom were real estate speculators[5] with connections to agent

---

[*] Six miles square is equal to six miles on each side or thirty-six square miles.

Oliver Partridge of Hatfield, Massachusetts. They obtained lots, paid expenses (for surveying), and then sold to other speculators or settlers. Sometimes land was given to veterans for military service or to legislators to influence legislation. Governor Wentworth and his relatives and friends obtained lots which they could then sell, the King collected quitrents (taxes) of one shilling per 100 acres to fill his always empty coffers, the speculators hoped to make profits, and the settler could buy a piece of land, which he then had to improve according to the charter's provisions. Governor Wentworth named the first town Bennington in 1749 and the second (ours) after the Earl of Halifax, a prominent supporter of the American colonies.

Shortly after Halifax was chartered in 1750, during the relatively quiet period before the start of the French and Indian War in 1754, there may have been an attempted settlement. Two historians note this little known event; Benjamin Hall states, "[S]ettlements [in Halifax] were commenced in 1751, but those who undertook them were not able to prosecute their plans on account of the hostility of the Indians."[6] Matt Bushnell Jones quotes a letter from Oliver Partridge to Lieutenant Governor Colden of New York, dated November 12, 1764, requesting confirmation of the Halifax grant. Partridge claimed therein, that settlement had been made in Halifax long before 1760 . . . "but we were drove off by the enemy"[7] [↪ 26]. If these two reports refer to the same unsuccessful settlement, they pose intriguing questions: First, could a settlement be initiated by circa 1751 before the resumption of war in 1754, considering that the town plat, which officially defined the grantees' lots, had not been registered until April 2, 1751? Second, would some of the grantees be ready to promptly settle or sell to others eager to settle? Regrettably, we do not have the records of the Halifax proprietors' meetings, starting in 1750. If we did we might be able to solve yet another Halifax mystery, the attempted and failed 1750s Halifax settlement.

The outbreak of the French and Indian War in 1754 resulted in a full-scale resumption of Indian raids from Canada. What protection would potential Halifax settlers have had at this time? Virtually none. Fort Dummer, near Brattleboro, had been built in 1724 to protect Connecticut River settlements, but was unable to maintain protection during this period. Also, it was too far from Halifax to respond quickly. A string of forts along the northern border of Massachusetts were built in 1744, and one, Fort Morrison, was located a few miles south of Halifax in the small town of Colrain, Massachusetts, but on the wrong side of the probable direction of attack. Western Abenaki Indians, from the protection of surrounding hills, had laid siege to the fort as late as 1759, resulting in a fierce struggle.

There apparently was a plan for the long-term safety of grants settlers. The Halifax charter reserves one acre in the center of town for each grantee. Rev. Eastman states:

> This reserved land at the geographical centre of town was
> designed to serve the purpose of a garrison in case there should be
> war with the Indians. Here each grantee might erect a block-house
> to which he might retire with his family on short notice in case of

danger while the country was new, having an acre of ground which he could cultivate as a garden. But the Indians gave no trouble to the early settlers of Halifax and the land reserved for purposes of defence has long since been otherwise disposed of.[8]

Therefore, Eastman outlines a defense plan but says it was never implemented [because there was no settlement until 1761 and by then Indians were no longer a threat].

By 1759, the tide of war turned dramatically in favor of the British. Rogers' Rangers carried out a retaliatory attack on the Abenakis in St. Francis, Quebec, destroying their ability to mount any further raids on the New England settlements and Lord Jeffrey Amherst occupied Fort Ticonderoga. These events, including General Wolfe's defeat of General Montcalm in Quebec, and earlier British victories at Fort Frontenac in Quebec and Fort Louisburg in Nova Scotia, effectively ended the French and  Indian War in America and the danger to the settlers of New England.[9] The floodgates of immigration could now open.

In 1761, the first settler arrived in Halifax.[10] This was Abner Rice, who located on Lot 7, which abuts the Massachusetts line, and was originally granted in 1750 to Gad Corse. Very little was known about Abner Rice until recently. The first concrete evidence of Rice in Halifax is a deed that records the sale of the westerly part of Lot 7 to Benjamin Henry of Colrain, Massachusetts, on December 16, 1762 [HLR 1A: 570]. This deed establishes Lot 7 as the location of the first Halifax settlement.

The first book of land records in the Halifax town clerk's office (Book 1A) starts in 1778 with the founding of the independent state of Vermont. Halifax town records for the entire period from 1750 to 1764 (under New Hampshire) and 1764 to 1777 (under New York) have been lost, with the exception of the 1750 Charter, which includes only the names of the original proprietors and a survey of their numbered lots. Research in the New Hampshire Archives revealed additional Halifax land transfers dating back to 1750.[11]

Rev. Eastman, in his article on Halifax, writes, "The grantees held meetings for business for several years, at such times and places as they saw fit to appoint. No connected record of proceedings of those meetings is in the possession of the town."[12] He refers to a vote on November 18, 1750, to raise a tax of five pounds per lot to defray specified expenses. This meeting may have taken place in Hatfield, Massachusetts, where principal proprietor Oliver Partridge and most of the original grantees lived. It is interesting that on November 19, 1750, one day after the above meeting, Joseph Barnard sold his Lot 26 to Oliver Partridge for five pounds.

An analysis of scant land transactions during 1750 shows approximately four purchases of grantee lots and one sale, all by agent Oliver Partridge, occurring on June 27, 1750, indicating that trading of lots had started.[13]

As noted earlier, there was an attempted settlement in Halifax in the early 1750s, which failed, but no further information is available. Whether any original grantees participated is unknown.

Just recently an early deed dated February 28, 1753, recorded June 30, 1788 [HLR 1A: 587], has been found. It transferred one half of Lot 61 from William Williams to Edward East, laborer, both of Deerfield. This may be the earliest deed following the flurry of trading in 1750.

There were a number of early New Hampshire deeds recorded in Book 1A including Abner Rice's 1762 deed to Benjamin Henry. Nathaniel Chipman of Vermont wrote to Alexander Hamilton of New York on July 15, 1788, of Vermonters willingness to enter the union ". . . if given assurance that the federal courts would not invalidate New Hampshire titles. . . . [The desire for this assurance may have accounted for the recording of early deeds in book 1A in 1788] Hamilton agreed that Kentucky's bid for independence from Virginia rendered this a 'favorable moment' for effecting Vermont's entry into the Union." Vermont finally entered the Union in 1791 as the fourteenth state.

©2008 *Stephen Sanders*

ENDNOTES

1. Colin G. Galloway, *The Western Akenakis of Vermont* (Norman, OK: University of Oklahoma Press, 1990) pp. 26, 141–143. The earliest permanent English settlement in the southeastern part of what is now Vermont was Fort Dummer, built in 1724 on the west side of the Connecticut River just south of the present town of Brattleboro, to provide defense during Grey Lock's War, 1723–1727. Two river towns, Westminster and Rockingham, were founded on the west side of the Connecticut in 1736, protected by small forts and blockhouses, followed by settlement in Putney in 1742 or 1743. Additional settlements were made on the east side of the river, including Fort No. 4 in 1744 at Charlestown, New Hampshire. For more on early forts and settlements along the Connecticut River see Benjamin H. Hall, *History of Eastern Vermont* (New York: D. Appleton, 1858) Chapters 1–3.
2. Frederic F. Van de Water, *The Reluctant Republic :Vermont, 1724–1791* (Taftsville, VT : Courntryman Press, 1974) pp. 40, 43. Reprint of the 1941 ed. (New York : John Day Company).
3. Walter Hill Crocket, *Vermont, The Green Mountain State*, vol. 1 (New York: The Century History Company, 1921) p. 182. For an enlightening list of the recipients of both New Hampshire grants and the subsequent New York grants, see pp. 175–200 therein.
4. Van de Water, pp. 36–59. A lively account of the land grant disputes between the govenors of New Hampshire and New York.
5. Ibid., p. 39.
6. Hall, p. 96.
7. Matt Bushnell Jones, *Vermont in the Making 1750–1777* (Cambridge, MA : Harvard University Press, 1939) p. 107.
8. Hemenway, p. 410.
9. Hall, pp. 89–92.
10. Thompson, p. 85.
11. Land Transfer Records, Division of Records Management & Archives, Concord, NH, vol. 77, pp. 27–30.
12. Hemenway, p. 411.
13. Land Transfer Records, Division of Records Management & Archives, Concord, NH, Vol. 77, pp. 27–30.

THE MAN WHO CHARTERED HALIFAX

COLONEL OLIVER PARTRIDGE

To dismiss, without further inquiry, the men named on the Halifax charter as mere land speculators who never actually settled the town closes a door to understanding how many of the earliest settlers found their way to Halifax. Land speculation was a common practice in the British colonies, especially as frontier land ceased to be the setting for warfare. The investors in the wilderness tract offered by New Hampshire governor Benning Wentworth in 1750, lived about thirty-five miles south in Hatfield and Deerfield, Massachusetts. One can read about their lives in the town histories of those places.[1] Oliver Partridge of Hatfield, age thirty-seven when he obtained the charter, was a Yale graduate who studied surveying and law and was active in town and state government. At the signing of the charter on May 11, 1750, Wentworth appointed Partridge moderator of the initial proprietors' meeting, to be held on the first Wednesday of August 1750, for choosing town officers. No record of that or any other proprietors' meeting has been found. However, the role of Partridge in shaping the early settlement of Halifax is clear and went considerably beyond buying and selling real estate.

In May 1750, Oliver Partridge was the Hatfield town clerk, an office he held from 1732 to 1784. As clerk, Partridge had continued the careful recording, begun by his predecessor, Dr. Thomas Hastings, of all Hampshire County incidents of Indian raids and casualties. The "Massacre Journal," so named by Hastings, is a record of specific Indian attacks that occurred from 1704 to 1746. The final entry written by Partridge is dated May 10, 1746, "The enemy fired upon Sergt. John Hawks and one Miles near the province fort at Hoosick and wounded them both. On the same day the enemy killed Matthew Clark, of Colerain, and wounded his wife and daughter."[2] Whereas some names on the Halifax charter are Partridge's political, military, and business acquaintances, and some are his neighbors, relatives, and in-laws, among the Halifax grantees are families that suffered losses during the French and Indian War—families, like the Hawks, whose names had appeared in the Massacre Journal.

The Massachusetts men named on the original charter were from families that had experienced several generations of frontier life. The settlement of Hatfield, Hadley, and Deerfield in the early 1700s was highly perilous and often involved life-and-death struggles for homes and fields.[3] In the *History of Hatfield,* Daniel Wells tells us, "The stress of the conflict with the French and Indians developed a group of leaders of strength and ability, who came to be known as the 'River Gods.'[4] He mentions Colonel Israel Williams and Colonel Oliver Partridge as two who succeeded Colonel Samuel Partridge (Oliver's grandfather) in political and military influence.

During the decade that preceded the charter of Halifax, Oliver Partridge, serving as a representative to the Massachusetts General Court, was enlisted by Colonial Governor Shirley to help secure the northwestern Massachusetts frontiers. Shirley appointed Oliver Partridge, Colonel John Stoddard of Northampton, and John Leonard of Springfield to construct a line of forts "from Colerain to the Dutch settlements."[5] In 1746, when word of the attack and burning of Fort Massachusetts reached Hatfield, Partridge took a party of men to investigate and to bury the dead. He also helped to rebuild the fort. In 1749, the year before he founded Halifax, Partridge was appointed by the General Court to oversee a resurvey of the tracts of land that would become Williamstown and North Adams. Many of the first settlers of those towns were soldiers who had been stationed at Fort Massachusetts.[6] The progression from frontier soldier to frontier settler, likewise, was a significant pattern in the settlement of Halifax.

THE NEW TOWNSHIP OF HALIFAX

In the spring of 1750, Oliver Partridge traveled to Portsmouth, New Hampshire, where, on May 11th, he signed the charter agreement as agent for the grantees. The date distinguishes Halifax as the *first* New Hampshire town chartered in Windham County and second of all the New Hampshire grants.

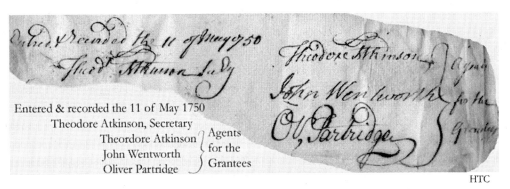

Entered & recorded the 11 of May 1750
Theodore Atkinson, Secretary

Theordore Atkinson ⎫ Agents
John Wentworth   ⎬ for the
Oliver Partridge ⎭ Grantees

HTC

"The Plan of the Township of Halifax,"[7] originally drawn in Portsmouth, included sixty-four equal shares or lots; however, sixteen acres from each of the four center shares were taken to form the sixty-four-acre center hexagon [↪ 504]. Thus one acre per each of the other shares was designated for use as common land. Lot 28, southwest and adjacent to the center common, was reserved for the "first settled minister," and the northeastern corner, Lot 64, was reserved for the school. Of the sixty-two available lots, twelve were chosen by Governor Wentworth and members of his family and council.[8] The remaining fifty lots were granted to Oliver Partridge and forty-nine others. "Entered by the Secretary of said Province upon this Plan. Each man taking his Chance whose name stands in the schedule annexed to the grant of said Township."[9] Theodore Atkinson, Secretary of New Hampshire; John Wentworth; and Oliver Partridge signed the document.

Back in Hatfield, Partridge hired a trio of rugged woodsmen[10] to drag chain and links through "six miles square" of wilderness, blazing trees, setting off roads, and, according to historian Benjamin Hall, "the lot of each owner was marked at the corners with 'lasting boundaries.'"[11] He filed the plat "made by Matthew Clesson, Surveyor and Aaron Denio and John Morrison, chain men under Oath" at the New Hampshire secretary of state's office on April 2, 1751.[12] According to Rev. Eastman, the total cost for "obtaining the survey, platting the lots and obtaining the patent was, £279, 11:6, or about $865."[13] Although he did not cite his source, apparently, Eastman viewed some original proprietor's records. He referred also to a vote, taken at the November 28, 1750 meeting, to defray the expenses of obtaining the charter and platting the lots by taxing proprietors and retaining any surplus funds in the treasury.[14]

Rev. Eastman wrote, "It is thought that Mr. Partridge became the original proprietor of nearly one-half of the town."[15] Land records of New Hampshire, Massachusetts, and Vermont confirm that Partridge ultimately owned sixteen lots, exactly one-fourth of the town. Lot 20, which on the town plat plan bears the name Oliver Partridge, became the original business center of Halifax. First settled by John Crosier, Lot 20 includes the intersection of the County and Jacksonville Stage Roads and Woodard Road. Partridge purchased fifteen additional lots in all.[16]

OLIVER'S HIGHWAY TO HALIFAX

In the Hampshire County Court of Sessions records at the Hampshire County Courthouse in Northampton, Massachusetts, is the following 1762 petition:

> Oliver Partridge in behalf of Himself and others Proprietors of the Township of Hallifax Vz which lies north of and adjoining to Colrain humbly showeth. That there are several Townships laid out northerly of Colrain particularly the Township of Hallifax where are some families settled and a number of Men at Work on the Lands in said Township and the Situation of the Land in sd Township is such it is quite necessary that there be a Communication between them and the County of Hampshire by the Way of Colrain which will be of public Service to this County as well as those people. And altho there be a County Road already laid out as far as Colrain Meeting House which is about four miles from the Line of said Township of Hallifax After repeated Applications to the Select Men of Colrain to lay out a Town Road from their meeting House to their North line they wholly neglect and refuse to lay out a road there. I would therefore humbly pray your Honors to appoint a Committee to lay a road from Colrain Meeting house to the north line of said Town so as best to accommodate the public. And as in Duty bound shall ever pray. Oliver Partridge. Read and Ordered that Elijah Williams Esq. John Hawks Esq. David Field gent. Joseph Barnard gent. and Seth Catlin gent. all of Deerfield in said County be a Committee to view and lay out the HighWay prayed for. . . . Copy & Warrant made Oct. 6th 1762[17]

One month later, the committee filed their survey, which the court approved and ordered "that ye Way therein described be herafter known as a HighWay."[18] Therefore, by November 1762, Oliver's highway offered settlers an accessible road from Hatfield, through Deerfield, Greenfield, Shelburne, and Colrain, into Halifax. The surveyors carved their initials on a tree located exactly one mile and three quarters and four rods west of the southeast corner of the township of Halifax, on the original province line. While blazes and other marked trees are long gone, the highway, now called, Route 112, is still used today.

A CHANGE IN PROVINCIAL GOVERNMENT

On July 20, 1764, by proclamation from the King-in-Council, all New Hampshire grantees were made subject to the authority of the province of New York. Partridge actively represented the town's grantees in a series of petitions, copies of which were provided by the New York State Archives.

Hatfield 12th of Nov[er] 1764 The Hon [able] Gov Colden[19]

Sir ~ Permit me to inform your Hon[or] that I have lately heard that
the King has fixed Connecticut River as the Western Boundary of
the Province of New Hampshire. From thence I conclude what was
Challenged West of the River by that Government is Under the
Jurisdiction of the Government where Your Honor is Commander in
Chief. ~ Suffer me further to inform your Hon. that in the year 1750 I
took out a Charter from Governor Wentworth in behalf of myself & a
Number of Others of a Township Six Miles Square known by the Name
of Hallifax, it lies About 12 miles west of Connecticut River & bounds
South on the Line of the Province of the Massachusetts Bay. ~ After
the Reduction of Canada we began to Settle it (yea long before but were
drove off by the enemy) and have now near forty persons who have
begun their Settlements & many of them Made good proficiency. We
are as well pleased to be Under the Jurisdiction of New York as New
Hampshire & Intirely willing to conform to their Orders what is
necessary to be done in order to secure Our possessions we are
Ignorant. Beg your Honor to Let the Hon William Smith Esq of New
York know your sentiments (as his [Justus] will Communicate them to
me) Of what must be done on our part and we shall be ready to do it.
Humbly Hope your Hon will not Suffer any Grant to be laid upon as we
have been at great expence to Settle the Kings Lands . . . ~
There are 12 rights or Shares in the Township containing about 360
acres each that were reserved by Gov. Wentworth & the Council of
New Hampshire for themselves & their friends upon which I think no
Duty has been done. We should be glad others were admitted in their
Stead who would promote the Settlement.
   I was emboldened to write to your Hon as I had once the pleasure
& Honor of an acquaintance with you. And beg leave to
      Subscribe my Self your Hon[or]
         Most Obed.~ Humbly Ser~.
                        Oliver Partridge [20]

On October 7, 1765, Partridge sent another letter to Colden:

CADWALLADER COLDEN
by Matthew Pratt   VHS

To the Honorable Cadwallader Colden esquire Lieutenant Governor & Commander in Chief of his Majesties Province of New York And to the Hon.ble his Majesties Council of the said Province.

Oliver Partridge in behalf of Himself & his Associates, Proprietors of a Township known by the name of Hallifax lying North of & adjoining to the North line of Massachusetts Bay & West of Connecticut River Most Humbly Sheweth.

That in the Year 1750 your Memorialist Obtained a Charter of the Said Township of Hallifax from his Excel.cy Governor Wentworth with the advice of his ~Your Memorialist caused the Said Township to be laid out into Sixty four equal Shares, run & well boundaries at the Corners of each Lot ~ And very soon after a Number of persons began the Settlement of Several Lots but were driven off by the Indian Enemy, And were never able to go forward with their Settlements until the Reduction of Canada Since which the Proprietors of more than forty Lots have begun their Settlements and are going forward with the Same.

Your Memorialist supposed when the Said Charter was granted that the Lands lay in the Province of New Hampshire but has been lately advised they fall into the Province of New York.

Your Memorialist begs leave further to inform your Honors that Governor Wentworth reserved sundry Lots for himself & his friends they with some others to the Number of Sixteen in the whole Neglect to do any duty [clearing and building] on Said Lands or pay any part of the Charges Arising thereon to great discouragement of the Setlers. A List of the said Lots herewith [↪ 28] presented together with a plan of the Township.

I would humbly beg in behalf of my Self & Associates that The Said Sixteen Lots may be assigned to some person who will do the Duty & Effectually bring forward the Settling on the Same. And that the Said Township may be Confirmed to your Memorialist & his associates and as in Duty bound shall ever pray.

New York Oct.o 7th 1765

Ol: Partridge

A List of the Lots in the Township of Hallifax on which the Proprietors have done no Duty.

No	1	Charles Coats	46	Jesse Heath
	8	John Wentworth, Esq[r]	51	Elnathan Graves
	10	John Wentworth Jun Esq[r]	52	Zech[er] Billing
	19	Eben[r] Wentworth	53	Abraham Bass
	34	Richard Wibird Esq[r]	55	Benjamin Munn
	35	Gov[nr] Wentworth	56	Meshack Ware Esq[r]
	40	Samuel Solly Esq[r]	61	Peter Boves
	44	Gov[nr] Wentworth	62	Oliver Graves [21]

In a letter, dated August 5, 1766, addressed "To his Excellency Sir Henry Moore, Barronet,"[22] Partridge reiterates most of what he said in letter two, and adds the following:

> May it Please your Excellency & Hon' s there is fifteen of the original prop's who utterly Neglect to do their Share of Duty
> on the Lands or pay any Taxes ~ Necessary for roads & other publick charges to the great discouragement to those who are Setling on Said Lands ~ And as I have been lately informed that the Said Township with other Lands lying West of Connecticut River are put under the Jurisdiction of the Government of New York, I beg leave to lay my Petition before your Excellency & his Maj'S Council of New York that you would be pleased to Grant the Said fifteen Lots to me that I may bring forward Settlements on them & so build up the Town. The Lots are particularly described upon a plan herewith presented. . . . Each Lot Containing 360 acres ~ I beg leave further to represent to your Excellency & Hons that at great Charge the Lots in whole Township have been laid out Marked & bounded and must be Continued in like form otherwise the Settlements will be very much Injured. The Said Town may in a Number of years prove beneficial to the publick tho it Intirely consists of mountainous Lands & is heavy Loaded with timber. And your petitioner as in Duty bound shall ever pray.
>
> Oliver Partridge [23]

Each of the preceding letters sounds the theme of promoting settlement. Since Partridge and his associates were not themselves potential settlers, their investment in Halifax resulted in their giving many acres to men who became the town's first residents. It was a condition of the New Hampshire Land Grants that five acres per every fifty acres must be cleared within five years or risk forfeiture to the Crown. Proprietors engaged in the practice of offering free land for what was known as "settling duty"—that is, clearing, building, plowing, planting, and occupying a lot. Such deeds say, "for consideration of duties being done" or "in consideration that the grantee hath cultivated and brought into improvement," or "for fully and completely performing the settling duty." Duty transactions sometimes appear as references embedded in other deeds. For example, a deed recorded in 1777, in which Oliver Partridge is grantor and Samuel Brown is grantee, describes the parcel as "North on the North line of the Lot, south on the South line of Original Lot 25, East on the Hundred Acres Given Elisha Pratt for Settlement and so far as to Make the Quantity of one Hundred and twenty five Acres" [HLR 1A: 19].

Other pioneer settlers to whom Oliver Partridge gave one hundred acres in exchange for improving the land, were: John Crosier, Lot 20; William Frazier, Lot 41; John Williams, Lot 5; Samuel Baker, Lot 54; Israel Guild, Lot 49; John Hall, Lot 50; Nathan Wilcox, Lot 39; Elijah Clark, Lot 30; Elisha Pratt, Lot 25; and David Rich, Lot 26.[24] Of his remaining lots, the records show that Oliver sold the entire Lot 11 to Robert Gillis and Lot 55 to Joseph Stebbins, who reconveyed it to Samuel Thomas. Both Gillis and Thomas settled their land and were counted in the 1771 census. Oliver's brother, Samuel Partridge, deeded one hundred acres in Lot 27 to Robert Crosier; and Dr. Jonathan Ashley, Partridge's brother-in-law, deeded one hundred acres in Lot 42 to Joseph McClure in exchange for settling. Ownership could transfer to a widow and minor children, as demonstrated in a record from 1780 in which Oliver Partridge "in consideration that Wm Frazier late of Halifax performed settling on #41," conveys "to Sarah Widow and Relict, James Petty Frazier, John, and Jabez Frazier, sons, 100 acres on East side the whole length north to south and at right angles reserving only the highway that crosses the land" [HLR 1A: 41]. The Partridge family's regard for the duty requirement promoted early settlement of the town. Eastman says it is not known if the claims of the grantees were ever questioned on this duty requirement.[25] If other proprietors conveyed land for settling duty, those records are not yet found in the Halifax books.

Among the cast of charter characters, the person least interested in the growth and prosperity of Halifax was avaricious Governor Benning Wentworth, who continuously violated the king's condition for granting land—that there be fifty families ready for immediate settlement. He foresaw when the wars ended, a land rush would begin. The idea of selling land bit by bit to individual settlers did not suit his opulent lifestyle. It would have been too much work for too gradual an income. Why not, instead, with the stroke of his quill pen, sell whole towns to men who could afford full, immediate payment, and let them assume the expense of a survey and the burdensome process of selling off individual lots? It is said Wentworth pocketed the per-share payments. Moreover, with each township granted, Wentworth could retain eight to twelve tax-free parcels for himself, his in-laws, and political allies in Portsmouth. On the Halifax town plan, the governor assigned himself adjacent Lots 36 and 44. His land was situated in what became known as Whitneyville. In 1795, Jedediah Stark, in a deed to James Bell, describes the property as "corner of Lot 36 generally known by being called the Governor's south rite or lot" [HLR 2: 305].

BENNING WENTWORTH
by Jos. Blackburn NHS

PUZZLING CHARTER QUESTIONS

o   How did Oliver Partridge and "his excellency, the realtor"[26] connect? One can only guess. After granting Bennington to a group of Portsmouth investors in January 1750, perhaps Wentworth, restless for another influx of cash, sent his prospectus to various town clerks or other prominent figures.

o   How did Governor Wentworth's council decide exactly where to locate Halifax? They placed the southeast boundary at a tree one mile west of the Green River on the New Hampshire–Massachusetts province line and ran the line west to a point approximately midway between Fort Dummer and Bennington. At the time the area was a vast wilderness criss-crossed by a few trails and two rivers.

o   How did Partridge meet and convey property to those who did settle? Much less guesswork is needed for this question: In 1754 [Oliver] was commissioned Colonel and sent back to Berkshire County by Col. Israel Williams with orders to strengthen the frontiers. In 1757, he succeeded Colonel Williams in command of the western forces. He commanded a battalion of light infantry or rangers stationed near Lake George in 1758 and was in the Battle of Fort Ticonderoga. "In the last years of the French and Indian War, Colonel Partridge was a recruiting officer for the County of Hampshire under royal authority, stationed at Fort Massachusetts."[27] Because of his service at the forts, his command of light infantry forces, and especially in his work as a recruiting officer, Colonel Partridge was in constant contact with young men from many Massachusetts and Connecticut sending towns. In a letter to his wife, Anna Williams, dated July 5–12, 1758, Partridge speaks of Rogers' Rangers leading his battalion through the wilderness between Lake George and the southern shore Lake Champlain[28] and describes, daily, the details of the campaign to take Fort Ticonderoga. The earliest settlers of Halifax were a diverse group from multiple towns. However, a common thread was, almost without exception, they all had been active either at the forts or in the final military campaigns of the French and Indian War.

o   Why didn't Oliver Partridge move to Halifax? Given the demands of his active political, military, and family life, the prospects of Oliver Partridge moving from Hatfield to Halifax were nil. Pioneering days were over for the Partridge family. They had lived in Hadley and Hatfield for four generations. William, Oliver's great-grandfather, had been a pioneer, active in the founding of seventeenth-century settlements on the Connecticut River. Oliver built an addition onto an already quite spacious family home where he and his wife, Anna, raised ten children of their own, as well as his widowed sister's three children. He was in public service his entire adult life—he was often sought after to represent the governor of Massachusetts, and often appointed to positions of trust. He was Hatfield town clerk, selectman, and representative to the General Court, and one of three Massachusetts delegates to the Stamp Act Congress. An account of his many accomplishments is given in the *History of Hatfield*.[29]

Oliver and Anna Williams Partridge lived and died in Hatfield, Massachusetts. It is difficult to imagine how Partridge found time in his active life to obtain the charter of Halifax, to communicate with New York governors on behalf of the proprietors and settlers, and to buy, sell, and promote settlement of at least a quarter of the town. It is not difficult to imagine that in his military activities, particularly those involving the border forts, Colonel Partridge may well have crossed paths with a number of men he encouraged to become early settlers of the town and to whom he gave or sold land. An interesting and somewhat ironic observation by historian Matt Bushnell Jones is that Partridge might have served as a role model for Ethan Allen. When Allen still lived in Salisbury, Connecticut on the Massachusetts–New York borders, it is thought that during the Anti-Rent War of 1766, he participated with the anti-New York forces, among whose leaders was Oliver Partridge.[30] That conflict was the model from which Allen developed the revolutionary style and strategies used by the Green Mountain Boys.

Photo courtesy Bob Drinkwater

Here lies interr'd,
the Remains of
Oliver Partridge, Esq.[r]
Who died the 21st of July,
A.D. 1792,
In the eighty-first Year
of his Age.
His usefulness in Church and State,
Was early known to men;
Bless'd with an active Life, till late,
And happy in his End.

At the time of his death in 1792, the New Hampshire tract of land Oliver Partridge had chartered forty years earlier had grown from wilderness to a community of 199 heads of families and a total population of 1,209.[31] King George III, Benning Wentworth, Cadwallader Colden, and Ethan Allen were no longer politically relevant. Halifax was now a thriving town, in a newly created county in a newly created state in a newly created country.

©2008 *Constance Lancaster*

ENDNOTES

1. Recommended sources for learning more about the men named on the Halifax charter, their families, work, and military service, are: George Sheldon's two-volume *History of Deerfield* (Deerfield, MA: Pocumtuck Valley Memorial Association, 1895–96 edition); and Daniel White Wells's three-volume *History of Hatfield, Massachusetts* (Springfield, MA: F. C. H. Gibbons, 1910).
2. Wells, p. 152.
3. Ibid., p. 160.
4. Ibid., p. 165.
5. Arthur Latham Perry, *Origins in Williamstown, A History,* 3rd ed. (Williamstown, MA: Published by the Author, 1904) p. 79.
6. Ibid. Another excellent reference is the Williams College archives Web page.

7. HTC, "Plan of the Township of Halifax," stored in the clerk's safe pending archival restoration. The surviving plan appears to be the actual raw draft and working copy used by Oliver Partridge. There are symbols and notations written on many of the numbered lots (w's and x's); however, no grantee names appear on this copy except for a note on Lot 5: "sold to Parish." The charter copies from the New Hampshire archives have grantee names inscribed on all the numbered lots and must have been a later recorded version of the plat plan. This offers a glimpse of the actual process of creating the plat plan. Whereas the grantees names are affixed to the charter, the assignment of specific lots happened later.

8. Benning Wentworth, Esq., was assigned adjacent Lots 36 and 44; Theodore Atkinson, Lot 3; Richard Wibird, Lot 34; Samuel Smith, Lot 21; Samuel Solley, Lot 40; Samson Shaeffe, Lot 16; Meshech Weare, Lot 56; Joseph Newmarch, Lot 14; John Wentworth, Lot 8; Ebenezer Wentworth, Lot 19; and John Wentworth Jr., Lot 10.

9. HTC, "Plan of the Township of Halifax."

10. Matthew Clesson of Deerfield was a scout and a lieutenant during the French and Indian War. Aaron Denio was born in Canada to Abigail Stebbins and James Denyo, who had been captured and taken to Canada in the 1704 attack on Deerfield. At the age of ten, Aaron was brought from Canada through the wilderness to Deerfield to visit and meet his grandfather Stebbins, with whom he chose to live. Aaron or his son Aaron could have been the chainman. Aaron Denio's name is on Original Lot 59 of Halifax. John Morrison, of the Colrain Morrison family, was the son of Hugh Morrison who, according to Lois Patrie, was a land speculator. In 1754, John Morrison was deeded the center section of Lot 1 in Halifax [HLR 1A: 135], which is the first known documented sale of property in Halifax to a non-original grantee or grantor.

11. Hall, p. 96.

12. New Hampshire State Papers, vol. 26.

13. Hemenway, p. 411. Eastman's total of $865 reflects the value of the dollar circa 1875.

14. Ibid.

15. Ibid.

16. From: Ebenezer Bardwell, Lots 5 and 33; Edward Partridge, Lot 11; William Bull, Lot 24; Jonathan Taylor, Lot 25; Joseph Barnard, Lot 26; Tim Childes, Lot 37; George Howland, Lot 39; Ebenezer Barnard, Lot 41; Eleazer Hawks, Lot 47; Daniel White, Lots 49 & 50; Obadiah Dickinson, Lot 54; Benjamin Munn, Lot 55; and Benjamin Shelden, Lot 60.

17. Hampshire County Court Records, *1762 Record Book for the Court of Sessions*, on microfilm, Book 7, p. 47.

18. Ibid., p. 69.

19. The addressee, per custom of the times, appears at the end of the letter but is placed at the beginning for clarity. Cadwallader Colden, scholar, physician, botanist, and political leader, was a lieutenant governor of New York who served as acting governor during the years 1760–1762, and 1763–1765, and was governor from 1769–1771.

20. New York State Archives, Albany, NY, *Letter from Oliver Partridge,* Series AO272–78: vol. 17, p. 67.

21. Ibid., vol. 20, p. 5.

22. Colonial Governor of New York, appointed by Lord Halifax in 1765. Moore died in office in 1769.

23. New York State Archives, Albany, NY, *Ol. Partridge's Memorial,* Series AO272–78: vol. 21, p. 106.

24. This is not an exhaustive list. Most of the earliest settlers did not record their first Halifax deeds.

25. Hemenway, p. 411.

26. Frederic F. Van de Water, *The Reluctant Republic: Vermont 1724–1791.* (New York: John Day, 1940) p. 36.

27. Wells, p. 174.

28. Massachusetts Historical Society, *Israel Williams Collection,* letter of Oliver Partridge to his wife.

29. Wells, p. 165.

30. Matt Bushnell Jones, *Vermont in the Making* (Cambridge, MA: Harvard University Press, 1939) pp. 280–281. Jones theorizes that from this land controversy between Massachusetts Bay, which made grants on lands claimed by New York patroons, east of the Hudson River, and New York civil authorities, whose attempts to eject the settlers on the debated lands, were flouted, Ethan Allen learned which techniques worked and which failed. "It would appear that in this Anti-Rent War we have the progenitor and the pattern of the revolution on the New Hampshire Grants." (p. 281). Jones refers the reader to Oscar Handlin, "The Eastern Frontier of New York," *New York History,* vol. xviii, no. 1, pp. 50–75.

31. First Census of the United States, 1790, Vermont (Washington, DC: Gov. Printing Office, 1907) p. 10.

First Four Families Myth

"There were but four families in the town of Halifax before 1766," Rev. Eastman said in Abby Hemenway's gazetteer. Those words have been endlessly repeated since first published in 1891 and may qualify as the most widespread myth of the chronicles of Halifax. Many more families were in town by 1766, but Eastman simply was not in a position to know about them or to have access to the records that document their presence.

While Eastman was researching and writing his Halifax history, about twenty years before the gazetteer's publication, he was interviewing people who were living in town decades after the deaths of the earliest settlers. Eastman's "four families" theory was based entirely on oral tradition. Zadock Thompson did not ask Rev. Wood for settler stories in 1823 when he set out to publish his much earlier gazetteer. Wood's circle of acquaintances surely included a large number of inhabitants who were sons and daughters of the pioneer settlers. Thompson, however, asked for statistical data; Wood responded accordingly, saying that Abner Rice settled in 1761 and the next settlers from Colrain and Pelham, Massachusetts, arrived in 1763 or 1764. Alas, he did not elaborate. If only Thompson had said, "Please send me your best bear stories!" [↵ 13]

About fifty years and another two generations later, when Hemenway requested for stories for her Vermont gazetteer, Eastman went right to work collecting them. One of his sources was "Widow Scott, Robert Crosier's daughter, now 94 years of age and able to give some statistics of the history of the first settlers."[1] Abel Scott's widow was Lydia Crosier Scott, who died at age ninety-five, just a year after Eastman interviewed her. Lydia's mother Jane Gault Crosier, died in 1850[2] having spent about eighty-five of her 105 years in Halifax. Jane was a young wife and mother during the pioneer settlement period; undoubtedly, she passed her memories down to her daughter who passed them along to Rev. Eastman. The few early surviving stories of Halifax may be attributed, in large part, to the longevity of these two women.

What Eastman actually said is, "The early records are sadly deficient, still, as nearly as can be ascertained, in the early part of the year 1766, there were but four families in the town. Mr. Rice in the east part, Capt. John Pannel and a Mr. Gaught in the southwest part (Pannel Hill) and a Mr. Pratt, who settled on the farm since occupied by Robert Collins. From the year 1766 the population of the town increased rapidly."[3] He simultaneously contradicted his assertion by saying, "Three brothers by the name of Crosier were among the first settlers in the year 1762 or '63."[4] Eastman's population tally for 1766, therefore, was off by at least three men named Crosier; moreover, he omitted more than a dozen others whose names are recorded in a nearby storekeeper's account book dating from 1764. That rediscovered ledger, in fact, now serves as an informal census of the 1766 Halifax families.[5]

THE REMARKABLE RICHARD ELLIS ACCOUNT BOOK

Known as the first settler of Ashfield, Massachusetts, Richard Ellis built a log house there and moved his family of nine from Deerfield in 1745. During the French and Indian War, Ellis served as an officer in the commissary department of the English or Colonial service in New England and New York. He was said to have been a man of strong will and remarkable memory.[6] Jane Phillips, his wife, died in 1760. In 1762, Ellis bought fifty acres in Lot 23 in Colrain where he "kept a country store and ashery."[7] He married widow Mary McCrellis Henry and played an active role in the town until about 1777, when he closed up shop and returned to Ashfield, where he died at age ninety-three. "His physical vigor and mental powers were retained in a high degree up to the last years of his life."[8] His grandson, Dimick Ellis, and great-grandson, Lewis Ellis, saved the accounting books, which they regarded as quite a curiosity for the view of articles bought, sold, and traded in pre–Revolutionary times. "In them are found the names of nearly two hundred persons who were residents of Colerain and adjoining towns."[9] In many instances, Ellis noted that a particular customer was "of Deerfield" "of Greenfield" or "of Hallifax." All transactions were dated by the month and year.

In 1956, Ruby Bruffee Austin transcribed and indexed many of the entries from the original ledger, which at that time was archived in Greenfield. Not every early settler necessarily traded with Richard Ellis, but his was the only store in the area during the first decade of Halifax settlement. The names of Halifax people recorded in the book from 1764 to 1766 are as follows:

Page 33   John Crosier of Hallifax Cr. June 1765 By 18 of Sugar.

Page 35   Samuel Clark of Hallifax Jan 1765 To paper of pins.
To Sundries, To 1 Silk Handkerchief, Dd Thomas.

Page 41   William Henderson Jr. of Hallifax. (a long list of debits and credits) Reference to Henry Henderson. A Credit in May 1765 was "By 30 pain of glass."

Page 42   Robert Pattison of Hallifax Dr Jan 1765 Nov 1766 & Feb 2 1767 paid to Aron Denio

Page 54   Abner Rice of Hallifax Dr. Jan Feb 1765 & Oct 1766 & June 1767 Cr by ashes 1765 2 Brooms 1766 R&B July 11 1768

Page 55   Deacon John Pennil Hallifax Dr Jan Feb & May 1765 Cr 1765 by 5 bu ashes

Page 60   Samuel Morison Dr Jan Apr Oct Nov 1765 Sept Oct 1766 & Aug 1. Cr 1765 By 2160 Brick

Page 68   Jeremiah Reed of Hallifax Dr Jan & Sept 1765 and no date rum by [William] Scott Cr Jan 1766 by 3 days thrashing July by Deacon Cochran Oct. by cash

Page 79   Joseph McCluer Dec. 1764 1 Testament 0 12 6 Feb 1 ax 2 12 6 Cr. Nov 27 1767

Page 80   David Bartlet of Hallifax Dr Feb 4 1765 1 ax Cr. July 1766

Page 81   James Hambleton of Hallifax Dr Dec 1764 I gauze Handkerchief 2-10-0

Page 93   Ezekiel Perrum Hallifax Dr Feb & July 1765 Cr
             July 1765 & Aug 1768
Page 94   John Clark of Hallifax Dr Feb 1765 1 ax
Page 96   Robert Crosier Dr Feb & May 1765
Page 101   David Rich May 1765 Dr To leather
Page 102   Elisha Prat Dr May & Dec. 1765 Cr July 17__
             & Bal July 12 1768
Page 114   Nathan Williams Oct 1766 Cr June 5,
             1768 by Abner Newton
Page 115   William Galt Dr Aug 1766 June 20 1767 Cr June 20 1767

From these records, it is evident within five years after the arrival of the first settler; at least twenty more families were active in Halifax. The names John Bolton, Isaac Orr, Deacon John Cochran, Abner Newton, Benjamin Henry, and William Wilson also appear in the Ellis account book, but there is no clear indication of whether they were still living in Colrain in 1765/66 or had moved to Halifax. By 1767, James Taylor and Benjamin Henry can be added to the confirmed "of Halifax" list. On page 103 of the ledger, dated July 1767, "James Taylor in Halafax" paid 14 shillings for a knife and pens. Patrie says Benjamin Henry "married at Greenfield, Feb. 17, 1767, Martha Ayers, dau. of Samuel, and soon removed to Halifax, VT."[10]

Oral traditions tend to be comfortable and cozy like old slippers. Chances are the oft-told settlement myths, including Eastman's story that there were only four families in Halifax in 1766, will prevail despite what the actual written sources show and what this history documents. Settlers arrived steadily during the 1760s, because it was now safe to migrate. Written records for Halifax Township during that period are missing. Boundary lines for that period are uncertain. More certain than the ledger "census" is the actual census count for Cumberland County taken in 1771. In that year fifty-five pioneer Halifax families were recorded by name.

Stories of several of these earliest families of Halifax are told in the pages that follow. Brief biographical accounts of some other families are included as well. And every family listed in the 1771 census appears in the "Early Settlers Chart." [↪ 132] We are indebted to a number of descendants of these families who have shared information from their personal records and research.

Of the original founding families, Crosier is the only family name that has continued to present-day Halifax. And in the words of the venerable Rev. Eastman, "as far as can be ascertained"* there are only three families[11] currently living in town that can trace their Halifax lineage back to the pre-1766 settlers. They are descendants of Arthur, John, and Robert Crosier; Elisha Pratt; John Pennell; and Jane Gault.

---

* At the time of this writing, it has not been possible to research every settler family for other possible connections to today's Halifax families. With the exception of the Crosiers, all such connections must be traced through maternal lines and involve multiple surnames. Thus the use of the phrase, "As nearly as can be ascertained."

Photo S. Sanders

This 18th century foundation built into the bank, typically known as a bank house, is located on the original Benjamin Henry property in Lot 7.

Those who journeyed to wilderness Halifax in the 1760s were hardy, courageous people. They overcame both natural and political obstacles in order to clear land, break soil, build foundations, and create community. Past, present, and future Halifax residents are under a lasting obligation to the men and women of this pioneer period.

~ *Constance Lancaster*

ENDNOTES

1. Hemenway, p. 408.
2. Ironically, both Jane Gault Crosier and her daughter, Lydia Crosier Scott, were neighbors of Thomas Wood and outlived him. Had he been asked to do so, Wood could have interviewed Jane Gault and recorded her stories firsthand.
3. Hemenway, p. 412.
4. Ibid., p. 408.
5. If Eastman's intention was to list only families and not include unmarried men, his count, nevertheless, still falls far short.
6. E. R. Ellis, *Biographical sketches of Richard Ellis: the first settler of Ashfield, Mass., and his descendants* (Detroit, MI: W. Graham Print, 1888) p. 13.
7. Ibid.
8. Ibid.
9. Ibid.
10. Patrie, p. 79-G.
11. The grandchildren of Bernice Burnett Barnett and Carrie Burnett Perna are eighth- and ninth-generation descendants of the following: Elisha Pratt through his daughter, Sally Pratt Learnard; Robert and Jane Gault Crosier through their daughter Lydia Crosier Scott; John Crosier through his daughter Martha Crosier Whitney. Lawrence (Larry) Crosier is a sixth-generation descendant of Arthur Crosier and a seventh generation descendant of Deacon John Pennell through his daughter Hannah Pennell Smith. Bernice, Carrie, and Larry are lifelong residents of Halifax.

First Settler
The Search for the Right Mr. Rice

All written accounts of the settlement of Halifax begin in 1761 with one man, Abner Rice of Worcester County, Massachusetts. Always known as "the first settler," Rice otherwise has remained a somewhat enigmatic individual—lacking a biography, a family, or a gravestone. In Hemenway's gazetteer, Rev. Eastman introduced the story that Rice was "shot for a bear while watching a field of grain" sitting under an apple tree "in company with others."[1] Further details of the incident and sources were not given. Not even a date. Mr. Rice's accidental death, if true, predates Halifax's earliest written records that began in 1778 and the earliest Vermont newspapers that began in 1781.[2] In 1788, when John Gault was accidentally shot in Halifax, the *Vermont Gazette* of Bennington published a report. More than a dozen newspapers through-out New England and as far distant as Pennsylvania, repeated the "Captain Gnault" story[3] [↪ 171]. Jonathan Kellogg's eyewitness account[4] and Captain Gault's gravestone provide vivid documentation of that event. In contrast, Rev. Eastman's account, written circa 1875, is the only known report of the accidental shooting of Abner Rice, and it appeared at least a century after the purported incident.

Photo S. Sanders
Ancient apple tree located on the Benjamin Henry portion of Lot 7 in Halifax, originally owned by Abner Rice.

Although records confirming Rice's tenure in Halifax are sparse, his presence is clearly documented. The name Abner Rice appeared on two 1770 settlers' petitions prepared in response to New York's claiming authority over all lands previously granted by New Hampshire. In 1771, when New York conducted a census of its "Vermont" territory, Nathan Williams, constable, identified Abner Rice as head of a family belonging to Halifax, Cumberland County, New York. A less formal but no less significant documentation of the man's presence in town was found in a ledger. Starting about the year 1764, and until 1777, Richard Ellis "kept a country store and ashery in the north-east part of Colerain"[5] and faithfully recorded his business transactions. Local folks, including Abner Rice, paid for goods such as nails, buttons, salt, and rum with ashes that Ellis would convert into pearl ash. Rice paid with ashes and brooms. "Abner Rice of Hallifax Dr [debit] Jan Feb 1765 & Oct 1766 & June 1767. Cr [credit] by ashes 1765 2 Brooms 1766 R & B [reconciled and balanced] July 11 1768."[6] His name appears in the ledger again under the date August 15, 1771.

In 1778, when the existing Halifax record books were set up, Abner Rice's family, evidently, had left town. Their names are missing from all Halifax records with one exception. Among pages of miscellaneous deeds at the back of the first town book is an entry, dated 1788, saying on December 18, 1762 Abner Rice, of Halifax, New Hampshire, quitclaimed a tract of 182 acres on the west side of Original Lot 7, to Benjamin Henry, of Colrain, Massachusetts. The agreement was acknowledged before Elijah Williams Justice of the Peace, Hampshire County, Massachusetts, in July 1765. This unique[7] deed appears without acknowledgement of a Halifax town clerk or Justice of the Peace [HLR 1A: 570]. A search for the Rice/Henry deed in Hampshire County proved fruitless, although several other deeds for the family of Benjamin Henry were discovered there. Nor did the Hampshire County Registry yield the most hoped-for original deed conveying Lot 7 from Gad Corse to first settler Abner Rice.

Until the current owner of the Benjamin Henry property, Stephen Sanders, published his articles for the Windham County and Halifax Historical societies, few if any additional details about our first settler had come to light. Sanders' articles refer to Andrew Ward's *Genealogical History of the Edmund Rice Family,*[8] which states that Abner Rice, born in 1726, youngest son of Daniel Rice and Judith Taylor "removed to Vermont and commenced the settlement of the town of Halifax in 1761." No further details are given in the Ward volume or its supplements. It turns out Ward credited the settlement of Halifax to the wrong Abner Rice.

FROM THE WRONG TO THE RIGHT RICE

The identity of Abner Rice was a priority verging on obsession for this writer, from that October evening in 1991, when I first met the town history committee and offered to help with genealogical research. For a decade, Rice was at the top of my research checklist on visits to historical societies and libraries. In 1994, when the computer joined our household, I joined the Rice-L Listserv at http://www.rootsweb.com, posted and monitored queries, and in 1996, requested and received a packet containing every Vermont Abner Rice census record and reference—all to no avail. Increasingly, it seemed that Sanders' lively and compelling account of the Henry/Rice families and exchange of property would be the full story. Stephen had searched records at Colrain and Greenfield, places I had not visited, and he, too, had fervently sought answers to the Abner Rice questions—identity, tenure in Halifax, family, home site, and manner of death. Both of us were disappointed that so little was known about the town's first settler, especially with this history book in progress.

In the autumn of 2001, our research fortunes changed. Bits of new and different information appeared simultaneously from Internet postings and the discovery of an old letter. The first of the Internet postings referred to the Abner Rice "identity unknown," who in 1754 had married Experience Shepard of Westfield, Massachusetts. The couple had "removed to Black River Country."[9]

Another posted message asked "whether the Abner Rice who had married Martha Daniels in 1752 was the Abner Rice born in 1726, son of Daniel and Elizabeth, or was he the Abner Rice, born in 1732, son of Charles and Rachel?" The message further stated, "It is known that Abner and Martha (Daniels) Rice removed from Spencer, Massachusetts to Halifax, Vermont (Bennington area) shortly after the birth of their daughter Thankful (b. 1758)."[10] The third source was a 1972 letter of inquiry on file at the Halifax Historical Society from a woman seeking help with her "Halifax Abner."

> Information recently received from the National Archives
> indicates that Abner Rice resided in Halifax from 1761 to 1774,
> approximately. Do your vital records for this period indicate the
> birth of any children to Abner (and Martha) Rice, especially by the
> names of Rachel, Sylvanus and John? If so, please give details.

The writer of the letter was sent a copy of Eastman's Abner Rice account from Hemenway's gazetteer. In her lightning fast reply, she said:

> What I'd like to know is when Abner was shot, was he killed? If
> so, he's not our Abner! For our Abner was living in Shaftsbury in
> 1790. So I'm hoping the shot just glanced off somewhere and he
> continued to sit there, watching that field of grain.[11]

The 1972 correspondence clearly indicated that information regarding the Halifax Abner Rice could be found in the National Archives; thus we scheduled a trip to the National Archives and Records Administration (NARA) in Pittsfield, Massachusetts. Meanwhile, I contacted both of the Internet posters.

Bonnie Wiley graciously shared her files for Abner and Experience Rice's descendancy. Their children were Experience, Lydia, Hannah, Abner Jr., William, and Daniel (births between 1757 and 1774). Abner Rice (1726), whom Ward had called the first settler of Halifax, was son of Daniel and had an older brother, William, so there were naming similarities. A close rereading of Ward's data for that family revealed that William had died, unmarried, in 1742, and his inventory included land in Westfield, Massachusetts.[12] Abner Rice (1726), as the youngest son, had inherited only his father's surveying tools and no land. It seems that William bequeathed his land in Westfield to his brother, Abner, who moved there, met and married Experience Shepard, raised a family, and eventually moved to "The Black River Country." A visit to the Hampden County Registry in Springfield, Massachusetts confirmed this theory.[13] Abner and Experience are recorded in the 1810 census for Edwards, St. Lawrence County, New York, through which the Black River flows. Their Rice descendants for at least five generations include sons named Abner, none of whom lived in or near Halifax. It seems certain that Abner Rice (1726) settled in Westfield, Massachusetts, not in Halifax, Vermont.

After ruling out Abner Rice (1726), there remained the job of confirming the presence in Halifax of Abner Rice (1732). For this information, I headed back to the Revolutionary War records at NARA. Pension file S14291 for RICE,

ABNER [Jr.] Continental (Vt), seventeen pages long, offered significant help but did not answer all questions. The most important details are found in the deposition given by Rice himself:

State of New York St. Lawrence County
On the twenty fifth day of September 1832, personally appeared in open court, before the Judge of the Court of Common Pleas in the said County now sitting, Abner Rice, aged 77 years the 18th day of November last, was a resident of Potsdam in said County and State who being first duly sworn according to law doth, on his oath, make the following declaration in order to obtain the benefit of the Act of Congress passed June 7th 1832. That he entered the service of the United States under the following named officers and served as herein stated. That in the fall of 1775 he went from Bennington, Vermont, his place of residence thence to Nottingham West in New Hampshire, that while there he enlisted as a volunteer for one year from the 1st of January 1776 under Capt. Varnum in what he understood to be Rhode Island Forces that immediately after his term of service commenced, he marched to Prospect Hill and joined Col. Varnum's Regiment where he remained until after the British evacuated Boston. . . . He marched from Boston to Providence to New London and New York where he remained about one month and then went to Long Island and was there through the battle at Brooklyn under the American generals, Putnam, Lee and Sullivan. . . . The Regiment to which he belonged passed from Red Hook near Brooklyn on Long Island to New York. He remained at New York a short time when the American Troops retreated from the City . . . and was with the sick at New York when his year expired on the 1st day of January 1777. . . . He returned home at the expiration of his term of service without any written discharge. . . .

He further saith that he was born in Brookfield, Worcester County in Massachusetts. At 4 years of age moved to Cold Rain in the State of New Hampshire, lived there 2 years and moved to Halifax, N. H. and lived there 13 years and moved to Bennington Vt. where he resided in the Revolutionary War. In 1777 he moved from Bennington to Shaftsbury Vermont and lived about thirteen years and moved to Cambridge, Vermont and lived there ten or eleven years and moved to Potsdam where he has ever since resided and now resides. He has no record of his age.

Subscribed & Sworn
this day & year aforesaid

Abner Rice

The file contains depositions from Abner's brother, John Rice of Locke in Cayuga County, New York, and from his neighbors, William Pike and Clement Carpenter. Abner Rice was on the pension rolls as of May 1833. What the pension file documents is Abner Rice, born on November 19, 1755, in Brookfield, Massachusetts, lived in Colrain, Massachusetts (1759–1760), Halifax (1761–1774), Bennington (1775–1777), Shaftsbury (1777–1790), and Cambridge, Vermont (1791–1802), had a brother named John, and resided in Potsdam, New York, from about 1802 until 1832, where he applied for his pension. Although his parents are not named in the deposition, there is ample evidence to conclude that the "Pensioner" Abner Rice was the son of the Abner Rice who "commenced the settlement of Halifax."

FROM WESTBOROUGH TO BROOKFIELD

Finding the right Mr. Rice made it possible to learn more about the background of Halifax's first settler. Abner Rice was born September 17, 1732 in Westborough, Worcester County, Massachusetts. He was the tenth and youngest child of Charles Rice of Marlborough and Rachel Wheeler, of Concord, Massachusetts. Abner Rice's grandfather, Thomas, a son of Edmund who came from England to Sudbury, Massachusetts in 1638, is thought to have been the first settler of Chauncy, a part of Marlborough that eventually became Westborough. According to the Edmund Rice Association, many generations of Rices were pioneer settlers.[14] This certainly has been true in Windham County. In addition to Halifax, the first settlers of Guilford and Somerset were Edmund Rice descendants.

Abner Rice's grandfather, Thomas Rice of Marlborough, Massachusetts, married his cousin, Anna Rice, and was a representative to the General Court at Boston. Their son Charles, father of "Halifax" Abner, was born July 7, 1684, the second of fourteen children. Worcester County was frontier territory, and in 1704, Charles's younger brothers, Ashur and Adonijah, and their cousins Silas, Timothy, and Nahor were working in the fields with their fathers when attacked by Utt Indians, who killed the youngest child, Nahor, and carried the others to Canada. Adonijah, Silas, and Timothy adapted to the culture of their captors and chose to stay in Canada. After four years, Ashur, the oldest of the kidnapped Rice boys, who did not adapt, was offered for ransom. Thomas redeemed his son and brought him home to Westborough. The story of the Rice boys has been subject of great interest in the annals of the Rice family.[15] For Abner Rice, his father, Charles, and grandfather, Thomas, and for Ashur, who never fully recovered from his ordeal, the saga was an ongoing part of their lives.

Charles farmed and built a house on land deeded to him by his father in Westborough and built a second larger house in 1737. In these homes, he and Rachel raised eight sons and two daughters. Ironically, even though the first settler of Halifax has no surviving home site, two of his boyhood houses still exist and are registered with the Massachusetts Historical Commission. The home that belonged to Abner Rice's grandfather, Thomas, is now the Westborough Country Club.[16] Rice's father, Charles, appears in Westborough town and church records, was a selectman, and served in the military nearly all his life. His sons Zebulon,

Adam, Adonijah, and Charles were soldiers in Fay's Company from Westborough. By 1757, after the death of Rachel, Charles and sons Zebulon, Abner, and Charles appear in Brookfield, Massachusetts. French and Indian War muster rolls of Brookfield note that Indians killed Abner's brother, Charles, in 1758. A week after his death, Charles's widow, Leah Jennings, gave birth to their first child. Later, she married Captain Jesse Burk, moved to Westminster, Vermont, and is buried in the Old East Parish Cemetery. One of Abner Rice's brothers, Oliver of Hardwick, Massachusetts, married Hannah Barrett and settled in Bennington Vermont. Another brother, Adonijah died in Revolutionary War service in 1777. Ward says "Abner Rice married Martha Daniel 1752, had one child at Westborough and moved away, probably to Brookfield, from which town he was a soldier in Maynard's company, Williams' regiment, in 1758."[17]

FROM BROOKFIELD TO HALIFAX - FRENCH AND INDIAN WAR CONNECTION

Without a deed from Original Lot 7 proprietor Gad Corse to Abner Rice or any deeds from Abner Rice or his heirs conveying the eastern half of Lot 7, one can only speculate about the Rice connection to land in Halifax. Charles Rice and his sons were active participants in the latter campaigns of the French and Indian War. This may have brought them in contact with some of the Massachusetts men from Hatfield and Deerfield whose names were on the original Halifax charter. A number of those men were second generation "Indian Fighters." Military service was, at times, rewarded with tracts of land. Fallstown (Bernardston) and Williamstown are examples of this practice. Expeditions at the close of the French and Indian War were populated with men from Brookfield, Pelham, and Ware. Many of these men actively manned the row of forts along the Massachusetts/Vermont border, including the fort at Colrain.

According to George Sheldon in his *History of Deerfield*, Gad Corse, born in 1723 in Deerfield, was "a tanner, soldier in French wars, was much employed in transporting military stores, driving cattle to the frontier armies and riding post for the commanders."[18] Brookfield supplied soldiers to the various campaigns, and in 1758, Abner Rice is on "the list of Brookfield men in the service" for the expeditions against Louisburg, Fort Duquesne, and Ticonderoga.[19] In addition to Rice, North Brookfield muster rolls for the last French and Indian War include the names Rainger, Bemis, Rich, Whitney, Baker, Kellogg, Hamilton, McClure, Bartlett, Smith, and Henderson—names that soon appear on deeds of landowners in Colrain and Halifax. It is conceivable that while in service in 1758, Rice met Gad Corse, or possibly even Benjamin Henry, who, according to Lois Patrie, was "present at the attempted storming of Fort Ticonderoga."[20] Gad Corse may have offered Rice settling rights or sold him the entire lot, if it was still in his name. Unless undiscovered records come to light, we may never know how, why, and precisely where Abner Rice and his family lived in Lot 7.

FROM HALIFAX TO BENNINGTON TO SHAFTSBURY

When Abner and Martha Rice) arrived in Halifax in 1761 they were about thirty years old. Peletiah was seven; Abner Jr., six; Archibald, five; and Thankful, three years of age. Abner Rice must have done the major share of land clearing and building. Chances are he had no more than an axe, adz and an auger with which to fell and limb giant trees, to build shelter, clear land, and make crude furniture for his family. Given their youthful ages, it is likely that more children were born to Abner and Martha, either in Colrain or Halifax, or both. Perhaps there was a daughter, Rachel, born in 1760. We know there was another son John, because of his deposition in the pension file. He may, in fact, have been the first male child born in Halifax. One wonders how close the Rice family lived to Benjamin Henry and his young family. By the time of the 1771 Cumberland County census, there were fifty-four other families in town. The Pattisons and Clarks would have been their neighbors. What kind of social life was possible for the older Rice children, especially as they neared marriageable ages? Did the family leave town, circa 1774, because Abner Rice was "shot for a bear"? His sons were old enough to hunt. Could it have been a domestic accident? Probably not. Such a story would have been more memorable and powerful than the one told by Rev. Eastman. If the shooting story is true, and the accident proved fatal, Rice would have been about forty-two years old at the time of his death under an apple tree in Halifax. Martha Rice would have relied on her three oldest sons, ages twenty-one, nineteen, and fifteen to help with the move to Bennington, where their uncle Oliver Rice lived. There is no Abner Rice probate record; there is no record of transfer of the Abner Rice property. There is no known Abner Rice gravesite.

In Bennington, Peletiah, and Abner Jr. volunteered to serve in the Revolution. Peletiah's earliest enlistment record is from January 1776,[21] as was Abner Rice's. On Christmas Eve, 1777, Thankful Rice married Robert Cochran, also a soldier of the Revolution. That same year, Peletiah married Mary Dutcher.[22] Robert Cochran was part of a Bennington proprietor's group that settled the northern Vermont town of Cambridge on the Lamoille River. Thus Thankful was once again a pioneer settler. Robert and Thankful's daughter, Martha, was the first death recorded in Cambridge, Vermont, in April of 1788. Colonel Cochran died in Cambridge, September 20, 1807, and is buried there.

After the Revolution, three of Abner and Martha Rice's sons served in the Vermont Militia. National Archives muster and payroll records for Captain Abbot's Bennington regiment include slips for Ensign Peletiah, and John and Abner Rice, who were serving in the same regiment in 1781. Abner Rice is listed on a militia roll with Winslow Perry for service in the alarm at Cambridge and Saratoga in July of 1781. In Shaftsbury, Winslow Perry married Rachel Rice, perhaps the daughter of Abner and Martha, born in 1760, two years after Thankful. Both Rachel Rice Perry and Thankful Rice Cochran were living in Milan, Huron County, Ohio, at the time they filed for and were granted Revolutionary War widows' pensions.

Traces of Abner and Martha Rice in Shaftsbury are scant. Leonard Deming's *Vermont Officers and Gazetteer,*[23] states that at the first Shaftsbury town meeting held on April 13, 1789, Abner Rice was elected constable. This might have been Abner Rice, Sr., if still alive; more likely it was his thirty-four-year-old son. Early records of the town are said to have burned in the home of town clerk, Jeremiah Clark. No land or cemetery records for this Rice family have been located.

Census records for 1800 indicate that Abner Rice Jr. and his brother Archibald Rice had joined Thankful and Robert Cochran in the settlement of Cambridge, Vermont. By 1803, when the first settlement of Potsdam, St. Lawrence County, New York, commenced, listed among the first group of settlers was "Abner Royce" from Vermont.[24]

Even though many of the missing pieces of the Abner Rice puzzle have been found, the first settler of Halifax continues to perplex and daunt researchers. It is good to have identified this man after years of searching. Born into a frontier family, he moved from frontier to frontier before finding his way to the Halifax wilderness where he made brooms and may have been accidentally shot. There is, of course, the second Abner Rice of Halifax—Abner, junior; at age six, he too was a pioneer settler. At age forty-six, like his father, he was clearing and settling wilderness land, this time in upstate New York. Without the words of his pension deposition, we may never have known for certain who was the right Mr. Rice.

©2008 *Constance Lancaster*

ENDNOTES

1. Hemenway, p. 415.
2. Elizabeth Cooley, *Vermont Imprints Before 1800* (Montpelier, VT: Vermont Historical Society, 1937) p. xiii.
3. *Early New England Newspapers 1690-1876*, online database by Newsbank, Chester, VT.
4. Hemenway, p. 420.
5. E. R. Ellis, *Biographical Sketch of Richard Ellis: The First Settler of Ashfield, Mass. and His Descendants* (Detroit, MI: W. Graham Print Co., 1888) p. 13.
6. HHS. Ruby Austin notes copied from *The Richard Ellis Account Books*, pp. 54–184 and located by Stephen Sanders in Colrain. This list includes the names of specific traders and dates of their trading activities.
7. The Rice/Henry deed is unique because no other record has been found documenting transfer of property between two settlers during the period Halifax was under the jurisdiction of New Hampshire.
8. Andrew Henshaw Ward, *A Genealogical History of The Rice Family: Descendants of Deacon Edmund Rice* (Boston: C. Benjamin Richardson, 1858).
9. Posted by Bonnie Wiley, http://rootsweb.com
10. Posted by Ryan D. Wood, http://genforum.genealogy.com
11. HHS, letters from Margaret Rotchford, 1972 (used by permission of Miss Rotchford).
12. Andrew Henshaw Ward, *A Genealogical History of The Rice Family*, (Boston: C. Benjamin Richardson, 1858) pp. 54–55.
13. Deeds located at the Hampshire County Courthouse in Springfield, Massachusetts confirm ownership of Westfield land by William, son of Daniel Rice, as well as Abner Rice and also Abner, son of Abner and Experience Rice.
14. Edmund Rice Association Web page, http://www.widomaker.com/igwklera/edmund.htm
15. For a full account, see "The Rice Boys Captured," posted by John Buczek on his Web site, http://freepages.history.rootsweb.com/~historyofmarlborough/thericeboys.htm
16. John Buczek, http://freepages.history.rootsweb.com/~historyofmarlborough/thomasrice1sthouse.htm
17. Ward, p. 254.
18. George Sheldon, *A History of Deerfield, Massachusetts, Vol. II* (Deerfield, MA:Potumtuck Valley Memorial Association, 1983) p. 134.
19. J. H. Temple, *History of North Brookfield, Massachusetts* (published by the Town of North Brookfield, 1887) p. 216.
20. Patrie, p. 79-H.
21. NARA, Pension Record #S14286, Pelatiah Rice (microfilm).
22. Pelatiah Rice was born April 1, 1753 in Westboro, Middlesex County, MA, son of Abner Rice and Martha Daniel. He married Mary Dutcher. His grave is in Union Cemetery, towns of Westfield and Portland, New York. His place of enlistment was Walloomsac, Rensselaer County, NY. Government marker at his grave: "Ensign Rice, Vt. Mil." He is on the pension list of 1831, aged 79 years, and residing in Chautauqua County, NY.
23. Leonard Deming, *Catalogue of the Principal Officers of Vermont 1778–1851* (Middlebury, VT: author, 1851) p. 180.
24. J. H. French, *Historical and Statistical Gazetteer of New York State* (Syracuse, NY: R. P. Smith, 1860) p. 582.

Journey of Origins
Elisha Pratt – the Progenitor

As research began on the Pratt lineage, curiosities led to a journey of origins. From where did this family come from and what brought Elisha Pratt to Halifax? Was there something in his background that motivated him to venture into undeveloped land? Was there a connection between his family and some of the other early families who came to Halifax? How much did their connections in the early militia and Revolutionary War influence them? The following findings principally include only those descendants who lived and reside in Halifax today some 240+ years later.

It cannot be determined from the early records precisely what year Elisha Pratt stepped into Halifax, but it appears that he arrived in the early 1760s. A deed dated the twelfth day of September 1753,[1] records that Elisha Pratt, from Westown, Massachusetts, purchased land in Ware, Massachusetts. He sold the

same property to David Pratt, quite likely his brother, which is recorded in a deed dated April 8, 1762.[2] It is clear from the pension record of Elisha's son, James, that "he was born in Ware, Massachusetts on March 25, 1763 and moved when very young to Halifax, Vermont."[3] Elisha may have arrived in Halifax as early as 1762 before James's birth, as it seemed to be a pattern that the men first explored new territory, prepared the land, built a home, then brought the family along. What James meant when he said "very young" is uncertain.

Evidence suggests there were other members of Elisha's family among some of the early settlers in Halifax. Elisha's sister, Elizabeth, born in 1733, married Simeon Blackmer on August 18, 1754 in Warren, Worcester County, Massachusetts. Simeon Blackmer is listed in Halifax in the Early Settlers Census of 1771 [↪ 132]. John Blackmer (possibly a brother or cousin to Simeon) owned property along the Ware River in Massachusetts, close to Elisha's property. Elisha's sister, Thankful, b. circa 1740, married a Peter Pattison (Patterson). During the grants controversies, Peter Pattison signed the 1770 and 1778 petitions. Another sister of Elisha, Hannah, who was born in 1746, married a Samuel Brown in 1767 in Ware, Massachusetts. A Moses Brown also owned property just east of the Ware River in 1786. On July 5, 1777, Samuel Brown purchased in Halifax one hundred and twenty-five acres from Oliver Partridge in Lot 25 [HLR 1A: 19] . . . East of the hundred acres given Elisha Pratt for settlement by Oliver Partridge [HLR 1A: 127]. On October 12, 1778, Brown sold a portion of Lot 25 to Andrew Rutherford from Ware, Massachusetts [HLR 2: 83]. Without doing a complete genealogical search on Samuel Brown, it is unclear as to whether the Samuel Brown who is listed as one of the original grantees on the charter in 1750 was connected to the Samuel Brown who married Hannah Pratt and is listed on the 1771 census on Lot 25. Given the evidence that Elisha was originally from Ware, Massachusetts, and that his sister, Hannah's marriage to Brown took place in Ware, there is strong evidence to suggest that this was the same Samuel and Hannah Brown who lived in Halifax. It is possible that the names of Elisha's sisters, Thankful and Elizabeth, did not appear on the early records because women did not generally sign documents. Elisha's wife's sister, Elizabeth Fletcher, married David Rich and lived for a time in Amherst,

Massachusetts before arriving in Halifax. Rich is listed on the 1771 census in Halifax as head of household. For his settling duty, Rich received from Oliver Partridge the north portion of Lot 26. In this case, both he and Elizabeth's signatures appear on the deed when the property was sold to John Sawtell on September 13, 1782 [HLR 1A: 198]. Elisha was in town in

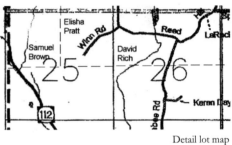

Detail lot map

1765 because his name is recorded in sequence with David Rich in the Richard Ellis account book[4] [⌐ 34]. Ellis kept records for his store in Colrain, Massachusetts, where he recorded the dates and transactions of customers from Halifax, Vermont, and Colrain, Deerfield, and Greenfield, Massachusetts. The fact that David Rich settled on the north half of Lot 26, Samuel Brown settled on the northwest side of Lot 25, and Elisha Pratt settled on the northeast side of Lot 25 provides additional support for their close ties.

It was common that the first names of families be carried on in subsequent generations. In many cases, it was important enough that when a child died early, the next brother or sister was given the same name. In Elisha's brother David's line a few of the common names were Elihu, Warner, Edward, and William. Those same names appeared in Halifax in later years on deeds and other records. Whether these are from David's line is unclear.

THE FAMILY HERITAGE FROM PLYMOUTH TO HALIFAX

> The Pratts were early settlers of this State. Among the outstanding
> characteristics of all pioneers are courage, self-reliance, ambition
> and initiative; and these attributes seem to have been passed on
> from one generation to another of Vermonters and wherever they
> went, these men made good on their own account.[5]

Elisha brought with him to Vermont a rich pioneering heritage left by his great-great uncle Phineas Pratt,[6] who was one of the first English inhabitants of the Massachusetts Colony,[7] and his great-great grandfather, Joshua Pratt,[8] who arrived in Plymouth on the ship *Anne* in 1623.[9] Just as Phineas and Joshua Pratt were influential in the beginnings of the New World, Elisha was instrumental in the founding of Halifax and the new state of Vermont. In 1662, Phineas Pratt submitted a paper of his narrations entitled *A Declaration of the Affairs of the English People That First Inhabited New England,* which is printed in the *Massachusetts Historical Collections.*[10] Both Phineas and Joshua are found listed together on various lists in both *The Great Migration Begins, Immigrants to New England, 1620–1633* and *Plymouth Colony, Its History and People, 1620–1691,*[11] along with familiar names such as William Bradford, the first governor of the Plymouth Colony and Captain Miles Standish,[12] who led the citizens' militia.[13] Joshua Pratt served in various capacities during the early settlement of Plymouth: Between the years 1623 and 1648 he was listed in the Division of Land and Cattle, was a messenger and constable, which in those days was similar to a minor governor rather than a policeman. He was repeatedly listed as viewer or layer of land, viewer of the hay grounds, an arbiter, sealer of weights and measures; he was listed among the men "Able to Bear Arms of the Plymouth Colony," and was twenty-fifth on a list of purchasers of large tracts of land that sold for a profit.[14]

Elisha, b. 1728, is the fifth generation and his son the sixth generation to venture out into undeveloped land, following in Joshua's footsteps some one hundred-plus years after his arrival in the New World.

> Elisha Pratt, son of Elisha b. 1729 [1728] & Lucy Fletcher and a friend "Cole" left Pawlet VT in 1801, each with an axe and a gun, and leading a cow and arrived on the east side of the Lake where there were only 2 or 3 houses. Elisha Jr. m. Elizabeth Saunders, dau. of Thomas Saunders and Elizabeth Cross. One week after the marriage he bought 100 acres of land for one pound of flour and nine pounds of pork per acre. They lived and died on that land and bult a house of Greek revival architecture.[15]

Only four of Elisha and Lucy's ten children remained in Halifax for any length of time. Two grandsons married Halifax girls. Elisha, son of James, married Lucy Sumner, b. 1800, in 1820. Lucy was the daughter of Joel Sumner and Elizabeth Warren Everett, who were married in 1786. Another grandson, James, son of Elijah Pratt, married a Sarah Wells.

Elisha and Lucy's Children

Lucy married Banks Bennet and resided on Lots 26 and 34. Although families sometimes did not record the details of their marriages, births, and deaths, fortunately they often recorded these details in their family Bibles or on a page of the land records. One could learn much from this type of record, as in the case of Lucy and Banks Bennet Their record spans eleven years, beginning with their marriage on December 21, 1776 and ending with Lucy's death the same day their daughter Lucy was born.[16] In 1795, Banks sold a portion of his land bordering "his dwelling house" to Joseph Swain [HLR 5: 103]. In 1801, fourteen years after his wife's death, while living in Pawlet, Vermont, he sold his remaining property to Cyrus Miner [HLR 3: 176].

JAMES continued to live in Halifax six years after his marriage to Sarah Gillis on February 7, 1788, before moving to Pawlet, Vermont in 1794. Although no written records of their children's births have been found in Halifax, it is likely the first three of their ten children were born in Halifax because in the census of 1790, James Pratt is listed as head of household with two boys under sixteen, one girl under sixteen, (along with his wife).

DORCUS married Nathan Loomis Jr. of Ashford, Connecticut. On July 3, 1780, Nathan purchased from a Samuel Holmes, also of Ashford, Connecticut, 100 acres in the southwest corner of Lot 17 [HLR 1A: 27]. Five years later, on September 30, 1785, he sold this piece to Dorcus' brother, Jonathan [HLR 1A: 444].

SALLY, as early-recorded history has it, was the first white female born in Halifax, in 1766 on Lot 25, later owned by Robert Collins,[17] which is in the vicinity of what is known as Winn Road. She married Moses Learnard and lived out her life on the Learnard Home Place[18] on Lot 19. With research, the help of more mature family members, and stories exchanged between neighbors, it is believed that Sally's birthplace has been located on the Winn property. Bertell (Burnett) Woods remembers the location of an old stone foundation while haying on the Winn farm with her father in about 1928. Neighbors recollect hearing that the original Winn house was moved from the top of the hill onto that old stone foundation. Over ten years later, in 1939, when her oldest brother, Malcolm Burnett was working on the same farm, Bertell remembers seeing the house after it was moved. After returning to the site in 2004, Malcolm verified the location of the Winn house after it had been moved. Another indication that ties this place to Sally is that just below this spot is a little brook, which extends down the mountainside and crosses the present Route 112 and the North River in the vicinity of the present day Stone Valley Farm. Fowler Brook runs by the Pennell house, down the mountain into the North River in the same vicinity. Given the preponderance of evidence, it seems reasonable to believe that Sally's mother, Lucy would have followed a trail along this little brook or along marked trees when she encountered a bear on her way to the Pennell place to obtain a hot coal. This popular bear story has survived from the early days of Halifax[19] [↪ 64]. Another account depicting the hardships Lucy faced follows:

PRATT HOME FOUNDATION   Photo Robert Rogers

> Pastures not being inclosed cows were suffered to run at large in
> the woods. It was often with difficulty that they were found. Mrs.
> [Lucy] Pratt on one occasion in searching for her cow just as night
> was setting in, became completely bewildered more than a mile

from home in a dense forest. Not knowing which way to direct her course she sat down and wept. Soon the thickening clouds began to pour down rain, and there was every appearance of a cold, stormy, October night. At this juncture, while she was casting about to know how she should spend the night, she heard the voice of her husband, of whose return she had known nothing, calling her name from a distance. She at once responded to the call and attempted to make her way in the direction of the distant sound, but being bewildered she took the wrong course and went in the opposite direction from the voice. Her husband perceiving that her voice grew fainter and fainter by distance, called upon her to stop till he could come to her. But she, confident that she knew the course she was taking quickened her speed, thinking that she might save him the trouble of coming all the way to her. She was overtaken at last in the border of Whitingham near where Mr. Barrington now lives on North river, at more than twice the distance from home than when she first made answer to the call of her husband. They then took their course homeward through the dark forest and drenching rain. Returning to their quiet home in their snug log-cabin, they doubtless rejoiced together, with their little ones, in the favorable issue of the enterprise.[20]

TOWN AND STATE AFFAIRS

Elisha was not only active in town affairs, serving as lister and surveyor of highways [HLR 1A: 408], but his name was the eighth on the list of freemen [HLR 1A: 399], signifying that he was one of the first Halifax residents to declare his loyalty to the newly created State of Vermont. For his loyalty, his name appears on the list of Vermont freemen together with other Halifax men who were granted land per "THE CHARTER OF TWO HEROES," dated October 1779. North and South Hero are located in the chain of islands called Grand Isle. A relevant portion of the Two Heroes charter reads:

Know ye, that whereas, COLONELS, ETHAN ALLEN, & SAMUEL HERRICK, and their associates our worthy Friends, have by Petition requested a Grant of a Certain large Island, lying, and being, situate in Lake Champlain, in this State, and know sometimes by the name of the Grand Isle Alias Great Island, in order for settling and Cultivating the same and thereon making a New Plantation; WE HAVE therefore thought fit for the due

encouragement of their laudable designs, and for other valuable
considerations us hereunto moving, and do by this Presents in the
name & by the Authority of the Freemen of the State of Vermont,
give and Grant the Tract of Land or Island aforesaid, hereafter
more fully described and bounded, unto them the Said Ethan
Allen, & Samuel Herrick, & to several persons hereafter named
their associates viz[t] . . . Hubbel Wells, Edward Harris, Silas
Hamilton, William Williams. . . . William Hill, Caleb Owen, Amos
Peabody, Thomas Hunt, John Hamilton . . . Silas Hamilton Ju[r],
Elisha Pratt, James Gray. . . [all Halifax men, among others]
Which Tract of Land, or Island, hereby given and Granted, as
aforesaid, is bounded & described as follows viz[t] BEGINNING . . .
And, that the same be & hereby is Incorporated into one district,
Township, or Incorporation by the name of the TWO HEROES. . . .
upon the following conditions viz[t] that each Proprietor in the said
Two Heroes, his heirs, or assigns, shall Plant & cultivate two acres
of Land, or have one Family Settled on each respective Right,
within the Term of one year next after the Conclusion of the
Present war, on penalty of the Forfieture of each respective Right
or Share of Land in said Island not so improved, or settled, & the
same to revert to the Freemen of this State, to be by their
Representatives, Regranted to such persons as shall appear to
Settle and cultivate the same, In Testimony, whereof we have
caused the Seal of this State to be affixed In Council this 27 day of
October AD 1779. And in the third year of the Independence of
this State.[21]

As stated in the charter, if a family did not settle on a "respective Right, within the
Term of one Year next after the Conclusion of the Present war . . . the same [was]
to revert to the Freemen of this State. . . ." Likewise was the case with Alburgh,
chartered on February 23, 1781[22] and Woodbridge, chartered on October 26,
1781,[23] except the term was three years. The name of Elisha's son James appears
on the list of freemen for both Alburgh and Woodbridge. Elisha's sons Jonathan
and James also served as freemen in Halifax. Elisha was listed as well on the
"PETITION OF EDWARD HARRIS et al. FOR A PORTION OF SOMERSET" dated
March 1780 [↻ 107–108]. "There is no record of legislative action thereon."[24]

PENSION RECORDS

Elisha served in the Revolution in Captain Josiah Boyden's Company, (1777). His
three sons, Jonathan (at the tender age of 16), Nathan, and James, who were not
much older, also served during the Revolutionary War. Detailed accounts are
wonderfully preserved in their pension records. When Jonathan applied for his
pension, his sister Dorcus Loomis, filed two affidavits on her brother's behalf
with the court, one of which follows:

Dorcas Loomis, wife of Nathan Loomis, of the town of Middlesex in the county of Yates and State of New York aged sixty four years, being duly sworn according to law doth depose and say that she distinctly recollects that on or about the time that the battle of Bennington took place, in the war of the Revolution her brother, Jonathan Pratt who has subscribed and sworn to the above declaration left home, at Halifax in the State of Vermont, where her father then resided for the purpose of entering the service of the United States that she then understood that he was absent several months and that she then understood that the said Jonathan Pratt was while so absent engaged in actual service as a soldier in the United States, nor has she ever heard any doubt thereof whatever expressed. And further the said Deponent saith not

Subscribed and Sworn to
This 31st day of Aug. 1832   *Dorcas Loomis*

JAMES' PENSION RECORDS

James' pension records provide an account (transcribed in part) of his service with the Green Mountain Boys under Ethan Allen.

That he entered the Service of the United States early in the Spring of the year 1780. And he thinks it was about the 15th of April 1780, that residing at that time at Halifax in the State of Vermont he voluntarily enlisted at said Halifax for the term of nine months under the authority of the State of Vermont in the Vermont State Troops, so called and went from that place through the town of Bennington, Manchester, Pawlet, Rutland . . . to the town of Pittsford, in the County of Rutland, viz State of Vermont, where he joined a company of Infantry commanded by Capt. Hutchins of Bennington, in which the other officers whom he remembers were Spencer of Bennington & Ensign Brookline. He remained at Pittsford . . . until the month of September or October, when he was marched in his company thro Rutland to Castleton in the County afd, a distance of about Seventeen miles, and there joined the regiment commanded by Col. Ebenezer Allen in which Isaac Clark was Major. . . .

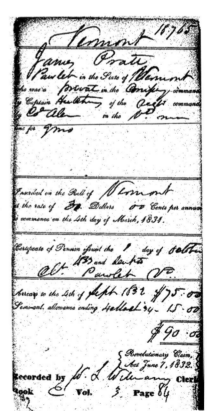

NARA, S14222

He remained at Castleton, a space of time in garrison . . . until some time in the month of October, when the British having landed at Skeensboro [now Whitehall] in the State of New York, & a distant from Castleton about ten miles, he well remembers that alarm guns were fired at Castleton in order that the neighboring Militia & other troops might assemble to repel the enemy. Immediately after this, he was marched in a detachment under the command of Maj. Clark, to Fort Ann, in the State of New York, at which place he arrived the morning on which the fort was surrounded by the Americans. The British then marched towards fort George & Ticonderoga; and Maj. Clark's detachment in which the declarant was then serving returned to Castleton. Gen. Ethan Allen had then, or soon after, arrived at Castleton, & who as the declarant thinks commanded the Vermont Troops. They were afterwards under the command of Gen Enos. The declarant served at Castleton about three months longer in garrison . . . and was dismissed in January 1781 without discharge in writing. . . . He refers, however, to the affidavit of his sister, Sally Larned, which will show that he was absent from his home & as she supposed in the service of his country.

And the declarant well recollects that while at Castleton the Troops were almost every morning, drawn up around a pine stump from which Gen. [Ethan] Allen used to make address to them. And he also remembers that one Asa Starkweather served there: therein facts are corroborated by the affidavit of Peter Stevens, who also swears to his belief that the declarant was at Castleton, as he has above stated.

And being interrogated, the declarant says, that he was born at Ware, in the County of Hampshire and State of Massachusetts, on the 25th day of March AD 1763. His age is recorded in an old Bible by the hand of his parents, which is now in his possession, but he knows of no other record thereof. At the time when he entered the service of his country he was resident at Halifax afa. & continued to reside there until the year 1794, when he removed to Pawlet, Vermont where he has ever since lived. He voluntarily enlisted. Capt. Allen & Sawyer commanded companies in the regiment to which he belonged. He never received a discharge & has no documentary evidence of his service. . . .

While residing at said Halifax, James Pratt volunteered about April 15, 1780, served as a private in Captain Hutchins' Company, Colonel Ebenezer Allen's Vermont Regiment, was stationed at Pittsford and Castleton: in October following, when the British landed at Skeensboro, he marched in a detachment under Major Isaac Clark to Fort Ann, in New York, but arrived after the fort surrendered. He returned to Castleton and continued to serve [under Gen. Ethan Allen] until in January, 1781, when he was discharged. . . . [25]

Sworn & Subscribed
The day and year afa   *James Pratt*

As James stated in his sworn statement, his sister, Sally provided an affidavit, which follows on his behalf.

SALLY (LARNED) LEARNARD'S AFFIDAVIT

THE MOVE TO PAWLET

Elisha and Lucy sold their property of 100 acres in Halifax to John Smead and followed their son James to Pawlet, Vermont, in 1794. Elisha's character is depicted as follows:

> While reading the Bible one Sunday morning his wife saw a fine buck in the cornfield. Handing him his gun, she said, "There is a noble buck out there and we are almost starving. Had you better not shoot him?" "No," he replied, "the Lord hath sustained us and kept us alive thus far, and if it is His will that we shall have that deer to keep us from starving He will cause it to come back some other day." His faith was well grounded, as the deer came back a few days later and was quickly killed.[26]

Elisha died on July 3, 1807 at the age of seventy-nine. Lucy died on May 1, 1827 at the age of ninety and both are buried at Mettowee Valley Cemetery in Pawlet, Vermont. James continued the family heritage serving as constable in Pawlet,

1804–1805, partaking in the military band and serving in the state legislature for two years. He died in Pawlet, Rutland County, Vermont, on September 15, 1854. It was said of James that he was

> . . . a fine specimen of the hardy, thrifty, intelligent farmer who laid the foundations of society in this town [Pawlet]. His home was ever a seat of hospitality and good cheer. His conversational and story-telling powers were unrivaled.[27]

Presently, Elisha's lineage lives on in Halifax through the grandchildren of Bernice Barnett and Carrie Perna, making up the eighth and ninth generation respectively.   ©2008 *Carrie Perna*

ENDNOTES

1. Hampshire County Courthouse, Springfield, Massachusetts, Book 1, pp. 338–339. HHS: Copy of the original deed between John Post and Elisha Pratt held by author.
2. Ibid., Book 17, pp 36–38.
3. NARA, Pension file S14222.
4. RBA.
5. Stone, vol. 4, p. 795.
6. Robert Charles Anderson, *The Great Migration Begins, Immigrants to New England, 1620–1633,* Vol. I, A-F Boston : New England Historic Genealogical Society) p. 1513. "Joshua Pratt and Phineas Pratt have many times been called brothers. Though there is no direct evidence of this relationship, much circumstantial evidence points in that direction. They received joint grants in the 1623 Plymouth division of land, and were listed consecutively in the 1639 Plymouth list of freemen. Bathsheba, daughter of Joshua, married in Charlestown, where her uncle Phineas Pratt was living at the time; she may have been placed in his household after her father's death." See also: *Phinehas Pratt and Some of His Descendants.* A Monograph prepared by Eleazer Franklin Pratt (Boston: Printed for Private Distribution, 1897) p. 36: "Joshua Pratt, who we believe was the brother of Phinehas."
7. Ibid., p. 1516.
8. Carrie Perna, Pratt Genealogy.
9. Anderson, p. 1511.
10. Massachusetts Historical Society, Collections of the Massachusetts Historical Society: Vol. IV of the Fourth series. Little Brown and Co., p. 487.
11. Eugene Aubrey Stratton, Fellow of American Society of Genealogist, Former Historian General of the General Society of Mayflower Descendants, *Plymouth Colony, Its History and People, 1620–1691* (Salt Lake City, UT: Ancestry Publishing, 1986).
12. Ibid., p. 76, 419–420, 427–429, 440.
13. Ibid., Appendix F, p. 22.
14. Ibid., Appendix G, pp. 415–417, 421.
15. http://genforum.genealogy.com/pratt/messages/2960.html Location where they settled was possibly Lake George.
16. Nathan Bennet, their Eldest son was born in Halifax the 18th Day of June 1778. Jemima their Eldest Daughter Born in Halifax 9th Day of August 1781. James Bennet their 2nd Son Born in Halifax June 6th 1785. Lucy Bennet their 2nd Daughter born in Halifax August 28th 1787. Lucy Bennet the Wife of Mr. Banks Bennet Died the 28th Day of August A.D. 1787. [HLR 1A: 377]
17. Hemenway, p. 413.
18. The "Learnard Home Place" has been known by the family since it derived its name from Sally and Moses Learnard. See *Journey of Origins, The Progeny Continues* in the second volume.
19. Hemenway, pp.413–414.
20. Ibid., p. 413.
21. Harry A. Black, ed., *State Papers of Vermont, Volume Two* (Bellows Falls, VT: Gobie Press, 1924), pp. 192–193.
22. State Papers of Vermont, Vol. II, pp. 4–6.
23. Ibid., Appendix A, pp. 235–238.
24. State Papers of Vermont, Petition for Land Grants, pp. 149–151.
25. NARA, Pension file S14222, pp. 0497–0500.
26. Stone, p. 30.
27. Ibid., p. 795.

Longest Continuous View
The Crosiers

Photo C. Lancaster

From the arrival of the first Halifax settlers, axes and muskets in hand, there has been one family name always present in the town. The Crosier brothers headed north to hew out wilderness clearings about 1762/1763[1] after the close of the French and Indian War. This was a time when the six miles square of uninhabited, densely forested land called "Hallifax" invited settlement. John, Robert, and Arthur Crosier, Abner Rice, and Elisha Pratt, all migrated from central Massachusetts frontier towns that supplied soldiers to the final war expeditions, including the campaign to capture Fort Ticonderoga. The Crosier men who came to Halifax were, most likely, the sons of John Crosier from Pelham, Massachusetts.[2]

John Crosier, it is believed, descended from families that had settled in Antrim County, Ulster Province, Northern Ireland, not far from Belfast. The name Crosier may have evolved from Anthony DuCrozat, a French Huguenot, who left France to escape the persecution of Protestants after revocation of the Edict of Nantes.[3] In Ireland, his name was spelled Crossett. His grandson, William Samuel Crossett, married Martha Hamilton, who was from one of the many Scotch–Presbyterian families that also had fled to Ulster because of religious intolerance. After the death of William in 1722, his widow entered the Colonies, probably at Boston, with her four sons, one daughter, and other members of the Hamilton family.[4]

Eventually, this group of Presbyterians settled in Worcester, Massachusetts, where the local Puritan people did not welcome them. In 1740, after hostile neighbors tore down, chopped, and burned the framework built for their church,[5] the Scottish families petitioned Colonel John Stoddard of Northampton for a new township. He granted them a tract of land east of Amherst, which they called New Lisburne.[6] In 1742, the town's name was changed to Pelham.[7]

According to manuscript records of Kings Chapel in Boston, John Crosier, son of Martha, and William Crossett married Martha Lindsay on January 13, 1735.[8] John and his family appear as "Crossett," "Croser," and as "Crozier" in various Pelham town records, which document that he and Martha lived out their lives there. He bought and sold land, paid property and school taxes, and was listed as a fence viewer in West Parish in 1761.[9] Three of John and Martha's four sons—John Jr. , Arthur, and Robert— were pioneer settlers of Halifax, Vermont. Alexander remained in Pelham.

Military records from the *History of Pelham* include a muster roll for men from Pelham who, with Captain Robert Lotheridge, marched to the relief of Fort Henry in 1757. Arthur Crosier, John Lynsey, and John Crosier Jr. are listed.[10] Another roll titled, "A Return of Men in Col Israel Williams Regiment to be put under the immediate command of Jeffry Amherst for the invation of Canada in 1759,"[11] includes John Crosier, Sr., age fifty-nine, and Arthur Crosier, age nineteen, and adds, "Each man furnished his own gun and enlisted April 2."[12] Arthur Crosier also appeared on a muster roll for April 1760 called "A return of men enlisted for His Majesty's service in the reduction of Canada"[13]

The Crosiers who arrived in Halifax two and a half centuries ago were: John, who married Thanks or Thankful (last name unknown); Arthur (called "Aaron" on the 1771 census), who married Elizabeth (last name unknown),[14] possibly his second wife; and Robert, who married Jane Gault. These three men are listed as heads of families in the 1771 Cumberland County census for Halifax.

CROSIER PROPERTIES

Given their presence in Halifax since 1763, Crosiers are, inevitably, mentioned throughout this volume in various contexts. It is the intention here to concentrate on the early years; those most obscured by time, and not attempt to provide a comprehensive biography of the family.

Recorded deeds for the original Crosier Halifax land transactions have not been found. However, references in subsequent deeds serve to identify the Crosier properties and confirm that John and Robert Crosier settled on Lots 20 and 27. These were the original charter lots assigned to Oliver and Samuel Partridge of Hatfield, Massachusetts. Oliver's name was on Lot 20 and Samuel's on Lot 27. The proprietors named on the charter knew that, according to terms of the Wentworth grants, unimproved lands might be subject to forfeit; hence they sought out rugged young men and offered them land in exchange for settling and laboring to improve it. Col. Oliver and his cousin, Lieut. Samuel Partridge gave John and Robert Crosier one hundred acres each.

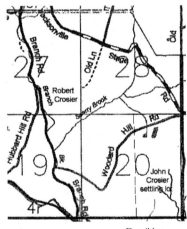

Detail lot map

JOHN: We know from Oliver Partridge deeds for Lot 20 and from a number of deeds by which John Crosier conveyed property to others, that his "settling lot" was the northeast quadrant of the lot. The northwest portion of Lot 20 was conveyed by Partridge to Elias Persons of Brimfield, Massachusetts in 1774 [HLR 1A: 218]. In 1779, Partridge conveyed the center portion of Lot 20 to Nathan Whitney of Brookfield, Massachusetts, located "on the West line of said Hundred Acres on Which John Crozier Dwells." [HLR 1A: 57].

Boundary references in later deeds confirm that it was John Crosier who first settled and "improved" the land in Halifax Center, south along Stowe Mountain Road and west along Woodward Hill Road. In June 1780, surveyor Hazael Shepard, per order of Halifax selectmen Hubbel Wells, Edward Harris, and John Sawtell, laid out the first recorded town road, which is described as a highway 176 rods long (.55 miles) and three rods (50 feet) in width, running from John Crosier's northeast corner, east ten degrees, south to the large spruce tree on the east side of the "Proprietor's Road" (Stowe Mountain Road) [HLR 1A: 25].

John Crosier appeared as grantor in many transactions relating to the Hamilton/Muzzy store and tavern property at the Center, which a century later was the Crosier's store and post office, run by descendants of John's brother, Arthur. In 1788, John Crosier sold a parcel to Benjamin Bemis of Spencer, Massachusetts [HLR 1A: 539], who reconveyed it to Amos Muzzy. He also sold property to Muzzy's partner, Reuben Hamilton [HLR 1A: 213]. Crosier sold small parcels in Lot 20 to the Chandlers, who owned a chain of stores in Massachusetts, and to Joseph Henry, when the newly formed Chandlers & Henry firm was acquiring the business assets from creditors of the bankrupt Amos Muzzy [HLR 2: 359]. Other John Crosier land transactions involved Thomas Farnsworth, Joseph Tucker, and David Wolley. His remaining Lot 20 holdings, conveyed by deed to his son John Jr. in 1818, consisted of about fifty-six acres [HLR 4: 34-35].

The 1820 census indicates that John and Thankful were living with or adjacent to their son John Jr. and his wife Polly Lee; however, in the 1830 census, neither John Crosier family is listed for Halifax. It is likely that John, Sr., died by 1823, even though there is no town death record for him. John and Thankful's other son, Phillip, and wife, Abigail Nichols, were listed in Whitneyville in 1820 with seven children, and Phillip deeded ten acres of Lot 44 to Thankful in February 1823, which suggests that she was now a widow. Of Phillip Crosier's sons, Abner, Amasa, and Augustus joined the huge migration of Halifax families to Susquehanna County, Pennsylvania. His fourth son, Benjamin, moved to property along the North River in Colrain, where his descendants still live today. In 1993, Benjamin's grandson, Ralph, with the help of his wife, Frances, and daughter, Judy, established the annual Crosier reunion.[15] John Crosier Jr.'s sons all eventually moved from Halifax; his son, William Lindsey, born in 1804, appeared on the 1830 and 1840 local census rolls but later is found in Adams, Massachusetts, in the Berkshires.

John and Thankful Crosier's family line has continued in Halifax for many generations through their daughter, Martha, born in 1768, who married Eleazer Whitney and raised a family of fourteen children in Whitneyville. Eleazer, probably a brother of Nathan Whitney who moved to the property just west of John Crosier, served in the Revolution from Brookfield, Massachusetts, and was granted a pension in 1819. After his death in 1840, his widow received pension assistance until her death in 1865 at age ninety-seven. Martha gave a deposition in support of Sally Pratt Learnard's application for a widow's pension, saying that she had been a guest at the wedding of Sally and Moses.

ROBERT: Land records place Robert Crosier in the southeast corner of Lot 27 on Branch Brook. He also bought and sold properties in Lot 19. Robert and Jane (Gault) had four children, two of whom married children of Thomas and Sarah Hale Scott: Lydia Crosier married Abel Scott and lived in the Thomas Scott homestead on Stowe Mountain Road. She is the Widow Scott whose help recounting stories of the early days was enlisted by historian Rev. Hubbard Eastman; Samuel Crosier married Sarah Scott, and in 1798, Robert conveyed fifty acres of Lot 27 to him [HLR 2: 588]. When Samuel left town, he conveyed the property to his sister Catherine, and brother-in-law, Jonas Brown. They gave a life lease to Robert, Jane, and to Jane's mother, Elizabeth Gault, who was living with them as of May 10, 1813 [HLR 6: 303]. Census records for 1830 show Jonas and Catherine, six children, and one female (Jane) more than eighty and less than ninety years of age.

Robert died on June 10, 1829, according to the recently discovered Jonas and Catherine Brown Bible, which was on display at the 2004 Crosier reunion.[16] There is no grave marker for him, but it is thought that he may be buried in Halifax Center Cemetery next to his wife. Her death in 1850 at age 105 makes her the woman with the greatest longevity in Halifax. As with John, Robert's descendants, who bear the Crosier name, are no longer present in Halifax. However, there are families in town who descend from Robert and Jane Gault Crosier through his daughter Lydia Crosier Scott, and her daughter, Sally, who married Nathan Learnard.

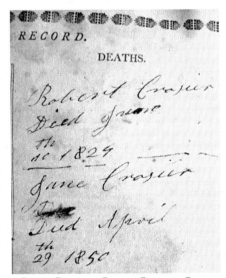

BROWN BIBLE   Courtesy Constance Omasta

ARTHUR: The third Crosier brother built his house east of the geographical center of town on property in Original Lot 38 along what is today called Deer Park Road. The charter name on Lot 38 is Timothy Woodbridge of Hadley, Massachusetts. In the earliest land record found for Arthur, dated 1780, he conveyed thirty-two and three-quarters acres located in the northwest corner of Lot 38 to Daniel Squire [HLR 1A: 32]. In those times, property often was one's only asset. Because early property transfers seldom involved strangers and often reflected family ties, it seems worthy of note that Daniel was the nephew of William Scott who had settled on Lot 37 before the 1771 census and of Thomas Scott, who migrated to Halifax from Ashford, Connecticut about 1779, the same time as Daniel. Their families may well have traveled together. The conveying of property from Arthur to Daniel strengthens the possibility that Arthur's wife may have been a Scott.

Early Halifax deeds often reference "the center road leading from Colrain to Marlborough" and the intersecting "highway, which leads to Arthur Crozier's farm" [HLR 1A: 266]. Deed references to Crosier neighbors along that road include

Jonathan Kellogg and William Stark, brother of lawyer and land speculator, Jedediah Stark. A family historian, L. Halsea Crosier, says Arthur lived at Morell Knoll,[17] farmed, and worked some in carpentry. On October 22, 1804, Arthur transferred ownership of his property to his son, James, who in turn gave a life lease to Arthur and his "present wife Elizabeth"[18] [HLR 4: 20].

After the marriage in 1805 of James to Polly, daughter of David Stow, both families lived on the same property, and census records designate James as the head of household. One of the Crosier family cemetery plots in Halifax Center includes graves of Arthur; Annah, his daughter; his son James and wife, Polly Stow; his grandson, James and wife Malona L. Brown; and his great-grandson, James Knox Polk Crosier, a member of Company K, 4th Vermont, who was killed at the Battle of Winchester, Virginia. The Lawrence Crosier family currently living in Halifax Center is descended from James and Polly.

Arthur, Robert, and John Crosier, through life-lease conveyances to their children, ensured continued family ownership of the home farm properties they had worked so hard to establish.[19] By 1810, the census shows six Crosier heads of households: Robert, Samuel, John, James, Phillip, and Joseph. In 1824, Joseph Crosier,[20] son of Arthur, seems to have caught the family pioneering spirit "and with his two eldest sons Joseph Jr. and David, from Halifax commenced clearing the southwesterly part of Searsburg . . . regarded as the first permanent settlement. . . . They cut a wagon road, cleared land, built a house of spruce logs and bark and moved their families from Halifax with a yoke of oxen and one cow."[21]

Crosiers in the census records from 1850 forward are Arthur's descendants. James, Moses L. , and Rufus are listed in 1850; and Moses and Rufus appear again in 1860; by 1880, Alson and Elmer, both sons of Rufus, appear on the list. Child's *Gazetteer and Business Directory* lists "Alson, (West Halifax) wool grower 43 sheep, sugar orchard 700 trees, and farmer having 196 acres. James Crosier, (Halifax Center) farmer 110 acres, age 74. Rufus Crosier (Halifax) farmer 166 acres, and Orval H. Crosier, (Halifax Center) assistant postmaster, general merchant, flour and feed."[22]

Anyone wishing to trace properties owned by the Crosiers of Halifax might be well advised to schedule more than one research session. Vera Crosier has been compiling a list from the index from Halifax land records, and to date there are more than two hundred Crosier deeds.[23]

CROSIERS IN THE COMMUNITY

The first documented Crosier activity in Halifax appears in the Richard Ellis account book: "John Crosier of Hallifax Cr June 1765 By 18 of Sugar at 3/. Dr June & Dec 1765" and "Robert Crosier Dr Feb & May 1765." It would appear that John bartered maple sugar for goods from the Ellis store. The next record is the 1771 Cumberland County census, which names all three Crosier brothers.

Evidently, members of this family refrained from involvement in the early Yorker/Vermonter political controversies. None of them signed the 1770 or 1771 petitions to the New York governor that circulated through town at that time, and the Crosier name is not included in any of the later accounts of Yorker mayhem in town. Robert and John Crosier's names appear towards the beginning of the list of freemen of Halifax started in 1778, which suggests they were Vermonters, not Yorkers; however, Robert's name does not appear on the list of town office holders during the first decade of town meetings. Of the brothers, John was the most politically active in the early years. He was chosen to serve as a tithing man, [overseer of community behavior] together with Elias Persons, for the year 1784 [HLR 1A: 425]. At several town meetings, including that of 1793, the freemen chose John Crosier for pound keeper [HLR 2: 176]. John had at least one meeting house pew, which he sold to Henry and Hastings in 1794 [HLR 2: 441]. Even though Arthur's name does not appear on the original freeman's list, he was chosen to be one of the five fence viewers in 1790, along with James Pratt, Nathaniel Streeter, Samuel Underwood, and Thomas Scott. In 1798 and 1799, Arthur served as a surveyor of highways, and in 1800 was a grand juror. Both John and Arthur are found on the list of sixty-three "subscribers and Inhabitants of the Town of Halifax" to support local tavern keeper and farmer, Amos Muzzy's colorful petition [↪ 509] to the Vermont State Assembly for relief from his financial difficulties.

One can place the Crosier families in neighborhoods according to the original 1784 school district lists. Arthur Crosier was named in Original District No. 2. His neighbors included half a dozen Wilcox families, the Sylvester and Elisha Worden families, as well as Benjamin Weeks. John and Robert Crosier appear in School District No. 10 together with James and John Woodard, Edward Harris, Rev. Goodall, Joseph Tucker, Isaac Orr, Stephen Gates, Thomas Farnsworth, and Nathan and John Whitney.

Samuel, son of Robert Crosier, involved himself in public service. It is Samuel, who, as town lister, undertook the Herculean task of recording the census of Halifax in 1810—the peak population year. Two years later, minutes from town meeting indicate that Samuel resigned his position in order to serve in the War of 1812. Later generations of Crosiers more frequently appear in the public eye. Rufus Crosier (1824–1903) served as constable after returning from his service in the Civil War. Perley Eugene (1869–1937) was appointed postmaster at Center Halifax in 1903 and served until his death in 1937, after which his son, Paul DeWolf (1894/5–1968), served until the Center post office closed in 1954. Perley served as Halifax road commissioner; his son, Paul, and grandson, Larry, also worked for the town. The Crosiers were merchants at Halifax Center for many years and held a variety of town offices, including, at times, health officer and auditor. Lillian Crosier oversaw the "Free Public Library." Clara Crosier served as a school director and was active in the historical society. Paul D. Crosier was a selectman in the years 1928–1930, 1934–1936, and 1957–1964. Margaret Hill Crosier served as town treasurer from 1947–1950 and for fourteen years, 1953–1967, was town clerk.

Larry Crosier is descended from Arthur Crosier through James (1783–1860), who married Polly Stow; Rufus Crosier, who married Chloe Ann Stacy; Perley Eugene Crosier, who married Lillian M. DeWolf; and Paul DeWolf Crosier, who married Margaret Ella Hill. Their son Lawrence Eugene Crosier[24] has two daughters with his first wife, and with his second wife, Vera M. Chase, has two sons, Michael Lawrence and Paul James. Families named Crosier have owned and lived on land in Halifax Center from approximately 1763 to date—a period of 240+ years. No other family in Halifax bears that distinction!

CROSIER WOMEN – KEEPERS OF THE TRADITIONS

Having the longest continuous view of the town of Halifax does not necessarily translate into a clear record of 240+ years of history and events. Nevertheless, it is interesting to note the special role of the women in this family, who have a long tradition of being keepers of events and stories of the town. The tradition begins with Jane Gault Crosier, whose life in Halifax spanned 105 years—from the earliest Cumberland County days, through the Yorker conflicts, statehood, and massive population growth, to the time of the great exodus from town. Jane outlived the town's first historian, Thomas Hough Wood. Her daughter, Lydia, Mrs. Abel Scott, passed along the stories and traditions she learned from her mother and from their neighbor, Sally Pratt Learnard, to an even later historian, Rev. Hubbard Eastman. By 1891, when Eastman's history was published in Hemenway's gazetteer, Lillian "Lilla" DeWolf, "Pearl" Crosier's wife, was a young woman. In addition to her duties as a mother, while assisting her husband in the store and post office at Halifax Center, she, too, preserved stories and events. Lilla culled newspapers for articles about local people; she clipped, dated, and pasted them onto the pages of old unused post-office books. The Crosier scrapbooks are one of her legacies to Halifax historians.

Halifax Center, as drawn by Lilla Crosier in 1887. The right side of the drawing shows every structure on the land that was originally owned and cleared by John Crosier.

Lilla's daughter, Clara Crosier Barnard, treasured the history and stories of her birthplace. Her written reminiscences of daily life in Halifax appear throughout this volume and have greatly enriched the town's history. Often it is said, "Clara would be able to answer that question. Clara would know." Her comments appear on many of the old photos at the historical society. She was the featured guest historian who spoke at the 1975 Vermont Bicentennial Celebration in Halifax. Clara's sister-in-law, Margaret Hill Crosier, assisted Harry E. Goodnough during his last years as town clerk, and in her role as his successor, had care and custody of the town records for many years.

A great-great granddaughter of Lydia Crosier Scott, who does not bear the Crosier name but certainly carries on the family tradition of story telling, is Bernice Burnett Barnett. She has been writing and publishing stories of her hometown for many years, telling many a lively tale, which has greatly enriched the chronicles of Halifax. Her niece, Carrie Burnett Perna, has taken up the tradition and become an important contributor to this town history. Another important contributor is Vera Crosier, the custodian of the Crosier scrapbooks, who has been a valuable resource for this publication. Thus the tradition of Crosier women as keepers of the stories of Halifax continues.   ©2008 *Constance Lancaster*

ENDNOTES

1. Hemenway, p. 408. Note: Eastman's source for these dates may have been Lydia Crosier Scott, daughter of Robert Crosier and Jane Gault.
2. Iris Wilcox Baird, *The Crosiers of Halifax, Vermont: Some Descendants of John Crosier c. 1714–c.1755* (monograph) (Lancaster, NH: 1996) pp. 1–3.
3. Iris Wilcox Baird, *Crossetts and Crosiers Some of the Descendants of Anthony Ducrozat c. 1624* (monograph) (Lancaster, NH: 1996) p. v.
4. Genealogical Notes and Queries, *Boston Transcript*, March 11, 1908.
5. William Henry Eldridge, *Henry Genealogy* (Boston: Press of T. R. Marvin & Son, 1915) p. 3.
6. For details of Lisburn, Ireland and its Huguenot population, visit http://www.lisburn.com
7. Josiah H. Temple, *History of Palmer, Massachusetts 1716–1889* (Springfield, MA: Published by the Town of Palmer, 1889) pp. 38–39.
8. Iris Wilcox Baird, *Crossetts and Crosiers Some of the Descendants of Anthony Ducrozat c. 1624* (monograph) (Lancaster, NH: 1996) p. 7.
9. Ibid., p. 7.
10. C. O. Parmeter, *History of Pelham, Mass. 1738–1898* (Amherst, MA: Carpenter & Morehouse, 1898) p. 343.
11. Ibid., p. 344.
12. Ibid.
13. Ibid.
14. Family genealogies say Elizabeth's maiden name was Stowe or Stone. Town records, however, do not support this theory. Stowe and Stone families did not arrive in Halifax until after the Revolution. The Scott and Shepard families were Arthur's immediate neighbors in 1770. Halsea Crosier believed Elizabeth was a Gault.
15. Halifax Crosier descendants actively research their family history. The reunions, held in Colrain until 1999, now take place at the Halifax Community Hall each July. Iris Wilcox Baird compiled a genealogy of the John and Thanks Crosier family of Halifax, first issued in 1996. She continues to update the material as new information and corrections are made known. The local coordinator of the Crosier reunion event is Vera Chase Crosier. Iris and Vera can be contacted through the Halifax Historical Society.
16. The Bible is in the possession of Constance Omasta. An extract of the complete family record is on file at the HHS and has been added to the Crosier genealogy.
17. "Morell Knoll" does not appear on Halifax maps; however, John Morrell is in the 1790 census and in that year sold to Joseph Wilcox, property in Lot 38, north of Arthur Crozier [HLR 2: 611].
18. Ruby Austin says the words "present wife" usually indicate a second marriage.
19. The tax valuation in pounds for 1792 shows Roberts's valuation at £19–10, John's at £ 21–15 and Arthur's at £22."
20. A descendant from this family, Ernest Upton Crosier, married Mensje Visser and has lived in Halifax since the 1950s.
21. Frank Pulaski, *History of Searsburg, Vermont*, http://www.geocities.com/RainForest/2068/ (From the homepage, click on the History of Searsburg link.)
22. Child, p. 415.
23. Some Crosier names in these records are: John, Robert, Arthur, Philip, Samuel, John Jr., James, James Jr., Rufus, Thankful, Benjamin, Zilpha, William L., Loin, Rodney, Moses, Alson, Lewis F., Elmer, Dora, O. Rufus, Perley, Chloe A., Paul D., Lilla, Hattie, Mrs. Myron L., Wayne, Edith A., Merton, and Margaret.
24. Lawrence and his brother, James Alson Crosier, were born in Halifax at the homestead recently owned by Douglas Riggs.

From Yorkshire, England
Deacon John Pennell

What drew John Pennell Jr. to the Halifax wilderness? He does not fit the pioneer profile. At age forty-three, Pennell was older than most first settlers. For more than a decade he had owned and operated the famous tavern his father built in the center of Colrain. He had served Colrain for many years as settler's clerk, and was chosen town clerk and selectman for the years 1761 and 1762. Nevertheless, shortly thereafter, probably during 1764, John Pennell Jr., his wife Eleanor Smith, and five children[1] moved north over the "province line" to start anew as one of the founding families of Halifax. Their relocation is documented in the ledger of Richard Ellis who recorded a business transaction with "Deacon John Pennil, of Hallifax"[2] in January 1765. Like most of the other earliest settlers, the sons and grandsons who carried on the family name disappeared from town records by 1830. Unlike most of the pioneer families, however, the legacy of the Pennells includes an original house, still standing, and a road and cemetery that bear the family name. Pennell (whether spelled, Panel, Pannel, Pennill, Pennel, or Pennell) is a name that will not be lost or forgotten in Halifax.

Born in 1721, John Pennell Jr. was a Yorkshire lad until age seven when he traveled with his parents and younger brothers Archibald and Isaac across the Atlantic from England to New England. They settled in Southborough, Massachusetts, where in 1737 John's mother, Margaret, died in childbirth, leaving his father with six children and a newborn infant to care for. By 1738, John had a stepmother, Sarah, and his father had purchased settling lots in newly opened Boston Township No. 2 (Colrain). John Pennell Sr. "spent the next two summers building a two story combination home and tavern with a large room above the tavern where travelers could spend the night."[3] In 1740, the Pennell family moved to their new home, and on March 21, 1741, Sarah gave birth to a son, Abraham, who is who is believed to be the first male child born in Colrain. Their tavern/home was located on Chandler Hill across the road and slightly south of the meeting house, and as the earliest public house in Colrain, it became the town's "first center of social activity."[4] Often the settler's meetings were held there. Its three fireplaces were said to have been "mammoth in size"[5] and on cold winter evenings, town meetings would adjourn to the Pennell Tavern.

Frontier life was especially perilous from the first settlement of Colrain until the end of the French and Indian War. During those years, various Pennell names appear on the garrison and muster rolls. According to Louise Patrie, "Five Pennill sons served as Indian Scouts."[6] John Sr.'s wife, Sarah Pennell, quite possibly was the woman mentioned in an account of "Indian Troubles" in Colrain. Early in the summer of 1747, John Mills, who lived next door to the tavern, was attacked by Indians and killed near his house. "About the same time a woman named Pennell disappeared from the settlement, and nothing being heard or seen of her after, the belief in general was that she had been carried into captivity by the Indians."[7] No further records of Sarah's life or death have been found.

In 1748, John Pennell Jr. married Eleanor Smith. In that year, John Sr. conveyed ownership of his town properties, including the tavern, in equal shares to his newly married firstborn son and to his youngest son, Abraham, then age six. The Pennell family continued to operate the tavern until April 1769, when they sold it to John Wood.

The fate of John Pennell Sr. is not evident. He provided property in Colrain for each of his sons. This included "second division" lots in the northern part of the township. Robert took up residence on Christian Hill near "the Vermont line but eventually moved to Salem, New York in 1778."[8] Isaac and Abraham also went to live in New York State. According to *The History of Colrain,* John Pennell Sr. donated land in 1745 for the Chandler Hill Cemetery, but there is no record of his burial there. Patrie says he died by 1767.[9] In later years he would have resided with one of his sons; this offers the possibility that he participated in the settlement of the Pennell Hill Halifax property and may well have helped his son construct the homestead that stands there today.

DEACON PENNELL HOUSE

THE PENNELLS ON PENNELL HILL

While the physical distance between Pennell Tavern in Colrain and Pennell Hill in Halifax may have been short, the difference in the settings of the two locations in 1764 was vast. Deacon John Pennell left his life at the core of a bustling, established town that had already amassed several decades worth of recorded history, much of which he had written while town clerk, and took up residence in a remote, isolated, densely wooded place. There is no recorded history for those early years of the Halifax settlement. Whatever dates and events were preserved would have been written in journals or recorded in family Bibles. Notes from the early years of John Pennell's life in Halifax, if recorded at all, have not been found. What remains from that period is one colorful story, recounted by Rev. Hubbard Eastman, who wrote:

> The late Widow LEARNARD, born in 1766, is thought to have been the first child born in town. Her father, Mr. PRATT, located on the farm now occupied by Robert COLLINS, when there were but four families in the town. Their nearest neighbor was Captain PANNEL who lived on PANNEL Hill four miles distant. Mr. PRATT had occasion to leave his wife and two small children at home in his absence of 10 days. The first or second night of his absence the fire

went out. Mrs. P. had no means of obtaining fire but from her neighbors. She took her two children, one in her arms, leading the other, and started for Captain PANNEL'S through a dense forest guided by marked trees. When she had gone a little distance from her home she roused a bear who ran up a tree. With self-possession she took her apron and tied it around the tree, and hanging her bonnet upon a stake she place it against the tree and passed on. Captain PANNEL returned with her and shot the bear, which had been kept upon the tree by the bonnet and apron. Those were days of female courage as well as hardship, inured as they were to life in the wilderness.[10]

This folklore has survived as the most popular bear story from the early days of Halifax [ρ 48]. Tradition has cast John Pennell in the role of rescuer. Most likely he is the one who wielded the trusty flintlock. It should be noted, however, in Halifax written records, starting with the original freeman's list, the Pennell who always was known, as "Captain" was James, the son of John, even though John, who always was known as "Deacon" served as a captain of the Cumberland County Militia and "led the Halifax Company in the Battle of Bennington, August 1777."[11]

Prior to Halifax written records, we find, in one of the few extant record books for Cumberland County, Elisha Pratt and John Pennell serving together as jurors in 1772. The book records that the court adjourned to Westminster at the "House of Ephraim Ranney, Esquire."[12] When court opened, jurors [of Halifax] sworn in were: "John Pannel, Asa Havens, Elisha Pratt, Robert Paterson, [Pattison] John Thomas, and John Barber."[13] Court sessions were held twice a year, usually late spring and fall, just after planting and harvesting times. One can assume the Halifax jurors traveled by horseback to the courthouse where they stayed for the duration of the hearings before returning home.

Pennell property in Halifax was located in Lot 2, an original Wentworth grant assigned to Selah Barnard of Deerfield. A local historian described Barnard as "prominent in war and in peace soldier, trader, farmer"[14] and a man who kept a tavern and store. Chances are Pennell, as a tavern keeper and a soldier in the French and Indian War, was acquainted with Barnard. A deed recording the property transfer of Lot 2 from Barnard to Pennell has not been found. However, the early Halifax land records show Deacon John Pennell as the sole "grantor" of land parcels in "Right No. 2." He conveyed by deed a total of 364 acres in three divisions, one to each of his three sons. The first two subdivisions occurred in May 1787: 150 acres to John III [HLR 1A: 530] and 100 acres to James [HLR 1A: 542]. In 1796, Deacon John conveyed 114 acres in Right No. 2 to his son, Andrew [HLR: 3: 393].

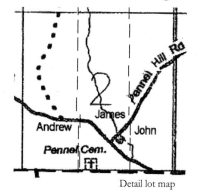

Detail lot map

At the time of the first two deeds, Deacon John was sixty-six years old, and his sons by then were married and had children. It is not certain how many Pennell family dwellings existed; probably three. The original Pennell homestead, completed circa 1764, may have been large enough for two small families. The federal census for Vermont in 1791 enumerates four Pennell families, as does the Halifax grand list for 1792, which values Captain James at £46, John III at £37, and Andrew and Deacon John Pennell each at £27. Deacon John, his second wife Sarah Breckenridge, and their daughter, Sarah probably lived in the original homestead with John III and his wife, Jane Holmes. Where did James and Andrew build their homes?

The census for 1800 lists three Pennell households: James, Andrew, and Widow Jane; the census for 1810 lists two, James and John; the 1820 census lists James only, and the 1830 census does not include the name Pennell at all. Since the Pennells did not record family births, marriages, and deaths in the town books, it is difficult to know who is who.[15] We know from gravestone and land records that "Widow Jane" was the, wife of John Pennell III "who was killed by the fall of a tree June 23d 1793 in the 35th year of his age"[16] Before 1830, Jane and her son, John IV, sold the Pennell homestead to Oliver Niles, who conveyed it to his son, James, who raised his family there with his wife, Sarah Tucker. Jane continued to live on Pennell Hill in Halifax with her daughter Eleanor Pennell Burrington and died in 1846, at age ninety. Even though the census of 1830 lists no one named Pennell, there were several Pennell daughters in town, and descendants continued in Halifax through Hannah, daughter of Deacon John and Eleanor, who married Joel Smith, son of Simeon Smith. After living for a few years in Walpole, New Hampshire, and Salem, New York, Joel and Hannah returned to Halifax by 1791. Currently, there are Halifax residents who can trace their ancestry to Deacon John Pennell through his daughter, Hannah, and granddaughter, Chloe Smith, wife of John Richardson Stacy. This couple is buried in the Pennell Hill Cemetery.[17]

The Pennells of Halifax were very active in military service and in Halifax town government. In politics, Deacon John appears to have been a moderate during the tug-of-war period between the Yorkers and Vermonters [↩ 154]. He was chosen to be one of the surveyor/measurers in 1779 but does not appear on the freeman's list until 1781, the year that most of the steadfast Yorkers in town changed their allegiance, took the Freeman's Oath, and first attended a town meeting. At that March meeting, Deacon John Pennell was elected selectman together with Benjamin Henry Sr., John Sawtell, Joseph Tucker, and Hubbel Wells. At the April 1781 meeting, it was voted that Hubbel Wells, Deacon John Pennell and Captain Robert Pattison "be the committee to provide a minister, on the town cost, to preach in the town for four Sabbaths on trial" [HLR 1A: 410]. At times, Deacon John Pennell served as moderator for town meetings and held various other offices over the years. John's son, Captain James Pennell, is named on page two of the freeman's list. He served several times as a lister, and like his father, served as a selectman of the town for a number of years.

In addition to the popular story about a Mrs. Pratt, an apron, an offending bear, and Captain Pennell's "trusty flintlock rifle," there is a lesser-known story that involves a Mr. Morgan, a famous horse, an offending sheriff named William Rice, and Captain Pennell's sons, James and Andrew. Lot 1, just west of the Pennells, was bought and sold in its entirety several times. Jonas Bond, of Petersham, Massachusetts, acquired Lot 1 in 1783 [HLR 1A: 245]. Bond did not settle on the property. Rather, he subdivided the lot and in 1786 and 1787 sold 112 acres each to William and Reuben Rice. William had the center lot, which he reconveyed in 1790 to Aaron Lamb. Reuben Rice conveyed his lot, the parcel abutting the Pennell's land, in June 1794. "Reuben Rice of Randolph in the County of Orange, State of Vermont in consideration of the sum of one Hundred pounds Lawfull money to me in hand paid by Justin Morgan of the Said County and State" etc. [HLR 2: 302]. Four months later, in October of 1794, Justin Morgan conveyed the same property to James and Andrew Pennell [HLR 2: 321]. Connecting the dots in this series of transactions suggests possible land speculation, or perhaps the operant term is "horse-trading." Justin Morgan's horse is not mentioned in the land records of Halifax; one must read between the lines of the deeds. A timeline from the *National Museum of the Morgan Horse*[18] shows that Morgan brought his unusual horse, "Figure," to Randolph, Vermont, around 1792. In 1793 and 1794, Morgan advertised Figure at stud in Lebanon, New Hampshire, and Randolph and Royalton, Vermont. No details of the whereabouts of the horse during those years are given. Also, "just when Figure passed out of Morgan's hands is not known, but it is known that Morgan no longer owned the horse in 1795."[19] It has been said that Figure was traded, sold, willed to, or taken to settle a debt by William Rice, sheriff of Woodstock.

Surely there is a connection between the horse, William and Reuben Rice, Justin Morgan, the property in Halifax, and the Pennells. Could the transaction in Halifax in 1794 answer the question of when, why, and how the horse passed out of Morgan's ownership? Justin Morgan died in 1798, and from that time on, as was the custom, his horse, Figure, was called Justin Morgan, the horse that became our Vermont state horse.

Back on Pennell Hill and the question of what drew Deacon John Pennell to the Halifax wilderness, it appears that the overriding consideration was land. John and his sons, James and Andrew, bought and sold property not only in part of Lot 1 and all of Lot 2, but also in surrounding Lots, 3, 9, 10, and 11. They sold to people whose names appear on the McClellan and Beers maps as residents in the mid-1800s, some of whom were: George Boardman, Elias Fowler, Ezra Gleason, Jonas Sanders, Elias Hager, Hezekiah Smith, and William Burrington. Sadly, the Pennells could not sustain their own lives and families on the beautiful hill property that bears their name. The premature death of John Pennell III, killed by a falling tree, may have been a factor. The wonderful house, however, still stands.

Charles McCune's recounting of the history of the original homestead says, "In 1818 a daughter-in-law of John Pennel [widow Jane] sold the property to a James Niles. Niles sold it in 1855 to a [James] Sheppardson. The property was handed down to a son, Norris Sheppardson, who had a blacksmith shop across the road from the house. In 1902, Norris died and his brother Clarence sold the property to the Kemp family. In 1930, the Kemp family sold it to Andrew and

Ruth Zagrubski. In August 1938, it passed to the McCune family."[20] In 2002, after more than sixty years caring for the Deacon John Pennell homestead, Charles and Edith McCune conveyed it to Donald and Diana Chase who reclaimed the pastures and constructed a new barn for their herd of Belted Galloways.

HHS

A reminder of the colorful early life of the town and of the families who dwelled in the venerable house on the hill is found engraved on a stone embedded in the wall in front of the Pennell place. This marker is attributed to Norris Shepardson, who during his years on Pennell Hill waged a campaign to erect road signs throughout the town. The marker literally points the way from the Deacon Pennell house to Halifax— four miles.

©2008 *Constance Lancaster*

ENDNOTES

1. Births of John and Eleanor's children recorded in Colrain are: Rachel, b.1749, m. Josiah Clark; Hannah, b.1751, m. Joel Smith; James b. 1753, m. Hannah Smith; John, b. 1758, m. Jane Holmes; Andrew, b. 1761, m. Sabrina Smith. Unrecorded children are Seth and Chloe, [no further information], who probably were born in Halifax. Recorded in Halifax is Eleanor, b. 1767, m. Joel Littlefield. Also the child of John and second wife Sarah (Breckinridge) Pennell recorded in Halifax is Sarah, b. 1772, m. William Work.
2. Richard Ellis account book, transcribed by Ruby Bruffee Austin. Typescript on file at the Halifax Historical Society.
3. HTC, Elizabeth Barber Lusk, *John Pennell of Yorkshire England, Massachusetts and Vermont: Genealogy and History,* folder with typescript and photocopies, compiled September 1996, p. 2 (hereinafter cited as Lusk).
4. Patrie, p. 180-H.
5. HHS, Floor plan of the Pennell Tavern.
6. Patrie, p. 20-H. For a detailed account of the period of King George and the French and Indian War and the Pennells' role in the town of Colrain.
7. Louis H. Evarts, *History of the Connecticut Valley in Massachusetts* (Philadelphia: J. B. Lippincott, 1879) pp. 747–748.
8. Patrie, p. 122-G.
9. Ibid., pp. 225, 121.
10. Hemenway, p. 413.
11. HHS, Charles W. McCune, *The Captain John Pennel House,* typescript undated.
12. Newfane County Court House, Book of Cumberland County Records, Vol. I, p. 26.
13. Ibid.
14. George Sheldon. *A History of Deerfield Massachusetts,* Vol. II (Deerfield, MA: Pocumtuck Valley Memorial Association, 1983) p. 69.
15. One source of confusion in tracing the Pennell family is the many marriages to Smiths. Deacon John married Eleanor Smith (parentage undocumented); his brother, Abraham, married a Smith; two of his sons married daughters of Hezekiah Smith; and his daughter, Hannah, married, Joel Smith, son of Simeon, an early Halifax settler, probably no relation to Hezekiah. A granddaughter married Jonathan Smith, whose son by a previous marriage was Austin Smith, both of whom are found in Halifax land records.
16. Pennell Hill Cemetery, gravestone record.
17. Prior to the summer of 2003, the burial site of Chloe Smith Stacy was a mystery. The persistence of Nancy Nims and Cathy Swett was rewarded when Nancy pulled back the sod next to John Richardson Stacy's marker in the Pennell Hill Cemetery to reveal her badly disintegrated yet still readable headstone. The Joel Smith family Bible record, discovered in the family files at the HHS, documents Chloe's parents. Thus there are, in fact, still Deacon John Pennell descendants in Halifax: the descendants of Sanford Smith Fairbanks and Rufus Crosier, for example.
18. Elizabeth A. Curler, *The Life and Times of Figure,* http://nmmh.tripod.com/figure.html
19. Ibid.
20. Charles McCune, *Halifacts,* no. 28, August 1998, p. 5.

CARVED IN STONE
GAULT / GAUT

A descendant of Captain John Gault, Gary Putnam, who has spent many years researching his ancestry, commented, "Of all the families I've researched, this one has to be the most challenging and frustrating."[1] Agreed. Frustration begins with the surname itself, which appears in Halifax town records variously as Gaut, Gatt, Goit, Gautt, and Gault. The elegant slate headstones at the Clark Farm Cemetery, where William is buried, bear the incised name "Gaut"; whereas, the engraver of the slate headstones at the Pennell Hill Cemetery, where Captain John is buried, carved the name "Gault." These two men were brothers, sons of James and Elizabeth Gault of Londonderry and Windham, New Hampshire.

The Halifax Gault/Gaut families, like many of the earliest settlers, descend from the Scotch-Presbyterian families who were living in Northern Ireland in the seventeenth century. William and Benjamin Galt's signatures appear on the Shute petition [↪ 499] that hangs in the Historical Society in Concord, New Hampshire; they arrived on one of the shiploads of petitioners who sailed to Boston between 1718 and 1726. Putnam believes the Halifax Gault families descend from William Galt of Londonderry, New Hampshire where many of the Scotch-Irish immigrants settled. The "Mr. Gaught," said by Eastman to have settled on Pennell Hill before 1766, has not been identified; nor is it likely that he was the grandfather of Captain John Gault who, in the spring of 1788, was shot on muster day.[2] Captain Gault's older brother, William, however, had arrived in town by 1766.

THE KNOWN AND THE UNKNOWN

There are certainties about the Gault families of Halifax. We know that both William and John dwelled and died in town. William arrived with his wife, Elizabeth, from Deerfield, Massachusetts in 1766 and took up residence in eastern Halifax. The Ellis account book [↪ 34] verifies William Gault's presence in June of 1766. Captain John, his wife Betty, and their son, Alexander, left Windham, Rockingham County, New Hampshire, and settled at Pennell Hill in southwestern Halifax by 1775.[3] Another certainty is Jane Gault married Robert Crosier, raised a family, and died in Halifax. Most likely William and John were her first cousins, sons of her father's brother James. Rev. Eastman wrote Jane's younger brother, Samuel, died in Halifax in 1761 and is buried on Christian Hill in Colrain. This is said to have been the first death in Halifax. However, there is no record of Samuel's birth or death, nor is there any record of his parents.[4]

Land records from the earliest Halifax books document the presence of other Gaults, who may have been Jane and Samuel's siblings. In 1784, James Gault of New Perth, New York, deeded to John Gault of Halifax, Cumberland County, New York, 100 acres, "being part of" Original Lot 3 and bounded by Alexander Gault's land on the west [HLR 1A: 177]. In 1786, John Phinton Gault of

New Perth sold to John Kirkley of Halifax, 100 acres, being part of Original Lot 3, which he received "by estate of inheritance" [HLR 1A: 91]. These deeds suggest the presence of James, John Fenton, and Alexander Gault in the Pennell Hill and Phillips Hill, Lot 3 area. Military records for these three men confirm they lived in Halifax, "of the York grants," during time of the Revolution.

Originally granted to Benning Wentworth's secretary, Thomas Atkinson, Lot 3 was conveyed to Hugh Bolton of Colrain on June 8, 1763. Hugh Bolton's daughter, Elizabeth married Samuel Morrison, who moved to Halifax before 1766. It is probably more than a coincidence that Alexander Gault is listed on a 1746 Londonderry, New Hampshire, muster roll[5] of men paid for fourteen days scouting at Canterbury, together with Samuel Morrison, Joseph Stewart, Hugh Thompson, and several Wilsons, all early settlers of Colrain and Halifax. Gary Putnam believes that the father of Jane, John Fenton, James, Alexander, and Samuel was Alexander Gault (b. circa 1726), and that he migrated to Halifax. Samuel Gault, Alexander's brother, may also have been in Halifax prior to settling in Bradford (formerly Moretown), Vermont. Jane Gault Crosier named her firstborn son Samuel— whether after her father or brother or both falls into the category of unknowns.

Further documentation of the connection between the Gaults and Colrain families is found in James Gault's pension record. In his affidavit made January 1, 1833, he states that in 1776 he "then lived in the town of Halifax, then state of NY but now in the state of Vermont," when he entered the service as a substitute for Jonathan McGee in the company of Captain of Hugh McClellan.[6] This enlistment took him to Deerfield, Northampton, and eventually to the Battle of White Plains. Other enlistments took him to Albany, Saratoga, Fort Edward, Fort Ann, and Ticonderoga. He then enlisted in the company called "The Green Mountain Boys" to join Colonel Warner's Regiment and was present when the Indians attacked.[7] Similar and overlapping military service is found for Alexander, John Fenton, and John Gault.

It is known the Gaults bought, sold, and inherited property in Lots 3, 11, 18, and 19. At the time of his death, Captain John Gault had recently wed Margaret and acquired property in Lot 11, where he planned to build a frame house. His inventory, taken in 1789, included "50 acres in the house lot, a new frame for a house, and 40 ¾ acres of land referred to as the Ferral [Jerrill] lot."[8] It is also known that by the time of the 1790 census the only Pennell Hill Gault still in Halifax was "Widow Gautt," listed as head of household. The name "John Gault" appeared on the "Vermont sufferers" list of July 11, 1786, as a recipient of 280 acres of land in Bainbridge, Chenango County, New York. Indications are that Captain Gault intended to continue to dwell in Halifax. It is not known what became of Margaret after her husband's death. Their only son, Alexander, who married Elizabeth Mixer of Colrain, lived and owned property in Whitingham before heading west to Ohio in 1814.[9]

William Gaut, a weaver from Londonderry, New Hampshire, married Elizabeth Leen on July 7, 1765 in Deerfield, Hampshire County, Massachusetts. This was William's second marriage. In 1766, the Deerfield selectmen warned William and Elisabeth out of town together with his sons, William, Alexander and

John and daughters, Jean and Lydia, "last from Londonderry in the province of New Hampshire."[10] Sons James and Archibald were born in 1770 and 1772. We know from a bequest in Gaut's will, that he had a daughter, Esther, who was the wife of Captain Donald Donalson of Colrain. William and Elizabeth lived on Original Lot 23 on the east side of Halifax. In addition, he owned part of adjacent Lot 31, which he purchased from Benoni Cuthbert. The Gaut gravestones are among the earliest slate markers in town and are located in what is now known as the Clark Farm Cemetery. Both of William's sons married Clarks. James died in 1771 in his twenty-first year and is buried in the farm cemetery. Thomas Clark was named guardian to Thomas Gaut, James's infant son. William Jr.'s wife, Jane Clark, is buried in the farm cemetery also, but only her footstone is visible. Jesse Clark was named guardian of Jane and William Jr.'s son William, born 1799, who remained in Halifax after his father remarried and moved to Madison, New York. William Sr. was awarded 210 acres in Bainbridge, New York, in 1791, but he did not relocate. His son Archibald appears to have gone to Jericho, New York, to claim the land; however, he was back living in Halifax at the time of the 1800 census. A number of property transactions involving this family appear in the town records. From time to time, William purchased property at sheriff's auctions, perhaps as an investment. In 1786, he bought from his nephew, Alexander of New Perth, fifty acres once owned by Thomas Baker abutting Captain John Gaut's land [HLR 1: 294], and he reconveyed that parcel to Captain James Pennell in 1792 [HLR 2: 210]. William Gaut died in 1801. On March 5, 1805, Archibald Gaut of Halifax deeded to Elisha Worden of Marlboro 120 acres of Original Lots 23 and 31 at Halifax, twenty acres to be taken off fifty acres of land deeded by Benoni Cuthbert to William Gaut who deeded it to Archibald [HLR 4: 54]. For more than a century, ownership of this farm property continued in the Worden family.

GAULTS IN THE COMMUNITY

Military service, as has been noted, was integral to the lives of the Pennell Hill Gaults. In town politics, John Gault's name is on the list of freemen, and he attended town meeting. He is referred to as Ensign, Lieutenant, and Captain. Ensign John Gault was chosen to serve as "Haward" (Hayward) in 1781, a lister in 1782, and as a "Surveyor of the Highways" from 1781–1784. He served as surveyor of highways in 1786, and he continued to serve as captain of the local militia until his death on training day. Politically, it would seem most members of the Gault families aligned themselves with the Yorker faction. For their loyalty, both William and John were granted land in Bainbridge, New York. Williams's neighbors Asa and Samuel Clark, William Shattuck, and David Lamb were granted sufferers' land. By 1783/4, most of the Pennell Hill Gaults, together with their neighbors, the Gillis family, who owned all of Lot 11, had moved to Salem, Washington County, New York. The Vermont State Assembly declared Yorkers, "enemies of the state," and their lands were subject to confiscation. A close neighbor, Lieutenant Thomas Baker, suffered confiscation of his property. In the census of 1800, there were far more Gaut/Gault names listed in New York State than in Vermont. In Windham County one finds Captain John's son, Alexander of Whitingham, and William's sons William and Archibald of Halifax. Jane Gault Crosier may be the only other member of these families to have remained in Halifax. She is buried in the Center Cemetery, having lived to the age of 105 years, five months, and nine days.

EPILOGUE

The Gault families were present in Halifax for about four decades; their most enduring legacy is carved in stone. Worthy of note is the fact that very few of the earliest settlers of Halifax have probate records. Many do not have cemetery markers. Captain John and William have both. Much can be learned about the character, families, and condition of their lives and deaths from these records. Captain John Gault's probate record is one of only five[11] from Halifax that predate the 1790 census. Without a stable currency during the grants period, business had to be transacted via a trading network of services and goods. The extensive list of those debits and credits found in probate documents provides a record of people in town during a period of great flux. Ironically, Captain Gault's long list of creditors includes Amos Muzzy, owner of the tavern where he was shot. It is interesting that although Captain Gault signed all his deeds with an X, signifying that he could not read or write, his inventory included, in addition to articles of clothing housewares, tools and livestock, "one old bible, one spelling book and one old Esop's Fables."[12]

In his last will and testament [HLR 2: 267], William Gaut says, "And whereas I have forty seven dollars and nine in cash now by me, my will is that out of that money there shall be purchased two pair of gravestones, one pair to be placed at my grave after my decease and the other at the grave of my late wife." Her headstone says, "In memory of Mrs. Elisabeth wife of Mr. William Gaut who died Aug. 14th 1800 in the 71st year of her age. Death is a debt to nature due/Which I have paid and so must you." His marker says, "In memory of Mr. William Gaut who died Jan. 24th 1801, in the 66th year of his age. Blessed are the dead / Which die in the Lord." These elegant slate markers were placed, originally, in a public cemetery and are no longer standing. Sadly, the violence done to them happened just a few years after they were erected. Ebenezer Clark was accused and convicted of "furiously plowing, breaking and knocking down stones" in the cemetery behind his home in October of 1807. He appealed his conviction [↪ 511] and in 1809 at a new trial, the local court found him not guilty. Testimony at that trial was not included in the court record. After the controversy, the cemetery was no longer used for burials nor cared for by the town, and most of the stone markers are still lying on the ground, partially buried with sod. Hopefully, the little Clark Farm Cemetery, now considered to be on private land, will one day be restored, enclosed by a wall, and its original beauty preserved.

The Captain Gault slate markers, on the other hand, still stand and are in good condition at the old Halifax cemetery on Pennell Hill. John's headstone tells the story of his violent death: "In Memory of Capt. John Gault Who was axedentely shot through the head by one of his soldiers on training May ye 6th, 1788 in ye 43rd year of his Age In health and prosperity/ Anon in eternity." and for his wife who, it is believed, died in childbirth, "Mrs. Bettey, Ye wife of Capt. John Gault who died March ye 9th, 1776 in ye 34th year of Age The morn of life I saw/Behold this world as vain/ Resined to natures law/ Imortal life to gain." No other Gault family markers are found on Pennell Hill. *~ Constance Lancaster*

Two Elizabeths – Elizabeth Morse, wife of John Gault and Elizabeth Leen, wife of William Gaut. Their carved slate markers are located in the Pennell Hill and Clark Farm Cemeteries.

 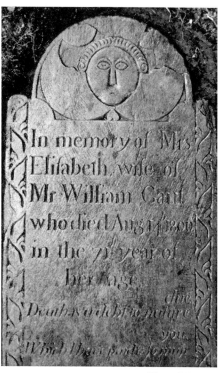

Photo C. Lancaster   Photo C. Perna

ENDNOTES
1. Gary Putnam, via e-mail to C. Lancaster, October 24, 2002.
2. Gary Putnam believes the ages and dates are not reasonable for John Gaut's grandfather to have been a Pennell Hill settler. From an e-mail, October 24, 2002.
3. John and Betty's marriage is recorded in Windham, New Hampshire, and there is no record of John Gault, son of James and Elizabeth, in Windham after December 1774, when he is listed as freeholder and taxpayer. http://wc.rootsweb.com/cgi-bin/igm.cgi?op=GET&db=garyputnam&id=I2208
4. If Samuel's family, whoever they were, did live in Halifax in 1761, it calls into question the designation of Abner Rice as first settler of Halifax. However, to date, no confirming records have been located.

5. Chandler Eastman Potter, *Military History of New Hampshire,* 1623–1861, Vol. 1 (Concord, NH: Adjutant General's Office, 1866–1868) p. 91.

6 NARA, pension file S15134. http://worldconnect.rootsweb.com

7. Ibid.

8. Estate of John Gautte [sic], Probate Records, District of Marlboro, Vermont, Vol. 1, pp. 246–247.

9. "In 1814, the Alexander Gaut family left Whitingham and headed west. The parents and their eight children, with all their possessions, traveled in a wagon pulled by oxen. Their progress was slow. They were compelled to stop by the illness of their youngest child, Lucy. She died, and was buried by the roadside. With saddened hearts, the family went on, anxious to reach their destination." Mildred Stearns, unpublished personal papers, including "The History of John Gaut Family." http://worldconnect.rootsweb.com

10. *Court of Sessions 1766–1771,* Hampshire County Courthouse, Northampton, MA. Book 10, p. 35.

11. The other pre-1790 Halifax probate records on file are for Philemon Stacy, Thomas Alverson, William Frazier, and Jonathan Harrington.

12. Estate of John Gautte, [sic] Probate Records, District of Marlboro, Vermont, Vol. 1, pp. 246–247.

* * *

"When men came to hack out homesteads in the forest before bringing their families here, they lived in the simplest fashion. . . . Three things were of absolute necessity for the early settler — his gun, a large iron kettle, and an axe."

Clara Crosier Barnard, Bicentennial address, May 10, 1975

BENJAMIN HENRY ARRIVES

In 1762, one year after Abner Rice's first settlement, a new figure appears on the Halifax scene. This is the young intrepid Benjamin Henry Sr. of Colrain, Massachusetts, who, upon returning from the French and Indian War, purchased the westerly part of Original Lot 7, containing 182 acres, from "Abner Rice of Halifax in the province of New Hampshire Husbandman in consideration of the sum of twenty three pounds thirteen shillings & four pence Lawful Money of the province of the Massachusetts Bay," by deed of December 16, 1762 (recorded April 10, 1788) [HLR 1A: 570]. When Benjamin Henry Sr. bought his property in Halifax, it was only two months before the 1763 Treaty of Paris officially ended the French and Indian War, and five years prior to his marriage to Martha Ayers of Colrain in 1767. Did the young man want a farmstead of his own in "the wilderness" close to his family in Colrain? During the 1760s, Colrain families were crossing the border to settle in Halifax, including John Pennell Jr. (1765) and Samuel Clark (1766).[1]

Benjamin Henry Sr. was born in Colrain on May 12, 1742, the son of Hugh and Mary Henry. The Henry family (descended from French Huguenots) can be traced back to Benjamin's grandfather, David Henry of Londonderry, Ireland. His grandmother was Scotch-Irish, as were many of the settlers of Colrain. Two of David's sons, John and Hugh, came to America and settled in Colrain in 1738. Hugh and his wife Mary were married in Ireland and had eight children, of which Benjamin was the youngest and the only one born in Colrain. (His birth closely followed that of Abraham Pennell, born March 21, 1742, the first white male born in Colrain.) Hugh Henry was the moderator of Colrain's first town meeting, which was held in his home. He died in 1746 when Benjamin was only four years old.[2]

Benjamin, together with his older brother James, are reported to have served as scouts with the elite British unit known as Rogers' Rangers during the French and Indian War.[3] Benjamin, who would have been sixteen years old at the time, was said to have been present at the attempted storming of Fort Ticonderoga. This would have been in 1758 when a superior British force under General Abercrombie was repulsed with heavy losses. In that same year, his brother John, then age twenty-eight, had an encounter with Indians near Fort Morrison in the northern part of Colrain.

> On March 21, 1758, John Henry and John Morrison had a narrow escape. Signs of Indians were discovered near Fort Morrison and the two men, probably members of the garrison there, set out for the other forts to warn them of the danger. The Indians, who were watching the fort from ambush, followed them and fired at the two men. One of the bullets broke Morrison's arm but he disregarded the pain and continued on the way to Fort Lucas. Fortunately they came across a colt in one of the fields which they were crossing on foot. It had never been broken to riding but

Henry held it and assisted Morrison to mount, and after mounting
it himself, without bit or bridle guided the colt across the river and
up the hill to Fort Lucas. The Indians, enraged by the men's
escape turned back to Fort Morrison, set fire to John Morrison's
barn which was south of the fort, and killed his cattle. . . ."[4]

BENJAMIN SETTLES IN HALIFAX

We have little information on
Benjamin's activities in the period
between his 1762 property purchase and
his 1767 marriage. But we can assume
that such an active, ambitious young
man would not wait to start clearing the
land and providing some rudimentary
shelter. He had relatives in Colrain,
including his widowed mother, who
died at an advanced age at his home in
Halifax; his uncle, John Henry, who
died in 1755; and aunt, Mary McCrellis.
John Henry's farm, which was in the
vicinity of Fort Morrison in the
northern part of Colrain, was only a few
miles from Benjamin's lot. John Henry
was Mary McCrellis's third husband. In
1772, she married her fourth husband,
Richard Ellis, who operated a store
from 1764 to 1777 [☞ 34], where much of
Colrain and Halifax traded, including
Benjamin. The indefatigable Mary
McCrellis, who outlived four husbands,
died in Leyden, Massachusetts, at the
home of her youngest son, Andrew
Henry, May 11, 1802 at the age of
ninety-six.[5]

Benjamin's house, originally a
one-room half-Cape, would have been
built sometime between 1762 and
February 17, 1767, the day he and
Martha were married and shortly after
moved to Halifax[6] Their first child,
James, born in Halifax, April 3, 1768
[HLR 1A: 383] was followed by nine more
children, all born in Halifax.

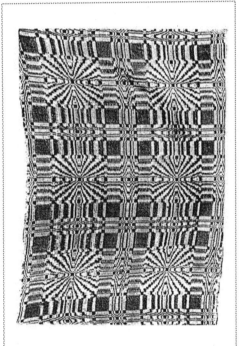

WOVEN *in 1720 by Mrs.
Benjamin Henry, Halifax,
Vt. The great age of the coverlet shows plainly in the picture,
the light spots being places where
the wool is worn off from the
linen foundation. This resembles
"Sunrise on the Walls of Troy,"
which is sometimes called "Jefferson's Fancy."*

Eliza Calvert Hall, *The Book of Handwoven
Coverlets* (New York: Dover Publications,
1988) p. 58–59.

I speculate that the date woven into the
coverlet was misread as 1720, but was
actually 1770.

Besides providing for a large family of ten children, Benjamin was active
in the politics of his time, which influenced his children to also be active in

Halifax life. He was justice of the peace for thirty years and also served as treasurer, town clerk, and selectman of Halifax. He served in the state legislature for twelve years and represented Halifax at the Constitutional Convention in Bennington in 1791 when Vermont entered the Union as the fourteenth state.

"Benjamin Henry A Man For All Seasons" in the next section, outlines Benjamin's role in the Yorker controversy of early Halifax and the part he played in the town's acceptance of the authority of the newly formed state of Vermont. You will also see the role he played, from a position of strength, in persuading the newly founded state of Vermont to fully pardon the insurgent Yorkers in the southeastern towns, including Halifax, in return for their acceptance of the legitimacy of Vermont.

HALIFAX BARN LOOM

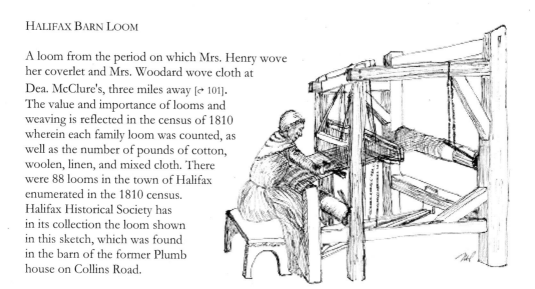

A loom from the period on which Mrs. Henry wove her coverlet and Mrs. Woodard wove cloth at Dea. McClure's, three miles away [↪ 101]. The value and importance of looms and weaving is reflected in the census of 1810 wherein each family loom was counted, as well as the number of pounds of cotton, woolen, linen, and mixed cloth. There were 88 looms in the town of Halifax enumerated in the 1810 census. Halifax Historical Society has in its collection the loom shown in this sketch, which was found in the barn of the former Plumb house on Collins Road.

WHAT BECAME OF THE HENRY FAMILY?

How was the Henry family faring at the start of the nineteenth century? Quite well, to judge by the 1810 census, which shows sixteen members in the robust Benjamin Henry household. But changes were taking place. By 1816, Benjamin, son James, and daughter Patty had died and were buried in the family cemetery.

The homestead was passed on to his second son, Samuel, whose wife Polly would die within the year. Samuel sold to Benjamin Jr., a member of the legislature 1820–1821, and tavern/innkeeper in Halifax, who eventually moved to Greenfield, Massachusetts. Considering the public offices that Benjamin Henry Sr. held, it is likely that his house served as a meeting place for the transaction of town business and possibly an early tavern [↪ 236]. By 1830, there seemed to be no members of Benjamin Henry's immediate family remaining in Halifax. Some of them had moved to other towns in New England, New York, or further west.

I always wondered why Martha, Benjamin's wife, is not buried with her husband. Just recently, I discovered that she survived Benjamin by sixteen years and is buried in Heath, Massachusetts, where she was living with her third son, David, and his wife Prudence (Fish), who had fourteen children. An interesting fact is that four of the six sons of Benjamin and Martha married Fish daughters, who were neighbors, and a Henry daughter married a Fish son. My research of the Henry family is from a composite of Halifax town records [HLR 1A: 383], the Henry genealogy, Henry tombstones, from Lester Warren Fish's *The Fish Family in England and America*,[7] and a letter dated January 3, 1996 from Mr. Charles Fish, author and Fish family descendant of Dummerston, Vermont.[8]

In 1876, an important event took place at the old Henry homestead in Halifax. It was now the sixtieth anniversary of Benjamin Henry's death and a large family gathered to honor their patriarch. The oldest survivor was daughter Betsy Clark, who was to die in 1879 at the age of ninety-five. Services were held under two venerable apple trees and homage was paid to the three buried Henrys. The Henry family must have been proud of Benjamin's service to his town, state, and country. His epitaph reads, "A useful man having represented his town 12 years in the legislature out of 13."

©2008 Stephen Sanders

Endnotes

1. Patrie, *Genealogy*. In the years following the settlement of Halifax in 1761 many Colrain people crossed the border to begin new lives. The family ties between Colrain and Halifax are strong to this day. A partial list of Colrain families, members of which immigrated to Halifax, has been culled from the Patrie genealogical section: Barber, Bell, Burrington, Breckinridge, Canedy, Clark, Dalrymple, Ellis, Fairbanks, Handy, Taggart, McCrellis, Mixter, Morrison, Pattison, Orr, Pennill, Holmes, Stewart, Thompson, Wallis, Wilson, Workman.

2. Ibid., p. 19-H.

3. Ibid., p. 41-G, p. 79. Patrie's sources are family records and *Henry Genealogy* by W. H. Eldridge, 1915. Patrie states "The rolls of Rogers' Rangers are unfortunately inaccessible for as colonel of the Rangers, Rogers served under commission from the Crown, and the rolls were sent to England." To date, my research has been unable to locate the rolls to which Patrie refers.

4. Patrie, p. 38-H.

5. Ibid., p. 62-G.

6. Ibid., p. 79-G. The list of marriages consecrated by the Rev. Roger Newton of Greenfield, Massachusetts, records, "1767 February 17, Benjamin Henry and Martha Ayres, both of Colrain." [Francis, M. Thompson, *History of Greenfield shire town of Franklin County Massachusetts* (Greenfield, MA: T. Morey and Son, 1904) p. 701.

7. Lester Warren Fish, *The Fish Family in England and America* (Rutland, VT: Tuttle, 1948).

8. The children of Benjamin and Martha Henry were: JAMES, b. April 3, 1768 d. July 27, 1815, Halifax, m. Katherine Fish, 2 children; SAMUEL, b. April 8, 1770, d. 1856, Syracuse, N.Y. m. (1) wife Polly Warner, 6 children, (2) wife, Annis Fish, m. December 8, 1818; DAVID, b. June 16, 1772, d. 1855, Heath, Massachusetts, m. Prudence Fish, 14 children; ROBERT, b. September 25, 1774, d. 1820, Salem, New York m. Fanny Colwell of Colrain; BENJAMIN, b. August 8, 1779, d. Greenfield, Massachusetts, m. Betsy Fish, April 21, 1803, 2 children; MARTHA, b. February 20, 1782, d. unknown; PATTY, b. 1783? d. 1813, Halifax, m. Dudley Fish; JOHN, b. June 4, 1781 drowned while a young man (in the Black River); BETSY, b. 1784, d. 1879, m. Ayers Clark; ELIZABETH, b. March 30, 1787, d. 1824, Oneida County, New York m. Amasa Spurr of Colrain. Where discrepancies exist, preference was given to the Halifax Town record, Book 1A, p. 383.

Captain Robert Pattison
Father of the First Male Child

Gone and mostly forgotten is the Pattison family. Robert Pattison, the pioneer settler, was of Scotch ancestry, born into the family of James and Margaret Orr Patterson of Dunlace County, Province of Ulster, Ireland. His route to Halifax is not precisely known, but it may have included Londonderry, New Hampshire, where his wife, Betsey Cochran was born. What is known is "Robert Pattison of Hallifax" is recorded [ρ 34] in the Ellis account book for purchases made in January

Detail Kyra Markham Mural, Community Hall

of 1765. By then, Robert and his wife had settled in the area now referred to as Grove. Later that year, on September 12, 1765, Betsey would give birth to their first child, a son, whom they named William. William Pattison was the first male child born in Halifax, Vermont.[1]

Robert Pattison, or Captain Pattison as he was known in Halifax, established a farm on his original hundred acres of land located in the northwestern portion of Lot 15. His property included a stretch of the Jacksonville Stage Road southeast of Halifax Center; the family homestead may have been the house at the corner where the Stage Road turns north. In 1778, Robert Pattison sold his farm to Benjamin Barber. In about 1860, the Barbers sold to Richmond and Daniel Sumner Worden, who operated the Grove post office from their home at that location. The period of Worden ownership ended with the death, in 1920, of Sumner Benjamin Worden, after which the property underwent several changes of ownership. Since 1948, the property has been owned and farmed by Gene and Pauline Gates. The original homestead may be gone, but the stonewalls still stand, and farming has continued on the land that Robert Pattison was laboring to clear more than two hundred years ago, a decade before the American Revolution.

During the grants controversies, Robert and his brother, Peter Pattison, signed the 1770 and 1778 petitions, seeking equitable fees, confirmation of their Halifax property rights, and declaring loyalty to the State of New York. Robert's name appears in the 1771 census as a head of family. Peter's name is not recorded, which suggests they were part of one household. Peter married and moved to Pawlet, Vermont, some time after 1778. In 1772, Robert Pattison served as a juror at the Cumberland Court in Westminster together with Deacon John Pennell, Elisha Pratt, and Captain John Thomas. Captain Robert Pattison was active in the militia and in Halifax town government; he was chosen to be

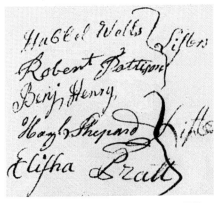

Lister's signatures – 1781   VSS, Vol. 23, p. 101B

moderator, selectman, lister, petit juror, and surveyor of highways at various town meetings. This father, like many others of early Halifax, devoted himself to farming, and sent offspring out into the world who became ministers, educators, doctors, including, in this case, a college president and a Civil War artist.

After Robert Pattison sold his Lot 15 property to Benjamin Barber in 1778 [HLR 1A: 84], he established a new farm further south through purchases of property in Lots 7 and 8 near the area that became the Amidon orchard. The trail of deeds is confusing.[2] What is known is the Pattison family, for the next decade or so, lived and farmed on the Colrain border, where their close neighbors were the Thomas Taggart family from Colrain, the Samuel Fish family from Groton, Connecticut, and the family of Dr. Jeremiah Everett from Westminster, Massachusetts. In 1790, Robert deeded one half share of his 160-acre farm (one hundred acres in Lot 8 and sixty acres in Lot 7) to William, his son. Another son, Robert Pattison Jr. and Sarah Everett witnessed the transaction [HLR 1A: 143] and in November 1791, William Pattison married Sarah Everett. The 1791 census indicates the Robert Pattison family included four males over age sixteen, one male younger than sixteen, and six females. None of the births and marriages of Robert and Betsey's children are found in the town records. In 1794, Robert and William Pattison conveyed their farm to John Green [HLR 2: 243]. The 1800 Vermont census lists as residents of Pawlet, Robert Pattison and his brother Peter's widow, Thankful Pratt who was from the Halifax Pratt families that had also relocated to Pawlet.

Much of what we have learned about the Pattison family of Halifax was found in a book by Henry Clay Fish, written to commemorate the golden wedding anniversary of his parents. Fish contacted the sons of Rev. William and Sarah Pattison. Dr. Samuel W. Pattison of Ypsilanti, Michigan sent a few biographical notes:

My father [William Pattison] often related a circumstance concerning his grandfather Cochrane. He had been educated and lived a Presbyterian till he was 99 or 100, having for more than 50 years been an elder in their church, and then received baptism as administered by the Baptists, making a clear address to the people at the water-side, explaining fully his change of views. He was the father of Colonel Cochrane, of Revolutionary memory [Could this be Robert Cochran of Bennington?]. . . . Robert Pattison, my grandfather, commanded a company in what was called the "Old French War," and was captured, but finally escaped, stripped of his clothes.[3]

William and Sarah Pattison's son, Robert Everett Pattison, educator, was born in 1800, graduated from Amherst College in 1826, and had an illustrious academic career, including twice holding the presidency of Colby College in Waterville, Maine, where he was also professor of intellectual and moral philosophy. Another, son, Samuel Warren Pattison, was the first physician to locate in the township of Fenton, Michigan. He followed Indian trails and blazed trees as a pioneer doctor serving several frontier towns. Dr. Pattison said of his father:

> William Pattison was born in Halifax, Vermont and was a minister of the Gospel for more than fifty years. Though brought up a Presbyterian, he became a Baptist when he married Miss Sally Everett. He became pastor of the church at West Haven, Vermont, drawing up the first petition presented to the Vermont legislature requesting the abolishment of church rates. Apparently, his efforts were not successful at first, and as the property of his parishioners was taken from them for nonpayment, he became highly displeased and moved to Warsaw in western New York. He resided in this locality for the rest of his life and died at the age of eighty-four years. He served as Chaplain in the War of 1812, and was often in great demand as a talented speaker.[4]

Rev. William Pattison's grandson, James William Pattison, at age nineteen enlisted in the 57th Massachusetts Volunteers. "He was at Petersburg, Virginia, during the siege and sent letters and illustrative drawings to *Harper's Weekly*, thus beginning his artistic career" as a painter, writer and lecturer.[5]

One often learns stories of early Halifax life from those who migrated to other places. From Washington County, New York, comes such a story told to the grandson of Dr. Peletiah Fitch and Robert's brother, Thomas Pattison. Their grandson, Dr. Asa Fitch, was an eminent entomologist as well as a dedicated nineteenth-century historian for his county. His journals and interviews fill seven volumes known simply as *The Asa Fitch Papers*. A sample of which follows.

> Grandmother Elizabeth [Ashton] Pattison told "In Burgoyne's time, we started from here [Stillwater] some time in August. I had but one child then, Rachel … we went to Bennington where we staid a week, and then on to Halifax, where we were when the Bennington battle was fought. We remained there till February, for there was nothing here for us to live on, the town having been so desolated by the war, and my husband finding employment enough there to support us. Glad was I to get back in sight of the North River again."[6]

Asa Fitch noted, "A number of Washington County New York settlers who fled from before Burgoyne's army were received into the Peletiah Fitch house in Halifax.[7] Dr. Peletiah Fitch built the house later owned for many years by

Ebenezer Clark [↪ 92, 336]. Fitch was a judge of the Cumberland County Court, and on the second floor of his home there was a large room sufficient to accommodate the public for court sessions. The Peletiah Fitch house was located just south of where Robert Pattison first settled. Today, Linda Gates Swanson lives on the Fitch property and her parents, Gene and Pauline Gates, live on the Pattison property.

There is only one Pattison death record in Halifax: Charles C., son of Robert and Rebecah Clark Pattison, who died August 28th, 1822, in his fourth year. His marker in the Pennell Hill Cemetery is inscribed:

> *This lovely bud so young and fair*
> *Call'd hence by early doom*
> *Just came to show how a sweet flower*
> *In paradise would bloom* [8]

Samuel Warren Pattison said Robert and Betsey Cochrane Pattison "lived to be over ninety and died in Heath, Mass."[9] Vital records for Heath, Massachusetts, document that a Captain Robert Pattison died there on January 5, 1821, at age eighty-nine.[10]

~ Constance Lancaster

ENDNOTES

1. From *Biographies of Notable Americans*, 1904, "Robert Everett Pattison, educator, was born in Benson, VT, Aug. 19, 1800; son of the Rev. William and Sarah (Everett) Pattison; grandson of Capt. Robert and Elizabeth (Cochrane) Pattison and of the Rev. Dr. Jeremiah and Elizabeth (Warren) Everett. Capt. Robert Pattison and his wife were both Scotch, but living in the north of Ireland, whence they immigrated to America, and settled in Vermont. Their son, the Rev. William Pattison, was the first male child born in Halifax, Vt.", www.ancestry.com

2. In December of 1779, Robert Pattison purchased thirty acres in Lot 7 from Joseph Stewart [HLR 1A: 38, 39]. And in 1783, he purchased sixty-five acres in Lot 7 from Samuel Avery of Preston, CT that Avery had purchased from Oliver Newall of Colrain in 1777 [HLR 1A: 119, 120]. Ebenezer Nims, whose wife was Margaret Pattison, sister of Robert and Peter, conveyed to Reuben Clark in April 1779, another 110 acres of Lot 7, and this same parcel was conveyed by Reuben and Agnes Clark to Doctor Jeremiah Everett of Westminster Massachusetts in March 1783 [HLR 1A: 192] Benjamin Henry claimed ownership of 182 acres or the entire western half of Lot 7. The overriding question is how the eastern half of Lot 7 properties, comprising about 178 acres believed to have been originally owned by Abner Rice, ended up in conveyances amounting to 305 acres plus a 60 x 2 rod road? All recorded transactions pertaining to Abner Rice's property occurred after his untimely death and after his family had disappeared from Halifax circa 1774. Further study is needed.

3. Henry Clay Fish, *Golden Wedding of Rev. Samuel & Mrs. Bersheba P. Fish* (New York: Wynkoop & Hallenbeck, 1867) p. 100.

4. R. S. Morrish, M.D. "Early Practitioners in Genesee County," *The Bulletin* [medical journal published circa 1940] found in folder at the Ypsilanti Historical Museum, Ypsilanti, Michigan, courtesy of Ray Henry.

5. Anonymous, *The Patterson & Pattison family association: A contribution of genealogical records 1963–1967*, publisher unknown, vol. 4, pp. 136–137. Retrieved from Heritage Quest via online link at a local library.

6. Laura Penny Hulslander, transcriber and editor, *Dr. Asa Fitch, Volume 2* (Fort Campbell, KY: Sleeper Co., 1997) p. 34.

7. Ibid., p. 29.

8. Regina Carr Hardgrove, Elaine Claire Fairbanks, *Epitaphs from Halifax, VT* (Brattleboro, VT: Self published. 1973) pages not numbered.

9. Fish, p. 101.

10. Heath, Colrain, and Montague, Massachusetts's vital records to 1850, p. 131.

EARLY CLARK FAMILIES

Studying the Clark families of Halifax has provided an interesting view of how both colonial and post–Revolutionary War families migrated to a particular region, established themselves, and intermarried with other families of that area. In later generations, some branches moved on to other parts of a growing country, while others remained in Halifax and continued to contribute to the growth of the community and surrounding towns and villages.

First of all, it is important to realize that Halifax had two large unrelated Clark families, one tracing its origins to Samuel Clark, formerly of Colrain, Franklin County, Massachusetts, and the other descending from Lieutenant James Clark, formerly of Westminster, Worcester County, Massachusetts. These two families eventually merged, but not until 1802[1] [HLR 2A: 49]. This article will explore the origins of these two Clark families, hopefully shed some light on where they lived in Halifax, and explore where succeeding generations migrated.

WHO WAS SAMUEL CLARK?

Samuel Clark was the son of John Clark and Agnes Adams. One of nine children, he was born in Coleraine, Londonderry, Ireland, circa 1716, and arrived in Boston harbor with his parents in either August or October of 1718 (sources vary as to the exact date). The family was part of a group of families traveling in a fleet of five small ships under the direction of the Rev. William Boyd. In March of 1718, Rev. Boyd had been sent by a group of Scotch-Irish Presbyterians living in Northern Ireland to Governor Shute of the Massachusetts Bay Colony. Samuel Clark's father, Lieutenant John Clark, was one of 319 men who signed a document, which is now known as the Shute Petition [↪ 499]. According to Lois McClellan Patrie,

> Lieutenant John Clark was born in Coleraine, Ireland, about 1660 . . . his ancestors having come to Ireland from Argyllshire, Scotland. He was the son of John and Ann (Horseman) Clark of Ballyruff and grandson of William Clark of Antrim, Ireland. He lived for some time in Londonderry, Ireland, and probably received his lieutenant's commission there at the time of the siege. He . . . lived in Worcester from 1718 and was in that town when the church was destroyed. He moved to Colrain and bought several of the first settling lots, 1739/40. He seems to have been one of the wealthiest of the first settlers. . . . He died at South Hadley about 1750, aged 90. His wife was Agnes Adams, whom he married about 1697, probably in Londonderry, Ireland.[2]

A detailed and more complete history of the Siege of Derry and the migration of the Scotch-Irish Presbyterians of Londonderry to Boston and thence to Londonderry, New Hampshire (and eventually Halifax), can be found in C. E.

Potter's *The History of Manchester, Formerly Derryfield in New Hampshire.*[3] Briefly, a number of the Scotch-Irish Presbyterian families migrated from Boston to Nutfield, New Hampshire, later renamed Londonderry (while others, including Lieutenant John Clark and his family, migrated to Worcester, Massachusetts). After numerous difficulties experienced by the Scotch-Irish community in establishing itself in New Hampshire, several of the families that had gone to Nutfield (e.g., the Halls, McClures, and Taggarts) eventually made their way to Halifax by way of Colrain, Massachusetts.

Samuel Clark married Margaret Paul in Colrain, circa 1743.[4] They lived in Colrain next to the lot that originally belonged to his parents, Lieutenant John Clark and Agnes Adams, and later to his brother George Clark. Samuel Clark also lived in Royalston, Massachusetts, and according to family legend, in Pawlet, Vermont, where he was a cabinetmaker for Ira Allen, Ethan Allen's brother. This, however, has not been substantiated.

Samuel and Margaret moved to Halifax a "short time before 1766, when he stated that he and his wife were residents of Halifax. In fact, they were among the earliest settlers there."[5] In 1778, Samuel sold a portion of his Halifax holdings

> [i]n consideration of 60 pounds lawful money of the Massa-
> chusetts Bay, to me in hand paid by Joseph Bell of said Halifax,
> cordwainer [shoemaker] . . . his heirs and assigns forever, 60 acres
> of land with a dwelling house and barn thereon standing, and in
> the southeast part of the original lot in said Halifax No. 16.
>
> [HLR 1A: 148]

As the years passed, and at the age of seventy, Samuel Clark sold another eighty acres of his land in Halifax for 200 pounds, this time to two of his sons, Thomas and Josiah Clark, on "this 22nd Day of April 1785 & in ye 8th year of our Independence" [HLR 1A: 223]. This property was located in the southwest corner of Original Lot 16 and bounded on the east by land owned by Joseph Bells and Samuel Clark Jr., bounded on the north by land owned by Josiah Clark, and bounded on the west by land owned by "one James Clark." The terms of this sale are most interesting by twenty-first century standards, as recorded in an addendum dated May 2, 1785:

> Be it forever hereafter Remembered that a condition of the Within
> Release is on this Special Condition Viz. that if the Within Named
> Thomas Clark and Josiah Clark, their heirs or assigns, Shall Do
> Well & provide for the Within named Sam[l] Clark & Margarett his
> Wife Everything that is Necessary for a Comfortable Support
> both in Sickness & in helth Both Meet Bread & Lodging Wearing
> apperril & a Comfortable Room by them Selves & keep three
> Cows Summer & Winter & a Horse Likewise & 12 Sheep.
> Likewise to keep polley abbot till she is Eighteen years of age.
>
> [HLR 1A: 225]

One can only assume that Thomas[6] and Josiah abided by these conditions. Samuel Clark died on May 25, 1789, "in the 74th year of his age." His wife Margaret died ten years later on July 11, 1799, "aged 72 years." Both are buried in the Clark Farm Cemetery on Stark Mountain Road, where their slate tombstones are still legible today. Their epitaphs read, "His/Her virtues might a monument supply, yet underneath this stone his/her ashes lie." We have no record of what happened to Polly Abbott.

Photo C. Perna

SAMUEL CLARK'S CHILDREN

Vital records for the town of Colrain show that Samuel Clark and his wife Margaret Paul had five children: Thomas, Josiah, Martha,[7] Samuel Jr., and Jerusha. In addition, several researchers acknowledge an additional and youngest son, Ebenezer.

THOMAS had three wives. His first wife, Elizabeth Gault, bore him eight children prior to her death on March 18, 1790. She is buried in the Clark Farm Cemetery on Stark Mountain Road. His second wife, Susannah Bell, died circa 1812 in Halifax; her place of burial is unknown. She bore Thomas Clark two children. Thomas's third wife, the widow Mary Otis, moved with Thomas to Jefferson County, New York.

JOSIAH married Rachel Pennell, daughter of Deacon John Jr. and Eleanor (Smith) Pennell. Josiah Clark died in Halifax on August 21, 1815, and is buried in the Clark Farm Cemetery with his son, Josiah Clark Jr. and his baby daughter, Naomi Clark. There were eight other children in this family.

SAMUEL JR. purchased the bulk of his father's farmland "for fifty pounds lawful money . . . one hundred and fifty acres" [HLR 1A: 484]. This transaction occurred on "this twenty fifth day of April in the year of our Lord one thousand seven hundred and eighty five" [HLR 1A: 484]. Samuel also is mentioned in the following transaction, in which his brothers purchased the previously documented eighty acres:

> The above said Thomas Clark & Josiah Clark is to have all the farming tools formerly belonging to the above named Samuel Clark. Likewise, the above named Thomas & Josiah Clark is to pay unto Samuel Clark, Jr. the sum of two pounds lawful money at the decease of the above named Samuel Clark & Margaret, his wife. [HLR 1A: 225]

JERUSHA was born on March 13, 1754, in Colrain. Sometime prior to 1771, she married, probably in Halifax, Robert Gillis, a veteran of the American Revolution. On June 3, 1777, Robert Gillis purchased from Oliver Partridge all of Halifax Original Lot 11, consisting of approximately 360 acres. The deed states that he is "of Halifax in the County of Cumberland and State of New York." It appears that in 1783 and 1784 that Robert Gillis "of New Perth, County of Charlotte and State of New York" conveyed all of his property in Halifax in four separate deeds. Jerusha bore Robert Gillis six children before her death sometime prior to 1787.

EBENEZER is somewhat of a mystery. Although not recorded in the Colrain Vital Records, it is generally accepted that Samuel Clark had a fourth son, Ebenezer Clark. It is curious that Ebenezer does not appear in Caldwell's compilation of Colrain records,[8] whereas the other five children clearly do. He does, however, appear in Lois McClellan Patrie's *History of Colrain, Massachusetts* as the child of Samuel Clark and Margaret Paul. The date attributed to Ebenezer's birth is 1752, placing him between Samuel Clark Jr. (born August 19, 1750) and Jerusha Clark (born March 13, 1754). Nor does Ebenezer appear in the various 1785 land transactions in which Samuel Clark transferred ownership of his property to his sons James and Josiah and to Samuel Clark Jr. One wonders why the omission?

According to Elizabeth Floyd, in 1808 Ebenezer Clark was "indicted for ploughing up & disturbing a public burying ground which was on land owned by the son of Samuel Clark."[9] Indeed, Ebenezer petitioned the Vermont General Assembly on October 5, 1809, asking for a new trial, indicating that he had "New and important evidence which was totally unknown to your Petitioner at the time of said Trial, which said Evidence, if your Petitioner had known and had at said Trial, Your Petitioner . . . believes would clearly and fully establish his Innocence relating to the offence complained of in said indictment."[10] Ebenezer Clark's petition for a new trial was granted and eventually his name was cleared [↺511].

Questions, however, remain. Is this public burying ground the Clark Farm Cemetery located behind the house on Stark Mountain Road that Ebenezer and his descendants later inhabited? If his parents were buried there, wouldn't he have known that? Also, the reference to "land owned by the son of Samuel Clark" is strange if Ebenezer Clark was also Samuel's son. Finally, there is a family legend that Ebenezer Clark's saddlebags are "in a museum in Montpelier, Vermont." Obviously, additional research is needed to solve the question of Ebenezer Clark's parentage, and perhaps to find the saddlebags of family lore.

Ebenezer Clark was, however, in Halifax as early as 1778, when he appears on the Baptist list [HLR 2A: 9]. We also know that on March 18, 1786, he added to the land he already owned in the upper part of Lot 15, which he purchased from J. Henry Henderson.[11] The purchase price was

> . . . three hundred and sixty pounds . . . Containing Eighty Acres
> with a House & Barn — orchard Standing and is Bounded as
> follows Southwesterly by Benjamin Henry's land Eastwardly —
> James Clark — [this is undoubtedly Lieutenant James Clark] north
> on Ebenezer Clark's — west on Nathan Fish's Land.[12] [HLR 1A: 371]

In 1802 he sold twenty acres of land in Original Lot 6 to Samuel Henry for $200 [HLR 3: 304].

Ebenezer Clark married Annis Meacham, the daughter of James Meacham and Lucy Rugg of Williamstown, Massachusetts. Ebenezer and Annis Clark lived in the large two-story house on Stark Mountain Road, the foundation of which can still be seen today.[13] They had six children, the oldest of whom was Clarissa Clark, who married Samuel Clark, the son of Lt. James Clark and Sarah Kent, thus uniting the two Clark families in Halifax. A letter written by Ebenezer to his daughters, Clarissa and Annis, on July 1, 1808, provides an interesting portrait of this enigmatic character from Halifax's past:

Continued

Ebenezer Clark served as a selectman for the town of Halifax in 1812 and died on August 24, 1824. He is buried in the Halifax Center Cemetery with his wife, his son, Dr. Ebenezer M. Clark, and his grandson, Benjamin Clark. There are descendants of this branch of the family living in Guilford to this day.

SAMUEL CLARK'S BROTHERS

In addition to Samuel Clark, at least one of his brothers also settled in Halifax.

JAMES, Samuel's older brother, "came to Halifax in 1777, locating upon the farm now [1884] owned by Joseph Worden."[14] This property was located on the western edge of Original Lot 32. According to longtime Halifax resident, Jeremy Freeman Jr.

> My father did extensive research concerning the history of this place and always told me the place was built by Jimmy Clark in 1777 . . . the hill below my house, which ends on the Halifax-Guilford town line, has always been known locally as Jimmy's Hill, named after Jimmy Clark. [HHS: Halifacts No. 24]

James Clark was the father of seven children, including James, Elisha, and Asa Clark. Asa Clark's sons were Archibald, Asa, Elisha, and Elias Clark. Asa Clark, and his four sons lived in Halifax until moving to Rutland, Jefferson County, New York, in 1805. While in Halifax, Asa Clark owned a farm located on the southwest corner of Original Lot 40. Jeremy Freeman Jr. says of this farm, later owned by the Evans family.

> This is my favorite of all the old farms now gone, partly because its meadows and pasture abut my property, partly because I have pictures of the old house, (a nice cape with a wing and attached shed), and partly because when it was all open it must have been a beautiful spot. This house was supposedly built by Asa Clark, son of Jimmy Clark, in 1779. [HHS, Halifacts No. 24]

James Clark, Asa's father, remained in Halifax until his death in 1786.

GEORGE remained in Colrain, where he died in 1792, but Hamilton Child asserts that four of his sons settled in Halifax.[15] One of these was Elijah Harroun Clark. "He is believed to be the 'man named Clark' who set out the first apple tree and the first currant bush near the geographical center of Halifax, probably in 1765 or 1766."[16] This reference by Patrie is most likely based on information found in the 1891 *Vermont Historical Gazetteer*.[17] Elijah Clark's farm was located in the northwest corner of Original Lot 30 and "bounded on the east by land owned by Sylvester Worden" [HLR 2: 505]. Elijah Clark, his wife (Patience Ellis), and their six children (all born in Halifax) [HLR 1A: 378] lived in Halifax until 1788 when they moved to Thetford, Orange County, Vermont. It appears, however, that Elijah Clark retained ownership of his Halifax property until as late as 1811 [HLR 6: 26]. He died in 1812, and is buried in Thetford.

WHO WAS LIEUTENANT JAMES CLARK?

Lieutenant James Clark, the head of the "other" Clark family in Halifax, was the son of James Clark and his wife, Jerusha Bullard, of Lexington and Medfield, Massachusetts. This family traces its origins to Wells, Somerset, England, where the will of "John Clarke, alias Kingman of the Liberty of the Cathedral Church of St. Andrews in Wells in the county of Somerset, yeoman . . ." was proved on September 25, 1641.[18] The first member of this family to arrive in the Colonies was James Clark (the son of the above mentioned John Clarke) of Braintree, Roxbury, and eventually Rehoboth, Massachusetts. The records for the Massachusetts General Court refer to, "James Clark of Braintree, Dec. 24, 1639, a lot for two heads" [indicating that the person was married, i.e., two heads, and therefore entitled to eight acres; single men were entitled to four acres].

Lieutenant James Clark was born August 25, 1735 in Medfield and died April 27, 1815, possibly in Halifax, Vermont. His intention to marry was recorded in Weston, Massachusetts, and he married Sarah Kent on September 9, 1762, in a ceremony conducted by Rev. Samuel Woodward. Apparently they only lived in

Weston for about five years. In 1766, James and his family moved to Westminster, Worcester County, Massachusetts, as documented in the *History of Westminster 1728–1893*:

> James Clark, with wife Sarah and 3 children came from Weston
> in 1766 and were received into the household of Elijah Gibbs.
> He soon became a soldier of R. E. [Regular Enlistment].[19]

James signed "A List of Souldiers under the command of Nathan Whitney, Capt., in Westminster, on Sept. the 8th, 1772." He was one of seventy to do so. This means, quite literally, that James was a British soldier here in America. Later, however, he joined the rebellion against British rule. On August 3, 1774, James Clark was one of forty-eight "Votable Inhabitants" of Westminster to "signe a Covenant that might be Drawn up and laid before the Town." The covenant was basically a boycott against Britain and British products. When the boycott failed, as did the colonists' efforts to win representation in Parliament, James Clark joined in the War of the Rebellion.

The lengthy *Massachusetts Soldiers and Sailors of the Revolutionary War* records Lieutenant James Clark's extensive record during the war. He participated in the alarm at Lexington and Concord (1775), the Battle of Bennington (1777), and the march from Westminster to East Hoosick, New York (1777). In addition, he was stationed at Fishkill, New York, under General Gates until the surrender of the enemy on the 17th of October 1777.[20] James was commissioned a lieutenant on July 17, 1777, and served in "Capt. Thomas Nash's company, of Col. David Cushing's regiment; engaged Dec. 20, 1777; service to March 1, 1778, for 2 months and 10 days, with Maj. Edward Procter's detachment of guards at Fort Hill."[21] This apparently was his last engagement in the war. He was forty-three years old.

In the *History of Westminster, Massachusetts*, the following notation is found: "Nothing has been learned of this family after its disappearance from the records in 1779."[22] After six generations of living in Massachusetts, the Clark family moved to Halifax, Vermont. In Halifax, Lieutenant James Clark and his wife Sarah, added two little girls to their already substantial family of ten children (Susannah, born on August 2, 1782; and Hannah, born on January 20, 1788)[23] [HLR 1A: 378]. James Clark and his family lived in Halifax School District No. 4, probably somewhere in the southeast corner of Original Lot 15. Where James and Sarah Clark are buried is unknown.

THE TWO CLARK FAMILIES MERGE

In December of 1802, Clarissa Clark, the eldest child of Ebenezer Clark and Annis Meacham,[24] married Samuel Clark, the eighth child of Lieutenant James Clark and his wife Sarah Kent.[25] Prior to her marriage, Clarissa was a schoolteacher in Halifax, probably teaching in School District No. 4, in which her family lived. The schoolhouse for this district was only a short walk from her father's farm on Stark Mountain Road and still stands. The family retains, to this day, a penmanship sample (ink on paper) prepared by one of her pupils, Benjamin Cuthbert.[26] This document is dated "Halifax, March ye 3rd 1802," and young Benjamin added, "My pen was rough upon the paper or else I would have wrote it better."

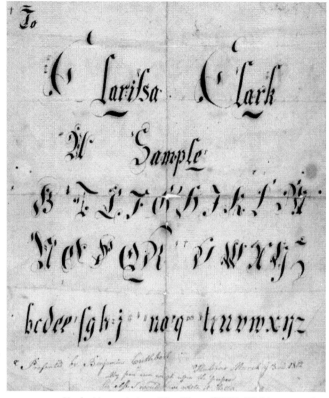

Clarissa's sister, Lucy,[27] also taught school in Halifax. In her letter of July 3, 1804, she writes to her sisters Clarissa and Annis Meacham Clark Newcomb:

> Ever loving Sisters . . . I have no news to write at presant only I
> am a keeping school this summer and it makes me lazy as ever,
> but it agres with me very well. I had as do it as any other work. I
> have gotten me a new gown pale blue [undecipherable] cambric &
> an pare of black morocco shoes & a white cambric bonet. I would
> send you a piece of my gown but it is to the tailors to be made and
> I do not have a piece at home . . . The ring is round it hath no
> end, So is the love to you I send.[28]

Clarissa and Samuel were married by the Rev. Jesse Edson, minister of the Congregational Church in Halifax Center. It is interesting that the young couple chose Rev. Edson to perform their marriage, especially since the bride's father was a member of the West Halifax Baptist Church since 1778 [HLR 2A: 9]. But this may have to do with Rev. Edson's abiding interest in the young people of his community.

SAMUEL AND CLARISSA CLARK LEAVE VERMONT

Shortly after their marriage, the couple moved to Winhall, Vermont, where they briefly lived either with or in close proximity to the bride's sister, Annis Meacham Clark, and her husband, Ephphatha Newcomb.[29] In 1806, however, Samuel and Clarissa Clark, their two children, and the Newcombs left Vermont for Madison County, New York. A Madison County newspaper clipping dating from 1929 provides insight into what their trip must have been like:

> In the year 1806 one Samuel Clark of Halifax, Vt., moved his family, comprising his wife and two small daughters, making the trip with a yoke of oxen, to the very northwest corner of the township of Madison, about November 1, settling on a part of Lot Number 1. They cleared away the virgin forest and made, during the winter, a place to raise crops the coming summer.[30]

Once established in Madison County, the Clarks eventually intermarried with families of another Scotch-Irish group with surnames like Tackaberry, Tooke, Kern, Fearon, and Marshall.[31] With the opening of the New Military Tract in 1806, land was plentiful in New York and many former citizens of Vermont ended up in this part of the country.

CLARK HOMESTEAD, Grove, Vermont. August 8, 1890.   HHS

Halifax, Vt.

Hattie, Sumner and May DeWolf; Almon, Minnie, and Clara Prouty; Lorinda and Benjamin Clark with Harold Prouty.

On Friday evening, between 9 and 10 o'clock, Benj. Clark's house and contents and an adjoining barn were burned. The main barns escaped. The fire is supposed to have started near the roof as Mr. Clark did not have any fire in the lower part of the house. The house was one of the old settlers having eaves on all four sides, a fashion once in vogue here.   *Gazette & Courier*, January 26, 1901

DR. EBENEZER M. CLARK

Ebenezer Meacham Clark was the son of Ebenezer Clark and his wife, Annis Meacham, and the brother of Clarissa Clark. He was born in Halifax on August 2, 1796, and was a physician and Thomsonian practitioner [↻ 336]. The photograph is one of several photographs taken of the Clark home on Stark Mountain Road on August 8, 1890. The photographs were taken at a gathering of the Clark family celebrating the ninety-second birthday of Ebenezer M. Clark's wife, Jerusha Bucklin Clark.[32] Ebenezer and Jerusha were married in Halifax on October 4, 1819 and were blessed with seven children.[33] Descendants of this family can be found in Guilford, Vermont, to this day.   ©2008 *Ray Henry*

ENDNOTES

1. The two Clark families merged on December 9, 1802 with the marriage of Miss Clarissa Clark, daughter of Ebenezer Clark and Annis Meacham, to Samuel Clark, the son of Lieutenant James Clark and Sarah Kent, both of Halifax. The marriage was performed by the Rev. Jesse Edson.

2. Ibid., p. 19.

3. C. E. Potter, *The History of Manchester Formerly Derryfield, in New Hampshire; Including that of Amoskeag, or the Middle Merrimack Valley.* (Manchester, NH: C.E. Potter, 1856), Chapters 7, 8, and 17.

4. Margaret Paul was born circa 1727, but her ancestry has yet to be established. The Agnes Paul married to James Stewart Jr. mentioned in the "Genealogies" section of Patrie could be Margaret's sister.

5. Patrie, p. 45-G.

6. On April 14, 1812, Thomas Clark, like his father, sold his land in Halifax to his sons Samuel and John Clark on condition that they provide for his needs. This was, however, before he married his third wife, the widow Mary Otis, and prior to moving to Jefferson County, New York. Thomas Clark served in the American Revolution in Capt. Page's company of Vermont Volunteers from August 17, 1781 to November 21, 1781, responded to the alarm on October 24, 1782, and to the alarm at Bennington on September 24, 1777. He died in 1824, and is buried in the Woodside (Mixer) Cemetery in Belleville, New York.

7. Martha Clark was the mother of Polly Abbott.

8. Frank E. Caldwell, *Colrain, Massachusetts, Births, Marriages, Deaths, and Cemetery Records (abt. 1741–1859),* (Retyped by the Genealogical Society, Genealogical Society of the Church of Jesus Christ of Latter-Day Saints, 4291: 1955); 1.

9. Elizabeth A Floyd, *Clues For Finding Your Vermont Clarks: A Master Index & Four Cross Indexes 1770's– 1880's* (Connecticut: The Society, 1979) pp. viii, 226.

10. VSS: MSVT SP, Vol. 47, p. 147. Ebenezer Clark's petition was filed in Montpelier on October 18, 1809.

11. This was not the only "transactions" the Ebenezer Clark family had with the Henderson family. In a rather long, three-page letter dated December 23, 1799, John Henderson wrote to Ebenezer's daughter, Clarissa Clark on woman's role in society. He directs that "the chaste Lucretia, and the faithful Penelope of 'ancient story' never thought it beneath their dignity to turn the spinning wheel or the heave the shuttle. And Homer, the elegant and accurate delineator of ancient manners informs us, that the immortal Hector on parting with his wife, the beautiful Andramache, at the gates of Troy, bid her 'hasten to her task at home; there guide the spindle and direct the loom.' How striking the contrast between the ancient and modern ladies of rank; while you admire and imitate the virtues of the one, learn to despise the views and fancied politeness of the other."

12. This particular deed does not give a lot number. In 1782, William Shattuck sold to J. Henry Henderson the same partial [HLR 1A: 71] and in 1779, Pelatiah Fitch sold to William Shattuck the same eighty acres [HLR 1A: 141], both of which clearly state this partial is located in Lot 15.

13. This large house burned to the ground on January 18, 1901. The Clark Farm Cemetery is located directly behind the foundation under a small grouping of trees.

14. Child, p. 221.

15. Ibid.

16. Patrie, p. 47-G.

17. Hemenway, p. 414.

18. Henry F. Walters, *Genealogical Gleanings in England,* Vol. II (Baltimore, MD: Genealogical Publishing, 1969) pp. 1256–1257.

19. William Sweetzer Heywood, *History of Westminster, Massachusetts: 1728–1893*, (Lowell, MA: 1893), pp. 581–582.

20. Heywood, p. 174.

21. Massachusetts, Secretary of the Commonwealth. *Massachusetts Soldiers and Sailors of the Revolutionary War.* (Boston: Wright and Potter Printing Co., State Printers, 1896–1908) 17 v. 27 cm; Vol. 3, p. 33.

22. William Sweetzer Heywood, *History of Westminster, Massachusetts: 1728–1893*, (Lowell, MA: 1893), pp. 581–582.

23. The other ten children in this family were: Nathan Clark (1763), Sarah Clark (1765), Jerusha Clark (1766), Silas Clark (1768), Elizabeth Clark (1770), James Clark (1772), John Clark (1774), Samuel Clark (1776; who married Clarissa Clark of the Scotch-Irish Clark family in Halifax), Josiah L. Clark (1777), and Josiah L. Clark (1779). All but Jerusha left Halifax for other parts of the young republic; the majority found homes in New York State.

24. Ebenezer Clark and Annis Meacham were blessed with six children: Clarisssa Clark (1780), Annis Meacham Clark (1783), Lucy Clark (1787), Harry Clark (1790), James M. Clark (1794), and Ebenezer M. Clark (1796).

25. According to family tradition, Lieutenant James Clark, Samuel's father, was off in the Massachusetts Militia fighting the British just prior to Samuel's birth. To be with his wife for the birth of their son, he had his eldest son, Nathan Clark, take his place on the battlefield. Nathan Clark's service as a private in Capt. Wm. Morean's company is well documented, but the dates (March 27, 1778 to July 2, 1778) do not quite match the birth date of his younger brother (June 29, 1776).

26. Possibly the son of Benoni "Cutboth" of Guilford, whose name appears in the Halifax Land Records (Book 1A, pp. 125 and 178) in land transactions involving Nathan Wilcox and William Gault.

27. Lucy Clark married David McClure on March 19, 1807, in Halifax. They both died quite young (she in 1814 at the age of 27 and he in 1813 at the age of 30). They are buried in the Halifax Center Cemetery. They left four young children under the age of six.

28. Used with permission of Ray Henry, ®2006. All rights reserved.

29. Annis Meacham Clark married Ephphatha Newcomb in Halifax on March 9, 1802.

30. G. L. Clark, "Clark Family to Meet at Eaton," newspaper clipping from Eaton, Madison County, New York (May 1, 1929).

31. This group of families migrated from Arklow, Wicklow County, Ireland, in a group of fishing vessels owned by William Kern. They arrived in Philadelphia in 1806, and soon settled in Pratts Hollow, Madison County, New York. Like the Clarks before them, and the Ulstermen who signed the Shute Petition, they were fleeing religious strife in Ireland.

32. Jerusha Bucklin was born August 8, 1798 in Guilford, Vermont. She was the youngest daughter of Benjamin Bucklin and his wife, Patience Horton. She died in 1892, two years after the photographs were taken, at the age of 94. She is buried with her husband, Ebenezer M. Clark, in the Halifax Center Cemetery.

33. Eunice J. Clark, born in 1822 and married to Henry C. Bell; Lucy Clark, born in 1824 and married to Mr. Babcock; Ebenezer Clark, born in 1828 and died in 1831; Annis P. Clark, born in 1833 and married to Alonzo Weatherhead; Susan Chloe Clark, born in 1834 and married to Abel Gilbert Yeaw; Benjamin Ebenezer Clark, born in 1835 and married to Lorinda Barton; and Clara Clark, born in 1839 and died in 1840.

A Quiet Man
Jeremiah Read

Young Jeremiah Read and his bride, Mary, traveled from Windham County, Connecticut, arriving in Halifax before January of 1765. They settled on the Old County Road north of Halifax Center in the area known today as Harrisville. His properties were located in adjoining portions of Original Lots 45 and 53 near where the old maps show the Allen homestead and where the former through road to Moss Hollow Road now ends. The Green River runs through Lot 53 and includes several mill sites. Richard Ellis recorded on page sixty-eight of his account book that, in "Jan & Sept of 1765, Jeremiah Reed of Hallifax" purchased goods which he paid for by "three days thrashing." [ρ 34] Despite numerous records documenting his presence in town, the name Jeremiah Read is not mentioned in any of the gazetteer histories. Attention to this man seems long overdue.

Jeremiah Read, born May 8, 1740, was the fifteenth and youngest child of Thomas Read of Windham, Connecticut.[1] In 1756, Indians killed Jeremiah's elder brother, Josiah, who was in service during the French and Indian War and on a march from Fort Edward. There may be a connection between the loss of Josiah and Jeremiah's acquisition of a settling lot in Halifax. Abner Rice lost his brother under similar circumstances and within a few years had property in town. On the other hand, perhaps Jeremiah participated in military activities himself and had seen the prospects for settlement in Vermont. There are no deeds or records documenting how he became a landowner in the town.

As one of its first settlers, Read had been active in Halifax for more than a dozen years before it became possible to record his property transfers, births of his children, and to register his earmark in the town records. In 1778, the minority party of "Vermonters" declared loyalty to the newly created state of Vermont and were holding the first town meetings and setting up the Halifax record books. "Jeremiah Reed" is the twenty-fifth name on the original list of freemen. His name does not appear on any petitions nor is he named in any of the various Yorker riots or other local political conflicts. Jeremiah seems to have been a quiet man.

James Gray recorded the births of Jeremiah Read's children as the first such entry, followed by birth records for his own children:

HLR 1A: 330

He was, however, the first member of the community to avail himself of the new record book purchased by the selectmen. The first deed on the first page of the first book of land records for Halifax documents the transfer in 1773 of fifty acres in Lot 45 from Jeremiah Read to William Scott. The first town clerk to write in Book 1A was James Gray, elected in 1778. There is another Halifax first to Jeremiah Read's credit. In a letter, handwritten in 1841 called "The History of the Baptist Church in Halifax" and sent to the Windham Association, the clerk of the church, quoting Mr. B. [Benjamin] Wilcox, wrote, "The first sermon of any denomination I heard preached in town was given by Elder Ewens. . . . He baptized the first person that was baptized in this town— his name was Mr. Jeremiah Reed." [2]

In May 1778, Read sold forty acres of Lot 53 "to Elias Rise [Rice] of Lime [Lyme] New Hampshire" [HLR 1A: 7]. On March 8, 1780, on behalf of himself, his sons, and thirty-six other Halifax residents, including Jeremiah Read, Edward Harris petitioned the General Assembly at Westminster for a two-thirds portion of "wild uncultivated land" in Somerset, Vermont. [3] There is no record of action taken on this request. In October of 1780, Jeremiah Read of Woodford, in the county of Bennington, Vermont "for consideration of two hundred and fifty Spanish milled dollars" paid by Edward Harris of Halifax in the county of Cumberland, and state of Vermont sold 60 acres on the west end of the hundred acres he received for settling Lot 53 [HLR 1A: 145]. Esther Read witnessed the deed by making her mark. [4] The wording of this deed provides the only known documentation that Jeremiah Read received his property in exchange for settling. [5] This is the last mention of Jeremiah Read in Halifax. It is not known why the man who had just two years earlier made certain that his family was first to be documented in the town records, suddenly moved away.

The Read family did not prosper in Bennington. The four children were warned out of town in December 1783, clearly an indication of hard times. Jeremiah died prior to June 24th, 1784, which is the date the inventory of his estate, was filed with the probate court. His estate was declared insolvent. [6] In addition to a few household items, Read's inventory included fifty-three-and-a-half acres of land [7] valued at 15£ 24 s. and "1 bible and 1 psalm, value 7s."

~ *Constance Lancaster*

ENDNOTES
1. Thomas Read's ancestry can be traced back to Somerset, England. His first wife, Rebekah Palmer, bore him seven children. His second wife, Easter Webb, bore eight children. As the youngest son, Jeremiah's prospects for inheriting land in Connecticut were poor.
2. UVM, carton 2 folder 15, Halifax, Vermont Baptist Historical Society Records.
3. State papers of Vermont, Petition for Land Grants, pp. 149–151.
4. That it was Jeremiah's daughter who witnessed the deed suggests that his wife, Mary, may have died.
5. Lot 53 was originally granted to Abraham Bass of Hatfield, Massachusetts.
6. Bennington, Vermont, *Probate Book of Records,* pp. 137 and 142.
7. Bennington Museum, Bennington, Vermont. His land is recorded on the Bennington map of 1785 as "The Read Farm." Lot 46A. A. D. Cutler to Jeremiah Read located near the northeast corner of the town on some of the highest elevation." Courtesy Tyler Resch, museum librarian.

First Town Clerk
Samuel Woodard

We know Samuel and his nephew, James Woodard, came to Halifax from Canterbury, Connecticut, by 1770, since they both signed petitions that year. Confirmation of their arrival is found in the Revolutionary War pension record of James's son, John, who was born in 1762. He said in his deposition that "in his 7th year his father, James, moved to Halifax, Vermont."[1] In 1824, in the first historical account of Halifax, the gazetteer historian, Rev. Thomas Wood, mentioned Samuel: "The time the town was organized is not precisely known, but was about the year 1770. The first town clerk, of whom any information has been obtained, was Samuel Woodard."[2] Corroboration that Woodard served in this capacity exists in only one known document. Samuel Woodard signed *A Petition of the People of Halifax* [↪ 278] on November 11, 1773, as "Districk Clerk."[3] This petition appears on a broadside housed in the New York State Library, and refers to a "legal town meeting."

Samuel, who was the youngest son of Richard and Mary Woodard, was born in Canterbury, Connecticut on January 29, 1725. In 1751, he married Margaret Cleveland, daughter of Timothy and Dorothy Hyde Cleveland. Seven of Samuel and Margaret's eleven children were born in Connecticut. The family left Canterbury some time after the birth of Samuel Jr. in 1763, and may have lived briefly in or near Shelburne, Massachusetts, before arriving in Halifax.[4]

Photo C. Perna
MR. SAMUEL WOODARD

Died Dec. 21st 1794
In the 75th year
of His age
Death is a debt to nature due
which I have paid and so must you

FAMILY PROPERTIES

Deed descriptions tell us even though Samuel and his sons bought and sold a number of parcels of land located in various lots, most of their property was located in South Halifax in Lots 5, 6, and 14 and included frontage on both sides of the North River. Several deeds refer to mill activities. In 1803, Timothy Woodard, son of Samuel, purchased from John Kirkley "south on the south bank of the stream known as North River, east on the brook . . . one acre containing a mill plan and yard with a mill dam and saw mill and grist mill standing thereon with all privileges and appurtenances being part of Lot 5" [HLR 3: 437]. In 1814, Artemas Woodard, son of Samuel, purchased property from Ashbel Mason "on the brook to Woodard's sawmill" [HLR 6: 319]. Artemas cosigned and held a mortgage for the mill owned by his son-in-law, David Fisher. Samuel's son, Joseph, sold Lot 5 river property to David Stow, another known mill owner.

Early town records and deeds refer to "The Samuel Woodard Bridge," and the town relied on the Woodards to take care of it. In 1787, for example, it was "Voted to excuse Mr. Samuel Woodard from working at the roads So long as he maintains the Bridge by his house" [HLR 1A: 496]. Not long after Samuel's death, a 1797 deed agreement between John Henderson and Art Woodard mentions "The Timothy Woodard Bridge." It is not certain exactly where the bridge was located. Some deeds refer to the "Woodard Brook" [probably the Vaughn Brook]. Route 112 was laid out on east side of the North River in 1831 [HLR 3A: 277–278]. Prior to that time, the Woodard Bridge may have provided folks traveling on one of the many old roads safe passage over the North River. Or it may simply have been the means to cross the Woodard Brook. Whatever its location and purpose, the Woodard Bridge is long gone; however, a nearby geological phenomenon, described by Rev. Wood in 1824, endures. "On the margin of North river is a curious cavern, called *Woodard's cave* . . . It is 25 feet in length, five in breadth and the same in height. The two sides are solid rock, and the covering a large flat stone. This is a resort for people, fond of exploring the wonders of nature"[5] [ᴩ 2, 3].

In 1789, Samuel Woodard conveyed to his son Art, a large tract of property in Lots 6 and 14, and Art reconveyed it to his son, Benjamin, in 1823[6] [HLR 6: 427]. We know three generations of Woodards owned and lived on that same 267 acres of land. We know also that in 1856 the Woodard property was identified as the George Boardman Dennison Farm on the McClellan map. Dennison was Benjamin Woodard's son-in-law. On the Beers 1869 map the property is labeled "E. Higley." Ownership continued in the Higley family for three generations, according to Mrs. Hartman, who wrote about the property for the Halifax Historical Society.[7] The homestead on 175 acres has just sold again. It is not clear which generation of Woodard's constructed the elegant home; however, the real estate listing said, "the impressive and beautifully laid stone foundation fits together like an exquisite jigsaw puzzle."[8]

THE SAMUEL WOODARD FAMILY IN THE COMMUNITY

Samuel Jr. was the first member of this Halifax Woodward family to fight in the Revolution. In July 1776, he served for five months as a substitute for Stephen Willcox.[9] Samuel wrote in his pension deposition that his company was "commanded by John W. Gort [Gault] who lived in Halifax" and Edward Harris was lieutenant. In August 1777, Samuel Woodard Sr. was drafted into "the Service of the United States for four months."[10] Samuel Jr. took the place of his fifty-two-year-old father. In 1777, his brothers, Timothy and Artemas, enlisted in a Massachusetts regiment and were present at the surrender of Burgoyne. Artemas's deposition, on behalf of his younger brother, says:

> [I]n the year 1777 my brother Samuel Woodard. . . . was drafted
> as a militia Man from Halifax and marched to Bennington and
> from there to Saratoga. I was in the regular service at the same

> time at the capture of Burgoyne. . . . these were men drafted
> from Halifax together with my brother Sam, viz. Joseph Willcox[,]
> Jonas Shepard[,] Job Williams & Joseph Williams they were half-
> brothers[,] John Cary[,] . . . Amos Peabody[,] Lieut Ned [Edward]
> Harris who was their Lieut. . . . & Jonathan Whitney. . . . at the
> same, Capt. Nathan Williams was one who volunteered, and he
> afterwards removed back to [Canterbury] Connecticut. . . . I
> returned home about the middle of July. Samuel had returned
> before and met me with a horse, my brother Timothy who was a
> regular with me went on home and sent Sam with a horse for
> me. I was then lame and could not keep up.[11]

Thus three sons of Samuel Woodard served multiple tours of duty and later filed for pensions. Their depositions provide valuable details about their own Revolutionary service and the service of their Halifax neighbors. Both Timothy and Artemas received pensions. Samuel's application was rejected. He moved to Bainbridge, Chenango County, New York, in March 1806. Timothy also left Halifax and died at age ninety in Eden, Erie County, New York. It was Artemas, always called "Art," who continued the Samuel Woodard family presence in Halifax.

In politics, Samuel Sr. was an active participant in the efforts to win confirmation of the township from New York. His name is on all the early petitions, and he donated a dollar in salts to help send a letter to the king in 1773. However, in 1778, he did not sign the petition in support of the New York governor. He was among the first group of townspeople to take the Freeman's Oath and to attend the new State of Vermont-sanctioned Halifax town meetings. Although he did not serve again as town clerk, Samuel did hold the office of selectman and often accepted the important positions of town treasurer and collector of taxes. Art's name appears as an office holder and juror for the town, and Samuel's grandson, Benjamin, continued the family tradition by serving many terms as a selectman and also as a state representative.

Art and his wife Elizabeth raised their sons, Benjamin and Richard, and daughter, Eunice, on the Woodard Farm (recently the Hartman property). Their son, Benjamin and his wife Asenath Orr, daughter of Isaac Sr. resided at the Woodard Farm and cared for Art and Elizabeth there. Richard settled on Stowe Mountain Road south of the Center where he raised a family and engaged in farming. The census of 1840 shows four prospering Woodard families, of the Samuel branch—Benjamin's sons, Benjamin and Luke, having married and established separate households. However, the next decade brought terrible misfortune in the form of disease and death.

Between 1842 and 1854, fourteen family members, spanning four generations, died: Art and wife, Elizabeth; their son, Benjamin and wife, Asenath; their sons Luke and wife, Harriet and Benjamin Jr. and wife, Annis; their son Benjamin E. and their daughters Susan, Eunice, Mary, and Elizabeth, wife of George B. Denison.

In that difficult decade, almost every Halifax descendant of Samuel and Margaret Woodard joined them in the Center Cemetery. The lone exception was Francis Luke Woodard, surviving son of Luke and Harriet Plumb, who was raised at the West Halifax home of his grandfather, James Plumb. The census of 1860 lists Francis as a sixteen-year-old farm laborer living at the James and Hollis Plumb Farm (currently the Addis House). Within two years, at age eighteen, Francis would enlist in Company F of the 16th Infantry Vermont Civil War Regiment, where he served for nine months. His record indicates "Distinguished Service." Carl and Clayton Woodard were his sons. Lucille Woodard Cook, retired postmaster for Halifax, is his granddaughter. She is a sixth generation descendant of first town clerk, Samuel Woodard.

THE JAMES WOODARD FAMILY

The other Woodard who appeared on the 1771 census with Samuel was his brother Isaac's son, James, who was born January 28, 1737 in Canterbury, Connecticut, and died April 10, 1820 in Halifax. Congregational Church records show that James married Abigail Harris in 1762 in Canterbury, and their first three children were born there.[12] Their sons, Titus and Israel, were born in Halifax in 1770 and 1776. In the first division of the town into school districts, James and his eldest son, John, were placed in District No. 10, and Samuel's family was assigned to District No. 6. James's farm was located in the western part of Lot 20 on Woodard Hill Road. The original homestead exists today. The 1792 property assessment lists James and his son, Titus Woodard, as owners, and the evaluation of 70£ makes it one of the most valuable properties in town. On nineteenth-century maps the site is labeled "L. M. Woodard." Lemuel Martindale Woodard (1821–1896) was the son of Israel Woodard and Persis Martindale and a grandson of James. In 1940, the original James Woodard homestead became the property of Norris and Pat Johnson, who took a great interest in its restoration and history.

FAMILY AND COMMUNITY

James signed the same petitions as Samuel and also donated a dollar in salts to help underwrite the petition to the king. His name is seventeenth and Samuel's eighteenth on the freeman's list. In the first election of town officers, James was chosen to be a tithing man [HLR 1A: 400], and the following year, a fence viewer [HLR 1A: 403]. Evidently, he served in the Revolution because at a Halifax town meeting in 1787 it was "Voted to allow James Woodard Seven Shillings for a Blanket that was taken from him in the Last War" [HLR 1A: 435]. Titus and Israel were too young to serve, but his son, John, described his own enlistment in Halifax and service in an application for a pension:

> From Halifax he was enlisted by Capt. Hubbel Wells in April 1780
> to serve for 9 months in the Vermont State Troops; he went to
> Bennington then to Pawlet then to Pittsford where he joined the
> company of Capt. Jesse Sawyer ... then with 11 others went to
> Castleton, Vt to keep the fort at that place; he stayed there until

the January following when he was discharged and returned home. . . .Titus Woodard of Halifax then aged 66 in April 1837 swore before Sanford Plumb, J. P. that his oldest brother, John Woodard, then residing with him in his father's home in Halifax, had enlisted into the Army of the Revolution and served out his term. James Pratt of Pawlet, Rutland Co. VT, on 15 Jan. 1838 deposed that he was 74 years of age and that about 15 Apr 1780 he and John Woodard, both of Halifax, enlisted, served together part of the time, with Pratt returning to Halifax in January 1781 and Woodard returned about a week later. The application for a pension was denied as no record could be found of Capt. Hubbel Wells Company.[13]

The following story is one of those told by Rev. Eastman in Abby Hemenway's gazetteer as an example of early settler "hardships and fortitude":

A Mrs. Woodward, the mother of Titus and Israel, wishing to weave a web of cloth, was under the necessity of going on foot three miles to Dea. McClure's. After she had performed the work of her family in the morning and having spent the day at the loom, she returned at night to do the work of her house. This practice she continued till she had completed her web.[14]

* See footnote

Looms were scare in those times [ᴑ 77]. To appreciate Abigail Harris Woodard's fortitude, one should know that Deacon James McClure owned property in Lots 42 and 43. His mill site was on the Branch Brook on land that for many years was part of the Plumb Farm and today is owned by the Addis family. Exactly where the loom was housed is not clear, but Mrs. Woodard needed to travel down Woodard Hill to the Branch Road, over the Branch through West Halifax, and up Collins Road to reach the McClures in order to start her day of weaving. Quite a trek!

Headstones for the graves of James Woodard and Abigail have not been found. The families of Titus, Israel, and Lemuel, however, have marked graves in the Center Cemetery. Lemuel, or "L. M." as he was known, served Halifax as a selectman, treasurer, state representative, superintendent of schools, and justice of the peace. An obituary in *Zion's Herald* calls him Rev. Lemuel M. Woodward, a local preacher of the Methodist Episcopal Church, who "died in the same house in which he was born and had always lived" and where he and his wife, Rosanna Eddy, raised their seven children.[15]

---

* Mrs. Pat Johnson, in going through the attic of the Woodard house, found an ancient "reed" which was actually made of reeds set into a wood frame. [modern reeds are of metal] The reed is used to separate the threads of the warp on the loom. The space between each reed sets the density of the cloth being woven. A weaver would have several made for different kinds of cloth. Mrs. Johnson donated the "reed" to the Pocumtuck Museum in Deerfield.

Of the few known surviving family registers created by Almira Edson is one commissioned by Israel Woodard, circa 1837, which records his family. The 16x18 ink and watercolor is on display at the Coggeswall Grant House in Essex, Massachusetts.[16]

Even though some records for these families say "Woodward," the preferred spelling is "Woodard." Samuel's father, Richard Woodward, migrated from Newton, Massachusetts, in 1708, to become one of the original settlers of Canterbury, Connecticut, and a founding member of the Congregational Church. Over time, the spelling in both church and civil records of Canterbury changed to Woodard. Richard's Halifax offspring adopted that spelling of the name. Descendants of Samuel and James Woodard, the settlers who journeyed from Canterbury to Halifax in 1769, continue to be a part of the community to the present. Though the Woodard Bridge over the North River washed away, and the road that bears the Woodard name no longer connects the Center to Branch Road, the historic houses built by these families have survived and are part of the Woodard legacy.

~ *Constance Lancaster*

JAMES WOODARD HOMESTEAD ON WOODARD HILL ROAD   HHS

ENDNOTES

1. Nicholson Ancestor Table by Jean Maack, http://awt.ancestry.com
2. Thompson, p. 149.
3. Broadside, Halifax, Vermont Town Meeting, A *Petition of the people of Halifax*, "Early American imprints. First series; no. 42449," Readex Microprint, Chester, Vermont, 1985.
4. Scott Bartley, ed. *Vermont Families in 1791, Volume 2* (Camden, ME: Picton Press, 1996) p. 219.
5. UVM, letter from Rev. Wood to Zadock Thompson, original document.
6. Additions to the original Samuel Woodard parcel of about 188 acres were acquired from Nathaniel Bennet Jr., 40 acres [HLR 2: 99]; Nathan Fish, 39 acres [HLR 3: 7].
7. HHS, House Book.
8. Berkley & Veller Greenwood Country Realtors, MLS listing, West Dover, VT, 2003.
9. NARA, Samuel Woodward, Pension file R11845.
10. Ibid.
11. Ibid.
12. Congregational Church records, Canterbury, CT.
13. Nicholson Ancestor Table.
14. Hemenway, p. 413.
15. Seymour C. Vail, *Zion's Herald* (1868-1910): Nov. 11, 1896; 74: 46; APS [American Periodical Series] Online (ProQuest Information and Learning Company, 2006) p. 739.
16. This magnificent family register was part of the private collection of Nina Fletcher Little, and now it is displayed in her former home, Cogswell Grant, which was donated to the Society for the Protection of New England Antiquities (SPNEA). The house is located in Essex, MA and is open to visitors during the summer months, http://www.spnea.org/visit/homes/cogswell.htm

WILLIAM SCOTT
SEALER OF LEATHER

Gazetteer and family historians begin the Scott family of Halifax story with Thomas (b. 1744), his wife, Sarah Hale, and six children arriving from Ashford, Connecticut circa 1781 and settling at Halifax Center, where four generations lived and farmed. Largely overlooked, however, is his older brother, William (b. 1733), the Scott who actually led the way to Halifax during the pioneer settler days. As early as 1765, Richard Ellis records that William charged rum to Jeremiah Read's account. William and Jeremiah appear on the first page of the existing Halifax land records. Read the grantor, conveyed to his brother-in-law, William Scott of Halifax, fifty acres in the southwest corner of Lot 45 [HLR 1A: 2].

Both men migrated from the town of Willington, Tolland County, Connecticut, where in 1757, William, son of Henry and Mary Scott, married Rebekah Read, daughter of Thomas Read and Esther Webb. They named their firstborn son Josiah in remembrance of Rebekah's brother, a soldier in the French and Indian War, who was killed by Indians in 1756 on the return march from Fort Edward.[1] Some time after the birth of their daughter, Esther, in 1764, William and Rebekah journeyed on wilderness trails north to Halifax, probably in the company of Jeremiah and his wife, Mary.

William Scott was the first to clear the land and build a dwelling in the area, which on current maps is where Tucker Road intersects the Old County Road in Whitneyville. William actively pursued confirmation of his property rights during the grants period. He signed both of the 1770 petitions. By 1778, he had aligned himself with the Vermonter contingent in town. He took the Freeman's Oath and attended the first town meeting, where he was chosen "Collector" and "Leather Sealer" [HLR 1A: 400]. In 1779, he held the offices of surveyor of the highways and again was chosen leather sealer [HLR 1A: 403]. Tanned leather for shoes and harnesses was an essential commodity and a major investment for eighteenth-century families. It was the responsibility of the leather sealer to inspect and certify the quality of all tanned leather goods sold or traded. His mark of approval was stamped on every pair of shoes sold in the town. It is likely William Scott was the first tanner and shoemaker in Halifax.

THOMAS SCOTT ARRIVES

Not much more is known about William other than what can be surmised from his property transactions. By 1780, he counted himself among those who, together with Edward Harris, petitioned the Vermont State Assembly for unsettled land in Somerset, Vermont. The petition was never granted. On October 26, 1781, William conveyed twenty acres of Lot 45 property to Joseph Tucker. That same year, William's younger brother Thomas and family arrived from Ashford, Connecticut, and apparently moved in with William or succeeded him at his dwelling. That Thomas originally located in Whitneyville, not the Center is confirmed by the placement of families in school districts in September

1784. William's name is not on the school list. His son, Josiah, and his brother, Thomas, both are listed in School District No. 3. Other Whitneyville families on the District No. 3 list were David Allen, Hubbel Wells, Elijah Clark, Israel Jones, Job Harris, and Jonas Shepard, whose wife was Esther Read. Another Scott relation on the school list was Daniel Squire from Ashford, whose mother was Ellis Scott, the sister of William and Thomas. (It is evident that the Read, Scott, Shepard, and Squire families constituted a "cluster migration" group.)

In February 1785, Thomas Scott sold property with a house and barn in the southwest corner of Lot 45 to Oliver Waters [HLR 1A: 211]. The property description matches the description of the parcel Jeremiah Read had conveyed to William Scott. Apparently, this was William's original homestead. In 1785, Thomas purchased from Edward Harris, twenty-two acres in Lot 21 containing a dwelling house, barn, and traders' store [HLR 1A: 284]. Thus it appears that Thomas relocated his family from Whitneyville and took up residence at Halifax Center during 1785.

What became of William? A deed dated October 1783, records that "Wm. Scott late of Halifax now of Canterbury, Connecticut" conveyed sixty-seven acres

in the northeast corner of Lot 51 to Jonathan Whitney [HLR 1A: 209]. This seems to be a rare instance of a Halifax settler reversing his migration. The customary pattern was to migrate further north in Vermont or to the west. At the time William returned to Connecticut, he would have been fifty years old. It is not known if his wife was still living. Her brother, Jeremiah Read, and his family had moved to Woodford, Vermont. William's son, Josiah Scott, appears on the 1791 census in Halifax before he moved west to Bennington. The timing of William's departure from Halifax in 1782 coincides with the date on a mysterious gravestone in the secluded Scott Cemetery located a little south of

Photo C. Lancaster

William's dwelling and tannery. Today the carved words on a fieldstone marker clearly say, "In Memory Mrs. Esther Scot who died Nov. 1782 Aged 85." Her footstone says, E. S. If these dates are accurate, that grave is the final resting place for a woman who was born in 1697. Could this perhaps have been the mother of William, Thomas, and Ellis Scott?

~ *Constance Lancaster*

ENDNOTES
  1. *Windham Vital Records 1692–1850* p.287 from the Barbour Collection; *Connecticut Town Birth Records, Pre-1870*, vol. 2, p. 8.[database online]. Original data: Provo, UT, USA: The Generations Network, Inc., 2006 Ancestry.com; Lorraine Cook White, ed., *The Barbour Collection of Connecticut Town Vital Records*, vols. 1–55 (Baltimore, MD: Genealogical Publishing Co., 1994–2002).

Edward Harris, Esq.
Green Mountain Renaissance Man

His name appears on countless eighteenth-century state, county, and Town of Halifax legal documents. He served as a representative to the General Assembly of the State of Vermont from 1778 through 1783. He served as a selectman, treasurer, auditor, moderator, and justice of the peace in early Halifax. Who was Edward Harris?

Born on July 17, 1739, in New London County, Connecticut, Edward was the ninth child of Dr. Samuel and Dinah Wilcox Harris. Edward was a young man when his father, who had "entered as a surgeon," died in August 1756 at Fort Edward, New York.[1] In 1763, Edward married Lydia Wight, and Ebenezer, their first child, was born in 1765. The family then migrated from Connecticut to Halifax, where Harris was an established resident by 1770. He signed the 1770 Cumberland County petitions and was enumerated as head of a household in the 1771 Cumberland County Census. By 1773, Edward Harris was an office holder in Halifax Township under the laws of New York State, County of Cumberland. His signature appears on a broadside titled *A Petition of the People of Halifax*, signed "at a legal Town-Meeting, November 11, 1773." The petition asks for assistance to build a meeting house and support the gospel "in this new and as yet uncultivated Country." Edward Harris signed as "Society-Clerk"[2] [↪ 278].

A second 1773 document reveals the early political sentiments of Harris, as well as the nature of his occupation in Halifax. His contribution, as a subscriber to sponsor a petition to the king "to confirm our lands to us, who settled them under New Hampshire charters, was "one dollar in smith work."[3] There is no land record for Edward Harris that mentions a blacksmith shop. We do know, however, he owned property in Halifax Center in Lot 21 along the common. In a deed dated October 1785, Edward Harris, for one hundred and forty pounds paid by Thomas Scott, conveyed "a certain tract or parcel of Land Scituate in Hallifax aforesaid Containing twenty two Acres precisely with a Dwelling House and Barn and Traders Store Standing thereon" [HLR 1A: 284]. This deed places the Harris Store near the intersecting roads of Halifax Center at the first business center of the town. It is useful to know the Harris family was offering goods and services to local residents in Halifax by 1773 at about the time Richard Ellis was closing down his traders store in Colrain.

Harris and Green Mountain Politics

Before, during, and after the American Revolution, Edward Harris, was an active participant in the political arena. In October 1774, Harris was the Halifax delegate to the First Cumberland County Convention held at Westminster, where he was chosen to be one of a select committee to review a strongly worded letter drafted in response to the British "Boston Port Bill," the act imposing a tax on tea.[4] At the Cumberland County Convention held in February 1775, Harris was voted to the Standing Committee of Correspondence to exchange views with other Committees of Correspondence on such subjects as British authority versus "Liberty, Property & every thing dear to the Inhabitants of this Colony & America."[5] In 1776, Harris served as an officer in the Halifax Militia. He joined Captain Josiah Boyd's Company with more than a dozen other Halifax men who served together on expedition to Bennington in 1777.

The name, Edward Harris, Esq., is second on the original Halifax freeman's list of 1778, a demonstration of his loyalty to the newly created State of Vermont. Harris was a leader of the minority group of residents who assembled at the first recorded town meeting on March 3, 1778. At that meeting, after voting to "Except the Constitution of the State of Vermont," those present "chose Capt. Hubbell Wells and Ens. Edward Harris to represent the town at a General Court at Winsor" [HLR 1A: 400]. This was the first of six terms Harris would serve in the general assembly.

By March 12, 1778, Wells and Harris were present at the meeting house in Windsor, Vermont, where the various town representatives "formed themselves into a House."[6] The representatives met and worked every day except Sunday, from March 12 through March 26. It was a marathon session of law and policymaking to set up Vermont State government. Many of Harris's committee assignments concerned fairly routine matters, such as selecting a day for annual town meetings, creating a procedure for appointing probate judges, and deciding what to do with timber on the Wentworth and related lots. However, a more daunting assignment was his appointment "to a committee to prepare a bill relative to Tories."[7] It was on the final day of the March session that three quickly enacted resolutions empowered the governor and council to judge and punish acts of "high treason, and treacherous conspiracies" and "to dispose of Tory estates, and to put the money into the treasury of this State."[8]

The general assembly reconvened in June at Bennington and in October at Windsor. Again, we see evidence of the leadership role of Harris when on the last day of that session, Saturday, October 24, 1778, the representatives "Resolved, that a committee of three be appointed, to prepare a bill, respecting the freedom of slaves, agreeable to the bill of rights. Committee chosen—Mr. Harris, Mr. Rowley and Mr. Cooper." According to historian, Wardner, "This was the first recorded notice of official recognition of the most famous provision in Vermont's Constitution."[9] J. G. Harris noted, "Our ancestors were mostly liberal Congregationalists. . . . Strongly opposed to human slavery and staunch Republicans."[10]

During his tenure as a state representative, Harris was appointed to many committees, and his opinion often was solicited. Volume three of *The State Papers of Vermont, Journal and Proceedings of the General Assembly,* has 267 pages of text, and Edward Harris is indexed to sixty-eight of them. He was a highly active and well-respected representative. In 1781, Edward Harris, Esq. was one of three men chosen to supervise the printing of 25,155 pounds in bills in various denominations that could be redeemed by the state treasurer. Harris served at every session from the opening of the assembly in 1778 through 1783.

HARRIS AND GREEN MOUNTAIN REAL ESTATE

The real estate transactions of Edward Harris pose a perplexing set of questions. In his hometown, he owned relatively modest parcels of property: the already mentioned small portion of Lot 21; plus a purchase from Jeremiah Read in 1780 of 60 acres, including a mill site on the west end of Lot 53 [HLR 1A: 145]; plus a part of Lot 54, which he sold after leaving town. However, Harris did acquire substantial amounts of property in other parts of Vermont. The state assembly appointed him to be one of the "commissioners of sales" in the 1778 procedures of confiscation of property. He is on record as having purchased 220 acres in Pittsford.[11] As an outspoken supporter of the newly created State of Vermont, the Allen family rewarded Harris, together with 596 proprietors, a tract of land in the grant of Two Heroes [p 49]. Furthermore, a petition from Edward Harris and sixteen associates to the governor, council, and general assembly of the State of Vermont in 1782 for a certain tract of land by the name of "Harris's Gore," containing 6,026 acres, was approved.[12] What Harris did with his Vermont real estate is a question beyond the scope of this work. It is interesting to note, however, census records for 1791 and 1800 describe the Gore as "uninhabited," and a Caledonia County map for 1858 identifies Harris Gore, "Population, 8."

One Edward Harris land-grant petition that is highly relevant to the Town of Halifax may have originated with the appointment of Harris to "the committee to take into consideration the situation of ungranted lands within the state which can be settled and petitions filed in the secretary's office." Edward Harris, together with a group of thirty-nine others (mostly residents of Halifax), filed a petition, dated March 1780, asking for a portion of Somerset. The text of this petition mentions that Harris had done "conciderable Labour . . . Preparing to make Settlement for himself and two sons."[13] There is no record of legislative action for his petition. It is significant to note people of Halifax, as early as 1780, were seeking new and different frontier land. Most of the disappointed signers of the Somerset petition, in fact, soon left Halifax for places further north within the state or moved westward into New York State.

PETITION OF EDWARD HARRIS ET AL.   149

* * *

PETITION OF EDWARD HARRIS et al. FOR A PORTION OF SOMERSET *

State of ⎫   To the Honourable General Assemble Now Seting at
Vermont ⎭ Westminister in and for Said State. The Petition of Edward Harris¹ & others of His Assotiates Humbly Sheweth. That

* * *

*State Papers of Vermont, (Mss.) vol. 21, p. 149.
   1. Edward Harris was four times member of the assembly from Halifax...

whereas there is a Cartain Tract of wild uncultivated Land in this State it being part or two thurds of the Township formerly Granted by the Governor & Councel of New Hampsheir and Knoon by the Nam of Sumerset Said two thirds of Said Sumerset being of the west part of Said town Setuate on the Green Mountain------Your Petitioner would obcerve to your Honours that Jest before the Present war the Governer and Councel of New York together with a Clan of Manopolissing Land Jobers Joined to parswaid the New Hampshier Grantees that ther Grants of Lands obtained from Said hampsheir ware Elegal and that the Said State or Goverment of New York would Never Defend Such grants and the Said Clan of manopelisers Did Imploy ther Toals in whedling the Just Grantees of Said Sumerset as well as many other Honnest New hampsher Grantes out of ther Just Rites of Land for Vary Vanity and after they had thus Don the Said Land Jobbers Gave up ther Pilfered Hampsher Titels to the Governer & Councel of Said New York. and Said authority of New York Conterary to Orders from the King of Grate britton Proceded to Regrant Said Tract of Land to a Cartain Clan of menopelisers, all which hes hetherto Hindred the Settelment of Said Lands, and Your Humble Petitioner would Pray Your Honours that as your petitioner Hes Don Conciderable Labour on Said Land Prepairing to make Settlement for himself and two Sons that your Honours would Grant the Same to Your Petitioner & Assotiates in Such Time and with Such Regulations as your Honours Grat wisdom Shall See meat and Just. And your Honours Petitioner as in Deuty Bound will Ever Pray------
Dated at Westminster March yᵉ. AD 1780--

Amos Peabody	Thomas Sterns	John Waldow
Elisha Pratt	Eliphelet Hyde	Reubin Harris
Reuben Hamilton	John Pirce	Elias Rice
Jonous Wheler	Benjamin Meges	William Hill
Josiah Locke	Jonas Shepard	Phillip Wood
William Williams	William Scott	John Sawtel
Edward Harris	Jeremiah Read	Elias Persons

* * *

Oliver Wilder	Ebenezer Harris	John Thomas
Silas Hamilton	James Hebert	Samuel Thomas
John Marks	Reufus Shephard	Benj. Blodget
James Roberts	Haret Shephard	Eliezer Harris
Jesse marks	James Mix	Presarved Gardener
John Hamilton	Zaceriah Waldo	Samuel Shepardson

Mary Green Nye, ed., *State Papers of Vermont: Volume Five: Petitions for Grants of Land, 1778–1811* (Brattleboro, VT: Vermont Printing, 1939) pp. 149–151.

EDWARD HARRIS AND THE TOWN OF HALIFAX

At home in Halifax, Edward Harris, Esq., held a variety of public offices: selectman, moderator, lister, and treasurer. In 1779, he was chosen a member of the "Committee to take care of minister and school lands" [HLR 1A: 403]. Often, it seems, the town appointed Edward Harris to committee work that required skillful negotiations involving difficult issues. For example, he was chosen, together with Hubbell Wells and Benjamin Henry, Esq., to petition the general assembly for an "elevation of their heavy taxes" [HLR 1A: 422]. Another time, it was the issue of Ira Allen's appointee, James Whitelaw, resurveying and mapping all Vermont town boundaries. In 1782, a committee made up of Philemon Stacy, Thomas Clark, and Edward Harris was chosen to "Settle with Deacon McCrelis for his Cattle taken to pay the Towns Debt" [HLR 1A: 421].[14] McCrellis of Colrain was a nonresident owner of multiple properties, who apparently had difficulty complying with the town tax. The compromise settlement, deftly worked out by the committee, resulted in Mr. McCrellis conveying to the town four acres of land in Halifax Center on which to build a meeting house, and that is exactly where the first meeting house, which served the town of Halifax for more than fifty years, was constructed.

At the March 1784 meeting held in the newly completed meeting house, a series of disbursements were voted. Some went for "carrying the chain" or surveying roads; some went for care of John Spencer, making his coffin, and digging his grave; and the final item was "Voted to Esq. Harris for Six Quarts of Rum" [HLR 1A: 430]. In accordance with the custom of the times, this may have been the town's cost for labor to build the meeting house. Another Harris building project is noted in the records: "Voted to build a pound on the south line of the meeting house common for the benefit of the town at large said pound to be forty feet Square built with logs" [HLR 1A: 433]. At the next meeting, it was "Voted to Except the pound that Esq. Harris has Built on the Meeting House Common." Thomas Scott was chosen pound keeper [HLR 1A: 434]. The last time Edward Harris appears in town meeting records is March of 1787 when he was appointed to the committee to audit the treasurer's records [HLR: 1A: 437].

The organization of school districts in 1784 placed Edward Harris, Esq., in Halifax Center, School District No. 10, and he was appointed supervisor for that district. His brother Job and family, having recently moved from Connecticut to Halifax, were listed for School District No. 3, which was located in the area on the Green River that would become known as Harrisville. Job purchased

```
Children of Samuel Harris and Dinah Wilcox.

    Samuel born Sept.26, 1722. Died July24,
1726.
    Paul, born Mar.21,1724. A benevolent
man and confidential friend.
    Ruth, born Mar.17, 1726. Married Cady.
    Samuel, born Dec. 18, 1727. A theoretic
physcian.
    Silas, born Jan.3, 1737. An honest
farmer.
    Dinah, born May 18, 1733. Married
Doubleday. A serious woman.
    Job, born Feb.10, 1735. Solemn but
cheerful. A poet.
    Lois, born Nov.20, 1736. Married Wrist..
Very solemn but social.
    Edward, born July 17,1739. Justice of
peace and legislator. Salem N. Y.
    Reuben, born Dec. 1741. Very athletic,
cheerful and good humored.
```

Notes by Edward's nephew, Jonathan Grant Harris[1]

Edward's Lot 53 property [HLR 1A: 161] and became owner/operator of the Edward Harris mill. Job's sons, Joshua and John, were young men at the time the family arrived in town, and by 1791, each was listed in the census as a separate family. More than four generations of the Job Harris family continued to live and work in Halifax.

In a series of transactions between 1784 and 1788, Edward Harris and his son, Ebenezer, sold their Halifax properties, the final transfer occurring in April 1788, when Ebenezer, sold to Burden and Josiah Wilcox thirty-three acres in Lot 29 "butting west on the meeting house common" [HLR 2: 28], and Edward sold fifteen adjacent acres to Burden and Josiah [HLR 2: 27]. Edward's wife, Lydia, signed his deed, so we know she was still living at that time.

In 1785, Ebenezer Harris of Halifax married Lydia, daughter of Halifax selectman, Captain John Sawtell. In February 1789, Ebenezer Harris traveled on foot from Halifax to Camden Valley, New York, with his wife on horseback, bearing an infant of six months. He taught in a pioneer school for eighteen years— one of his students, Jared Sparks, became president of Harvard in 1849.[15] He also worked as a carpenter and joiner, and for forty years was a Methodist minister. Apparently in his later years, Edward Harris moved to New York State to be near his son, Ebenezer. The federal census of 1790 places Edward Harris in Salem, Washington County, New York, next door to his son. Little is known about Edward's life and activities in New York, exactly when he moved there, or exactly when he died. Somewhat of a Renaissance man, Edward Harris, Esquire, in addition to all his other accomplishments, is said to have written the dirge sung at the funeral of Captain John Gault.

~ *Constance Lancaster*

ENDNOTES

1. Jonathan Grant Harris, *Record and Genealogy of the Harris Family*. (Rome, PA. March 5, 1869). Typed pages tied with ribbon, [typist unknown]. Digital copy courtesy of Gordon Agren by e-mail, May 2, 2004, p. 5.

2. Halifax, Vermont Town Meeting, 1773, "Petitions of the People of Halifax," broadside, microfilm #42449, Readex, Chester, VT.

3. VHS, Charles Phelps papers, loosely bound folder.

4. E. P. Walton, ed., *Records of the Council of Safety and Governor and Council of the State of Vermont, to Which are prefixed the Records of the General Conventions From July 1775 to December 1777. Volume 1* (Montpelier, VT: J. M. Poland, 1873) p. 318.

5. Ibid., pp. 329–330.

6. William Slade Jr., *Vermont State Papers: Being a Collection of Records and Documents, Connected with the Assumption and Establishment of Government by the People of Vermont* (Middlebury, VT: J.W. Copeland, 1823) p. 255.

7. Ibid., p. 263.

8. Ibid., p. 267.

9. Henry Steele Wardner, *The Birthplace of Vermont: A History of Windsor to 1781* (New York: Privately printed by Charles Scribner's Sons, 1927) p. 472.

10. Harris Bible, p. 3.

11. Mary Greene Nye, ed., *State Papers of Vermont: Volume Six. Sequestration, Confiscation and Sale of Estates.* (Published by authority Rawson C. Myrick, Secretary of State, 1941) p. 388.

12. Harry A. Black, ed., *State Papers of Vermont, Volume Two* (Bellows Falls, VT: Gobie Press, 1924) pp. 92–93.

13. VSS, State Papers of Vermont, (Mss.) Vol. 21, p. 149.

14. William McCrellis of Colrain acquired a number of the Halifax properties that were forfeited by Governor Wentworth's New Hampshire proprietors. When the town placed a tax on nonresident landowners, apparently McCrellis did not comply until some of his cattle were attached.

15. Marda Suliga Gedcom, http://www.awt.ancestry.com/

HENRY HENDERSON
HE BROUGHT HOME THE CHARTER

In February 1989, the *Brattleboro Reformer* announced a significant discovery. "A book of land records more than two centuries old lay undisturbed for years in the dark brick vault of the Newfane Courthouse until the recent day when an amateur historian pulled it out of its cubby hole." The discovery was Volume I of the Cumberland County records. The first deed entered in the book was from 1766, "while the colonies were still under the rule of England's King George III."[1] Months later, when the archivists had completed work preserving the aged leather volume, Elaine Fairbanks and I headed to the Newfane Court House to examine the records. Our excitement at the prospect of finding gems of Halifax history within the old Cumberland County deeds soon abated. The writing was tiny, the ink was faded, and there were only a few relevant records. Elaine delivered six pale gray, grainy photocopies to the files at the Halifax town clerk's office. It was nearly impossible to decipher the words on the deeds and very disappointing none of the familiar earliest settler names appeared in those records.

However, a recent revisit to study the deeds has proven quite interesting. Four of the six Halifax transactions involve William Henderson of Halifax. The earliest is 1766, and of special interest is a deed date 1767, in which Henderson conveys a parcel of land "with a dwelling house" in Lot 22. It does not appear that the grantees—in these deeds, Isaac Gibson, Levi and Abijah Willard of Lancaster, Massachusetts—ever took up residence in Halifax. In fact, several of them had settling lots in Walpole, New Hampshire. The transactions suggest William Henderson may have been involved in land speculation, or the deeds may have been mortgages. It also suggests William had already constructed a house by this early date.

William Henderson Sr. was born about 1718 in Ireland and married Sarah Smith in 1740 in Worcester County, Massachusetts. Their children—William, Henry, John, Sarah, James, and David—were born in Lunenburg, Massachusetts, between 1744 and 1757. William Henderson appears as a head of household in the Halifax census of 1771. Five years earlier, however, his sons William and Henry appeared on page 41 of the Richard Ellis account book. The following record reveals how the traders store operated:

[Account of]
William Henderson Jur. Of Hallifax

Jan 1765 To 3 yds of ferret	*Cr May 1765 By 30 pain of Glass
To Everlasting Dr. Henry Henderson	By tea & Scarlet Shallone
Feb. 1 To 1 ½ Yard drab cloth	By 3 yds Brown Shalone
To 1 Silk Handkerchief DR Henry	By 7 Quarts rum
To 10 hornsbuttons	By James Wallace
To 2 ½ yds ferreting	Cr Jan 1766 By cash
To 1 Jack knife 1 Stick Mohave	Cr. By John Stewart 2d

To 2 ½ yds plush & silk handkdf	Cr May 1767 By my order on you favr Abner Newton
Feb 2 To 1 yard drab Cloth	Feb 1767 Cr to an order upon Jas Clark
To 1 linen handkerchief	
1766 To melting potash	[Dr =Debit; Cr=Credit]

The Henderson credit, "By thirty pain of Glass," seems worthy of note. There was very little glassmaking in the colonies until 1810; most occurred in New Jersey and Pennsylvania. How and where did William Henderson acquire glass for trading? Was this surplus from building one or more of the Henderson homes? It seems likely the family built some of the earliest frame dwellings in Halifax.

William, John, James, David, and Henry bought and sold property in Lots 45, 27, 22, 21, 19 14, 15, 7, 6, and 5. Henry's name appears most often. Even though all the Henderson men signed petitions, Henry is the only family member who signed the freeman's list. In 1778, James, Henry, and David Henderson, together with forty-five other Halifax residents, signed a petition declaring their loyalty to the governor of New York. In September that same year, James Henderson sold property in the northwest corner of Lot 21 to Joseph Tucker of Townsend, Massachusetts, and moved to New Perth, New York. In 1792, David Henderson of Kingsbury, New York, sold property to John Little of Halifax in Lot 14, located south of Isaac Orr, west of "Orr's Road." The 110-acre property included a house and a log barn [HLR 2: 150]. The 1791 Halifax federal census lists the families of William, William Jr. , and Henry. In 1800, William, and William Jr. appear with James in the federal census records for Salem, Washington County, New York, and only Henry Henderson is still listed for Halifax.

ABOUT HENRY

Henry Henderson was just twenty years old when he first arrived in Halifax, and thus was able to help with the labor of clearing land and constructing a home. Some time prior to the fall of 1772, he married, Mary (last name unknown), who gave birth to a daughter, Betty, in July of 1773, followed by births of five sons: John, Henry, Levi, Chester, and Jesse born between 1773 and 1788. Henry's signature on the freeman's list follows Benjamin Henry, which means, in politics, he was a Yorker like the majority of the town and boycotted town meetings until March of 1781. Lt. Henry Henderson, as he was known at town meetings, was several times chosen to serve as a selectman and held various other town offices, such as surveyor, measurer, and juror. In 1785, Henry Henderson, Nicholas Dyke, and Dr. Jeremiah Everett were appointed to serve as the committee to make recommendations concerning the new meeting house. At the Halifax annual meeting in 1790, "it was voted that Mr. Henry Henderson have Seven Schillings for obtaining a Coppy of the Charter of the Town of Halifax & Lodge the Same in the Town Clerk's office" [HLR 1A: 177]. According to oral tradition, Henderson retrieved the 1750 document from Oliver Partridge in Hatfield, Massachusetts, and carried it in a bucket back home to Halifax. Considering the fact that for nearly two hundred years the venerable parchment was rolled up and tucked away in various homes of various Halifax town clerks, and considering that it was on occasion displayed with the old relics and curiosities in the hall at the notoriously rainy agricultural fair, it is astonishing the charter survived until the latter years of the twentieth century when, courtesy of Roger McBride, it underwent archival conservation.

THE HOME FARM

Photo courtesy Alice Hebard Lively. Photo restoration by Patric DuBreuil

HENDERSON HOUSE
Rear view of the State Line Tavern from the Hebard period of ownership (1924–1969). The ell to the right of the chicken brooder in foreground is the original Henry Henderson home, later co-owned by Dudley Fish and Benjamin Henry Jr. James Landon Stark constructed the tavern building beyond the ell facing Route 112, circa 1832. Emory Hebard tore down the ell during the 1960s. A floor plan of the interior, as recalled by Alice Lively, can be viewed at the Halifax Historical Society Museum.

Henry Henderson bought and sold a number of Halifax properties. In 1782, he bought from William Shattuck a house, barn, orchard, livestock, and furnishings on eighty acres for 380 pounds [HLR 1A: 71] and sold the property with house, barn, and orchard in March 1786 to Ebenezer Clark for 360 pounds [HLR 1A: 371]. It is not known if Henderson lived on that property between the two transfers of ownership, but the deed description for 1782 states that the southern boundary abutted property belonging to Benjamin Henry and James Henderson. This was the former Dr. Peletiah Fitch homestead, which continued under Clark family ownership.

In partnership with Philemon Stacy, Henry Henderson bought and sold several properties in 1783. After Stacey's death, Henderson purchased at auction the Stacy millplace, dam, sawmill, and mill irons on the North River. Deeds for other properties in the area refer to the brook running into the North River by "Henderson's Mill." Presumably, by then Henderson and his family were living south of his mill in the house he had built on the Colrain line. Later deeds refer to the property as "Henderson's Home Farm." This is believed to have been the site of the future State Line Tavern. Henderson owned the land both north and south of the province line on the North River.

On May 30, 1885, in an address delivered before the G. A. R. (Grand Army of the Republic), Colrain historian, Charles H. McClellan, related the following anecdote:

> I will add an account of the building of a bridge across North River in 1789, by one Henry Henderson as it appears in the records. A meeting was held April 6, 1789, and a committee chosen to "treat" with Mr. Henderson regarding the building of the bridge. Their report under date of May 11, of that year, embodies the proposition of Henderson regarding the matter, and is as follows:

> To the Gentlemen, Selectmen of Colrain and other inhabitants concerned, would inform you that Deacon Riddle and James McColluck hath been talking with me respecting building a bridge over the river known by the name of North River, just below Abraham Avery's [Probably near Elm Grove] in said town, and I have agreed with the above named men to build the frame of a bridge over said river, and maintain said frame seven years from the completing of said bridge, and that on special condition that the said Selectmen above mentioned, pay me fifteen pounds lawful money's worth; one barrel of New Rum by the 15th day of June next, as cheap as it can be bought in Greenfield, by the barrel, and the remainder of said fifteen pounds to be paid in grain or suitable neat stock, at the completing of said frame; and as I have a subscription paper which will be void if said bridge is not planked and passable by the first day of November; therefore must have the inhabitants of Colrain bound on their part to plank said bridge by the time above mentioned, This from your friend, *Henry Henderson, Halifax, May 8, 1789.*

> The town voted to build the bridge, and chose Oren Smith, William Stewart, and Jonathan McGee, a committee to give and take bonds of Henderson. I have introduced this to show the bridge builders here of the present day, what the *motive power* was that built bridges 100 years ago, and that it would seem that the *New Rum* was a more important part of the remuneration than neat stock. I trust it staid in the contract required; though it would

seem from the quantity of *"stimulant"* that Henderson was getting near, that it was in imminent danger of being floated down stream before the frame was even raised.[2]

Perhaps it was his penchant for "stimulant" that led to Henry Henderson's financial woes. Writs of attachment were levied by several of his neighbors. In 1799, James Henry, the merchant, attached Henderson's property and threatened him with the Newfane jail. After settling the claims, Henry Henderson and his son, John, sold off their Halifax and Colrain property. Book 3 records in nearly sequential pages the following transactions: Henry Henderson sells his meeting house pew to Benjamin Henry Esquire. Henry Henderson sells pew number ten and twenty in the gallery to Thomas Clark and Josiah Clark. Henry Henderson sells his Philemon Stacy pew. The same pattern occurred with his other properties, including the Henderson Farm. Henderson's final deed on record, whereby he transfers ownership to John Kirkley [HLR 3: 127] refers to "all my home farm" in Lot 6—bounded south by Colrain, west on the highway and on land belonging to Art Woodward, north on lands belonging to Nathan Fish, and east on the highway that leads from Colrain to Guilford containing one hundred acres. This deed firmly establishes that the Henderson family resided on the property James Landon Stark eventually would purchase and where he would build the State Line Tavern.

   After the torrent of selling, the Hendersons disappear from town records. In the 1800 Halifax census, the Henry Henderson family is listed as having five males less than ten years of age. The family was counted a second time and listed in the 1800 census for Kingsbury, Washington County, New York: Kingsbury. For a man who lived and worked in Halifax for thirty-five years, very little evidence of his presence remains. Evidently, his was rather a hearty family, for there are no Henderson gravestones or death records in town. About 150 years after Henry Henderson left his "Home Farm," Emory Hebard, who owned the Stark Tavern building and property, tore down the ell that was originally constructed by Henderson. Hebard stored the surviving twelve-over-twelve windows in the barn. Quite possibly those old windows, built with panes of glass acquired by Henderson, may be the only remaining trace of the man who brought the charter home to Halifax.

~ *Constance Lancaster*

ENDNOTES
1. Theresa M. Maggio, "Recovered Records Offer Glimpse of Colonial Life," *Brattleboro Reformer,* February 27, 1989, Brattleboro, VT.
2. Charles H. McClellan, *The Early Settlers of Colrain, Mass.* (Greenfield, MA: W. S. Carsen printer, 1885) p. 31–32.

WILLCOX FAMILY REGISTER

Register
Of Mr. Joseph Willcox's Family.
He was Born April 19, 1760, and was married to Miss Pruden
ce Dalrymple March 22, 1793. She was Born March 23, 1773,
and by her had the following Children, viz.

Names	Births	Deaths
Joseph Willcox jr	Born September 8, 1793	
Tylor Willcox	Born May 4, 1795	
Lovisa Willcox	Born March 28, 1797	
Mary Willcox	Born July 18, 1799	
Samuel Willcox	Born November 19, 1801	
James Willcox	Born April 10, 1804	
Lewis Willcox	Born July 27, 1806	
Elizabeth Willcox	Born February 10, 1809	
Anna Willcox	Born January 19, 1813	
Mr Joseph Willcox Departed this life November 29, 1829		

"I Tylor Willcox of Halifax in the County of Windham and State of Vermont, of lawful age, testify and say that the accompanying Register is a true copy, as far as regarding names and dates of an old record contained on the blank leaf of a family Bible, which is now destroyed, and which had been in the family from my earliest recollection to the time when the copy was made to wit sometime in the Spring of the year 1830 –

I further depose and say that my father Joseph Willcox died on the 29th day of November A. D. 1829 – and that my mother Prudence Willcox now of Halifax Afsd is his widow and has not intermarried since his decease and further this deponent Saith not." *Tylor Willcox*

NARA, R11526

From Richmond, Rhode Island
William Wilcox

According to Rev. Eastman, "The northeast part [of Halifax] was settled by people from Rhode Island, among whom were the families of Wilcox and Thomas."[1] William and Elizabeth Baker Wilcox with their family of nine children, migrated to Halifax from Richmond, Washington County, Rhode Island, before 1770. Among those who signed the 1770 petitions as landowners in Cumberland County, were William and his eldest son, Nathan. Each was listed as "head of a family" in the 1771 Cumberland County Census. Also, on that census list were Captain John Thomas from Exeter, Rhode Island, whose wife was Catherine Wilcox, and Samuel Baker, Elizabeth's brother. The earliest Wilcox, Baker, and Thomas properties were located near the Halifax–Marlboro border line in Lots 62 and 63 and along the Green River in Lots 54 and 55. The first Wilcox reference found in the Halifax land records, dated May 31, 1769, is a deed from Jeremiah Read conveying the whole of Lot 62, except fifty acres in the southwest corner, to "William Wilcox, of Hallifax . . . Yeoman" [HLR 1A: 171].

William Wilcox served as a private in the Vermont Militia for twelve days in Captain Boyden's Company on expedition to Bennington in 1777. At the time, William was about fifty-eight years old.

HHS, Ruby Bruffee Austin. *Records of the Wilcox Family of Rhode Island.* Undated, unpaginated spiral bound booklet.

He appears on the original freeman's list of voters in Halifax, and his son, Joseph, was added to the list in 1799. Other than jury service in 1781, William did not hold public office; however, his sons, Stephen and Joseph, held various offices. Stephen appears on the first page of town meeting records, having been chosen a surveyor of the highways. The 1784 organization of school districts places the families of William's sons, Stephen, Nathan, Benjamin, Joseph, and Taber, all in District No. 2. The 1791 federal census lists Stephen, Nathan, Benjamin, William Jr. , and Taber, as well as Burden [Borden] and Josiah, who were sons of Jeremiah from Little Compton, Rhode Island, and from a different Wilcox family line.[2] In 1800, the census records the William Wilcox families of Benjamin, Joseph, Stephen, Taber, and William. Also on the list is Weeks, the son of William's brother Thomas, who had emigrated from Ashford, Connecticut, together with his brother Stutley, and settled on Lot 44.

In 1775 and 1778, William Wilcox conveyed his Lot 62 property in two parcels to Rhode Island emigrants Thomas Alverson and Joseph Pierce [HLR 1A: 11 & 47]. Subsequent deeds place William's residence in Lot 39 north of the Weeks Cemetery on the Deer Park Road in an area where maps show multiple Wilcox properties. Elizabeth Baker Wilcox died in 1788, and according to the town records, "Mr. William Willcox departed this life in Halifax, July ye 2nd, 1805. This is the Old Gentleman" [HLR 2: 15]. No gravestones have been located for William or Elizabeth. The following is from a Massachusetts newspaper:

> In Halifax, (Vt.) Mr. *Wm. Wilcox*, Aet. 85; he has left 9 children, 81 grand-children, and 62 great grand-children, 10 of which, in the arms of their parents, attended his funeral.[3]

WILCOX PROGENY

At the time of his death in 1805, not all of William's 152 descendants were residing in Halifax. Deaths and departures to other states diminished the size of the family. The known 1805 Wilcox death toll in Halifax from early August to late December of 1805 included, in addition to William, his sons William and Taber, his granddaughter Phoebe and his daughter Alcy's husband, Benjamin Weeks.

NATHAN, William and Elizabeth's first son, married Rebecca Moon who bore sixteen children in Halifax between 1769 and 1784. Remarkably, all sixteen children survived to adulthood, but their mother is unaccounted for in the census of 1791. Their father cleared portions of two hundred acres of Halifax wilderness. Nathan's original property consisted of one hundred acres in the northeast corner of Lot 39, conveyed by Oliver Partridge in exchange for the labor of settling, plus a contiguous one hundred acres in the northwest corner of Lot 40, which he received from William Clark "by virtue of the labor done on said land" [HLR 1A: 498]. Nathan disappeared from Halifax land and census records after 1791. Most of the six sons and ten daughters of this sturdy couple married in Halifax and migrated to the counties of Cortland, Jefferson, and Oneida in New York. First-born daughter Elsie may have raised her youngest sister Elizabeth, the sixteenth child. Elizabeth apprenticed as a tailor to Elsie's husband, Ephraim Brown, in Homer, New York, and died in Brigham City, Utah, in 1881. At age sixty-six, Elizabeth, who was born in 1784 in Halifax, was the oldest in a company of 261 Mormon overland pioneers who departed Council Bluffs, Iowa by wagon train early in June 1850 and arrived in Salt Lake four months later having, during the final weeks, traveled through hub deep snow.[4] The *History of Elizabeth Wilcox Mead Noakes* is available at Daughters of Utah Pioneers Museum in Salt Lake City, Utah.[5]

STEPHEN, their second son, married Elinor Ewing, daughter of, William, the first Baptist minister in Halifax, and they are listed as residents of Halifax, together with their ten children, in the 1800 census. Stephen owned property in Lots 47 [HLR 2: 491] and 48 [HLR 3: 177]. The latter, which he purchased in 1801, included grist and saw mill sites on the Green River. Land records refer to Stephen Wilcox as "gentleman" instead of "yeoman," which suggests he engaged in trade rather than agriculture. Not a lot is known about the children in this family. Several moved to Guilford. A daughter, Harriet, married Joseph Nye in 1818 and moved to Ellington, Chautauqua, New York. In 1807, "for goodwill & natural affection," Stephen conveyed 100 acres in Lot 47 to his first two sons, William and Joshua [HLR 4: 235]. This Wilcox farm, located on Houghton Road, is where Joshua and his wife, Eunice McClure raised their seven children. Joshua and Eunice Wilcox have marked graves at the Center Cemetery. Stephen died in Ellington, New York, on August 4, 1844 at age 92 years and 4 months, according to his gravestone record in the Joseph Nye family plot at the Pioneer Cemetery.[6]

JOHN, their third son, married Catherine Woodard, probably the daughter of Samuel of Halifax, and moved to Pawlet, Vermont, before 1781. They were parents of eleven children.

TABER, their fourth son, owned property in Lots 39 and 40, where he lived with his wife Elizabeth, who by 1804 had given birth to eight children. He died in 1805, and his widow married Benjamin Matthews of Thomas Hill.

JOSEPH, their fifth son, married Prudence Dalrymple, daughter of William and Mary Streight Dalrymple, in 1793, and they made Halifax their permanent home. A register from the Joseph Wilcox family Bible recording the births of their nine children is on file at the National Archives as part of the application from

Photo C. Lancaster

Prudence seeking a widow's pension. In her deposition, Prudence states: "she is the widow of Joseph Willcox who was private in the Army of the revolution and enlisted at said Halifax in the winter of 1781 into Capt. Fish's Company of Infantry in Col. Fletcher's Regiment and went to Castleton in the State of Vermont and served in said company as she thinks was the term of one year."[7] Joseph's sons, Tyler (b. 1795), Samuel (b. 1801), and Lewis (b. 1806) perpetuated the Joseph Wilcox line in Halifax. Samuel and his wife, Martha Gould, lived on the original family homestead until their deaths. Their markers are adjacent to those of Joseph and Prudence in the Center Cemetery.

DEACON BENJAMIN was the sixth son of William Wilcox. He married Thankful Worden, daughter of Sylvester, lived in Lot 46, had twelve children, and died in June 1843, at age eighty. Gravestone records for Benjamin and Thankful have not been found. Their children connect by marriage to the Cook, Wicks, Stanclift, Bardwell, Cole, and Shepardson families. Philena Wilcox and James Shepardson, son of Zephaniah Shepardson of Guilford, raised their family in the Deacon John Pennell House in Halifax. The property passed down to their son, Norris Henry Shepardson, who took special interest in the history of Pennell Hill.

Most Wilcox families of Halifax were active Baptists, as shown by the names Benjamin, William, Stephen, Wickes [Weeks], Taber, Joseph William, and William 3d on the church list by 1800. The earliest account of Halifax Baptist Church history found in a letter from Luther Edwards,[8] clerk, written in 1841, quotes Mr. B. (Benjamin) Wilcox, who is able to describe the earliest services held in log homes. This Mr. Wilcox, whose life spanned the years 1763 to 1843, was the primary source for the Baptist history that predates the society's written records. Benjamin was present at the first sermon preached in town and the first baptism, that of Jeremiah Read.[9]

WILLIAM JR., the seventh son of William. and Elizabeth, married Relief . (last name unknown). Births of their nine children were recorded on the same day in July 1805 that William recorded the death of his father, as "The old Gentlemen." Written below the list of children is, "Mr. William Willcox deceased in Halifax October, 24, 1805" [HLR 2: 15]. William's niece, Phoebe., daughter of Taber and Elisabeth, died two days later, and Taber, died a few months later in December of 1805. Perhaps they all succumbed to the same disease, which may have been cholera, given the number of dead livestock itemized in William's probate inventory.[10] Widow Relief Wilcox. married Capt David Town of Marlboro and died January 17, 1813, "ae 45," according to her gravestone at the Weeks Cemetery. The family of William and Relief continued in Halifax through the union of their son, Willard and Polly Scott, daughter of Abel, until that couple moved to Stamford, Vermont, about 1840. Eventually, their son, Royal Quincy Wilcox, returned to the area and for many years was proprietor of the Glen House in Jacksonville. R. Q. Wilcox appears in the 1892 Halifax town report, "For Support of Poor…keeping Ira Learnard." In 1886, he sold Halifax property to William and Laura Niles [HLR 15: 269–70]. The census for 1900 lists Royal Wilcox, age fifty-seven, general store merchant, his wife, Ruth (Starkweather) and their twenty-one–year-old son, William, general store clerk. R Q. Wilcox died in 1904.

ALCY, their first daughter, married Benjamin Weeks Jr., gave birth to ten children in Halifax, and was a widow by 1805.

ELIZABETH, their second daughter, married James Pierce of Halifax and moved to New York State.

DECLINE OF THE WILCOX DISTRICT

Six of William's sons owned property in Halifax before 1800, and even though Nathan left town, his Lot 39 property continued under family ownership. The Wilcox families owned enough property to qualify as their own district. Reference is made in a town meeting record from 1880 when it was "Voted to discontinue the highway leading from the dwelling of Orrin F. Wilson [Elisha Worden farm] to the place where formerly stood the School House in the "Wilcox District" so called, and when a district, designated as No. 13."[11]

Therefore, it is not surprising that three generations from the original settlers, a handful of aging descendants, still farming more than five hundred acres, faced financial hard times. Four Wilcox properties are identified on the McClellan map in 1856, and three are listed on the Beers map in 1869. The 1870 census lists families of Chester Wilcox 500/500 Samuel, 1000/1000 and Tyler & Lewis 4000/6000. (The figures represent the value of real estate and personal property.) Lewis, a bachelor, lived with his brother Tyler and family. By March 7,

1874, Chester M. Wilcox had moved to Guilford when he deeded 30 acres of land to Samuel of Halifax on the road by Samuel's dwelling [HLR 14: 134]. On February 26, 1875, Lewis Wilcox of Brattleboro filed his last will and testament, naming his nephew, Lewis H. [Hart] Wilcox, beneficiary to his estate. "The said Lewis H. Wilcox shall retain the Real Estate of the old Wilcox Homestead in Halifax and bequeath the same to one of his heirs that it may remain in the family where it has been for the last hundred years" [HLR 14: 212]. In 1876 Tyler and Lewis H. Wilcox took a mortgage with the Vermont Savings Bank for that 500-acre farm, excluding the small farm of 28 acres owned by Samuel Wilcox. The

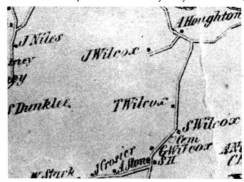

Detail McClellan
The Wilcox five hundred acres were described: *northerly* by lands of Sarah M. Lynde, the farm of A. J. Kenney and the farm of Rufus H. Houghton; *easterly* by lands of Daniel DeWolf and the Charles & Emery Evans farm and land of I. & I. H. Worden; *southerly* by lands of I. & I. H. Worden, Samuel Wilcox, A. H. & H. F. Stone and the James Crosier Farm; *westerly* by lands of Samuel Wilcox, A. H. & A. F. Stone, the James Crosier farm, the Jesse Dunklee place, now owned by James G. Howard, and the farm now owned by Alson Crosier.

property was mortgaged two more times in 1879, the year Tyler Wilcox died, and L. H. Wilcox and his wife, Emma declared bankruptcy. A number of legal filings ensued vying for mortgage property rights. The 1880 Halifax census lists two Wilcox households: Samuel, . age 78 and wife Martha, and Lewis H. age 32, Emma, and four children with the notation "Injuries" by Emma's name. In an article called "Gleanings from the Town Reports," written for *Halifacts*, Norris Johnson noted that reports from 1879–1886 make repeated references to litigation expenses in connection with "the Wilcox case."[12] Details regarding the nature of the Wilcox lawsuit, which cost the town more than $2,500, are not included. However, from the Greenfield *Gazette & Courier*, of September 22, 1779 we learn:

> As Mr. and Mrs. L. H. Wilcox were returning from Brattleboro,
> on Saturday evening, the 13th, they met with an accident by which
> Mrs. Wilcox nearly lost her life. In the darkness they were both
> precipitated down a high embankment badly injuring Mrs. Wilcox
> internally. At first her life was despaired of, but she is now
> improving.[13]

The following week's paper reported that Mrs. Wilcox, who was thrown from a buggy, was still in critical condition. The paper, of February 16, 1880, reported, "L. H. Wilcox has sued the town for $15,000 damages for injuries received by his wife on the highway last fall."[14]

The Wilcox name does not appear in the 1884 Hamilton Child business directory for Halifax or in the Halifax census of 1900. However, the 1900 census for Hastings, Dakota County, Minnesota, lists Lewis H. Wilcox, "occupation farmer, age 52," with wife, Emma A., son, Charles, daughter-in-law, three grandchildren, and a servant. A Minnesota biographer describes Lewis H. Wilcox as "a well-known resident of Hastings . . . a New England man who in early life had studied for the bar, but whose career in Minnesota was chiefly identified with farming and dairying . . . proprietor of the Lakeside Dairy Farm . . . a man of no little prominence in that section of the state."[15]

Examples of Wilcox family lore are few. One undocumented story appears in the Worden genealogy, compiled by John Worden of Colrain.

> . . . many came from Massachusetts, Connecticut, and Rhode
> Island and made permanent settlements. The "Indian scare" and
> the wolves disappeared. The last wolf that was killed in Halifax
> was shot by Samuel Wilcox, in a "drive" some distance west from
> the Dennison-Worden cemetery, on the steep bank, —lower or
> south side of the road to upper green river.[16]

The bounty for this wolf was paid to Samuel, born in 1801, son of Joseph and Prudence who is buried in the Center Cemetery. Among the laws passed by the General Assembly in February 1779 was "An Act to encourage the destroying of Wolves and Panthers."[17] The 1840 census lists this Samuel as a teacher at a district schoolhouse having forty-eight scholars! In 1885, the newspaper reported, "Henry Goodnow has moved into town on to Charles Hicks' farm known as the Samuel Wilcox place."[18]

A story told in a family letter sent by a descendant of Willard Wilcox refers to two Wilcox brothers (probably Weeks and Stutley) who moved to Halifax and built a brick house, having made all the bricks themselves.[19]

There is a perplexing dearth of marked Wilcox gravestones in Halifax. Within all cemeteries, there are exactly eight markers bearing the name Wilcox. Markers are missing for William and Elizabeth, Taber and Elizabeth, Benjamin and Thankful, and William Jr. from the original generations whose deaths are recorded in the town. Many acres of former Wilcox property have, over the years, been heavily logged, and it has been said that loggers at times used gravestones in that remote area to help gain traction in the mud. The Weeks Cemetery, we are told, at one time included more gravestones. Of course, it is possible families simply could not afford to hire stone carvers. William's probate record, however, documents he did not die insolvent. His estate easily paid six different doctor's bills, amounting to $88.68, and $2.50 to Jacob Hastings for his coffin, among other debts, leaving assets of more than a thousand dollars.[20] Given the reported size of the William Wilcox funeral, one wonders why his memory was not preserved in stone, or if it was, has been lost.

Epilogue

It was the William Wilcox family that brought Ruby Bruffee Austin to the town archives circa 1965 to pursue the ancestry of William Bruffee, who married Nathan's daughter, Elsie. While studying Halifax records to accomplish her own research objectives, Ruby began the laborious process of extracting the vital statistics—school, church, warning, and census lists, in addition to all Wilcox deed references from the early record books. She created a cemetery list from Harry Goodnough's note cards on file and from personally copying gravestone inscriptions. During hunting season, she would offer a ten dollar reward to any hunter who would return to her a "most wanted" cemetery stone location and inscription.[21] Ruby typed up her notes. Her work is of enormous value to any person wishing to find family information from the earliest records and has served as a quick reference tool for the Halifax town clerk. Her notes have been an invaluable resource for the writers of this town history.

* * *

Ruby Evelyn Bruffee was born in Springfield, Massachusetts, in 1898, graduated from Middlebury College, class of 1920, and died in Northampton, Massachusetts, in 1986. She married Clyde H. Austin, a commander in the U. S. Navy who died in 1948. They witnessed the attack on Pearl Harbor.[22] When I learned that Iris Wilcox Baird had known and worked with Ruby, I corresponded with her, and she shared these memories:

> I knew Ruby Austin when she was living in Colchester, Vermont. We corresponded for several years, and I owe her a great debt for the mass of carefully researched and typed materials she sent me. Along the way, we exchanged a lot of comments about her and my current activities, the weather and so on, always from her with a wry and positive outlook, no matter how bad the weather, or how she felt. After a while we were able to arrange to meet in Montpelier, whenever I could get away, and I benefited even more from her vast knowledge about how to find information, and how to evaluate it—she also showed me the cafeteria in the basement of a state office building where we could get a good lunch cheap! In cold weather she usually wore a wool poncho which I believe she had acquired somewhere in South America—I wish I could recall exactly how that came about, but I think it had to do with

some wartime work she had done. When we finished for the day, we usually went across the street from the Pavilion to have tea and a snack before we parted ways. She is one of the people I am truly grateful to have known. I do recall as characteristic of her helpful commentary, after a very long assessment of all that she had been able to pull together on one particularly knotty problem, that after laying out all the facts and suppositions, and her evaluation, she said in parting, "these are your ancestors—you figure this out!"[23]

* * *

~ Constance Lancaster

ENDNOTES

1. Hemenway, p. 412.
2. In 1785, Borden married Eleanor McCrellis, whose father, William of Colrain, conveyed his Halifax property in Lot 44 to them. These two brothers and their families relocated to New York State before the census of 1800.
3. Mortuary notice, *Newburyport Herald,* August 6, 1805, vol. IX;, Iss. 34, p. 3. *Early American Newspapers,* Series I (Chester VT: Newsbank).
4. Edward Hunter Company 1850, http://www.lds.org/churchhistory/library/narrative
5. Nona Freeman Farrer, http://www.lds.org/churchistory/library/sourcelocations
6. Dee Davidson posted on rootsweb L New York, Chautauqua, http://boards.ancestry.com
7. HHS, Ruby Bruffee Austin. *Records of the Wilcox Family of Rhode Island.* Undated, unpaginated spiral bound booklet.
8. Edwards, for many years clerk of the Baptist Church, was married to Mary Wilcox, daughter of Joseph and Prudence.
9. UVM, *Vermont Baptist Historical Society Records,* carton 2, folder 15, Halifax.
10. William Willcox Probate Record, Marlboro District Probate Court, Brattleboro, VT, Vol. 3, pp. 351–352.
11. HTC, town meetings records, unnumbered pages.
12. HHS, Norris Johnson, ed., "The Wilcox Case," *Halifacts,* No. 12, December 1978.
13. Halifax, Vt. *Gazette* & *Courier,* Greenfield, Massachusetts. Monday, September 22, 1879, p. 2.
14. West Halifax, Vt. *Gazette* & *Courier,* Greenfield, Massachusetts. February 16, 1880, p. 2.
15. Ancestry.com Minnesota History and Biography, 1915, [database on-line]. Provo. UT, USA: My Family. Com. Inc., 2004. Vol. 3, p. 1315. Accessed August 18, 2006.
16. HTC, John Worden, *Worden Family Genealogy,* typescript, p. 36.
17. William Slade, *Vermont State Papers* (Middlebury, VT: J. W. Copeland, 1823) p. 322. This law offered a bounty of eight pounds for any grown wolf or panther and half that amount for whelps. The head of the killed animal was to be brought to the selectmen or constables, who would cut off both of its ears. There were antifraud provisions built into the law, and any person who was found to have poached animals from another person's pit or trap was subject, for each offence, to "be whipt on the naked back, not exceeding ten stripes."
18. HHS: Niles, p. 41.
19. HHS, *Halifacts,* No. 14, 1980, p. 3.
20. William Willcox Probate Record, pp. 351–352.
21. Recollection by Barbara Bruffee of Greenfield, MA, phone conversation, May 2003.
22. Ibid.
23. Iris Wilcox Baird, e-mail, March 18, 2003.

THE ENIGMATIC ISAAC ORR

The name Captain Isaac Orr weaves its way noticeably through early Halifax records and Yorker episodes; yet there are many respects in which his story is a puzzle. For many years, William Orr, a direct descendant of Isaac's son David, has searched for Isaac's parents. The Orr family, first of Colrain and then of Halifax, must have been part of the Scotch-Irish migration. The Orr surname appears multiple times on the Shute Petition [↻ 499] and in a variety of Maine, Massachusetts, and New Hampshire locations; but without knowing their first names, it is difficult to trace the exact route Isaac's parents took to Colrain. Land and marriage records, as well as the Richard Ellis account book [↻ 34], link Isaac Orr to the families of Hugh Henry, John Bolton, Deacon John Cochrane, and the Pattisons, all of which strongly suggests the Orrs migrated with those families from Londonderry, New Hampshire. The Ellis account book mentions the "Widow Orr" in 1772; Deacon Cochrane[1] paid her account. The widow and her former husband, whose identities are not yet known, and who were the parents of Isaac, pose the first Isaac Orr puzzle.

Isaac married Elizabeth Carswell, the daughter of Nathaniel Carswell and Esther Henry, who was an elder sister of Benjamin Henry, Esq. The second Isaac Orr puzzle is although he is named in land records for 1770 and 1771 as Isaac Orr "of Hallifax," and he signed the Gloucester and Cumberland petitions of 1770[2] as a Halifax resident, Orr is not named on the list of heads of families for the 1771 Cumberland County Census. A deed dated March 1771 refers to him as "Isaac Orr of Halifax in the County of Cumberland and Province of New York."[3] The census was taken in April 1771. Without exception, every other Halifax individual whose name appears on those petitions is also listed in the 1771 census. Perhaps this was a census-taker error. Another puzzle.

ISAAC AND POLITICS

In politics, Isaac Orr sided with the Halifax majority Yorker faction. He was named by William Hill as one of the club-wielding rioters who disrupted the Vermont court in 1778, after John Kirkley and his wife Hannah were arrested for assault and battery against David Williams.[4] Isaac Orr was one of the forty-five Halifax residents who signed a petition in support of the state of New York in 1778. This was a transition time in the Yorker/Vermonter controversy. Most men who signed that petition left Halifax and moved to New York State prior to the 1791 census. Among those who, like Isaac Orr, chose to stay and get involved in town government under the laws of the newly created state of Vermont, were Deacon John Pennell, the Clarks, Henry Henderson, Benjamin Henry, and Robert Pattison.

Isaac Orr was active in the local militia. In records of town meetings, he is referred to variously as Ensign Orr, Captain Orr, and Lieutenant Orr. He is called Capt. Isaac Orr on the gravestone of his wife, Elizabeth, and in Vermont military records, he is listed as a first lieutenant in the Vermont Southern Regiment from Halifax in 1782.[5] Over the years, Orr was chosen town moderator, selectman, lister, constable, surveyor of the highways, and was voted to be part of a committee of three in 1781 to send for the preacher, Mr. Goodale, and provide his board. Oddly, in 1802, Isaac's name appears as one who did "not agree with the majority religious opinion of the inhabitants of the town" [HLR 2A: 46], and Isaac Jr. expressed the same view, which was recorded a year later, in November of 1803. Isaac Orr participated extensively in local politics, which brings us to puzzle number three. His name is nowhere to be found on the freeman's list! Taking the Freeman's Oath appears to have been the basic requirement for voting at town meetings and holding public office. If Isaac did take the oath, his name was never added to the list.

PROPERTY AND FAMILY

The Halifax grand list for 1772 assessed Isaac Orr's more than three hundred acres of property in Halifax Center at £53, making it one of the most valuable holdings in town. His lands were located in Lots 21 and 22, with dwelling houses along what was then called "Orr's Road."

Today this is the dead end Vaughn Road, but in his time, Orr's Road was a well-traveled thoroughfare leading to a point on Route 112 south of the intersection of Stowe Mountain Road. Much effort has been made to pinpoint Isaac Orr's homestead site, since he operated a "public house," which was the first known tavern in Halifax. Orr received his tavern-keeper's license from the Cumberland County Court in 1772 and 1773[6] [↪ 237]. William James, a current property owner in the area, has walked

Detail lot map

TO BE SOLD.

Fifty or Sixty Acres of choice

LAND;

LYING about 80 rods South of the Meeting House in *Halifax*, and on the great road to *Bennington*, consisting of Mowing, Ploughing, Pasturing, and Wood Land, with an excellent Clay bank, suitable for Brick.—The terms of sale will be easy for the purchaser. For particulars, apply to the subscriber in Halifax

ISAAC ORR.

HALIFAX, Nov. 22, 1796.

Greenfield Gazette, November. 24, 1796

the Vaughn Road and noted several substantial foundations. He believes that remnants of the original farmhouse may have been standing as recently as the 1930s. On the Stowe Mountain Road portion of Orr's property, some of the acreage where the family's merino sheep once grazed is still maintained as meadow. Further down Stowe Mountain Road, one can find traces of the Amos Muzzy pearl ash works along the brook on land he purchased from Isaac Orr in 1790.

Daughters of Elizabeth and Isaac Orr married the sons from neighboring families. For example: Betsey married Joseph Henry Esq., Polly married Salmon Hunt, Asenath married Benjamin Woodard, and Annis married Benjamin Green Jr. Isaac's son David married Sarah Fish, daughter of Nathan and Phoebe Packer Fish, and Isaac Jr. married Susannah Sumner, daughter of Daniel and Lydia Fairbanks Sumner. Both Sarah and Susannah were widowed at a young age. Neither remarried. Susannah raised her children on the Orr family farm in Halifax and is buried with her husband, Isaac Jr. in the Center Cemetery. Sarah Fish Orr took her children back to live at her parents' farm, and eventually, they moved to Heath, Massachusetts, to the farm where her sister, Prudence, and husband David Henry were raising their fifteen children. A son, John

Courtesy William W. Orr
Handwritten on back of picture by my Grandfather, William H. Orr. Circa 1860 Sarah Fish, widow of David Orr of Halifax with her sons, [left to right] George David Orr of Colrain, MA John Henry Orr Sr. of North Adams, MA and Isaac Orr, Jr. of Brooklyn, NY.

Henry Orr, settled in North Adams, where his family has continued to live for many generations. The following article appeared in the *Vermont Phoenix* on May 28, 1886.

> John H. Orr, a prominent and respected business man of North Adams, Mass., died on Wednesday at the age of 75. Mr. Orr was a native of this town [Halifax], and lived here until he was ten years old. He removed to North Adams from Heath in early manhood, and for forty years had lived in the house he bought at that time. He represented the town in the legislature in 1850, and had been town sexton for 26 years. He was the oldest resident member of the Congregational church and a prominent Mason, being chaplain of Greylock lodge.[7]

The last Orr land transactions in Halifax appear in 1829/1830 and involve Isaac's grandsons, Henry Orr and George Green. These records pertain to settlement of the complicated and intertwined estates of Nathan Fish and Benjamin Henry. The final Orr and Green deed to "Colman & Nims," dated May 1830, is a precise description of the original Benjamin Henry property currently owned by Stephen and Mariette Sanders. In that deed, the family retains the "liberty of ingress and regress from the north" to the gravesite of the late Benjamin Henry, Esquire and the right to visit, bury the dead, erect monuments or fence the same if desired" [HLR 7: 277].

Isaac Orr's wife, Elizabeth, died in 1813 and is buried in the Center Cemetery. In the family plot there are headstones for Isaac's two sons, Isaac Jr. , and David; a grandson, Nathan; and daughter-in-law, Susannah. Isaac's second wife, the widow Miriam Stewart Bullock, was buried in 1825 at the Blanchard Cemetery in Guilford with her first husband. The 1818 probate record[8] for Isaac Jr. includes the information that Justus Hall was paid three dollars "for making a Coffin for the deceased" and John Crosier was paid two dollars "for digging the grave." The cost for his monument is not mentioned. Isaac Jr.'s probate remained open until after the death of Isaac Sr. because he had transferred ownership of all his property to his sons in exchange for care in his old age, but then he had outlived them both. His son-in-law, Joseph Henry, administrated the estate, and paid Isaac Orr Sr. one hundred dollars per year. The final payment was made in April 1827, and report of the sale of real estate was dated April 1828, which means Isaac Orr died in 1827/1828.

The fourth Isaac Orr puzzle is there is no date of death, cemetery card, or any other death record for him. An erased but still readable note on the cemetery card for Elizabeth Orr says there appears to be no marker for Capt. Isaac or the stone has disappeared [HTC: VR]. The D. A. R. listed Isaac Orr Jr. as one of the gravesites to be decorated, even though Isaac Jr. did not serve in the military. The assumption can be made that Captain Isaac Orr is buried somewhere in the family plot, and the flag is intended to mark his grave. We do not know. Even in death, Isaac is a puzzle.

~ Constance Lancaster

ENDNOTES

1. Nearby neighbors, and perhaps relatives of the Orr and Pattison families, were John and Sarah Fulton Cochran from Colrain. They purchased from Abner Newton, who was on the 1771 Cumberland Census, a hundred-acre property between the Isaac Orr and the Pattison farms. "Deacon John Coghran" and "John Coghran jr." are early names on the Halifax freeman's list but do not appear on the 1771 or 1791 census rolls. They probably left town in January of 1779 when they sold their one hundred acres, dwelling house, and barn in Lot 14 to John Little [HLR 1A: 65]. John Cochran Jr. and Sarah signed the deed.

2. Jay Mack Holbrook, *Vermont 1771 Census,* copyright 1982 by Jay Mack Holbrook, p. 62.

3. Record of fifty acres from John Bolton, Hampden County Registry of Deeds, Springfield, MA, Book 4, p. 417.

4. VSS, Vermont State papers, vol. 17, p. 9.

5. Unpublished notes on the *Descendants of Isaac Orr, Sr.,* courtesy of William Orr.

6. Windham County Courthouse, Newfane, VT. Cumberland County, vol. I, Court of Common Pleas, 1772–1773.

7. HHS: Niles, p. 55.

8. Marlboro District Probate, Brattleboro, VT, vol. 9, p. 248; vol. 12, p. 223.

Halifax Families in 1771
The Cumberland County New York Census

The debate between the royal governors of colonial New Hampshire and New York contesting borders and claiming the land, lying between the Connecticut and Hudson Rivers, affected the lives of pioneer settlers residing throughout the New Hampshire Grants. During the controversy, Halifax inhabitants became fiercely divided. They debated and signed petitions. This struggle, in effect, was a thirty-year-long gestation leading to the birth of the state of Vermont. Without the prolonged controversy, the town of Halifax might now be a part of the state of New York.

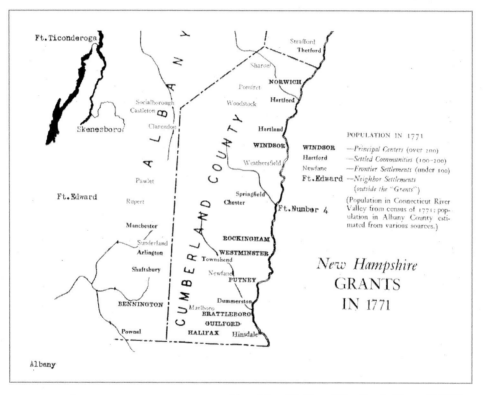

Adapted from *The Vermont Story*, Frontier Map, p. 39, VHS

One of the most significant documents originating from the grants conflict is the Cumberland County Census. The New York governor's need to know who populated the territory he was claiming prompted him to issue an order to Daniel Whipple Esq., High Sheriff of the County of Cumberland. Whipple, in turn, sent the following message to each township:

> In pursuance of a warrant to me from his Excellency The Right
> Hon. John, Earl of Dunmore, Captain General, and Governor in
> Chief of the Province of New York, bearing date, the 16th day of
> January 1771: you are herby required and commanded forthwith to

Number and Take an Account of all the Inhabitants within your District, Distinguishing therein the age, sex, and whether Black or White, as in the scheme at the foot hereof; which you are to do with as great exactness as possible, and to return the same to me under your hand, as soon as conveniently may be, together with a list of the names of the head of every Family within the same District. Given under my hand and seal, at Brattleborough, in the County of Cumberland, the 26th day of March 1771. [Seal] Dan'l Whipple, Sheriff.

The Brattleboro *Semi-Weekly Eagle* published Whipple's declaration in the 1850 series entitled "Antiquarian Documents," and subsequent issues included census reports from Cumberland County towns. Halifax appeared fourth in the series. This record shows that more than half of the total population of 329 residents consisted of males and females less than sixteen years of age, while the smallest portion of the population consisted of people above the age of sixty. There were 174 children in Halifax and only eleven senior citizens. Three towns on the east side of the mountains had larger populations: Westminster with 478; Guilford with 436; and Brattleboro with 403.

Antiquarian Documents.

Census of Cumberland County.
No. 4.

A List of the names of the heads of families, which belong to HALIFAX, is as follows:

Seth Knowles, John Pannel, Wm. Gault, James Taylor, John Gautt, Simeon Smith, Simeon Smith, Jr., Elisha Pratt, Elisha Pratt, Jr., David Rich, Sam'l Brown, Jos. McClure, Simeon Blackmore, David Bartlett, Ezekiel Perham, Rufus Harrington, Ebenezor Sabin, John Goodrich, Jonas Sheperd, Wm. Scott, Jeremiah Reed, Jacob Sheperd, Elijah Clark, Robert Crozier, Aaron Crozier, Tho's Sabin, John Crozier, James Woodward, Sam'l Woodward, Wm. Henderson, Nathan Williams, Joseph Williams, Eben'r Parish, James Carey, Benj'a Henry, Sam'l Morrison, Wm. Cooper, Abner Rice, Robert Patterson, Jona. Safford, Sam'l Clark, Robert Gilles, Thomas Clark, Abner Newton, Edward Harris, William Wilson, James Clark, Nathan Wilcox, William Wilcox, Sam'l Thomas John Thomas, Benj'a Thomas, Sam'l Baker Joseph Stuart, George Lyon.

WHITES.	
Males, under 16.	100
Males, above 16 and under 60,	83
Males, 60 and upwards,	4
Females, under 16,	74
Females, above 16,	61
Females, above 60,	7
	329

BLACKS,   None.

No. of the heads of families, 55

A true list—Test—pr me—

Nathan Williams, *Constable*, 1771.

Semi-Weekly Eagle, January 7, 1850

1771 FAMILIES

To visit and interview all Halifax households from Pennell Hill to Thomas Hill in less than two weeks during mud season seems rather a daunting assignment for Constable Nathan Williams. By then, however, there must have been a network of trails and pathways connecting the settlers, many of whom were still dwelling in log houses. No doubt as the census-taker made his rounds, his neighbors provided food, lodging, and the warmth of a fire.

That Halifax had a constable in 1771 suggests the existence by then of town government, elected officers, and a protocol for community decision-making, despite the absence of written town records from the period. There are frustrating gaps in what we know about proprietors' decisions during the first two decades after the Halifax town survey of 1751, and nearly all recorded deeds for lands conveyed to the earliest settlers are missing. Thus, the Cumberland County Census is of special value to historians.

The first documented transfer of property to a 1771 census family is for Ebenezer Parish. Oliver Partridge wrote "Parish" on Lot 5 of the original plat plan drawn up in 1751.[1] However, from 1751 until the census-taker's record, no references dating Parish's efforts to settle their property have been found. The second known land transfer to an actual settler[2] is on record in the current Halifax town books. On May 15, 1754, Hugh Morrison conveyed Lot 1 to John Morrison [HLR 1A: 135]. The Ellis account book confirms that Samuel Morrison was living in Halifax by 1765 [ρ 34]. Other 1750s transactions may have occurred, and some property owners may have tried to clear and settle their land before 1761, the date of the confirmed first settler, Abner Rice whose original record of ownership has never been found. The Parish Lot 5 property included the Gorge and some of the best mill sites in town. It was the obvious choice for first settlement. Historian Walter Crockett wrote, "An attempt made in 1751 to settle Halifax, the second Vermont town granted by Governor Wentworth, was frustrated by the hostility of the Indians."[3] The likely candidates for those early attempts would have been families already living in northern Colrain who appear in the Ellis account book and in the 1771 list of inhabitants.

EARLY SETTLERS CHART

The following chart tracks what is known to date about each of the 1771 census families of Halifax through the first federal Vermont Census of 1791. Settlers names appear in the order reported by Constable Williams. To date, there are several unidentified men on the census list. If the year of a settler's arrival in Halifax is confirmed the information has been included. The process of settling wilderness land, however, was exactly that—a process. For most families settling probably occurred over a period of several years and cannot be precisely dated. The key to the symbols ($ †) in column one appears on page 137. The 1773 subscriptions document referred to in column three appears on page 381.

~ Constance Lancaster

ENDNOTES

1. HTC, original plat plan kept in the town vault, badly deteriorated and in need of archival restoration. What was written in 1751, presumably with a quill pen and ink, is clear and readable.

2. Records for a number of lot transfers among original proprietors who did not actually settle in Halifax have been located in New Hampshire and Massachusetts archives.

3. Walter Hill Crockett, *Vermont: The Green Mountain State*, vol. 1 (New York: The Century History Company, 1921) p. 208.

1771 CENSUS CUMBERLAND COUNTY NEW YORK HEADS OF HALIFAX FAMILIES (Listed in original order & spelling)	MIGRATED FROM TO LOT NUMBER(S) YEAR OF ARRIVAL (If known)	1773 SUBSCRIPTIONS raised to petition king "to confirm lands to us who settled them under New Hampshire Charters"	MARCH 1778 HALIFAX DECLARES LOYALTY TO NEW YORK SIGNATURE ON LETTER TO GOV. COLDEN	MARCH 1778 ORIGINAL FREEMANS LIST *NAMES ADDED (Annually)	SEPTEMBER 1784 FIRST TEN SCHOOL DISTRICTS CREATED (Listed by Families)	1790–1791 FEDERAL VT CENSUS WINDHAM CTY Table: 1 . 2 . 3 = Column 1/males 16 and older Column 2/males under 16 Column 3/females
1. Seth Knowles †						
2. John Pannel $	Colrain, MA 2 1764/65		John Pennell	Dea. John Pennell *Capt. James Pennell	No. 1 Dea. John, John, Jr. & Capt. James Pennell	1 . 0 . 2 / John 2 . 2 . 2 / James 2 . 3 . 2 / John, Jr. 1 . 2 . 2 / Andrew
3. Wm. Gault $†	Deerfield, MA 15 1766		William Gault		No. 4 William Gault	2 . 0 . 1 / Wm 1 . 1 . 0 / Wm-2nd
4. James Taylor $	Deerfield, MA by 1767					
5. John Gault	Londonderry, NH 3, 11, 18, 19			* John Gault	No. 1 Lt. John Gault	1 . 1 . 1 / Widow
6. Simeon Smith † (In Walpole NH by 1773)	Brookfield, MA	1 dollar in pails				2 . 3 . 3 / Joel 1800 Census (Returned by 1792)
7. Simeon Smith, Jr.	Brookfield, MA	s3 in salts				
8. Elisha Pratt $†	Ware, MA 25 1764/65	s3 in salts		Elisha Pratt *James Pratt *Jonathan Pratt	No. 9 Elisha Pratt Jonathan Pratt	1 . 1 . 2 / Elisha 1 . 2 . 2 / James
9. Elisha Pratt, Jr.						
10. David Rich $†	Amherst, MA 26 by 1766				No. 5 Joshua Rich Jathenial Rich	2 . 2 . 2 / Thaddeus 1 . 2 . 2 / John 1 . 1 . 2 / Jathenial

Name	Origin			Persons	No.	Census
11. Sam'l Brown †	Ware, MA 25 after 1767					1 . 4 . 5 / Joseph
12. Jos. McClure $	Brookfield, MA 42, 43 1764			Thos. McCluer * Joseph McCluer	No. 5 Joseph McCluer	
13. Simeon Blackmore	Warren, MA					
14. David Bartlett $	1765					
15. Ezekiel Perham $ (*May have gone to Athens, Vermont*)	Middlesex, MA by 1765					
16. Rufus Harrington	Scituate, RI 58			* Dⁿ Jn. Herrington	No. 4 Timothy Harrington No. 8 Mr. Herenton	1 . 0 . 1 / Widow 1 . 2 . 2 / Daniel
17. Ebenezer Sabin †	Pomfret, CT 43					Ebenezer & Ebenezer, Jr. (*Returned before 1800 census*)
18. John Goodrich	Tolland, CT					
19. Jonas Sheperd †	Plainfield, CT 6, 37, 45			Jonas Shepard Capt. Hazael Shepard Rufus Shepard	No. 6 Jonas Shepard	4 . 0 . 2 / Jonas
20. Wm. Scott †	Tolland, CT 37, 44, 45 by 1766			William Scott * Dr. Phillip Scott * Josiah Scott * Thomas Scott	No. 3 Josiah & Thomas Scott	4 . 4 . 3 / Thomas 1 . 2 . 2 / Josiah 1 . 1 . 3 / Phillip
21. Jeremiah Reed	Tolland, CT 45, 53 1764/65			Jeremiah Reed		

1771 CENSUS CUMBERLAND COUNTY NEW YORK HEADS OF HALIFAX FAMILIES (Listed in original order & spelling)	MIGRATED FROM TO LOT NUMBER(S) YEAR OF ARRIVAL (If known)	1773 SUBSCRIPTIONS raised to petition king "to confirm lands to us who settled them under New Hampshire Charters"	MARCH 1778 HALIFAX DECLARES LOYALTY TO NEW YORK SIGNATURE ON LETTER TO GOV. COLDEN	MARCH 1778 ORIGINAL FREEMANS LIST * NAMES ADDED (Annually)	SEPTEMBER 1784 FIRST TEN SCHOOL DISTRICTS CREATED (Listed by Families)	1790–1791 FEDERAL VT CENSUS WINDHAM CTY Table: 1. 2. 3 = Column 1/males 16 and older Column 2/males under 16 Column 3/females
22. Jacob Shepard †	Plainfield, CT 37		Jacob Shepard			
23. Elijah Clark †	Colrain, MA 30, 37	1 dollar	Elijah Clark	* Elijah Clark	No. 3 Elijah Clark	
24. Robert Crozier $	Pelham, MA 19, 27 1763/64		Robert Crosier		No. 10 Robert Crosier	2. 0 . 4 / Robert
25. Aaron Crosier	Pelham, MA 38				No. 2 Arthur Crosier	2. 2 . 4 / Arthur
26. Tho's Sabin	Pomfret, CT 20 1763/64					
27. John Crozier $	Pelham, MA 20 1763/64			John Crosier	No. 10 John Crosier	2. 1 . 4 / John
28. James Woodward †	Canterbury, CT 20 1769	1 dollar in salts		James Woodard		2. 2 . 3 / James
29. Sam'l Woodward †	Canterbury, CT 5, 6 1769	1 dollar in salts		Samuel Woodard * Art Woodard * Timothy Woodard * Samuel Woodard, Jr.	No. 6 Samuel Woodard	2. 0 . 2 / Sam'l 1 . 1 . 3 / Art 1 . 1 . 3 / Tim

Family	Origin	Payment	Names	*	No.	Census
30. Wm. Henderson $ †	Leicester, MA 6, 21, 22, 45 before 1765		Henry Henderson David Henderson James Henderson	* Henry Henderson	No. 6 Henry Henderson	2 . 0 . 1 / Wm 3 . 0 . 1 / Wm, Jr. 1 . 5 . 2 / Henry
31. Nathan Williams $ †	Canterbury, CT 5 by 1766	1 dollar, salts	Nathan Williams	David Williams	No. 6 David Williams	
32. Joseph Williams †	Canterbury, CT 5, 12, 13	Thos. Williams 1 dollar, in boards			No. 6 Joseph Williams	
33. Dr. Eben'r Parish †	Canterbury, CT (named on Lot 5 in 1751)					
34. James Carey †	Newport, RI 14		James Carey John Carey			
35. Benj'a Henry $ †	Colrain, MA 7 1767	1 dollar	Benjamin Henry	* Benjamin Henry	No. 4 Benj. Henry, Esq.	4 . 2 . 4 / Benj.
36. Sam'l Morrison $ †	Colrain, MA 1 by 1766					
37. Wm. Cooper †						
38. Abner Rice $ †	Brookfield/ Colrain, MA 7 1761					
39. Robert Patterson $ †	Colrain, MA 7, 8, 15 1764/65		Robert Pattison Peter Pattison	* Robert Pattison	No. 4 Capt. Robert Pattison	4 . 1 . 6 / Robert

1771 CENSUS CUMBERLAND COUNTY NEW YORK HEADS OF HALIFAX FAMILIES (Listed in original order & spelling)	MIGRATED FROM TO LOT NUMBER(S) YEAR OF ARRIVAL (If known)	1773 SUBSCRIPTIONS raised to petition king "to confirm lands to us who settled them under New Hampshire Charters"	MARCH 1778 HALIFAX DECLARES LOYALTY TO NEW YORK SIGNATURE ON LETTER TO GOV. COLDEN	MARCH 1778 ORIGINAL FREEMANS LIST *NAMES ADDED (Annually)	SEPTEMBER 1784 FIRST TEN SCHOOL DISTRICTS CREATED (Listed by Families)	1790–1791 FEDERAL VT CENSUS WINDHAM CTY Table: 1.2.3 = Column 1/males 16 and older Column 2/males under 16 Column 3/females
40. Jona Safford †	Preston, CT 15		Jonathan Safford, Daniel Safford		No. 2 Daniel Safford	1 . 0 . 2 / Dan'l
41. Sam'l Clark $†	Colrain, MA 16 1765		Samuel Clark	* Samuel Clark, 2nd	No. 4 Samuel Clark, Samuel Clark, Jr.	1 . 0 . 4 / Eben^r, 1 . 1 . 3 / Sam'l, 1 . 1 . 1 / Sam'l 2nd
42. Robert Gilles	Colrain, MA 11		Robert Gillis, Joseph Gillis, Thomas Gillis			
43. Thomas Clark †	Colrain, MA 16, 23	s4 in butter	Josiah Clark	* Thomas Clark, * Josiah Clark	No. 4 Thomas Clark	1 . 2 . 3 / Thos, 3 . 2 . 4 / Josiah
44. Abner Newton $†	Colrain, MA 14					1 . 0 . 0 / Zaphon, 1 . 2 . 2 / Shadrach
45. Edward Harris †	New London, CT 21, 53	1 dollar in smith work		Edward Harris, Esq., * Eliezar Harris, * Joshua Harris, * Ebenezer Harris, * John Harris	No. 10 Edward Harris, No. 3 Job Harris	1 . 1 . 1 / John, 1 . 0 . 2 / Job, 1 . 0 . 1 / Joshua
46. William Wilson $	Londonderry, NH Colrain, MA				No. 7 John Wilson	
47. James Clark $	Colrain, MA 32		James Clark, James Clark, Jr., Asa Clark	* James Clark, * James Clark, Jr., * Asa Clark	No. 7 James Clark	1 . 4 . 5 / Asa, 1 . 3 . 4 / Elisha

Name	Location	Notes	Names	Names	No. / Census	Numbers
48. Nathan Wilcox †	Richmond, RI 39, 40				No. 2 Nathan Wilcox	2 . 4 . 4 / Nathan
49. William Wilcox	Richmond, RI 39, 40, 62			* William Wilcox	No. 2 William, Stephen, Benjamin, Joseph & Taber Wilcox	1 . 2 . 3 / Benj[a]; 2 . 3 . 3 / Stephen; 1 . 0 . 5 / Taber; 3 . 2 . 3 / Wm., Jr.
50. Sam'l Thomas	Exeter, RI 46	s7, Lawful money		* Samuel Thomas	No. 8 Samuel Thomas	3 . 3 . 3 / Wm.
51. John Thomas	Richmond, RI 63	s6 Lawful money Peleg Thomas s6 in Lawful Money		Capt. John Thomas * John Thomas, Jr.	No. 8 Capt. John Thomas John Thomas, Jr. William Thomas	2 . 1 . 3 / John; 1 . 2 . 2 / John, Jr.
52. Benj'a Thomas	RI 63			Benjamin Thomas	No. 8 Benjamin Thomas	2 . 3 . 5 / Benj[a]
53. Sam'l Baker	Exeter, RI 3, 32, 54	s6 in salts	Samuel Baker Thomas Baker	Thomas Baker		
54. Joseph Stuart †	Colrain, MA 8	1 dollar John Stewart, s3 in salts	Alexander Stewart Joseph Stewart, Jr.			
55. George Lyon †	Colrain, MA 8		George Lyons Joseph Lyons			

KEY: **$** = traded with Richard Ellis 1764–1774. Ellis kept a country store and ashery in the northeast part of Colrain In his ledger book of accounts are found the names of nearly two hundred persons from Colrain and adjoining towns.

† = signed the 1770 petitions to the Governor's Council of New York and to the King of England for confirmation of lands granted by Benning Wentworth.

APPARENT CENSUS TAKERS ERRORS:

Line 9: Elisha Pratt, Jr. was not old enough to be considered the head of a family. No explanation available.

Omissions: John Bolton, Isaac Orr and Peter Pattison. Each signed the 1770 petitions as a resident of Halifax.

~ *Constance Lancaster and Carrie Perna*

Section Two

Politics on the Path to Statehood
1771 – 1791

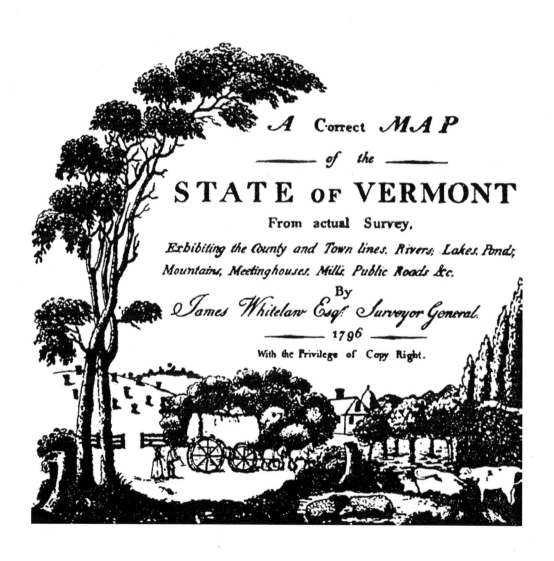

A Correct *MAP*

of the

STATE of VERMONT

From actual Survey,

Exhibiting the County and Town lines. Rivers; Lakes. Ponds;
Mountains, Meetinghouses. Mills. Public Roads &c.

By

James Whitelaw Esq.r Surveyor General.

1796

With the Privilege of Copy Right.

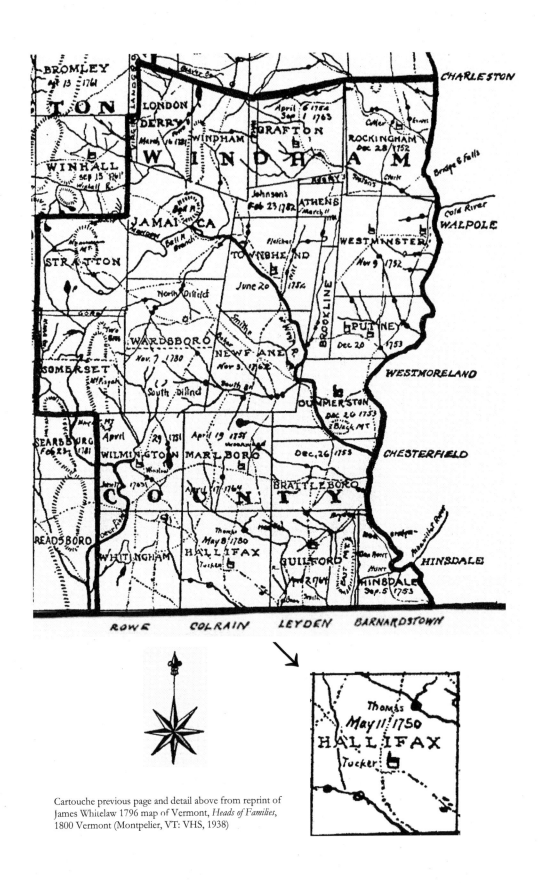

Cartouche previous page and detail above from reprint of
James Whitelaw 1796 map of Vermont, *Heads of Families*,
1800 Vermont (Montpelier, VT: VHS, 1938)

Halifax Discovered
Patterns of Early Migration

Changes in the population of Halifax Township during its first century were dramatic. The periods of greatest growth occurred after two periods of war, and the families arriving in Halifax often included men who had participated in these military activities. In 1771, the first census taker counted 329 residents distributed among fifty-five heads of families. These pioneer emigrants began settlement of the town at the conclusion of the French and Indian War. Their hardiness and fortitude prepared the way for the huge influx of emigrants who arrived following the Revolutionary War, swelling the town's population to its peak by 1810. Where these people came from shifted as Halifax evolved from a frontier wilderness to a civilized settlement and as footpaths and bridle trails became roads and highways connecting Halifax to other places in New England.

FRONTIER MIGRATIONS

In 1761, when first settler Abner Rice relocated from what his son later would describe as "Cold Rain," Massachusetts, across the province line into "Halifax, New Hampshire" both towns were part of New England's northern frontier.[1] There was no road to Halifax. Nor was there a road through sparsely settled north Colrain to Fort Morrison, the post occupied by Lieutenant John Hawks from 1754–1757 while in command of all the Massachusetts border forts.[2] Hawks and his men would navigate a network of difficult trails along the high ridge east of the North River to get to the fort. Abner probably utilized these old military trails while finding his way to Lot 7 in Halifax, where he established the first permanent settlement in the town.

Oliver Partridge petitioned the Hampshire County Court in 1762 for a highway from the meeting house in Colrain north four miles to the Halifax line, the court suitably appointed Colonel John Hawks chief surveyor,[3] assisted by other veterans of the French and Indian War, to lay out the highway. No longer fearing Indian raids, they chose a more accessible valley route. From the meeting house, they laid a road heading west, across the river, north, past the farms of John Clark, John Morrison, and Hugh Bolton Jr., east, back across the river, north along the east side of the river, crossing into Halifax at the site of what in later years would serve as a stage stop and state-line tavern. Oliver's highway, currently Route 112, continues to be the main north-south road connecting Halifax to Colrain [↪ 505–507].

FIRST WAVE AFTER THE FRENCH AND INDIAN WAR

With the close of the war and the opening of a new highway, the first wave of migration into Halifax began. Two routes would dominate. One was via military service. Soldiers recruited from Worcester and Hampshire counties in central

Massachusetts and Tolland and Windham counties in central Connecticut served with colonels Oliver Partridge, William Williams, John Hawks, and other Hatfield and Deerfield military officers who were proprietors named on the Halifax charter. Many of the first men to arrive in Halifax had been soldiers whose names appear on garrison lists and muster rolls or who had a brother or father on the mortality lists from the final campaigns of the war. Often, military service, stamina, and a sharp axe were all the payment needed for one hundred acres of land in the New Hampshire grant called "Hallifax."

The second foremost early migration route was the push north from Colrain over the Massachusetts/Vermont border. Most early Colrain families shared a common origin—the Scotch-Irish settlement in Northern Ireland. The Shute Petition [↵ 499] brought the first of the boatloads of Presbyterian families and their minister, Rev. William Boyd, to Boston in 1718. "In a seven year period fifty-four vessels arrive in Boston harbor from Ireland with companies of immigrants. These immigrants were encouraged to move to the frontiers. The Scotch were trained to hardships and as Indian fighters they proved to be among the best."[4] Many of these families went to Londonderry (Nutfield), New Hampshire; others went to Worcester, and then to Pelham (New Lisburne), Massachusetts. A number of the Ulster migration families eventually settled in Colrain and later moved north into Halifax.

> **For Ireland.**
> JOHN LITTLE, takes this method to inform his Countrymen and others, that he will sail for LONDONDERRY, or BELFAST, in *Ireland,* about the middle of *January* next.—Those who wish to write to their friends, may now have an opportunity, by applying to him ; and as he purposes to return in about two years, he will, probably, have it in his power to bring them answers to their letters.
> HALIFAX, (*Vermont,*) Nov. 3, 1794.

Greenfield Gazette, November 6, 1794

Others moved directly to Halifax. One third of the heads of families in the 1771 Halifax census were from this population of Scotch-Irish immigrants [↵ 132].

One other notable migration into Halifax before the 1771 census was a group of Baptists from Rhode Island who settled in the northeast part of town. They were the Baker, Harrington, Thomas, and Wilcox families. Samuel Baker served during the French and Indian War, and John Thomas who "served as Ensign in Richmond, RI in 1758, and was made Lieutenant in 1760,"[5] may be the same Captain John Thomas, early settler of Halifax. It is not clear, whether these Thomas Hill settlers migrated as part of the Baptist group that settled in Leyden, Massachusetts, or if there was a military connection.

SECOND WAVE AFTER THE AMERICAN REVOLUTION

Population growth in Halifax between the first and second census counts was not just a second wave; it was a tidal wave. The number of residents quadrupled, increasing from 329 to 1,309 people during those two decades. The town would never again experience such growth. In 1800, the population increased to 1,600, and in 1810, it reached a record high of 1,758.

Several Halifax settler myths derive from this period. For example: One hears it said, by local residents, that Halifax once had the largest population in

Windham County. The census numbers, however, belie this claim. In 1771, Halifax had the fourth largest population in the county; in 1791 and 1810, it was fifth; it was sixth in 1800, 1820, 1830, and 1840. By 1850, it had dropped to fourteenth place [↪231]. While never, in fact, the most heavily populated town in the county, the town's populace during those years was considerably larger than it has been ever since.

CONNECTICUT SETTLERS

Another example, and among the most persistent Halifax myths, is the claim that most of the early settlers came from Stonington, Connecticut. This notion may have developed from the Halifax description published in Child's 1884 *Windham County Gazetteer*. Of the fourteen family biographies included in that gazetteer write-up, twelve emigrated from Connecticut with four listed from Stonington: Niles, Plumb, Green, and Wheeler, who settled after the 1791 census. The Worden and Fish families, who arrived soon after the Revolution, are profiled in the gazetteer without mention of their Stonington connections. Other Halifax Stonington family names were: Boardman, Brown, Burdick, Collins, Crandall, Dennison, Grant, Minor, and Whipple.

Nevertheless, a great many Connecticut families arrived from other towns: Canterbury, Tolland, Willington, Pomfret, Norwich, New London, Preston, Colchester, Plainfield, Groton, Enfield, Lebanon, Scotland, Durham, Windsor, Litchfield, and Ashford, to name a few. Some of the non-Stonington family names were: Avery, Barber, Lamb, Stark, Ransom, Dean, Stanclift, Safford, Kellogg, Sabin, Hatch, Mason, Tucker, Wells, Shepard, Hall, Hunt, Gore, Otis, Kingsbury, Harris, Scott, Smith, Squires, and Holmes.

The first two elected representatives to the state assembly for Halifax were Connecticut-born Hubbel Wells from Colchester, and Edward Harris from New London. The area from which Halifax settlers originated, if drawn on the Connecticut map, would include the entire counties of New London, Windham, and Tolland. All are located east of the Connecticut River and due south from the part of central Massachusetts that was the other major source for Halifax population growth during the last three decades of the eighteenth century. What these Connecticut emigrant families had most in common was not geography; rather, it was their service in the Revolutionary War [↪ 178].

MASSACHUSETTS SETTLERS

The post–Revolutionary War population boom included a few families from nearby frontier towns, but most new arrivals came from more highly developed Massachusetts towns back east. Again, what these families had in common was service in the war. Their stories are documented in dozens of pension files.

Private Eleazer Whitney enlisted at Brookfield, Massachusetts, in February 1777, and his final discharge came in December 1782.[6] During this time, his parents, Nathan and Abigail, migrated to Halifax, settling on property in Lot 20 adjacent to John Crosier. After five years of service, Eleazer joined his family in Halifax, married the girl next door, Martha Crosier, and settled about a mile and a half north of the Center. By 1850, there were six Whitney families recorded on the Halifax census, all progeny of this couple. One hundred years and four generations after Eleazer arrived in town, his descendants occupied numerous farms in the neighborhood that continues to be known as Whitneyville.

From Concord, Middlesex County, Joseph Swain, artificer, who served in both the army and the navy[7] emigrated to Halifax in 1783 with his celebrated bride, Meliscent Barrett, who, according to family lore, had learned from him how to craft cartridges for use by the Concord troops on April 19, 1775. The Swain farm was located on Sprague Road. He set up a blacksmith shop; she converted one room of their home into a school [↪ 407].[8]

From Raynham, Bristol County, Private Israel Jones,[9] migrated to the banks of the Green River in Halifax where he set up a mill at Reid Hollow. Jones would live to the age of ninety-nine; his grandson, Ansel, served as Halifax town clerk. During this period, another veteran of the Revolution, Daniel Sumner, from Princeton, Worcester County, arrived and set up the first of the Sumner family mills near his Pennell Hill property. The surge in population must have created enormous demand for lumber, grain, and textiles—thus the need for multiple mills in a township abundant in waterpower.

FAMILIES FROM WESTMINSTER

A Massachusetts town that seems to have escaped notice of the gazetteer historians and is comparable to Stonington, Connecticut, for the copious number of families that relocated to Halifax, is Westminster,[10] located in Worcester County, east of Fitchburg off today's Route 2. Beginning in 1780 with Lieutenant James Clark, the following Westminster men and their families contributed to the growing population and community life of Halifax: Moses Learnard, Asa Brooks, Samuel Wood, Nicholas Dike Jr., Thomas Farnsworth, Solomon Fessenden, Dr. Jeremiah Everett, Joseph Perry, Darius Sawyer, Stephen Calef, Amos Conant, Benjamin Treadaway, and Rev. Abner Bemis. Revolutionary soldiers from this town included minutemen and enlisted men. Many participated in the Lexington alarm of 1775 and in the defense at Dorchester, under the command of Colonel Nicholas Dike, during the siege of Boston in 1776. Westminster regiments responded to the invasion of Burgoyne and to the Bennington alarm in 1777.[11] An example of the parallels and close connections of these Westminster veterans is found in land and military records. Listed among the nine Westminster men who enrolled in January 1779 and were stationed at Claverack, New York, were Joseph Perry, Asa Brooks, Samuel Wood, and Moses Larned [Learnard]. The town voted them each a bounty of £ 22.[12] In 1883, Joseph Perry bought Halifax property from Darius Sawyer, adjacent to Asa Brooks, and Samuel Wood bought 104 acres, half of the property Moses Learnard had purchased in 1781. Their children would attend the same district schools.

Halifax early School District No. 4 included the Westminster families of Amos Conant, Lieutenant James Clark, and Dr. Jeremiah Everett. Dr. Everett had been the first practicing physician in Westminster, while at the same time serving as a schoolmaster. The town historian referred to him as "the only knight of the saddle bags in town."[13] He was appointed surgeon of Colonel Nicholas Dike's regiment, on duty at Dorchester Heights. About 1784, he migrated with his wife, Elizabeth Warren, and family to Halifax where they resided on the 120-acre former Pattison farm, which included the Abner Rice first settlement site.

About 1794, Dr. Everett's father, Jeremiah, of Attleboro, Massachusetts, also a veteran of the Revolution, joined his son in Halifax. He died in 1798 and was buried at the Clark Farm Cemetery near his granddaughter Polly. Later family interments took place at the Fish/Bell Cemetery in Grove. Everett daughters married into the Sumner, Pattison, and Hall families,[14] and two sons migrated to the Midwest. Dr. Everett's son, Jacob W. and wife, Mary Fish, daughter of their neighbor, Samuel Fish, continued the family farm in Halifax. Dr. Everett, age ninety-one, and Elizabeth, age eighty-three, had been married for sixty-five years at the time of their deaths in August 1831. Their house and orchards, known more recently, as Benjamin Barber's farm and grove, often served as the meeting site for the Halifax Agricultural Society.

The pension file[15] for yet another Westminster Revolutionary War veteran who migrated to Halifax, describes multiple enlistments. Thomas Farnsworth, a minuteman at Lexington, served also at the Battle of Bennington and at Dorchester under the command of Colonel Dike. In Westminster, Farnsworth operated a blacksmith shop diagonally across from the Everett Tavern. He married Anna Estabrook in the fall of 1778, and by 1783, they had joined the rapidly growing Township of Halifax, where eight of their eleven children would be born. Captain Farnsworth, as he was called in the town records, soon was elected to positions of trust. He served as selectmen, together with Benjamin Henry and Darius Bullock, in 1787. In 1788, the voters chose him constable and tax collector, and re-elected him for many years of service. Thomas Farnsworth died on August 10, 1836. Although headstones in the Center Cemetery mark the burials of his first wife, Anna, and second wife, Catherine Northam, Captain Farnsworth is one of many prominent citizens of Halifax for whom there is no visible carved gravestone.

The Farnsworths operated a blacksmith shop and eventually owned two adjacent farms with dwelling houses on Woodard Hill Road. Their property extended from the Joseph Henry Store, later the Stephen Niles Store, south to James Woodard's land, north to the Jacksonville Stage Road, and west to the Branch Road and Nathan Learnard's land. The 1856 McClellan map shows both Farnsworth houses, which at the time belonged to Captain Farnsworth's son Thomas and grandsons Elijah Bordwell and Luther Ransom Farnsworth. The older of the two houses remains.

In 1871, Horace Stowe bought from Luther R. Farnsworth the former Thomas, Experience, and Elijah B. Farnsworth house located on property that abutted the store at the Center, together with the blacksmith shop operated by Luther's son, George, and 125 acres along both sides of Woodard Hill Road [HLR 13: 635]. Luther and George appear in the 1884 business directory[16] for Whitingham, Vermont as owners of an apple orchard, sugar grove and blacksmith shop in Jacksonville. The fate of this second Farnsworth house, later called, "The

Stow Place," is unclear, and there is no known photograph of it. However, a photograph taken by a Capt. Farnsworth descendant in July 1928 shows the barn, which Larry Crosier says was located across from the cellar hole of the house (facing page). During the years the Crosiers cared for the town's horse-drawn hearse, it was stored in this barn.

FARNSWORTH BARN, WOODARD HILL ROAD   Photo Lois Rabe, courtesy Wm. Farnsworth

Postcard C. Lancaster

Probably constructed by Nathan Whitney circa 1778, who sold all his land and dwelling in 1785 to Captain Thomas Farnsworth of Halifax [HLR 1A: 215], the property remained in the Farnsworth family for several generations until January 1860 when Luther R. Farnsworth sold it to Sanford Fairbanks, who died in 1864 while serving in the Civil War. Rufus Crosier purchased the farm from widow Almira Fairbanks as part of the estate settlement. Presently owned by David Jones, the dwelling is commonly known as the Rufus Crosier House.

The preceding account of migration into Halifax does not presume to be more than an overview of the subject. Rather, one hopes by identifying specific early patterns of emigration, some of the people who did the emigrating, and places they emigrated from, the reader will have a better understanding of the character of the town during its formative years.

Currently, the population of Halifax is on the increase. People often choose the area for retirement life. Another current trend is people who can work out of a home office or commute to work in other places are moving into town. Some are restoring or renovating old houses and farms. The office of the town clerk is a beehive of activity. Town clerk, Laura Sumner, who nevertheless manages to stay ahead of the phenomenal mound of paperwork, has been heard to say, "Halifax has been discovered!"

~ Constance Lancaster

ENDNOTES

1. Fifty years earlier, the general courts of Massachusetts and Connecticut had designated certain places official "frontier towns": Brookfield, Hatfield, Hadley, Westfield, and Deerfield in central Massachusetts, and Colchester, Windham, and Danbury in central and western Connecticut, began as fortified towns on the edge of wilderness. The frontier line steadily moved north and west as towns evolved from frontier to settled status. During the first half of the eighteenth century, the status of a town often was defined by the course of the French and Indian War.

2. George Sheldon, *A History of Deerfield, Massachusetts*, vol. II (Deerfield, MA: Pocumtuck Valley Memorial Association, 1983) p. 190.

3. Edward Brooks, in *A Glimpse into the Personal Life of Col. John Hawks,* points out that Hawks had completed building the western half of the road from Crown Point to Fort No. 4, and, therefore, had been appointed chief surveyor by the General Court of Hampshire County to lay highways from smaller towns to connect with larger towns in Western Massachusetts. History and Proceedings of the PVMA 1930–1938, vol. VIII (Deerfield, MA: The Association) p. 32.

4. Charles H. McClellan, *The Early Settlers of Colrain, Mass.* (Greenfield, MA: W. S. Carsen, 1885) p. 11.

5. HHS, Baker and Thomas family files.

6. NARA, Pension File W22611. Eleazer Whitney was inscribed on the pension roll of Vermont at the rate of $8.00 per month to commence on April 2, 1818. He died in June 1840, age 85 years. Martha applied for widow's benefits in 1843. She died in Halifax on November 29, 1865, age 97 years.

7. NARA, Pension File W20079. Swain enlisted as a blacksmith and armorer. During 1776, he marched with twenty- four artificers to Crown Point, New York. These smiths were sent ahead of the troops to Chambleau, Canada and back to Fort Ticonderoga until their discharge in 1777. In 1778, Swain enlisted in the Continental Navy, and served four months on "The General Gates," a privateer out of Marblehead, Massachusetts that captured half a dozen enemy brigateens.

8. HHS, *West Halifax as written up by Blanche E. Legate Sumner,* typescript given by Ellen Hill Powers, 1982.

9. NARA, Pension File S15486.

10. Participants in King Phillip's War and their families petitioned Governor Dummer for land grants to reward service done for the Commonwealth in the Narragansett wars. After six years of petitions, the township of Westminster, first named Narragansett no 2, was one of six grants issued by the general court of the Commonwealth.

11. William Sweetzer Heywood, *History of Westminster, Massachusetts.* (Lowell, MA: Vox Populi Press, S.W. Huse, 1893). Names and details of Revolutionary War service of Westminster men appear on pages 172–179 of the History of Westminster.

12. Ibid., p. 175.

13. Ibid., p. 640.

14. Firstborn Elizabeth Everett married Joel Sumner, son of Daniel, who died in Bradford, Pennsylvania, having gone to visit the grave of his son, Jesse. Sarah Everett married Rev. William Pattison, the first child born in Halifax, son of Captain Robert. Sally Everett, daughter of Jacob, married Judge Obed Hall, son of Lotan Hall, superintendent of schools and state representative for Bennington County.

15. NARA, Pension File S22236.

16. Child, p. 523.

Setting Up Town Government

A set of Halifax written records prior to 1778 has not been found. Nevertheless, local government in some form must have existed in the town by 1770. During November and December that year, more than forty-five Halifax residents signed petitions to the governor of New York and the King of England asking for confirmation of ownership of their properties. Their names joined those of more than 350 other Cumberland County residents who had settled and improved lands originally granted by the New Hampshire governor only to find themselves now under the jurisdiction of New York. Given the number of Halifax signatures, a gathering or meeting may have taken place at a local home where folks could hear the issues, discuss strategies, and sign the petitions. On January 16, 1771, New York governor Lord John Murray Dunmore, doubting the veracity of so many petitioner names, decreed that the sheriffs of Cumberland and Gloucester counties should take "an enumeration of the inhabitants of their respective bailiwicks."[1] This Cumberland County census offers the first evidence of local government in Halifax. Nathan Williams, serving as an elected or appointed town constable, signed the return in April 1771. His tally for Halifax heads of families exceeded the number of names on the petitions just six months earlier. Lord Dunmore had his answer.

Nathan Williams' name appears again on one of the few known documents to have survived from the earliest years of Halifax town government. The 1773 broadside titled, *A Petition of the People of Halifax*,[2] seeks financial support for Halifax to build a meetinghouse [↻ 278]. Confirmation that a town meeting was held appears at the end of the petition as follows.

N. B. *Halifax* is one of the Towns granted by *New-Hampshire*, and now claimed by *New York* ; it joins *Colrain*, of the *Maffachufetts*.

Signed by us at a legal Town-Meeting, November 11th. 1773.

JOHN BOLTON,   } Committee for
JOHN THOMAS,   } the Diftrict of
BENJ. LYMAN,   } *Halifax.*

We do hereby Certify, all whom it may concern, That the Petition from the Diftrict of *Halifax*, in the Hands of the Rev. Mr. WILLIAM EWING, is fent out at the Defire of the Inhabitants in Town-Meeting affembled, and *John Bolton*, Efq; and Lieut. *John Thomas*, with Mr. *Benjamin Lyman*, were by the Town appointed to fign faid Petition in their Behalf. As Witnefs our Hands at *Halifax*, November 11. 1773.

NATHAN WILLIAMS, Moderator.

SAMUEL WOODARD, Diftrict Clerk.

EDWARD HARRIS, Society-Clerk.

See endnote 2

1773 Town Officers

Biographies of Samuel Woodard, district clerk, and Edward Harris, society clerk, appear in Section I of this volume. Nathan Williams, like Woodard and Harris, migrated to Halifax from Windham County, Connecticut, where he was born in

1723, the son of Joseph Williams and Susanna Lawrence. Between May 1765, when his ninth child was born, and October 1766, when Richard Ellis recorded purchases by Williams at his Colrain trading store, Nathan and his family[3] moved to Halifax. His two oldest sons, Joseph and David, were young men capable of helping with the labor of clearing land and building a home. The family settled in South Halifax and owned properties in Lots 5, 12, and 13 through which the North River flows. The 1771 census includes three related Williams households: Nathan, his son Joseph, and his brother-in-law Ebenezer Parish. The location of these families is significant. Written on Lot 5 of the Halifax plat plan, drawn up in 1750/1751 are the words "sold Parish."[4] The first survey would have identified the potential for mill sites in Lot 5, which includes the Gorge on the North River. Mills were the foremost priority for any frontier settlement. With its abundance of waterpower, Lot 5 was the first property in Halifax to transfer from a proprietor to a settler and is the only lot that bears a written name on the original lotting plan, now stored in the town vault.

Biographical details are sparse for the first identified town official. Most derive from military records. A transfer to his brother David in 1781 of Lot 13 property inherited by Joseph refers to "my honoured Father Nathan Williams Deceased" [HLR 1A: 526]. Reference is made to "the late Capt. Williams." In his pension deposition Nathan Williams, stated "his father, Captain Nathan Williams, commanded a company of militia and was killed in a battle with the Indians in the retreat from Ticonderoga."[5] Details of his death on July 6, 1777 and burial in a shallow grave on the battlefield in east Castleton were reported in 1820 when Capt. Williams's body was exhumed and buried in the church yard with full military honors and speeches on Independence Day [↻182].

Captain Nathan Williams' sons, David, Joseph, Job, and Nathan, served in the Revolution from Halifax. Nathan Jr. signed the petition to the New York governor in March 1778 and returned to Canterbury, Connecticut, before 1782. Joseph and David Williams held public office in town and appear on the 1784 list for School District No. 6. Constable William Hill filed a complaint to the governor in September 1778, saying he had "to arrest the Bodys of John Kirkley and Hannah his Wife . . . for asault and battery perpetrated in the highway on the body of David Williams in Hallifax,"[6] and when he delivered the Kirkleys to the court in Westminster, an unruly mob of Halifax men, wielding clubs, disrupted the proceedings[7] [↻172]. During the tumultuous decade of civil strife arising from the Yorker/Vermonter enmity, many Halifax residents chose to leave the town. Among the early Halifax settlers missing from the 1791 Halifax census are members of the family of Nathan Williams.

The three men called the "Committee for the District" on the 1773 broadside, were most likely acting in the capacity later known as selectmen. Benjamin Lyman, who was born in 1734 in Lebanon, New London County, Connecticut, was active in Halifax for about ten years, serving as a town officer, and moved to Whitingham before the 1791 census. In 1799, at Bolton, Washington County, New York, a falling tree killed him. His sons Isaac, Benjamin, and Eleazar served in the Revolution from Halifax, and each received a pension.

In 1763, John Bolton, son of Hugh, first physician of Colrain,[8] purchased Lot 3 in Halifax from Theodore Atkinson in Portsmouth, New Hampshire. The date on his deed, as often was the case, does not indicate the year he took up residence. Bolton's presence in town is apparent from his signatures on petitions in 1770 and 1773 and on land records he witnessed, as justice of the peace. In 1776, "John Bolton of Hallifax, New York,"[9] purchased fifty acres in Colrain with a house and two barns and moved back to that town. Bolton is one of four Colrain men active in Rogers' Rangers. At age nineteen, he served under General Wolfe at the decisive Battle of Quebec.[10] He died in Warren, New York, in 1807.

John Thomas, the third member of the 1773 committee, on the other hand, played an active role in Halifax throughout his life. Born in 1727 in Rhode Island, Captain John Thomas and his wife Catherine Wilcox settled in northeastern Halifax in the area still known as Thomas Hill and are buried in the Thomas Hill Cemetery.[11] His property contained a sawmill and a gristmill; an early map of Halifax prominently displays the name Thomas with a mill symbol on the Green River. His stature within town government is evident in the placement of the name, Capt. John Thomas, third on the freeman's list just after the names Hubbel Wells, Esq., and Edward Harris, Esq., the first two representatives to the state assembly. John Thomas was chosen to serve as a selectman in 1779.

HALIFAX IN THE CUMBERLAND COUNTY, NEW YORK RECORDS

From 1763 to 1766, the jurisdiction of Albany County courts extended to the banks of the Connecticut River and included all the land that would become the state of Vermont. Public officials, east of the mountains, were hard-pressed to serve the court some hundred to two hundred miles distant. "With difficulty could the sheriff of Albany County serve a process in the northern part of his bailiwick; and not without a guard of a dozen men, could he with safety convey a prisoner or a debtor through the woods and over the mountains to the jail at Albany."[12] Thus on July 3, 1766, the governor and council of the province of New York created Cumberland County on the east side of the Green Mountains, which encompassed most of present counties of Windham and Windsor. Chester became the county seat, home of the courthouse, jail, and semi-annual sessions of court. In 1772, the Cumberland Court moved from Chester to Westminster, which was thought to be a more convenient and accessible location for residents of the county.

As noted in "Henry Henderson: He Brought Home the Charter," an old leather-bound record book discovered in a safe at the district courthouse in Newfane, Vermont, revealed property transfers not documented in the Halifax town records. Volume I of Cumberland County Deeds 1766–1774, contains about ten pages of Halifax transactions. These records were begun just sixteen years after the town received its charter. Names on the deeds are Giles Alexander, Joseph Stewart, William Henderson, Isaac Gibson, Jacob Stewart, Levi Willard, Abijah Willard, and George Lyons, and their property transfers date from 1767 through 1769. Deeds of this vintage rarely appear in the Halifax town records because the set of books that exists today was placed in service in 1778. This means transfers of land in Halifax that occurred before 1778 were recorded, in some instances, many years after the actual agreements took place.

In addition to Cumberland County deeds, the Windham County courthouse is the repository for volume I of the Cumberland County Court of Common Pleas, with records of sessions held from June 1772 through December 1773. These include "Lycences for Retailing Spiritous Liquors and keeping Taverns pursuant to the Directions of the Act of Assembly"[13] In 1772, tavern licenses were granted to Jonathan Safford and Isaac Orr of Halifax, and James Wild was issued a license for retailing. The records include names of jurors from all towns in the county. A grand jury list for December 1772 records from Halifax, "those appeared and sworn: John Pennell, John Thomas, Elisha Pratt, Robert Paterson, John Barber. Default: Abner Newton, Nathan Williams, Silas Hamilton."[14] No explanation is provided for how these men were selected, whether by election or appointment, to serve at the court.

The volumes preserved in the vault at the Windham County Courthouse offer details of pre–Revolutionary life in Halifax that would not otherwise have been known. County court records for the years 1775 to 1778 have not been found, probably due to a hiatus in court activities. On March 13, 1775, the Cumberland County, New York court sessions ceased as the result of rioting that led to the so-called Westminster Massacre [↻ 166]. In March 1778, the organized government of Vermont established a new court system. Found in the New York state manuscripts relating to Revolutionary records are the minutes from two 1776 Halifax town meetings shown below.[15] These reflect local resistance to the creation of a new state and document yet another Halifax town clerk who served during the Cumberland County period.

At a Town Meeting Regularley warned, held at Halifax yᵉ 2ᵈ Day of September Anno Domini 1776, Lieut John Thomas chosen Moderator, Put to Voat whether they would choose a Deligate to meet the Green Mountain Boys. Voated in the Negative.   A True Copy Test,
                                                    PELATIAH FITCH, *T. Clerk.*

[Miscel. Pap. 36: 233.]
At a Town Meeting Regularly warned held at Halifax 18ᵗʰ Day of October Anno Domini 1776, Mr James Gray was chosen Moderator. Then it was put to Voat, who Present are for Setting up a New State in this Difficult and Distressing Time; and who for continuing through the present Troubles, still to the State of New York. Voated to continue still to the State of New York, as above, Nemine Contradicente.   A true Copy Test,
                                                    PELATIAH FITCH, *T. Clerk.*

See endnote 15

ORGANIZATION OF THE EARLY TOWN RECORD BOOKS

The earliest Halifax record books, stored in the vault at the town clerk's office, contain a great variety of material. People recorded their deeds, marriages, births, and deaths, earmarks for identifying livestock, and even lost and found horses. When the official town church was declared to be Congregational/Presbyterian, anyone not wishing to pay the church tax would record that he was a member of the Baptist Church or that he "did not agree with the majority religious opinion of the town" [⟶ 513]. The town clerk and selectmen recorded road surveys, lists of school districts, and those who had taken the Freeman's Oath. "Warnings Out," to absolve the town of the obligation to support those new to town who might not succeed in becoming self-sufficient, was recorded, as were provisions for care of the poor and indentured (those in what is now called foster care). Constables who were both peace keepers and tax collectors recorded properties to be sold "at vendue," or public auction, for nonpayment of taxes or other debts, and warned meetings for the citizens to gather to vote in state and national elections. And, of course, there were recorded minutes for all town meetings.

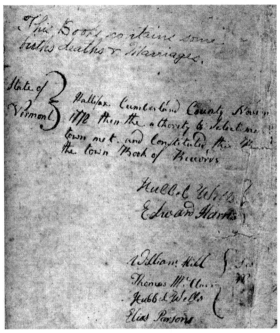

HLR 1A flyleaf

Twenty-eight years after the ink dried on the charter parchment in New Hampshire, pen met paper in the Town of Halifax, State of Vermont in the first existing[16] Halifax town record book. This image shows the actual writing.

Inscriptions copied from inside the covers of Books 2 through 4 of the Halifax town records are:

- Book 2 (1790): "Alphabet [Index] for 2nd Book Nathan Fish" "This Book Purchased at the Cost of the Town of Halifax and Dedicated to the Use of said Town for Recording Deeds. No. 2"

- Book 2A (1791): "No 2 This Book Purchased at the Towns Cost and Dedicated to the Towns Use for Recording Town Votes Earmarks Marriages Births and Deaths. Halifax, March the 7th AD of 1791."

- Book 3 (1799): "The third book appropriated to the use of Land records in the Town of Halifax in September in the year 1799. Attest Darius Bullock Town Clerk."

- Book 3A (1821): "Halifax Town Book No 3 for recording Marriages births deaths Survey Bills ear marks [ ] AD 1821 and division of [ ] and is the first book for recording Attachments made on real estate in the Town of Halifax and also assignments of Real Estate Personal Property —No 1."

- Book 4 (1804): "No 4 The fourth book of Land records applied to that use Halifax in September in the year of our Lord AD 1804. Attest Darius Bullock Town Clerk"

The A books were discontinued after Book 3A and placement of the records in Book 1A answers the question of why there is no Book 1. On close examination, it becomes apparent the first volume of records manages to combine 1 and 1A into a single book. The town clerks used books 2 and 3 for recording deeds. They used the 2A and 3A books to preserve vital records and minutes of meetings. The first recorded town meeting in 1778 is entered on page 400 of Book 1A, more than half way through the book, as if it were the beginning of a separate volume 1A. Consecutive town meetings are recorded in Book 1A, forward from page 400 through page 439, covering meetings held from March 1778 through March 1788. Deeds are recorded at the beginning of Book 1A, perhaps intended to be Book 1, and continue through page 398 where the freeman's list and town meetings begin. Deeds resume on page 439 after the first decade of town meetings.

Page 399 of Book 1A carries the title "A List of the freemen in Hallifax." Even though pages 398 and 399 each contain two columns of names of the men who took the Freeman's Oath, by cross-referencing each name with the town meeting records and observing the changes in penmanship, it is clear this was an ongoing list. Apparently, the list began with the first thirty names in the left column of page 399, a portion of which is shown here. As needed, a second column was added and continued on page 398. The list continued on the lower half of page 62 in the section of deeds where there was half a page of space available. The lists on these three pages include the Halifax freemen recorded annually from 1778 through 1796. Changes in penmanship make it possible to tell when each new group of freeman was added at an annual meeting, even though the names are not dated. Starting in 1797, in Book 2A, each person who became a legal town voter or freeman is listed in the town meeting report for that year. Each of the first freemen shown here took his oath in order to participate in the March 3, 1778 meeting. These names would have been recorded in November of that year after the town acquired the first record book.

HLR 1A: 399

Paper was scarce and books were valuable. At a meeting legally warned in 1781, it was "Voted that the five law Books in the Town be in the Care of the five Select men and they to be accountable for them at the Years End" [HLR 1A: 411]. On the top half of page 25, Book 1A is a record dated June 18th, 1780 "that the Select Men of the Town of Hallifx Laid out a road . . . [surveyed by Hazael Shepard] on the east side of the Proprietors Rode." Shepard, of Halifax, was the first Windham County surveyor appointed by the state of Vermont, through an act passed at the general assembly meeting in October 1779.[17] This may be the earliest authorized Halifax town road survey. The bottom half of the survey page contains birth records for the family of Daniel Squire. A similar example of filling in every bit of blank space is found on page 341, where the births of Henry and Mary Henderson's family were recorded vertically on the edge of a page where several surveys were recorded. The vertical writing says: "A record of the birth of the children of Mr. Henry Henderson: Mary his Wife. Betty Henderson their daughter Born in Halifax July 10, 1793 John Henderson their son Born in Halifax Oct. 5, 1776 Henry Henderson their son born in Halifax Jan. first 1780 Levi their son born in Halifax April 7, 1784 Chester their son born in Halifax Jan. 28, 1786 Jesse their son born in Halifax Sept. 23, 1788" [HLR 1A: 341]. On the same page with the births of his children, Henry Henderson signed the survey as selectman along with Samuel Woodard, Daniel Isham, and Jonathan Wells.

Other survey records and the original school district list appear among the pages of deeds in the front half of Book 1A. The town meeting and vital records resume in Book 2A. Deeds are continued throughout Book 2. The same organization occurs in Books 3A and 3. From Book 4 on, only deeds, mortgages, and a few estate distributions are recorded in the land record books. Other books were set up for other types of records.

Book 1A was put into service about eight months after the first recorded town meeting held in March 1778. James Gray, town clerk, wrote the minutes for meetings held in March, April, June, August, and September of 1778 and February of 1779. Hubbel Wells was elected town clerk in March 1779, and the penmanship style changes for the next sets of minutes. While reading town records, one gets to know the distinctive hand of the various town clerks, that is, until the advent of the typewriter.

THE POLITICAL PENDULUM VIEWED THROUGH TOWN MEETING RECORDS

THE MINORITY

In 1778, a faction of the town set up the "recorded" town government of Halifax. Politically, these were "Vermonters." The majority of the townsmen were "Yorkers," who boycotted the first three years of town meetings. The political split in the town is clear from the minutes. The first group of names on the freeman's list, about thirty in all, included scarcely enough men to fill all the positions needed to conduct town business, and many of the men were chosen for multiple offices. Evidently, a majority of the men in town were unwilling, in 1778, to declare allegiance to the new state of Vermont and take the Freeman's Oath. It was only after the governor and general assembly had convincingly proven their authority and offered full-scale amnesty to those who would declare allegiance to Vermont the cast of town meeting characters changed dramatically. The freeman's list grew appreciably by 1782. Prominent residents, such as Benjamin Henry, Robert Pattison, Isaac Orr, Henry Henderson, and Lieutenant James Clark, do not appear in the records of the first three years of town meetings until the dramatic turning point in March 1781.

A record of the first town meeting follows.

(400)

At a town Meeting Regularly Warnd & held
at Hallifax on tuesday the third Day of March 1778 —
Chose Capt Hubbel Wells moderator — — —
it was Put to a Vote whether the town would Except
the Constitution of the State of Vermont
it Pased in the affirmative
Chose Capt Hubbel Wells and Ens Edward Harris
to Represent the town at a General Court at Winsor
                              Attest James Gray town Clerk

at a meeting of the freemen of the town of hallafax Legally
warnd & Held in Hallifax afore st on the 9 Day of April 1778
Chose Capt Hubbil Wells moderator
Chose Lieut John Thomas as a Deligate to Cary the Votes
for a Judg of Probates to Gilsion — — —
Voted to adjurn this meeting to the third tuesday in
June at Eleven oclock in the foure Noon — — —
June 16th 1778 the freemen of this town met according
to adjurnment Chose James gray town Clerk
Chose Capt Hubbel Wells Doct Wm Hill & mr
Israel guild Select Men — —
Chose James gray town treasurer — — — —
Chose mr Amos Pebody & Doct Wm Hill Constables
Chose mrs Benjamin Lymon Jonas Shepard Lieut Caleb
Owing Elias Parsons & Stiphen Wilknox Survayors
of high ways
Chose messjars John Hall & Elias Parsons fence Viewers
Chose mr Thos mClure & Capt Hubbel Wells Lifters
Chose messjars James gardner & Wm Scot Colectors
Chose mr Wm Scot Leather Seallor — — —
Chose mr John Hall & Doct Wm Hill grandjurors
Chose Lieut Caleb Owing & James Woodward
tithing men —
Chose Rufus Shepard & Jol Peas hogy howards
Chose Capt Hubbel Wells Sealtor of waits & measurs
Chose Lieut Caleb Owing Doct Wm hill bear Reefs
Chose Elias Parsons Brandor Chose Benjamin Lymon
Pound Keeper & his Barn yard for a Pound
                    Attest James gray town Clerk

Continued

(401)

At a meeting Leagally warn'd & held at Hallifax July 7th 1778
Chofe meet Elias Parfons & Thos Mcluer felect men in
adition to the former for the year Enfuing
the freemen Broght in there Votes for a Judg of Probates
Chofe Capt Habbil Wells & Enfign Edward Harris Juftiss of
the Peace for the town for the time Being . . . .
                                    Atteft James Gray town Clerk

[HLR 1A: 400–401]

The freemen reconvened on September 1, 1778 and chose Hubbel Wells and Edward Harris to again "Represent the town for the time Being" [HLR 1A: 401]. On February 8, 1779, at a legally warned meeting of the freemen, Benjamin Lyman moderated a discussion regarding the issue of the "Circumstances of the State of Vermont in Regard to the Union Containing Sixteen Towns East of Conecticut River . . ." [HLR 1A: 401]. They voted unanimously to instruct the town representatives to carry a vote of disapproval of the union to the next general assembly session in Bennington.

At the second annual meeting of the Town of Halifax held on March 13, 1779, the freemen chose "Capt. Hubbel Wells, Mr. Israel Guild, Capt. John Thomas, Doctor William Hill and Edward Harris, Esq." to be selectmen. It was voted that the selectmen would take care of the "Minister and School Land in the town of Hallifax" [HLR 1A: 403]. New names appearing on the list of officeholders in 1779 were: John Sawtell, Thomas Alverson, Dr. Peletiah Fitch, Deacon John Pennell, Joseph Tucker, and David Williams. After all the town offices were filled the only other business was "Voted that Hogs Shall run at Large from the fifteenth of October to the first of may." These minutes were recorded by Hubbel Wells, town clerk.

The third annual meeting warned and held in Halifax took place on March 30, 1780. James Gray was chosen town clerk and selectmen chosen were: Hubbel Wells, Edward Harris, James Gray, John Sawtell, and Israel Guild. New names added to the roll of officers were: Jonathan Wells, Stephen Gates, John Gault, James Hebard, and Deacon Eliphelet Ellis. From these minutes, we learn where town meetings were taking place.

> Voted that this meeting be adjurnd to the Last Thursday in April at one
> o clock to meet at Mr. Jos Tuckers for the further Business of this
> meeting and to Raise, if the town think it proper, mony to Provide Seals
> Brands Weights measures and any other business Proper to Be Don on
> Sd Day. [HLR 1A: 405]

Until 1785, and when the first meeting house was complete, meetings were held at "Landlord Tuckers." Joseph Tucker owned various properties in Halifax Center, and at the March 1779 meeting it was "Voted a Place to Erect a Pound Be on the Common or Side of the Road at the Parting of the Roads Between Joseph Tuckers & Elias Parsons" [HLR 1A: 405]. Both men owned property in Halifax

Center. Also at that meeting it was:

> Voted that a Larram [alarm] Post Be erected on the width of Land near
> Elias Parsons. Voted that whenever a Larrum of four guns is fired at the
> Larrum Post, By any Sworn officer of the Town that all who here the
> Same Shall Repair to the Post with all speed. [HLR 1A: 405]

On April 27, 1780, the adjourned meeting was reopened, and it was voted to
dismiss James Gray from his three offices (town clerk, selectman and leather-
sealer) to be replaced by Hubbel Wells, town clerk, Doctor William Hill,
selectman and William Scott, Sealer of Leather. In other business, Doctor Hill and
Joseph Tucker were chosen to "Represent the State of the Town to his Ecellency
Governor Chittenden and report to the town" [HLR 1A: 405]. In May, the town
meeting "Heard the Report of their Committee from the Governer" [HLR 1A: 406].
No details of the report appear in the minutes. The next entry is the listers'
report, recorded on November 1780, and what may possibly be the first grand list
for the town of Halifax.

> The Sum Total of the Fourfolded is   1171-0-0
> The Sum Total of them that were not four folded[18]   689-0-0
> NB the above Sum is them that we have Warned
>   Edward Harris, John Sawtell, Joseph Tucker - Listers [HLR 1A: 407]

Taxes The Catalyst For Change

The 1780 grand list appears to coincide with the turning point in participation in
town government. The provisions tax levied on the towns by the state of
Vermont at their October 1780 assembly became the catalyst for change as
demonstrated by the following sequence of events.

> This Act for the purpose of procuring Provision for the Troops, to be
> employed in the service of this State, for the year ensuing [set up the
> following quota for Halifax:] *Pounds of Flour, 4,500; Pounds of Beef 1,500;
> Pounds of Salted Pork 750; Bushels of Indian Corn 126; Bushels of Rye 63.*[19]

Forty-three Halifax freemen voted on the state's demand for these commodities
to help feed the troops. The terse minutes from that Halifax town meeting tell the
story.

> At a Town Meeting Legally Warned and Hold at Landlord Tuckers in
> Hallifax on the 8th day of January 1781.
> At the Meeting aforesd Voted Dr. Wm Hill Moderator for the Meeting.
> Put to Vote Whethor the Town would pay the provision Tax Laid by
> the General Assembly at their Last Session. Past in the Negative of
> thirty against it[,] thirteen for it. [HLR 1A: 407]

Nothing else is reported in the minutes for this meeting nor did Hubbel Wells
sign his report. On February 5, 1781, a petition, which describes the political
climate in Halifax as on the edge of full-scale anarchy, and announces the
resignation of all the town and militia officers pending redress of grievances, was
delivered to the governor and the General Assembly of Vermont.

To His Excelency Governer Chittenden together With the
Honourable Councill and General assembly of the Representatives of the free men of the State of Vermont Greeting
The petition of the Authority Melitica Officers
Select men and Others Inhabitants of the Town of Williston
Humbly Sheweth that the Situation of Your petitioners
at present is such that Renders it impracticable for
us to Discharge our Duty in our Respective Offices
for to prosecute the Orders Which we Receive From our
Superiors Officers and in perticular our Raiseing
our proportion of provisions for the armey Your petitioners therefore pray the Collection of the provision may
be postponed for the preasent for the following Reasons
(vez) first Because we are not able to Inforce one
Single act by Reason of our Devision Secondly Because
at a Legal Town Meeting there ware but 13 in the
Town that Voted to Raise it 3dly Because Many that
Were friends — — the State Do Declare they will re-
volt if they are ablidg'd to pay it under the ineason
administration of Goverment 4thly Because the York
ers have Invited all those who are Oposed to the
to take protection under them and Some have Gone
Already and Signd their articles and we are Confident
if it Must be Raisd at this time that the Inhabitants
in General Will sling of Goverment —
Whenever we have Sent our under officers to warn them
of a Draught the Yorkers have Confin Beat and abused
them Made them Burn their Orders and promis never
to Return on such Busines in this Manner we have
Bin Treated for this Many Years without any Redress
Which Renders Goverment a Burden to us insted of
Secureing our Lives and properties under this Situation Your petitioners pray they may not be Called on
for men or Money untill they have their Greavences
Redress and are able to Soport Goverment —

For as all Goverment ought to be Institut
ed and Soported for the Security and protection
of the Community as Such and to Enable the
Individuals who Compose it to Enjoy the Natural
Rights and the other Blessings Which the Great
Author of Existance hath Bestowed on Man.
and Whenever those Great Ends of Goverment
are not Obtained the people have a Right
by Common Consent to Change it and Take
Such Measures as to them may appear Necessa
ry to promote their Safety and Happines

and as your petetioners are friend to Goverment
for the affore Said purposes and the Natural
tendency a Disregard of this adrss may have
in the Weakening this Riseing State we Cannot
But Hope and Expect that Your Excelency and
Honours in Your Great Wisdom Will Redress our
Greavences or those of us in Commission
Must of Necessity Resign our office and Do
Hearby Resign untill we see our Greavences
Redress'd

This May Certifie to the Honourable assembly
to Whom it is addrest that Dr William Hill and
Mr Joseph Tucker Were Chosen (by a Large
number of the Inhabitants of Hallifax Concern
for Raiseing Men) to present this petition With
the State of the Town to your Excelency and
Honours Hallifax February ye 5th 1781

Hubbel Wells ⎱ Select   Hubbel Wells Justes of peas
Israel Guile ⎰ Men   Caleb Owen Capt
John Sawtell   Stephen Gates fut
Wm Hill   David Williams. Jus

A public record of action or response to the petition has not been found. One wonders what actions and negotiations transpired behind the scenes.

ENTER THE NEW MAJORITY

The fourth recorded Halifax town meeting, legally warned for March 26, 1781, was attended by many former Yorkers, and a number of new names appear as office holders. The full listing follows:

Moderator:	Mr. Joseph Tucker
Town Clerk:	Hubbel Wells
Selectmen:	Benjamin Henry, Deacon John Pennell, John Sawtell, Joseph Tucker
Town Treasurer:	Hubbel Wells
Constables & Collectors of Taxes:	Philemon Stacy and John Sawtell
Listers:	Capt. Robert Pattison, Hubbel Wells, Benjamin Henry, Elisha Pratt, Capt. Hazael Shepard
Sealer of Weights & Measures:	Nathaniel Swain
Grand Juror:	Lieut James Clark
Tythingmen:	Nathaniel Swain and Thomas Clark
Haward:	Ensign John Gault
Surveyors of Highways:	Jonas Shepard, William Wilcox, James Clark, Jr. Lieut. James Clark, Lieut Stephen Gates, Ensign John Gault, Elisha Pratt, Zebulon Ames, Jonathan Wells, Nathaniel Swain, Nathianel Bennet, and Benjamin Thomas.
Fenceviewers:	Lieut. James Clark, Lieut. Henry Henderson, Lieut. Stephen Gates

At the reconvened meeting the next day the following were chosen:

Petty Jurors:	Joseph Tucker, Capt. Robert Pattison, Capt. Caleb Owing, Henry Henderson, Jonathan Wells, Capt. John Thomas, William Shattuck, Nathaniel Swain, Stephen Gates and Thomas Clark
Committee to take into Custody and Sell Two Rights of land "called Ned East's Rights:	William Hill, Hubbel Wells, Benjamin Lyman, Joseph Tucker, and Capt. Caleb Owing.

The freemen met again in April to "take into Consideration the Expedience of Building a Meeting House and Calling a Minister and Taxing the Town for the purpose aforesaid" [HLR 1A: 410] and appointed Hubbel Wells, Deacon John Pennell, and Captain Robert Pattison a committee to "provide a Minister on the Town's Cost to preach in the Town for four Sabbaths on trial."

In May, the legal town meeting appointed the town's selectmen to a committee to "have the Care of Raiseing 13 men that are Called for in the Town" [HLR 1A: 411]. It is likely this was a call for militia service.

At the next meeting held in June, it was voted to "Build Said Meeting House by the Great Road North of Joseph Tuckers on the rode North of the Brook in the Most Convenient place.". . . It was also decided to fund the building of the meeting house by raising one hundred pounds, based on the polls and rateable estates of the "Inhabitants of Hallifax that are not of a Different principle in Matters of Religion from the Established Religion of the Land Which is Congregational or presbyterian" [HLR 1A: 413].

Finally, six months and six productive meetings after the town rebellion, the letter of appeal to the governor and resignation of the town officers, the provision tax issue was reconsidered. At a town meeting legally warned and held on August 10, 1781, it was "put to vote. Wither they will pay the Whole provision taxes in Beef if the Commesary will Take it and passed in the affirmative. Voted to Chose a Committee of two to provide Beef for sd [said] Rate. Voted that Capt. Hazal Shepard and Lieut William Shattuck be the Committee for the purpose aforesaid. Voted that Said Committee purchase a Quantity of Beef Not Exceeding Sixty Hundred Weight upon three Months Credit in Behalf of the Town for Vermont Currency" [HLR 1A: 413]. One month later the town met to raise a tax of twenty pounds "for the paying for preaching in Said Town" and decided to send for Mr. Goodale for a two-month trial period. "Lieut [Philemon] Stacy, Ensign [Isaac] Orr and Lieut [Joseph] Tucker" were appointed the committee "to Send for Mr. Goodale and provide his board" [HLR 1A: 414] [↪ 280]. By December, the town decided to "give the Rev. Goodall a Regular Call to Settle with us in the Gospel Ministry" [HLR 1A: 415]. Another tax issue arose in 1781, which fell on the shoulders of constable and tax collector Philemon Stacy, who received the following notice:

> To the Constable of the Town of Hallifax. Greeting
> Whereas the General assembly at their Sessions in Winsor in April 1781 Did Grant a Tax of ten Shilings on Each Hundred acres of land in the Town of Hallifax Except publick Rights & the College lands this is therefore to Command you to Collect of the Several persons owning lands in sd Town of Hallifax ten Shilings on Each Hundred Acres and in the Same proportion a greater or a lessor Quantity . . . & pay of same into the Treasury on or Before sd first Day of April Next and if any person or persons shall refuse or Neglect to pay his or her Just proportion of Sd Tax You are Commanded to Distrain his her or their Goods or Estates and them Dispose of the las Direct & also Satisfy your own fees . . . Given at the Treasury office in Sunderland 2nd Day of November 1781. [HLR 1A: 62]

This statement is repeated on various pages of Book 1A, and below each is the word "Duplicate," followed by a description of a tax sale: For example:

> In Obedience to ye above Warrant I have posted part of ye Lot No fifteen & Sold so much of the North East Corner of sd Lot to Highest Bidder as to pay Nine Shilings & Eleven pence tax & ten Shilings & five pence Cost the Highest Bidder is Oliver Waters and it Covers thirty Acres & one half on sd North East Corner in one Compact Body it being Known by William Shattocks Lot
> Hallifax September ye 25th 1783   Test
> Jos. Williams   Philemon Stacy Cons.   Joel Sumner [HLR 1A: 131]

Other properties sold were: Seven Acres of Lot No Forty— John Williams and Others to William Wilcox; Six and one quarter Acres of Lot No fifty five— Samuel Thomas to Oliver Waters; Nine and three quarter acres of Lot No Fifty— John Torrey to David Mclain; Forty Nine Acres and a quarter of Lot No Sixteen—Joseph Bell to Oliver Waters; Fourteen and one quarter acres of Lot No Twenty five—Nathan Pratt to Oliver Waters, and two hundred thirteen acres of Lot ten, an unassigned Wentworth Right, to Henry Henderson.

Early in 1782, the town met and decided to petition the "Comesary General of this State to have the Liberty to pay the provision Tax for this year in beef next Summer," and Hubbel Wells, Hazel Shepard, and Philemon Stacy were appointed to draft the petition [HLR 1A: 417]. A committee of three was chosen to settle accounts with the selectmen, and the first Monday in March was set for the annual meeting.

Between March of 1781 and 1782, the town held ten meetings, focusing on fiscal conciliation with the state and raising funds to build a meetinghouse and hire a minister at home. Over the next decade leading to Vermont federal statehood, the Halifax town government, in addition to responding to the general assembly mandates, would busily work to build and shape the community.

* * *

In March 1782, the town voted in the affirmative "they will Raise the Seven men Sent to by the Board of War." It was "Voted that the Select Men Hire Seven men for the Service of the State of Vermont from said 15th of April to the 15th of December Next as Cheep as they Can and assess the Inhabitants according to their Respective Lists, in 1781 for sd payment of Said Men" [HLR 1A: 419]. The seven men hired to help defend the frontiers were paid the rate of forty shillings a month [HLR 1A: 420].

In 1782, it was "Voted to Raise a Tax of two pence on the acre of Non Residents Land in the Town of Halifax. . . Voted to apply the Whole of Said Tax to the Building a Meeting House in Sd Town on the South Side of Deacon McCreles Lot No. 29" [HLR 1A: 421]. The nonresident tax resulted in the town's acquisition of a more suitable property for the meetinghouse that had not yet been constructed according to the previous plan. Upon seizure of his cattle for nonpayment of taxes, Deacon McCrellis of Colrain "sold" a part of his Lot 29 property to the town. By 1785, a meetinghouse had been built and town meetings were held there.

In December 1782 the town

> Voted that Mr Thos Scott & Mr Watters be a Committee or ajants
> to procure a Charter of Coppy of the Charter of Hallifax at Col
> Partridges in Hatfield[.] Voted that if Col Patridge Charge for the
> Coppy of the Charter to make Report to the Town. [HLR 1A: 422]

Apparently, this did not work out. No further mention is made until 1790: "Voted that Mr Henry Henderson have Seven Shilings for obtaining a Coppy of the Charter of the Town of Halifax . . ." [HLR 2A: 177]. According to Laura Sumner, town clerk, the charter was in disrepair when she took office, but Roger McBride underwrote the cost of its restoration.

Politics and taxes made the news at some meetings. In February 1783,

> Voted that we will pay no more Taxes to the State of Vermont till the Matter is Settled by Congress Dissenters from afforesd vote Philemon Stacy Caleb Owen Jonathan Wells Joseph Tucker Hubbel Wells Thomas Scott Edward Harris Oliver Waters.
>
> [HLR 1A: 423]

At the September 3, 1783 town meeting they voted "the Representatives be Directed to use their Influence in preventing the Tories Returning to this State." The "Tories" in this case were Yorkers who where loyal to New York and to the American cause, and mislabeled by the Vermont government. And then after reconsideration, they "Voted to Nullify and Make Void a Certain Vote passed in Town Meeting heretofore Respecting their not paying any More taxes to the State of Vermont until the Matter was Determined by Congress" [HLR 1A: 424]. Locally, the listers rated property each year, and a simple form of taxation often was the norm. It was "Voted to Raise a Tax of one penny on the pound Ratable Estates of the Inhabitants of Halifax on the List for the Year 1790 to be paid into the Town Treasury by the first Day of Sept. next" [HLR 2A: 177]. In 1786, it was "voted to take the School Rent for this year in Grain, that is to Say, Wheet at four Shilings pr Bushel and Indian Corn at two Shilings and five pence pr Bushel" [HLR 1A: 434].

In February of 1785, it was decided to procure weights and measures for the town. These would have been used by the town sealer of weights and measures and today are displayed at the town clerk's office.

Halifax residents are also proud to have in their possession the original weights and measures which have been preserved and passed down for generations. The early settlers used these in their commerce and also when they measured their produce to pay their taxes, as was the custom of their time.

These weights and measures were made in England and date back before the year 1750. Close examination reveals the insignia of the British crown. It is little wonder that they have endured centuries of use. They are made of solid copper, and are very heavy and durable.

These historical items are now being kept at the Town Clerk's Office.

HHS Scrapbook clipping dated 1979   Photos C. Perna HTC

At the 1786 meeting, the people "Voted to Chose a Committee of three to Confer with a Committee from Colrain Respecting a Bridge over North River." Benjamin Henry Esq., Edward Harris Esq., and Mr. Nathan Fish were elected to a committee for this purpose [HLR 1A: 433]. Concern about the surveyor general's plan to have James Whitelaw survey the state resulted in a vote "that Esq Benj Henry Esq Harris and Hubbel Wells Be a Committee to Draught a petition to the assembly Respecting the Surveyor General Surveying this Town" [HLR 1A: 429]. The Whitelaw map includes some information supplied by the town [↵ 139, 140].

Halifax was growing, and in order to provide education for its youth, they voted at a town meeting held August 30, 1784,

> to Chose a Committee from Several parts of the Town proposed
> for School Districts accordingly Chose Esq Henry Lt Orr Capt
> Sawtell Lt Tucker Jasper Hunt David Allen Stephen Willcox
> Thomas Scott Lt Henderson James Clark Jur Capt James Pennel
> Joseph McCluer & Hubbel Wells to preprose a plan of Divideing
> the Town into School Districts and Make Report to a later Town
> Meeting. [HLR 1A: 427]

On September 7, 1784, the report was accepted. It was "Voted that the districts be recorded in the Town Book with each man's name belonging to the representative districts [↵ 324]. Each school district kept its own records and a trustee reported to the Town Clerk" [HLR 1A: 428]. Ten school districts were created. In 1786, School District No. 11 was established and in 1787, it was "Voted to Divide the NW District into two Divisions" [HLR 1A: 437].

On the lighter side, the animals were occasionally mentioned in the old records.

> Halifax, November . . . 1789, then James Pratt of Halifax
> Exhibited an account of Two Stray Colts Taken into his Custody
> Some Days past that he the James Judged was Manifestly Strayed
> from the owner viz one two year old Mare Colt of a Chestnut
> Culler with a White Strip in the face and Black Mane and Tail
> undocked also a Last Spring Horse Colt of a Bay Culler Black
> Mane . . . [HLR 1A: 387]

From 1778 to 1788, the first decade of recorded town government, Halifax town meetings were held often more than once a year. Voters met whenever issues needed to be addressed. They provided for representation at the state assembly; voted on national, state, and county issues; provided local officials for the town; and treated issues of roads, bridges, boundaries, districts, taxation, religion, education, defense, health, welfare, and animals, for which they built at least three pounds on the south line of the common, on which they had succeeded in building a meetinghouse. Town clerks James Gray, in 1778; Hubbel Wells, from 1779 through 1786; Nathan Fish, in 1787; and Hubbel Wells, in 1788 kept records of what transpired during that decade. By 1788, Halifax town government was up, running, and duly recorded. The cornerstone was in place.

~ Elaine Fairbanks and Constance Lancaster

EARLY TOWN OFFICERS

Between 1771 and 1777, due to missing records, the only known town officials and representatives were: John Bolton, James Gray, Dr. Peletiah Fitch, Edward Harris, Dr. William Hill, Benjamin Lyman, Nathan Williams, Captain William Williams, and Samuel Woodard. On January 15–16, 1777, Vermont declared independence from Great Britain and from New York.

DATE	SELECTMEN	CONSTABLE	TOWN CLERK	REPRESENTATIVE
1778	Capt. Hubbel Wells Dr. Wm Hill Israel Guild Thos. McClure Elias Parsons	Amos Peabody Dr. Wm Hill	James Gray	Edward Harris Hubbel Wells 2 sessions
1779	Capt. Hubbel Wells Dr. Wm Hill Israel Guild Capt. John Thomas Edward Harris, Esq.	Amos Peabody Dr. Wm Hill	Hubbel Wells Amos Peabody	Edward Harris Hubbel Wells
1780	Hubbel Wells Edward Harris James Gray Dr. Wm. Hill John Sawtell Israel Guild	Dr. William Hill Joseph Tucker	James Gray Hubbel Wells	Edward Harris Hazael Shepard
1781	Hubbel Wells Benjamin Henry Deacon John Pennell John Sawtell Joseph Tucker	Philemon Stacy John Sawtell	Hubbel Wells	Edward Harris Benjamin Henry
1782	Lt. Thomas Taggart Lt. James Clark Capt. Robert Pattison	Samuel Woodard Capt. Caleb Owen	Hubbel Wells	Edward Harris
1783	Edward Harris, Lieut. Henry Henderson Daniel Isham Jonathan Wells Samuel Woodard	Oliver Waters Joseph Williams	Hubbel Wells	Edward Harris Joseph Tucker
1784	Benjamin Henry Lt. Joseph Tucker Thomas. Scott Hubbel Wells Lt. Thomas Clark	Isaac Orr Joseph McClure	Hubbel Wells	Hubbel Wells
1785	Hubbel Wells Benjamin Henry Thomas Taggart David Allen Capt. James Pennell	Thomas Scott	Hubbel Wells	Hubbel Wells
1786	Hubbel Wells Benjamin Henry Thomas Taggart James Pennell Nathan Fish	Oliver Waters	Hubbel Wells	Hubbel Wells
1787	Nathan Fish Joel Hall Thomas Farnsworth Thomas Scott Judge Wells	Thomas Scott Jasper Hunt	Nathan Fish	Hubbel Wells
1788	Benjamin Henry Nathan Fish Hubbel Wells	Lt. Thos. Farnsworth	Hubbel Wells	Hubbel Wells
1789	Benjamin Henry Nathan Fish Hubbel Wells	Lt. Thos. Farnsworth	Hubbel Wells	Benjamin Henry
1790	Capt. James Pennell Benj. Henry, Esq. Nathan Fish	Lt. Thos. Farnsworth	Hubbel Wells	Benjamin Henry

Above town officers served during the Republic of Vermont years (1777–1791). On March 4, 1791, Vermont was admitted as the fourteenth state.

WHO WAS DOCTOR WILLIAM HILL?

Today, young people in Halifax learn about what is referred to as "The Westminster Massacre." On that fateful day, March 13, 1775, the Cumberland County Court session was disrupted by protestors and ended in violence and bloodshed. "Eight of the Rioters were taken prisoners [including William French, who later died] and the wounded were taken care of by Doctors Day, Hill and Chase. The latter of which was immediately sent for on Purpose." Doctors Day and Hill may have been present at the court to serve as jurors or representatives for their towns. Doctor Hill lived in Halifax and served as a army surgeon during the Revolution.

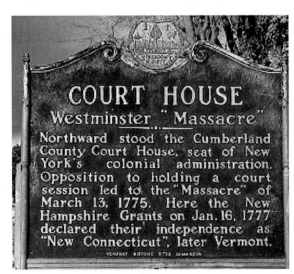

Photo courtesy Dan Axtell

Doctor William Hill is fifth on the Halifax original freeman's list, and he was the second man voted to be a town selectman in 1778 under the laws of the new state of Vermont. The early town meetings document his energetic participation in setting up the town government and negotiating with Governor Chittenden and the state assembly. For three years he served as town selectman and constable. After the 1781 change in leadership, his name is no longer found in the meeting records. He moved to White Creek, New York. In 1818 he joined his son, John, in Eden, New York where he kept a tavern until his death. William Hill lived in West Halifax on property in Lot 43, which was owned originally by Jonathan Wells and later deeded to James Plumb. It is not known if Doctor Hill practiced medicine in Halifax; but it is known, for at least a few years, he did practice politics.

School children might enjoy knowing that Halifax, then a hotbed of Yorker sentiments, participated in the naming of Vermont. Doctor William Hill represented Halifax at the convention of the New Hampshire Grants held in Windsor on June 4, 1777.[20] The convention acknowledged in January, when it declared the New Hampshire Grants to be "a free and independent state," to be known as "New Connecticut," it was not aware that a district on the Susquehanna River already bore the name "New Connecticut," and thus it was resolved the New Hampshire Grants district would be known by the name of "Vermont." Doctor Hill's name is on the list of those who voted for the resolution. The vote was unanimous.

~ Constance Lancaster

ENDNOTES

1. Hall, p. 188.
2. *A Petition of the People of Halifax*, American Imprints Series, #42449, microform, courtesy Readex, Chester, Vermont.
3. Nathan Williams married Grace in 1745, who died in 1755. Their children were Joseph (b. 1745), Grace (b. 1747/48), and David (b. 1752). In 1755, Nathan married Waightstill Davenport. Their children were Olive (b. 1756), Job (b. 1758), Nathan (b. 1760), Waitstill (b. 1762), Abraham (b.1765), and Isaac (b.1765). Source: Judy Buss posted at WorldConnect.com.
4. HTC. This fascinating document, currently in pieces, is stored in a cigar box in the town clerk's safe. It is scheduled for archival restoration. Apparently used as a "working" draft by Governor Wentworth and the Partridges, it seems to record the process of divvying up the land. Some lots are annotated with tiny Ws, (for the governor) some have Xs, and others have a mark that faintly resembles an elongated letter p. Probably, these represent the choices made by the original grantor and grantees. More than half of the lots are blank. The names of the original proprietors must have been added and duly recorded in Portsmouth, New Hampshire, at a later time. Perhaps Henry Henderson retrieved this document from Hatfield, Massachusetts when he went there on behalf of the town to pick up the Charter.
5. NARA, Nathan Williams pension file # W26029.
6. VSS, MsVtSP,(Manuscript Vermont State Papers) vol. 17, p. 9. From his position in this incident and his participation in the first town meetings, often serving as an officer, it is clear that David Williams was a Vermonter.
7. Ibid.
8. Patrie, pp. 17–18-G.
9. Franklin County Registry of Deeds, Greenfield, MA, Book 3, p. 121.
10. Patrie, p. 41-H. The 1759 Battle of Quebec, according to Patrie, "made Colrain safe from Indians for all time." In 1777, John Bolton entered Revolutionary service second in command to John Wood and later succeeded him as Captain. They trained a company of Colrain men as engineers or artificers and were assigned to West Point, where they remained until the end of the war in 1783. Under Bolton's direction, they constructed a chain across the Hudson River to prevent passage of British ships; Bolton also engineered construction of the Croton River Bridge. When the government failed to pay his men, Bolton mortgaged his property and paid them himself. Never reimbursed, he ended up a homeless pauper at the close of the war and lived out his days with his children in Warren, New York. Patrie, pp. 70–71.
11. From Thomas Hill Cemetery: Capt. John Thomas died Sept. 25, 1815 Aged 88 *Friends depart dry up your tears, / Here I must lie till Christ appears.* In Memory of Mrs. Catherine Thomas Wife of Capt. John Thomas who died April 17th 1805 ae 79 years *Don't mourn for me dry up your tears/ I shall arise when Christ appears;/ And like his Glorious body be,/ And reign with him eternally.*
12. Hall, p. 136.
13. *Volume I Cumberland County Court of Common Pleas*, Windham County Courthouse, Newfane, Vermont, p. 4.
14. Ibid., p. 27.
15. Ancestry.com, New York Historical Manuscripts: Revolutionary Papers [database on-line]. Provo, UT, USA: MyFamily.com, Inc., 2003. Original data: Calendar of Historical Manuscripts, Relating to the War of the Revolution, In the Office of the Secretary of State, Albany, N.Y., vols. I-II (Albany, NY: Weed, Parsons, and Co., 1868).
16. It is presumed that records were kept prior to 1778, however those records have not been found.
17. Aaron H. Grout, *State papers of Vermont Volume Three* (Bellows Falls, VT: P. H. Gobie Press, 1924) p. 86.
18. Four-folds were the penalties for a man's not listing all his property (many were later crossed out).
19. William Slade, *Vermont State Papers* (Middlebury, VT: J. W. Copeland, 1823) pp. 409–410.
20. E. P. Walton, ed., *Governor and Council Vermont,* vol. 1 (Montpelier, VT: Steam Press of J. Poland, 1873) p. 53.

Photo C. Lancaster

Early Militia and the Revolutionary War

The shattered remains of an old iron howitzer bear witness to an active militia at one time in the town of Halifax. In the 1950s, while digging to create a foundation for a garage next to his house in Halifax Center, which was a store and post office for many years, Paul Crosier found pieces of the old weapon. The origins of the gun are obscure; however, artillery experts say that these weapons, dating back to the Revolutionary period and before, were often well used before falling into the hands of the local militia men and were known on occasion to blow apart in the field. If only this howitzer could tell its story!

Photos C. Perna HHS

It is not known just when a militia force was organized in Halifax. There appeared to be rapid settlement of the town between the mid-1760s when about twenty families were settled here until the census of 1771, which listed the population as 329. It is quite likely that some sort of militia force was organized to defend the town, particularly since a number of the heads of households at that time were men who had seen action during the French and Indian War and were experienced fighters. The first town meeting under the auspices of the newly found state of Vermont that can be found in town records took place on March 3, 1778. Records from this point on often refer to men by their military title, which would seem to confirm that a militia force existed and continued for some time after the Revolutionary period. This history of the militia is pieced together from a variety of sources and is focused particularly on the personnel involved. The political setting of the period is key to understanding the militia, and I have attempted to integrate this aspect of our history here as well.

The earliest reference to a militia force in Halifax is found in the records for Cumberland County, New York (Halifax then being considered part of New York State). In 1774, the Provincial Congress of New York authorized raising a militia, and in January 1776, the nominations for the officers for Halifax were approved as follows:[1]

> Captain David Rich
> First Lieutenant Benjamin Henry
> Second Lieutenant Robert Patterson [Pattison]
> Ensign Edward Harris

These men presumably had volunteers who trained under them. It was the custom that the officers were elected by their men and then officially commissioned by the government of New York; however, it was often the case that New York commissioned those who were outspoken loyalists to New York. Of these four men, Benjamin Henry was known to be an experienced fighter, having served with Rogers' Rangers during the French and Indian War, and was present at the storming of Ticonderoga during this period. Prior to coming to Halifax, Benjamin Henry lived in Colrain, Massachusetts. He appears on the 1771 census as living in Halifax.

Edward Harris also appears in the census of 1771. Harris served as a delegate from Halifax to the assembly at Westminster, Vermont, on October 19, 1774, which was called to determine the sentiment on Britain. The report of this assembly stated "He who has nothing but what another has power at pleasure lawfully to take away from him, has nothing that he can call his own, and is, in the fullest sense, a slave."[2] In addition to his role as a militia leader, Harris led an active political life. In 1775, he appealed to the state of New York as part of a loosely organized group opposed to British rule called "Friends of Liberty," expressing their desire of having more town autonomy. At a town meeting on March 3, 1778, the town voted to accept the Constitution of the State of Vermont, and Edward Harris and Hubbel Wells were appointed "to represent the town at the General Court at Winsor" [HLR 1A: 400]. It should be pointed out that this vote represents the sentiment of those present at this town meeting who had signed the Freeman's Oath pledging allegiance to the state of Vermont. The majority of those living in town at that time were loyal to New York. Harris was appointed by the Vermont State Assembly in 1779 to serve on one of their committees. The Vermont Revolutionary Rolls list Harris on the rolls of Captain Josiah Boyden's Company.

Robert Pattison came to Halifax from Colrain and David Rich came from Amherst, Massachusetts. Both are listed as heads of households in the census of 1771.

While the State of New York approved these early militia officers, their loyalties did not necessarily lie with that state. Loyalties among townspeople were very much divided, with some identifying with New Hampshire, some with New York, and still others with the as-yet-unrecognized state of Vermont. A review of the political status of this area during the period prior to 1791, when Vermont finally received recognition as a state, reveals constant feuding and much confusion over who actually had jurisdiction over the New Hampshire Grants. During the Revolutionary War years, it appears that all these forces were united in opposition to Britain.

In addition to these officers recognized by the state of New York, there are references in the Vermont Revolutionary rolls to Sergeant John Gault, who is listed in Captain Josiah Boyden's Company of Colonel William Williams Regiment of Militia (Vermont Militia). There are several references to John Gault on various expeditions, including one to "the Lake" (Champlain) in 1780.[3] There is some confusion as to which John Gault is referred to here as there were several generations of John Gaults in Halifax, the earliest being head of one of the first families that settled the town in the early 1760s. Captain John Gault was accidentally shot and killed by his own company and is buried in the Pennell Hill Cemetery. Apparently the Captain and his men gathered at the nearby drinking spot after training exercises. The story behind this incident appeared in the *Vermont History Magazine* and was related by Jonathan Kellogg, a member of the local militia trained by John Gault.

Captain Gault . . . just as he left the store of Hamilton and Muzzey, in an attempt of some of his company to honor him by firing according to the custom of those days, was shot through the head, a part of his skull hitting the door of the store.[4]

Vermont.

BENNINGTON, May 12.
We hear from Halifax, in Windham county, that on Tuesday last, after Captain John Gnault, of that town, had dismissed his company, the soldiers, as is too common among *militia men*, began firing round their captain in order to *honor him*, when unfortunately one of their guns, being less elevated than the soldier was aware of, was fired close behind Capt. Gnault, the contents of which entered his skull and instantly deprived him of life. *Thus in the prime of life, through mere carelessness and unsoldier like boyish folly fell a very valuable officer ; in whose death the public have to lament the loss of a citizen whose conduct, in every particular, does honor to his memory.*

REGIMENTAL ORDERS.
Bennington, May 26, 1788.
To the Captains of the different Companies of the First Regiment in the First Brigade.

WHereas frequent accidents happen by disorderly firing on the parade, on field days &c. You are hereby required strictly to forbid your men to presume to fire a gun on muster days, or on the parade, without special orders from you, or the officer commanding, for the time being, on pain of a trial by Court Martial.

PORTSMOUTH, May 31.
We learn from Halifax, in Vermont, that Capt. John Gnault, of that town, having dismissed his company, the soldiers, as is too common among militia men, began firing round their Captain, in order to honour him; when unfortunately, one of the guns, being less elevated than the soldier was aware of, was fired close behind Captain Gnault, the contents of which entered his skull, and instantly put a period to his existence.

1. *Vermont Gazette or Freemen's Depositor,* May 12, 1788
2. *Vermont Gazette or Freemen's Depositor,* May 26, 1788
3. *New-Haven Gazette, and the Connecticut Magazine,* June 12, 1788, Courtesy Readex

We have no early diaries to describe the training or to give us a more complete picture of the early militia, but if Halifax muster days bear any resemblance to those of other towns, we can surmise that these occasions offered men the opportunity to come together, imbibe the spirits, and generally to enjoy one another's company, while at the same time learning defensive strategies.

Early references to the militia in Halifax indicate that the men mustered at Halifax Center. In addition to the howitzer mentioned earlier, an old bayonet and cannon balls have been found in Halifax. Town records from March 3, 1781, state, "The militia of this town voted to divide into two companies in the manner following: West and East companies by area" [HLR 1A: 407]. According to Grace Stone, the militia trained in a field currently owned by the Stones on Hatch Road next to the field owned by the Putnam family (Lot 54). Grace relates that this information has been passed along through the years; however, no evidence has been found to support this. It is possible that one of the militia companies trained on this site after the division referred to above.

Officers for the Cumberland County New York Militia, commissioned on August 18, 1778, for the town of Halifax were as follows:

Captain John Pennell
Peletiah Fitch Jr.
Ensign Joseph Stewart Jr.

John Pennell was listed in the census of 1771. He came to Halifax from Colrain where he served in a variety of town offices. He is referred to as one of the earliest settlers in Halifax, having settled in the mid 1760s in the southwest corner of town, referred to today as Pennell Hill. In

Bayonet fragments found in West Halifax

the history of Colrain, it is stated that John Pennell Jr.'s father came from England and settled in Colrain in 1739. John Jr. and his brothers were Indian scouts and served in the French and Indian War.[5] John Pennell Jr., died in 1797 at the age of seventy-six and is buried in Pennell Hill Cemetery. His son, James, was a member of Captain McClellan's Company and marched from Colrain to Boston in April 1775. James is also listed at Charlestown and Winter Hill from August to October 1775. He was called to Bennington on August 16–19, 1777, and to Saratoga September 20 to October 18, 1777, where he is listed as Sergeant Pennell. It should be noted that the dates for his duty in Bennington correspond with that well-known Battle of Bennington.

Dr. Peletiah, father of First Lieutenant Fitch, is recorded in history as being a strong and vocal supporter of New York and was listed as one of the petitioners to Governor Clinton of New York for relief from the attacks of the independent (Vermont) forces. In 1778, Governor Clinton of New York wrote the following in a letter to his friend Fitch:

> . . . still as on a former occasion, [I] earnestly recommend a firm
> and prudent resistance to the draughting of men, raising taxes, and
> the exercise of every act of government, under the ideal Vermont
> State; and in such towns, where our friends are sufficiently
> powerful for the purpose, I would advise the entering into
> association, for the mutual defence of their persons and estates
> against this usurpation.[6]

That same year, Peletiah Fitch Jr. was involved in a notorious incident in the history of Halifax. In 1778, it is recorded that John and Hannah Kirkley, loyal Yorkers, met David Williams, a supporter of Vermont, on the road. The encounter apparently led to blows. Justice of the Peace Hubbel Wells issued a warrant for the arrest of the Kirkleys "for perpetration of an assault and battery on David Williams." A trial was called; however, the proceedings were interrupted by a rowdy group of Yorkers who declared the trial out of order and denounced the justice of the peace. The fact that the Vermont assembly appointed Hubbel

Wells was cause for some dismay by those loyal to New York who refused to recognize his authority. It is said that the Yorkers arrived with bludgeons and "attempted to take prisoners." In addition to Peletiah Fitch Jr., the following people were listed as disrupting the trial: Thomas Clark, Thomas Baker, Isaac Orr, Henry Henderson, Alexander Stewart, Jonathan Safford, Elijah Edwards, and sixteen others.[7] It should be noted that both Baker and Orr were officers in the New York State Militia, and Henry Henderson is listed in the Revolutionary War rolls as being a private in Captain Levi Goodenough's Company of Rangers for the state of Vermont.

On August 18, 1778, Dr. Fitch was commissioned (by the state of New York) to be Judge of Inferior Court of Common Pleas and made chairman of the Committee of Safety for Cumberland County.

The Committee of Safety took a poll in Cumberland County in August 1778, to determine where citizens' loyalties lay. The results in Halifax were:

> For New York 63
> For Vermont   36
> Neutral   20
> Total polled   119[8]

Despite these numbers, which would indicate strong loyalty to New York, at the first town meeting in Halifax, which took place on March 3, 1778, the assembly voted to accept the Constitution of the State of Vermont. Perhaps this merely reflects the loyalties of those who were in attendance at this particular meeting. Over the next several years, a shift in loyalties occurred so that by 1784 the Yorkers were considered a minority. In the meantime, however, they were very vocal and active.

During February 1779, the Vermont General Assembly adopted the Militia Act to allow for the drafting of troops. The state was divided into militia districts, which were to furnish soldiers when called upon. If the men were not forthcoming, fines were enacted, and if not paid, property was confiscated accordingly. Needless to say, given the divided sentiments and loyalties in Halifax and other nearby towns, this act caused quite a stir. It was in the financial interest of the newly established state of Vermont to target Yorkers for the draft in order to derive the much-needed income from the resulting fines and confiscations. The *Official History of Guilford* describes a meeting in Brattleboro with committees of several towns represented, including Halifax, in July 1779, for the purpose of defending themselves against the Vermont loyalists.

> Much feeling was aroused by reason of the drafts by which
> Vermont replenished its militia, especial effort appearing to be
> exercised to secure those from the New York faction. In Halifax
> 5 Yorkers were drafted, but no Vermonters.[9]

The militia of Cumberland County, New York, was organized into northern and southern regiments in 1778. In July 1782, the following officers were chosen for the southern regiment, Halifax Militia:

> First Major William Shattuck
> Captain Thomas Baker
> 1st Lieutenant Isaac Orr
> 2nd Lieutenant Daniel Donaldson
> Ensign David Lamb
> Quarter Master Elisha Pierce[10]

William Shattuck was a very active Yorker and was involved in a number of confrontations with the Vermont forces. In May 1782, an incident occurred in Guilford when a deputy of the state of Vermont was sent to levy fines against Yorkers who had refused to be drafted by Vermont. The deputy took a cow as payment. Meanwhile a large group of Yorkers, including Shattuck, assembled at Hezekiah Stowell's tavern in Guilford, presumably to discuss the seizing of the cow. The deputy was intercepted by this mob, and the cow was returned to her original owner.[11]

Shattuck figured in another incident in Guilford later that year when he heard that the Green Mountain Boys were on their way to Guilford to "dispossess" Daniel Shepardson of his worldly goods. Shepardson, another loyal Yorker, had apparently refused to be drafted into the Vermont Militia or to pay his fines. Shattuck, according to the *Official History of Guilford,* organized "two companies of men" to confront Colonel John Sargent of the Vermont forces and forced him to back down.[12] In September 1782, Ethan Allen, reportedly with a force of 400, marched to Brattleboro, Halifax, and Guilford to take prisoners (twenty in all, including Shattuck, Baker, and Lamb). The prisoners were marched to Westminster where they were imprisoned. It was determined they should be banished and all their property confiscated. Shattuck's worldly goods were described as follows in the Guilford history:

> About 80 acres of land in Halifax, with the buildings thereon
> standing, about 10 tons of hay, a small quantity of rye in sheaf, a
> considerable quantity of flax spread on the ground, and about 2 or
> 3 acres of Indian corn standing on the ground. . . . All goods sold
> except his wife's apparel, the beds, and one cow.[13]

Shattuck, like the others, was banished to New Hampshire; however, despite the severity of the sentence, he and the others returned to Vermont shortly thereafter. The United States Congress on December 5, 1782, made a strong statement against the Vermont forces and their mistreatment of Shattuck and the others banished in the aforementioned incident. The following is excerpted from that act of Congress:

> That the people inhabiting the said district claiming to be
> independent, be, and they are hereby required without delay to
> make full and ample restitution to Timothy Church, Timothy
> Phelps, Henry Evans, William Shattuck, and such others as have
> been condemned to banishment and confiscation of estates, or

have otherwise been deprived of property, since the first day of September last, for the damages they have sustained by the acts and proceedings aforesaid, and that they be not molested in their persons or properties, on their return to their habitations in the said district.[14]

These men petitioned the state of New York for compensation for their loyalty; however, because of the New York authorities' preoccupation with the war with Britain, their pleas were initially ignored. In 1786, the state of New York finally awarded property to these men as well as other loyal Yorkers (144 in all). The land awarded was in Clinton Township, later to become Bainbridge, New York. The Halifax parties who received property included Shattuck, Baker, Lamb, and William and John Gault.

Another colorful incident in the political history of Halifax, which is related in Hall's *History of Eastern Vermont*, occurred in January 1784, when a group of Yorkers kidnapped an officer of Vermont, Ensign Oliver Waters, in Brattleboro and took him to Northampton, Massachusetts. When news of the event reached Halifax the following day, a group of men loyal to Vermont led by Joseph Tucker, followed the kidnapping party. As the story goes, this party reached Northampton the next day, rescued Waters, and took his guards captive. This suggests that the rescue party was high in spirits (probably brought on by alcohol as well as their victory), and thus pumped up, decided to capture Timothy Phelps (a strong opponent of the Vermont forces) who was visiting his family in Hadley, Massachusetts. After kidnapping Phelps, the Halifax party headed homeward; however, a sheriff who had been sent in pursuit by the Phelps's family soon overtook them. Tucker and his men were arrested and taken back to Hadley where they were later found guilty and fined. In addition to Joseph Tucker, the following Halifax men participated in this incident: Thomas Scott, Stephen Gates, Timothy Woodward, David Williams, Elijah Phillips, Gorham Noyes, Joel Sumner, Philemon Stacy, Daniel Walworth, Rufus Fisk, Samuel Dennison, John Noyes, Caleb Owen, Thomas Farnsworth, and Nathaniel Whitney.[15] It is not known whether this was an official militia body; however, several of these names appear in town records with military titles. Stephen Gates and Caleb Owen appear as "Lieutenant" in town meeting records.

In *The Reluctant Republic*, Frederic Van de Water makes the following statement about the militia, which would seem to summarize these incidents:

> The regiments were formed on paper, but never approached actuality. The technical members thereof were more intent on fighting each other than in combining against a common foe.[16]

~ *Susan Rusten*

BIBLIOGRAPHY

Crockett, Walter H. *Vermont: The Green Mountain State*. New York: Century History Co., 1921.

* * *

STATE MILITIA AND THE REVOLUTIONARY WAR

The list of men who served in the Revolutionary War was compiled by cross-referencing those who appeared as heads of households in the 1771 census with lists from town records written in the 1780s, NARA pension files, and the Vermont Revolutionary War rolls. Many Halifax men were found on the payroll lists for Captain Josiah Boyden's Company in Colonel William Williams' Regiment of militias on expedition to Bennington, during August and September of 1777.[17]

The 1777 constitution of the State of Vermont provided for a state militia. The Green Mountain Boys were the militia of Vermont from 1777–1791. During this period, New York formed the Cumberland County Militia and commissioned officers into service. Halifax men served in the Revolutionary War from both militias.

LIST OF MEN WHO SERVED FROM HALIFAX

NAME	(RANK) COMPANY/ DETAILS
Thomas Alverson	Capt. Boyden's Co., 1777.
John Baker	Capt. Hugh McClellan's Co. of minutemen, Col. Samuel Williams's Regt., 1775; Capt. Riddles's Co., Col. Foster's Mass. Regt., 1776; Capt. Williams's Co., Col. William Williams's Regt., Green Mountain Boys, and Capt. Lee's Co., Col. Seth Warner's Regt., 1777; Capt. Smalley's Vermont Co., 1778.
Peleg Baker	Capt. Boyden's Co., 1777.
Thomas Baker	Capt. Hugh McClellan's Co. of minutemen at Lexington Alarm, Col. Samuel Williams' Regt., 1775; Capt. Robert Oliver's Co., Col. Ephraim Doolittle's Regt., at Bunker Hill, 1775; (Capt.) Halifax Co., Cumberland County Militia, 1782.
Banks Bennet	(Sergt.) Capt. Boyden's Co., 1777.
Ebenezer Clark	Capt. Boyden's Co., 1777.
Elijah Clark	Capt. Boyden's Co., 1777.
James Clark	Capt. Boyden's Co., 1777.
Thomas Clark	Capt. Boyden's Co., 1777; Capt. Peter Page's Co. of Volunteers, 1781; Capt. Elijah Galusha's Co., 1782.
Daniel Donaldson	Capt. Robert Oliver's Co., Col. Ephraim Doolittle's Regt., at Winter (Bunker) Hill, 1775; Capt. Sam Taylor's Co., Col. Nicholas Dike's Regt., Roxbury, 1776; (Sergt.) Capt. Goodenough's Rangers, Sam Herrick's Regt., 1777; (2nd Lieut.) Halifax Co., Cumberland County Militia, 1782.
Peletiah Fitch Jr.	(1st Lieut.) Halifax Co., Cumberland County Militia, 1778.
William Frazier	Capt. Boyden's Co., 1777.
Preserved Gardner	(Sergt.) Capt. Boyden's Co., 1777.
Stephen Gates	(Lieut.) Halifax Co., Cumberland County Militia, 1781.
Alexander Gault	Capt. Boyden's Co., 1777.
James Gault	Capt. Hugh McClellan's Co., Col. Mosley's Regt. Battle of White Plains 1776. Capt. John Wells' Co., Col. Robinson Ticonderoga. 1776-1777. Serg. Nathan Williams Co. Green Mountain Boys, Col. Warners Regt. Hubbardton 1777.
John Gault	(Sergt.) Capt. Boyden's Co., 1777; Capt. Wm. Hutchins's Co., 1779.
John Fenton Gault	Capt. John Wells' Co. Col. Robinson. Ticonderoga 1776-1777.
Israel Hale	Capt. Josiah Fish's Co., 1781.
John Hall	Capt. Boyden's Co., 1777.
Edward Harris	(Ensign) Halifax Co., Cumberland County Militia, 1776; Capt. Boyden's Co., 1777.
Benjamin Henry	(1st Lieut.) Halifax Co., Cumberland County Militia, 1776.

David Henderson	Capt. Levi Goodenough's Co. of Rangers, Col. Herrick's Regt., 1777.
Henry Henderson	Capt. Levi Goodenough's Co. of Rangers, Col. Herrick's Regt., 1777.
James Henderson	Capt. Boyden's Co., 1777.
David Lamb	(Ensign) Halifax Co., Cumberland County Militia, 1782.
Benjamin Lyman	Capt. Levi Goodenough's Co. of Rangers, Col. Herrick's Regt., 1777.
Isaac Lyman	(Ensign) Battle of Bunker Hill, Co., Regt. Unknown, 1775; (Adjutant) Col. Fletcher's Unit, 1781.
Joseph Lyon	Capt. Hall and Capt. Allen's Co., Col. Seth Warner's Green Mountain Boys, 1776; Capt. Levi Goodenough's Co. of Rangers, Col. Herrick's Regt., 1777.
Isaac Orr	(1st Lieut.) Halifax Co., Cumberland County Militia, 1782.
Thomas McClure	Capt. Boyden's Co., 1777.
Caleb Owen	(Capt.) Halifax Co., Cumberland County Militia, date unknown; (Lieut.) Capt. Boyden's Co., 1777.
Robert Pattison	(2nd Lieut.) Halifax Co., Cumberland County Militia, 1776; Capt. Boyden's Co, 1777.
Solomon Pease	Capt. Boyden's Co, 1777.
Andrew Pennell	Capt. Levi Goodenough's Co., 1777.
James Pennell	Capt. Hugh McClellan's Co. of minutemen at Lexington Alarm, Col. Samuel Williams' Regt., 1775; Capt. Hugh McClellan's Co., Col. David Fields Regt., Bennington Alarm, 1777.
John Pennell	(Capt.) Halifax Co., Cumberland County Militia, 1776.
Ezekial Philips	Capt. Boyden's Co., 1777.
Elisha Pierce	(Qtr. Mstr.) Halifax Co., Cumberland County Militia, 1782.
Joseph Pierce	Capt. Boyden's Co., 1777.
Elisha Pratt	Capt. Boyden's Co., 1777.
James Pratt	Capt. Wm. Hutchins's Co., Col. Ebenezer Allen's Vermont Regt., Maj. Isaac Clark, Gen. Ethan Allen, 1780–1781.
Jonathan Pratt	Capt. Goodenough, Col. William Herrick's Regt., 1777; Capt. Fish's Co., Capt. William Herrick's Regt., 1778; (2nd Sergt) Gen. Samuel Fletcher, Lieut. Eastman, 1778; Substitute for brother, Nathan, date unknown; Substitute for brother, James, Capt. Blakesley's Co., 1779.
Nathan Prate (Pratt)	Capt. Levi Goodenough's Co. of Rangers, Col. Herrick's Regt., 1777.
David Rich	(Capt.) Halifax Co., Cumberland County Militia, 1776; Capt. Boyden's Co., 1777.
Thomas Rutherford	(Corpl.) Capt. Boyden's Co., 1777.
Hazael Shepard	(Capt.) Halifax, Vermont Militia, 1781–1782.
Jonas Shepard	(Capt.) Halifax Militia; Capt. Boyden's Co., 1777.
William Shattuck	(1st Maj.) Southern Regt. Cumberland County Militia, 1782.
Joseph Stewart	Capt. Boyden's Co., 1777; (Ensign) Cumberland County Militia, 1778.
John Thomas	(Lieut.) Halifax, Vermont Militia, prior to 1778–1782.
William Thomas	Capt. Boyden's Co., 1776; Halifax Militia, 1779.
Oliver Waters	Capt. Benjamin Whitney's Co. at Guilford and other parts, 1783–1784.
Hubbel Wells	(Capt.) Halifax, Vermont Militia, 1778–1780.
John Wilcox	Capt. Levi Goodenough's Co. of Rangers, Col. Herrick's Regt., 1777.
William Wilcox	Capt. Boyden's Co., 1777.
David Williams	Capt. Joseph Tyler's Co., 1780; Capt. Bigelow Lawrence's Co., Col. Walbridge's Regt., 1781; Halifax, Vermont Militia, 1781–1782.
Nathan Williams	(Capt.) Killed by Indians in the retreat from Fort Ticonderoga, 1777.
Nathan Williams Jr.	Capt. Keith's Co., Col. Michael Jackson's Mass. Reg., 1779–1780; (Serg) Capt. Blakesley's Co., Col. Malcolm's Regt., 1780.
Artemas Woodward	Capt. Toogood's Co., Col. Nixon Regt., Hampshire 5th Co. Continental Line, 1777.
John Woodard	Capt. Jesse Sawyer's Co. of Rangers, Ebenezer Allen's Detachment, 1780–1781.
Samuel Woodard	Capt. Boyden's Co., 1777; Capt. Joseph Tyler's Co., 1780.

MILITARY TITLES used in the Halifax town meeting records, 1778–1790:

(Lieut.) Thomas Clark, (Lieut.) Thomas Farnsworth, (Capt.) Stephen Gates, (Ensign, Lieut., (Capt.) John Gault, (Lieut.) Thomas Taggert, (Capt.) John Hamilton, (Lieut.) Henry Henderson, (Lieut.) Jonathan Kellogg, ("Major") Amos Muzzy, (Ensign, Capt.) Isaac Orr, (Capt.) Pattison, (Capt.) John Pennell, (Ensign) Elijah Phillips, (Lieut.) Jonathan Rich, (Capt.) John Sawtell, (Lieut.) William Shattuck, (Ensign) Hezekiah Smith, (Lieut.) Philemon Stacy, (Ensign) Nathaniel Swain, (Capt.) John Thomas, (Lieut.) Joseph Tucker, (Ensign) David Williams.

MEN WHO SERVED BEFORE MOVING TO HALIFAX

The following individuals served in the Revolutionary War in the state or states identified before coming to Halifax. David Niles was killed at the Battle of White Plains in 1776; after which, his widow and four sons came to Halifax.

Adams, Levi, CT, VT	Green, John, CT	Perry, Joseph, MA
Adams, Thomas, MA	Guild, Jesse, CT	Phelps, Francis, MA
Alexander, Jonathan, NY, VT	Hall, Joel, CT	Pike, Elijah, VT
Allen, David, CT	Hamilton, John, MA	Plumb, James, CT
Babcock, James, CT	Harrington, John, NH	Ransom, Newton, CT
Barrington, William, RI	Harris, John, CT	Sawyer, Darius, MA
Bemis, Rev. Abner, MA	Hatch, James, CT	Shepardson, William, VT
Brown, Oliver, MA	Hatch, Nathan, MA	Smith, Asa, MA
Bullock, Darius, MA	Hewes, William, MA	Smith, Hezekiah, MA
Bush, Moses, MA	Hotchkiss, Elihu, CT	Smith, Joel, NH
Calef, Stephen, MA	Hunt, Charles, CT	Stacey, Philemon, MA
Carpenter, Asaph, VT	Jones, Israel, MA	Stone, Elias, MA
Cary, John, NY, VT	Kellogg, Jonathan, MA	Sumner, Daniel, MA
Clark, James, MA	Learnard, Moses, MA	Sumner, Joel, MA
Collins, Daniel, CT	Lamb, David, CT	Swain, Joseph, MA
Cole, Benjamin, CT	Larrabee, Timothy, VT	Swain, Nathaniel, NH
Cutler, Joel VT	Marble, Jonathan, MA	Town, David, MA
Dike, Nicholas, MA	Mason, Ashbel, CT	Whipple, Abraham CT
Everett, Jeremiah Sr., MA	McCarger, Thomas, MA	Whitney, Eleazer, MA
Everett, Dr. Jeremiah Jr., MA	Miner, Ephraim, CT	Whitney, Jonathan, MA
Farnham, John, MA	Mullett, James, VT	Whitney, John, MA
Farnsworth, Thomas, MA	Muzzy, Amos, MA	Wood, Samuel, MA
Fish, Samuel, CT	Nye, William, MA	Worden, Thomas, MA
Goodall, Rev. David, MA	Otis, Stephen, CT	

~ Constance Lancaster and Susan Rusten

* * *

REVOLUTIONARY WAR HEROINE MELISCENT BARRETT SWAIN

Photo C. Lancaster

History books are full of heroes and heroines. However, this story is about an unsung heroine of the Revolutionary War. As I walked amongst the gravestones of an old cemetery in my hometown of Halifax, the inscription on a bronze marker caught my eye: *Revolutionary Heroine Placed by Milly Barrett Chapter D.A.R.* next to the stone for *Meliscent, Wife, of Joseph Swain. Died August 16, 1838, aged 78 years.* Being a lover of history, this prompted me to do some research. I did not have to go far. The information was in *Halifacts,*[18] our local historical society newsletter. It seems Meliscent Barrett Swain demonstrated her ability to follow directions explicitly and in so doing earned her place in American history. Her father was Colonel James Barrett, who was commander of the colonial troops at the first battle of the Revolutionary War at Concord Bridge on April 19, 1775. One of Meliscent's first acts of loyalty to the colonies was that of escaping into the woods and hiding her father's important papers and the family silver in the baby's cradle just as the British arrived to search their home. She was then only sixteen years of age. Other times, she, along with her parents and grandparents, would conceal the stores of rebel ammunition from the British. But her claim to becoming a heroine was the fact that she carefully took note of the directions shown her for making cartridges.

Colonel Barrett and his son James had furnished farm provisions, such as oatmeal, to the military forces, through the commissary department in Boston. Quite often, young staff officers would be sent up to Concord on this business and, while waiting for its conclusion, would amuse themselves by talking "loyalty" with James' daughter Meliscent, to hear her rebel replies.

One of these young officers was Joseph Swain, a blacksmith, later in charge of the rebel armory, who repaired and made guns for the Concord soldiers. He asked Meliscent what they would do if it became necessary for the colonies to resist the British since there was not a person in Concord who even knew how to make cartridges. She replied that they would use their powder horns and bullets just as they shot bears.

"That," said the young man, "would be too barbarous. Give me a piece of pine and I will show you how."

After whittling the stick to the proper form, Swain took a pair of scissors[19] . . . and cut the paper for the pattern cartridge.[20]

Concord Free Public Library

During the war, the young ladies of Concord made all the cartridges under Meliscent's supervision. But why does Meliscent's name appear on a grave marker in a Vermont cemetery you ask? At the age of twenty-three, she married her blacksmith-teacher, Joseph Swain, who had bought 100 acres of land in Halifax, where he established his farm and smithy. The Swains lived all their married life in Vermont and raised a family of nine children.   ~ *Bernice Barnett*

DEPOSITION FOR PENSION JONATHAN PRATT

Provision was made for persons who were in service of the United States to receive a pension by an act of Congress on June 7th, 1832. The following is a transcription of a handwritten deposition of Jonathan Pratt, when he applied for his pension in 1832 at the age of seventy-one years for his service in the Revolutionary War. The signatures are scanned from the copies of original documents obtained from the National Archives in Pittsfield, Massachusetts.

> State of New York
> Ontario County, _____ _____
>   On this twenty seventh day of August in the year, eighteen
> hundred and thirty two, personally appeared in open Court before the
> Judges of the Courts, of Common Pleas, of the said County, now
> setting, Jonathan Pratt a resident of the town of Gorham in the County
> of Ontario aforesaid, aged Seventy one years who being first duly sworn
> according to law doth on his oath make the following declaration in
> order to obtain the benefit of the provisions of the Act of Congreſs
> paſsed June 7, 1832.
>   That he entered the service of the United States under the
> following named officers, and served as herein stated. On the 10th day of
> August 1777 he joined a company of State Troops, or Militia of the
> State of Vermont, in actual Service under the command of Captain
> Goodenough and Lieut. Eastman in Col. William Herricks Regiment at
> Bennington in the State of Vermont. Deponent was soon after marched
> with the said Regiment to Arlington in the same state, where they were
> stationed a few weeks and were thence marched to Manchester – and
> thence to Pawlet in the same state –and thence immediately to Saratoga
> in the State of New York where they arrived and joined the army under
> Gen. Gates on the day preceding the surrender of Gen. Burgoyne.
>   The whole regiment to which Deponent belonged stood at
> guard with arms in their hands during the whole night of the 16th of
> Oct. and on the following day were present when the British army laid
> down their arms
>   One the same evening the Regiment in which deponent served
> was march to Battenkill, and on the following day a detachment of sixty
> men of whom deponent was one was selected to guard a company of
> Torries under Capt. Adams and Lieut. Adams, as prisoners to Fort
> George at the head of Lake George. The said detachment of sixty men
> as aforesaid was under the command of Capt. Allen. After safely
> conducting the said prisoners to Fort George, the said detachment
> marched to Pawlet in the State of Vermont, and at that place rejoined
> their said Regiment under Col. Herrick as aforesaid and in the month of
> December of the same year the said Regiment was discharged.
>   In the month of April of the next year (1778) the deponent was
> hired by a Claſs of Militia of the town of Halifax in the state of

Vermont (who were required to furnish a soldier for the state troops) to serve as a soldier for the term of nine months. Deponent immediately proceeded to Fort Warren at Castleton, Vermont and was there mustered in a company under Capt. Fish, Lieut. Lyman, Ensign Higley, and orderly serjeant Nichols – in Col. William Herricks Regiment.

A few days after the said deponent so commenced his said term of service at Fort Warren several scouting parties or parties of rangers were organized by order of Gen. Samuel Fletcher their commanding that post. Deponent volunteered to serve as one of such scouts or rangers and was appointed Second Serjeant – and a part of Seven men was placed under his command. During the said term of nine months he was occupied with the soldier so placed under his charge, a great proportion of the time, in ranging and traversing the Country from Fort Warren to Crown Point – Otter Creek and Middlebury in Vermont. On one occasion while proceeding with the men under his order towards Crown Point to relieve a scouting party under Serjeant Blackman, he met a soldier of the said party who informed him that the said Serjeant Blackman and party had that morning been attacked and destroyed by the enemy excepting that he the said soldier had escaped. Deponent immediately gave notice to his superior Officers, of the said attack and volunteered with a company under command of Lieut. Eastman to march on the following day in quest of the enemy and to bury the bodies of the killed. On proceeding to the place of the attack five dead bodies were found, and reterned.

In the summer of the year 1779-(but in what month deponent cannot recollect) he went as a substitute in place of his brother James Pratt who had entered in the state troops of the State of Vermont for the term of six months at Fort Warren above mentioned and was there enrolled as a soldier in a company of the said troops commanded by Capt. Blackesley or Blakerlee who was said to be a continental Officer. The said deponent while there in service in the said company marched in a detachment of five hundred men to attack a British Post on Diamond Island. The enterprise was succe∫sful but before its accomplishment and while on the march deponent was taken sick with measles and was conveyed back to Fort Warren.

At the expiration of his term for which the said James Pratt had so enlisted, deponent was dismi∫sed having served as such substitute according to the best of his recollection, more than three months. He further declares that he was in actual service as a soldier as above stated on his first term four and a half months: on his second term nine months and on his last term more than three months.
The said deponent further saith
1st The he was born in the town of Weston in the State of Ma∫sachusetts in the year 1761.
2nd That at the times when he was so called into service as aforesaid he lived at Halifax in the State of Vermont, from whence he removed a few years after the close of the revolutionary war to Kingsbury in the State of New York and that in the year 1801 he removed from thence to the town of Gorham in the County of Ontario where he has since resided and now resides.

3rd That he has no other record of his age than a memorandum there of in his family Bible

4th He went first into the service as a substitute for Nathan Pratt. On the next tour he was hired as above stated. He subsequently went as a substitute for James Pratt as aforesaid.

5th Recollects Gen. Eno or Enos at Fort Warren – Gen. Gates at the Surrender of Burgoyne. Col. Seth Warner, Col. Samuel Robinson and Capt. John Warner at Manchester and Bennington in Vermont in addition to those before mentioned.

6th Never received any written discharge

7th S____ Blodget and Timothy Mower Esq. Are persons who are well acquainted with him and who reside in the town of Gorham aforesaid and who can as he believes certify as to his character for veracity and their belief of his services as a soldier of the revolution.

He has no documentary evidence whatever nor does he know any person now living who has personal knowledge of his said services.

He hereby relinquishes every claim whatsoever to a pension or annuity except the present and declares that his name is not now on the Pension Rolls of the Agency of _____ State.

Sworn and subscribed the day
And year aforesaid in open Court   *Jonathan Pratt*
State of New York
Ontario County, ∫S

Jonathan Pratt the above named applicant being duly sworn doth depose and say in addition to his forgoing declaration that the clergyman to whose society and church deponent belonged, died some months since and that he knows no other clergyman in the vicinity who could probably testify of their knowledge of his reputation in the neighborhood where he resides.

Sworn and Subscribed to this
3rd day of January 1833 before me   Jonathan Pratt

Chester Loomis

Judge of the County Court of said County[21]

                                                    ~ *Carrie Perna*

* * *

Captain Nathan Williams Remembered

Captain Williams was slain on a Sunday morning, July 6, 1777, in a field near the site of Fort Warner, east of Castleton Village, while repelling the attack of a party of British and Indian forces. In the rush of retreat, "his body, after being scalped, was left on the ground until evening, when by the arrival of American troops from Ticonderoga, it was taken, and in the morning, with no funeral obsequies, or winding sheet, than an Indian blanket, buried eighteen inches deep by a few soldiers."[22] There it lay undisturbed for forty-three years.

As the citizens of Castleton planned the forty-fourth observance of American Independence, Lieutenant Elias Hall, who had witnessed the deaths of Nathan Williams and his own father and had been taken prisoner the same day, urged the town "to remove the remains of Capt. Williams, if to be found, from the site of Fort Warner, and give them an honorable and suitable sepulcher in the burial yard of the parish."[23]

Thus, on July 4, 1820, General Isaac Clark led a military procession to the burial site. They disinterred a fully formed skeleton, laid it in a coffin, which was carried to the village meeting house. The poem inscribed on the coffin was read. After prayers and patriotic speeches, the procession moved to the churchyard. "The coffin was strewed with evergreens by 13 young lads, and the minute guns and the knell added seeming sensibility and gratitude on all who were present to witness the final discharge of a debt long due to worth and valour heroically, displayed in the cause of freedom and country."[24]

Captain Nathan Williams came to Halifax from Canterbury, Connecticut, and was among the early settlers and town officials. As the first town constable, he was responsible for compiling the census of 1771. His sons, Joseph, David, Nathan, and Job were members of the Halifax Militia, and all four served in the Revolutionary War. Nathan Williams was fifty-five years old when he was killed.

~ Constance Lancaster

ENDNOTES
1. Hall, p. 257.
2. E. P. Walton, ed., *Records of the Council of the State of Vermont*, vol. 1 (Montpelier, VT: E.P. Walton, 1873) pp. 318–319.
3. It is likely this is a reference to Fort Ticonderoga.
4. Hemenway, p. 420.
5. Patrie, p. 121-G.
6. Samuel Williams, *Vermont During the War for Independence, 1794* (Burlington, VT: reproduced by Free Press Printing, 1944) p. 187.
7. Hall, p. 316.
8 . State of New York, *Public Papers of George Clinton*, vol. 3 (Albany, NY: Jones B. Lyon, 1900) pp. 16–17.
9. *The Official History of Guilford*, p. 52.
10. Hall, p. 773.
11. *The Official History of Guilford*, p. 59.
12. Ibid., pp. 65–66.
13. Ibid., p. 67.
14. E. P. Walton, ed., p. 249.
15. Edward Hoyt, ed., *State Papers of Vermont*, vol. 3 (Montpelier, VT: Lane Press, 1952) p. 92.
16. Frederic Van de Water, *The Reluctant Republic* (New York: John Day Co., 1941) p. 162.
17. In many cases, more than one man with the same name served in the same time period, thus there is always room for error.
18. Dorothy Christie, *Halifacts*, vol. 1, no. 9, March 1977. *Revolutionary Heroine, Meliscent Barrett Swain.*
19. Concord Free Public Library, Concord, MA, by permission. Scissors carried to Halifax by Meliscent Barrett Swain.
20. HHS. Copy of presentation letter written by James P. Swain when he donated the scissors to the Concord Free Public Library, March 1875.
21. NARA, pension file # 24,145, pp. 1240–1245.
22. *Vermont Journal*, Windsor, VT, July 24, 1820, courtesy Readex.
23. Ibid.
24. Ibid., The churchyard is located on Route 4A in Castleton Village beside the Federated Church.

EARLY EMIGRATION
POLITICAL DISCORD AND POWER STRUGGLES

When migration historian Stilwell said, "Vermont before it was half settled experienced its first emigration movement"[1] he was referring to the confiscation of property and banishment of Loyalists or Tories—those who supported the British during the Revolution. "It was an emigration carried out under duress, with bitterness and in poverty."[2]

In Halifax, however, British sympathizers were not an issue. The issue was Yorkers—those who remained loyal to the authority of New York versus Vermonters—those who were loyal to the newly created independent state of Vermont. When the Republic of Vermont was established in 1777, a majority of Halifax residents continued to be loyal to New York. As the Vermont General Assembly increasingly enacted punitive loyalty laws enforced by Ethan Allen's troops, many changed their allegiance. *The Vermont Journal* of November 20, 1783 announced the dramatic conversion in Halifax, and newspapers in Massachusetts, Connecticut, New Hampshire, New Jersey, and Pennsylvania spread the word.

> **WINDSOR, (Vermont) Nov. 20.**
> Advices from the lower part of Windham county, mention, that the inhabitants of the town of Halifax, who have heretofore refused to support the authority of Vermont, and acted in opposition to its government, have lately come in, almost to a man, and acknowledged themselves subjects of this State, taken the oath of allegiance, discharged their arrearage taxes, and appear desirous to assist in quelling those disturbers of the public peace, who have long infested the southern part of this State.

Vermont Journal and the Universal Advertiser, November 20, 1783 Courtesy Readex

Amid this period of political discord and bitter power struggles, Halifax experienced its first emigration movement. Ironically, it was both Vermonters and Yorkers who left town.

In 1778, a small group of loyal Vermonters of Halifax began holding town meetings, electing local officials and representatives to the General Assembly, and they recorded their activities in Book 1A of the town records that exist today. Several years and many meetings later, a large group of residents, probably both Yorker and neutral in sentiments, showed up at the March annual meeting and voted themselves into office. Many of the unseated original officials soon left town; this emigration included the first town clerk, James Gray; the first constable, Amos Peabody; and three of the first selectmen, Dr. William Hill, Israel Guild, and Elias Parsons, whose names are inscribed on the flyleaf of the first book of town records. Despite the increasing authority of the independent state of Vermont, these and other local Vermonters, including Edward Harris, a six-term Halifax representative and a dominant figure in the General Assembly, did not stay.

Of the loyal Yorker families who left town during the turbulent 1780s, there was never a question of patriotism. Dr. Peletiah Fitch, who himself served, is said to have "at his own expense equipped four sons for service in The Revolution."[3] Fitch also served New York as a judge of Cumberland County (the future Windham County), and at times, court sessions took place at his home in Halifax. However, the new Vermont General Assembly established its own court system. Letters from Fitch to New York governor George Clinton, offer vivid observations of the local political conflict and escalation of violence, including erection of a whipping post near the jail in Marlborough for people who refuse to pay their fines.[4] In 1779, Dr. Fitch sold his Halifax home [↪ 217] and moved to Salem, Washington County, New York. Over the next few years, others followed.

Benjamin and Thomas, sons of early Halifax settler Samuel Baker, suffered confiscation of property because of their New York adherence. Captain Thomas Baker and Ensign David Lamb in a 1782 affidavit[5] [↪ 174] describe their arrests by Ethan Allen, imprisonment, trials and fines for "treasonable conduct against the authority of the State of Vermont."[6] The Bakers, several of whom had notable service in the Revolution together with other Halifax veterans, emigrated to Washington County. Land records document that Robert, Samuel, and Thomas Gillis; David James and William Henderson; James, John Fenton, and Alexander Gault; Samuel Murdock; and Daniel Squire[7] sold properties in Halifax after having relocated to the Washington County, New York towns of Salem, White Creek, Hebron, Fort Ann, and Kingsbury. The Baker, Gillis, and Gault families had been Pennell Hill neighbors and in-laws. This seems to be the first sizeable cluster migration out of Halifax.   ~ *Constance Lancaster*

ENDNOTES

1. Lewis D. Stilwell, *Migration from Vermont* (Rutland, VT: Academy Books, 1983) p. 89. Originally published by the Vermont Historical Society, 1948.

2. Ibid.

3. Rosco Conkling Fitch, *History of the Fitch Family,* 1930, p. 64, citing the *New York Genealogical and Biographical Record*, vol. 34.

4. *Public Papers of George Clinton, First Governor of New York 1777–1795—1801–1804*, vol. 3 (New York: James B. Lyon, State Printer, 1900) p. 672.

5. E. P. Walton, ed., *Records of the Governor and Council of the State of Vermont*, vol. 3 (Montpelier, VT: Steam Press of J. & J. M. Poland, 1875) pp. 240–266.

6. Ibid., p. 89. David Lamb, a veteran of three enlistments in Norwich, CT, remained in Halifax until 1807 when he moved to Mexico, NY. His fine was reimbursed by the state in 1785.

7. HHS, Ruby Bruffee Austin, typescripts 1957. pp. 34–35.

Benjamin Henry
A Man For All Seasons

Could Halifax's first settler Abner Rice, and Benjamin Henry, who purchased half of Rice's Lot 7 in 1762, have imagined that within two years New York would have legal claim to the New Hampshire Grants, forcing them to live with the uncertainty of how this would affect the validity of their deeds? [↪ 79] Already, in December 1763, New York had ordered the sheriff of Albany County to forward the names of those who possessed lands under the New Hampshire Grants "so they might be proceeded against according to law." In rebuttal, Governor Wentworth, in March 1764, declared the New York 1664 grant obsolete, but if the jurisdiction should be altered, the Crown would confirm the existing New Hampshire grants.[1] He advised the settlers not to be intimidated by threats of New York, and that civil officers should continue to exercise their jurisdiction and punish all disturbers of the peace.

New York, for its part, had applied to the Crown for confirmation of the original 1664 grant to the Duke of York. This application was supported by a petition supposedly signed by many settlers, favoring annexation to New York, which may have influenced the king to rule in July 1764 that New York's border was to be the west bank of the Connecticut River.[2] Further disputes arose. To New York, this ruling meant that all New Hampshire grants were invalid, whereas New Hampshire's interpretation was that grants made prior to July 20, 1764 were valid.

In November 1764, Halifax agent, Oliver Partridge wrote Lieutenant Governor Colden of New York requesting a confirmation of the 1750 Halifax grant. "Partridge expressed the hope that in any confirmatory grant made by New York these shares [originally assigned to Governor Wentworth and his council] might be allotted to others to promote settlement. [The confirmation was postponed.] In October 1765 a formal petition for confirmation of Wentworth's grant was filed, and in due time it was granted by the New York Council,[3] but no patent was taken out[4] [↪ 26]. A printed document located at Vermont Historical Society, entitled "Subscriptions raised to send a petition to the King to confirm our lands to us, who settled them under New Hampshire charters" lists contributions from several southeastern towns including residents of Halifax. [↪381]. Benjamin Henry subscribed for one dollar. Unfortunately, this single sheet is not dated.

It is hard to tell how the internal strife of the land grant disputes affected Benjamin Henry's life. He had faced real danger and hardship during the French and Indian War. In 1762, when he was barely out of his teens, he bought and paid for a lot in the wilderness. He had to clear the land and plant, and build a shelter for himself, while constructing a home for his future wife, whom he would marry in 1767, and who would give birth to their first child in Halifax in 1768.

New York had prevailed over New Hampshire in 1764. One would think the controversy might have been settled, but what followed were years of uncertainty, petitions and counter-petitions, riots, and directives that were frequently ignored.

One advantage of the British system of jurisprudence is the right of ordinary subjects who feel aggrieved to petition directly to the king. By 1770, many of the inhabitants of the New Hampshire Grants, who by now felt comfortable and protected under the stable administration and court system of New York, petitioned the Crown for relief from the rioting of New Hampshire adherents in the town of Windsor who may "expose them to the difficulties and hardships with which they so lately had contended."[5] Benjamin Henry and other Halifax settlers, who signed this petition of November 1, 1770, must have felt more secure as loyal adherents to New York, even though New York still had not confirmed the Halifax grant. A second petition for "Confirmation by New York of certain New Hampshire Grants"[6] dated December 3, 1770 and directed to Governor Dunmore of New York, addresses this issue. The petitioners state that they have settled on the lands granted to them,

> . . . cultivated and improved the same . . . conceiving their title to be good . . . and are now desirous of holding the same under the government of New York, if they can obtain a confirmation of the lands . . . improved on for moderate fees . . . as they have expended their worldly substance upon the premises . . . wholly unable to pay the patent fees demanded . . . and ask the Governor to tender compassion. . .[7]

to present their case to the King so he will give relief to them. Henry and Rice also signed this but confirmation was still not forthcoming. This proved to be a good thing because towns whose grants were not confirmed did not lose their properties and avoided New York's exorbitant fees.

In 1774, the provincial congress of New York authorized a militia, and in January 1776, Benjamin Henry was approved as first lieutenant of the Halifax Company of Cumberland County and commissioned on February 26, 1776.[8]

The year 1777 was of tremendous significance to the land grants. New Hampshire had renounced all political connection with the grants. Meanwhile, the forces in favor of an independent Vermont met in Westminster in January and resolved to form a new state briefly known as New Connecticut. Among towns not represented were Halifax, Guilford, Stamford, Wilmington, Brattleboro, Vernon, Woodford, Marlboro, and Putney.[9] The inhabitants of these towns, comprising the southeast section of the grants, were considered "Yorkers," because they favored allegiance to New York and opposed the formation of the "pretended" state of Vermont. An appeal to Governor Clinton of New York resulted in the usual promises of help, apparently reassuring Halifax, which sent a message of thanks on March 10, 1778 signed by forty-six inhabitants, including Benjamin Henry.[10]

PUBLIC PAPERS OF GEORGE CLINTON.
[No. 1161.]

THE SECESSION OF VERMONT.

Halifax, Cumberland County, Declares Its Allegiance to New York.

We the Subscribers Inhabitants in the Town of Hallifax, in the County of Cumberland, and State of New York, having viewed His Excellency Govourner Clinton's Proclamation, Dated the 23d Day of February Last, Respecting Dificulties and Disputes Subsisting in Part of the County of Albany, and the Counties of Charlotte, Cumberland and Gloucester, and having Duly perused the said Proclamation and the Matters therein Contained, Do Return our hearty Thanks to his Excellency, to the Honourable Senate and Assembly, for the Salutary Measures taken for Settleing the Peace and Unity of these Northern Counties, and notwithstanding the uneasiness of many Disaffected Persons; we do freely Comply with the Terms of said Proclamation and Rejoice to find Such Pacific Sentiments therein Contained, Not in the Least Doubting but, on Suitable application we may have Redress of all Greivencies.

Dated in Hallifax March ye 10th A. Dom. 1778.

* * *

Alexander Stewart,	Asa Clark,	Robert Patison,
Peter Pattison,	Elisha Clark,	Moses Kimball,
Robert Gillis,	Josiah Clark,	William Potter,
Thomas Clapp, jun'r,	James Henderson,	Benj. Henry,
Jonathan Safford,	Isaac Orr,	John Pennel,
Daniel Safford,	Elijah Clark,	James Clark,
Benoni Cutbeth,	Matthew Gettie,	Saml. Clark, Ju'r.,
James Clark Jun,	Joseph Gillis,	Joseph Stewart, Ju'r.,
William Gault,	Thomas Gillis,	John Cary,
Elijah Edwards,	Samuel Clark,	Thomas Baker,
George Lyons,	Pelatiah Fitch,	Nathan Freeman,
Elijah Edwards June	Henry Henderson,	James Cary,
Joseph Bell,	Pelatiah Fitch, Ju'r,	David Henderson,
Joseph Lyons,	Elisha Fitch,	Samuel Baker,
Dan Rude,	John Avery,	Nathan Williams,
Asa Clark,	Samuel Stanton,	

Nevertheless, at the first meeting in Halifax on March 3, 1778, it was voted to accept the constitution of the state of Vermont, perhaps reflecting the loyalties of those in attendance at this particular meeting. Only a few months later, in August 1778, the Committee of Public Safety took a poll in Cumberland County. Halifax results: for New York, 63, for Vermont, 36, neutral 20, total 119.[11] Although polls are not always accurate, this one seemed to indicate that, in spite of the vote in favor of Vermont at the March town meeting, a majority in Halifax still favored New York.

Benjamin Henry did not maintain his commission in the Cumberland County Militia after 1778, when Vermont outlawed membership in the New York Militia.[12] Peletiah Fitch, an ardent Yorker, replaced him.

As late as 1780, the Yorkers in Cumberland County were still concerned for their safety and fearful of confiscation of their property by Vermont. In September 1780, Congress, which had its hands full dealing with the Revolutionary War, resolved to postpone any further consideration of jurisdiction of the New Hampshire Grants.[13] Faced with the reality that neither Congress nor the governor of New York, despite his exhortations to resist the abuses of Vermont, would come to their rescue, loyal Yorkers of Cumberland County were forced to propose their own political solution. To that end, a convention of town committees was called for October 31, 1780, at which time a select committee of thirteen members, one of whom was Benjamin Henry,[14] was chosen to consider the feasibility of following Vermont's example by forming a new government to include towns on both sides of the Connecticut River. "The idea this brought forward of establishing a western line of a new district at the ridge of the Green mountains [i.e., eastern Vermont seceding from Vermont, merging with towns on the east side of the Connecticut River to form a new state], manifested clearly the unwillingness of the New York adherents to acknowledge the jurisdiction of Vermont, provided they could ensure their own safety in any other way."[15]

Vermont, which was under pressure from New York, New Hampshire, and even Congress because of its bold annexation of counties in both western New Hampshire and eastern New York, to say nothing of its negotiations with the British in Canada,[16] may have taken the threat of secession of Cumberland County seriously enough to offer complete amnesty to all Yorkers for judgments against them, including fines and forfeitures for offenses against the authority of Vermont committed prior to October 1, 1780.[17] These important concessions, quite possibly resulting from the pressure exerted by the thirteen-member select committee, including Halifax's Benjamin Henry, may have eased the apprehension of the inhabitants of southeastern Vermont to the extent of accepting the authority of the state of Vermont. In 1781, Henry appears in Leonard Deming's *Catalogue of the Principal Officers of Vermont 1778–1851* as representative of Halifax in the General Assembly of Vermont.[18]

As a sidelight to all this, on February 11, 1782, Governor Chittenden laid before the House a letter from General George Washington, advising Vermont to relinquish annexed counties of New Hampshire and New York in order to facilitate its admission to the Union. On the same day there was also a letter from Benjamin Henry dated Halifax, January 21, 1782[19] (contents unknown). One may speculate that this letter may have contained Benjamin Henry's resignation as Halifax representative to Vermont, for whatever reason, possibly resulting in the 1782 blank slot for Halifax in Deming. See discussion in endnote 18.

On October 23, 1783, in another act of reconciliation, the Grand Committee of Vermont asked the governor to offer a pardon for all offenses committed against the state by persons in the southern part of Windham County who have previously opposed the government and shall take an oath of allegiance before any justice of the peace. Benjamin Henry resigned his position as justice of the peace on October 21, 1783,[20] two days before the above proclamation was issued. Is this a pure coincidence or are the two events connected?

By November 27, 1783, the *Vermont Gazette* (Bennington) stated, "We are informed (by letter from persons in Brattleboro) that Governor Clinton of New York has refused any further encouragement to the disaffected in Windham County, and advises them to pay their taxes to Vermont. In consequence to which numbers have actually paid their taxes, and there is the highest prospect of their full submission to the government of this state."[21]

On December 8, 1783, intelligence was received at Windsor that the inhabitants of Halifax, heretofore opposed to Vermont, were almost to a man paying their taxes and appeared willing to aid in quelling the disturbances of the peace. It seems it took three years from the first offer of amnesty for most of the inhabitants [♭ 175] of Halifax to finally be reconciled to the authority of the state of Vermont.

©2008 *Stephen Sanders*

❦

ENDNOTES
1. Hall, p. 129.
2. Thompson, Part II, p. 13.
3. Matt Bushnell Jones, *Vermont in the Making 1750–1770* (Cambridge, MA: Harvard University Press, 1939) p. 108.
4. New York Land Papers, vol. 20, p. 5.
5. Hall, p. 169.
6. Ibid., p. 170.
7. Ibid.
8. Ibid., p. 772.
9. Ibid., p. 269. ". . . in Halifax [1776], where the inhabitants voted not to send a delegate 'to meet the Green Mountain Boys,' no disposition was shown to throw off the jurisdiction of New York. "
10. State of New York, *Public Papers of George Clinton, Vol. III* (Albany, NY: James B. Lyon, 1900) pp. 16–17.
11. Hall, p. 755.
12. Ibid., p. 773.
13. Ibid., p. 400.
14. Ibid., p. 401. The other members of the committee were Luke Knowlton, Hilkiah Grout, Oliver Lovell, Col. John Sargeants, Micah Townsend, Maj. Jonathan Hunt, Simon Stevens, Charles Phelps, James Clay, Maj. Elkanah Day, Thomas Cutler, and Barzillai Rice.
15. Ibid.
16. Rowland E. Robinson, *Vermont – A Study of Independence*. Rutland (Rutland, VT: Charles E. Tuttle, 1975) pp. 203–224.
17. Hall, p. 402.
18. Leonard Deming, Catalogue of the Principal Officers of Vermont 1778–1851, pp. 17–18. Deming's listing of Benjamin Henry as 1781 Vermont Representative is not shown on some other lists. It was not until eight years later that his name reappeared in Deming. He then served 1789–1797 and again 1799–1801. These later terms add up to twelve years out of thirteen, which appears in the epitaph on his 1816 tombstone. Interestingly, the 1781 slot in Deming that Henry occupied is blank in 1782. The year 1781 was immediately after Henry served on a select committee of Yorkers.
19. *State Papers of Vermont, General Assembly*, vol. 2, p. 44.
20. Records of Govenor and Council, of the State of Vermont, vol. 3, 1782–1791 (Montpelier, VT J. and J. M. Poland, 1783–1780) p. 29.
21. Ibid., p. 307.

HALIFAX UNDER SIX FLAGS

A little of the history of the New York/Vermont controversy is in order here to understand how the present political persuasion of Halifax came about. The focus will be only on those parts of the controversy that affected the history of Halifax.[1] Of course there are extensive histories written about the evolution of Vermont's statehood.

Vermont was originally divided into four counties. The northeastern half of Vermont was initially named Gloucester County. The southeastern half, called Cumberland County, established a second time in 1768, encompassed, approximately, the present counties of Windsor and Windham. The western half of Vermont was Charlotte County in the north and Albany County in the south, with the north/south dividing lines being roughly the chain of the Green Mountains, and the east/west dividing line for Albany County being the northern borders of Arlington and Sunderland.[2] The very early settlers of the far southeastern corner of the New Hampshire Grants lived under the flags of Massachusetts, New Hampshire, New York, and Vermont, all under the king of England, and later the United States. Vermont was divided geographically and politically by each of these governments until 1791.

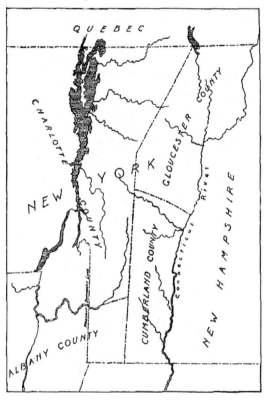

Miriam Irene Kimball, *Vermont for Young Vermonters* (New York: D. Appleton, 1904) p. 89.

WEALTH/LAND THE HEART OF THE YORKER/VERMONTER DISPUTE

Why did the residents of southern Cumberland County (now Windham County) remain loyal to New York, and why did those settlers hold out so long? How did it happen that the residents of Cumberland County on the east side of the state came to be enmeshed in the disputes of Albany County, located on the west side of the Green Mountains? The Yorker/Vermonter controversy might be considered the first civil war in the American colonies and possibly the longest-running dispute. The debate over loyalties among the men supporting New Hampshire, New York, Massachusetts Bay, and later Vermont, within the New

Hampshire Grants encompassed a span of more than forty years—from 1749, when Bennington was the first town to receive a charter, to 1791, when Vermont achieved statehood.

The primary factor motivating the fight was economic, not freedom from Great Britain, because by 1776 freedom had been declared. Colonial men, then, were subsistence farmers who purchased land, cleared it, and developed it for agricultural purposes. For them, there was little or no cash flow, but there was a system of bartering. Another way of generating wealth from the land was by buying cheap and reselling at a profit. Because of the ambiguous land titles in the grants, there was the potential for substantial profits for speculators. Therefore, their wealth, at that time, was land, and that land was the basis of the economic system.

The disputes during the years 1760 to 1791 were about the control, the ownership, and the use of the land known as the New Hampshire Grants. It is unlikely that the motivation of the brothers Ira and Ethan Allen was, initially, about such lofty notions as "freedom from tyranny of New York," or defense of the "poor against the rich," or of the "weak against the strong," as touted by some of our history books. The Allens were land developers. Their concern was economic, for the 60,000 acres of land they owned and were developing, called the Onion River [Winooski] Land Company. They had reason to be concerned: New York was eyeing the fertile and militarily and strategically important Champlain Valley. In 1779, in a polemic titled "A Vindication," Ethan Allen says, "that the spring and moving cause of our opposition to the government of New York was self-preservation; viz. [namely] First, the preservation and maintenance of our property."[3]

Appeals had been sent to England in 1767, requesting King George's judgment on the proprietorship of the New Hampshire Grants. Both New York and the Bennington Boys[*] were willing to await the ruling. However, persons in Cumberland County, the southeastern half of the New Hampshire Grants, were not represented initially. The Bennington men felt sure King George's decision would not threaten their present position, which had been the status quo since 1764, when the king had declared "the west bank of the river Connecticut" as the boundary between New Hampshire and New York. The western boundaries between Massachusetts and Connecticut had been settled with New York by 1773. Negotiating around the grant with the Duke of York, New York's position was that, while it had ceded land to those two states, that compromise did not include or affect ownership of land lying to the north of Massachusetts.

> And that the grant to the Duke [of York] was valid has been
> certified by high authority. In 1933, the Supreme Court of the
> United States, called upon to determine the exact division between
> Vermont and New Hampshire, found it needful "to consider the
> history of the subject from the creation of New York and New

---

[*] So-called because the first meetings were held in Bennington; later they were to be known as the Green Mountain Boys.

Hampshire as adjoining Royal provinces to the admission of
Vermont into the Union as an independent state."[4]

Clearly, this should be indisputable: The territory presently known as Vermont
was in the state of New York at that time. The people of Vermont were surprised
but willing to submit to New York, according to William Slade Jr. Secretary of
State, because

> . . . they had no apprehension that it could . . . affect the *title* of
> their lands. Having purchased, and paid for those lands, under
> grants from the crown, they did not understand by what
> perversion of justice, they could be compelled, by the same
> authority [i.e., New York under the aegis of King George] to
> repurchase [those lands], or to abandon them.[5]

In another boundary dispute, Charles Thompson evinces the following
history of the northern boundary of Massachusetts. In 1741, New Hampshire and
Massachusetts decided that the line followed the Merrimack River curve for
curve, but three miles to the north. However, Massachusetts reasoned

> . . . it could claim for its own all the land as far north as the line
> that the Merrimac had so long kept from going west. Indeed,
> Massachusetts had for years been treating a part of the
> Connecticut Valley as its own. It had granted land on both sides
> of the river in the general neighborhood of Fort Dummer.[6]

Since 1724, when Massachusetts established Fort Dummer, followed by
several other Vermont settlements, Massachusetts assumed its boundary ran "due
west [from its northern most point] until it met his majesty's other governments
or twenty miles east of the Hudson River."[7] If Massachusetts had prevailed,
several tiers of southern Vermont towns would be in Massachusetts. Further,
Thompson asserts, the Yankees of Massachusetts disliked the "Yorkers whose
public affairs were managed by a patrician class whom they thought arrogant."
The New England farmers, he continues, "owned their own farms, had their own
form of government, and called no man master."[8] The western boundary of
Massachusetts and Connecticut, no doubt, was the basis for New Hampshire's
contention that its western border also extended to twenty miles east of the
Hudson River.

BENNINGTON THE FOCAL POINT FOR THE REBELLION

Why did Bennington emerge as the focal point of the Vermont rebellion while
Halifax and most of present day Windham County remained staunchly loyal to
New York? One reason may be the isolation of those towns to the east, separated
as they are by the chain of the Green Mountains. Fort Dummer and the
settlements along the Connecticut River, granted by Massachusetts Bay, predated

the 1749 charter of Bennington by more than twenty-five years. The first town east of the mountains to be chartered was Halifax, the second town in the New Hampshire Grants to receive its charter, on May 11, 1750. Thus, Halifax held considerable status in the early history of Cumberland County.

The Yorkers in the southeastern part of the grants were not persons from New York who had come into the New Hampshire Grants to usurp properties of Vermonters. Those New York sympathizers in Halifax had been on their land since 1761, nearly twenty years, and even much earlier along the Connecticut River. They were middle-aged emigrants from Massachusetts and Connecticut who had lived on their land grants from Governor Wentworth for some five years before the youthful Allen brothers migrated from Connecticut, and for some twenty years prior to the confiscation proceedings against their land by the state of Vermont.

Other factors in the controversy might be the proximity of New York State, as it bordered Bennington in the western part of Vermont, or the fact that New York had designs on the prime lands in the Champlain Valley and the strategic waterway of Lake Champlain. Another reason was likely the very lay of the land, as well as the isolation of eastern Vermont. The mountainous terrain of the east lay between the fertile Connecticut River Valley and the Green Mountain chain. When compared with the fertile valleys of Lake Champlain or the Hudson River, the hilly, wooded terrain was likely less desirable for cultivation or development. At any rate, New York first tried to oust homesteaders along the western side of Vermont.

The Grand Committee and Militia in Bennington, the first company of the Green Mountain Boys, was formed at Bennington on October 24, 1764. It was the precursor of the Committee of Safety; furthermore, the first roster did not contain a single person named Allen, Baker, or Warner. Later, Ira and Ethan Allen and other brothers, along with cousins Remember Baker and Seth Warner, became officers in the militia, and, ultimately, leaders in the formation of Vermont. As a result of several incidents, the Grand Committee and Militia reorganized in 1771, with Seth Warner as commander. In 1772, Ethan Allen was chosen colonel of the regiment.

In order to build a military force, in 1775, the Second Continental Congress urged all towns in the original thirteen colonies to set up committees of safety. Their function, in addition to defense, was to carry on the interim governments after the colonial governors were overthrown in the Revolution and before state governments were officially formed. Early meetings of the Committee of Safety were held at Bennington and Dorset on the west side of the mountains. The Committee of Safety, perhaps one more factor that contributed to the dispute, evolved from the earlier militia of the Green Mountain Boys. These military officers from the west side of the mountains emerged as leaders in Vermont's revolution, with the power to govern. At least at first, the eastern residents certainly did not accept this government of Vermont as a fait accompli.

Yet, the inhabitants of Bennington in Albany County still did not think they had a problem. That is, until surveyors began laying out land for New Yorkers in the Battenkill Valley—the very land granted by Governor Wentworth;

the very land that had been newly cleared of woodlands by the sweat of a brow and a pair of strong hands. At this time, perhaps the most compelling reason emerged: economics. To pay again for the land or to abandon the land which represented wealth was inconceivable to the settlers. The fees charged by New York to confirm land claims granted by Wentworth might be affordable to the small landowner, but the wealthy large landholders considered it disproportionately onerous. Enter the Committee of Safety with certain governing powers, and Ira and Ethan Allen, who had a large tract of land in northern Albany County called the Onion River Company. The Allens saw the potential to become rich as land speculators but at the time had no resources to pay New York to confirm their land titles, because they had purchased that land on credit. The stakes were very high. If they won, they became very wealthy; if they lost, they became paupers, or worse, debtors sent to prison.

Of Ira Allen's holdings, which ultimately amounted to 200,000 acres, Thompson points out:

> We have to smile a little when we learn that Ira let much of the
> land on perpetual leases, some of which, at least as late as 1927,
> were paying rent to [his] heirs. You see, the long-lease system was
> much used by the York proprietors and was much disliked by
> Vermonters. It was one of the reasons why they did not want
> Yorkers to control the land.[9]

THE FIGHT FOR VERMONT STATEHOOD

How were the Allen brothers and a few men from Bennington area able to form a coalition that, ultimately, included all the residents of the New Hampshire Grants and that resulted in the state of Vermont? The earliest settlers in Halifax, as in many towns, were from Massachusetts[10] and maintained ties to that state. Besides the obvious family ties, there were the philosophical, political, and economic ones. The accepted currency of that time was the British pound, considered, as can be seen in the wording of the early Halifax deeds, the "lawful money of the province of Massachusetts Bay." They preferred the autonomy of the town meeting form of government that gave them local control rather than the county form of government favored by New York. Indeed, Walter Crockett tells us, "Most of early meetings [1761 to 1777] were held in Connecticut and Massachusetts towns in which some of the principal proprietors resided.[11] This may account for the absence of any records of Halifax town meetings prior to 1778.

Although they had an established government under New York, there was a group of men who wanted to be reunited with Massachusetts Bay. From 1770 to 1780, Phelps was active representing a group that tried to establish a government under Massachusetts Bay. In the special collections at the University of Vermont is a copy of a petition dated May 28, 1777,[12] presented by Charles Phelps to the Massachusetts legislature in which he asked that state to lay claim to the southeastern corner of the New Hampshire Grants. He cited an Indian treaty of 1720 to support his argument for the predominant ownership of the grants by Massachusetts.[13]

Thompson tells us that in 1780, Charles Phelps was really a "prickly thorn" in Ethan Allen's side. Allen took a letter to Samuel Adams, president of the Council of Massachusetts,

> [u]rging the General Court to abandon claim to territory in Vermont and not to oppose its independence. Unfortunately, Charles Phelps of Marlboro was there to fight Ethan at every point. . . . [H]e [Phelps] was copious in talk, irritating and pertinacious in argument, not without knowledge and ability, and Ethan's master in dealings.[14]

> Charles Phelps of Marlboro, [was] the garrulous and able foe of Vermont who at a memorable hearing on Vermont affairs before the Massachusetts legislature so annoyed Ethan Allen, his opponent, by proving himself to be physically as big as Allen, in dress as resplendent, and in speech even more fluent.[15]

Thomson tells us that Adams answered, espousing the same old Merrimac River boundary line as the northern Massachusetts line, and he "roundly asserted the right of Massachusetts to Southern Vermont. . . . However, the claim was advanced apparently with no serious intention."[16]

The necessary ingredients in this mix were the visionary Allens and the Bennington Boys, who were able to bring the various political factions together using eloquence and armies. A most important weapon for the Allens was the use of words. They extensively published polemics to support their political views, while discrediting the politics of their perceived enemies. They frequently contradicted themselves when it seemed expedient. When it was to their benefit, they invoked the laws and methods of Congress, but when Congress issued an order to allow William Shattuck of Halifax and other dispossessed Yorkers to return home and have their property restored to them, the Vermonters declared sovereignty, complete independence, and self-rule. The Allens were able to publish frequently and widely disseminate their political views after they astutely brought Judah P. and Alden Spooner and their printing press to Vermont and designated them the state printers.* This, then, enabled Ira and Ethan to publish their views to the audience they wanted to influence at the state's expense.

It is well documented in the various early histories of Vermont and New York that, for fifteen years, a flurry of letters flew between the settlers on both sides of the New Hampshire Grants controversy and the governor in Albany, as well as between the governors of Massachusetts, New Hampshire, and New York, to King George in England, and, later, to the Continental Congress. Each proposed possible divisions of the grants or supported their claims to

---

* The Assembly voted, on October 1778, Judah P. and Alden Spooner as the official printers. In October 1779, 300 pounds was voted to move the Spooners' press from Dartmouth, New Hampshire, to Westminster to print the state laws for dissemination.

proprietorship of the grants, and each defended their individual claims to the boundary lines. The majority of the people of the New Hampshire Grants were satisfied to be under the government of New York. William Shattuck from Halifax and others with seats in the New York legislature represented the people of the grants living in Cumberland County. Zadock Thompson, in his *History of Vermont*, notes, "The courts for Cumberland County were held at Chester for four or five years. . . ." Regarding Cumberland County under the aegis of New York in 1772, he continues, " . . .upon the recommendation of the supervisor of the county, the county seat was removed to Westminster, and a courthouse and jail erected."[17]

The Vermonters took advantage of an incident that became known as the "Westminster Massacre" when they took possession of the courthouse in order to disrupt the court proceedings of New York. The Yorkers believed that a secondary aim was to prevent them from collecting outstanding debts, which they needed to do in order to raise the cash to pay taxes assessed by Vermont. It happened in Westminster because that was the seat of the New York government in the eastern part of the New Hampshire Grants, and it became one focal point of dissention between New York and Vermont. And it happened in Westminster because Vermonters were determined to do, by strong-armed techniques, that which they had not been able to accomplish using political persuasion. Although New York was recognized by Congress as a state in the United States and Vermont was not, those who remained loyal were branded as "enemies of this and the United States" by Vermonters.[18]

Add C. Niles, a resident of Halifax and a correspondent for the *Vermont Phoenix* and possibly other local papers, wrote and compiled a collection of his newspaper articles. In 1884, he published the following little known fact under the headline, "THE HIDING PLACE of Ben Baker, the Tory who shot William French":

> Although not generally known, there is a place in Halifax that brings to mind an event that is historic in the annals of our state. Within the limits of the old Calvin Bucklin farm there is a depression in the ground that was once the cellar to a small log house, and that cellar was for more than a week the hiding place of Ben Baker the tory who shot William French at Westminster court house, March 13, 1775. French's blood is supposed to be the first bloodshed in the Revolution.[19]

Benjamin Baker was listed among the Vermont Sufferers who were recipients of land in Bainbridge, New York.[20]

Benjamin Hall discussed the pledge of allegiance of several towns in the Bennington area of Albany County, west of the mountains. The men began a move towards a "separate and independent state" in the fall of 1776 at a meeting of the Committee of Safety at the second Dorset convention. Among a variety of irregularities, there were disparities with the representation of towns, particularly east of the mountains. "In some [towns], however there were two parties, and in a few, as in Halifax,[*] where the inhabitants voted not to send a delegate 'to meet the Green Mountain Boys,'[21] no disposition was shown to throw off the jurisdiction of New York.'[22] At this juncture the Green Mountain Boys realized the precariousness of their neophyte government and the need to increase the strength of their position by recruiting men of the eastern towns. They held the next convention in Windsor on the east side of the mountains.

Meanwhile, prior to the 1775 takeover of the courthouse and the now famous events at Westminster, there was an established and functioning government in place with courts of law and representation in the New York State legislature. In Hall's history[23] are civil and military lists that include many Cumberland County residents as the "Representatives in the Colonial General Assembly of New York Elected By The People;" "Deputies in the New York Provincial Congress, and Convention for the State of New York"; the latter listed William Williams of Halifax as serving in the 1775–1776 Congress, for three terms. William Shattuck, a strong Vermont opponent from Halifax, was a member of the 1783–1784 Assembly. William Williams was also a justice of the peace in 1772, and a deputy in 1775 and 1776 in the New York Provincial Congress.

In 1775, Congress established a quota and assigned the number of men for each state to contribute to the Continental army. ". . . [T]he quota assigned to Cumberland County, on the 7th of June [1776], was one hundred and twenty-five . . ."[24] The New York Provincial Congress made the following military assignments. According to Hall, these persons from Halifax served for New York. In 1775, Major William Williams "offered his services as Colonel of a [New York] regiment of militia"; he was named a Colonel in the Lower Regiment in 1776, while he is listed as First Major of the Southern Regiment in 1782. The Committee of Safety submitted a list of military officers for 1776. For Halifax, they were Captain Daniel [David] Rich,[†] First Lieutenant Benjamin Henry, Second Lieutenant Robert Paterson, and Ensign Edward Harris.[25] Yes, the latter was without doubt the same person who became a prominent Vermont supporter, and who, along with Hubbel Wells, became the first representative from Halifax, serving from 1778–1783 on many important committees in the Vermont Legislature.[26]

At the July 2, 1777, meeting of the Bennington Committee of Safety, Ira Allen was appointed to discover a way of funding a regiment. After reportedly thinking about it all night, at sunrise, he proposed "the policy of sequestration and

---

*   The first Dorset meeting was held July 24, 1776, and adjourned to meet again September 25, 1776. The earlier meeting was poorly attended, with no representation from the eastern side of the state. Slade says, "For the purpose of ascertaining the views of those residing east of the Green mountains, upon the measures suggested by the committee from the Dorset convention, the people of each town were invited to assemble in town-meeting and express their opinions as to the course they should deem it best to pursue." Slade records show that eleven attended from the east side of the mountains, while forty-six represented the west. Bennington had six delegates, while most towns had one or two. Although Halifax had voted specifically not to send a delegate, Colonel Benjamin Carpenter of Guilford is listed as the Halifax representative. That fact likely did not entitle him to two votes. Benjamin Carpenter was a landowner in Halifax and Guilford.

†   Hall lists him as Daniel while Crocker lists him as David. Since no other Rich men appear in Halifax, it is assumed they are one and the same [↪ 169].

sale of the property of Tories. . . .Through Ira's financing the people of Vermont, unlike the people of any other New England State, paid almost no taxes."[27] At its March 1778 session held in Windsor, the governor and council made this recommendation:

> Whereas no provision has as yet been made to supply the
> Treasury of this State seasonably to Answer the present demands
> on the Treasury And Whereas this Council are informed that the
> Honorable the Continental Congress have recommended the
> Measure of disposing of Estates of Enimical Persons within each
> state and whereas this Council are of the opinion that it is
> necessary some measure be Adopted to Assertain the Particular
> Estates which are or may in the future be Confiscated before sale
> be made thereof this Council would therefore recommend to the
> Honorable Assembly to propose some suitable method for such
> purpose that the Treasury may thereby be supplied.[28]

Remember, Vermont was not yet a state and repeatedly proclaimed itself a sovereign territory, independent of the United States. Remember, too, that the "Enimical Persons" that Vermont was targeting were very loyal to the "American cause," but were considered enemies and threats to a small number of Vermonters because of their political principles. To enable the confiscation of the properties of the Yorkers required constitutional changes. As adopted in July 1777, the first Vermont Constitutional law, Article IX, under "Declaration of Rights . . ." states:

> That every member of society hath the right to be protected in the
> enjoyment of life, liberty and property, and therefore, is bound to
> contribute his portion towards the expense of the protection, and
> yield his personal service, when necessary, or an equivalent
> thereto; but no part of a man's property can be justly taken from
> him, or applied to public uses, without his own consent, or that of
> his legal representative's . . . nor are any people bound by any law,
> but such as they have in like manner, assented to, for their
> common good.[29]

Article XIII states that in "controversies respecting property, and in suits between man and man, the parties have a right to a trial by jury. . . ."[30]

The heavy-handed men in the legislature, it appears, did not give the political dissenters the same rights they would have given if the disputes had been between neighbors. The laws were written with the notion that the land disputes would be with the Yorkers. No doubt the Yorkers questioned why the Vermonters, contrary to their own law, were usurping their civil rights just because they were New York adherents and why Vermonters were not paying a fair share of the needed taxes. Also contrary to this law, persons who had voted their allegiance to New York were being "bound" by Vermont laws even though they had not "assented to" those Vermont laws. There is a certain irony, too, in the wording that prefaces every law, which says, "Be it enacted, and it is hereby enacted, by the representatives of the freemen of the state of Vermont. . . ." Contrary to the principles of a democratic society, the new government was an oligarchy—a minority of Vermonters had assumed the role of lawmaker, judge, jury, and executor of a myriad of laws, made up as they were needed to legalize their actions.

The use of economics was a very astute move on the part of the Vermonters. They increased their treasury by acquiring and selling, often to prominent Vermonters, the land of the Yorkers who were generally wealthy landowners. At the same time, they increased the number of landholders sympathizing with their government, and they strengthened the authority upon which the land titles they were reissuing depended. Likewise, they were decreasing the numbers and the power, as well as the wealth, of their perceived enemies, the Yorkers [⌒ 210].

Before the Spooners' press, there was a very limited communication system in those days. Mountains and distance from the seat of government at the home of Governor Thomas Chittenden in Arlington isolated the towns in the far southeastern corner of Vermont. One can imagine that the county sheriff might have knocked on a door with a warrant to sell the property of the inhabitants for taxes before they knew that Vermont had levied those taxes, and with little or no time to raise the cash. It is probable the taxes would have seemed exorbitant to farmers rich in land but destitute of cash money, which is exactly what the state wanted.

The whole political climate must have been one of confusion and distrust. It would be difficult to turn away from an established and familiar government system under the recognized state of New York. These men considered themselves loyal to the American cause, and they viewed the Vermonters as the rebels or even traitors to the American movement towards freedom at a time when it was necessary to band together and put all their energies and resources into fighting the Revolution. The government of the Vermonters was perceived to be a threat to the cause of liberty, not only by the Yorkers, but by the United States Congress as well. Over and over again, the Vermonters proclaimed their independence from any authority and claimed sovereignty, accusing the Yorkers of treasonous activities when they carried out their elected or appointed duties under New York. The Yorkers believed that because New York, Massachusetts Bay, and New Hampshire were recognized states in the American cause, and Vermont was not a state, persons who rebelled against those states were rebelling against America. Civil war clouds were gathering force over the northeast even as the first thirteen states fought the Revolutionary War.

All manner of storms were brewing that July 8, 1777, when the Committee of Safety met in Windsor. The Revolutionary War winds had been blustering for two years. That very day, thunderheads were darkening western Vermont as Burgoyne's army marched southward from Canada towards the homes of some of the delegates. Fearing for their property and families, those Vermonters were nervous and wanted to end the convention early to return home. It is said that because of a violent thunderstorm, the convention delegates could not leave Windsor, and so reluctantly went back to work on revisions to the proposed constitution. The Vermont Constitution was born during a thunderstorm and faced several much larger local, regional, and national political nor'easters. Like the earlier conventions at Dorset, Manchester, and Bennington, all poorly attended, by only eleven to seventeen men, with very few or none of those from the east side of the Green Mountains, the Windsor convention was still poorly attended, with representation heavily favoring the west side of the mountains. When the delegates were instructed to poll the people of their towns, seven of the towns in Cumberland County came out for New York, including Halifax, Guilford, Brattleboro, and Marlboro.

Touting the constitution, (which had not been ratified by the people because Ira "doubted whether a majority would have confirmed it"[32]), and the elected officers as the only official government of Vermont, the Green Mountain Boys began imposing their unilateral rule with a very heavy hand to bring the eastern inhabitants around to their political point of view. It mattered not whether the Yorkers wanted the Vermont political structure. A conflict between the Vermonters of the new Vermont government and the Vermonters who were unwilling to change their established government was a formula for civil war. Many friends and family members were pitted against one another when they disagreed over the politics of New York or Vermont. Notable in Halifax was the Williams family, but perhaps, the most surprising of these was the Allen family. Ethan Allen reported his brother Levi to the Vermont authorities and had his land confiscated for his "Tory" politics.[33]

A group of Yorkers, members of the County Committee, met in Westminster in September 1777, and decided that

> as members of said committee and well wishers to the Common
> Cause of America and this State think it our duty to send some
> suitable person to the Convention or Legislature of the State of
> New York with the votes of the County Committee, in order to
> give them a true representation of the Difficulties of the County
> of Cumberland. . . .[34]

To answer, Governor Clinton issued one of many proclamations in which he promised,

> The several branches of the Legislature of the sate of New York
> will concur in the necessary measures for protecting the loyal
> inhabitants of this state, residing in the counties of Albany,
> Charlotte, Cumberland and Gloucester, in their persons and
> estates. . . .[35]

The Yorkers in Vermont were most thankful for Clinton's promise of relief from a situation that was becoming intolerable.

Just one week after the first Halifax town meeting for which a record was kept, presumably by the Vermont faction, a petition was presented by the Yorkers to the state of New York. Under the heading, "The Secession of Vermont: Halifax, Cumberland County, Declares Its Allegiance to New York," more than forty-six persons signed the petition dated March 10, 1778, a document that can be found among Governor Clinton's papers. They "heartily thanked his Excellency as well as the Honorable Senate and Assembly" for the proclamation of February 23 that promised them support from New York [p 184]. Had they known that support would never materialize, perchance history would have been rewritten, and the Yorkers might not have persisted in the direction they were headed. Regarding a separation from New York in 1778, Hall records the following votes in Halifax: "For New York 63, for Vermont 36, neuters 20."[36] It should be noted, too, that Halifax had applied to New York for confirmation of their New Hampshire charter in 1765.

THE POLITICAL CLIMATE HEATS UP

Why didn't the Vermont sufferers simply change their allegiance in favor of Vermont? For many reasons: First, a group led by Charles Phelps wanted to be reunited with Massachusetts when they perceived that New York "was not coming over to the Revolutionary cause;"[37] second, they did not yet trust the Vermonters, especially in light of negotiations between Ira Allen and Governor Haldimand in Canada. The Yorkers considered themselves supporters of "the common cause of America."[38] They suspected the Allen brothers were not above considering the usefulness of the proximity of their land holdings to Canada if that allegiance proved most advantageous fiscally and politically. Quoting from Governor George Clinton's papers, Hall espouses this theory:

> The New York party in Vermont, though reduced to a minority, was still unwilling to abandon their cause. Startling reports of negotiations between the Governor and Council of Vermont on the one hand, and the agents of the British ministry in Canada on the other; the flight of Luke Knowlton of Newfane, and Samuel Wells of Brattleborough, on the receipt of information of the passage by Congress, in secret session, of a resolution authorizing their arrest by the Commander-in-chief, in consequence of "a dangerous correspondence and intercourse" in which they were said to be engaged "with the enemy;" the constant passing and repassing of messengers; the fact that passports could be obtained from Governor Chittenden which would give the bearer a safe-conduct among the British in Canada—these and other circumstances induced many to believe that Vermont was preparing to desert the American cause, and influenced some to seek protection from New York.[39]

In several towns, Hall reports, the citizens recanted their allegiance to Vermont and addressed Governor Clinton, "that they might be considered 'not as those who had rebelled against the best governments,' when the district of the New Hampshire Grants should again become subject to New York."[40]

A petition to Congress, dated July 23, 1779, was signed by the Cumberland County Committees of the towns of Hinsdale, Guilford, Halifax, Brattleboro, Fulham, Putney, Westminster, Rockingham, Springfield, and Weathersfield in the state of New York. The petition expressed the predicament of the New York sympathizers and their persecution by the Vermonters. The heavy-handed tactics of the Vermonters were working to create a climate of fear, as shown by the petition, which states in part,

> . . .That in almost or quite every town throughout the District, there are Persons who disapprove of the Government attempted to be established by those who have revolted from New York; but that many of them for fear of popular Rage durst not publicly oppose it; and that Since October last almost the whole County of Gloucester have fallen off from Vermont and are now in open opposition to it.
>
> That those who continue allegiance to New York have refused entering into this unprovoked and unreasonable Rebellion against lawful authority . . . because they conceive that an internal Revolution undertaken at this Juncture, must be attended with bad consequences to the common Cause of America.[41]

The petition relates that "the Vermont Faction" had, in 1777, applied to Congress for representation as "an Independent State." Congress replied, "that it was composed of Delegates chosen by and representing, the Communities respectively inhabiting the Territories of New Hampshire . . . and New York . . . as they stood at the time of its first institution" and that Congress would not interfere in the internal affairs of any of the states.[42]

The petition asks Congress to dismiss a former plea of Jonas Fay and the Vermonters. The petition also accuses the leaders of the Vermonters of deceiving the people, when they established a constitution and elected officers, into thinking "that Congress was in favor of the plan." Remember, the people of Vermont had not been asked to ratify the Vermont constitution. The Vermonters had omitted that important detail, because they knew that the New Yorkers would be able to overrule it.

The petitioners argued that they did not have representation because they had not chosen the elected officials. They asserted that

> [They] who continued subjects of one of the United States have not been allowed the Privilege [to choose their government], but the Insurgents both by their civil and military authority have at every opportunity attempted to control them to submit to their usurped Government, and very lately many of their principal

officers declared in the most publick manner that their
Government was determined to enforce submission by arms until
Congress should otherwise direct and to leave no doubt of the
Sincerity of this Declaration they were then in the Act of
Compelling Submission to their Government at the head of about
two hundred armed men. That beside this, their pretended
Legislature in June last passed an Act declaring that if any person
within this pretended State shall after the first day of September
next accept hold or exercise any office, civil or military, other than
shall be derived from the said pretended State, he shall for the first
Offence, pay a fine not exceeding one hundred pounds [second
offence, be whipped; third, have his right ear nailed to a post and
cut off and be branded on the forehead with a *C* on a hot iron][43]

The petition continues to point out how loyal they have been and how
brutally treated by the Vermonters. They assert that to prejudice the Vermont
cause, they have been labeled by the Vermonters "in the odious light of Tories
and Enemies to the Country." They remind Congress that they have served their
country well whenever there has been a call for men and that they will do so in
the future when called by the proper authority.

They conclude that, if Congress should "be so inattentive to the rights of
one of its members as to declare the New Hampshire Grants an independent
State," the climate of animosity in Vermont would be so intolerable as to force
them "to sell their interests (if that privilege is allowed them) and remove to some
other state." They strongly assert, that they "are in the fullest sense as unwilling to
be under the jurisdiction of Vermont, as [they] can conceive America would be to
revert back under the power of Great Britain and they [members of Congress]
should consider their lives and properties equally insecure."[44] By order of the
committee, Samuel Minot, chairman, signed the petition.

In early 1779, Yorker Micah Townsend (who would eventually change his
loyalties to become secretary of state for Vermont[45] and a British loyalist) wrote to
Governor Clinton,

Ethan Allen had remarked that the trials of the Yorkers had not
been held for the purpose of distressing individuals, but that they
were intended as a challenge to the government of New York "to
turn out and protect their subjects." He [Townshend] also stated
that Allen had publicly declared that the supporters of the new
state had, for a long time, been engaged in making preparations
for a contest with the Yorkers, that they were now prepared to
receive their opponents, and were desirous that Governor Clinton
should be informed of their readiness to fight.[46]

It was also a ploy to determine to what level or even whether, New York would
provide support for the Yorkers in the Grants. Governor Clinton's replies and
support for the New Hampshire Grants were always only on paper. The

Vermonters' view was that "for New York to delay taking arms, however specious the reasons is the same as to yield the point."[47] After the convention of May 25, 1779, the County Committee, under Samuel Minot as chairman, sent another plea to New York. Hall wrote,

> The prayer for relief was of a nature not to be mistaken. If aid is not rendered, 'our persons and property must be at the disposal of Ethan Allen, which is more to be dreaded than death with all its terrors'[48]

In June, Governor Chittenden again began to draft men in southern Cumberland County for the Vermont Militia. Of course, the Yorkers refused to serve or pay to hire someone to serve in their place, a common practice at that time. Remember, they were being counted as part of New York's quota of militia and were already in the service of New York; but they were now being asked to serve the Vermont Militia or pay Vermont. Vermont raised the penalties. They began confiscating property to "be sold at vendue," such as a cow, a heifer, or both, or a load of hay, which in some cases was "more than twice the amount needed to discharge the obligation."[49] Vermont's primary goal never aimed to force the Yorkers to serve in the militia, but to have a reason to appropriate their property to supply the treasury.

On October 22, 1779, the legislature enacted a law and appointed commissioners, any three of whom were authorized to make decisions concerning "controverted titles of lands." Edward Harris of Halifax was named one of the commissioners. Members of this committee were given the authority to review and condemn the property of anyone considered an enemy of Vermont and to sell that property at public auction. However, transactions preceded the above law. One such transaction on December 8, 1778, appears in the State Papers of Vermont. Edward Harris of Halifax, a prominent member of the legislature, bought 220 confiscated acres for 500 dollars or two dollars and twenty-seven cents an acre.[50]

The change in law to accommodate confiscation of lands of Yorkers came in 1780 in Article V. Those who refused to pay taxes levied would have property of equal value seized and sold: ". . . regarding the collection of provisions for the Commissary allowing him to seize so much of the Delinquent's Property, as will pay said Cost and rate, being sold at Vendue."[51] This law was extended to include anyone who professed allegiance to New York.

It appears that the Yorkers were, by and large, a wealthy group of men. To supply its treasury, the Vermonters, again and again, levied fines or bonds on the Yorkers for various offenses against the sovereign territory of Vermont. William Shattuck of Halifax, Timothy Phelps and Timothy Church of Marlboro, and Henry Evans of Guilford had their properties confiscated, and they were banished from the state under penalty of death upon their return.[52] Shattuck, Phelps, and Church were arrested, tried, and imprisoned in Bennington. Clearly, the Yorkers felt that they were serving the Congress of the United States as seen in their letters from prison. On December 5, 1782, Congress decreed:

That the people Inhabiting the said district claiming to be
Independent, be, and they are hereby required without Delay to
make full and ample restitution to Timothy Church, Timothy
Phelps, Henry Evans, William Shattuck and such others, as have
been condemned to Banishment and Confiscation of Estate, or
have otherwise been deprived of Property, . . . for damages they
have sustained by the Acts and proceedings aforesaid; And that
they be not molested in their persons or properties on their return
to their habitations in the said District.[53]

Ira's response was that: "[Vermont was] governed by Committees of
Safety and Conventions, which was their highest Judicature for the Security of
their just rights against Oppressions of the (then) Province of New York . . ."[54]
He used the argument that Congress had used when it declared British rule null
and void. Because Congress would not recognize Vermont as a state, it had put
the banished persons under the jurisdiction of Vermont and Congress had no
right to order Vermont to reinstate the Yorkers.[55]

Later on, after paying heavy fines for his incarceration in addition to other
expenses, Shattuck was allowed to return home to live and work (as long as he
didn't engage in any annoying activities), but he was required to keep the treasurer
of the state of Vermont informed of the income and expenses of his estate. Hall
also pointed out that whenever the state became strapped for money, they
invariably laid more taxes on the Yorkers to restock their coffers.[56] Vermont was
doing exactly that which they had accused New York of doing, but were making
up the laws to support their actions. They designated a person as an enemy of
Vermont and the American cause and then summarily confiscated their wealth—
their developed land—to fill the state treasury. Yorkers were the only ones taxed,
while Vermonters paid virtually no tax. One can only guess how that level of
discrimination might be onerous if not downright oppressive. Why, then, did
Halifax, Guilford, Marlboro, and Brattleboro, led by lawyer Charles Phelps of
Marlboro, continue to remain staunchly New York supporters?

Slade relates that "Vermont was now reduced to a situation extremely
embarrassing" because of the claims being made by New York, New Hampshire,
and Massachusetts on the territory. At this juncture in 1779,

> . . . events took place, in Cumberland County, which gave a new
> impulse to the controversy with New York. The Vermont
> Sufferers petitioned Governor Clinton that he take immediate and
> effectual measures for protecting the loyal subjects of this part of
> the state in their persons and properties, and to convince the
> honorable Congress, of the impropriety of delaying a publication
> of their sentiments . . .[57]

A militia had been formed by the Yorkers on the advice of Congress and
Governor Clinton in support of the American cause, but possibly with the intent
to resist the government of Vermont. Perhaps the Vermont leaders were afraid

the New York faction was gaining sympathy in Congress, as well as political and military strength.

THE STATE OF VERMONT EMERGES

Another event that conspired to shape the government of Vermont and that of Halifax was the notion of a "valley state" made up of towns along both sides of the Connecticut River. Independent of New York and Vermont, it was engineered by Ira Allen and proposed by Luke Knowlton,* who was believed by the Yorkers to be supportive of their cause. C. M. Thompson gives this analysis:

> Luke Knowlton began his task with the Yorkers of Cumberland County with advocating a valley state. Of course they found the proposal seductive for they hated Ethan Allen on the one hand and on the other were tired of looking to New York for adequate help that had never come. . . [58]
>
> He [Ira Allen] kept in the background while Luke encouraged the idea, but he came promptly to the front when the idea of uniting with Vermont took place. . .

Thompson, expanding on the novel possibility, tells us that at this point the Yorkers seemed ready for a break with New York. They foresaw a state much larger than Vermont with the balance of power in their favor and diminished power for the Allens, even limiting Vermonters to the area west of the chain of the Green Mountains. The Vermont leaders saw very different possibilities. Thompson, reporting a conversation between Ira Allen and Justus Sherwood, a Vermonter and a British agent, states, ". . . Ira furthermore declared that Ethan's Vermont had taken in a great slice of New Hampshire 'with a view to embarrass Congress and to strengthen themselves for a revolution.'" Thompson continues to say that, "the Allens and their friends," many of whom were Loyalists and British sympathizers, had several options. They could unite with the United States or with Canada.[59]

Finally, on September 24, 1779, Congress recommended that Massachusetts, New Hampshire, and New York "forthwith pass laws, expressly authorizing Congress to hear and determine all differences between them, relative to their respective boundaries."[60] When this reached Vermont, a committee was appointed to "form.... a plan.... [of] defence against the neighboring states, in consequence of the late acts of Congress, for that purpose."[61] It was decided that, "this state ought to support their right to independence, at Congress, and to the world, in the character of a free and independent state."[62]

---

* Knowlton's political affiliation, first with the Yorkers, swung to the Vermonters after he established a rapport with Ira Allen in September 1779, when they appeared before Congress (Allen representing Vermont interests and Knowlton representing the Yorkers) to request that the boundary disputes between New York and Vermont be settled. It was about that time that Knowlton changed his New York loyalty and became a double agent for Vermont, or even a triple agent based on the charges by Congress that all the while he was in actuality a Tory, a British agent. Knowlton was captured by Major William Shattuck of Halifax and taken to General George Washington. Eventually he escaped to Canada.

In the Assembly Journal of Proceedings, February 14, 1781, the Vermont governor, Council, and House of Representatives took "into consideration the matter of laying jurisdictional claim east and west."[63] According to the papers of William Slade, conventions had been held with representatives from a group of thirty-five New Hampshire towns lying alongside the Connecticut River and with a group of New York towns along the disputed western boundary of Vermont, lying as far west as the Hudson River.[64] This annexation of bordering towns would have resulted in a state larger than New Hampshire or New York. Edward Harris of Halifax served on the committee of five that met with the Committee appointed by the convention at Charlestown, New Hampshire.

Slade, ignoring the fact that many of the Vermont leaders proved to be British loyalists, called the move the "peculiar genius of her statesmen," and he said, "none have more effectually contributed to sustain her independence." He continues, "By this bold and decisive policy, she had augmented her resources— compelled the respect of her enemies—gained upon the confidence of her friends—quieted disaffection at home—invited emigration, and thus laid the foundation for a large and powerful state." But, he asserts, there was an even more important "advantage resulting from this policy, which produces a still higher conviction of its importance." He was referring "to the influence produced by this policy upon the negotiations with the enemy in Canada."[65] Indeed, those negotiations with the British may have had the most impact on the decisions of Congress because of the threat posed by the "British Colony of Vermont," not to mention the strategic command of that all-important waterway Lake Champlain. Control of the Hudson and Connecticut Rivers was equally important. Through Vermont, Great Britain would have several direct routes into the United States, including the borders of New York, New Hampshire, and Massachusetts. Furthermore, those states would be isolated, creating a serious security breach by weakening the defense of the entire northeast.

In the years 1781 to 1783, that which history calls "The Haldimand Negotiations" took place, primarily between Ira Allen, representing the state of Vermont (though Ethan Allen was later involved), and Governor General Frederick Haldimand in Quebec for the British government. Haldimand, when he was stationed in New York at the beginning of the Revolutionary War, became well aware of the infighting between New Hampshire, New York, and Massachusetts Bay over proprietorship of the New Hampshire Grants. He was also aware of the refusal of Congress to accept Vermont as a state. Slade notes that there is little history and no documentation on paper of the Haldimand Negotiations (though another source says it is well documented in Canada, albeit, undoubtedly, from another point of view) except that of Ira Allen himself in his *History of Vermont*.[66]

In April 1781, Colonel Ira Allen, though in Canada ostensibly to negotiate the release of war prisoners, displayed great courage by going, alone, to Quebec to meet with Governor Haldimand. However, this was not the first contact with the British, for Colonel Beverly Robinson had contacted Colonel Ethan Allen on more than one occasion in 1780 and 1781 with invitations to negotiate with the British. The question remains as to why Ethan Allen held those letters for over a year before reporting them to Congress, and only then when he used them as a negotiating tool.

In July and September 1781, negotiations with Ethan Allen and British agents continued in Sunderland where he lived and in Skeensboro, New York. One wonders how a contingent of six to eight British agents was able to travel such a long way so openly through the state from Quebec in Canada to Sunderland in southern Vermont. Slade relates "In these times, party spirits ran so high against tories, or any correspondence with the British" that in one incident a group became aware of the British agents and their mission with Ira Allen. When a mob threatened to tear down the Allen house (Ethan and Ira shared the house), Ira diffused the situation. Slade continues, "It is worthy to remark, that Sunderland, where they lived, was more than sixty miles from the frontiers; yet a sergent and six or eight men frequently passed with their arms, in 1781 and 1782, without being discovered by any that would inform against them."[67]

On the plus side, while these negotiations were taking place in secret, an armistice was in effect keeping British troops immobilized in Canada, obviously aiding the American cause until surrender at Yorktown. Of the September meeting Slade reports:

> The British Commissioners insisted that Vermont should declare itself a British Colony, offering [an entire army with the leaders to be named by Vermonters], with other advantageous and lucrative offers, proposing an expedition against Albany; that by uniting the British troops and the Vermontese, they would form a strong barrier, and be able to defend themselves against the States; that the Commander in Chief was determined not to lose the campaign inactively; that something effectual must be determined on, before they parted, or the armistice must cease.[68]

Meanwhile at their June session, the Vermont Assembly decided to send agents to Congress. Slade, referring to Allen's *History of Vermont*, said that while on their way to Philadelphia the men read a newspaper article with the following:

> . . . a letter from Lord George Germain to Sir Henry Clinton dated Whitehall February 7, 1781, which was taken by the French and carried to Paris, and by Dr. [Benjamin] Franklin, forwarded to Congress, who had ordered it to be printed, containing, among other things, the following: "The return of the people of Vermont to their allegiance is an event of the utmost importance to the King's affairs . . . General Haldimand, who had the same instructions as with you, to draw over those people, and give them support, will, I doubt not, push up a body of troops, to act in conjunction with them, to secure all avenues through their country into Canada; and when the season admits, take possession of the upper parts of the Hudson's River and Connecticut River, and cut off the communication between them. . . ." This information had

greater influence on the wisdom and virtue of Congress, than all
the exertions of Vermont in taking Ticonderoga, Crown Point,
and the two divisions from General Burgoyne's army, or their
petition to be admitted as a state in the general confederation, and
offers to pay their proportion of the expences of the war.[69]

The Allens were always intellectually sharp and slick of tongue. Slade
reports another interesting incident that took place during the legislative session
in October 1781 held in Charleston (at that time in Vermont, not New
Hampshire) when a letter from a British general arrived for Governor Chittenden
apologizing for having killed a Vermont soldier and explaining that he had sent
the soldier's clothing home to his widow. "The messenger not being in on the
secret [negotiations with the British] failed not to proclaim the extraordinary
message of General St. Leger through the streets of Charleston, till he came to the
Governor." Meanwhile, the government of New Hampshire had sent Major
Runnals to Charleston with 200 troops, presumably to disrupt the proceedings.
As Governor Chittenden was reading the letter, Major Runnals asked Colonel Ira
Allen why General St. Leger was sorry to have killed one of his enemies in a time
of war. "Mr. Allen said that he could not tell." When Runnals repeated the
question, "Mr. Allen observed, that good men were sorry when good men were
killed, or met with misfortune." When the "enraged" Runnals pressed the
question again, "Colonel Allen then requested Major Runnals to go at the head of
his regiment, and demand the reasons of his sorrow, and not stay there, asking
impertinent questions, eating up the country's provisions, doing nothing when the
frontiers were invaded. Very high words passed between the Major and Colonel
Allen, till Mr. Runnals left the room. This maneuver drew all the attention from
said letters."[70]

This is how Governor Chittenden and Colonel Allen managed to
continue their duplicity, according to Slade:

> It was then proposed that the Board of War should be convened;
> and the Governor then summoned members of the Board of War
> to appear, as soon as possible, in his chamber leaving Mr.
> Hathaway [the messenger] to deal with the populace, — the War
> Board being all in secret. New letters were made out from the
> [British General's] letters, and, for the information and satisfaction
> of the public, read in council and assembly, for the originals, and
> then returned to the Governor. Those letters contained everything
> but the existing negotiations, which prudence and policy dictated
> to be separated from the other part of said letters.[71]

Still quoting from Allen's history, Slade brings to a close his description of
the Vermont negotiations in 1781, by noting that Colonel Ethan Allen had
suggested the capture of Lord Cornwallis and his army.

The packet containing Colonel Allen and Major Fay's letter was delivered at Ticonderoga about ten o'clock in the morning. About an hour after, an express arrived from the southward, which was supposed to contain the news of the capture of Lord Cornwallis and his army; for before evening the troops, stores, etc. were embarked, and, with a fair wind, returned to Canada. —Thus ended the campaign of 1781, with the accidental loss of only one man, on the extensive frontiers of Vermont exposed to an army of ten thousand men; yet she did not incur any considerable debt. — Such were the happy effects of these negotiations.[72]

The surrender of Lord Cornwallis at Yorktown, Virginia, on October 19, 1781, effectively ended the Revolutionary War. Still, the leaders of Vermont persisted in continuing negotiations with the British in Canada in 1782 as they continued to pressure Congress. In Slade's judgment,

Thus terminated a negotiation, by which Vermont, abandoned, and exposed, was protected, as if by magic, from the overwhelming power of the enemy; while at the same time, and by the very same means, she added to her importance in the estimation of Congress, and secured a more respectful hearing of her claims to independence![73]

While the involvement of the Allens was most significant, for positive and negative reasons, in the early formation of Vermont as an independent state, making it what it was in the 1780s, their duplicity may have been just as much a hindrance to the final cohesion of the inhabitants of the New Hampshire Grants into a cogent state. Aaron Grout, the secretary of state in Vermont, perhaps a bit too strongly asserts, "there was never any question of the loyalty of the Allens and the Vermont leaders."[74] Nevertheless, those who had been punished by Vermont for much less serious acts considered those negotiations to be acts of treason. For their refusal to serve in the Vermont Militia, resulting in unfair taxes levied only against the property of those who disagreed politically with the Vermonters, the Yorkers had suffered the loss of their wealth through the confiscation and sale of their estates. Through their inability to protect their assets or to do business, they were financially ruined.

Part of the negotiated peace treaty to end the Revolutionary War stipulated that the properties confiscated from loyalists be returned. Apparently that did not happen in Vermont. In 1786, a petition, dated February 24, addressed to the governor and legislature of New York and signed by Colonel Timothy Church, Major Shattuck, and Major Henry Evans complains:

That your petitioners and those they represent are Inhabitants of Cumberland county and by their attachment, zeal and activity in Endeavoring to support the Just and Lawfull authority of New York Incurred a Displeasure from those who stiled themselves

freemen of Vermont, But by the encouragement from the several
Resolutions of Congress and Particularly that of the fifth of
December 1782, and the laws and Resolutions of the state of New
York, your petitioners were induced to believe that the Lawless
and ungrateful usurpers would be brought to submit to its Lawfull
authority, or at least to permit your petitioners to remain
peaceably on their Farms, under the Jurisdiction of New York,
But notwithstanding the Resolutions and Laws, these lawless
usurpers, raised in Arms to the number of four or five Hundred,
Drove some of your Petitioners from their habitations,
Imprisoned others, killed one, and wounded others, confiscated
their Estates and sold their Effects.

      Your petitioners cannot but hope that having thus
sacrificed their all, suffered such exquisite Tortures, Banishments,
Imprisonments in loathsome Goals, half starved, and threatened
with Ignominious Deaths, But, that your Honors will take their
case into your most serious Consideration, and grant them some
relief in their Deplorable Situation, and your Petitioners as in duty
bound will ever be good Citizens of the State of New York.[75]

Attached to the above petition and with the same date was "A List Of
The Civil and Military Officers," noting those who had been commissioned by
the state of New York and the amount of the losses they had suffered.

On March 1, 1786, the New York Senate responded that the above
petitioners and the people they represented had, indeed, suffered greatly for no
other reason than that they supported the "lawful authority of this state in the
said County [Cumberland] which from time to time have done in pursuance of
sundry Resolutions of Congress. . . ." That they had been

deprived in a great measure of the means of subsistence and
having become odious to the present Government of the said
Assumed state by reason of supporting the Laws of this state in
the said County are unable to continue longer in the said County
without the greatest inconvenience to themselves and families and
are desirous of removing immediately into the western parts of
this state, Provided they could procure vacant lands fit for
cultivation, That in the Opinion of your committee the said
Petitioners and others whom they represent have a Claim on the
State for some compensation for their sufferings and Losses, and
that it will be proper for the State to Grant the Petitioners . . .[a]
quantity of vacant land equivalent to a Township of Eight miles
square.[76]

The resolution passed the New York State Assembly and the House. The
Vermont Sufferers were given the township of Clinton (now Bainbridge) in
eastern New York. Because it was the frontier, at that time it was in the western

part of the state. Timothy Church was the largest recipient of land, holding 3,840 acres in six parcels, while William Shattuck received 3,200 in five parcels. Among the other recipients from Halifax were William Gault, 210 acres, and Joel Bigelow, 350. And remember Benjamin Baker who is purported to have spent a week in a Halifax cellar hole? He received 97 acres. Vermont paid New York State $30,000, which was divided among seventy-six claimants. Samuel Partridge received $49.91.[77]

HALIFAX AND VERMONT UNDER ONE FLAG

In conclusion, New York settled the boundary line and Congress made Vermont a state in 1791. Benjamin Henry, from Halifax, was among the one hundred and five Vermont representatives who ratified the Constitution of the United States in Bennington on January 10, 1791. On March 4, 1791, Vermont was admitted the fourteenth state in the United States of America.[78] With the political dissidents removed, Halifax was at last able to achieve a Vermont majority. Thus, while there was never a formal Massachusetts[79] government, only political "wannabes," residents of Halifax had familial, economic, philosophical, and/or political dealings with governments, flying the six flags of Great Britain, New Hampshire, Massachusetts, New York, Vermont, and finally, the United States of America.

But, as a footnote, there are three more notable incidents in the political history of Halifax. On October 24, 1791, a petition was put before the Vermont Legislature for a new township. Perhaps it was a result of lingering Massachusetts or New York sympathies or lingering dissention among the Vermonters and those Yorkers who changed their political viewpoint and remained in Halifax. The petition asked for a new town to be taken from Halifax, Whitingham, Wilmington, and Marlboro. The petition states:

> A petition for incorporation of a town from two miles square of
> the northwest corner of the town of Halifax, two miles square
> from the northeast corner of Wilmington [N.B., this was an error
> and should have read Whitingham], two miles square from the
> southeast corner of Wilmington, and two miles square from the
> southwest corner of Marlborough, was read and referred to
> Messrs. Robinson, Bigelow and Cutler, to state facts and report.[80]

At this time, all that is known with certainty is that the petition was not enacted, as no new township was incorporated from these four towns. However, this petition may have been a culmination of repeated efforts over at least a ten-year period of time to organize a separate government in Halifax, possibly, one might speculate, emulating the government of Massachusetts, since New York adherents had been removed; but there was still a Massachusetts faction that had been active under the leadership of Charles Phelps of Marlboro. Likely Vermont made no distinction between persons preferring either Massachusetts or New York forms of government. If they were not for Vermont, they were against it and were made to suffer the same consequences.

Kathy Watters, administrative assistant at the Vermont State Archives, shared the following information via e-mail on July 10, 2003, regarding two earlier petitions that show the continuing dissatisfaction of this group in this area of northern Halifax. She writes:

> There are two petitions for a gore of land as you describe. [She is referring to my request for the final outcome of the 1791 petition.] The first, entitled "Petition of Jonathan Knight et. al. for a Gore Between Marlboro, Guilford, and Halifax," filed February 14, 1781, signed by Jonathan Knight, Isaac Miller, Jr., and John Williams. The land as described in this petition is located in the northern portion of the town of Halifax. There is no record of legislative action on this petition.
>
> The second petition, entitled "Petition of Amasa Shumway for Lands now Included in Whitingham" was filed October 20, 1783. It was read and action postponed until the next session in order that the petitioners could cite the heirs of Colonel Whiting to show cause why the prayer of the petition should not be granted. No further record is found. In 1787 and 1796 portions of the lands described in this petition were granted to Jonathan and Arad Hunt, and Amos Green and Company.[81]

There were no new townships incorporated from northern Halifax, and the names of these petitioners do not appear in the list of Vermont Sufferers removed to Bainbridge, New York. It may be assumed then, that, like it or not, the last dissenters of the Vermont government and their followers gave their loyalty to their respective towns and to the state of Vermont, thus resolving the affects of the many controversies that stimulated the transformations that effectively resulted in the Halifax, Vermont of today.   ©2008 *Molly Stone*

ENDNOTES

1. Almost no Halifax town records exist prior to 1778, possibly because they were New York records and might have been destroyed when Vermonters came into power. Those records in existence are located in New Hampshire, New York, Massachusetts and, possibly, Connecticut in the towns where the earliest meetings were held by the first proprietors. A great deal of information can also be gleaned from the earliest Vermont State papers, as well as records of those states involved in the controversy. S. R. Hall, L.L.D., in *The Geography and History of Vermont* (Montpelier: C. W. Willard, 1868), explains the absence of early documents from 1784 to 1791: "From this time to 1791, both parties held public and secret meetings. The Yorkers, though they had the town books, dared not enter records in them. During this confusion and jealousy one party stole the records of the other and hid them together with their own, and many deeds and proprietor's papers, under the earth in the pound, where they remained till none of them could be read" (pp. 164, 165).

2. Aaron H Grout, Secretary of State, *State Papers of Vermont, Volume Three: Journals and Proceedings of the General Assembly of the State of Vermont*, March 1778 to June 1881, vol. 1 (Bellows Falls, VT: P. H. Gobie Press, 1924) p. 15. Hereinafter cited as Grout, vol. 1.

3. J. Kevin Graffagnino, ed., "A Vindication of the Opposition of the Inhabitants of Vermont to the Government of New York, and of Their Right to Form Into An Independent State," in *Ethan and Ira Allen: Collected Works In 3 Volumes*, vol. 1 (Benson, VT: Chalidze Publications, 1992) p. 226 (originally published in 1779 by Alden Spooner).

4. Charles Miner Thompson, *Independent Vermont* (Boston: Houghton Mifflin, 1942) p. 42. Hereinafter cited as C. M. Thompson.

5. William Slade Jr., ed., Secretary of State, *Vermont State Papers, Records and Documents, Journal of the Council of Safety, Laws From 1779–1786* (Middlebury, VT: J. W. Copeland, 1823) p. 19. Hereinafter cited as Slade.

6. C. M. Thompson, p. 39.

7. Ibid., p. 40.

8. Ibid., p. 43.

9. Ibid., p. 531.

10. Halifax was located a short distance north of Fort Morrison in Colrain, MA. It is said that men followed the North River into Halifax, settling on land there. Indeed, the first Vermont settlements tended to be located near Massachusetts forts for protection.

11. Walter Hill Crockett, *Vermont, The Green Mountain State,* vol. 2 (New York: Century History, 1921) p. 168.

12. University of Vermont, Special Collections, Charles Phelps Papers, 1754–1781, box 1, folder 45.

13. Ibid., box 1, folders 46 and 47.

14. C. M. Thompson, p. 410.

15. Ibid., p. 493.

16. Ibid., p. 411.

17. Thompson, p. 20.

18. Hall, pp. 750–751. I used primarily Benjamin H. Hall's *History of Eastern Vermont from its Earliest Settlement to the Close of the Eighteenth Century* (New York: D. Appleton, 1858) as a source. His perspective is that of eastern Vermont and the Yorker point of view. One can read opposing Vermonter viewpoints in Hiland Hall's *History of Vermont, From its Discovery to its Admission into the Union in 1791.* (Albany, NY: Munsell, 1868).

19. HHS: Niles, 1884, pp. 23, 24. A. C. Niles did not reference the publisher, but as we read the Halifax book of newspaper clippings, we can make some assumptions. From 1881–1887, it appears that he wrote primarily for the *Vermont Phoenix.* He may have published the same pieces in the *Brattleboro Reformer* or other newspapers in publication at that time, since identical articles are reprinted in a different typeface. He also included items of interest written by other correspondents. Some articles have the initials Z., S., or L. at the end, indicating other correspondents submitted them. These and other newspaper articles have contributed a great deal of history.

20. E. B. O'Callaghan, *The Documentary History of the State of New York*, vol. 4, Hon. Christopher Morgan, Secretary of State (Albany, NY: Charles Van Benthuysen, 1851) pp. 1017–1018. Hereinafter cited as O'Callaghan.

21. Slade, p. 66.

22. Hall, p. 269.

23. Ibid., pp. 763–770.

24. Ibid., p. 256.

25. Ibid., pp. 761–773.

26. Grout, vol. 1, p. 3, March 12, 1778, "The representatives of the freeman of the several Towns in this state, met at the meeting house in said Windsor, agreeable to the Constitution, and formed themselves into a House."

27. Mary Greene Nye, ed., *State Papers of Vermont, Volume Six, Sequestration, Confiscation and Sale of Estates,* Rawson C, Myrick, Secretary of State (Montpelier, VT: The Modern Printing Co., Barre, VT., printer, 1941) p. 6–7. Hereinafter cited as Nye.

28. Ibid., p. 13.

29. Allen Soule, ed., *Laws of Vermont, State Papers of Vermont*, vol. 3, Howard E, Armstrong, Secretary of State (Montpelier, VT: Vermont Printing Co, 1964) p. 9.

30. Ibid., p. 10.

31. Grout, vol. 1, pp.26, 93.

32. C. M. Thompson, p. 341.

33. Tories were those persons who professed allegiance to Great Britain and were considered enemies of the American patriots. Presumably, by 1776, when the thirteen colonies declared independence, all Tories had been prosecuted for treason and involuntarily or voluntarily left the United States. Residents of Vermont, like many other states, escaped to Boston or New York. Some later returned to their homes and took the oath of allegiance to the United States or to Vermont. Those who retained their true Tory political passions presented to the British government claims for their services and losses. They were granted money to establish new homesteads in Canada.

34. *Public Papers of George Clinton, First Governor of New York 1777–1795—1801–1804*, vol. 3 (New York: James B. Lyon, State Printer, 1900) pp. 16–17.

35. O'Callaghan, p. 949.

36. Hall, Appendix J, p. 755.
37. C. M. Thompson, p. 181.
38. O'Callaghan, p. 983.
39. Hall, quoting from George Clinton Papers in New York State Library, vol. xvii, documents 4939, 5055, p. 485.
40. Ibid., p. 486.
41. O'Callaghan, p. 983.
42. Ibid.
43. Ibid., pp. 984–985.
44. Ibid., pp. 981–987.
45. C. M. Thompson. p. 445.
46. Hall, p. 354.
47. Ibid.
48. Ibid., p. 340.
49. Hall, p. 536.
50. Nye, p. 388.
51. Ibid. p. 215.
52. C. M. Thompson, p. 500.
53. Graffagnino, p. 87. "A Copy of A Remonstrance, of the Council of the State of Vermont, Against the Resolutions of Congress of the 5th of December Last, which interfere with their internal Police," by Ira Allen and Thomas Tolman.
54. Ibid., p. 89.
55. Ibid., p. 93.
56. Hall, p. 506.
57. Slade, p. 106.
58. C. M. Thompson, p. 438.
59. Ibid., p. 439.
60. O'Callaghan, p. 993.
61. Grout vol. 1, p. 83.
62. Ibid., p. 193.
63. Ibid.
64. Slade, p. 141.
65. Ibid.
66. Slade, p. 142.
67. Ibid., p. 150
68. Ibid., p. 151.
69. Ibid.
70. Ibid., p. 154.
71. Ibid.
72. Ibid.
73. Ibid., p. 156.
74. Grout, vol. 1, p. 145.
75. O'Callaghan, p. 1015.
76. Ibid., pp. 1016–1017.
77. Ibid., pp. 1018–1019.
78. Slade, pp. 194–195.
79. Halifax Land Records record properties purchased and sold by William Shattuck. Several of the earliest Halifax deeds are filed in Massachusetts at the Hampden County Registry of Deeds, Springfield, MA.
80. John A. Williams, ed,. *State Papers of Vermont, Volume Three, Part V, Journals and Proceedings of the General Assembly of the State of Vermont, 1791–1792*, Richard C. Thomas, Secretary of State (Montpelier,VT: no publisher listed, 1970) p. 35.
81. *State Papers of Vermont*, vol. 5: Petitions for Land.

William Shattuck
A Flash of Glory

There is no written history of the William Shattuck family, particularly in the Halifax years, yet much can be pieced together, like a pioneer patchwork quilt, from family and land records as well as the historical papers of Vermont, New York, and the Library of Congress. The trail of his life wound through three states and Canada, with the Halifax years from 1779 to 1786 being the most notable because of his Yorker activities, which so irritated the early Vermont leaders.

William Cutter wrote of the Shattuck family: "A brave, hardy, patriotic and liberty-loving race in America have sprung from early colonists of this name in Massachusetts."[1] William Shattuck began his life in Deerfield, Massachusetts on August 31, 1747, the son of Samuel Shattuck and Sarah Clesson. At the age of twenty-four he married Lydia Allis in Montague, Massachusetts. His educational background is not available at this time, but his ancestors and descendants include a long line of well-educated, prosperous men in Massachusetts, Vermont, and New York, some of whom were included in the westward movement. William and Lydia's first child Eliphalet was born in Ashfield, Massachusetts, where William is said to have been a blacksmith.[2] Naming their fifth child, born in 1786, George Clinton Shattuck, for the governor of New York, made a bold, opinionated statement given William's status and the political climate of the time. In addition to Halifax, the Shattuck family is known to have lived in several Vermont towns, including Guilford and Brattleboro, as well as several New York towns. This pattern of moving the family from town to town and even state to state is evident throughout the rest of William Shattuck's life. Along with farming and blacksmithing in the years 1779 to 1781, he incorporated a very busy political life.

Although he lived in Halifax for barely seven years, Shattuck bought and sold several properties,[3] in Lots 1, 15, 19, and 23.[4] Where he lived is speculation, but a good guess is that it was the property in Lot 15, consisting of eighty acres with a house and barn that he purchased for "Two Thousand, One Hundred Pounds" from Dr. Peletiah Fitch in April 1779, placing the family in Halifax at that time. The November birth of Sophia, the second child, also confirms the family's residence. The deed reads in part: "Peletiah Fitch of Hallifax in the County of Cumberland and State of New York, Esq. To William Shattock of Ashfield in the County of Hampshire and State of Massachusetts Bay. . . Eighty Acres in southwest corner of Lot No. 15, With Dwelling house and barn thereon standing . . .Recorded in Hampshire [County in Massachusetts] June 24th 1779"[5] [HLR 1A: 141]. On June 23, 1782, that property in Lot 15 was transferred to Henry Henderson and included "all his household furniture and Two Cows Two horses and ten sheep together with all the [   ] and appurtenances. . . ." It appears that this was the property confiscated and sold by Vermont in retaliation for Shattuck's Yorker activities. The 1782 deed reads in part: "William Shattock of Hallifax, in the County of Windham and State of Vermont, Gentleman, in consideration of Three Hundred and Eighty pounds for consideration paid by

Henry Henderson of Hallifax, being part of the Lot of land lying in Halifax, part of Original Lot No 15 with Dwelling House and Barn thereon Standing all his Household furniture. . . ." [HLR 1A: 71]

What is of particular interest is that the location of the first deed (1779) was in "County of Cumberland and State of New York," while the second was "County of Windham and State of Vermont." This is one of the earliest deeds that reflect the manner in which Vermonters merely transferred properties from the state of New York to the state of Vermont. Several deeds to and from Shattuck now generate more questions than answers. If this was the property confiscated in October, why was this June land transfer recorded three months before Shattuck's September trial and conviction by the Vermonters? How were the properties handled that were confiscated and sold by the Vermonters? How were those deeds transferred and recorded when one party would have been in disagreement? History tells us that the state of Vermont confiscated land with this same description, yet why does this deed sound as though William Shattuck sold the land and received the proceeds from the sale with no hint that the money went into the Vermont treasury?[6]

Shattuck emerged as the most important leader of the Yorkers in Halifax when he became embroiled in several incidents in the controversy between New York and Vermont. In 1782, Shattuck was commissioned First Major under Lieutenant Colonel Commandant Timothy Church of the Southern Regiment of the New York Militia in Cumberland County [ↄ 174]. Among the New York adherents, all of whom were ardent American patriots, there was an aura of fear and distrust of the new, unstable, and unpredictable Vermont state government. Shattuck may have been among those who wished to align themselves with the State of Massachusetts, yet he supported the government of New York [ↄ 174].

On May 10, 1782, a group of Yorkers, including William Shattuck, was meeting at the home of Hezekiah Stowell in Guilford when Barzillai Rice, a local sheriff's deputy, was ordered to seize several properties in the amount equal to, or sometimes double, that of the cost of hiring someone to serve in place of those who had refused to serve, as was the custom of that time. Hall wrote of this incident:

> Opposition to the unjust demands of Vermont was loudly
> proclaimed, and it was plainly evident that words were to be but
> the prelude to action. William Shattuck, of Halifax, a leader among
> the Yorkers, failed not on this occasion to strengthen the minds of
> his friends. Mingling in the crowd, he counseled them to protect
> their rights; to stand by their liberties; and to repel the invasions of
> a usurped power. "I am a supporter of the opposition," he
> declared, "both in public and private. I deny the authority of
> Vermont. The cause that I maintain is just, and I have done and
> will do all in my power to uphold it." With Shattuck the majority
> coincided.[7]

A cow was seized by the deputy and promptly returned by the Yorkers. However, according to Hall, "While the supporters of the claims of New York exulting in the success which had attended this effort . . . the citizens of Vermont were rejoicing that this forcible resistance had placed them in possession of an argument which would henceforth warrant them in punishing their opponents as disturbers of the peace and contemners of lawful jurisdiction."[8] Thus the stage was being set for the confiscation of Shattuck's Halifax property. Vermont needed to fund its treasury without levying taxes against Vermonters. Shattuck and other wealthy Yorkers became that source of revenue.

Because they needed to make the fines and confiscation of property legal and acceptable in the minds of the Vermont supporters, the legislature spent a busy few weeks passing laws that addressed the "punishment of conspiracies" and that empowered Ethan Allen to unite the Vermont Militia on the west side of the state with volunteers from Cumberland County. On September 9, 1782, Ethan Allen and about two hundred mounted and armed men "were under full march," according to Hall. They went first to Marlboro where they targeted Timothy Phelps, who particularly enraged the Vermonters, then on to Guilford. By this time, with the added Windham County Militia, the troops numbered 400. Meanwhile, Hall reported, "Col. Walbridge, who with a party of men, had been sent into Halifax, succeeded in arresting Maj. William Shattuck, Capt. Thomas Baker, and Ensign David Lamb, three of the leading Yorkers in that town, and conducted them under a strong guard to head-quarters . . . and although resistance was offered, yet the Vermonters were not only too numerous, but were also too free in the use of powder and ball to be overcome by their surprised and unarmed opponents."[9]

The New York prisoners were taken on September 10 to the jail in Westminster where they were held under heavy guard. Vermont hurriedly convened a session of the Superior Court the next day, when they tried the "principal offenders" first, including William Shattuck. According to Hall, they were charged with a variety of seditious acts on several occasions, and, in addition, "that they did 'with force and arms treacherously conspire an invasion, insurrection, and public rebellion against this state, by their treacherously assembling together, consulting and advising together of the means to destroy the constitution of this state, and subvert the freedom and independence of the government thereof.'"[10] Fifteen witnesses testified in support of the various charges against the Yorker leaders. Hall continued:

> It was proved that Shattuck . . . boasted that he should obtain assistance from [New York] government, and would 'drive the matter warmly' . . . that he had counseled the people to continue their opposition to Vermont; had declared that he would do all that he could both public and private to oppose the state; and had verified this declaration of his acts. . . . It does not appear that any attempt was made by the defendants to disprove the statements of the opposing witnesses.[11]

A judgment of guilty was pronounced. Shattuck and the other Yorkers were to remain in jail until October 4, 1782, when they were to be escorted by the sheriff to the state line and

> . . . forever banished from this state, not to return thereto on
> penalty of death; and that all their goods and chattels, and estates
> be condemned, seized, and sold, as forfeited to the use of this
> state. . . . Of the effects of Shattuck, a constable made return that
> he had attached 'about 80 acres of land in Halifax, with the
> buildings thereon standing; about ten tons of hay; a small quantity
> of rye in sheaf; a considerable quantity of flax spread on the
> ground; and about two or three acres of Indian corn standing on
> the ground.'[12]

This appears to be the property transferred to Henry Henderson on June 23, 1782, three months prior to Shattuck's trial and conviction. Hall noted that, with the completion of the trials and sentencing of the other Yorkers, a small group of Vermonters had enforced its civil laws using military force. Their treatment was, "in some instances, unnecessarily severe and cruel." While incarcerated, a couple of men went eleven days with only four meals. Hall did not specify which men. "Ethan Allen himself acknowledged, that the method which had been pursued by him was 'a savage way to support government.'"[13] When the situation of the Vermont Sufferers became known, some men in Massachusetts were inclined to provide the Yorkers with assistance,[14] including the provision of armed troops. Hall quoted one message from these supporters to the south: "You and I are, with all the United States, bound by the confederacy to protect them from all such violence."[15] Yet, no such protection ever materialized to help the Yorkers in their cause.

Shattuck and Henry Evans were ejected from Vermont with no funds, only that which they could hastily raise from friends or family. They took their troubles first to Governor Clinton in New York, then to Congress in Philadelphia in October 1782. Hall shared the contents of the petition Shattuck and Evans presented to Congress on October 28, in which

> . . . they briefly rehearsed the history of the difficulties which they
> had been obliged to encounter; referred to the 'fifty persons
> having families,' who had been driven from their homes, and who
> were then 'wandering about in the utmost distress;' mentioned the
> forbearance which the sufferers had exhibited in refraining from
> 'acts of retaliation;' and asked for aid and for the restoration of
> their possessions to those who had been deprived of them by the
> late transactions of the people of Vermont."[16]

Congress advised New York to revoke all civil and military commissions, while recommending that Vermont make full restitution, allowing the sufferers to return to their homes and to remain unmolested. Vermont's reply was that it was an independent territory and in no way bound by the Congress of the United States. The threat of interference from Congress, possibly with sympathy and tangible support on behalf of the sufferers, may have influenced the Vermonters to begin to change their stance.

While they had accomplished some of their objectives, Shattuck and Evans' distress continued because of escalating travel expenses and a lack of funds. They tried to borrow 100 dollars from the State of New York. Hall quoted James Duane's plea on their behalf: "If this plan fails, it is more than probable they will lose their liberty, as they have already done their property. . ."[17] They were awarded the loan, thus avoiding debtor's prison. Audaciously, Evans immediately returned home to Guilford, while Shattuck continued to comply with the banishment. Upon his return to his home in Halifax on December 15, 1782, Shattuck was, according to Hall, informed of Vermont's plan to "dispossess Daniel Shepardson of Guilford or pull his house down. Shattuck and a number of Yorkers met on the 17th, determined to protect Shepardson from violence."[18] He went to Guilford, where he raised two companies of men, resolving to retaliate by detaining two prominent Vermonters. When that foray was unsuccessful, they tried on the December 20 to capture John Bridgman, one of the court judges, whom they released on parole with messages for the Vermont Governor. The result was another assault by the Vermonters who now feared a civil war. Shattuck and his men waited in ambush, but the expected attack never happened. On their way to Guilford, the Vermont Militia, startled by a detachment of what they thought were Yorkers, scattered in all directions. They later learned they were their own men.[19] Often, the men hesitated to use force because it was difficult to distinguish an "enemy" who was a relative, friend, or neighbor and who had no distinctive uniform.

In January 1883, Governor Clinton summoned Shattuck to Poughkeepsie, perhaps to ask him to serve in the New York legislature. He returned home, according to Hall, to the same old problems:

[I]n early February . . . he was informed that a party, "employed by
the express order of the pretended Superior court, in that district
called the New Hampshire Grants," were on the alert to arrest
him. He accordingly fled to Guilford . . . [where] he continued
under the protection of his friends in that town. But he did not
remain long there . . . [H]e again visited Poughkeepsie, where on
the 22d of February, he made a formal deposition . . . of such
facts he deemed important. A few days later he was sent with
dispatches to Philadelphia. Although [there was] a warrant for his
arrest . . . so long as he prudently refrained from rendering himself
obnoxious to the laws of Vermont by special acts of disobedience,
he was allowed to hold communion with his family without being
molested.[20]

Several incidents in 1783 may have increased the credibility of the Yorkers
in the estimation of the Vermonters, and that may have caused the latter to soften
their position a bit. Congress directed New York, New Hampshire, and
Massachusetts to give their permission to settle the boundary disputes that had
plagued the New Hampshire Grants for so long. In January 1783, William
Shattuck, in addition to being well-known to Congress in Philadelphia, was
elected to the assembly of New York State.[21] Vermont leaders began to
understand that the Yorkers were gaining political stature, sympathy, and support
from the surrounding states and Congress as well.

Another event that boosted Shattuck's political importance was an
assignment issued by General George Washington. In his capacity as First Major
of the Southern Regiment and as second in command of the Yorkers, Shattuck
was directed to carry out the capture of Luke Knowlton and Samuel Welles,
Vermonters who were considered Tories and enemies of the United States. The
following is a letter, located in the Library of Congress, with this heading, "To
Mr. Willm Shattuck: Instructions to apprehend Knowlton and Welles. By His
Excellency George Washington, Esqr, General and Commander in Chief of the
Armies of the United States of America."[22] Washington wrote from headquarters
on March 11, 1783:

Whereas Congress by their Resolutions, have especially
authorized and requested me, to take such measures as I shall
think proper to apprehend and secure Luke Knowlton and Samuel
Welles, two persons supposed to be within the Territory called
Vermont, and who are charged with high Crimes and
misdemeanours against the United States of America.

You are therefore hereby authorized and impowered, to
use your diligent Endeavours, in such way as shall be thought
proper to secure and apprehend the said Knowlton and Welles,
[or either of them], and him safely keep, that they may be
conveyed to Congress. Taking care, that in the Execution of such
measures as you shall adopt, no means shall be used that may tend

to excite or procure any general Commotions, Broils, or Contentions among the People of said Territory, or any Inhabitants of these United States.

And all Officers civil and military are hereby requested to aid and assist the said Wm. Shattuck in such reasonable and proper Measures as may be adopted by him, for the apprehending, safe keeping and conducting the said Knowlton and Welles, or either of them [to the Hd. Qrs.] of the Army; that they may be delivered over to the Orders of Congress, to be dealt with as they shall judge proper.

In the writing of Jonathan Trumbull, Jr. The words in brackets in the draft are in the writing of Washington, and his abbreviations are here followed.[23]

Located at the Library of Congress is the following document that tells more of the story and confirms that Knowlton was detained by Shattuck, but it does not mention Welles. This interesting entry also shows the language of the time as well as the accusations coming from both sides:

The Board of Treasury to whom was Referred the Memorial of William Shattuck and Timothy Church, Beg leave to Report:

That it appears from the Journals of Congress of the 5th. December, 1782, That the Memorialists were Condemned to Banishment and Confiscation of Property by certain persons assuming to Erect themselves into and Independent State, within that District of Country on the West side of Connecticut River, commonly called the New Hampshire Grants, in violation of the Resolves of Congress of the 24th of September, 1779, and the 2d June, 1780; that the United States Congress required of the Persons exercising such Authority, to make full and ample Restitution to the Memorialists for the Damages by them sustained, and not to molest them in their Persons or Properties on their Return to their Habitations in said District.

That the Memorialists state, that in defiance of this Resolve they were on their return to the District above mentioned confined in Jail, where they were loaded with Irons and suffered all the hardships of a rigorous Imprisonment for the space of five months.

That it appears from a Certificate of His Excellency Governor Clinton that William Shattuck (one of the Memorialists) in consequence of a Warrant from the late Commander in Chief delivered to him in the Spring of 1783, apprehended a certain Luke Knowlton (an Inhabitant of the District abovementioned) charged with keeping up a Correspondence with the Enemies of the United States, and brought him to the Head Quarters of the American Army in the latter end of the year 1783.

That the said William Shattuck Swears, that he has only received on account of the said Service from His Excellency General Washington, the Sum of Fourteen Dollars, and that the just balance due him for his Services and Expences is Forty eight Pounds, two Shillings and ten Pence Current Money of New York.

Under these Circumstances the Board Beg leave to Observe: That although they doubt not the Sufferings of the Memorialist have been such as they Represent, yet inasmuch, as their Banishment, Confiscation of Property, and the Imprisonment they suffered in consequence of it, proceeded from their holding Commissions under the State of New York and from their zealous Attachment to the Jurisdiction of that Government, it would be improper for the United States to Apply any part of the General Funds in making that Compensation which the Memorialists may with Confidence expect from the Justice of the State, in whose Cause their Sufferings have been sustained. With respect to the Claim made by William Shattuck for his Service and Expenses in apprehending Luke Knowlton, in consequence of a Warrant from His Excellency the Commander in chief, the Board beg leave to report the following Resolve, Viz.

That there be allowed William Shattuck, such a Sum as the late Commander in Chief shall certify to be a proper Compensation for his Services and Expences in Apprehending Luke Knowlton, in pursuance of the General's Warrant for such purpose; and the Board of Treasury take Order for paying the same, or producing such Certificate.
April 10th, 1786. [24]

Among the financial papers of George Washington is a receipt from William Shattuck to General Washington for "Five pounds, Sixteen shillings, York Currency, to help pay my expences in locking up Luke Knowlton."[25]

At this point in history, Yorkers in southeastern Cumberland County were causing serious concerns for the Vermonters who feared for the very survival of the new state if the Yorker activities and influences were not terminated at once and for all time. William Shattuck was arrested again on December 25, 1783, and remanded to Bennington jail. Hall notes, "Though William Shattuck had not been released from the penalties from which had been imposed upon him by the decree of banishment, yet so long as he refrained from inimical acts he was allowed to live in the undisturbed possession of his house and farm [although now in Guilford]. Still he was obliged to render to the treasurer of the state of Vermont [Ira Allen] an account of the income and expenses of his estate."[26] By 1784, as evidenced by the birth of son William on December 26, the Shattuck family was living across the town line in Guilford, having been dispossessed of their Halifax home, household furnishings, and property.

Meanwhile, Governor Chittenden offered a pardon to those Yorkers who pledged their allegiance to the state of Vermont within thirty days by taking the Freeman's Oath, and the town of Halifax changed its loyalty by voting its allegiance to the state of Vermont. Shattuck petitioned for a pardon. The following appears in a Vermont Assembly Journal: "February 24, 1784, A petition signed William Shattuck who is now in Bennington [Jail] praying for pardon &c. was read and referred to a Committee of five to join a Committee from the Council. . . . The members chosen Mr. [Gideon] Ormsby, Mr. [Edward] Harris, Mr. [John] Shumway, Mr. [Matthew] Lyon and Mr. [Noah] Sabin." [27]

On February 26, 1784, the committee "brought in their report which was read and *ordered* Myrick's quote to lie on the table."[28] Although William Shattuck's name appears on the Halifax freeman's list, yet when the committee presented its report on March 1, 1784, he was denied the pardon.[29] Still the harassment of the Yorkers continued. In early 1784 the Vermont legislature was petitioned on behalf of the Yorkers arrested, requesting their release and the opportunity to make "an amicable settlement of past misunderstandings . . . upon just and equitable terms."[30] Governor Chittenden's reply was his certainty that the assembly would have no compassion for those who had caused them so much trouble. The only acceptable outcome from Vermont's standpoint would be complete submission of the Yorkers.[31]

Hall gave this account of a later petition:

> On a subsequent occasion Shattuck petitioned the Council for his release, acquiescing in the justice of the sentence of banishment which had been passed upon him by the Superior court in September, 1782, and praying for pardon. His prayer was granted on the 12th of April, 1784, and a resolution was passed, restoring him to partial citizenship, and declaring his estate free from the ban of confiscation. The conditions on which these favors were bestowed, were that he should pay to the sheriff of Bennington county £25 lawful money, to meet the costs of prosecution; satisfy the "just demands" of Nathan Fay, the jail keeper for board; and give to the treasurer of the state bonds for £100, lawful money, with sufficient sureties, that he would not "enter or presume to go into the county of Windham, without liberty therefore first had and obtained" from the Council. With these terms he complied, and thus obtained his discharge. A few weeks later he notified to Governor Chittenden the "distressed circumstances" of his family, and his inability to relieve them, except in person. A passport, signed by the Governor and Councillors, was accordingly granted to him on the 8th of June, 1784, by which permission was given him to visit his family unmolested. [32]

Hall mentions yet another petition from Shattuck that was presented to the assembly on October 14, 1785, requesting, "that he may be relinquished from paying a bond of £25, which he had given this state, which was for cost for keeping him in Goal, [jail]."[33] This petition was dismissed on October 18, 1785.[34]

The two Halifax representatives to the Assembly, Edward Harris and Hubbel Wells, served on the two committees.

Shattuck was active buying and selling properties in Halifax, according to land records, until 1786. It appears he may have remained in Vermont until 1794, where he lived in Guilford and Brattleboro. Other Shattuck children included Phylinda, the third child born in Vermont, in December 1781, though it is unclear where she was born; then William, born in Guilford in 1784, and George Clinton, born in Brattleboro in 1786. Four more children, mentioned by Robert Kline, are Mary, Phylinda, Sabra, and an unnamed son, all of whom died young and whose dates of birth and death are unknown.[35]

Those Yorkers, 125 families, who did not take the Freeman's Oath or who were denied a pardon by Vermont were rewarded by New York for their loyalty. In response to a petition, "in behalf of the 'Sufferers,' the New York Legislature voted to assign to the petitioners and their associates eight miles square in the area newly acquired from the Iroquois; and this was definitely located by the Land Office Commissioners, in May 1776, in Clinton Township."[36] Carlton Hayes described the hardships encountered by the sufferers as they moved their families and household possessions by horseback, canoe, and on foot to this remote area of New York that was, at that time, the western frontier. After first negotiating over thirty miles of Green Mountains between Halifax and Bennington [Hogback Mountain, Searsburg Mountain, and Woodford Mountain], the jumping off point for their journey was Hoosick, New York. From there they trekked over trails to the Mohawk River that took them to Cooperstown. After another distance along wilderness trails, they canoed down the Susquehanna River to Township Number 2, Clinton, named for George Clinton. The town later merged into Jericho, but today the area comprises the towns of Bainbridge and Afton.[37]

William Shattuck was the second largest recipient of land, receiving five lots totaling 3,200 acres in Lots 36, 53, 65, 82, and 78. However, like many of the Vermont Sufferers he never settled there, but most likely sold the property to land speculators. New York census data lists the family in Romulus in 1800. The life of Eliphalet, a successful physician, can be traced through the births of his children in Ovid, Seneca County, New York; then Benton, in Ontario (later Yates) County, New York, before he moved to Indiana. William Jr. lived in Prattsburg, Steuban County, New York and in Romulus, New York. He studied law, was admitted to the bar, and "engaged in the profession for three years in Romulus, and nine years in Penn Yan, Yates County. He was appointed master in chancery, captain of an artillery company, and had a colonel's commission offered him, which he refused. [The 1820 New York State Census, page 413, confirms his residence.] In 1821 he relinquished the profession of law and united with the Friends' Society."[38] He was mentioned in the history of Yates County as living in Benton in 1824, where he built the courthouse at the county seat, Penn Yan.[39] George Clinton Shattuck appears in the 1810 census in Steuban County, but he left Romulus in 1817 and moved to Indiana.[40]

The life of William Shattuck, ever the wanderer searching for the new frontier, ended in Canada in 1810. Robert Kline writes that: "As early as 1791 or

1792, he obtained from the government of Canada West (now Ontario, Canada) a grant of land, but, not complying with the settling duties, it became forfeited. About 1809 or 10 he petitioned for a renewal of the original title, and while his petition was pending he made a tour of exploration through Ohio and Kentucky, when he wrote to his family the last letter they ever received from him. It is said that he returned to Canada to ascertain the result of his petition, and that he was there accidentally thrown from a horse and killed, in 1810."[41] Subsequently, Lydia Shattuck received property from William Shattuck in 1822, according to the Ontario County Deeds Index.[42] However, it is unclear whether it was from William Jr. or from her husband's estate. She is not listed as a head of household for the census years 1820 or 1830, although her sons and other Shattuck family members are included. She died on September 28, 1833, at Prattsburg, Steuben County, New York.[43] Descendants of William and Lydia Allis Shattuck continue to populate Vermont, New York, and points west.   ©2008 *Molly Stone*

ENDNOTES

1. William Richard Cutter, A. M. *Genealogical and Personal Memoirs Relating to the Families of the State of Massachusetts,* vol. 3 (New York: Lewis Historical Publishing, 1910) p. 1834.
2. Robert Kline, "Modified Register for Samuel Shattuck," an excerpt from his database, sent by e-mail on November 26, 2003, that includes children and grandchildren of Samuel Shattuck, compiled from vital records from the towns mentioned in Massachusetts, Vermont, New York, and from Lemuel Shattuck's *Memorials of the Descendants of William Shattuck* (Boston: Dutton & Wentworth, 1855). Hereinafter cited as Kline.
3. Halifax Land Records record properties purchased and sold by William Shattuck. Several of the earliest Halifax deeds are filed in Massachusetts at the Hampden County Registry of Deeds, Springfield, MA.
4. November 10, 1794, a deed [HLR 2: 293] shows "William Shattuck of New Ipswich in the County of Hillsborough, State of New Hampshire for the consideration of Thirty One pounds lawfull money received of James Peirce and Benjamin Weeks, Junior both of Halifax . . . part of the Original Right Number fifty two . . . eighty six acres." Although William Shattuck was still in Vermont, probably living in Guilford as late as 1794, still it is uncertain that this was our William Shattuck.
5. That house burned in 1902, and on the property today is the home of Linda Gates Swanson.
6. Shattuck next bought one hundred acres, part of Lot 19, on Hubbard Hill, from Henry Henderson on July 17, 1781, "in the fifth year of American Independence" [HLR 1A: 44]. However, in November 1781, 208 acres of land in Lot 19 was sold to Moses Learnard with the deed recorded in "Hampshire Greenfield May 7th 1782." It is unclear just how one hundred acres doubled in four months. In November 1783, Shattuck sold to Jonas Bond for two hundred pounds [HLR 1A: 146] property located in Lot 1 that he had purchased for five pounds from Charles Coats of Bernardston, MA in June [HLR 1A: 147]. Curiously, there is an identical version of this deed recorded seven years later on January 2, 1790, appearing on the last page of Halifax Land Records, Book 1A.

     The final piece of land bought and sold by Shattuck was located in Lot 23. William Gault, David Lamb, and Jonathan Safford, all ardent Yorkers, owned neighboring lots. Lamb lived in a home on the site now occupied by the Roddys on the Jacksonville Stage Road near the Guilford town line. In this transaction, Shattuck purchased sixty acres from John Linn of Colrain for one hundred pounds on December 20, 1786, which he resold on December 25 to William Gault for sixty pounds. For the second time he suffered a loss on the resale of a property, although he did realize a handsome profit when he purchased land from Coats for five pounds that he sold for two hundred pounds.

     An interesting petition, dated July 3, 1780, presented by John Corrick, et al., reads in part: ". . . whereas there is within said state, in different places, large tracts of vacant Lands, not granted by any state; And Petitioners are desirous of cultivating and settling some part thereof, pray your Excellency and Honours to grant them a sufficient quantity of said Lands for a Township, six miles square, in such place, and under such restrictions, reservation and regulation, as your Excellency and Honours Wisdom shall direct. . . . [signed at] State of Massachusetts Bay July 3d 1780 Billirica." Included in the list of sixty names are William Shattuck Jr. and Lemuel Shattuck. It is unlikely that this William Jr. is the Halifax William, and it is not possible that it was his son, William Jr. since he was not born until 1784. Shattuck family histories list two men named Lemuel. The Lemuel living in 1780 was the son of a William Shattuck. This Lemuel was born in Hollis, New Hampshire in 1773 and would have been seven years old. There is no record that this petition was enacted. Rawson C. Myrick, Secretary of State. *State Papers of Vermont, Vol. Five; Petitions for Grants of Land 1778–1911* (Bellows Falls, VT: Wyndham Press, 1939). p. 173.

7.   Hall, p. 425.
8.   Ibid., p. 426.
9.   Ibid., p. 444.
10. Ibid., pp. 446–447.
11. Ibid., pp. 447–448.
12. Ibid., p. 448.
13. Ibid., p. 455.
14. Ibid., p. 450.
15. Ibid., p. 451.
16. Ibid., p. 465.
17. Ibid., p. 468.
18. Ibid., p. 474.
19. Ibid., p. 475.
20. Ibid., pp. 487–488.
21. According to the Web site, http://politicalgraveyard.com/bio/sharpenstein-shaver.html, accessed February 23, 2004, The Political Graveyard: Index to Politicians, William Shattuck was a member of the New York Assembly from Cumberland County 1783–1784.
22. George Washington Papers at the Library of Congress, 1741–1799: Series 3b, Varick Transcripts, http://lcweb2.loc.gov, accessed February 23, 2004.
23. Ibid.
24. *Journals of the Continental Congress, 1774–1789,* Monday, April 17,1786, Library of Congress, Manuscript Division, http://lcweb2.loc.gov, pp. 196, 197, accessed February 23, 2004. The following footnote is part of this text: "All which is humbly Submitted.1 [Note 1:1 This report, signed by Samuel Osgood and Walter Livingston, is in the Papers of the Continental Congress, No. 138, II, folio 351. According to indorsement if, (probably a typo that should read of) was read April 17.]"
25. *George Washington Papers at the Library of Congress, 1741–1799: Series 5 Financial Papers,* William Shattuck to George Washington, November 26, 1783, Revolutionary War Accounts, Vouchers, and Receipted Accounts 2., http://lcweb2.loc.gov/cgi-bin/query/P?mgw:2:./temp/~ammem_LPOn::, accessed on February 23, 2004.
26. Hall, pp. 505–506.
27. Rawson C. Myrick, Secretary of State. *State Papers of Vermont, Vol. Three, Journals and Proceedings of the State of Vermont;* February 1784 to February 1887. Vol. 1 (Bellows Falls, VT: Wyndham Press, 1939) p. 14.
28. Ibid., p. 19.
29. Ibid., p. 30.
30. Hall, p. 507.
31. Ibid., pp. 507–508.
32. Ibid., p. 526.
33. Myrick, p. 170.
34. Ibid., p. 189.
35. Kline, p. 153.
36. Carlton J. H. Hayes, *Story of Afton: A New York Town on the Susquehanna* (Deposit, NY: Valley Offset, 1976) p.6.
37. Ibid., p. 7.
38. Kline, p. 153.
39. J. H. French, *Gazetteer of the State of New York: Embracing a Comprehensive View of the Geography, Geology, and General History of the State* (Syracuse, NY: R. Pearsall Smith, 1860) p. 717.
40. Kline, p. 3.
41. Ibid., quoting from *Memorials of The Descendants of William Shattuck,* p. 153.
42. *Ontario County Deeds Index Letters SH to SL, 1789–1845,* http://raims.com/DeedsSH.html, accessed November 25, 2003.
43. Kline, p. 3.

THE MEDIATOR
HUBBEL WELLS

The name of one man resonates throughout the early political dynamic in Halifax as a patient guide and dedicated leader who helped shape a viable town government. Hubbel Wells appears to have earned the respect of both factions and helped heal the rancorous wounds from the great division between Yorkers and Vermonters. From the beginning, his allegiance was to the state of Vermont. During the years 1771 through 1791, while Vermont declared its independence and achieved statehood, Halifax saw a number of town officers come and go. Hubbel Wells, however, stayed the course. He served as town clerk, moderator, selectman, militia captain, state representative, and judge, through it all.

Born in Colchester, Connecticut, in 1730, to Jonathan Wells and Mary Hubbel Newton, his great-grandfather, Thomas Wells, was an early settler and military commander of Deerfield, Massachusetts, who experienced the struggles and hardships of frontier life. In one raid, Indians scalped three of his three daughters, two of whom survived, and his widow, Hubbel's great-grandmother, died a captive on march to Canada.[1] Understandably, some of the progeny of Thomas Wells chose to move south to Colchester.

Hubbel was the eighth son in a family of fifteen children. In 1754, he married Zerviah Chandler. After the birth of their twins, Hubbel Jr. and Mable in October 1770, the Wells family of ten moved to Halifax where two more children were born. In 1773, Deacon McCrellis conveyed Lots 43, 51, and 52 to Hubbel Wells [HLR 1A: 18]. The 1784 school district list places Hubbel Wells in District No. 3 and his son Jonathan Wells in District No. 5.

The 1830 census, tells us Hubbel Jr. and two of his sons, Levi and Horatio, had joined the group of Halifax families who migrated to Jackson, Susquehanna County, Pennsylvania. Darius, another son of Hubbel Jr. was still living on Collins Road in Halifax in 1830. A full genealogy of the Wells family is available in the family files of the Halifax Historical Society. Without death records in the town books for Hubbel and his wife, Zerviah Wells, and without

> **DIED.** In Halifax, Vt. the 3d. inft. Deacon HUBBEL WELLS, in the 74th year of his age. He had fustained the office of deacon with high reputation, for nearly fifty years; first in Colchefter, Con. fince in Halifax. He was among the early fettlers of Halifax, a very useful member of fociety, as well as promoter of religion: improved in the town bufinefs, as a militia officer, a civil magiftate, and judge in the county court—all which flations, he filled with dignity and reputation; and always fustained an unblemifhed character; exhibiting an uniform pattern of undiffembled, cheerful piety—was univerfally beloved and refpected by his acquaintance.

Greenfield Gazette, January 16, 1804

cemetery markers, the question of where and when they died had been unanswered until his recently discovered obituary.

"Capt. Hubbel Wells, Esq." is the first name recorded on the freeman's list. The preceding Early Officers Chart shows his dominance on the Halifax political scene during the first decade of recorded town government. He served in high-level positions during both the minority and the majority town meeting periods. It is interesting to note on that colorful confrontational 1781 petition to Governor Chittenden and the state assembly, his signature appears twice, once as selectman and once as justice of the peace. It is likely the bill that was read and passed—entitled "An Act for the purpose of granting an Abatement on the Provision tax in the Town of Halifax as assessed for the Year 1781"[2]— was a result of Hubbel Wells leadership and initiative with the provisions tax petition.

His contribution during that difficult turning point year is noted at the August, 1784 meeting. It was "Voted to allow thirty Shiling a peace to Benj. Henrey, Esq. Capt. John Sawtell, Lt. Joseph Tucker & Hubbel Wells, Selectmen for ye Year 1781 for their Extraordinary Trouble in Settling their Town affairs" [HLR 1A: 426]. That the Vermont state assembly held Wells in high regard is evident in his appointment in 1778 to serve as one of five judges for the Westminster shire and his appointment as judge of the County Court in 1786. It would be fitting to show a photograph of Hubbel Wells's gravestone, but its existence is not known. Nor do we have a portrait of him to view. However, we do have examples of this man's distinctive record-keeping as shown in the following minutes for a town meeting.

HLR 2A: 173

The Hubbel Wells legacy endures in the robust script that graces countless pages of the town record books.

~ *Constance Lancaster*

ENDNOTES

1. George Sheldon, *A History of Deerfield Massachusetts*, vol. 2 (Deerfield, MA: Pocumtuck Valley Memorial Association, 1983) p. 356.

2. Aaron H. Grout, *State papers of Vermont Volume Three* (Bellows Falls, VT: P. H. Gobie Press, 1925) p. 212.

CENSUS – POPULATION GROWTH AND DECLINE

TOWN	*1771	1791	1800	1810	1820	1830	1840	1850	1860	1870	1880
Athens	....	450	459	478	507	415	378	359	382	295	284
Brattleboro	403	1589	1867	1891	2017	2141	2623	3816	3855	4933	5880
Brookline	....	....	472	431	391	376	328	285	243	203	205
Dover	....	....	....	859	829	831	729	709	650	635	621
Dummerston	189	1501	1692	1704	1658	1592	1263	1645	1021	916	816
Grafton	....	561	1149	1365	1482	1439	1326	1241	1154	1008	929
Guilford	436	2432	2256	1872	1862	1760	1525	1389	1291	1277	1096
HALIFAX	**329**	**1309**	**1600**	**1758**	**1567**	**1562**	**1399**	**1133**	**1126**	**1029**	**852**
Jamaica	....	263	582	996	1313	1553	1586	1606	1541	1223	1252
Londonderry	28	362	330	637	958	1302	1216	1274	1367	1252	1154
Marlboro	50	629	1087	1245	1296	1218	1027	896	741	665	553
Newfane	52	660	1000	1276	1506	1441	1043	1304	1192	1113	1031
Putney	301	1848	1574	1607	1547	1510	1382	1425	1163	1167	1124
Rockingham	225	1235	1684	1954	2155	2272	2330	2837	2898	2854	3797
Somerset	....	111	130	199	173	245	262	321	195	80	67
Stratton	....	95	271	265	272	312	341	286	366	294	302
Townshend	136	676	1083	1115	1406	1386	1345	1354	1376	1171	1099
Vernon	**	482	480	521	627	681	705	821	724	764	652
Wardsboro	....	753	1484	1159	1016	1148	1102	1125	1004	866	766
Westminster	478	1601	1942	1925	1974	1737	1546	1721	1300	1238	1377
Whitingham	14	442	868	1248	1397	1477	1391	1380	1372	1263	1240
Wilmington	71	645	1011	1193	1369	1367	1296	1372	1424	1246	1130
Windham	....	....	429	782	931	847	757	763	680	544	536
Total	2712	17693	23581	26760	28457	28748	27442	29062	26982	26036	26763

* New York census of Cumberland county, January 16, 1771.

** Hinsdale, of which Vernon was a part, contained 107 inhabitants.

Windham County Census, Child, p. 304

TOWN	1890	1900	1910	1920	1930	1940	1950	1960	1970	1980	1990	2000
HALIFAX	**702**	**662**	**635**	**504**	**390**	**352**	**343**	**268**	**295**	**488**	**588**	**782**

Courtesy Vermont Department of Libraries, Montpelier, VT

HHS

STATE LINE TAVERN

Photo C. H. Liebs, Vermont Div. of Historic Sites

SECTION THREE

TAVERNS AND MEETING SITES

Photo C. H. Liebs, Vermont Div. of Historic Sites
TAVERN ENTRANCE

SQUIRE JOSEPH HENRY STORE/ TAVERN   HHS

SQUIRE JOSEPH HENRY HOUSE   HHS

TAVERNS AND TAVERN KEEPERS

As Halifax grew in population, so did the need for stores, post offices, and public gathering places. A tavern served a variety of community needs under one roof. The local taproom was the place to hear news, discuss politics, and transact business while imbibing "ardent spirits." Eye-catching broadsides papered the walls, together with notices of town meetings, elections, laws, ordinances, and auctions. In 1778, when Dr. Amsden rode into Halifax Center to deliver a single handwritten copy of the latest proceedings from the Vermont General Assembly,[1] chances are it was posted for all to read at Joseph Tucker's tavern. At the time, the town had not yet built its first meeting house, and early meetings to organize and launch the town government took place at "Landlord Tucker's."

When Vermont achieved statehood in 1791, most roads were not wide enough to accommodate wagons or stagecoach passage; people traveled and transported goods on foot or by horseback over narrow trails and pathways. In 1796, the initial transportation act by the Vermont legislature established a turnpike corporation, authorizing construction of a road from Bennington to Brattleboro, with plans to include five tollgates. Lucie Sumner and Bernice Barnett hiked and documented two of the earliest east/west southern Vermont roads. Maps in their book, *Roads in the Wilderness*, show that, except for one mile of the Albany Road, the early turnpikes did not pass through Halifax.[2] On well-traveled roads between larger cities, "the tavern sign swung at frequent intervals,"[3] about every eight miles, which was the customary distance a traveler on foot in winter could manage before needing warm shelter. In newly settled frontier areas, accommodations were available in

Detail C. J. Sauthier Map, Old Maps, West Chesterfield, NH
ALBANY ROAD AS IT CROSSES NORTHWEST HALIFAX

private log homes or family farmhouses, where a few rooms might be given over to meals and lodging for travelers and barn space provided for horses or oxen. Tavern fare varied widely. Often, the meal was whatever the family had prepared for the day—which is the origin of the term, "pot luck."[4]

Early tavern beverages often were produced on the premises. Beer was home-brewed from grain crops; homegrown fruits were used to make apple cider and pear brandies, and honey was fermented to become mead. The Starks of South Halifax maintained a large apiary at their tavern farm.[5] Settlers carried apple tree cuttings and seed with them "so apple orchards were usually the first permanent crop planted."[6] Cider was most in demand for that potent distillation known as "applejack" or apple brandy.[7] When available, imported rum was one of the more popular spirits.

On a cold night, the tavern keeper would brandish an iron, blunt-nosed poker, called a loggerhead, which he first heated in the fire, then plunged into a mug of "flip" to create a sizzling potent treat. On a cold day, the tavern fireplace served those who gathered at the unheated meeting house for lengthy church services and town business meetings. At the midday break, folks could "warm up" in the tavern and replenish their foot warmer pans with fireplace coals. By 1784, Halifax had raised its meeting house on the common by the Center Cemetery. Town records for the annual meeting held in March 1791,

"Pewter mug used by landlord Henry of South Halifax, Vermont." Collection of Memorial Hall Museum, Deerfield, MA. Used with permission. (Landlord Henry was possibly Benjamin Sr., Benjamin Jr., James, or

FLIP – a warm-up drink popular in colonial days. Recipes vary but were usually a combination of rum, beer, or ale; cream; egg; and spices, stirred with a hot poker, causing it to sizzle and foam, as the sugars caramelized.

note, "Voted to adjourn this Meeting to the dwelling House of Col. Amos Muzzy, for half an Hour" [HLR 1A: 177]. Muzzy kept a tavern nearby. How long the half-hour warm-up actually lasted is not recorded, but when the meeting reconvened, it was immediately "adjourned to the 29th Day of March Instant at one o'clock afternoon at the Meeting House in Halifax."

There is no local tavern building, past or present, open to the public today. The most familiar sites are the Crosier Store at Halifax Center and Stark's Tavern at the state line in South Halifax, now both private homes, but for many years, they served as stage stops and post offices. Licensing records document many more tavern keepers than known tavern buildings. Further study of land records, cross-referenced with names of the individuals who held licenses, might eventually confirm the presence of additional surviving taverns in the town.

YORKER TAVERN KEEPERS FIRST HALIFAX PUBLIC HOUSES

During the tumultuous tug-of-war between New York and New Hampshire over "the Grants" and the effort to forge an independent state of Vermont, taverns often were the setting for the ongoing drama. Decisions and plans of "The Vermont Council of Safety" were created during seventeen meetings held between July 1775 and December 1777 in Bennington at Stephen Fay's Catamount Tavern, known also as "The Inn of the Green Mountain Boys." East of the Green Mountains, Yorker resistance to those decisions and plans often took shape at meetings held at the tavern house of Hezekiah Stowell on the road leading from Halifax to Guilford Center. Significant Yorker/Vermonter militia confrontations occurred at Stowell's Tavern as well as at the Packer Family Tavern at Packer Corners in Guilford.[8]

ISAAC ORR: A colorful tavern incident appears in Hemenway's *Vermont Historical Gazetteer*. Citing as an example of "political strife," Hubbard Eastman writes:

> There were other occurrences, which showed the party feeling. Mr. Orr, a Yorker, who kept a public house on the place where Deacon Williams now resides, was visited by two Hampshire men who sought admission to his house, and being refused, they entered by force, and seizing Mr. Orr, demanded of him that he should say *New Hampshire*, and despairing of help otherwise from their firm grasp, he cried out *New Hampshire* to their satisfaction.[9]

This is mild-mannered "political strife," compared to what transpired when the conflict shifted from New York versus New Hampshire ownership of the "Grants" to the more hazardous issues of loyalty to New York versus loyalty to the newly created state of Vermont. Yorkers increasingly suffered punitive reprisals carried out by Vermonter Ethan Allen and his Green Mountain Boys.

If Isaac Orr operated his public house at his home, the fracas with the bullies from New Hampshire took place just "beyond the sharp easterly turn" heading south on Orr's Road [HLR 6: 360]. The dwelling is identified as J. Vaughn on the Beers map of 1869. Deacon Park Williams, who later owned the Orr property, conveyed it to his son-in-law, John Vaughn. "Orr's Road" became "Vaughn Road." The original dwelling is now a cellar hole.

Documentation that Orr hosted a pre–Revolutionary Halifax tavern exists in one of the few surviving Cumberland County, New York, record books. In 1772, the court issued "Lycenses for Retailing Spirituous Liquors and for keeping Taverns"[10] (court record shown below). In June 1773, he was again listed with

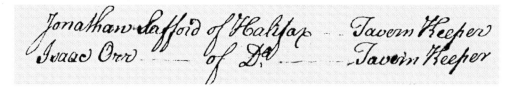

Jonathan Safford "of the same place," with Daniel Whipple and John Bolton providing their "Securities." Court records from 1774–1780 are missing, so it is not certain if his license was renewed during those years; but it seems likely it was.

JONATHAN SAFFORD, who was licensed to keep a Halifax tavern in 1772 and 1773, is less well known. Apparently, a pioneer settler, Jonathan Safford, signed the 1770 petitions and is listed as head of a household in the 1771 census; yet his name does not appear in the index of the Halifax land records.

In June 1773, John Bolton, a Halifax selectman, sent a note to newly elected New York General Assemblyman Colonel Samuel Wells of Brattleboro, asking for reimbursement of the "nine Shillings and Six Pence Lawful money" paid to Jonathan Safford "for Nesesares the People of Halifax had when they Come to Lextion [election].[11] No further explanation is offered; however using alcohol as an incentive to gain a vote was and is not an uncommon practice. Because Safford was licensed that year, people may have read about the election from notices posted at his tavern and may have voted there as well.

A clue to Safford's location exists in a boundary description for land conveyed by Robert Pattison to Benjamin Barber in 1781. The parcel, located in the northwest corner of Lot 15, was bounded by Jonathan Safford on the south [HLR 1A: 521]. Jonathan Safford, perhaps the son of Jonathan Safford the tavern keeper, married Esther Worden, daughter of Elisha; their son Richmond was killed by lightning in 1802 at the age of fourteen. He is buried at the Worden Cemetery, and his is the only Safford marked grave in Halifax. There is no further record of the Jonathan Safford family in Halifax. Knowing his property location and his connection to the Worden family suggests that Safford may have been the proprietor of "Junction House." Jeremy Freeman Jr., in an article written for *Halifacts*,[12] says Bub Visser recalls that the large foursquare two-story homestead at the intersection of the Jacksonville Stage Road and Amidon Road was once known as "Junction House." He saw the fifteen-by-thirty-foot dance floor on the second level of the building some years before the house collapsed. Epaphroditus S. Worden (known as "Seymour") purchased this property in 1828. It is not clear who actually constructed the house. The building was opposite what became the

post office, owned and operated by Seymour's brother, Richmond Worden, and was on the stage route to Brattleboro. It would have been a convenient location for an early tavern. In 2002, an archeological dig at this site in search of tavern artifacts unearthed remnants of clay pipes and mochaware bowls used to serve flip.

The Orr and Safford licenses from 1772 and 1773 are unique for three reasons: the early dates, so few were granted, and they were granted[13] to Halifax individuals by the provincial government of New York under the authority of King George III, "In the Twelfe Year of the Reign of our Sovereign Lord George The Third by the Grace of God of Great Britain France and Ireland, King Defender of the Faith and so forth."[14] No additional tavern licenses were found for Halifax until 1781, after the Vermont General Assembly, in 1779, passed "An Act for licensing and regulating houses of public entertainment, or taverns; and for suppressing unlicensed houses."[15] The act required that "selectmen, constables and grand-jurymen, shall, some time in the month of March annually, nominate the person or persons whom they think fit and suitable to keep an house of public entertainment in the town for the ensuing year."[16] From the list of nominees, a judge and his assistant at the county court would select innkeepers and retailers of spirituous liquors annually. Under the newly constituted Halifax Vermont town government, neither of these two Yorker tavern keepers would have been deemed "suitable" by the selectman. Both had signed the petition of 1778 expressing their loyalty to New York, [⟳186] and both were named by Halifax constable William Hill as part of the group of Halifax rioters·who disrupted the court at Westminster in 1778.[17]

Neither man would have been granted a license. The penalties were severe for unlicensed sale of "strong beer, ale, cider, perry, [pear brandy] metheglin [mead wine, rum, or mixed drink, or any strong drink, whatsoever."[18] Clearly, Isaac Orr and Jonathan Safford were forced out of the tavern-keeping business because of their political loyalties.

VERMONTER TAVERN KEEPERS

During the post–Revolutionary War years, Halifax tavern life reflected the population boom. County court records show that licenses and renewals were

Windham County Courthouse, Newfane, VT, Proceedings of the County Court, 1793, p. 251.

granted to: Joseph Tucker; Thomas Scott; Amos Muzzy; Reuben Metcalf; Philemon Stacy; Philemon's widow Mary Fairbanks Stacy; Jonathan Rich; Joseph McClure; William Forbes; James Henry; Ebenezer Clark; Joseph Cobb; Calvin Ransom; Levi Hall; Henry Henderson; Isaac Martin; Abel Shepard; and Joseph Henry, among others. It is not surprising to find many of those licensed to dispense "ardent spirits" also were mill owners [↗ 276]. The correlation is that grinding grains and corn was step one in the distilling process. "As increasing populations boosted the volume of agricultural surpluses that could be grown yet not transported, breweries and distilleries emerged to convert the grain portion of the surplus into a 'cash crop' for local as well as more distant markets of thirsty consumers."[19]

Windham County Courthouse, Newfane, VT, Court of Common Pleas and General Sessions of the Peace, Cumberland County Courthouse, 1781–1792, vol. II, p. 52.

Worthy of notice is the tavern license granted to a Halifax woman in 1785. Mary Stacy, widow of Philemon, would not be allowed to vote in her lifetime; yet, the court licensed her to serve rum slings and apple brandy for at least three years after her husband died, until the probate court approved the auction of his properties.

COLONEL AMOS MUZZY – Probably the most vivid reference to a tavern in post–

MUZZY TAVERN   HHS

Revolutionary War Halifax appears in Hemenway's *Vermont Historical Gazetteer*. Apparently, it was the custom after militia musters to gather at the local store or tavern. On this particular occasion, Captain Gault was shot while leaving Hamilton and Muzzy's store[20] [↗ 171]. Captain Gault's shooting happened in May 1788. According to the Halifax town records, Amos

Muzzy "Trader" purchased from Benjamin Bemis of Spencer, Worcester County, Massachusetts, a tract of land in the northeast corner of Lot 20 in July 1788 [HLR 1A: 586].[21] Muzzy's first license was issued in November 1788. At the time of the Gault shooting, Muzzy was not licensed to keep a tavern, although he may have been in the process of setting up his tavern operation. This raises questions. Joseph Tucker and Thomas Scott, who were licensed through 1788, did not renew for 1789. The location of their tavern activities is not certain, but both lived at the Center. Scott had purchased a trading post and house near the common from Edward Harris in 1781. In 1791, he conveyed property to Muzzy.

Muzzy's tenure in Halifax was brief and dramatic. Born in Spencer, Worcester County, Massachusetts in 1762, he was son of John Muzzy II and Abigail Reed. He died in May 1831, at aged seventy, in Attica, New York, and his obituary calls him "A soldier of the revolution."[22] Muzzy's great-grandfather, Benjamin Muzzy, designed the "Buckman Tavern," which he had built as a dwelling for his son John and which was the first public house in Lexington, Massachusetts. John's granddaughter, Ruth Stone, and her husband, John Buckman, managed the tavern when it served as the rendezvous of the minutemen. It was there that Paul Revere came to give the alarm that the British were coming. Several members of the Muzzy family participated in the fighting and gave their lives at Lexington, including a cousin, Amos Muzzy, for whom there is a monument on the green at Lexington.

Amos Muzzy was the fourteenth of sixteen children. What brought him to Halifax in 1787 with his wife, Sarah Snow, their children, and his brother, Benjamin[23] is not known. He entered into partnership with Reuben Hamilton, a relative of Silas Hamilton, the Whitingham tavern keeper. Upon arrival, Amos Muzzy involved himself in the business of the town and the militia. He served as a constable, and in 1790, according to town records, "Major Amos Muzzy was Chosen lister" [HLR 1A: 175]. He appears on the freemen's list as *Col. Amos Muzzy*.[24]

On September 12, 1792, he mortgaged his Halifax and Whitingham properties to Timothy Williams of Boston, Massachusetts, for 300 pounds to be repaid with interest by January of 1797 [HLR 2: 212]. On September 21, 1792, Muzzy and Hamilton were delivered to the courthouse in Newfane by Benjamin Henry Esq., whereupon the sheriff took them into custody.[25] In 1794, Amos Muzzy petitioned the State of Vermont "for an act of insolvency." His petition, published in the Vermont State papers, describes his struggle with debt, imprisonment in the Newfane jail, loss of property, and work as "a Common Day Labourer to support his Wife and Six small Children" [↪ 509]. Muzzy blamed Reuben Hamilton for the tavern debt. Apparently, the "Colonel" had won over the town. Sixty Halifax residents supported him by signing the petition. His final Vermont tavern license was issued for the year 1795. Muzzy defaulted on his mortgage to Williams and disappeared from the Halifax scene.

However, the colorful "Colonel Muzzy reappeared about 150 miles west. Abner Livermore (1777–1857), a Waterville, New York, early resident and school teacher penned the following letter in 1851, recording his memories of local people and events from the 1790s through the early 1800s. The original document is in the collection of the Waterville Public Library.

It has already been mentioned that in May 1799, we had the first view of Sangerfield Huddle . . . of log cabins, some roofed with long cedar shingles but mostly covered with slabs. Major Benj. White had an unfinished frame house. . . . His nephew, Col. Amos Muzzy, had also an unfinished frame house, had raised a signpost and was a tavern keeper. A man of great pomposity, he had been a Lieut. Col. Commander of a regiment of militia in Vermont had been a country merchant and a broker merchant, too, as well as myself. He was the first tavern keeper in the place. He could make (so he said) a brandy sling or a rum sling a shade better than any other man. Likely it was even so. . . . Amos Muzzy was also the first postmaster in the town. With his pompous manner, he was not a bad sort of a man; almost every one he spoke of was his intimate personal friend. He was Supervisor [mayor] of the town. . . . There were not literally giants in those days but little great men and great little men. Many a good fellow worked for White in building his mills and on stormy days and leisure hours they told stories and sang songs and drank sling with Col. Muzzy.[26]

A street map of the Waterville village as it was in1805 shows the Colonel Muzzy Tavern and Post Office, built in 1796, located at an intersection of several roads, not at all unlike the layout of Halifax Center, Vermont.[27]

DEACON JOSEPH TUCKER arrived in Halifax after the Revolution and immediately became prominent in town affairs. He held a tavern license from 1781 through 1788. According to town records, landlord Joseph Tucker hosted most, if not all, of the early town meetings, starting in 1778 soon after the time he arrived from Townsend, Massachusetts. Tucker's brother, Reuben, had operated a tavern in Townsend, but because of his Loyalist sympathies, sold his property and moved his family to Nova Scotia. Another brother, Moses, was a patriot who served in the Revolution. Joseph Tucker and his wife, Abigail Emerson, left their politically divided family and settled in the politically divided town of Halifax, where he became an active player in setting up the town government. Tucker was a leader of the local minority Vermonter faction. He was chosen by the town to accompany William Hill to meet with Governor Chittenden and report on the "situation" in Halifax [↪ 159].

Deacon Tucker served as selectman in 1781 and 1784, lister in 1791, town moderator in 1782, and he represented Halifax in the Vermont Legislature in 1783. He owned a number of Halifax Center properties. The James Whitelaw "correct map of the State of Vermont," printed in 1796, using "Plans forwarded by the Selectmen . . . in pursuance of an act of the General Assembly," includes a symbol for the meeting house, four symbols for mill sites, and two names, Tucker and Thomas. Later maps show a Tucker tannery located on Sperry Brook, below the Jacksonville Stage Road. Historic houses associated with the Deacon Tucker family are the Christie's Tucker Road home, which dates back to Joseph, and the Crosby house on Jacksonville Stage Road, originally the George C. Tucker farm [↪ 373]. Deacon Joseph Tucker died in 1808 and is interred in the Center

Cemetery. Century Farmer, Henry Merton Scott, son of George and Sarah Tucker Scott of Halifax Center, was a fourth generation descendant of Deacon Joseph Tucker.

LIEUTENANT PHILEMON STACY moved to Halifax with his family from Grafton, Massachusetts, in 1778 or 1779 and purchased the mill complex located in Lot 5 on the North River. He set up a blacksmith shop, and operated a sawmill and a corn mill just below the Gorge. He purchased additional parcels of property in Lots 13 and 30, and at the time of his premature death, he owned what he called "a winter house" in the Center to be close to the new meeting house.

> **TO BE SOLD,**
> ONE half of the Sawmill and Gristmill, owned in common, with Lieut. Henry Henderson, situated about two miles south of the meeting house, in Halifax, on the county road.—The situation of the place, both for custom and convenience, needs no recommendation —Pay will be made easy, and a good title given.—For further particulars inquire of
> **MARY STACY,**
> Halifax, Sept. 1, 1794.

Greenfield Gazette, microfilm, PVMA Library, Deerfield, MA

Stacy, a loyal Vermonter, was licensed as a tavern keeper from 1781 until his death in 1784, during which time he was in partnership with Henry Henderson, who also was licensed to keep a tavern. As noted earlier, the widow Mary Fairbanks Stacy was issued a license in June of 1785 that was renewed until Stacy's properties were sold at auction in 1789 to help pay his debts. One of the buyers of Stacy's property was William Forbes, a Greenfield, Massachusetts merchant who moved to Halifax and from 1790 through 1796 held tavern-keeper's licenses. He was actively involved with the part of the former Stacy mill properties on the North River, located south of that portion owned and operated by Henry Henderson. In 1799, Forbes conveyed his property to James Henry, son of Benjamin Henry Sr. [HLR 2: 608]. James Henry's first license was issued in 1797, about the time he took over from William Forbes. His brother Robert shared in the business. Henry's licenses were renewed until 1800, after which there are no further recordings of tavern licenses until 1815. There are no Forbes or Henry descendants still active in town; however, the Fairbanks families of Halifax descend from Philemon Stacy through his son, John Richardson Stacy.

JOSEPH MCCLURE, (1744–1817) pioneer settler, came to Halifax from Brookfield, Massachusetts, in 1764 with his brother, Thomas, and set up one of the earliest mill operations in town. Thomas served as selectmen in 1778, during the first year of Vermont town government in Halifax. Joseph's settling lot of 100 acres, conveyed by Jonathan Ashley, was on the east side of Lot 42 [HLR 1A: 486]. He also owned a hundred acres on the west side of Lot 43, along the Branch Brook where the mill yard was located. His properties included the sites of the current Addis and Sommerfeld houses. McClure was licensed to keep a tavern from 1784 through 1787. Could his tavern building have been a log house or ell that later was incorporated into one of the existing hip-roofed homes standing on Collins Road? In 1823, James and Benjamin McClure of Pompey, New York, deeded their father's Lot 43 property to James Plumb Jr.,[28] who is credited with constructing the building since known as the Plumb House.

MAJOR REUBEN METCALF held licenses for five years, starting in 1790 through the Amos Muzzy period and may have worked with him. Metcalf was a lister in 1792 and appears in the 1790 Halifax census, but was of Brattleboro by the 1800 census.

EBENEZER CLARK, who was licensed starting in 1795, did his tavern keeping at the Clark homestead on Amidon Road. On the second floor of his large foursquare house was a very large ballroom, which served originally as a Cumberland County courtroom,[29] later as a place for religious revival meetings, and eventually became the Thomsonian medical practice [↵ 336] run by Clark's son, Dr. Ebenezer M. Clark. Ebenezer Sr. renewed his license for six years until 1800. There are no court license records from 1800 to 1815, but it seems likely he would have continued to operate his "place of publick entertainment" for a few more years. In 1808, he wrote to his daughter, "Our ballroom has turned into a place for preaching" [↵ 88].

OTHER POSSIBLE TAVERN SITES

Jonathan Rich owned property in Lots 50 and 58, and conveyed ownership to James Hatch. The Hatch homestead shown in old photos was massive [↵ 298]. Abel Shepard often served as town constable. He was the son of blacksmith and pioneer settler Jonas, who owned property at the mouth of Woodard Brook on the North River. His name also appears in various land records associated with Joseph Cobb and Calvin Ransom in Lot 29.

Calvin Ranſom,
IS now in readineſs to begin the MALTING BUSINESS, a few rods eaſt of the Meeting Houſe, in *Halifax,* (Ver.) where any commands in that line will be punctually attended to, and every favour gratefully acknowledged.
HALIFAX, Nov. 25, 1795.

Greenfield Gazette, microfilm, PVMA Library, Deerfield, MA

EARLY NINETEENTH CENTURY INNKEEPERS AND RETAILERS

A list was obtained from the Vermont Secretary of State's office that documented licenses granted "to innkeepers and retailers of spirituous liquor." These licenses, issued by the Windham County Court, cover a period from 1816 until the mid-1830s. It became the responsibility of the town selectmen to authorize licenses after this time; however, only two instances of this practice have been found in the Halifax land records. The selectmen authorized James L. Stark "to keep an Inn or victualizing House" for the year 1855 [HLR 3A: 445] and issued similar approval to Benjamin Eames [↵ 298] in 1861 [HLR 3A: 525] Recently found licensing records at the Windham County Courthouse in Newfane add to the list, but do not include ones issued from 1800 to 1815. The clerk of the court during those years did not enter licenses into the court records.

Thompson's 1824 *Gazetteer of the State of Vermont* notes the presence of four taverns in Halifax. The 1842 edition of the gazetteer reports Halifax has two stores and does not mention a tavern. A considerable number of Halifax town grand lists, which might identify stores and taverns, are missing; so the few licensing records that are available are of special value. A pattern emerged in the early nineteenth century. There tended to be three licenses to sell or serve "ardent spirits" in Halifax issued per year, and they were repeatedly issued to the same business owners: one in Halifax Center, one on Pennell Hill, and one in South Halifax. The lone exception was a few years' succession of tavern licenses for an establishment at Reid Hollow in north central Halifax on the Green River

SQUIRE JOSEPH HENRY – More than fifty years of store keeping makes Joseph Henry's business one of the longest in continuous operation in the history of the Town of Halifax. Joseph Henry (no relation to Benjamin)[30] was born in 1775 in Rutland, Worcester County, Massachusetts, the son of William and Susannah Phelps Henry. When he moved to Halifax about 1797, he was young, single, and able to devote all his time to managing the Chandlers & Henry Halifax store and tavern, his first residence in town. By 1806, when he married, he lived south of the tavern on property later known as the Charles Learnard place. Joseph Henry's first license was issued in 1798.

John Chandler, a merchant of Petersham, Massachusetts, who purchased the former Amos Muzzy and Reuben Hamilton properties from their Boston creditor, Timothy Williams, may have recruited Henry.[31] In 1791, at age twenty, John Chandler's son, Clark, had moved to Colrain to set up a branch of his father's chain of general stores.[32] Reference is made to the fact Chandler

Chandlers & Henry, HAVE, FOR THE UTILITY OF THE PUBLIC, OPENED IN *HALIFAX,* AT THE STORE FORMERLY OCCUPIED BY COL. *AMOS MUZZY,* *A most complete and elegant assortment of* ENGLISH, INDIA, HARD WARE & W. I.

Greenfield Gazette, microfilm, PVMA Library, Deerfield, MA

also had an interest in a store in Halifax for a few years "with Joseph Henry as partner and manager."[33] A biographical sketch of Major Clark Chandler states, "in addition to his large business in Colrain, he was interested in the firm of Chandlers & Henry in Halifax, Vt., – at the store formerly occupied by Col. Amos Muzzy."[34] The earliest Chandlers & Henry reference found in Halifax land records is from 1798 when they purchased one-and-a-quarter acres in Lot 28, between the roads "leading from the County Road running through said Town to Captain Farnsworth's . . . to the road leading to Wilmington" [HLR 2: 536]. This is the V-shaped parcel at the intersection of Old County and Jacksonville Stage Roads in Halifax Center. In 1799, Chandlers & Henry bought from John Crosier a piece of land in Lot 20 on which Amos Muzzy had once lived [HLR 2: 59].

The Chandler family's interest in the Halifax business was decidedly short term. In 1804, they sold a parcel to Henry Burdick[35] that appears to be the Chandler portion of the Chandlers & Henry tavern property. Burdick, who came to Halifax from Stonington, Connecticut, by way of Leyden, Massachusetts, around 1802, is said to have kept a farm and tavern in Halifax until his death in February 1807. In 1810, Burdick's widow, Lydia Crandall, married Constable Isaac Day, who had been a merchant in Keene, New Hampshire, before coming to Halifax. Isaac and Lydia continued the operation of Burdick's Tavern. Their property is difficult to pinpoint from the deed descriptions, but it was in close proximity to Joseph Henry's store. Because there are no records of licenses between 1800 and 1815, the first innkeeper's license on record for Isaac Day is

1816, and it was renewed until 1823. During those same years, Joseph Henry obtained retailer licenses. This suggests that the Days were operating the tavern, and living there; and at the same time, Henry was operating the store in the same building but resided a few doors away in his house. In 1824, Lydia and Isaac Day moved to Ithaca, New York.

By 1806, when Joseph married Elizabeth "Betsy" Orr, daughter of Isaac Sr., he may have already constructed the elegant house that still stands today. In 1818, Isaac Orr deeded his considerable property, on the east side of Stowe Mountain Road, to Joseph Henry, under the conditions that he be allowed to continue to live in his home during his natural life [HLR 6: 156]. Essentially, this perpetuated the agreement Orr had made with his sons, David and Isaac Jr., who predeceased him. Joseph's interests included not only his retail store and the tavern, but also his farm (he co-owned Merino sheep, which were raised by Isaac Orr Jr.) and his participation in Halifax town government. He served as selectman for many years, intermittently between 1807 and 1832, and represented Halifax in the legislature in 1849. His son and business partner, Rufus King Henry, who took over operation of the store, represented Halifax in the legislature from 1840-41 and served as town clerk from 1834 until his death in 1852 at age forty-five. The administrator's notices announced all the store goods would be sold to settle his estate. On May 10, 1852, Joseph Henry placed an advertisement offering the sale of all his Halifax property.

Real Estate for Sale.

The subscriber, being about to leave the place is desirous of selling all his Real Estate, consisting of one good Dwelling House, Barn, Carriage House, and other out buildings: the Store lately occupied by R. K. HENRY, deceased: and about 200 acres of improved land. It will be sold in lots to suit purchasers, on a liberal credit, and at a low price......The above Lands and Buildings are situated at the centre of the town of Halifax, and there is an excellent opening for any enterprising man to embark in the mercantile business.

I am also desirous of selling all my personal property, Household Furniture, &c., consisting of 3 good Horses, 3 Cows, 14 Sheep, 1 Yearling, 1 Buggy, 1 Double Wagon, Carts. Sleds, Plows, Farming Tools, 1 Good Cutter, and a large lot of Household Furniture.   JOSEPH HENRY.
Halifax, Vt., May 10th, 1852.   78

Semi-Weekly Eagle, Oct. 28, 1852. Courtesy Readex

The buyers were Elijah, Ira, Hannah, and Caroline Corse of Whitingham. In his deed to Elijah Corse, Joseph Henry refers to the "house built by me and in which I have lived many years," and the parcel "on which the shop stands and has been occupied for a long time by myself and my son" [HLR 10: 459 and HLR 11: 23]. This confirms that Squire Joseph Henry constructed the large white house on Stow Mountain Road, [⌂ 234] currently owned by David Brewster and Gregg Orifici, and that he did not build the Center store building. In 1855, the Corses reconveyed the Henry properties to Stephen Niles, who with the help of his son, Albert, kept the store and post office open to the public.

After the death of Rufus, leaving behind three of their sons buried at Center Cemetery, Joseph and Elizabeth Orr Henry moved to Warren, Pennsylvania, where their son Francis lived. Francis Henry operated a store in partnership with his cousin, Richard Sumner Orr, a grandson of Isaac. Rufus Henry's widow resided on the V-shaped parcel at the Center in a house later known as "The Harriman Cottage." The name "Mrs. Henry" appears at that location on the McClellan map in 1856, but she and her children moved to Warren, Pennsylvania and are found in the 1860 census records for that town. We know of no descendants of Squire Henry who reside in Halifax today; however, the elegant house he created continues to prosper and bears testimony to his fifty-four years as a successful Halifax merchant.

SAMUEL GOODNOW (1785–1845), son of Jesse Goodnow and Polly Bond of Sudbury, Massachusetts, was licensed as a retail merchant and innkeeper from 1816 until 1830. Jonas Bond, Polly's brother, owned Halifax Lot 1 in 1783. Bond subdivided the lot into three parcels: The eastern third was conveyed in 1794 by Justin Morgan to James Pennell, who conveyed a portion to Charles Burrington. In a deed from Charles Burrington to Samuel Goodnow dated 1816, the property is said to be bounded by James Pennell and located on the "highway leading from Whitingham to Colrain," minus one acre designated as a burial ground [HLR 6: 46]. The dot that marks the Goodnow/Burrington building on the Beers map rests right on the Vermont/Massachusetts border. The Goodnow tavern neighborhood would have included residents of Pennell Hill in Halifax and Christian Hill in Colrain. On today's maps, it is McMillan Road on the Halifax side and Ed Clark Road on the Colrain side of the boundary.

    Three of Samuel and Sally Reed Goodnow's eight children are buried in Pennell Hill Cemetery, the burial ground mentioned on the deed. Their sons Walter and Joseph moved to Whitingham, Vermont, and their son Jesse married Dianne Thompson and continued ownership of the tavern property. Samuel Goodnow's license for 1826 includes Henry Plumb as a partner, but Henry Plumb was licensed in Whitingham that year also. The following year, the Whitingham license was issued to Saxton Plumb & Co., and Samuel Goodnow is listed without a partner. Samuel's older brothers, William and Joseph, built the first store in "Center Village" Whitingham, in 1804, [36] so it is possible that Samuel learned merchandising by working with his brothers before setting up his own store in Halifax. Taking into account the missing license records, his business was in operation for about twenty years. Sadly, more is not known about the Samuel Goodnow tavern and store, nor is there a photograph of the building, which today is just a cellar hole.

BENJAMIN HENRY JR. (no relation to Squire Joseph) obtained a retailer's license from the county court in 1816 and remained on record in this capacity until 1824, when he was licensed as an innkeeper. Benjamin, son of Benjamin Henry Sr. , who built the house where the Sanders currently live, was born in Halifax in 1779. He married Betsey Fish, daughter of Nathan and Phoebe, the girl next door, and entered into a business partnership with her brother, DUDLEY FISH, whose wife was Patty Henry, Benjamin's sister. Fish & Henry enterprises were located on the property, which several decades later would be sold to James Landon Stark, who would build on the site of the house known today as Stark's Tavern. Two deeds to Fish & Henry from John Kirkley, one in Halifax and one in Colrain, document their ownership of the property on the state line. In the Halifax deeds, John Kirkley conveys to Benjamin Henry Jr. of Colrain and Dudley Fish of Halifax, the farm of Henry Henderson that he purchased in 1800. [37]

Fish & Henry engaged in a variety of business activities that catered to stagecoach and other travelers on the popular thoroughfare connecting Colrain and Halifax. In 1808, they purchased a potash works from Moses Jackson. Blacksmith shop tools and 400 "bu" (bushels) of "coals" (ash) are mentioned in a transaction in 1809. The census of 1810 lists Fish & Henry as a single household. Later deeds mention the store, the signpost, and the tavern stand. A number of Colrain transactions from 1807 through 1818 refer to Fish & Henry during the years Dudley was living, and after his death in 1814 from "Spotted Fever," refer to, "Benjamin Henry, of Halifax, trader."

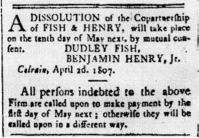

A DISSOLUTION of the Copartnerfhip of FISH & HENRY, will take place on the tenth day of May next, by mutual confent.   DUDLEY FISH,
BENJAMIN HENRY, Jr.
Colrain, April 2d. 1807.

All perfons indebted to the above Firm are called upon to make payment by the firft day of May next ; otherwife they will be called upon in a different way.

NOTICE.

ALL who are indebted to the Subfcribers will find their Notes & Accompts in a proper place for collection, if not prevented by payment previous to the tenth day of Oct. next—without further ceremony.   FISH & HENRY,
Halifax, Sept. 21, 1812.   85

Greenfield Gazette, April 3, 1807   *Franklin Herald,* Sept. 29, 1812. Courtesy Readex

Evidence of tavern activities is found in the announcement the probate court sessions will be held "at the dwelling House of Fish & Henry in said District on 20th of Feb. 7, 1812."[38] Court sessions of the period customarily were held in places that offered food, drink, and care of horses. Benjamin's son, Nathan Fish Henry, was said to have been born "in the Stage Tavern in Halifax"[39] about 1804. When Benjamin's license lapsed in 1824, his son Nathan had reached the age of maturity and was licensed as an innkeeper from 1825 through 1829. In 1830, after Nathan became an innkeeper in Greenfield, James L. Stark obtained his first license, which he renewed through 1833. By then, he had purchased the State Line Tavern property, which was contiguous with the Nathan Fish homestead where he was living.

During his latter years of ownership, Benjamin Jr., mortgaged to Martin Field part of Original Lot 6, and referred to "my old sign post" in describing the boundaries [HLR 7: 53]. It was required by law "That every person who shall keep an inn, or house of public entertainment, shall, within thirty days after his or her license, put up a proper sign, upon or near the front of his or her house with his or her name thereon, and keep up such sign during the time he or she shall keep such house of entertainment, under penalty of forfeiting and paying two dollars for every month's neglect."[40] Other mortgage deeds refer to the shop, horse shed, "goods room" old sign (tavern sign), and the "tavern house and tavern stand formerly owned by Benjamin Henry" [HLR 7: 247]. In Books 6 and 7 of the Halifax land records, several suits against Benjamin Henry Jr., Samuel Henry, and Simeon Fish were filed that seem to indicate they were forced to sell off their property or deed portions to various individuals, including the Starks. The Henrys apparently left Halifax during this period, as they are not listed in the 1830 census. More about Nathan Fish Henry is found in the *History of Greenfield, Massachusetts* from "Sketches of Former Citizens."[41]

Simeon Fish, who had assumed the role of his brother, Dudley, in the Fish & Henry partnership, continued to live in Halifax. He too, was forced to sell off his Lot 6 properties, including his father's farm, which he conveyed to James Landon Stark. A transaction, dated March 19, 1829, sums up the chain of ownership of the Stark Tavern land. Simeon Fish quitclaimed to Jedediah Stark

> [his] right and interest in all that part of Right No. 6 being called
> The Henderson Farm on which Nathan F. & Benjamin Henry
> now live—further reference to the deed of said Benjamin Henry
> and Dudley Fish. Also all my right & title to said Stark of 45 acres
> lying in Colrain. . . adjoining the said Town of Halifax which was
> once a part of the said Henderson Farm and now owned by the
> said Dudley Fish & the said Benjamin Henry. [HLR 7: 221]

It seems likely that James Landon Stark built the new tavern building after he bought the property in 1833 and a few years after the construction of Vermont Route 112. Emory Hebard, who lived in the Stark homestead for forty-five years and worked to analyze the numerous old foundations and cellar holes "is quite sure that the house now standing is not the 1792 house but was more probably built . . . at a later date."[42] The prominent architectural fan detail over the front door is typically found in buildings constructed in the 1830s [↗ 233].

JARED PIERCE, in 1819, was granted a retailer's license. Jared was the son of Polly Weeks and Allen Pierce, whose father's family had migrated to Halifax from Killingly, Connecticut, before 1774. Jared Pierce married Louisa Wilcox in 1815 and bought a tract of land in Original Lot 54 at the site of a sawmill in 1817 [HLR 6: 258]. In 1820, he purchased another parcel in this vicinity by a gristmill. His father passed along to Jared more property at this site during the same year [HLR 6: 307]. Jared Pierce maintained his license through 1822. In about 1824, he moved to Antwerp, Jefferson County, New York. Halifax land records show that John Reid purchased at least part of this property in 1824 [HLR 6: 455]. Reid's innkeeper licenses have not been found; however, references to Reid's Inn appear in various newspapers, and an 1849 business directory lists as a public house, "John Reid, Railroad House, Green River."[43] When Reid offered his place for sale in 1856, his advertisement said, "Farms and Mills for sale, consisting of a large, new and well-built Dwelling or Tavern house, calculated for public or private use; two barns and a full-suite of out-Buildings; also several second-hand Dwelling houses."[44] This tavern and inn was most recently the home of Tom O'Brien, located on the Green River Road. It is a large home with a dome ceiling "ballroom" on the second floor. It was also the site of two mills along the Green River, one of which was in operation until the 1930s. One of the dams that powered the sawmill between the bridges was washed out in heavy rains during the 1970s. Susan Rusten recalls that she and her brothers used to swim above this dam. The stone foundation, canal bed, and some of the water pipes from this mill still remain as monuments to its former stature. Later owners at Reid Hollow were Willard, Stockwell, Gates, and Warren [HLR 10: 163; 11: 387, 420].

The elaborate ceiling medallion in the public meeting room on the second story of the John Reid/Thomas O'Brien House bears witness to the wealth and ambition of the man who constructed it. Reid claimed in his for sale ad that Reid Hollow would become the "site of a village." The intricate plaster floral design shows its age; nevertheless, as one enters the room, the medallion draws the eye upward. Bryan Warren, a later owner, said his parents told him there were benches around the perimeter of the ballroom and a glass sounding bell, which hung from the medallion for acoustical effects. The flooring still springs. It is not certain when music last was heard from the closet-sized fiddler's nook adjacent to the ballroom.

The highly unusual ceiling in this house calls to mind the rare and beautiful curved ceilings found in two Pre-Revolutionary houses of Halifax built in the 1760's. The Deacon John Pennell and Benjamin Henry, Esq. Houses both have curved ceilings on the second floor. The rooms, now used as bedrooms, may have originally served for political gatherings and tavern activities. Similar ceiling exists in the Hall Tavern at Historic Deerfield as well as what was known as "Tory Hollow" tavern in Arlington, Vermont.

REID HOUSE DOMED CEILING
Photos C. Lancaster

BENJAMIN HENRY HOUSE

BENJAMIN HENRY HOUSE CURVED CEILING
Photos S. Sanders

PENNELL HOUSE   HHS

At a recent auction, someone found an invitation, dated 1857, announcing a "New Year's Ball" at Stockwell and Warren's Hall. Tickets were $1.75 "including Supper, admission to the hall and Horse keeping." The Beers atlas for 1869 refers to the "Reid Hollow Hotel," operated by Gilman Warren.[45] The Warren family operated the mills at this location for many years. During the height of their mill operation, they employed many men and used both the old inn and the house above it to house their workmen and their families. Mary Sumner lived in one of these homes when she was a child and her father was working at the sawmill.

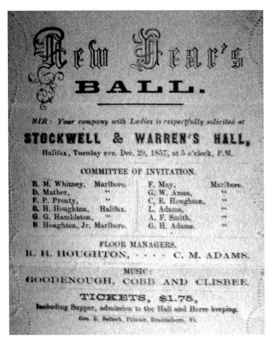

HHS

TAVERN TIDBITS

It is important to note here land ownership was not essential for a farmer or merchant. Lease arrangements were not uncommon, so land records are not necessarily indicative of where an inn was located.

JOHN PENNELL IV who was licensed for the year 1828, was the grandson of Deacon John Pennell and came from a tavern-keeping tradition. His great-grandfather, John Pennell, built the first tavern in Colrain, which his grandfather, Deacon John Pennell, had operated for many years prior to moving to Halifax. His father, John Pennell, was a farmer who died young, having been killed by a falling tree. According to descendant Elizabeth Lusk, John Pennell IV was unsuccessful at farming and tried tavern keeping, mostly in the Readsboro/Bennington area, after leaving Halifax. However, his 1827 account with Charles Thomson at the old Chandler Store in Colrain, lists multiple purchases of rum, wine, and brandy by the gallon, and his Windham County license for 1828 suggests he tried to set up a tavern operation in the Pennell Hill area. John's friend Austin Smith, after whom he named his son, paid for an innkeeper's license in 1826; however, no record exists for him after this year. Their inn keeping may have in some manner been connected. Smith's property was located in original Lot 28 at Halifax Center. The Deacon Pennell house was no longer in the family by 1828, but the spacious Burrington house, where John's mother Jane lived, poses a possibility.

ABEL SCOTT was licensed in 1829 and 1836. A Halifax tavern reference appears within the militia training records of the Fourth Company of the Third Vermont Regiment. The roll and return of the company was originally kept by Russell Bascom and is currently archived at the New England Historic Genealogical Society in Boston, Massachusetts. The record appears in the back of Bascom's journal. "Be it remembered that upon the 20 day of May 1829 William M Brown issued his orders to Sergeants Russell Bascom and William B Wheeler to warn the Company under his command to appear at Abel Scotts Inn in Halifax on the 11 day of June 1829 at nine of the clock. All for the purpose of inspection and Discipline."[46] How many years Abel Scott operated an inn is not known. He obtained licenses in 1829 and 1836. Ebenezer Pratt, who was Able Scott's son-in-law, was issued innkeeper licenses from 1832 through 1834; it is not known where the inn was located. Pratt owned property in Original Lots 61 and 62 on the border of Halifax and Marlboro; however, this does not seem an obvious place for an inn. Pratt married Able Scott's daughter, Cynthia, in 1829. It is likely that he obtained his licenses for a few years to run the tavern business for his father-in-law in Halifax Center. This theory is supported by the minutes from an 1832 town meeting that the meeting would adjourn for an hour to Col. Ebenezer Pratt's house.

STEPHEN GATES of Halifax Center obtained an innkeeper license in 1830. His son, Jesse Edson Gates is listed in the 1884 Beers business directory as operator of a mill at Reid Hollow, and it is likely that the Gates Inn was operating at the former Reid Tavern.

According to the late James Stone, his family owns a property on Reed Hill Road that is the site of an old tavern that he referred to as the "Hicks Tavern." The cellar hole is all that remains, and it is not clear when this business was in operation. Jim said that he had an old earthenware "grog bottle" which was found at this place and stamped with the year 1793. Several other people dug up these same bottles, which would seem to corroborate this as the site of a tavern. A Hicks family did own land in this area east of Hall Road and on the northeast side of Reed Hill Road.

STATE LINE TAVERN – Located on the old "province" line, between Colrain, Massachusetts, and Halifax, Vermont, the State Line Tavern, with rooms in both states, became the destination for eloping couples during the nineteenth century. Proprietors JAMES LANDON, "the old judge," and son, Jedediah Hyde Stark, Esq., justice of the peace, are said to have solemnized nearly four thousand marriages in a fifty-year period. The Starks were proud of their farm, apiary, orchards, and horses, and the grounds were beautifully landscaped. At various times the property was known as the State Line Tavern, Stage House, South Halifax Hotel, Temperance House, and Stark's Inn. Ultimately, it was widely known simply as " Jed Stark's Place."

Jed, "the marriage man," was a genial, mischievous, charming chap. A lifelong bachelor, he was known throughout Franklin County, Massachusetts, and Windham County, Vermont, as a man who would marry couples who came to him at any hour, day or night. There was a line drawn across the parlor floor, and depending on which side of the line the couple stood, they were pronounced man and wife in either Vermont or Massachusetts. After Jed's death in 1888, when the new survey showed the state line ran south of the ceremonial spot, many Massachusetts couples, it turned out, had been married in Vermont.

Now a private home, this handsome old building once boasted a fine spring dance floor above the carriage house. You could park your horse, climb the narrow stairs, and dance jigs and reels until well after midnight. In the summer, horses and buggies passed under a fragrant arch of cascading cinnamon roses on the road leading to the tavern. Equally romantic in winter, an invitation to take a moonlit sleigh ride to Jed Stark's was tantamount to a wedding proposal. Accommodations included overnight in the bridal chamber and in the morning, the traditional wedding breakfast.

THREE GENERATIONS OF HALIFAX STARKS

Previous Stark family biographies on file at the Halifax Historical Society include details and anecdotes well worth preserving; however, they also include some false assumptions that have been passed along as facts. Correcting details of the story does not diminish, in any way, the role of Jed, the amiable tavern keeper, justice of the peace, and practical joker, who enjoyed marrying couples in both Vermont and Massachusetts, depending on which side of the room the ceremony took place. Mainly, it is the stories of his father, James Landon Stark, and his grandfather, Jedediah Hyde Stark that suffer from embellishment. Two of the most commonly held misconceptions are:

> MYTH ONE: *Jedediah Hyde Stark moved to Halifax in 1793 and built the Stark Tavern.* The First Jedediah Stark settled on the County Road northwest of Halifax Center and never resided at the State Line property [↪ 312].
>
> MYTH TWO: *Jedediah Stark was related to General John Stark of Revolutionary fame.* The Halifax Starks were not even distant cousins of General John Stark.
>
> The Starks of Halifax descend from Aaron Stark, who settled in Groton, Connecticut, in the 1600s. General Stark of the "Molly Stark Trail" descends from Scotch–Irish immigrant parents who settled in New Hampshire in the 1700s. To date, genealogists have found no connections between these two families.

The Starks of Halifax came from Colchester, Connecticut, where Jedediah was born in 1764, son of Silas Stark and Jerusha Hyde. Jerusha's brother, Captain Jedediah Hyde, "was 1st lieut. in Capt. Coit's company at Bunker Hill and afterwards a captain in the regular line. He settled in Hyde Park, a new town which he named, and in which he was an original proprietor."[47] His son surveyed the lots to be given as rewards to the Green Mountain Boys in Two Heroes, Vermont. Jedediah Hyde Jr.'s log cabin in Grand Isle is a Vermont historic site, open to the public during the summer months[48] [↪ 49].

The first Jedediah Stark lived north of the Center, and his property included an apple orchard [↪ 386]. His brother, William, lived nearby on the Deer

Park Road, where he was a neighbor of the Arthur and James Crosier families. During his first forty years in Halifax, Jedediah (Diah) Stark was engaged in land speculation and the practice of law. In one deed, he purchased seventeen different parcels of land. It is challenging to trace Diah's own residence because the land records are so crowded with deeds where his name appears as mortgage broker. Census records, however, confirm he resided in Halifax Center and was a neighbor of Rev. Thomas Wood. His fascination with tracking the original proprietors' holdings prompted him to hire surveyor Samuel Shepardson to survey the center land (that hexagon in the center of town containing one acre per each original grant). The survey is in the Vermont Historical Society archives.

In 1826, James Landon Stark (1792–1868), known as Landon, was living on the former Stephen Hotchkiss farm in Whitneyville, bounded by James and Stephen Tucker, Captain Jonas Scott, and Luther Waters [HLR 7: 32–33]. It was James Landon Stark who acquired the properties that would become known as Stark's Tavern between 1828 and 1833 in a series of transactions involving the heavily mortgaged Henry and Fish parcels. James, his wife, Sybil Smith, and their seven young children moved into the former Nathan Fish home uphill from the tavern property. Probably it was after the 1831 construction of Route 112 that James added onto the original Fish & Henry Tavern building the new elegant structure known as Stark's Tavern. This addition is what survives today; the original tavern no longer exists. The census of 1830 shows Jedediah, his wife, Abigail Camp, and unmarried daughters, Caroline and Harriet, still living in Halifax Center. Within a few years, Jedediah was dead, his daughters were married, and his wife had moved to Bennington.

From 1830 to 1833, innkeeper licenses were issued to James L. Stark. Unlike his struggling predecessors, James L. Stark, the lawyer, was financially able to build and maintain the hotel, which may have the longest consistent operation in Halifax. In 1849, in keeping with the times, James L. Stark is referred to as proprietor of "Temperance House." His son, Jedediah Hyde Stark (1819–1888) became the legendary Halifax hotelkeeper.

James Landon Stark had an active political life, serving in the state legislature for eight years, as judge of probate for nine years, and justice of the peace for more than twenty years. He also served as South Halifax postmaster. In March 1863, James L. Stark conveyed to his son Jedediah Stark for $2,000, all of his property in Halifax and Colrain, including all livestock and tools, except for his gold watch, the horse named Jemmy and harness, and with specific detailed provisions regarding the care of himself and his wife during their lifetime [HLR 12: 439–441]. James and Sybil were to have a "separate table room with fire" of their choosing, a place to entertain, choice of produce from the garden, whatever might be necessary for their full comfort and convenience, and be given pocket money. Jed would manage the farm, and pay debts and taxes. There was no mention of tavern life in the three-page 1863 agreement. Sibyl died in 1865; Landon in 1868.

Ada Worden Wilcox, who was born at the State Line Tavern and lived there as a child wrote,

Jedediah operated the Estate as the State Line Tavern throughout his adult life while his younger brother Horace followed the trades of a carpenter and brick mason. With the help of Mrs. Mary E. Hall the housekeeper the place was well maintained and gained a wide and favorable reputation. The grounds were beautifully landscaped, the stage coach horses were shifted here, and it had quite a reputation as a mecca for eloping couples from Massachusetts and Vermont to come here to be married. Jed, Esq. was Justice of the Peace, and it is said that he married a lot of people.

[HHS Unpublished typescript. Ada Wilcox, 1980]

Maude Hebard, who also lived in the former Stark homestead, elaborates:

Following the ceremony the couples were always treated to a wedding breakfast. Prior to 1896, the state line ran through the house, but in the above year the line was re-surveyed and moved about a rod to the south so that now the dwelling is wholly in Vermont. During the Tavern days, Jed Stark had a line painted across the parlor floor and Massachusetts couples while exchanging vows stood on their side of the line and Vermont couples stood on their side. Jed Stark claimed Vermont as his legal residence while Horace Stark claimed Massachusetts as his. There is a story that a mother and a daughter while traveling that way put up for the night at the Tavern. The next morning as they were about to continue by stage coach, Jed in his most gracious manner, thanked them for stopping there and turning to the daughter said, "And as for the young lady—when you come this way next time, bring a fine young man and I will marry you." And she, smiling her prettiest, replied, "But if I don't bring that fine young man, then will you marry me?"

[HHS Unpublished typescript. Maude Hebard Undated.]

Halifax, VT.
There was quite a collection of people last Sun-Day at the place formerly known as Stark's hotel and South Halifax postoffice. By the death of Horace Stark it is supposed the pleasant and productive farm will have for an owner and occupier some one whose name is not Stark. Rev. Horace Fowler preached an excellent sermon, as he usually does on similar occasions. Remarks were made relative to its being rather an unusual occurrence, for not a relative was present and only one absent (direct), that of a niece, who was detained by illness of a near friend. Mr. Stark's age was 52 years, and was the last of a family of five sons and two daughters. *Gazette & Courier*, August 1, 1891.

Jed willed the property to his younger brother, Horace, whose ownership lasted only a few years. Horace, who died in July 1891, willed the property out of the family to Elsie Donelson, who lived on the Colrain part of their farm and who, over the years, had helped and cared for him during his frequent bouts of alcoholism. Horace bequeathed his tools to her son, Carl [HLR 16: 82–83]. The *Vermont Phoenix* reported in November 1891 the Colrain portion of the Stark home farm had sold at auction to Lewis Brigham of Colrain, Massachusetts, for $900 and the Halifax portion had sold to Charles Worden for $2,550 Jed and Horace are buried in the Stark family plot at the Niles Cemetery.

Various members of the Worden family farmed the property until selling to Emory Hebard in 1924. Jed Stark's old tavern no longer existed, but, the Wordens held dances on the old spring dance floor every two weeks and served a midnight meal. After Emory Hebard bought the Stark homestead, according to Ada Wilcox, he farmed some, specializing in registered Ayrshire cattle and representing the Town of Halifax in the state legislature. Emory and his family were there many years and made numerous structural changes to the buildings. The Stark Tavern was a classic example of the multipurpose tavern—inn, post office, and stage stop—that was typical during this era. Today it is a private home owned by Susan and Frank Maltese.

Photo C. Perna HHS

TEMPERANCE LECTURE THURSDAY "RAIN OR SHINE"

One of most heavily quoted rhymes celebrating tavern life is found in Samuel Clough's *New England Almanack* for the month of December 1702.

The days are short, the weather's cold,
By tavern fires, tales are told,
Some ask for dram when first come in,
Others with flip or bounce begin.

Less often quoted is the following rhyme criticizing tavern life for the month of January.

Ill husbands now in taverns sit,
And spend more money than they get,
Calling for drink and drinking greedy,
Tho' many of them poor and needy.

The influence of alcohol was both the boon and bane of Halifax society. The local economy thrived on the proceeds from the sales of distilled beverages, despite the fact that the problems resulting from over-imbibing were everywhere. In 1823, Rev. Thomas Wood sent to Zadock Thompson information about Halifax for inclusion in his gazetteer. He mentioned that at that time in Halifax, there were three taverns, two stores, and five distilleries.[49] The number of distilleries would indicate that the demand for alcoholic beverages was high during this period. From the late 1700s to early 1800s, rum was one of the chief items of trade and figured most prominently in the sales for local merchants.[50] "Before 1850, the State of Vermont led the nation in hop production."[51] Norris and Pat Johnson have found a shed believed to have been used for drying hops at the old Woodard place. Many local farmers maintained apple orchards for the production of hard apple cider. Apple brandy was one of the items produced in the mills at Reid Hollow. The importance of alcoholic beverages was emphasized in a report to the Vermont General Assembly in 1817 that stated "a sum of $1,000,000 was expended annually for strong drink."[52]

No other element seemed so capable of satisfying so many human needs. It contributed to the success of any festive occasion and

inspirited those in sorrow and distress. It gave courage to the
soldier, endurance to the traveller, foresight to the statesman, and
inspiration to the preacher. It sustained the sailor and plowman,
the trader and trapper. By it were lighted the fires of revelry and
devotion. Few doubted that it was a great boon to mankind. [53]

During the 1820s, the temperance movement began to gain footing.
Temperance societies were agitating in the state legislatures for prohibition laws.
These groups continued to grow and gain support so that the "evils of
intemperance" were regular topics in the newspapers and in the sermons of
various churches. In 1852, a prohibition law passed the Vermont State Legislature
and became law. The bill severely curtailed the manufacture and sale of alcohol
but did allow for its use "for medical, mechanical and chemical purposes."[54]
Despite the fact that this bill was enacted into law, it remained controversial. In a
referendum vote held that same year, Windham County voted 1,830 in favor of
prohibition and 2,275 against. [55] The social and economic impact of this law was
considerable. "Distilleries, long considered a necessary adjunct to a well-run farm,
were forced to close either as a result of diminished patronage or through the
action of a conscience-stricken owner."[56] How this played out in Halifax
specifically is not known; however, Halifax residents, to stop the sale of alcohol
within town limits, filed several petitions [↻ 515]. One of the petitions was from the
women of Halifax. At a time before women's suffrage, the signing of a petition
was, in effect, the only voting right available to female members of the
population. Despite these measures, it is clear from historical data that prohibition
did not stop everyone from distilling or imbibing alcoholic beverages. In 1864,
Walton's listed Russell Warren as manufacturer of cider brandy, and an 1865
edition lists Calvin Bucklin as distiller of cider brandy. [57]

From the *Greenfield Courier & Gazette*, Monday May 16, 1870 (Colrain)

> Our usually quiet village was startled Sun. aft. May 8th, by the
> report that a team from Halifax would soon pass through with 3
> dead young men. We felt great anxiety, and when the team passed,
> sure enough, there lay on the bottom of the wagon, three young
> men, dead drunk. It is reported that they went to a hotel at S.
> Halifax, and there loaded so heavily that before they had got into
> Massachusetts, they all fell from their wagon, and were found by a
> gentleman who procured a team and assistance & loaded them
> back in wagon and carried them home. [58]

Today there are few opportunities for townspeople to gather together for
fellowship except for clubs, organizations, and churches. There are no taverns or
stores in town where folks can exchange greetings and share stories about family
and other events of the day. Dances are a rarity. Sadly, the passing of these
institutions represents a thinning of the fabric that holds us together as a
community, and we think fondly of "the good ol' days."

~ Constance Lancaster and Susan Rusten

ENDNOTES

1. VSS, certain acts and precepts of the General Assembly, copied and delivered to the town of Halifax by Dr. Thomas Amsden, member of copying committee of the assembly, 1778, vol. 8, p. 309.

2. Bernice Barnett and B.B. Woods, *Roads in the Wilderness*, 2nd ed. (Halifax, VT: published by authors 1993). A delightful narrative that combines careful research with the adventures and discoveries while hiking.

3. Stone, vol. II 1, p. 98.

4. D. Michael Ryan, *Colonial Phrase to Modern Idiom: It's Pot Luck*, www.concordma.com/magazine/octnov99/toc.html

5. Child, p. 418. Also, the number of swarms of bees is noted in the Halifax grand list. At the auction of the property of Jed Stark, in 1888, five swarms of bees and eighteen empty hives sold for $13.

6. Stone, vol. 1. p. 98.

7. Ibid.

8. Detailed accounts of these incidents appear in section 1 of the *Official History of Guilford, Vermont 1678–1961*, published by the Town of Guilford and Broad Brook Grange No. 151 in 1961 and in Section II of this volume.

9. Hemenway, pp. 412–413.

10. *Cumberland County Court of Common Pleas and General Sessions of the Peace*, vol. 1, 1772–1773, Windham County Courthouse, Newfane, VT, p. 4.

11. Hall, p. 719.

12. Jeremy Freeman Jr., *Halifacts*, no. 24, untitled, undated.

13. A total of only thirteen tavern licenses were granted in 1772. Others were: Joseph Woods of Rockingham, John and Daniel Kathan of Fullam [now Dummerston, Vermont], John Serjeant and Josiah Arms of Brattleboro, Hezekiah Stowel and Samuel Nichols Esq. of Guilford, James Cumming of Putney, David Lindsay of Townsend, and Azchariah Gilson and Bildad Andros of Westminster.

14. *Cumberland County Court of Common Pleas and General Sessions of the Peace*, vol. 1, p. 1.

15. William Slade, Jr., *Vermont State Papers, Records and the Early Journals of the General Assembly* (Middlebury, VT: J.W. Copland, 1823) p. 370.

16. Ibid.

17. VSS, Manuscript Vermont State Papers, vol. 17, p. 9.

18. Ibid., p. 371.

19. Michael Sherman, Gene Sessions, and P. Jeffrey Potash, *Freedom and Unity: A History of Vermont* (Barre, VT: Vermont Historical Society, 2004) p. 136.

20. Hemenway, p. 420.

21. A petition on behalf of Amos Muzzy states he arrived in Halifax in 1887. Perhaps the date of the deed serves to formalize an arrangement with Bemis. The date of the Gault shooting is documented from his gravestone.

22. Sylvia Hasenkoph, *Patriot's Death Notices*, extracted from the three Catskill newspapers 1811–1849 (*Recorder, Messenger, Republican*) located at the Vedder Research Memorial Library, *Recorder*, May 24, 1832.

23. Benjamin Muzzy located in Jamaica, VT. He was the first of many Muzzy generations in that town.

24. D.A.R. records for Amos Muzzy accord him the rank of Massachusetts private. His pension was based on service as a private. Abner Livermore depicts Muzzy as "pompous of military titles." *Recollections of Abner Livermore, Waterville, NY, 1851*, http://www.midyork.org/Waterville/Archives/livermor.htm A letter in his pension file at National Archives [W16351] says, "In 1821 he was referred to as a colonel, but no explanation is given to said title." This title refers to service in the Vermont Militia after he came to Halifax. (hereinafter cited as Livermore.)

25. Windham County Courthouse, *Book of Common Pleas*, 1792–1795, p. 1.

26. Livermore.

27. Communications with Waterville, NY historians has not yielded a sketch or photograph of the tavern Muzzy built in that town. Such a document might provide clues to the construction of the Crosier Store.

28. McClure family Bible records and other information courtesy of Martha Ann Messinger are on file at HHS. Her information says James McClure, son of Joesph, "left his home in Halifax, Vermont at the age of 21 (in 1791) and walked to the Syracuse, New York area. James was one of 16 children and his father was a drummer in the American Revolution."

29. The Ebenezer Clark house was constructed by Dr. Peletiah Fitch, first judge of the Cumberland County Court.

30. Joseph Henry's paternal ancestors were William, father; Andrew, grandfather; and Malcolm, great-grandfather, who arrived in this country before the Scotch–Irish immigration of 1718, when Benjamin Henry's family arrived.

31. Timothy Williams, a merchant of Boston, conveyed to merchant John Chandler, of Petersham, Massachusetts, "a certain dwelling house, shop and barn and the land under and garden spot adjacent thereto, containing about half an acre more or less being part of the estate . . . of Amos Muzzy late of Halifax" and another piece of land containing about half an acre held by deed from Reuben Hamilton" [HLR 2: 609].

32. Patrie, p. 39-G.

33. Ibid., p. 127-H.

34. Charles McClellan, *Greenfield Gazette,* centennial edition, Greenfield, MA, 1892.

35. The details of the deed are worth repeating: "beginning at the Southeast corner of the garden formerly owned by Col. Amos Muzzy, thence running North on the west line of the road to the center of the second door from the south part of the house standing on said land thence West by a line drawn through the center of the shop chimney and through the building called the shop twenty two feet thence North to the south end of the shed thence twenty-two feet to the line of the road, East to the north end of the barn thence to the southwest corner of said garden thence East four rods to the first bounds containing 77 rods and a half of land" [HLR 2: 255].

36. Hemenway, p. 698.

37. "A certain tract of land in the Original lot number six in said Town of Halifax bounded beginning on the south line of said lot and on the west side of the highway that leads up the hill to Ebenezer Clarks thence northerly on the right side of said road till it comes to the land belonging to the estate of Mr. Nathan Fish deceased thence westerly on the south line of the last mentioned land till it comes to Art Woodard's land thence southerly on the east side of said Art Woodward's land to the North river thence down said river to the south line of said lot, thence easterly on the south line to the place of beginning" [HLR 4: 307–308].

38. District of Marlboro Probate Records, Brattleboro, VT, Book 11, p. 228.

39. Francis M. Thompson, *History of Greenfield: shire town of Franklin County, Massachusetts* (Greenfield, MA: Press of T. Morey & Son, 1904–1954) p. 862.

40. John C. Wriston Jr., *Vermont Inns & Taverns, Pre-Revolutionary to 1925* (Rutland, VT: Academy Books, 1991) pp. 15–16.

41. Thompson, *History of Greenfield,* vol. 2, p. 862. "1884, November—Nathan F. Henry, president of the Packard National Bank, died. Mr. Henry was born in the old stage tavern in Halifax, Vt., and kept hotel all his business life. In the old boating days, he kept the hotel at Cheapside, and in after years purchased the house at Montague City, now the residence of B. N. Farren, where he accumulated much money. He came to Greenfield and purchased a farm in the Meadows where he lived a few years, and then moved to Conway Street in this village. 'He was a careful, conservative man, possessing rare good judgment and sound common sense.' During the period before railroads replaced the river for transporting freight and passengers, there was a thriving port in the section of Greenfield called Cheapside. After leaving Halifax, Nathan F. Henry kept a riverside tavern there for several years until The Abercrombie brothers took over in about 1830 and it became the Abercrombie tavern. Nathan's cousin, Charles Henry, a native of Halifax, who also lived in Greenfield was "one of the stage drivers on the old line extending from Hartford to Hanover, N.H."

42. Claire Hebard Dill, *A State-Line Tavern and Farm,* HHS, unpublished manuscript, July 1985, p. 1.

43. HHS, Pat Johnson, single typed page of list from 1849 business directory.

44. *Semi-Weekly Eagle,* Brattleboro, VT, January 1856.

45. Beers Map.

46. R. Stanton Avery, Special Collections Dept., NEHGS [New England Historic Genealogical Society] Boston, MA.

47. Fred B. Perkins, *Perkins Family of Connecticut,* NEHGS Register, 1860, p. 117.

48. Hyde Log Cabin, Vermont State Historic Site, http://www.historicvermont.org (acessed June 3, 2003).

49. UVM, letter to Zadock Thompson from Rev. Thomas Wood.

50. David M. Ludlum, *Social Ferment in Vermont,* 1791–1850 (New York: AMS Press, 1966) p. 63.

51. Daniel H. Weiskotten, *Eidos Magazine* , summer 1978.

52. Ludlum, *Social Ferment,* p. 64.

53. John A. Krout, *The Origins of Prohibition,* (New York: Alfred A. Knopf, 1925) p. 38

54. Walter H. Crockett, *Vermont, The Green Mountain State,* vol. 3 (New York: Century History, 1921) p. 405.

55. Ibid., p. 408.

56. Ludlum, p. 72.

57. *Waltons',* S. M. Walton, Ed. (Montpelier, VT: Walton's Steam Press, 1864 & 1865).

58. Franklin County Publication Archive Index, http://fcpai.umassp.edu/archive.cfm?archive_article_ID=3061 (accessed April 5, 2004).

On the Hill and In the Hollow
Town Meeting Sites

In wilderness towns, settlers first attended to the basic survival needs of clearing land, planting crops, constructing dwellings, and setting up mills. Attention then turned to the community needs of government, religion, and public gathering places. Those who found their way to frontier Halifax were from established New England settlements, where the most prominent architectural feature of the town common was the meeting house, a symbol of political and religious authority. In September 1784, at the Center common, Halifax freemen first gathered to conduct town business at a meeting house instead of at a home or tavern. True to colonial tradition, this house served as a place for worship as well as a place to conduct town business. Since 1784, the people of Halifax have known seven meeting houses, four of which are still in public use. Only one was planned and constructed by the town; the others were built by church societies.

Halifax is not unique in its history of relocating meeting places from higher to lower ground. The neighboring towns of Marlboro and Colrain moved their early meeting house sites downhill. In 1825, Newfane, the shire town for Halifax, moved its entire original Newfane Hill settlement, which included the meeting house, county courthouse, jail, stores, academy, and private residences down to Fayetteville in the valley of the West River. This added another four miles to the Halifax constable's round-trip journey when escorting a debtor or horse thief to the jailhouse.

Nor was Halifax unique in controversy regarding meeting house locations. New Englanders often disagreed about where to locate schools, churches, and town halls. According to Colrain historian Lois Patrie, the factions of an ongoing meeting house dispute ended up in a final "pitched battle on the bloody ground" while tearing down the old house, after which a new house was amicably constructed at a new location.[1] Halifax town and church societies framed and completed their meeting houses with relatively little fanfare. Factions and discord developed half a century later when it was time to rebuild and refurbish the old buildings. No blood was shed. The battles were verbal, and the outcome was a peaceful progression from the hill to the hollow, with one notably painful exception. Unique in meeting house history is the degree of influence wielded by one individual, Judge James Stark, in this instance, whose personal vendetta deprived Halifax of a treasured historic public building, the original meeting house and landmark known as "The Old South."

HALIFAX BUILDS A TOWN MEETING HOUSE 1781–1784

What did such a monumental project require? Residents of four neighboring towns itemized the materials and manpower needed to frame and construct an early meeting house. Subscription papers dated "Halifax Dec'r ye 20th 1780" and "June ye 24th, 1781"[2] list donations of labor and materials to frame and cover a building for public worship "in the Senter Four mile Distant Part of Halifax, Whitingham, Wilmington, & Marlborough. . . . As may be a Convenient spot found."[3] Twenty men pledged their support.

June ye 24th, 1781.

*SILAS HAMILTON six days work & one Thousand Boards.
*LEVI HALL six days work & one Thousand Boards.
 JAMES ROBERTS two days work.
*JAMES GARDNER four days work.
*JONATHAN RICH six days work.
*JOHN HALL six days work.
*JOEL HALL six days work.
*ISRAEL GUILD six days work.
*JASPER HUNT four days work with a team & three Thousand
 Shingles.
 JAMES COSE four days work.
 RUFUS COSE four days work.
*LEVI ADAMS four days work.
*HAZAEL SHEPARD six days work & one Thousand Boards.
 BENJAMIN BARTON two days work.
 REPLEY MERRIL two days work.
*ISAAC LYMAN four days work.
*AMOS PEABODY ten days work.
 JOHN WOOD one gallon Rum.
 ZEBULON AMES Six days work.
 THOS. HUNT five days work.

* Halifax subscribers   *Green Leaves from Whitingham, Vermont* [3]

Each of the Halifax subscribers owned property in the northwest part of town. The proposed four-town meeting house was not built. However, about the same time, meeting house plans were emerging in the town of Halifax.

On April 16, 1781, the freemen introduced the subject of voting to build a house for the town [HLR 1A: 411]. Actual construction began after July 1782, and the first gavel pounded in the pulpit of the new house to call to order a meeting on September 7, 1784.

References to choice of site and funding for the new house appear sporadically in the records. At the June 4, 1781 meeting, it was voted to build a meeting house "by the Great [County] Road North of Joseph Tuckers [the southerly side of Lot 28] on the Rode North of the Brook in the Most Convenient place." The house was to be fifty-six feet long and forty-four feet wide "with Suitable Length of poasts to the Bigness of the house" [HLR 1A: 412].

This is the only physical description of the proposed meeting house found in town records, and there are no known photos or drawings of the actual building. However, the oldest surviving Vermont meeting house, built in 1787 by the Town of Rockingham, is the same vintage and identical in length and width;[4] therefore, photos of that house offer an idea of how the Halifax structure may have looked. A building committee of ten was appointed: "Hubbel Wells, Joseph McCluer, Captain John Sawtelle Esq., Benjamin Henry, Lieutenant William Shattuck, Captain James Pennell, Lieutenant James Clark, Ensign Nathaniel Swain, Lieutenant Philemon Stacy; and Sergant Jonathan Kellogg" [HLR 1A: 412].

> Voted that one Hundred pounds Lawfull Money be Raited on
> the poles and Rateable Estates of the Inhabitants of Hallifax
> that are not of a different principle in Matters of Religion from
> the Established religion of the Land which is Congregational or
> presbeterian for the purpose of providing Necessary Utensils for
> Building a meeting house in Said Town for publick Worship to be
> paid by the Respective inhabitants in any of the articles necessary
> for Said Building that the Town's Committee Can use for that
> purpose by the first Day of June Next. [HLR 1A: 413]

These plans changed. There is no account of necessary building materials (utensils or articles), construction activities, meetings, or votes. The next mention of the meeting house occurred more than a year later, in July 1782, and reveals a new site had been chosen near the intersection of the roads at Halifax Center (Lots 20, 21, 28, and 29). The July town meeting decision coincides with a deed from William McCrellis of Colrain, a nonresident landowner whose holdings in Halifax, at times, amounted to more than a thousand acres, including Lot 29.

On July 25, 1782 the town

> Voted to Raise a Tax of two pence on the acre of Non Residents
> Land in the Town of Hallifax agreeable to act of assembly.
>   Voted to apply the Whole of Said Tax to Building a Meeting
> House in Said Town on the South Side of Deacon Macrilles Lot
> No 29. Chose Mr. Samuel Woodard Collector to Collect said two
> penny Tax and pay the Same into the Town Treasury.
> Meeting Disolved — [HLR 1A: 421]

On July 26, 1782, William McCrellis conveyed by deed to the Halifax Society

> in Consideration of the Just sum of Eight pounds Lawful Money,
> four acres of land at the southwest corner of Lot 29, free of all
> Incumbrances. . . . During the Time the Sd Society or their Heirs
> Shall Meet on said Land for publick Worship or have a Meeting
> House Standing on the Sd Land and appropriate the Use of the
> same to the Congregational or presbiterian publick Worship.
> [HLR 2: 67]

On September 3, 1782, Edward Harris Esq., Philemon Stacy, and Thomas Clark
were chosen:

> to Settle With Deacon Mccrelis for his Cattle taken to pay the
> Towns Debt . . . Voted to pay Deacon McCrelis Eleven pounds
> twelve and Six Shillings Dn M. [HLR 1A: 421]

> Voted that a Tax of one penny on the pound be Laid on the poles
> and Rateable Estates of the Inhabitants of Hallifax on the debt in
> order to pay Deac'n McCrelis. [HLR 1A: 421]

The actual cost of the meeting house construction is never itemized in town
records. Moreover, there are no surviving written committee reports regarding
materials and donations of labor or design, nor do we know who was the master
builder in charge of the project. The next entry that mentions the issue was
recorded a year later, on September 2, 1783:

> Voted that all former Votes passed in Town Meeting Respecting
> Building a Meeting House in Hallifax and Taxes Voted for that
> purpose be hereby Nullified and Made Void. [HLR 1A: 424]

No new funding resolution was recorded at that meeting.

> On July 6, 1785, ten months after the meeting house first opened,
> it was Voted that the Meeting House in Hallifax Become the
> property of the Town at Large of all those that are of Similar
> Sentiments with those that Built the Same,

and a committee was appointed to devise some reasonable terms. The actual
committee report from Lt. Henry Henderson, Mr. Nicholas Dyke, and Dr.
Jeremiah Everett, is not included in the minutes from the reopened meeting on
August 29, 1785, but the meeting minutes begin:

> Voted that the former votes of this meeting held on the 6th day of
> July last respecting the meeting house be reconsidered Negative or
> Repeated.

> Voted to Relinquish all former Votes Respecting the Meeting
> House and Minister in Hallifax. [HLR 1A: 435]

With this perplexing decision, the subject of meeting house funding and
ownership disappears from the early Halifax town records. This change, perhaps,
was in response to laws enacted by the state regulating support of building
meeting houses and hiring ministers. From 1780 to 1807, variations of the Act
Supporting Ministers of the Gospel were in effect. In accordance with this law,
non-Congregationalists were required to register with the town clerk; therefore,

records exist stating who did not pay taxes to support the Halifax meeting house. Between 1785 and 1806, about 175 men are entered in the town records as Baptists, or "not in agreement with the majority" in religious sentiments and, therefore, not subject to the tax.[5] This was a sizeable portion of the town's taxable property holders [↝ 513]. By 1807, the Vermont Assembly ruled that support of all denominations must be financed by voluntary contributions, thus the Congregational minister's salary could no longer be raised through property taxes.

Several additional references to meeting house ownership exist in early land and probate records: Dr. Samuel Richardson conveyed land in Lot 28 to the society to enlarge the common [HLR 2: 515]. Joseph Tucker, in 1792, conveyed one acre at the corner of Lot 21 for a common to "the Inhabitants of the Town of Halifax that are of the Congregational and presbiterian [sic] Denomination of

Postcard courtesy C. Lancaster

Pewground, Rockingham, Vermont Meeting House. Built in the same time period as the Halifax meeting house. Both structures were fifty-six by forty-four feet. Pews were purchased and family members would sit together in their pew box and could share a foot warmer in the winter.

Christians" [HLR 2: 169]. John Crosier conveyed his right to "Pewground No. 15" to Joseph Henry and Jacob Hastings on April 17, 1797 [HLR 2: 441]. Philemon Stacy bequeathed to each of his five sons a choice of pew from among the dozen he owned.[6] A deed from Nathaniel Swain to Mr. Thomas Farnsworth in March 1788 conveys, "a pew or pew Ground in the New Society Meeting House in said Halifax the North Side of the West Door" [HLR 1A: 474]. Henry Henderson conveyed to Benjamin Henry Esq., for forty dollars, his right to "one half of a pew in the meetinghouse . . . designated by number one. . . . [A]lso one half of a pew . . . designated number twenty two in the Gallery of said House" [HLR 2A: 63]. These deeds offer clues regarding the structure of the house such as "West Door" and "Gallery." The existence of a gallery suggests that the building was at least a story and a half, perhaps two stories tall. The Rockingham Meeting House is forty-four feet tall, two stories, with a gallery, and three entrances.

The name of the town's original meeting place on the common at the Center was first recorded as "South Meeting House" in the minutes for September 1789, just five years after its completion [HLR 3: 173]. From 1782 until 1862, with the exception of a single meeting held in West Halifax in July 1852, every Halifax town business meeting took place at the Old South, a tenure of eighty years!

In the first order of business at the inaugural gathering of freemen held in the new meeting house on September 7, 1784, the voters approved the important proposal to divide the town into ten school districts. The first town moderator chosen to preside from the pulpit was Captain Caleb Owen. Other moderators during the initial decade of town meetings convened at the Old South were Thomas Taggart Esq., Dr. Jeremiah Everett, Lieutenant Joseph Tucker, Benjamin Henry Esq., and Nathan Fish Esq. The earliest preacher from the same pulpit was Rev. David Goodall, followed by Rev. Jesse Edson, and Rev. Thomas Hough Wood, who was a dominant presence in the town until his death in 1842.

For many decades, the Old South Meeting House common was where Halifax residents gathered for community events, and it was literally the heart of the town. The militia drilled there on muster days. Part of the yard was used as a burial ground, the first burial said to have been in 1785. Silhouettes of slate and marble gravestones were visible from the pews in the meeting house. By 1816, the view out the windows included the newly completed brick schoolhouse.

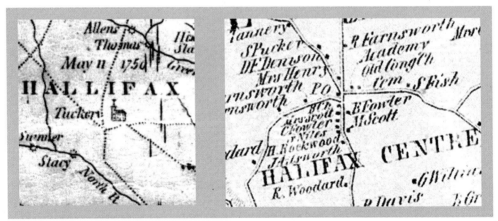

Detail Old Maps, West Chesterfield, NH

The earliest [Whitelaw 1796, left] and latest [McClellan 1856, right] maps showing the Old South Meeting House and its location at Halifax Center

MEETING HOUSES IN THE HOLLOW – MEETINGS ON THE HILL

In Halifax, the shift from the Center uphill to the Village downhill[7] was most dramatic in the decade from 1843 to 1853, during which time four new meeting houses were constructed.[8] Three were located in Plumb Hollow, now the village of West Halifax. The voters of Halifax, nevertheless, chose to continue meeting at "The Old South." They decided to invest in the upkeep of the original town meeting site, as shown by the minutes of 1844, wherein the town voted, "a Sum of money to repair South Meeting house, that a part may be used as a Town House." By 1854, there was no church society in residence at the Old South. Still, the house on the hill continued to serve the town for civil meetings, with occasional services conducted by a visiting clergyman.

Change was in the air, and some residents decided to test the degree of sentiment in favor of moving town government to "The Hollow." A vote taken at the March, 1852 town meeting:

Resolved that in the future Town & Freeman's meeting shall be holden at the Village of West Halifax, provided a suitable house be provided for holding said meeting without a town tax.
If the Town adopts the above resolution, the undersigned engage that a "Suitable House" shall be provided for holding said Meetings without a Town Tax. signed, Nicholas Clark, Sanford Plumb, Luther Bascom, W. J. Hitchcock, William Guild, Jonas Haven.[9]

The selectmen's warning for the next meeting was posted on June 21, 1852 at West Halifax, Old South, and at Green River.

Warning: Cong. Meeting House in W. H. July 5, 1 o'clock
Item: To See whether the town will accept of Said Meetinghouse to hold in future the town and freemen's meetings provided by the applicants without a town tax as a Suitable place for holding said meetings agreeable to a resolution on this subject passed at our last annual March meeting. Item: To see if the town will designate the place or places for notifying the town meetings.

At the town meeting held at West Halifax on July 5 1852, Jonas Scott was chosen moderator.

Voted. Not to accept the Congregational Meeting house to hold in future the Town and freemen's meetings.
Voted That in future our town Meeting Shall be warned by posting a notice at the following places viz—On the Congregational meetinghouse at West Halifax —at the North Meeting[10] house - At the South Meeting house also at South Halifax.

It would be another six years before the town would reconsider this issue and another eighty-five years before the voters would approve a similar motion.

RECYCLING A MEETING HOUSE

By 1854, the South Meeting House increasingly was referred to as "Old South," the church societies were gone, but the town was still holding six or more meetings a year at the building. Just up the road, in Whitneyville, a house built by the Baptists in 1801 and no longer in regular use was about to set an example and precedent for meeting house ownership and disposal. Given the somewhat convoluted nature of investment in a nineteenth-century meeting house, condition and old age were not necessarily sufficient grounds for abandoning or demolishing such a structure.

Even though the Town of Halifax had no proprietary interest in this meeting house as with the Old South, there are parallel legal issues and parallel recycling practices regarding treatment of an out-of-date community gathering place. Building materials, especially hand-hewn beams, glass windows, and blacksmith wrought iron had value and would be reused rather than burned, buried, or left to rot and rust. What happened to the old Whitneyville Baptist Church did not go unnoticed and set the stage for the fate of the Old South. An account of the

> **Journeymen Joiners**
> *WANTED.*
>
> THE subscriber wishes to hire Two Journeymen JOINERS during the summer, to be employed on the Meeting Houses in New Fane and Halifax.
>
> He wants, also, two or three active Lads, from 15 to 18 years of age as Apprentices to the Joiner's Business.
> STEPHEN OTIS, jun.
> *Marlboro*, *March 21, 1801.*
>
> *Federal Galaxy*, March 30, 1801.
> Brattleboro, VT. Courtesy Readex

deliberations by the church society, ruling by the state supreme court and eventual disposal and sale of the building appears in "Churches" in this volume. As noted in that article, Henry Clay Plumb bought the building at an auction held on January 18, 1854. Who was Henry Plumb, and what did he do with the wood from the old Baptist house that had been originally constructed by Stephen Otis?

Plumb was born in Halifax in 1831. His parents were William and Olive Eames Plumb, whose farm was on Reed Hill Road, south of the entrance to Hall Road. H. C. Plumb is generally acknowledged to have been the carpenter who, in 1853, constructed the new Baptist Meeting House, still in use in West Halifax today. In keeping with the notion of gathering up the fragments, that nothing be lost, young Mr. Plumb put his 1854 purchase of the Old Baptist Meeting House to good use. During the weeks following the auction, while the ground was still frozen, beams, boards, and other materials would be hauled, probably by oxen, from Whitneyville to West Halifax Village, where Henry had purchased from W. J. Hitchcock, a parcel of land located between Hitchcock's store on west Main Street and the center of the brook by the tannery bridge [HLR 11: 128].

On March 22, 1854, Plumb's brother-in-law, Russell Bascom, records in his diary that he "went to the hollow to work for H. C. Plumb."[11] From that date through June, nearly every diary entry refers to daily hours of work helping Henry build a new house. He mentions Thomas Minor, a neighbor and blacksmith, who also worked on the house, and John Fowler, the Pennell Hill stonecutter, did the "setting and underpinning" of the foundation stones. Henry Plumb was, at the time, twenty-three years old. The house he built in West Halifax, using, in part, materials from the old meeting house, may have been in anticipation of his wedding to Eliza Graves the following November. By 1860, he had sold the house to Albert F. Worden and moved to Amherst, Massachusetts. The house appears on the McClellan map as II. C. Plumb in 1856, on the Beers map as Geo. P. Worden, in 1869 and on the Halifax Historic Homes map of 2002, as Cook.

On August 5, 1861, at age thirty, Henry Clay Plumb enlisted as a sergeant in Company H, Twenty-first Infantry, Regiment Massachusetts. His regiment served on expedition with the Second Brigade under General Burnside. Henry died of disease on April 20, 1862, in New Berne, North Carolina.[12] The house he built, incorporating materials from the original Baptist Meeting House, stands on the corner of Main Street, facing the Community Club. In recent years, this historic and picturesque Halifax structure has been the residence of the late Lucille Cook. It is located within view of Henry Plumb's other building, today the West Halifax Bible Church.

H. C. PLUMB HOUSE   Photo Porter Thayer. Postcard HHS

During the time Russell Bascom was working on the Plumb house, he also served as town constable. His diary includes, in addition to his farm labors, carpentry work, notes on family matters and town politics, notes on his frequent travels in the company of lawyer Sanford Plumb and lawyer James Stark to various hearings and trials at court sessions in Newfane, Jacksonville, or Greenfield. Bascom, as town constable, was required to attend and assist at trials. After traveling to a trial in Greenfield, he usually would spend the night at Starks and have his horse shoed there. It is likely that James Stark was well aware of Bascom's carpentry work for H. C. Plumb, including integration of the meeting house materials. Within the year, similar questions arose regarding ownership and materials of the old Congregational Meeting House.

THE OLD JUDGE VERSUS THE OLD SOUTH

If the story of how James L. Stark maneuvered the town out of its first meeting house was ever widely known, it was also widely suppressed. Rev. Eastman did not even hint that there was a messy ongoing meeting house dispute, although he was working on his history of Halifax at the time. Without benefit of a file of loose papers and documents pertaining to the Halifax Congregational Meeting House, archived at the Vermont Historical Society, the fate of the Old South might not have surfaced. In the VHS pamphlets file are copies of circulars written by James L. Stark, printed for distribution to the residents of Halifax, dated March and August 1857. The first, entitled "Dea. William M'Crellis' Estate, who died in Batavia, N.Y. 1813" opens, "To the good citizens of Halifax, old and young, male and female:–That you may learn the facts in relation to the premises on which stand the old South meeting-House, and brick School House, I present you as follows:"[13] What follows, unfortunately, can best be characterized as a lengthy diatribe, which will not be repeated here. A copy is on file at the Halifax Historical Society. The text is replete with verbal assaults, innuendo, raving, ranting, and sprinkled with Latin and biblical quotations for dramatic emphasis. These printed booklets say more about the contentious character of the man who wrote them than they succeed in justifying his claim to ownership of the Old South Meeting House.

His main argument appears in the first two pages, where Stark states, because the Congregational Society has ceased to occupy the meeting house, ownership of the premises reverts to the heirs of Deacon McCrellis. He further states Charles Handy of Colrain, husband of Lovinia, daughter of Jane Ross, who was daughter of Deacon McCrellis, took possession of the Old South by posting a notice on the house:

> Notice is given that possession of this building is taken together
> with the premises on which it stands, as described in a deed
> executed by William M'Crelis dated July 26th 1782 & recorded, and
> all persons will be treated as trespassers who shall disturb the
> possession thereof,
> Halifax 2nd Feby 1855 Geo. B. Kellogg, Atty For Lovina Handy
> & Chas. Handy, husband of said Lovina. [HLR 11: 227]

Furthermore, according to Stark's circular, the Handys, on February 17, 1855, sold the meeting house as personal property, together with the stoves and pipe inside, underpinning stones, and door stones, to Jas. L. Stark and received payment, and on February 28, 1855, the Handys sold all their rights in the real estate to Jas. L. Stark. Charles Fowler, town clerk recorded both transactions on October 25, 1855 [HLR 11: 228].

Judge Stark's claim to ownership of the meeting house apparently was challenged or just plain ignored by local officials. Meeting minutes document that Town of Halifax meetings continued to be warned and held at the Old South Meeting House through 1861. Stark said, "The old south meeting-house on the hill in which town meetings have been holden, I have purchased and paid for."[14] He said also he offered it to various individuals at the Center, for what he paid for it, but he would give the meeting house to the citizens of West Halifax, "on the condition that they move the building from Halifax Center to West Halifax." His remarks indicate distain for Halifax Center residents, town officials, and businessmen, as well as the Center Baptist Church Society. As recently as 1850, according to town meeting minutes, Stark had been in conflict with the selectmen regarding his charges for services to the town. At some point, date not mentioned, he initiated a lawsuit against L. M. Woodward, town treasurer, who lived near the Center, demanding the key for opening and shutting the door to the Old South Meeting House. From all indications, James Landon Stark never offered to donate or to sell the Old South to the Town of Halifax, nor did he acknowledge the town's equity and interest in the building or its historic significance to the entire community.

After his public manifesto of 1857, Judge Stark rounded up several non-Halifax residents to assist him in filing a Vermont probate for the estate of Deacon McCrellis who died in 1813. On September 4, 1858, Leonard Brown of Whitingham was appointed administrator "upon the estate of William McCrillis late of Batavia, Genesee County in the State of New York, deceased giving bond of $500" with James L. Stark Surety.[15] In December 1858, Amos A. Brown and James Roberts of Whitingham appraised the estate, and in March 1859, Leonard Brown asked the court for license to sell the property at private sale after posting a notice in the local newspapers. No notice of this probate has been found in the *Vermont Phoenix*, which was the paper read by most Halifax residents at the time. The inventory, real and personal property, was listed by the appraisers:

4 acres of Land with an old meeting house standing thereon	$57.00
1 stove and a quantity of pipe[16]	9.00
	$66.00

Leonard Brown then sold the four-acre property, in 1859, quitclaiming the right and title to the churchyard or burying ground, to James Landon Stark for $65 [HLR 12: 195]. There is no mention of the prior sale of the same property by the Handys to Stark in 1855.

The case was considered by the district court at Fayetteville (Newfane), and as shown in this news report, the burden of rescuing the Old South fell on the shoulders of the Congregational Society at a time when the society was struggling to support preaching at the church in West Halifax.

In September 1862, and April 1863, the final mention of the meeting house appears in Halifax land records in deeds from James L. Stark to Charles Fowler and from Charles

HALIFAX, VT.—The Congregational Church in Halifax, Vt., and the land upon which it stands is in dispute. At the late term of the Court at Fayetteville, the following decision was rendered according to a report in the Vt. Phoenix:

Congregational Church of Halifax, vs. James L. Stark et al.—Judgment for defendants reversed and case remanded for a new trial. A condition in a deed to a religious society, in these words, to hold the land "During the time the said society shall meet on said land for public worship, or have a meeting house standing on said land for public worship, and appropriate the use of the same to the congregational public worship," contains two separate things to be done by the society, the fulfillment of either of which will save the forfeiture; and there was error in the County Court treating the condition as one indivisible obligation. And though it appears in this case that the society no longer "meets on said land for public worship," yet they have a right to show if they can, that they have a meeting house standing on said land and appropriate the use of the same to the congregational public worship." And proof that another society, not legal successors to the grantee, by permission of the grantees, occupying the meeting house on said land and maintain therein congregational public worship, will save the forfeiture. If such proof be not made, the land will revert to the heirs of the grantor, but the stoves and pipe in the meeting house are personal property, and will not pass to the heirs of the grantor as part of the reversion.

Gazette & Courier, March 6, 1861, Greenfield, MA.

Fowler to School District No. 6. Stark sold the property to Fowler for $75, and Fowler sold to the school district for $63. Both deeds "Reserve the right of Stark and Dutton to take away the old meeting house on said land as per contract" [HLR 12: 444, 452]. The property descriptions provide enough detail regarding the former meeting house sheds and the line of the cemetery wall and rebuilt wall to pinpoint the location of the Old South.

These stone steps, probably from the Old South Meeting House, are embedded in wall at the Center Cemetery entrance. The horse sheds for the meeting house were moved to the Center store circa 1855. More stonewalls were added to enlarge the churchyard along Stage Road. Thus all burials on the east side of the cemetery date from the mid-1800s.

Photo C. Lancaster

Able Dutton set up a sawmill, mill yard, and built a house[17] across the road from the Stark Tavern [HLR 12: 439]. Dutton could have hauled the pieces and parts of the meeting house down Stowe Mountain Road to Stark's land or to his mill. It seems likely that some or all of the materials were incorporated into buildings on Stark property. The combination carriage house and ballroom, constructed west of the main house on the tavern property, is approximately forty-four by fifty-six feet. The dismantling of the Old South took place after the final deed agreements of 1863 and before publication of the Beers map in 1869. Judge James Stark died on March 14, 1868, at age seventy-five.

MEETING SITES AFTER THE OLD SOUTH

Possibly in response to Stark's claim to the meeting house, at the March 1858 town meeting, a vote was taken to see if the town would hold future meetings in West Halifax. Results were "nays 116, yeas 101." Perhaps the closeness of this vote prompted a warning prepared at the August 1858 meeting for a special meeting to be held in September at the

> Old meetinghouse To see if the Town will vote to hold their
> Town freeman's meetings hereinafter in the Village of West
> Halifax and if so to see what course the town will take to
> secure a suitable place to hold said meetings in said village.[18]

At the September 1858 special meeting, the proposal received 102 nays and 130 yeas. The last meeting held at the Old South was in September 1861. From 1862 through March 1865, town meetings were warned for the Baptist Meeting House in Halifax Center. The meeting of September 5, 1865, was held at the high school room at Halifax Center, which is where it continued for many years. The words on the warnings were to meet at the "Town Hall at Halifax Center," or in the

"Center Hall over the School House," or at the Brick School House, and after school was no longer held in the building, it was referred to as the "Town House."

In 1884, another vote was taken to hold the meeting in West Halifax and again it did not pass. In 1939, at the Community Hall, it was voted (yeas 40, nos 6) to hold the annual March town meeting at West Halifax Community Hall every year. Norris Johnson, editor of *Halifacts* (no. 12, December 1978) summarized the final progression from hill to hollow.

> [Classes in] the Brick School house ended after 1909 but it served for town meetings continuously down to 1930 and also in 1932, 1934 and 1936 and 1938. During the 1930's the Town meetings alternated between the Town House in the Center and West Halifax. The meetings in 1931 and 1933 were held in the old schoolhouse (later firehouse) in West Halifax. The meetings in 1935, 1937 and 1939 were held in the Community hall which had been given to the Community club by the Universalist Society in 1935. The Community hall continued to be used for town meetings down to 1961 when the meetings moved to the new schoolhouse in West Halifax.

Since 1961, town meetings have been held at this West Halifax site.

POSTSCRIPT

It is not clear whether Judge Stark had any legal right to the meeting house built by the town, based on the original deed for the land. The Congregational Society was struggling to survive and was not in a position to test its ownership rights in the building. The final stages of J. L. Stark's takeover of the Old South played out against the shadows of events of the Civil War. Halifax town officials were preoccupied with funding soldiers' pay, and, in fact, borrowed $4,000 to be able to cover the needed $300 per soldier. Residents were preoccupied with news of the war and awaiting news of their sons and husbands. Meanwhile, James L. Stark obdurately sent his own sons, Jedediah and Horace, together with Able Dutton to dismantle and remove the building that, just a few years earlier, had played a prominent role in a patriotic day for the people of Halifax.

On Independence Day 1861, more than a hundred members of the Light Guard led the procession of residents to the Old South Meeting House, where they heard "The Star Spangled Banner" sung by the choir, speeches by the clergy, followed by dinner and toasts. "The Light Guards then went through with their drill in a soldier-like and military manner."[19] The news reporter commented that it seemed certain that "one good company of able and patriotic men can be furnished from this town"[20] should the government need them. More than a hundred were needed and served, and those who were fortunate to return home, discovered vacant ground where the meeting house once stood. Judge Stark had prevailed in his personal civil war.   ©2008 *Constance Lancaster*

Courtesy Saxtons River Historical Society
ROCKINGHAM, VERMONT MEETING HOUSE
How the Old South Meeting House may have looked.

ENDNOTES
1. Patrie, p. 93-H.
2. Clark Jillson, *Green Leaves from Whitingham, Vermont: A history of the town* (Worcester, MA: Printed at private press of the authors, 1894) p. 132.
3. Ibid., pp. 132–133.
4. Rockingham Meeting House, USDI/ National Register of Historic Places Registration Form, p. 4.
5. The detailed complete list compiled by Alden M. Rollins, CGRS, can be found in *Vermont Religious Certificates* (Rockport, ME: Picton Press , 2003) pp.144–152. See Appendix for list by names only.
6. District of Marlboro Probate Records, Book 1, pp. 35, 36 and 39; HHS, the last will and testament of Philemon Stacy; Stacy family file.
7. A provocative study of the uphill/downhill cultural concept can be found in Paul M. Searls, *Two Vermonts, Geography and Identity, 1865–1910* (Durham, NH: University of New Hampshire Press, 2006).
8. These were the Universalist Chapel in 1843, now the Historical Society building; the Congregational Church, in 1844, now the Community Club; and the West Halifax Baptist Church in 1853. The other Baptist Church, now the Union Society, was built at the Center, also in 1853.
9. HTC, Book of Town Meeting Records, untitled and unpaginated.
10. Little is known about the North Meeting House. It was located along the Green River at Reid Hollow, probably, at the former Tom O'Brien House. References to the Reid Inn, Gates Tavern, dances, social activities, and lectures suggest use of in the large second-floor meeting room. In recent years, the building on this site has been a private home.
11. Ibid.
12. HHS, Catherine Nims Swett, Susan Nims Scott, Nancy Nims Mullins, *A Nims Family Genealogy Project*, spiral-bound monograph, March 2004, p. 92.
13. VHS, James L. Stark, *Dea. William M'Crellis' Estate*, South Halifax, March 1857, p. 1.
14. Ibid., *Letter to Mr. William Mowry*,. p. 2.
15. District of Marlboro Probate Court, Brattleboro, VT, Book 21, p. 612.
16. Ibid., p. 651.
17. Ada Worden Wilcox referred to this house in her taped interview. Her mother's parents, Elihu and Mary Pratt lived there, and because of frequent flooding, the house was drawn across the road to the main property. She used it as a playhouse as a child. HHS, *Audio Autobiography Vol. 15. May 7, 1982.*
18. HTC, Book of Town Meeting Records.
19. *Phoenix*, July 18, 1861.
20. Ibid.

"No town perhaps has been more famous for rum selling and rum drinking in by-gone days, but for the last 30 years no merchant, or inn-keeper has sold alcohol as a beverage in town." [Written circa 1880 by Rev. Hubbard Eastman]   Hemenway, p. 408.

On May 7, 1952, Clara Crosier Barnard and Elaine Fairbanks interviewed Ada Worden Wilcox who lived at the Stark tavern during her childhood. Her parents, Laura Pratt and Charles Worden held dances there every two weeks. Ada recalls she helped serve the midnight supper to the guests. All the foods were homemade, baked beans, home-cured ham, pie and cake. When asked if she recalled the brick schoolhouse at the Center, she replied, "That's what my fireplace is made out of—those bricks. Lincoln Haynes brought them to me from Wilmington. Did she ever attend town meetings at that brick building? "I didn't go to Town Meeting. I wan't old enough to go——just my father and my oldest brother." Do you remember what they would bring home from the meetings? "I remember what they used to go with—a jug of hard cider. They used to have long sessions—my father and brother stayed the better part of the day. The folks all had a good time. . . each one of them took a jug of hard cider. I've got my father's jug downstairs now.   HHS, *Audio Autobiography, Vol. 16*

This brick [school] building [at the Center] was noted for the scene of town meetings and elections for many years. There are amusing stories told about those town meetings. Here is one of them. One year the votes were continually a tie, and the meeting was held all night. The voters becoming hungry, bought out the village store, and supplies brought in from West Halifax likewise vanished. At last overcome by fatigue and excitement, nature came to the rescue, and as sleep descended, those awake and able, quietly lifted the slumberers over the cemetery wall, and laid them down. Morning came. Inertia wore off. One of the villagers, surprised to see heads popping up here there in the cemetery, exclaimed, "must be it's the "Resurrection Morning."   HHS, *History of Halifax Vermont*, Maude Hebard, 1961, p. 8.

1909 Universalist Church   Porter Thayer HHS

1935 Steeple removed   HHS

SECTION FOUR
COMMUNITY LIFE

Photo, Chester H. Liebs, Vermont Division of Historic Sites

COMMUNITY HALL

THE BAPTIST
CHURCHES
Both Built
in 1853.

HALIFAX CENTER
Established by Elder Samuel Fish
and his followers. Currently the
Union Society at Halifax Center.

WEST HALIFAX
Established by Amos Tucker and
committee. Currently the West
Halifax Bible Church.

Photos, Chester H. Liebs, Vermont Division of Historic Sites

CHURCHES

In Halifax, as it was in early America, the banner of the Christian church either led the way, or followed closely behind the first settlers. Freedom to worship God independently and the furtherance of the spread of the Christian Gospel was forefront with the devout, God-fearing, early settlers, who laid the foundation of the young and vibrant nation. For many settlers, their precious Bibles and songbooks were among their most prized possessions as they traveled the dark wooded pathways, some perhaps only game trails or Indian passageways, and boated the sparkling swift streams leading to their new horizons. One must consider the mixed emotions of these brave souls, some leaving family behind forever and entering these forested hills of the disputed territory of Vermont in search of a new life and planting their roots into this rocky land. These settlers represented a cross section of the various Christian faiths, which sprang up in the receptive soil of the new world, shedding the bondage cords of the repressive British Anglican Church, the official state church of Britain.[1]

The timing of the earliest settlement of Halifax in the 1760s was on the heels of one of the greatest Christian "revivals" in history. This was the "Great Awakening," which began in the conservative middle colonies but quickly spread to our immediate south in Northampton, Massachusetts, and the northern Connecticut regions. Inspired by the preaching of such luminaries as George Whitefield and Jonathan Edwards, this movement spread throughout the settled lands of colonial America during the 1740s and 50s.[2] The effects felt on the early Halifax settlers isn't fully known. However, by the haste with which the settlers established their religious underpinnings, it can be assumed that this was a very important part of most of their lives.

The church buildings were more than mere "religious" meeting places. Through the faithful congregants, they also served as the center of social life, and even the social-service agency of the community. Most congregations took seriously Biblical references as to the care of "widows and orphans" (James 1:27). However, those that refused to work were given short shrift because of the biblical warning "if they don't work they should not eat" (II Thessalonians 3:10).

"After homes had been built, churches erected, civil governments set up, and means of livelihood secured, education was one of the earliest concerns of the colonists."[3] The church was the driving force of this initiative, as the need for people to be able to read their Bibles, and to train civil servants was in the tradition of early Christian reformers such as Calvin and Luther. It required education. One of the major tenets of the Mayflower Compact of 1620 was to create schools "so that their children would be taught to read and write."[4] The churches of Halifax were no exception but were an integral part of the community. An example of the great store that the settlers placed in their Christian foundations was stated in the following entry from the early town fathers and signed by the ruling committee at one of the earliest town meetings.[5]

A Petition of the People of *Halifax*.

WE the Inhabitants of the District of *Halifax*.   To all charitable and well disposed Christians of every Denomination, send *Greeting*.

Beloved, wishing Grace, Mercy and Peace, from God our Father, and our Lord Jesus Christ, may be multiplied unto you, and abound more and more. ———

We beg Leave to lay before you our Condition in this new, and as yet uncultivated Country : Our Complaints are not for want of Bread, but for want of Food for our immortal Souls.   We hope you may never experience what we have done some Years past ; no Meeting or Preaching upon the Lord's Day ; our Children growing up without Instruction ; Religion sinking, and Vice and Immoarlity abounding.   A Consideration which must affect every sincere Heart to hear of, and more to feel and see the dreadful Effects !   And now the Lord has been pleased to afford us the Means, we find ourselves unable to communicate that Support to our Minister, which we look upon to be our Duty, and his Due.

Our Petition therefore is, That you would take our Case into your charitable Consideration, and grant us such Assistance to build a Meeting House, and support the Gospel amongst us, as you would be willing to receive from us, were you in our Condition. . And we have appointed the Rev. Mr. WILLIAM EWING, to wait upon you with this our Request, and to receive from you such Assistance as you are pleased to favour us with ; and may He who has the Hearts of all Men in his Hands, enlarge your Possessions, and reward you a thousand Fold in this World : And at last may you shine as the Sun and as the Stars for ever and ever.   AMEN.

N. B. Halifax is one of the Towns granted by *New-Hampshire*, and now claimed by *New York* ; it joins *Colrain*, of the *Massachusetts*.

| Signed by us at a legal Town-Meeting, *November* 11th. 1773. | JOHN BOLTON, JOHN THOMAS, BENJ. LYMAN, | Committee for the District of *Halifax*. |

We do hereby Certify, all whom it may concern, That the Petition from the District of *Halifax*, in the Hands of the Rev. Mr. WILLIAM EWING, is sent out at the Desire of the Inhabitants in Town-Meeting assembled, and *John Bolton*, Esq; and Lieut. *John Thomas*, with Mr. *Benjamin Lyman*, were by the Town appointed to sign said Petition in their Behalf.   As Witness our Hands at *Halifax*, November 11. 1773.

NATHAN WILLIAMS, Moderator.

SAMUEL WOODARD, District Clerk.

EDWARD HARRIS, Society-Clerk.

American Imprint Series #42449 microform. Used with permission, Readex, Chester, VT. Courtesy C. Lancaster

BAPTISTS

In the history of Halifax, the Baptist churches have been the most prominent. It seems that the first ministers to emerge and preach to the Halifax settlers were Baptists. Elder William Ewens [Ewing] (1773) made an honest effort to establish a Baptist Church in town; however he was never officially settled as the minister.

WHO WAS REV. WILLIAM EWING?

This colorfully worded broadside called "Petition of the People of Halifax" from a town meeting held on November 11, 1773, implores "Christians of every Denomination" to grant "charitable Consideration. . . . and Assistance to build a Meeting House" and settle a minister in what is as an uncultivated, spiritual wasteland. Names of six town and church officers plus the Rev. Mr. Ewing, whose denomination is not stated, appear on the document. Rev. William Ewing, a former British soldier, moved from Wilmington, Pennsylvania, to Sturbridge, Massachusetts, in 1768, where he served as a Baptist minister and later preached regularly in Shutesbury. He is said to have "traveled widely in Massachusetts,[6]" It seems likely he distributed copies of the 1773 broadside and accepted donations for the earliest Halifax town meeting house that was never finished.

In a handwritten history of the Halifax Baptist Church archived at University of Vermont, Benjamin Wilcox states, "Rev. Ewing was probably the first minister of any denomination that preached in this town. They raised a meeting house for him. He stood in the place for a door . . . and made a prayer. The meeting house stood a few rods or feet from the center of the town. Elder Ewins held a number of meetings in the body of the frame, which was in the woods. But they [the town] failed to settle him, and the frame rolled down without any more's being done to it."[7]

This unfinished meeting house was near the old Scott Cemetery in the woods northeast of the intersection of County and Deer Park Roads. Larry Crosier recalls an enormous pine with a red-blaze that marked the geographic center of Halifax. The tree was clearly visible from the cemetery. Rev. Eastman called Elder William Ewing the first minister who preached in the town but failed to connect him to the Baptist Meeting House" frame in the woods. Records document that the Town of Halifax proposal to build a Congregational Meeting House did not occur until the fall of 1781, with a plan to start building in June of 1782. Eastman observed:

> The geographical centre of the town is three-fourths of a mile
> north of what is now known as the Centre. The frame of a
> meeting house was erected within a few rods of the geographical
> centre previous to 1780. But a few enterprising citizens established
> the business of the town at the place now called the Centre, so
> that the original frame of a meeting house was abandoned, and the
> present Congregational meeting house at the business centre was
> erected in 1782, but was not completed till several years
> afterwards, though it was occupied as a place of worship.[8]

Bits and pieces of Elder Ewing's story suggest that he chose Halifax and was welcomed by the town's leaders in 1773. The rapidly growing and changing population of Halifax, as constituted in 1778, did not agree with the choice made by earlier town officers. The "enterprising citizens" encouraged, perhaps, by Joseph Tucker, who hosted Halifax town meetings at his tavern and who favored the Congregational denomination, chose Rev. David Goodall in 1781 to serve as the town's first appointed minister.

In March 1778, Rev. Ewing, who had devoted about five years to preaching in town, sold his share of the minister's lot, which "a Committee of the Town of Hallifax in ye State of Vermont Now so Called"[9] had conveyed to him. The property contained one hundred acres on the southerly side of Lot 28, and Joseph Tucker of New Ipswich, New Hampshire was the grantee [HLR 1A: 22].[10] In 1782, this property was quitclaimed to Tucker by Rev. David Goodall. [HLR 1A: 202]. Ewing struggled to retain the Gov. Wentworth Lot 36 property in Whitneyville, where he had settled with his wife, Elinor and family.[11] In June 1778, he petitioned the newly established Vermont State Assembly for confirmation of ownership.[12] No action on the petition was recorded. He approached the new town officers of Halifax with a request, the details of which are not specified. The papers referred to in the minutes might have pertained to Lot 36 or to his conviction that he was to have been the town's settled minister.

> August 11, 1778, Chose Capt. Hubbel Wells moderator — Upon Perrusing Said papers we find a charge & Demand of Settlement with the said Mr. Ewing — But we Know not as we are any waise indebted to the said Mr. Ewings as a town, By Note Bond, Deed Promises or otherways & as he has made no Demand of any of the Perticulars we take it as an imposition & would Be Sory to Be troubled any more with So Unjust a Request; this Vote passed Unanimously. [HLR 1A: 401]

In January 1779, and November 1780, William Ewing, who by then had returned to Shutesbury, sold his remaining property in Halifax [HLR 1A: 51–52] where he had lived, across the County Road from his unfinished meeting house. " Buildings and building material seldom were left unused. Thomas Scott incorporated the original framework into a barn he built on his property in 1790. A carved weathered board, from that barn, is all that remains of this meeting house.[13]

In his account, Wilcox said how long Ewing stayed was uncertain but it was a number of years, and he baptized quite a number. "He preached in parts of the Town in log Houses and barns. They convened together the best way they could. Principally on foot on Horseback, Horse and ox sled in the winter. They had no other means of conveyance. Then Elder [Obed] Warren succeeded Eld Ewens. He was a smart Orthodox man. Under his labors a number were converted and baptized. He formed a small Chh. [church] in the North part of the town . . . after a short time the Chh. was dissolved [1792]"[14] For a few years he also attended Elder Littlefield's church in Colrain, Massachuetts.

"The Baptist Church was 'ecclesiastically constituted' July 3, 1793. The earliest meetings were held in homes but on December 18, 1800, gathered at the home of Jared Shepards[on], it was voted 'to build a house 35 x 45 feet, with a porch in front, sufficient for three doors, and two pairs of stairs (to a gallery)." [15]

Elder Abner Bemis settled in Halifax in 1795 and remained until his death in 1809.

> [His] death was due to a cancer on his lip, from which he had suffered with great patience and fortitude. He was invited to counsel with his brethren, when they were weighing the important question of his successor. They met at this residence to consider the matter prayerfully. With one or two exceptions, they were unanimous in accepting his choice of Elder Mansfield Bruce, A young brother whom he had recently baptized. Just then, brother Bruce unexpectedly entered the room. Father Bemis warmly grasped his hand and said 'My son in the gospel, I leave you in charge of my sheep and my lambs; take good care of them.' Already this young man had proved himself a workman that needeth not to be ashamed. This prayerful and evidently wise choice was defeated by the two dissenting members, who immediately wrote to Elisha Hall to visit them on trial. . . . He came . . . and in a short time he scattered the flock. [16]

Bemis and his wife are buried in the churchyard cemetery, known today as Whitneyville Cemetery. In his will, his twenty-acre property in the Whitneyville area was left to the Halifax Baptist Church. The present West Halifax Bible Church parsonage now nestles on this property.

Elder Paul Hines (or Himes) also settled here in 1813 and remained for seven years. He served at the first Baptist Church in Whitneyville. He compiled a book of hymns with Jonathan Wilson of Colrain, who was serving in Guilford at the time. This hymnal is believed to include, for the first time in publication, the hymn, "We Are Climbing Jacob's Ladder." It was said that the congregation in Halifax was not pleased with Himes because of his emphasis on singing during the services.

SELECTION OF

HYMNS,

FROM THE BEST AUTHORS;

BY ELDERS
PAUL HIMES AND JONATHAN WILSON.

Let the inhabitants of the rock sing.
ISAIAH, XLII. 11.

O Let the Nations be glad and sing for joy, for thou shalt judge the people righteously and govern the nations upon earth. Selah
PSALM lxvii. 4.

GREENFIELD, Mass.
PRINTED BY ANSEL PHELPS.
1817.

Courtesy David Hummon

JUST received, and for sale at the office of the YEOMAN, (price 58 cents,)
"A SELECTION OF HYMNS,
FROM THE BEST AUTHORS.
By Elders
PAUL HIMES & JONATHAN WILSON."
Let the inhabitants of the rock sing. Isaiah xlii. 11.—O let the Nations be glad and sing for joy, for thou shalt judge the people righteously and govern the nations upon earth. Selah. Psalm lxvii. 4."
☞ The above work may also be had at Mr. John Chase's Store, Guilford, where it is constantly kept for sale.

American Yeoman, vol. 1, issue 19, p. 1, June 10, 1817. Courtesy Readex.

Elder Samuel Fish (1788–1883), a native of Halifax, served as pastor of the Whitneyville Baptist Church beginning in 1820. He was the most prominent figure in the Halifax Baptist Church, known as a man of great piety and much loved by his parishioners. He was the pastor for sixty-six years and raised a large family on his farm adjacent to the Center Cemetery on a salary of $100 a year. On one occasion, when his salary was not paid promptly, he called a church meeting and asked to be dismissed. The church passed over the article regarding his request and appointed a committee to go visit with Elder Fish. There was no record of further trouble regarding this issue.[17]

Rev. Samuel Fish HHS

"While the population of the town, from a peak of 1758 in 1810, was declining, the membership of the church rose from 139 members in 1829 to a peak of 180 in 1838. Every few years there were revivals when large numbers of new members were 'extended the hand of fellowship.'"[18] "The various objects of moral reform received the attention of the [Baptist] Association [in Vermont]. . . . The Halifax Church had, in 1837, a temperance society, numbering two hundred and eighty-eight members, and an Anti-Slavery Society, numbering one hundred and sixty-two members."[19]

How Halifax Came to Have Two Baptist Churches

"By 1849, the original [Whitneyville] meetinghouse was in a poor state of repair and it was unanimously voted to build a new church in Halifax Center as soon as $800 could be raised for the purpose."[20]

Stephen Niles (1803–1886), clerk of the church, was a life-long resident of Halifax and a leader in the enterprise. Along with Warren Lafayette Fish (son of Elder Fish), Oliver Perry Niles, and Lemuel Martindale Woodard, Niles served on the committee to select a plan and site. The money was set-aside in 1852 and eight dollars of it was paid to Charles Fowler for a plot previously occupied by the Jonas Scott blacksmith shop. The minister, Elder Samuel Fish, was strongly in favor of the move. As the project to build in the Center got under way, some members of the church had second thoughts about location.

In December 1852, it was decided to build a meetinghouse in West Halifax and to seek subscriptions for the purpose. Stephen Niles . . . presented a petition asking the church to decide 'Which is the Baptist Church? —Those who have located and are about to build a House of Worship in the vicinity of the Center village or those who have located and are about building in West Halifax.' No immediate action was taken on the petition but at a meeting a week later it was resolved to call the Ecclesiastical Council to advise which House of worship should be built for the Baptist Church and Society of Halifax. The Council of five members, of whom three were ministers 'from abroad,' reported at a meeting on January 17, 1853 that, 'from the state of feeling exhibited by the different members of the Church and the preparation already made for building two houses of worship that our advice merely would result in no particular benefit to the Church.' . . . Elder Fish, who cast his lot with the church in the Center was, on request, dismissed. On August 25; after considerable discussion of the propriety of granting the request' it was voted that dismission be granted thirty-five members 'for the purpose of forming another church of the same faith and order in the center of the town'.[21]

> . . . . 100 years ago in our own little church in our own West Halifax there was a fight as to where to build this very Church. In Halifax Center or W. H. The old history of the Church states that the fight was so hot that blows were almost struck and the cuss words almost flowed. But just in time they decided to appoint a Committee of outsiders which were to come all the way over the mountains from a town called Brattleboro.
>
> Old Home Day Sermon, 1953, 100th Anniversary, HHS Notebook.

One church, which now stands in Halifax Center, became the Halifax Center Baptist Church; the other, built by the thirty-five members who were "dismissed," built the West Halifax Baptist Church in the village. They employed Henry C. Plumb as carpenter, a lad not twenty-one years old, to build the church, which still stands in the present West Halifax Village and is called the West Halifax Bible Church. Both Baptist Churches were constructed the same year, 1853.

Early in December 1853, a three-man committee of the West Halifax church was appointed to consider what to do with the old Baptist Meeting House now that two new houses had recently been completed. On December 24, 1853, William Plumb, James Niles, and Joshua Harris gave a lengthy report, a portion of which follows:

> As the said Meeting House has been abandoned a question arises as to what to do with it, whether it shall stand there, rot down, and go the way of all the earth, or be sold and converted into other property and uses. We think it as much a duty . . . to save property as it is to work and earn it . . . gather up the fragments that nothing be lost. . . . The Supreme Court of this State in 1846 ruled, "that the owner of a pew in meeting house … holds his pew subject to the right of the owners of the house, to take down, and rebuild, in case of necessity, without making him compensation . . . that the right of a pew holder to a pew in an meetinghouse is subordinate to the rights of the owners of the house. . . . The house in question is the property of the Baptist Chh. in Halifax, and they have the sole, and exclusive right to dispose of the same. …[Y]our comm. recommend that the Church, order and direct that sd house, together with the stoves and pipe and the land or common which it stands, be sold . . . and

if any person can substanciate a good & legal claim to any part of sd house it is but just that they should be renumeratd for same.[22]

It was voted to accept the report, and Wm. Plumb, Robt. Collins, A. M. Wheeler, Tho. H. Grant, and Joshua Harris were appointed "to sell the old meetinghouse, stove pipe, land it stands on and common around it and to settle all just legal claims if any are brought against the church."[23] No further report is found in the church records. However, the line-a-day diary of a local farmer, Russell Bascom, notes for January 18, 1854:

> Snowed five inches. The Old Baptist Meeting house sold in auction for $46.62 to H. C. Plumb. The Stoves and pipe sold to Joshua Harris for $11.00. The land sold to Jesse S. Dunklee for $6.75.[24]

Confirmation of the sale of the meeting house land is found in Halifax records [HLR 11:31]. One-and-a-half acres located east of the "land occupied as a graveyard," west of Emery Whitney, south of Dunklee, west of the "highway leading from Halifax Center to Marlboro" and north of the highway "leading by the dwelling of Emery Whitney" was conveyed by the Baptist Society to Jesse Dunklee. The deed, dated January 1854, was witnessed by Sanford Plumb and his daughter, Mary Ellen Plumb. "The Old Church" poem was "found in the key-hole of the old Baptist church in Halifax in 1858."[25] The authorship is unknown.

The Old Church's Lament

I wandered forth one summer morn,
  As wont, in musing mood,
Where stands an old deserted church
  Mid nature's solitude.

I stood and gazed, so strange the scene
  That on my vision broke;
When from the old and mossy walls
  A voice in echo spoke;

"Stranger, although deserted now
  And ruined I appear,
I've treasured many a memory
  Of hours that were more dear.

Kind faces oft before me flit,
  Sweet sounds the old haunts fill,
And friends that I so long have loved
  I dream are with me still.

But in the lonely churchyard near,
  Beneath the mountain shade,
Sleeping their long, last, dreamless sleep,
  My dearest friends are laid.

Down by the gushing fountain there,
  Sparkling so pearly bright,

Have many through long years gone by,
  Received the sacred rite.

And here, within these sacred walls,
  Once sacred held and dear,
Where assembled multitude
  Have bowed with hearts sincere,

Have youth and beauty often met,
  Where love joined heart with heart,
And at this alter breathed their vows
  That death alone can part.

Oft has the stricken mourner come,
  With anguish none can tell,
And of the loved one lost on earth
  Here bid a last farewell.

But now alas! I'm left alone,
  My sad fate to deplore,
And sigh that union once so true
  Has fled forever more.

And thus the old mansion spoke
  Of former days, it seemed;
When from the vision I awoke,
  And lo! 'twas all a dream.

1853–1885 Two Baptist Churches

The minutes from the nineteenth anniversary in 1854 of the Windham County Baptist Association include letters from both churches, as follows: [26]

> **West Halifax.** The past year has been one of mingled trials and mercies, yet we can see the kind hand of God overruling all for good. In attendance upon the stated preaching of the gospel and the means of grace, there has been an increasing interest. Our Sabbath School is prosperous. Most of the congregation, both old and young attend. During the year have completed our house of worship at an expense of $1700.
>
> **Halifax Centre.** During the year have completed our house of worship, and our congregation has exceeded our expectations. Our Sabbath School promises well. Three have been baptized and added to the Church.

Courtesy C. Lancaster

The "prudential committee" of the church in West Halifax—James Niles, Amos Tucker, and J. Tucker—obtained the services of W. N. Fay. In October 1853, the new church was dedicated and Rev. Fay was ordained and installed as pastor. His salary was raised by renting pews and by a tax levied on the grand list of members. In June 1855, Rev. Fay resigned. A succession of ministers served comparatively brief periods from this point on. In October 1857, George O. Atkinson was ordained and installed as pastor. He remained until July 1861.

Except for a short stint in Guilford from 1868 to 1869, Rev. Samuel Fish continued preaching in the new church in Halifax Center through the second Sunday in June 1871, rounding out fifty years of preaching in Halifax. "In his autobiography, written when he was about ninety years of age, he says: 'The whole that I baptized into both churches, east and west, was two hundred; I preached, I dare say, four hundred funeral sermons. As I preached three times one-half the Sabbaths, I think for nearly sixty years, I might have delivered eight thousand sermons.'"[27] His was a most productive ministry, indeed. One son, Henry Clay Fish, DD, was a noted Baptist clergyman.

Both churches suffered financial difficulties. After the retirement of , the two churches shared the services of Rev. Horace Fowler for two years, from 1873 to 1875. The Baptist Church in the Center voted on August 25, 1883 to disorganize. On February 28, 1885, the West Halifax Church likewise voted to disorganize "and unite and consolidate with the 'Centre' Church under the name of the Halifax Baptist Church."[28] Thus, after thirty-three years, the split was mended.

Some of the pastors who labored here from 1861 to 1970 are:
S. A. Blake, 1862
George F. Fay
Ephraim H. Bartlett
Horace Fowler
H. M. Hopkinson
(some dates unknown).
W. Goodenow, 1887–1892
A. A. Smith, 1893–1897
S. J. Smith, 1898–1901
J. E. Berry, 1902–1905
W. J. Vile, 1905–1907;
W. J. Hitchcock, 1908–1912
W. R. Tinker, 1912–1918
M. Telfer, 1919

Both meetinghouses were in a state of disrepair, and in 1886, the Church confessed to the Baptist authorities that it was unable to support itself. With the help of a revivalist the membership was increased and money was raised to repair the West Halifax house in 1887. To take over the meetinghouse in the Center, a Halifax Union Society was formed by people interested in saving the structure as a place for liberal, nonsectarian worship. At a meeting on August 22, 1891, the Halifax Baptist Church voted, 'to give their Church building at the Centre of the Town of Halifax to the Halifax Centre Union Society, provided they will repair and keep in repair, and use for evangelical purposes only.'

The meetinghouse in the Center found a benefactor in the person of Nabbe Allen (1816–1893) who left several thousand dollars to the Halifax Union Society for the 'repairs on the church buildings at Halifax Center and for the support of preaching therein according to directions of the said Society.' [29]

While the Baptists survived longest, there have been other religious groups, gathering in people's homes or schools if not in their own meeting houses.

CONGREGATIONALISTS

"Most of the early settlers came from Massachusetts and Connecticut where Congregationalism was dominant. Thus, the first church in Halifax was Congregational, constituted July 24, 1778."[30] Initially, they planned to erect their meeting house on land they acquired on the west side of Old County Road. However, they ended up choosing a site on the Centre Common on what is today near of the Center Cemetery [↩ 162, 261].

The early ministers of the Congregational Church were David Goodall, 1781–1796, a graduate of Dartmouth and a veteran of the invasion of Quebec by the British General Montgomery. Apparently, some of his sermons were published as well. He was

Photo Porter Thayer HHS
SECOND CONGREGATIONAL MEETING HOUSE

probably the first settled minister, but not the first to arrive here. That honor belongs to the Baptist minister, Elder Ewens. Next to serve was Jesse Edson, 1796–1805, a beloved preacher, also a graduate of Dartmouth. During his term, ninety-nine people were added to the church. He had a way with the youth, occasionally addressing them in his sermons. Next came Thomas H. Wood, who served from 1806–1842. A graduate of Williams College, he was credited with

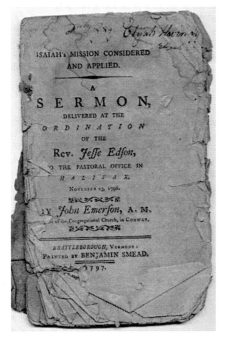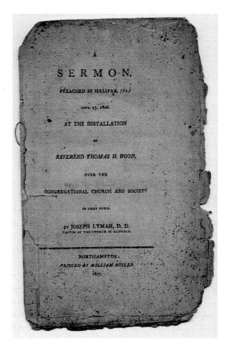

PUBLISHED SERMONS 1797 AND 1807   HHS

adding 154 members to the church. He is buried in the Halifax Center Cemetery. During his tenure, six young men entered the ministry. The next minister, Alpheus Graves , who served from 1843–1851, added thirty-eight to the church in his ministry, but was dismissed for unknown reasons, and made his way to Heath, Massachusetts, where he served for a time and was dismissed from there as well.[31]

In 1844, the Congregationalists moved to a new meeting house in West Halifax, the building today known as the Community Hall. Some members who disapproved of the move carried on services for a time in the old meeting house under the name of the Central Church. After the death of Rev. Wood, the Congregationalists declined in importance and the Universalists used the building on alternate Sundays and purchased the building in 1872.

* * *

This scripture was the basis for Jesse Edson's nineteen page "Discourse to the Young People of Halifax, October 17th, 1799", which was made public at the young people's request and published.

Whatsoever things are true, whatsoever things are honest, whatsoever things are just, whatsoever things are pure, whatsoever things are lovely, whatsoever things are of good report; if there be any virtue, if there be any praise, think on these things.

PHIL. IV. 8.

Early American Imprints, Series I: Evans, courtesy Readex

HALIFAX AUXILIARY FOREIGN MISSIONARY SOCIETY

About twenty-five years before the decline of the Congregational Church, an organization named the Halifax Auxiliary Foreign Missionary Society was formed. The purpose was to further the Christian church beyond the shores of America by sending missionaries to share the Gospel of Jesus Christ.

There were six articles adopted into this constitution: Article one was to appoint the officers to be filled and their duties. The second article stated, "Any person of any age or either sex may become a member of this society by paying to the treasurer semiannually the sum which he shall subscribe to this constitution." The third article stated, "Any member may withdraw from this society in six months after he has made known his intentions to the Clerk of the Society."

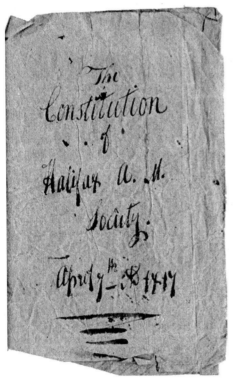 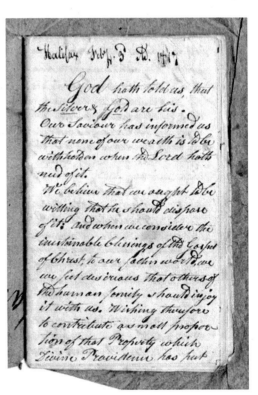

AMERICAN MISSIONARY SOCIETY CONSTITUTION 1817   VHS

Article four had to do with when they should meet. Article five stated that for a vote to be valid, it must be made "by two thirds of the whole number of Members." Article six gives the date of the first meeting of the society "on the first Monday in April [ ] 1817 at the South Meeting House at 2 o'clock P.M." And then this document lists eighty-five signers as "transcribed from the Constitution. Viz" and the amount of their donations.

This society was dissolved in 1825, according to their constitutional notes, but it was indeed a very early missionary endeavor and speaks volumes for their faith in Jesus Christ and their willingness to share in that faith by adding hands, feet, and their hard-earned funds to their prayers.

UNIVERSALISTS

THE BALLOUS AND THE UNIVERSALISTS IN HALIFAX
As it appeared in *Halifacts*, vol. 1 March, 1978, No. 10

Among the boys and girls raised in Halifax, none went on to a more distinguished career than Hosea Ballou II (1796–1861). While he himself moved to Connecticut at the age of 21, the Ballous had large families and were prominent in the town for a century beginning in 1800. The old Ballou homestead, now owned by Verna Canedy and her children, is on the Green River Road. It faces precisely south, looking out upon Ballou Mountain, a 2000-foot high memorial to the family.

The story begins with Maturin Ballou, a Baptist minister, who moved from Rhode Island to Richmond, New Hampshire, where his youngest son, Hosea I (1771–1852) was born. Attracted to Universalism, Hosea Ballou I became a preacher as Universalist societies sprang up in New Hampshire, Vermont, Massachusetts, and Connecticut.

The eldest son of Maturin Ballou had an eldest son, Asahel, who married Martha Starr of Guilford, Vermont. They had nine children, all boys, including two pairs of twins. Asahel, three months older than Hosea I, greatly admired his uncle and named his eldest son Hosea (II) after him.

Hosea II was born in Guilford, October 18, 1796. In 1799 his father bought a tract of land with a log house in Halifax and in 1800 built the present house. Asahel not only farmed but gained additional income making spinning wheels and chairs. It is said that he was such a fine penman that he could write out the Lord's Prayer in the space of a square inch. He served the town as justice of the peace and lister.

At age four young Hosea entered the Hatch School and each day walked the mile to the west. There he met Clarissa Hatch, later (in 1820) to become his wife. At age 14 he rode four miles on horseback to the elegant and respected brick school in Halifax where he was tutored in Latin by the Rev. Thomas H. Wood who was minister of the Congregational Church, that was then, located close by the school in the center. He was fifer in the Halifax militia during the war of 1812.

At age 15 Hosea Ballou became a public school teacher, serving at Marlboro two years and at Green River for one. For two years he was assistant to his great-uncle Hosea I at a private school in Portsmouth, N. H. He himself studied theology under the tutelage of Hosea I. At age 20 he began preaching, mostly in schoolhouses, in his home area.

In 1817 Hosea II was appointed pastor of a new Universalist Church in Stafford, Connecticut and preached around that state. In 1821 he moved to a new Universalist Church in Roxbury, Massachusetts, and he finally settled in Medford, Massachusetts in 1838. He wrote and edited religious books and magazines, sometimes in collaboration with Hosea I. He served a term as overseer of Harvard University and was granted the D. D. degree by that institution. Always devoted to the promotion of education, Hosea II was one

Continued

of the founding fathers of Tufts College at Medford; he became its first president in 1853 and held that post up to his death, May 27, 1861.

Meanwhile Hosea II's father Asahel carried on farming the old homestead in Halifax and after him his youngest son, Almon, born in 1816. Almon represented the town in the State legislature, 1867–68. Among the other sons Asahel Jr. farmed in Marlboro, Pearly farmed in Halifax, Levi and William became ministers in Orange, Massachusetts and Illinois respectively, Alvin became a doctor and moved to Illinois and Martin studied law at Wilmington and Harvard Law School and later became a circuit judge.

Asahel Ballou was at the head of the list of thirty founders of the Universalist Society of Halifax, January 25, 1839. He served as Treasurer until his death in 1851. His son Almon took over the job and carried on down to 1891. The last Ballou mentioned in the minutes of the Universalist Society of Halifax was Landon H. Ballou who was moderator in 1891, 1896 and 1898.

The early meetings of the Universalist Society were held at the home of Sanford Plumb. In March 1843 the Society appointed Sanford Plumb, Nathan W. Halladay and Addison Fowler, a Committee "to locate and superintend the building of the new chapel in connection with a new school house about to be erected in School district No. 15 . . ." The chapel was built quickly, at a cost of $346.93, and the Society met there for the first time October 3, 1843. Hosea Faxon Ballou (1799–1881) of Whitingham, eldest son of Hosea I, was engaged as minister on a half-time basis. He preached alternate Sundays for fourteen years, down to March 29, 1857. In 1850 his salary was $150, raised by subscription.

Hosea F. Ballou was a schoolteacher and farmer up to age 32. He married the eldest daughter of his cousin Martin Ballou and fathered ten children. To the great satisfaction of his father, he joined the ministry and was pastor of the Universalists at Whitingham for 25 years, 1831–56, at Halifax for 14 years, 1843–57, and at Wilmington for 15 years, 1856–71. He served 17 years, 1840–57, as town clerk of Whitingham and two terms in the State legislature, 1845 and 1855. After retiring from the ministry he was elected President of the Wilmington Savings Bank and held that post the last seven years of his life. One of his sons, Hosea Berthier Ballou, succeeded his father as town clerk in Whitingham and served for 42 years, 1857–99.

After Hosea F. Ballou resigned and moved to Wilmington, the Universalist Society of Halifax appointed Rev. J. Gifford to preach, again on alternate Sundays.

During the 1860's the minutes of the Society frequently mentioned needs for repairs to the chapel. The sturdy Congregational Meeting House in West Halifax, which had been build in 1844, was suffering disuse and the Universalists arranged to hold their alternate Sunday meetings there. In January 1872 it was voted that "A. F. Worden be instructed to investigate with the Congregational Society to see what their Meeting House can be bought for." It was further voted "That this Society occupy this House 'till the 1st of April next, then we go to the Chapel if we do not buy the

Continued

Congregational House by that time." The purchase was accomplished and in January 1873 a building committee to see to repairs was appointed.

In their new quarters the Society did well. At the annual meeting in 1879 two ushers were elected in addition to the regular officers, a moderator, clerk and treasurer, a prudential committee of three, and a collector.

There was a question of disposing of the chapel. In 1875 the prudential committee was authorized to lease or sell it. On September 45, 1880 a special meeting was called to see about selling the chapel and a committee was appointed "to put it up at auction in connection with the School District and sell or buy, or sell at a private sale at their discretion." There was a legal difficulty resolved by a special Act of the Vermont State legislature, approved December 18, 1880, authorizing "The First Universalist Society of Halifax" to dispose of its chapel and the interest of the said society in the lot upon which it stood. On June 8, 1883 it was deeded to George P. Worden and Landon H. Ballou for ninety dollars.

Succeeding Almon Ballou, Eli S. Cook became clerk and treasurer in 1892 and continued in those offices through 1911. Annual meetings became irregular after 1900 and there is no record of meetings between 1911 and 1926.

The interest of men declined and the ladies became more active. The original Rules and Regulations adopted in 1839 offered membership to "every man of the age of twenty one years and upwards of good moral Character on signing the foregoing Constitution . . ." At a meeting on February 5, 1898 the first mention is made of a Ladies Society. It was voted that the Treasurer might turn over the $7.75 in his hands, less $3.50 for tuning the organ, to Mrs. Elly Allen, the "Ladies" Treasurer. On May 31, 1909 it was voted to paper the church and two ladies, Mrs. Anna Ball and Mrs. F. T. Miner, were included on the committee to get the paper and see to having it put on.

Membership lists of the Ladies of the Universalist Church are available for 1910, 1914, 1915, 1916 and 1917. There were around twenty-five members. Regular religious services were suspended. George A. Chase was briefly given the use of the building for a store after a fire in 1923 destroyed the Chase home that also housed the store and post office.

In 1926 an effort at revival was made. On September 5 of that year there was an annual meeting after a preaching service at which eight people, including five ladies, were added to the membership rolls. The final services of the Universalist Society were held six years later, on July 10 and July 31 of 1932 with 21 persons present in each case.

The November 24, 1934 issue of the *Universalist Christian Leader* reported from West Halifax that: "At a recent meeting here it was voted to give the use of the church building as a community center, with the reservation of the right to hold religious meetings by the Convention or parish at any time, and on the understanding that the building shall be kept in good condition and that it be used for meetings, and not for storage or commercial purposes, and likewise that the grounds be well kept."

Continued

The *Leader* further reported, February 23, 1935: "The offer of the church building for a community center, with reservation of right to hold religious meetings, was accepted by the community. The steeple was removed, as it was not considered safe, and a birch floor was laid."

The Universalist ladies held a strawberry festival to raise money for the new floor to accommodate dancing. In 1951 an auction and food sale provided funds to reroof the building. At that time the belfry was removed. Much earlier the bell had been taken out and put to use as a watering trough on the Branch Brook Road near Homer Sumner's farm.

Since 1935 the meeting house, under the care of the Community club, has been used for dances, receptions and other events. It was used for town meetings in 1934, 1936, and from 1938 to 1959.

It is interesting that the Universalist Church in Sadawga Springs, Whitingham, was similarly given to a community organization, the Green Mountain Club, and now houses the Whitingham Historical Society museum.

Norris Johnson

METHODISTS

Rev. Hubbard Eastman was a Methodist minister who never lived in Halifax but was enlisted to write a historical account of the town for Abby Maria Hemenway's gazetteer. At the time of Eastman's death in 1891, a Methodist Church had been established in Halifax. Very little is written of the Methodist denomination in town; however, there were enough references in the newspapers to know that they were active and even had a church building in the Reid (often misspelled Reed) Hollow area. At times they used the school and church buildings at the Center.

> The Methodists are preparing to erect their church in the north part of the town. Baptism is expected to be performed next Sunday.[32]

> March 1881: The M.E. [Methodist] Church at Reed Hollow will be dedicated next Thursday, Nov. 10th. Services to commence at 2 o'clock. Rev. A. B. Truax of Brattleboro will preach. Other ministers are expected to be present. Afternoon and evening meetings will continue through the week. Quarterly meeting on the Sabbath at 11 o'clock. All invited.[33]

> The children connected with the Halifax Centre M. E. Sunday school are requested to meet at the schoolhouse next Sunday at 11 o'clock.[34]

> Rev. D. [Daniel] DeWolf will preach in the chapel at Reed Hollow next Sunday at 2 P.M.[35]

Halifax, May 15, 1885: Rev. H. Eastman of Jacksonville will preach on "The Works of Nature" at Read Hollow on Sunday, the 24th inst. at 2 p.m.[36]

Halifax 1886: Quarterly meeting service at Halifax, June 13th at 2 pm—A. J. Martin will preach at Reed Hollow Sunday, June 13th at 5 pm.[37]

June 1894, Baptists report: Halifax. One man and woman have recently been baptized at Halifax; also two excellent workers have been received by letter. Others are awaiting baptism. Held a week's meetings last winter, preaching every evening. . . . I preached at the Centre last Sabbath, at 3 o'clock. I could not get in before, as the Methodists held the ground. This suggests that church buildings were used by multiple sects.[38]

One of the prominent ministers of the Methodist/Episcopal (ME) persuasion was the Rev. Lemuel M. Woodward. Born in Halifax in December 1821, he died in the same house in which he had always lived on October 10, 1896. It was written about him in his obituary, "[A]s a preacher he was full-souled, instructive and earnest, enjoying a rich experience of full salvation." It was also said of him in the same piece "his name was a synonym for living Christianity." It was mentioned that even "Scoffers" at the mention of his name would note, "he is a Christian."[39]

Rev. Woodward wrote an interesting and touching piece that appeared in the *Zion's Herald* entitled, "Eighteen Months with the Comforter." In this article he shares his "conversion" experience at age fifteen during a neighborhood "revival." This conversion, he states, was at the home of Rev. Samuel Fish, the prominent Baptist minister, during a conference. It was then he knew that "a voice within me tells me that I am born a child of God." Rev. Woodward was a great friend and classmate of Rev. Samuel Fish's son, the Rev. Henry Fish, who became a prominent New Jersey theologian.

SUNDAY SCHOOLS

1881   A series of singing schools are to be held at the West village by A. C. Bickford.

1881   A singing school will be held at the school house in the Niles district to-morrow evening.

1882   The officers of the Halifax Center Baptists Sunday School for the year following are as follows: Superintendent, Add C. Niles; Asst. supt., Oscar B. Dix; Sec'y, and Treas., Mrs. J. L. Harrington; Librarian, Miss Hattie M. Clark; Ass't. Librarian, Miss Grace Worden.   HHS: Niles, 1881, pp. 2, 4; 1882, p. 2.

ONE HUNDRED YEARS 1953

Let's try for a moment to imagine what it would have been like to have been in W. H. the first Sunday after the building of this church here.

This Church was built during the hot summer of 1853 by a lad not yet 21, Henry C. Plumb. Early in October the Church was joyously completed and the first service was held by Rev. May [Fay]. It was a bright sunny day on the 9th of Oct. 1853. A cool crispe Sunday morning with the golden leaves etched against the deep blue sky. The buggies, wagons and horses lined the roads all the way from where Hardgroves live down to the bridge over the creek this all important Sunday.

For Many miles around the grinding of the buggy wheels on the hard frozen dirt road could be heard as first the Niles, the Harrises, and the Halls, the Collins, the Thurber and Tuckers and many, many, many more arrived. The women in their high necked black lace dresses and the men in their beards and some in Derby hats look very somber this bright Sunday morning.

Finally when all the families had taken their own pews that were rented at the much grumbled about price of 5 dollars per year, Rev. Fay stood up and started to talk in his deep heavy voice. He dedicated the Church. He even said 100 years from now this Church of God will stand as Mr. Plumb has built it but the world will be so changed you won't even recognize it. Then after the dedication he prayed May God bless the Congregation and the President of our Country, Franklin Pierce. May we all fight for the stopping of the black practice of slavery in this Country.

Finally Rev. Fay preached his Sermon on the evils of the day. When his eyes finished flashing and his last Amen rolled across the Congregation and on the Church doors there was fear of the Lord and of the fiery brimming pits of hell deep in the hearts of that Congregation on the 9th of Oct. 1853. . . . Now let put on our red turbans . . . and look deep into its mysteries as Mr. [Wayne] Kenyon tells us about the future. . . .

Let us transcend time for the span of ten decades and attend this church the West Halifax Church in the era of which we speak. We cruise along in our convertibles, helicopters with our Sunday best gleaming in the sun. Where one of Dalrymples goats grazed we spy a landing field and descent gracefully to our parking stand. A white coated attendant hands us a clamp on loudspeaker. We clamp it on, turn up the volume and listen to the sound of hymns, the old favorites that are still being sung. We see the choir on the screen and hear it from our speakers. This is only one of the millions of fly in Churches in the world. Soon the minister will appear on the screen and send forth to the hundreds of helicopters his message. . . . Buggies are replaced by mile a minute automobiles, fashions have changed toward comfort, electric lights blaze and illuminate where once candles and later lamps dimly lit a crowded room. Radio, telephone, telegraph, television link together in a world 25,000 meters in diameter a world that has become smaller as speed of communication has become great. If progress marches on as we celebrate one hundred years of its lifetime, let each one of us assembled here in the Church hope and pray that the candles on its anniversary cake be not extinguished but rather grow in number and glow with an undying light throughout the years.

Conclusion by Wayne Kenyon
Taken from HHS Notebook, pp. 3–4, 12–13, 16–17, 19,
Old Home Day Sermon, 1953, 100th Anniversary

WEST HALIFAX THE LATER YEARS

According to notes in the clerk's reports, Lucie Freeman was pastor at the Whitingham Community Church and also started serving the West Halifax Baptist Church in 1957. It was remembered how the three Lucies—Lucie Freeman, Lucie Sumner, and Lucie Cook—held weekly Bible classes after school at the schoolhouse. Lucie Freeman retired in October 1967 after ten years of service in West Halifax. In May 1970, the name of the church was changed to West Halifax Community Church.

In 1971, Lucie Sumner challenged Homer Smith, a dairy farmer from Buckland, Massachusetts, to start a Good News Club for children in West Halifax, since there were no regular Sunday service or Sunday school classes being held. Homer suggested Sunday school instead. Sunday school was started at the West Halifax Community Church about February or March 1972.

In 1973, several townspeople had an informal meeting with Homer Smith and asked him if he could hold regular church services as well as officiate at the weekly Sunday school. Homer replied, "You get ten people to come and I'll preach." Lucie Sumner asked, "Why do we need ten?" Homer replied, "We don't, I'll come for even one!" His first Sunday morning service was held on Easter Sunday in 1973. The furnace blew up that following week and the Grange graciously permitted the church services to be held in the Grange Hall until the church was cleaned. Fortunately, the church was covered by insurance.

One very faithful member was Raymond Ouelette, who regularly attended both morning and evening services. When he died in the middle of winter, the funeral was held in the church in sub-zero weather. Salamander heaters were brought in to help the furnace, which was incapable of heating the whole church.

Under the leadership of Pastor Homer Smith the church grew in members, services, and outreach. Midweek evening services, morning Bible studies, midweek prayer meetings, youth programs, and AWANA (Approved Workmen Are Not Ashamed) Club meetings were started. Many new members, on profession of Christ as Savior, joined the church. Twenty-one were baptized at Ryder Pond in Whitingham; many others were baptized at Smith's Pond in Buckland, Massachusetts, and still others were baptized in the church baptistery. This baptistery was removed in 2000 because of the decay in the floor under it.

Many improvements were made to the church building covering a span of time between 1975 and 1985 through work bees and donated labor. In June 1980, the name of the church was officially changed from the West Halifax Community Church to the West Halifax Bible Church; it became nondenominational, and membership to the American Baptist Convention was terminated.

In September 1984, Homer Smith resigned as pastor. The church members gave Pastor Smith and his family a unique gift to show their love and appreciation for his many years of tireless dedication and hard work—a handmade quilt with an appliquéd picture of the church in the center, surrounded by blocks of signatures embroidered by each church family. The ordination service for Homer Smith took place at the church on May 19, 1985, with several ministers from surrounding churches taking part. Rev. Homer Smith passed on during the spring of 2003 in New York State. Memorial services were held in

New York and Colrain, Massachusetts, with full houses in both locations. He and his wife Helene and family will be long remembered for their tireless work in our community.

A FEW ROUGH YEARS

It was difficult for the church to be without a pastor for that year and a half. The church invited guest speakers to fill the pulpit from 1984 until June 1986, when Alan Swanson, affiliated with American Mission for Opening Churches (AMOC), was called from Florida to serve as pastor. After a great beginning to his ministry, a schism developed between Pastor Swanson and some townspeople when the family of the deceased requested that a woman pastor from Guilford officiate at the funeral. Several months of unsuccessful attempts at reconciliation ensued, which was highly publicized (even reaching the *Boston Globe* and other regional newspapers). This emotional struggle eventually culminated in a lawsuit being brought against the "Bible Church" by those who identified themselves as members of the former Baptist Church. Pastor Swanson decided to tender his resignation as part of the court settlement. He resigned as of August 1988 and moved on to a church in Maine.

Another Florida pastor, Rollin Moranville, was called to Halifax in September 1988. After a disagreement ensued over doctrinal issues, he resigned April 2, 1989, taking some of the members with him to worship at the former Universalist Church, now the Community Hall. This caused a temporary split in the already split church. The remaining members arrived that Sunday morning, shocked to find the building unheated and both his and a church deacon's resignation letters on the back table. In September 1989, the two groups agreed to unite for a scheduled Bible conference with Harold Duff. This resulted in the church being reunited and Rollin Moranville moving back to Florida. The church continued to have a ministry with various guest speakers.

A TIME OF REFRESHING

During the winter of 1993/94, the church decided to have the lumber on their twenty-acre lot in the Whitneyville area appraised, cut, and sold to make room and pay for a parsonage on that lot. This was done on faith that a pastor would occupy it in the near future.

Village Missions, with whom the church became affiliated, sent James Dresser and his wife Wanda, who were the first to live in the new parsonage. Pastor Jim started preaching at West Halifax Bible Church on September 25, 1994. During their time in West Halifax, the Dressers held several Bible studies and also directed a kids' club for a short time. Because of ill health, Village Missions transferred the Dressers to Nebraska in May 1999, where life could be easier for them.

In November 1999, Village Missions sent Mark Monroe, his wife Leslie, and their three children. They continue at this present time in the ministry. Under Mark Monroe's direction, many improvements have been made to the building, including leveling the floor, changing the pews, and refurbishing the fellowship room.

In the earlier years, singing was taught in the schools using the hymns. Sunday schools were also held in the school buildings. All the churches housed libraries where anyone could come and check out a book.

The churches have been in Halifax from the town's inception and still have a special place in the community. Many have had life-changing experiences through the churches in Halifax. They remain at the heart of the community in more ways than one.

* * *

PARSONAGE

Located on the 1854 McClellan map, on Main Street in West Halifax, just east of the new Congregational Church, the building is identified as "Congregational Parsonage." Within ten years, there was no Congregational minister in residence in Halifax and it is unknown what happened to this parsonage.

The Beers map of 1896 shows the building uphill, or west of the Larrabee house on Collins Road, and it is identified as the home of Mrs. A. [Amos] Tucker. In 1870, her grandson, Harry Amos Tucker, was born in this house, the son of Levi Murray and Josephine Hosmer Tucker. Amos Tucker had been a key figure in the move to build a Baptist Church in West

Photo Porter Thayer, Postcard courtesy Charles Marchant

Halifax in 1853. In 1855, the Baptist Society discussed building a parsonage, but the minutes do not show that action was taken. Starting in 1907, Rev. William Hitchcock and family lived at the parsonage during his ministry at the Baptist Church. In 1978 it was under private ownership of Warren and Elizabeth Dalrymple when it burned. They placed a modular home on the original foundation.

~ *Constance Lancaster, Rev. Donald and Carrie Perna*

HALIFAX, VERMONT CHURCH RESOURCES

Ballou, Hosea Starr. *Hosea Ballou, 2nd, D.D., FIRST PRESIDENT OF TUFTS COLLEGE His Origin, Life, and Letters.* Boston: E. P. Guild, 1896.

Comstock, John M. *The Congregational Churches of Vermont and Their Ministry, 1762–1942*

Crocker, Henry. *History of the Baptists in Vermont.* Bellows Falls, VT: P.H. Gobie Press, 1913; St. Johnsbury, VT: Cowles Press, 1942.

The Constitution of Halifax A.M. Society: April 7th 1817. VHS

Universalist minutes, continuous from January 1839–January 1902. Also 1909, 1911, 1926 and 1932. Lists of church members and Ladies Society members, newspaper clippings, photographs, and copies of Windham County Church Association minutes, Book Two Baptist Church minutes; 1825, list of Baptist Church membership.

Rollins, Alden M., CGRS, compiler. *Vermont Religious Certificates.* Rockport, ME: Picton Press, 2002.

HTC, Books 1A and 2A.

Vermont Baptist History, Special Collections, UVM.

ENDNOTES

1. Howard F. Vos, Th. D., Editor, *Religions in a Changing World* (Chicago: Moody Press, 1959) pp. 410–421.
2. Earle E. Cairns, *Christianity Through the Centuries* (Grand Rapids, MI: Zondervan Publishing, 1981) pp. 366–367.
3. Ibid., p. 365.
4. D. James Kennedy, *The Rebirth of America* (Philadelphia: The Arthur S. Demoss Foundation, 1986) p. 121.
5. The petition was a broadside that would have been posted in more affluent communities for public view for the purpose of raising funds for the furtherance of spiritual work in Halifax.
6. http://www.newenglandancestors.org from a database called *Chapter 3, The Legislator*, available online to members only. Material cited as follows: George Colesworthy. *Historical Sketches of The Baptist Church in Shutesbury, Massachusetts*. (New York, 1882) pp. 4–6.
7. UVM, carton 2 folder 15.
8. Hemenway, p. 412.
9. Quitclaim deed from David Goodall to Joseph Tucker, dated January 9, 1782 and recorded by Edward Harris, Justice of the Peace on January 24, 1785. [HLR 1A: 202].
10. At the December 17, 1781 meeting, a committee comprised of Deacon John Pennell, Hubbel Wells, and Benjamin Henry was appointed to "treat with Mr. Goodall Respecting the Hundred Acres of Land Liet Tucker Lives on." [HLR 1A: 115] And the formal call to settle Rev. David Goodall includes the condition that he quit-claim one hundred acres on the southerly side of Lot #28, the minister's lot. [HLR 1A: 419]
11. Known children were Elinor Ewing, born Nov. 2, 1759 in Wilmington, PA, who married in Halifax about 1778; Stephen Wilcox, son of William. Stephen and Elinor were parents of at least ten children born in Halifax [see Halifax vital records]; And William Ewing Jr., who was age sixteen and of Shutesbury, Massachusetts, in 1779 when he enlisted in Capt. Dickenson's Co., Col. Porter's regiment of Hampshire County, Massachusetts [see *Massachusetts Soldiers and Sailors in the War of the Revolution.*, vol. 5, p. 442]. Wright and Potter Printing Co., Boston, MA 1896.
12. Rawson C. Myrick. State Papers of Vermont. Volume III. General Assembly 1784–1787. p. 18
13. The massive, weathered board hangs in an attached barn/shed at the Thomas Scott home, now owned by Anne DeWitt. Carved on it are the numerals 1790–1902. When Scott first came to Halifax, he occupied property close to the unfinished meetinghouse and Scott cemetery. The property for many years was a Scott family woodlot. After Scott moved to Stowe Mountain Road, he may well have incorporated materials from the abandoned Ewing meetinghouse when building his barn in 1790. Family tradition says the boards were from the Congregational House. However, Thomas himself was a Baptist, and the only unfinished meetinghouse in 1790 was the one by the Scott Cemetery.
14. UVM, *Vermont Baptist Historical Society Records*, carton 2, folder 15, Halifax.
15. HHS: Johnson, *The Baptist Churches of Halifax*, p. 1.
16. Rev. Henry Crocker, *History of the Baptists in Vermont* (Bellows Fall, VT: P. H. Gobie Press, 1913) p. 181.
17. HHS, *Halifacts*, No. 19, December 1985, p. 2.
18. Ibid., p. 2.
19. Crocker, p. 189.
20. HHS: Johnson, *Halifacts*, vol. 1, no. 7, March 1976, p. 2.
21. Ibid., p. 2, 5–6.
22. HTC, *Records of the Baptist Church in Halifax*, p. 84
23. Ibid., p. 85.
24. *Diary of Russell Bascom,* Russel Stanton Avery Manuscript Collection *NEHGS*. Boston.
25. HHS: Niles, p. 63.
26. Origen Smith, Clerk, Windham County Baptist Association, minutes from September 1854 (Boston: J. Howe Press, 1854).
27. Crocker, p. 191.
28. HHS: Johnson, *Halifacts*, vol. 1, no. 7, March 1976, p. 7.
29. Ibid., p. 8.
30. Ibid., p. 9.
31. *Phoenix,* March 17, 1860.
32. Ibid., November 13, 1879.
33. HHS: Niles, p. 5.
34. *Phoenix*, Sept. 28, 1883.
35. *Phoenix*, May 25, 1883.
36. Ibid., p. 38.
37. HHS: Niles, p. 5.
38. UVM, carton 2, folder 15.
39. Seymour C. Vail, Zion's Herald, November 11, 1896, p. 739. Retrieved from APS online database, document ID: 775532902.

EDUCATION AND SCHOOLS

THE CHARTER LOT

When the early settlers came to Halifax in the mid-1700s, their first priority was building shelters and planting gardens. At first, the children were home schooled, using books and Bibles their families brought with them. Rev. H. Eastman, wrote:

> In the original grant of the town one lot of 360 acres was appropriated for the benefit of schools. This lot is in the northeast corner of the town, commonly called Thomas Hill. The land is sold with the reserve, that the interest of two dollars a year per acre shall be annually paid into the town treasury in the month of ___ [May] for the benefit of the schools.[1]

The school charter land is first mentioned in town meeting records for March 1779. Selectmen, Capt. Hubbel Wells, Capt. John Thomas, Mr. Israel Guild, Doctor William Hill and Edward Harris, Esq., were voted to be the "Committee To Take Care of Ministers and School Land in the town of Hallifax" [HLR 1A: 403]. Initially, the minister's land received priority attention, and it was not until March 1784, as construction of the meeting house neared completion and a minister was in residence that the selectmen took up the matter of the "School Lot." A committee of five was selected to set up the terms and conditions for leasing the school land to benefit the town. In May, it was voted to "Leas the School Lot as Long as Wood Grows and Water Runs...at the tenth part of a Dollar per Acre Rent...that the Rent be paid in Money . . . that the Select men Give Mr. Benjamin Treadaway a Leas of s'd School Lot" [HLR 1A: 426].

> This Indenture Covenant Lease & agrement Made by & Between us Hubel Wells Benjamin Henry Thomas Taggert James Pannel & Nathan Fish Select Men for the Town of Halifax in the County of Windham and State of Vermont for year 1784 on one part & Benjamin Treadway of the aforesaid Town County & State . . . that Whereas there is a lot of Land No. 64 in the town Which said Inhabitants of said Town hold by Charter as a school Lot and agreeable to said Voters of said Town Reference thereto being had the Select Men of Town Were to Leas out said Lot No 64 for benefit of schools in said Town as Long as Wood Grows & Water Runs. [HLR 1A: 311]

Treadway conveyed portions of the school lot to Nymphas Stacy, David Allen, Solomon Fessenden, Stafford Horton and Edmund Fisher. Their deeds specified the property could be improved and dwellings constructed, but each Lot 64 lessee must pay annual rent to the town "on the sixth day of May so long as Wood Grows & Water runs." In 1786, the town "voted to take the school rent for this year in grain, that is to say wheat, at four shillings per bushel and Indian corn at two shillings and five pence per bushel" [HLR 1A: 434]. School rents are documented annually in Halifax town reports through 1970, when state law permitted the town to tax Lot 64 property the same as all property in town.

ESTABLISHMENT OF THE FIRST SCHOOL DISTRICTS

On August 30, 1784, the voters chose a committee "from Several parts of the Town . . . Esq. Henrey, Lt. Orr, Capt. Sawtell, Benj. Thomas, Lt. Tucker, Jasper Hunt, David Allen, Stephen Willcox, Thomas Scott, Lt. Henderson, James Clark Jr., Capt. James Pennel, Joseph McCluer & Hubbel Wells to prepose a plan of Dividing the Town into School Districts and Make Report to a later Town Meeting" [HLR 1A: 427]. The committee's report was heard and approved on September 7, and recorded in the town book on September 16, 1784.

Following is a list of "Men's Names that are annexed to each district" [HLR 1A: 181–183]. For clarity, punctuation has been inserted and the family names have been spelled as commonly known.

DISTRICT NO. 1: Samuel Holmes, Darius Sawyer, Dea. John Pennell, Capt. James Pennell, John Pennell Jr., John Kirkley, Mr. Loomis, Mr. Brooks, Lt. John Gault, Mr. Underwood, Aaron Sanderson, Mr. Sumner, and Joseph Horsley, with Lt. Stacy's farm.

DISTRICT NO. 2: Stephen Wilcox, William Wilcox, Nathan Wilcox, Benjamin Weekes, Tabor Wilcox, Joseph Worden, Arthur Crosier, Elisha Worden, Silvester Worden, Daniel Safford, Mr. Peters, Benjamin Wilcox, and Joseph Wilcox.

DISTRICT NO. 3: Hubbell Wells, Elijah Clark, Nathaniel Pribble Hayward, Josiah Scott, Thomas Scott, Oliver Waters, David Allen, Job Harris, William Shepardson, Israel Jones, Daniel Squire, and Ebenezar Hayward.

DISTRICT NO. 4: Thomas Taggart, Esq, Capt Robert Pattison, Dr. Jeremiah Everett, Lt. James Clark, Joseph Bell, Samuel Clark Jr., Samuel Clark, Josiah Clark, Thomas Clark, William Gault, David Lamb, Samuel Fish, Timothy Harrington, Benjamin Barber, John Little, Amos Conant, Nathan Fish, Benjamin Henry, Esq., and Thomas Fowler.

DISTRICT NO. 5: Jasper Hunt, Joel Hall, Joshua Rich, Joshua Lamb, Jethaniel Rich, John Hall, Levi Hall, Zerah Brooks, Daniel Delano, Jonathan Rich, Joseph McCluer, Jonathan Wells, Jonathan Kellogg, Benjamin Lyman, Benjamin Tilden, James P. Frazier and Azariah Hall.

DISTRICT NO. 6: Henry Henderson, Samuel Woodard, old Mr. Gates, Nathan Gates, Jonas Shepard, Philemon Stacy, David Williams, Elijah Phillips, Ezra Tubs, Samuel Sanders, Benjamin Sanders, Andrew Dunikan, John Joyner, John Berry, Elias Washburn, and Joseph Williams.

DISTRICT NO. 7: John Wilson, Daniel Doneldson, Elisha Clark, Asa Clark, James Clark, Matthew Ellis, Nicholas Dyke, William Farly, Paul Nickels, Samuel Nickels, Stephen Slaughter, and Elijah Taber.

DISTRICT NO. 8: David Allen, Joseph Pierce, Mr. Phillips, Aaron Slade, Capt. John Thomas, Benjamin Thomas, William Thomas, John Thomas, Jr., Thomas Alverson, David Alverson, Samuel Thomas, Mr. Harrington, Nymphas Stacy, Mr. Horton, Benjamin Treadway, Mr. Streeter, and Mr. Fisher.

DISTRICT NO. 9: Elisha Pratt, Capt. Caleb Owen, Banks Bennet, Elijah Thomson, Capt. John Sawtell, Joseph Swain, Joel Goodall, Samuel Wood, Moses Learnard, Jonathan Pratt, and the Rutherford Farm.

DISTRICT NO. 10: Rev. David Goodall, Joseph Tucker, Edward Harris Esq., John Crosier, Nathan Whitney, Thomas Farnsworth, John Woodard, James Woodard, Capt. Stephen Gates, Ensign Isaac Orr, Isaac Baldwin, Elias Persons, Israel Hale, Daniel Isham, John Whitney, Robert Crosier, and Daniel Brown.

DISTRICT NO. 11 was added in 1788. John Joyner, Andrew Dunikan, Hugh Canady, and David Stow.

To keep pace with population growth, additional schools were established. In 1809, a peak population year, town clerk Darius Bullock recorded the number of scholars as returned by the several district clerks: No. 1–56 scholars; No. 2–49; No.3–53; No. 4–70; No. 5–38; No. 6–24; No. 7–43; No. 8–55; No. 9–98; No. 10–64; No. 11–25; No. 12–23; No. 13–25; No. 14 –39; and No. 15–23 [HLR 2A: 92]. One wonders how these 685 school children fit into their schoolhouses.

HOW THE COMMON SCHOOL DISTRICTS OPERATED

Since people settled around places of industry, such as tanneries and saw mills, each little hamlet had its own one-room schoolhouse. The children walked to school, thus the schoolhouse was built as close to the center of the settlement as possible. Teachers, some quite young, boarded at homes of students in the areas where they taught. Within each district, schooling and schoolhouses were owned and funded by neighborhood families. At annual town meetings, voters could approve placement of families in specific districts, and could create new districts and consolidate old districts; but the business of each local school was overseen by a trustee or clerk who was expected to report to the town clerk once a year.

Each school district warned and held annual meetings, elected officers, kept records, collected taxes, and made decisions about every aspect of education. From hiring teachers; setting the number of terms and days of school; purchasing texts, flags, and dictionaries; to maintaining the building and supplying firewood, the local school committee decided all. Details of how a school district operated can be viewed at the Halifax Historical Society Museum in the original handwritten book of business meeting minutes, dating from 1830 to 1877 for the Hall School District.

Local autonomy continued until 1845, when the state set up a system of state, county, and local superintendents. In Halifax, a minister, physician, or lawyer customarily held the office of superintendent, and his primary duty was to certify teachers by means of an annual examination.[2] In 1892, when the Vermont Legislature abolished the system of district common schools, Halifax became one school district governed by a town elected board of directors and an appointed superintendent.

Thompson's 1824 *Gazetteer of Vermont* speaks of fourteen school districts in Halifax. There were, however, fifteen districts before 1824, and the sixteenth district was first mentioned in the town records of 1830. In that year, grades 11 and 12 were combined, and there were four scholars attending school in Marlboro [HLR 3A: 50]. It is likely there were never more than fifteen schools active in the same year. Schoolhouses are noted by SH on the 1856 McClellan map plus the Academy is so noted at the Center.

RENUMBERING THE SCHOOL DISTRICTS

Echoing Horace Mann's initiatives for school reform,[3] Vermont passed an "Act Relating to Common Schools" in November of 1945. This legislation created a system of county and state superintendents. In a regular front-page feature called "Educational", the *Semi-Weekly Eagle* examined issues of the common schools. A major contributor to this column was James Tufts, superintendent of Windham County, who visited more than a hundred schoolhouses, including four winter-term schools in Halifax.

> West Halifax, Dec. 25, 1849. *A Walk in a Blustering Day*. There are few roads in the county more bleak and hilly than the one from Guilford to this place. Though brought up on the hills, I never had such a battle with the wind and snow as passing over these hills today, the wind blowing almost a hurricane in my face, and the snow flying in the air, so I could hardly discover the direction of the road. . . . When I entered the school room in this place, half froze, I found the usual number of scholars, pursuing their business in a quiet, cheerful manner, and the teacher, with his coat off, conducting them rapidly up the hill of science.

Superintendent Tufts extended his hill metaphor to sound the theme of combining small school districts into larger ones, even though the children might have to hike more hills to reach a "good school," and their parents might have to conquer "hills of prejudice" to give up "small backward, cheap schools at their own door." He concluded his commentary:

> There can be no doubt at all, that it is the policy of all our towns, especially of the poorer and more hilly towns, to maintain good schools. The farmers on these cold hills cannot accumulate much wealth for their children, and therefore they should educate them as well as possible in the district school. The bleak winds of winter, that render their farms less productive, do not render the minds, or the bodies of their children less active and vigorous. . . . I have seen no brighter children in the County than in the school houses on the bleak hills where corn will not grow, and if there are any children in the world worth educating, these are the children. . . . We would say to the farmers in our County, the children you raise on these hills, if you only educate them properly, will be worth to you, and to the world more than any gold you could dig in the mines of California.[4]

The educational column in the March 18, 1850 issue featured a letter from the Halifax Teachers' Association reporting on twelve well-attended meetings held at various schoolhouses in town to examine both curriculum, and the school buildings. They recommended uniting some districts and stressed the need to repair or rebuild and winterize schoolhouses. "December's cold and pelting blasts" make it "necessary to raise a heat within that will roast one side, while the other is shaking and completely chilled. . . . A teacher may profess the wit of a Sheridan, and wisdom of a Solomon, and under these circumstances, his scholars will make but little proficiency."[5]

At the March 1850 town meeting, a committee was appointed to review the school districts and "propose such alterations. . . . as they shall deem expedient and proper." The committee members were: Rev. Alpheus Graves of West Halifax, Rev. Samuel Fish of Halifax Center, and John Reid, a merchant and mill owner at Reid Hollow on the Green River. Their recommendation for reorganizing and renumbering the districts was approved on April 8, 1850. The minutes from that meeting contain a series of votes to change the numbers of most of the school districts and reduce the total number from sixteen to thirteen. Number 16 [Harrisville] became Number 10; District Number 15 [West Halifax] became Number 7; original Districts 2, 3, and 14 were dissolved. Districts 1 [Pennell Hill] and 4 [Grove] kept their original numbers. Below is the revised list of Halifax school districts as of April 1850:

Dist.	1	Pennell Hill	Dist.	8	Hall
Dist.	2	Niles	Dist.	9	Hatch
Dist.	3	Fisher	Dist.	10	Harrisville
Dist.	4	Grove	Dist	11	Reid Hollow
Dist	5	Worden	Dist	12	Thomas Hill
Dist	6	Halifax Center	Dist	13	Whitneyville
Dist	7	West Halifax			

The 1869 Beers map shows fourteen numbered schoolhouses in thirteen districts. District 11 on the map includes two numbered schoolhouses, Wilcox and Reid Hollow. Apparently, they were in the process of merging. At times, students, who resided close to the town lines attended school in Guilford, Marlboro, or Colrain for one or more terms; nevertheless, thirteen school districts were active in Halifax until 1897.

RESCUED SCHOOL REGISTERS

Norris Johnson, a founding member of the Halifax Historical Society, studied the available school registers that were rescued from an old town safe, which was opened at the town clerk's office in 1973. The list of registers appears to be consistent with the 1850 district numbering and with the 1869 Beers map. However, his committee "found 14 Registers for 1859, 1862, 1863, and a District 14 Register for 1868 also. In all 540 Registers were salvaged in at least partly legible condition."[6] The list of registers compiled by Ruth Ellis, Mary Burnett, and Norris and Pat Johnson follows with correct dates of each school's closing added. The names of the numbered districts are: 1. Pennell Hill, 2. Niles/Valley, 3. Fisher, 4. Grove, 5. Stafford/Worden, 6. Center, 7. West Halifax Elementary (presently open), 8. Hall, 9. Hatch, 10. Harrisville, 11. Reid Hollow, 12. Thomas Hill, 13. Whitneyville, 14. unidentified.

District	Closed after
1. 1859–63; 1867; 1872–78; 1880–82; 1892; 1894–99	1914
2. 1859–63; 1867; 1872; 1874–76; 1880–82; 1887–89; 1891–99	1949
3. 1859–63; 1867; 1873–75; 1878; 1880–82; 1887–89; 1892–93	1907
4. 1859–63; 1867; 1871; 1873–74; 1876; 1878; 1880–82; 1887; 1890; 1892; 1895; 1898–99	1938
5. 1859–63; 1867; 1867; 1871; 1873–74; 1876; 1878; 1880–82; 1887–90; 1892–94; 1896–97	1897
6. 1859–63; 1867; 1867; 1870; 1872; 1874–76; 1878; 1881–82; 1889–90; 1892–99	1909
7. 1859–63; 1867; 1867; 1872–74; 1876; 1880–81; 1887–90; 1892–99 [Presently W. Halifax Elementary]	
8. 1859–63; 1867; 1872–74; 1876; 1878; 1881–82; 1887–90; 1892–99	1912
9. 1859–63; 1867; 1872–73; 1874–75; 1878; 1880; 1882; 1887–90; 1892–98	1923
10. 1859–63; 1872–74; 1876; 1878; 1881–82; 1889; 1892–96; 1898–99	1922
11. 1859–60; 1862–63; 1872–76; 1882; 1888; 1894; 1896–97	1929
12. 1859–63; 1872; 1874–76; 1878; 1880–82; 1887; 1892–99	1910
13. 1859; 1861–63; 1872–76; 1878; 1880–82; 1887–90; 1892; 1895–96; 1898	1915
14. 1859–63; 1868	1868

CONVERSION TO THE TOWN SYSTEM AND CONSOLIDATION

In 1870, the legislature passed "an act permitting schools to reorganize under town authority rather than in independent districts."[7] Halifax was one of many Vermont towns that resisted changing to a single district. In March of 1886, the local reporter chided,

> Despite the example of other towns, . . . it is not to be expected
> that this town will reform, but continue in its "pod auger ways,"
> its frequent community broils, sometimes spending valuable time,
> which would be unnecessary under the town system. We sincerely
> hope that the state will compel towns to support *public schools*, not
> community broils.[8]

The vote to adopt the town system was defeated 63 to 18.[9]

The key victory for reform came in 1892, when the legislature abolished local school districts. "This new law, called by its critics 'the vicious act of 1892,' gave towns sole authority for defining and enforcing educational policy within their boundaries."[10] Since enactment of that law, Halifax schools have been governed by a town board of directors aided by local and district superintendents. In his report for 1893, Superintendent Worden said, "It is hoped that the new school law will be given a fair trial and will be judged by its results . . . doubtless it will be found advisable to discontinue several schools and this in some cases will be an inconvenience, but the benefits may greatly outweigh the advantages in time."[11]

Norris Johnson described the process of school consolidations based on findings in the town reports. An edited version of his 1979 *Halifacts* article follows.

The number of schools in operation slowly and irregularly declined. The town report for 1892, for the first time, included a report by the school superintendent, noting, "[S]chools of two or three scholars are seldom profitable ones." F. Herbert Worden urged consolidations. F. Herbert Worden and Emory F. Evans were dominant figures in the school system for ten years, serving alternately as superintendent and clerk of the school directors. Mr. Worden also was a teacher until 1901, and after retirement from teaching, he kept the wood fires burning to heat the schools. He also maintained the school buildings as late as 1921.

The process of consolidation was slow. The two schools on what is now Route 112, Niles and Fisher (Nos. 2 and 3) were replaced in 1895 by a new school called Valley School. This was built on the other side of Route 112, from the original Niles School. The 1895 town report stated that schoolhouse No. 2 was entirely unsuitable. It was the first school the town offered for sale in 1896 under the new law.

SUPERINTENDENT VISITS VALLEY SCHOOL   HHS

Depending on numbers of students and availability of teachers, particular schools were closed for a year or more, and later reopened. Neighboring schools, such as Grove and Worden (Nos. 4 and 5) and Hatch and Harrisville (Nos. 9 and 10), were sometimes used alternately. Worden School, last used in 1897, was finally merged into Grove. The school directors at that time were E. F. Evans, R. J. Phillips, and S. B. Worden.

It was noted in the 1900 town report, "it is evident to all that the cost per scholar in our small schools is more than in our larger school, other things being equal, and the more schools we have the more expensive to the town; therefore, we have consolidated schools (Nos. 4 and 5, 9 and 10, 11 and 12" [HTC: TR 17].

Photos HHS

The picturesque Cape-style Whitneyville schoolhouse (above left) was located on the Old County Road just north of the cemetery. During 1899, one of the final years of classes here, Superintendent, F. Herbert Worden taught all three terms. Eventually, children from this district were sent to West Halifax. Zora Whitney sold the property to Dr. James Philand Niles, who made extensive plans to operate a slate quarry nearby. In a taped interview with the Cody brothers, Oscar said, "I tried to buy that [school house], but I didn't get a hold of the man in Boston and got beat out by old Mr. Lewis Sumner, the father of Ken and Homer." According to Joe Cody, the building was stripped of its clapboards, rotted out, and fell down.   Audio Autobiography, vol. 5, 1976.

In 1905, there were still nine schools in use. The Fisher and Worden schools had disappeared; students from the Whitneyville district (No. 13) were being sent to West Halifax (No. 7) and those from Reid Hollow (No. 11) to Harrisville (No. 10). Meanwhile, the Pennell Hill School (No. 1) had been discontinued after the spring term of 1915 because there were not enough scholars to maintain a legal school. The Hall school (No. 8) was closed after 1912, the Thomas Hill School (No. 12) after 1910. [Sadly there are no known photographs of Fisher, Worden, and Thomas Hill schools.]

REID HOLLOW SCHOOL   HHS   HARRISVILLE SCHOOL   HHS

The Harrisville school district of Halifax had very few pupils for the term of 1925–1926, while the Reid Hollow district near Warren's mills had a good number; so the two districts were consolidated at the Reid Hollow schoolhouse, and for one year the old schoolhouse was used, but it was found to be inadequate as to accommodations and badly out of repair, as well as unsightly.

In 1923, there were as many as six schools in operation, but Hatch and Harrisville schools were closed the following year. Reid Hollow, which had been closed some years earlier, continued in use through 1930. The school enrollment in 1935 varied from Valley School with nineteen students to West Halifax with forty-three and Grove with twelve. Grove survived until June 1939 and was briefly reopened for the school year 1953–54. At that time, there were only two other schools in town, West Halifax and Valley. [The new West Halifax School, erected in 1958, was enlarged in 1992.]

* * *

RECURRING THEMES

Several themes recur over the years throughout newspaper accounts, school directors' reports, and superintendent reports. The poor condition of many of the school buildings was a problem mentioned in a newspaper article dated 1849:

> Many of these old school houses will remain, until twice as much
> money is wasted in them, as it would cost to build new ones, to
> say nothing of the health and comfort, of both teacher and pupils
> which are sacrificed.[12]

The cost of maintaining so many small schools presented a tremendous burden to the town and is a theme that continues to plague rural education to this day.

Poor school attendance presented yet another challenge. In an 1899 report from Superintendent F. Herbert Worden, he states:

> If parents and guardians fully realized the necessity for prompt and steady attendance, it would greatly increase the efficiency of the schools. I think it would be well to require teachers to inquire into every absence, and unless satisfied that it was necessary to promptly report the fact. Many times a visit by the teacher will have the required effect. The appointment of a truant officer would have a good effect in cases where the absentee is entirely wilful. [HTC: TR 28]

Another theme that was frequently cited and that continues to resonate today is the need for parent involvement in the schools. Superintendent Worden had this advice:

> Parents should visit the schools often enough to be able to form an intelligent opinion of them. Spare harsh criticism of teachers and methods, especially in the presence of pupils, for it never helps in any good way, and often is unfair and unjust to the teachers, from not understanding all the facts and circumstances in the case. Encourage teachers by your presence and show interest in all school work. As a rule, all teachers do the very best they can under the circumstances in which they are placed. Teach your children to understand that the schools are for them, to fit them for business and for positions their country has to fill.
>
> [HTC: TR 30]

Unidentified school group   HHS

GRADUATION EXERCISES

In 1917, Superintendent stated, "Enough children graduate from the Halifax schools yearly to warrant holding graduation exercises at some central place, as a means of showing the town's appreciation of the success of its pupils and learning what is being accomplished in the schools" [HTC: TR 23]. Moffit wrote, "I plan to hold such a graduation this June . . ." In his 1918 report, Moffit said, "Last June, the first graduation was held at the Baptist Church in West Halifax and it was a demonstration of what can be done. The exercises reflected great credit upon the pupils and teachers" [HTC: TR 26]. That tradition has continued since 1992 to this day with exercises held in the multipurpose room at the school.

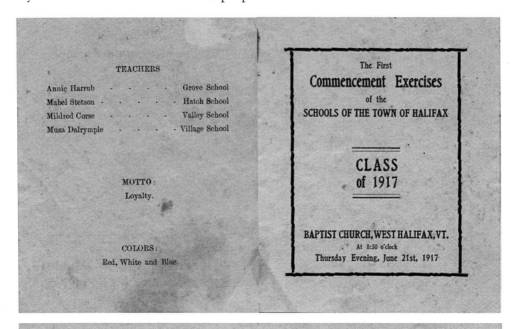

HALIFAX CENTER SCHOOL

The picture (right) shows the last days of what was mentioned in many old accounts "as a fine old academy." It served also as the district schoolhouse for the Center.

Picture taken circa 1898. 1st row front L to R, Ernest Fairbanks, Back row from left, 2nd boy, Dan Fairbanks, 3rd boy, Harry Goodnough, from right, 3rd boy, Mervin Fairbanks.   Photos HHS

Florence Fisher, former teacher at the Halifax School, wrote in a letter to Elaine Fairbanks, "When I was seventeen I taught at the Halifax Center schoolhouse. I drove from my home daily, [Thomas Hill] and

Florence Fisher

when school was over I headed home, not much time to spare. . . . When I was teaching at the center, I used various ways to drive over (horse and buggy) many times coming past the Deer Park." Fisher was born in Halifax on March 28, 1891.

PENNELL HILL

In the news 1899: "Extensive improvements are being made with the Pannell Hill school house. It was not only terribly cold in the winter, but dangerous from huge chunks of falling plastering. The raised floor for one part of the school room was a great nuisance." Fred Barnard, who, as a boy, lived in the Hagar homestead, speaking to the HHS in 1979, recalled the schoolhouse. "T'was like most of those district schools, had wooden pews and a big box stove, so you was half-baked which is how most of 'em turned out to be, but we survived. Course the water, we had to get from the brook. In them days it was safe to drink the water. years later, I heard the Woodards

HHS

[originally, the Thompson property] had a fire and the grass hadn't been cut, so it spread and burnt down the school." Pictured in front of the district 1 schoolhouse (above) on Pennell Hill are Sanford and Flora Plumb, children of Sidney H. Plumb. They attended in the 1870s.

COMMEMORATING THE HATCH DISTRICT SCHOOL

The Halifax Historical Society began the 2004 annual meeting with a rededication ceremony held at the foundation of the former Hatch School house. Little has changed at the dirt crossroads only slightly wider than those the children walked, at times in bare feet, to attend classes two hundred years ago. Mrs. Judy Jones, owner of the property, read the original deed, displayed photos, and presented notes on the history of the school.

This article of agreement witnesseth that I Calvin Olds of Marlboro of the first part do covenant and agree to build a schoolhouse in Halifax in school district No. five [later nine] near the corner of the roads where the old school house now stands of the following dementions viz: twenty eight feet by twenty on the ground and nine fut posts to be timbered and divided in the following manner viz. schoolroom twenty feet square wood room at the end occupying the rest with posts at the corners and between the partition and timbers overhead near enough to both upon and braced and studed with the out side of the house to be enclosed with three quarter boards clapboarded and shingled with two plain double doors one outside the other inside with seven twenty lighted windows lid by eight glass the joist and cornish to be suitable to the size of the house the body of the house to be well painted with Spanish brown and oil and trimed with white. The school room to be constructed and done off as near as the situation will admit like the one in the center of this town with the

HATCH SCHOOL   HHS

exception of the seats and seating to be spruce instead of hard timber and the wood room to be lined with ¾ planks all around the end. The schoolroom to be boarded to the ridge and a plank floor of two inch plank to be laid through the room without pinning or spiking. The above said house to be completed by the first of November next.

In witness whereof we have hereunto interchangeably set our hands and seals at Halifax this twenty first day of Jan. one thousand eight hundred and twenty three.

Signed sealed and delivered in presence of Timothy Larrabee, Nathaniel Goodspeed, Erastus Hall, Amos Tucker.[13]

Courtesy Jacques Tucker

Thus, District No. 5 of Halifax planned a new schoolhouse in 1823 at the cost of $152 dollars. Calvin Olds, the contractor, was the brother of Cynthia, wife of Timothy Larrabee, who lived about half a mile east of the schoolhouse on Green River Road. A full mile east of the schoolhouse was the Asahel Ballou farm at the junction of Brook Road. His son, Hosea, II, from age four to fourteen had attended the old Hatch School, whose frame was to be incorporated into the new school and moved slightly closer to the road. Walking the mile to the old red school and back morning and afternoon, he imagined the days when Ethan Allen and his Bennington men marched along this same road in the summer of 1783, on the expedition to subdue the Yorkers in Guilford.[14] As a young man, Hosea returned from working in another state to marry Clarissa Hatch, a schoolmate of his childhood, who lived a few rods beyond the school. Early photo views of the schoolhouse include a portion of the imposing James Hatch homestead and barns.

The ceremony concluded with a poem written for the occasion and read by Halifax poet, Wyn Cooper.

POSTCARD FROM HATCH SCHOOL

One of the first things I learn
is that in winter the school
is warmer than my house.
I try not to miss a day,
but sometimes it snows so much
I have to stay home.
Sometimes I'm needed
for planting or harvesting,
sometimes I'm sick,
but I never grow sick
of learning new words,
new ways to put numbers
together and take them apart.
I see places on the map
so far away I know I won't
get there: Russia, France, Ohio.
I would like to travel, but
only if I could come home
to Halifax, because my teacher
has taught me to be proud
to live in the second oldest town
in the great state of Vermont.

Courtesy Wyn Cooper

HATCH SCHOOL   HHS

HATCH SCHOOL GIRLS   HHS

HALL SCHOOL

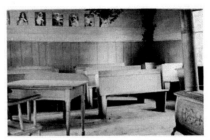

LEFT: Photo taken about 1905. Child is Beatrice T. Warren, two yrs. old. ABOVE: Hall classroom. HHS

Mrs. Florence (Phillips) Maxam taught school in the Hall district . . . in the summer of 1878. She was only 15 years old then, and attended high school the next four winters. W. S. Allen notes that in 1850 there were 18 families in the district who sent children to school. Hard feelings developed over the question of the location of the schoolhouse. This went on for a few years until 1855 when the district voted to build a schoolhouse nearer the center. This was done by measuring the distance from the Perry Hall house to each family in the district. The location agreed upon was 1,901 rods north and 1,899 rods south of the Hall building. The present site was chosen by a committee consisting of Benjamin Eames and Lemuel Hall. Perry Hall gave the land.

It was voted to adopt Elijah S. Allen's plan for a new schoolhouse 18 by 24 feet; to instruct the committee to dispose of the old schoolhouse at best advantage. The building committee let the job of building the new schoolhouse to Philo Brown of Whitingham for $150 and what he could salvage from the old schoolhouse.

The building was used for a school until 1912. It has been used as a camp since then. On display [at the Halifax Historical Society] are the old bookcase and teacher's desk and many of the pupils' desks. The two "outdoor facilities" are still standing and are used for woodsheds.   Excerpts from *Halifacts*, No. 36, July 2005.

HHS

Mrs. Berry
as she appeared
on this front of this
graduation program.

HALL : SCHOOL
VERMONT
1905

Presented By
Mrs. J. E. Berry
Teacher

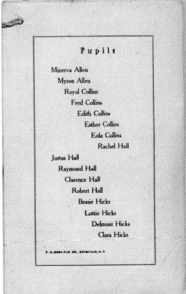

Pupils

Minerva Allen
Myron Allen
Royal Collins
Fred Collins
Edith Collins
Esther Collins
Eola Collins
Rachel Hall
Justus Hall
Raymond Hall
Clarence Hall
Robert Hall
Bessie Hicks
Lottie Hicks
Delmont Hicks
Clara Hicks

GROVE SCHOOL
A New Day For An Old School in Halifax

The Grove School in South Halifax, abandoned for years and rapidly becoming a total ruin, has been rebuilt and is reopening this week with Mrs. Gloria Brooks of Brattleboro, a former student at Marlboro College, as schoolmarm. With the co-operation of the Halifax School Board, Fred Bowen, Mrs. Mary Burnett and Mrs. Jane Grant, and the volunteer labor of two families of local residents, the decaying old building has been transformed at almost no cost to the town into a spruce "little white schoolhouse." Almost all the work was done as a contribution to the community by Mr. and Mrs. Eugene Gates and Mr. and Mrs. Richard Winston. Halliday Evans of West Halifax has donated a teacher's desk to the school, and also helped with the reconstruction. Charles Miller, formerly of Ripton, Vt. and now of Brattleboro, also donated a day's labor. Even the prospective pupils helped with the sweeping and oiling the floor and the new teacher wielded a paint brush, too.

Decision to re-open the old school was a difficult one to make in these times, when the trend is toward centralization of schools. Grove had been closed for some 15 years, due to the decline in the population of the area. But in recent years the number of children in South Halifax has increased rapidly, and the problem of transporting these children long distances over bad winter roads has given concern to the School Board as well as to the parents involved. The only alternative to transportation was to re-open Grove School, but the cost of reconstructing the old building seemed prohibitive. Co-operative volunteer labor solved this difficulty.

Brattleboro Reformer, October 2, 1953

STUDENTS GREET THE SUPERINTENDENT   HHS

DOWN MEMORY LANE REMEMBRANCES OF VALLEY

The wind whipped across Dean's Flat as we pushed our way to school along the wind-swept road. In the 1940 era, there was less traffic on the road. The wind drifted across the Flat, and walking in the tire track was often the only path. Even

on wintry days when it didn't snow, the frosty conditions chilled us as we walked the mile or more to school. I can remember the headscarf wrapped around my face and tied at the back of my neck and trying to breathe through the air hole. As we rounded the top of the hill beyond Niles Cemetery, we could see the school in the distance. The white building blended with the snow and

VALLEY SCHOOL   HHS

seemed farther away than it was. The school had a small porch, which allowed us some protection as we stomped our boots going up the wooden steps. The snow was light as a feather and sometimes for art we made snowflake designs out of construction paper to stick on the windows.

Our teacher taught eight grades in our one room. Just inside the school door there was a long bench and we slid our metal lunch pails under there for storage. During the winter, we had hot lunch. Sometimes the parents came with the lunch all ready to serve. At other times, in an adjoining kitchenette, which had a stove, dish cupboard, and washbasin, the teacher could be seen stirring something on the stove as she conducted a class. She read us a story every day. One book I especially liked was the one about birds. There was an exit door leading to the porch, but of course we always had a door which lead out to the woodshed and side lawn. There was a small mirror hanging on a string over the basin in the kitchen, tipped at most any angle to accommodate any height.

When school began in September, we always got to sit in the different desks to find the right one to fit us. We were all in the same one-room schoolhouse. We sat in rows with our backs to the door, facing the teacher. Everyone liked being near the window where we could be distracted at our convenience. There was a morning and afternoon recess and about an hour for lunch.

The front lawn at the school was large, and we made snow forts and had lots of snowball fights in the winter. We played games such as, Prisoners Base, Fox and Geese, softball, and hide-and-seek. We learned at an early age that when a parent visited the school, their conversation could be heard at an outside vent at the back of the school. There was a swing, which hung from the old oak tree. There were shade trees on one side of the building, which helped in the summer, but inside there were no fans to cool us when it was hot. The area around us was open, farms were nearby, and a lumber mill was across the road from the school. The Stone family operated this mill, and the mill whistle blew every day at noon.

There was no running water at school. Two children took turns carrying a pail of water from the Stone family home. No doubt, we made more than one trip, as this was used for drinking, hand washing, and lunch dishes. The toilet facilities were outside and the trips to the facility in the winter were quick and dreaded.

Holiday time was exciting for us. On Memorial Day, we marched from our school to the nearby cemetery to place handpicked flowers on soldiers' graves. Several parents attended the afternoon program, which included poems and songs. Lining up to march was fun. Niles was the nearest cemetery to our school. At Christmas time, we had plays and several recitations. All desks were turned to face the door and a sturdy wire stretched across the room with sheets pinned to it. The parents sat in our desks, and all children looked forward to Santa's visit. No doubt the parents were glad when it was over; they had to help us remember our parts for the play. The teacher stood behind the curtain to prompt us, especially when the curtain opened and stage fright set in.

I remember the big pictures on the wall. One of these was George Washington. Our country's flag was near the blackboard, and we pledged our allegiance to the flag each morning.

Several family members worked at the nearby mills and often moved on to other work. This affected our school enrollment. At times, we had as few as ten students.

As students we had chores to do. We had a flag by the porch to put up each day, and we had erasers to clap and blackboards to erase. There was no modern heating system. We had a big wood stove with a tin jacket around it. We spread our wet mittens and clothes on the tin under the stove. We took turns getting the wood in from the wood shed. My sister, Joyce, as well as other students, were janitors at the school one year. She got up early to start the school fire so it would be warm when the other children arrived. There were many cold days and the schoolroom was chilly. We pulled our desks close to the stove, so our faces were red and our backs were cold. There were large windows on one side of the room but without storm combinations, as we know them today. The cracks around the door let in a lot of cold. There were closets for our coats and boots.

Some books were available to us on the shelves, but we looked forward to seeing the "book wagon" come. Two librarians, who came with the book wagon, made scheduled visits to our schools in the

HHS

Back row L to R: Charlotte Miner, Carl and Lucille Stone, Regina Carr, Helen Harris, Bruce McQuirey, Front row: Joyce Fairbanks, Claire Dean, Elaine Fairbanks, Bernice Burnett

area. They helped us as we took turns going out to select our books. They were dedicated and opened up the world of learning for all outlying schools.

In back of the school was a large open field. At the far end was a brook, and that is where we got our pollywogs that we put in jars to watch them grow. On nice days we enjoyed being out of doors. Often the teacher would take us for nature walks to study flowers, birds, trees, and so on. As a bird lover, this was of great interest to me. These walks and the stories our teacher read about birds was helpful in the chart she had us make that told of their nesting habits, where they could be found, what they looked like, and the songs they sang. I used to sit in the apple orchard above my parents' house for hours watching the many birds that were there. Bluebirds were not endangered then, but today I get excited to see one. One of my grandmothers gave me a special book on birds, and even though it is worn with use and age, I gave it to my nephew, Warren.

I spent a lot of summer vacations in the hay field helping my grandparents. By myself, I hitched the horse "old Dan" to the whipple tree[15] and took the hay wagon down to the field where Gramp was tumbling hay with his hand rake. In the fall, when we returned from our summer vacation, one thing that impressed me was the shiny floor as we stepped in the door to begin in another grade. It was polished and shiny to the point where you could almost see your reflection.

The first day back at school was full of excitement. I got to wear a new dress and see my friends again. Of course, those students who were in the eighth grade had left for another school, and they left a big hole in our enrollment. In 1948, it was my turn to graduate and leave the school I loved. Graduation programs were a tradition, at which time parents and friends joined for an evening program by the students. At the time I graduated, we combined graduations with the West Halifax School.

The Baptist Church was the gathering spot for the occasion and a dance [at the Community Hall] was held in honor of the graduates following the program. The girls received corsages and the boy's boutonnieres, and as special guests of the occasion, we received free refreshments. The children loved the slippery dance floor and skated around in between parents who were dancing. The butterfly feeling we had earlier had disappeared and the evening was ours to enjoy.

My grandfather, Rolland, and daughters Arlene and Helena, as well as my brother Jerrold, sister Joyce, and cousin Regina, all attended Valley School over a span of several years. My mother said that when she and Helena walked to school, they often met Ed Niles. He had a horse and sleigh and with it he traveled Route 112 to below the Gorge to gather children and transport them to school. My mother and sister, Helena, hooked their sleds to the runners of the sleigh and got a ride to school. What fun!

Two of my best friends were Helen Harris (Floyd and Edith Harris's daughter), and Charlotte Miner (Henry and Sarah Miner's daughter), who both lived on Route 112. During our vacations, Charlotte walked early in the morning to visit me for a few hours. One morning I slept late and Dad woke me. As I stood in the door with blinking eyes and the sun beaming at me, Charlotte sat on the porch railing laughing at me. Helen lived the furthest away from my home, but we all got to see each other at school. Their grandparents and mine had lived in the area for a long time, so it was only natural that another generation would be friends also. Both girls went on to college and settled in other states. We still see each other at class reunions and talk about the "remember whens."

My grandfather told me that at the Valley School there is old ink well buried beneath the trees on the bank that runs parallel with Route 112. The ink well contains the names of the school children, including his.   *~ Elaine Fairbanks*

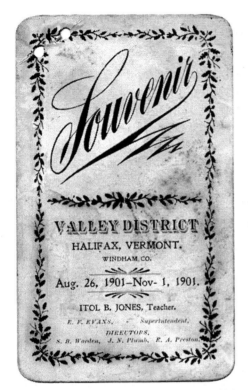 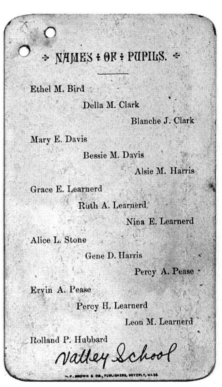

FALL TERM SOUVENIR   HHS

MEMORIES FROM MARY DAVIS

Some of my brothers and sisters attended school by the brook down by the Bender place [Fisher]. At one time young Fred May and his wife lived there. Gertrude Galvin, who married Merrick Harris, drove a white horse from where she lived on Pennell Hill down to teach at that school house. I attended Valley School and remember my teacher Rufus Brown [↩ 321]. He was quite a good size teacher . . . He had to be in order to wallop those big boys every day. There were a lot of Learnard children at the school, and a number of children whose parents worked at the Stone Clark mill. They boarded in the big house at the foot of Hubbard Hill.   HHS, Audio Autobiography, vol. 6, February 1, 1974

WEST HALIFAX ELEMENTARY / PLUMB HOLLOW SCHOOL

1903   HHS

Front Row Left to Right: Eugene Berry, Calista Worden, Pauline Adams, Alice Baxter, Mildred
Baxter, Bessie Ryder, Charles Morton Baxter, Delmont Hicks.
Second Row Left to Right: Sadie Clark, Roy Scudder, Ethel Clark, Mable Bessie Hicks, Laura
Phillips, Alice Phillips, Lottie Hicks, Alice Allen, Guy Ryder.
Back Row Left to Right: Harry Goodnough, Lovina Phillips, Mrs. Berry (teacher), Edith
Phillips, Nina Clark

Circa 1911 WEST HALIFAX BOWS   Photo Porter Thayer
                                                           Courtesy C. Lancaster

Circa 1911 WILFRED HITCHCOCK AND HARRY MAY   Photo Porter Thayer HHS

FROM THE OLD TO THE NEW

From the old to the construction of the new

Photos HHS

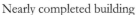

Nearly completed building

Building completed 1958

I remember when the construction for the new school building was completed and that cool October day when we walked together from the old school to the new. There was sadness and yet there was excitement about what the future had in store. It was a bittersweet day.

Halifax Elementary is bicentennial school

By BERNICE BARNETT
Reformer Correspondent

HALIFAX — About 140 townspeople turned out Monday evening for a program dedicating Halifax Elementary School as a Bicentennial School.

After a supper, Lavern Corey, chairman of the town's Bicentennial Committee, opened the program and presented gifts to Leah Thayer for designing the logo for a Bicentennial T-shirt, which will be sold. Jeffrey Longe also received a gift for designing a button.

Thomas O'Brien, a member of the state Bicentennial Committee, then presented the certificate designating the school as a Bicentennial School

to Daniel Corey, an eighth-grader. He also presented the Bicentennial flag to William Ackemann, a teacher.

The audience was then treated to a historical program by the schoolchildren. Grades 1 and 2 recited a poem by Robert Frost and danced an old dance called the Virginia Reel. Grades 3 to 5 presented a skit in which 10 different people of town history was represented. These included people who had been born in Halifax and those who had moved in but contributed to Halifax history.

After the program, the assemblage was served a Bicentennial cake, made by Corey.

Reformer, July 1991

Bicentennial float, "A Part of Our Past," Mariette Sanders, with school children.

"A Look at Our Future," with model of proposed building.

William Ackerman and Tom O'Brien holding the Bicentennial School Flag. Above photos HHS

Photo C. Perna

The new school, which includes an all-purpose room used for town events. Front right of the older building now houses the town offices.   ~ *Carrie Perna*

FLAG DAY AT VALLEY SCHOOL 1898

HHS

Teacher, Rufus L. Brown; Student enrollment as follows, youngest to oldest; not all named children are included in above photo (some children's ages unknown): Ruth Learnard [5], Bessie Davis [ ], Grace Learnard [6], Ervin Pease [ ], Blanche Clark [7], Nina Learnard [8], Rolland Hubbard [ ], Della Clark [ ] Mary Davis [9] Alice Stone [ ], Leon Learnard [10], Percy Pease [10], Leslie Davis [ ], Percy Learnard [11] Carl Stone, [11] Minnie Pease [ ], Harry Clark [ ], Horace Fowler [ ], Carl Ware [ ], Arthur Pike [12] Mabel Learnard [13], Stephen Strong [13], Bertha Clark [ ], Earl Brown [14], Benjamin Learnard [15].

Superintendent's flag references from the town reports:

1897 "Patriotism should be encouraged in all our public schools and the good work of unfurling the flag above them should go on until the stars and stripes wave over every schoolhouse in town." E. F. Evans

1898 "During the past year schools No. 2, 4 and 5 and 6, have unfurled new flags and it is hoped that others will be added during the coming year until each school shall have the stars and stripes waving above it. . . . I am glad to note the increased interest taken by the schools in Memorial Day exercises."
[Note: School No. 2 was Valley, and this is the year the picture was taken, presumably to show the new flag]

1899 "School No. 10 unfurled a new flag, making five schools having flags. May others be added until no school is without one." F. Herbert Worden, Superintendent of Schools p. 29

1900 "School No 1 unfurled a new flag, making six school houses having flags."

~ Bernice Barnett, Elaine Fairbanks Constance Lancaster,
Carrie Perna, Susan Rusten and Mariette Sanders

Beyond The Common School

Secondary education flourished in Halifax during the nineteenth century. Even though the classroom record books have vanished, confirming evidence is found in newspapers and other paper ephemera. From advertisements, we know the academy program at Halifax Center was one of the first offered in Windham County. In 1802, *Brattleborough Academy* was established in West Brattleboro.[16] About 1817, *Halifax Academy* opened its doors, initially to male students, and within a few years, to female students as well. By 1845, nearly every Windham County town advertised a secondary school program. However, Brattleboro and Halifax were the only towns in the county that operated two high school programs concurrently.

The Academy

The most enduring symbol of higher education in Halifax is the brick Academy Schoolhouse built on the common at the Center. It was located by the Old South Congregational Meeting House and Center Cemetery. Town records include plans to build the first meeting house in 1782; however, there is no mention of an effort to build a school nearby. In September 1784, at the first meeting held in the new meeting house, the voters decided to divide the town into ten school districts. Each district would keep its own sets of records. If the clerk's book for District No. 10, Halifax Center, were found, the records

THE ACADEMY   HHS
The original structure was two stories tall. Photographs show the line in the bricks from when the second story was removed in 1891.

might tell who built the academy and perhaps reveal the origin of its handmade bricks, a material rarely used on the exteriors of buildings in Halifax. The probate file for Isaac Orr Jr. tells us when the academy was constructed. Itemized together with payments for his medical care, his coffin, and digging his grave is a payment, "To Stephen Bullock, collector of the tax under the list of 1816 on school District No. 10 in Halifax, to finish building the schoolhouse."[17]

Vermont Phoenix, May 12, 1865

> The past season the Centre District have thoroughly repaired their brick schoolhouse, at an expense of about $500. The first floor is used for a District School, and the second story has been used for a select school for the last thirty years. These rooms are large and commodious, and command a full view of the Green mountains and surrounding country.

Vermont Phoenix, September 4, 1891

> Repairs on the old schoolhouse in district No. 6 are progressing
> finely. The second story is being taken out and the roof let down
> onto the first story.

In 1850, the town voted to change District No. 6, Fisher/Stowe, to
District 3, and District No. 10 was to "hereafter be known as and called District
No. 6" [HTC: TM 2]. The academy and the meeting house appear as adjacent
structures on McClellan's 1856 Halifax map. The mapmaker marked fourteen
school houses with the initials, "S. H.," but he labeled the school building at
Halifax Center "Academy." The Beers map published in 1869 identified the
academy as "Town Hall and School No. 6." The meeting house does not appear
on this map, since by then, James Landon Stark had torn it down.

With the founding of the academy circa 1816, local young men who
aspired to professional life could study Greek, Latin, and advanced mathematics
within those brick walls. By 1823, an academic program for young women had
been established. Rev. Wood's description, written for Thompson's initial
gazetteer, tells us.

> At the center is an elegant brick schoolhouse, 42
> by 24 feet on the ground, in which the languages
> and higher branches of literature are taught during
> most of the year. There is also a school for young
> ladies, in which, besides the higher branches of
> English education, are taught, drawing, painting
> and music.[18]

HHS

During this period, painting and ornamental needlework were considered
proper school subjects for girls. It is believed the gifted folk artist Almira Edson,
painter of family registers,[19] taught calligraphy and drawing at the academy. Her
father, Congregational minister Rev. Jesse Edson, died in 1805 when she was two
years old, but in 1819, she was living next to the schoolhouse in Halifax as the
ward of her father's successor, Rev. Thomas Wood.[20] Wood, like his predecessor
Edson, took an active interest in the youth of Halifax. He tutored young men
preparing for college. His pupils, usually from local farm families, would perform
farm chores in the predawn hours, followed by a horseback ride or walk to the
Center for lessons. Evening chores preceded more study. It was a rigorous
program.

Detail from James Tucker family register. Collection of the New-York Historical Society, Courtesy Janet Soyer
ORNAMENTAL CALLIGRAPHY BY ALMIRA EDSON

The education of young men received [Rev. Wood's] special attention, nine of whom from his own society fitted for college with him, besides several from adjoining towns. Six entered the ministry under his pastorate.[21]

Notable young men of Halifax who trained with Rev. Wood were: Congregationalists Elijah Plumb, DD; Rev. Sumner Everett, missionary to Constantinople; and Rev. Charles Scott; Baptists Rev. Henry Clay Fish, DD; Rev. Ross Burdick and Rev. Judson Tucker; and Universalists Rev. Hosea Ballou, "2d" and brothers, Levi and William Starr Ballou. In a biographical sketch of Yale College graduates, it is said that James Landon Stark "was prepared for College by his Pastor, the Rev. Thomas H. Wood (Williams Coll. 1799)."[22]

In his description of his grandfather's education, Hosea Starr Ballou[23] called attention to the financial hardships of obtaining education beyond the common school. When one son in a farm family aspired to advanced studies, resources were stretched thin, but usually, a way would be found to support further education for that son. Of the nine sons of Asahel and Martha Starr Ballou five sought advanced study. Hosea, Levi, and William prepared for the ministry, Almon, for medicine and Martin, for law. All five sons labored on the family farm (right) located on Green River Road and in the machine shop to help support the family that supported their education. Hosea Starr continues,

Built by Ashael Ballou, 1799   HHS

Four miles away, at Halifax Centre, lived Rev. Thomas H. Wood, who was glad to supplement his salary as Congregationalist minister by tuition fees as teacher. At fourteen years of age, Hosea began reciting Latin to him. From the beginning, he became a proficient Latin scholar. It was while studying Latin at home, late evenings after the labors of the day, that he first acquired the habit of putting bits of tobacco into his mouth to stimulate him to keep awake, a habit which, though scarcely observable, went with him as long as he lived. He also attended a "select school" at Halifax Centre. What he learned there he never forgot. It was not a wide curriculum, but it ploughed deep. He secured an average preparation for college, but, above all else, he learned there how to study. The aged daughter of Mr. Wood wrote a few years ago from a distant State that she remembered well seeing, as a child, three of the Ballou boys—Hosea, Levi, and William Starr, no doubt—one after another coming on horseback on a black mare with three white feet to recite to her father.[24]

Through this type of narrative, gazetteer accounts, and gleanings from newspapers, we can sketch the history of higher education in Halifax. Classified advertisements document some of the high school programs offered.

HALIFAX CENTER FIRST HIGH SCHOOL

HIGH SCHOOL.

THE first Term of the HALIFAX HIGH SCHOOL, will commence on MONDAY the 14th inst. The proprietors have erected a commodious Building, and engaged a Teacher as competent as any one in the State of Vermont.

Terms of Tuition, for all branches of study, $3,00. Board in good families, washing included, $1,25.

SAMUEL FISH, Jr. } *Agents for the*
JOSEPH HENRY, } *Proprietors.*
BENJ. WOODARD, }

Halifax, Sept. 3, 1835.

Halifax High School.

THE FALL TERM of the Halifax High School will commence the first Monday of September next, under the Superintendence of W. G. BROWN.

Tuition in all branches, $3,00.
Board in good families at   1,25.

JOSEPH HENRY, } *Agents*
SAM'L FISH, Jr. } *for the*
BENJ. WOODARD, } *Proprietors.*

Halifax, July 13, 1836.   7w45

HALIFAX HIGH SCHOOL,

UNDER the superintendance of DANIEL SHEPARDSON, Jr. The sixth term of the Halifax High School will commence September 4th.

Board and Tuition.

On most reasonable terms.

JOSEPH HENRY,
SAMUEL FISH, Jr.
BENJAMIN WOODARD.

Halifax, July 28, 1837.   5w   28

Halifax High School.

THE Spring Term of this hitherto liberally patronized Institution will commence February 21st, under the care of DANIEL SHEPARDSON, Jr. Terms as usual.

JOSEPH HENRY, }
SAMUEL FISH, } *Agents.*
BENJ. WOODARD, }

Halifax, Jan. 12, 1838.   6w20

Halifax High School.

THE Fall term of this Institution will commence on the second Wednesday of September next, under the instruction of Mr William Miller. A. B., whose experience and success as a teacher, enable the Trustees to promise all who patronize it, a first rate school.

Tuition,—Greek and Latin, $4,00.
Other Academic studies,   3,00.
Board as low as at any other place.

CHARLES FOWLER, Sec.

SAMUEL FISH, }
R. K. HENRY, } Trustees.
6w. STEPHEN NILES, }

Halifax, August 9, 1845

HALIFAX HIGH SCHOOL.

The Fall term of this School will commence on Wednesday September 3d, and continue eleven weeks; under the superintendence of Mr William J. Harris of West Brattleboro:— No pains will be spared on the part of the Teacher and friends of the school to render it pleasant and profitable to all who may attend.

Tuition in all branches, $3,00.
Board may be obtained as low as in any place. Rooms and accommodations furnished to those wishing to board themselves.

SAMUEL FISH, }
STEPHEN NILES, } Trustees.
R. K. HENRY, }

Halifax, July 30th, 1851.

Classified ads from Brattleboro newspapers, the *Phoenix* and the *Semi-Weekly Eagle*, as dated.

The first term of the Halifax Center High School was advertised September 3, 1835. Similar notices appeared for the winter, spring, and fall terms of 1836, and in July 1837, a notice appeared both in the *Vermont Phoenix* and the *Greenfield Gazette and Mercury* announcing, "The sixth term of the Halifax High School will commence September 4th." The agents in these notices were: Joseph Henry, who operated a large general merchandise store at the Center; Samuel Fish Jr., long-time Baptist minister and later a superintendent of the Halifax common schools; and Benjamin Woodard (grandson of first town clerk, Samuel), who served as a Halifax selectman and a representative to the state legislature. Rev. Thomas Wood, though still living at the time, was in declining health and probably no longer actively involved in the academy he had founded.

In 1835, the *Vermont Phoenix* ran notices for high schools in only two Windham County towns—Brattleboro and Halifax. Townsend, which had offered an academy program from 1826 to 1833, was in the process of building the high school that would become Leland & Gray.[25] The academy movement grew steadily throughout the decade, judging from the proliferation of advertisements. Usually, the preceptor for a term would be a recent graduate of Amherst, Middlebury, or Dartmouth. Daniel Shepardson, W. G. Brown, Lorenzo Blood, and D. M. Kimball, some of the instructors mentioned in the Halifax High School notices, are not recognizable Halifax names. These men would have "boarded around."[26] The typical academy guaranteed admission at low cost to pupils fresh from the common schools, whether they wished to prepare for college, for teaching, or for business. Students also could board near the school. "Mrs. Lilla Crosier said that boys who came from a distance boarded at the Stowe [Capt. Thomas Farnsworth] place (now a cellar hole) down Woodard Hill Road."[27]

The decided change in tone and wording in the notice for the 1839 winter term at Halifax High School (right), perhaps indicates a response to increasing competition.

To boast of a "pleasant and interesting" school program seems surprising for the period. Even more surprising is the appearance, a few years later, of a second Halifax high school, situated just over two miles from the brick academy. The *Vermont Phoenix* for August 15, 1845 contains nearly a full page of school ads, including Whitingham, Chester, Townsend, Guilford, and Brattleboro Academies, Saxtons River Seminary, Dummerston

Halifax High School.

THE *Winter Term will commence on TUESDAY*, the 11th of December, under the charge of its present Instructor. Mr. Kimball has been here during the past term: his success in teaching has been such as to entitle him in an eminent degree to the confidence of the community. No pains will be spared on the Teacher's part to make the School pleasant and interesting. We confidently hope that the friends of the school will concentrate their efforts for sustaining it, by sending us their scholars: we shall do our best to benefit them.

Board can be had here as cheap as at any other place. Accommodations can be had for boarding themselves. No extra charges for tuition in Mathematics or Languages.

JOSEPH HENRY, }
SAMUEL FISH, } Trustees.
BENJ. WOODARD, }

Halifax, Nov. 26, 1833.   4w13

Vermont Phoenix as dated

and Halifax High Schools, and the newly established West Halifax Select School. The presence of two high schools in Halifax, at a time when the total population had receded to fewer than thirteen hundred residents, is astonishing.

West Halifax Second High School

Exactly where was the second Halifax high school located? In the absence of surviving school records, we turned to land records to answer that question. During the early decades of the nineteenth century, the hamlet of West Halifax experienced steady residential and industrial growth, in part due to its abundant waterpower. In January 1739, a group of Halifax inhabitants formed a Universalist Society. In 1843, they constructed a building to serve as a combination chapel and schoolhouse. Subsequent land records confirm that the building in District No. 15, later known as Schoolhouse No. 7, and which today is home to the Halifax Historical Society, was also the original Universalist Chapel. Presumably, the religious meetings were held on the second floor and school activities on the ground floor, with high school and common school sessions offered, perhaps, during alternating terms. It is not known precisely when the original District No. 15 common school house[28] closed and the younger students began to attend classes at the new Plumb School.

Early photo Plumb School   HHS

West Halifax Select School.

THE Fall Term will commence on Wednesday September third, and continue eleven weeks.

The Trustees have engaged the services of Mr B. Sanford, member of the present graduating class in Amherst College. Mr Sanford is highly recommended as an experienced and successful teacher.

Pupils who design to become teachers will receive special attention to qualify them for the employment.

TUITION in the common English studies, $3,00 ; in the higher branches, $3,50.

Board may be obtained in good families on as reasonable terms as in any place in this vicinity.

By order of the Trustees.
W. J. HITCHCOCK, Secretary.
West Halifax, Aug. 9, 1845.   3w51

First advertisement for West Halifax High School.

The West Halifax School.

THE FALL TERM of this School will commence on Wednesday, Sept. the 6th, and continue eleven weeks. Mr. IRA CASE, A. B. a recent graduate of Amherst College, has been engaged as teacher.

He is highly recommended as an experienced and successful instructor. Tuition, $2,25 for the term including the higher branches.

Board can be had in good families as reasonable as in any other community in this vicinity. Appropriate instruction will be given to those who wish to qualify themselves for teaching.
W. J. HITCHCOCK, Clerk.
Aug. 17th. 1847.   tf107

WEST HALIFAX SCHOOL.

THE FALL TERM of this institution will Commence on Thursday, the 2nd day of Sept., next, and continue eleven weeks, under the superintendence of LORENZO P. BLOOD, A. B., who is well recommended as an experienced and successful teacher.

Board may be obtained in respectable families, on as low terms as at any other place.

Arrangements have been made to reduce the price of Tuition in all branches, including Latin, Greek, French, &c., to $2,00 per term.
E. S PLUMB, Clerk.
West Halifax, Aug. 16. 1848.

Classified ads from Brattleboro newspapers, the *Phoenix* and the *Brattleboro Semi-Weekly Eagle*, as dated.

Halifax was a two-high-school town for about half a century. In addition to advertisements for both schools found in various Brattleboro and Greenfield papers, Walton's register for 1867 lists a "Literary Institution, Halifax High School, G. E. Wheeler, Principal."[29] Nearly all documentation of the high school classes offered in Halifax Center and West Halifax are found in various newspaper announcements of openings and closing:

> October 1879 Halifax Center:
> The select school in this place is still flourishing. The students support a lyceum in which a good deal of native talent can be found.
>
> November 1879
> West Halifax: The fall term of the select school, E. J. Temple, principal, closed a highly successful session the 14th, but by request of his scholars, he gives them another week. The whole number of scholars has been 51, 40 of whom attended the extra week.
>
> Sept 1880 Halifax Center
> The select school began with 26 scholars.
>
> 1882   The West Halifax high school commences a three months term Wednesday, Aug. 31, with H. C. Davis, principal[.]

A more personal documentation of Halifax secondary education is found in Nellie J. Tucker's autograph album, which encompasses her high school years and is dated 1879 Halifax Center, Vermont. Nellie, the daughter of George and Cynthia Larrabee Tucker, collected signatures and sentiments from members of her family and from her circle of schoolmates. Autographs from the fall term of 1881 and winter of 1882 include the initials W. H. H. S. for West Halifax High School. Signatures from 1883 and 1884 include B. H. S. or Brattleboro High School. References to algebra, Latin, "participles and infinitives," and Shakespeare Club indicate a rather full academic life for this Halifax young woman. Some Halifax classmates who signed and wrote sentiments in her book were: Sarah Anne Hall, Israel Hall, Eleanor A. Griffin, Charlie L. Griffin, Alice M. Thurber, Nettie M. Weeks, Laura D. Worden, J. M. Hagar, Mary G. Stone, Grace A. Plumb, Mary Follett, F. E. Hagar and Orsamus Plumb.

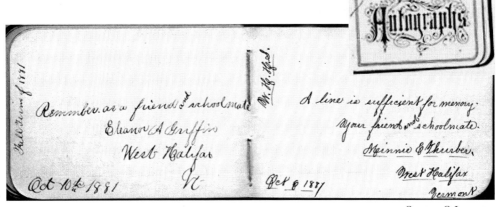

Courtesy C. Lancaster

It is likely that Halifax high school programs ceased about 1892 when the state legislature abolished autonomous school districts and made school buildings the property of the town. The town now operated as a single school district.

The brick academy building, home of Halifax High School, the symbol of "music, art and the higher branches of learning," and for most of a century the setting for political debate and the business of the town, did not survive. The town sold the property in 1954 for the sum of $50 to Lincoln Haynes of Wilmington [HLR 25: 153].[30] He dismantled it for the old bricks.

The four cornerstones of this revered historic structure are still visible on the original town common. Currently, there is no high school in Halifax.

~ Constance Lancaster

ENDNOTES

1. Hemenway, p. 412. Eastman said the rental income was $43.20, but Halifax town reports usually list the annual school lot income as $42.26, though various amounts appear through 1970, after which the town reclassified the school land as privately owned property. The Halifax town report of 1971 is the first that does not include a line item income from "glebe rent." James Stone, town treasurer for many years, said the legislature passed a law allowing the school glebe land to be taxed at the town's regular rate.

2. Halifax school superintendents before the town-wide district system: 1850–1851, Rev. Alpheus Graves; 1852, Rev. Samuel Fish; 1853–1854, Rev. Salmon Bennett; 1855, Rev. W. N. Fay, A. H. Stone, John Reid; 1856, Rev. Lemuel M. Woodward; 1857, S. S. Arnold, Rev. Samuel Fish, Rev. W. Pay; 1858, Dr. Henry Rockwood; 1859, Rev. Geo. M. Atkinson; 1860, Rev. Lemuel M. Woodard; 1861, Dr. H. E. Johnson; 1862–1863, Rev. Chas. W. Emerson; 1865, Rev. S. A. Blake; 1866–1867, Rev. L. M. Woodard; 1868, Dr. J. L. Harrington; 1870, W. H. Follett; 1871–73, Att'y. W. H. Follett; 1874, Dr. J. L. Harrington; 1875, Rev. H. Fowler; 1876–1878, Geo. L. Clark; 1879–1880, Rev. H. M Hopkinson; 1881–1883, A. C. Jones; 1884–1885, Dr. W. C. Whiting; 1886, Herbert Worden; 1887–1889, Chas. E. Thurber; 1890–1892, F. H. Worden.

3. Known as "Father of the Common School," Horace Mann promoted the concept of public education for every child, supported by local taxes. He worked to upgrade standards for teacher training and textbooks.

4. James Tufts, "West Halifax, Dec. 25, 1849" and "Concluded, West Halifax," the *Semi-Weekly Eagle*, Brattleboro, VT, January 3, 1850, p. 1; and January 7, 1850, p. 1, vol. III, nos. 42 and 43.

5. Letter from L. W. F., "Educational Halifax Teachers Association," *Brattleboro Semi-Weekly Eagle*, vol. III, issue 63, March 18, 1850.

6. HTC, Johnson report and file of school registers.

7. Michael Sherman, Gene Sessions, & P. Jeffrey Potash, *Freedom and Unity: A History of Vermont* (Barre, VT: Vermont Historical Society, 2004) p. 319.

8. HHS: Niles, p. 52

9. Ibid.

10. Sherman, et al., p. 319.

11. HHS, *The Annual Report of the Auditors of the Town of Halifax, VT for the Year Ending February 14, 1893*, Wilmington, VT, *Deerfield Valley Times* Print, 1893, p. 12.

12. Tufts, "Concluded West Halifax, Dec. 25, 1849," the *Semi-Weekly Eagle*, vol. III, no. 43.

13. Original document in the possession of Jacques Tucker, a fifth-generation descendant of Amos Tucker of Halifax.

14. Ballou, p. 49.

15. *Webster's New World Dictionary*, second college edition, "a wooden bar swung at the center from a hitch on a plow, wagon, etc. and hooked at either end to the traces of a horse's harness."

16. Mary R. Cabot, *Annals of Brattleboro: 1681–1895*, vol. 1 (Brattleboro, VT: E. L. Hildreth, 1921) p. 188.

17. Estate of Isaac Orr Jr., District of Marlboro Probate Court, no. 525, book 9, p. 411, March 24, 1819.

18. Thompson, 1824, p. 150.

19 Arthur B. and Sybil B. Kern, "Almira Edson, painter of family Registers," *Antiques Magazine*, September 1982, pp. 558–561.

20. Marlboro District Probate File No. 215 for Rev. Jesse Edson, who died intestate, shows that Rebecca Taylor Edson administered the estate [vol. 3: 144]. On August 26, 1806, she was assigned the widow's dower and appointed guardian of their three daughters, Rowena, Almira, and Susan [vol 3: 262]. In September 1810, Rebecca married Edward Adams Jr., a merchant and mill owner, after whom Adamsville, Colrain, Massachusetts was named. Adams had three daughters by his first wife, and in May 1811, a son, Edward, by Rebecca. It is not clear if or for how long the Edson daughters lived with the Adams family in Colrain, but in 1817, Rowena married, and Almira and Susan were living in Halifax as wards of Rev. Thomas Wood [HLR 6: 248]. One surmises they were teaching school. In 1821, Susan married Sylvester Bishop of Marlboro. Little is known of Almira's whereabouts until 1841, when she moved to Putney, Vermont. She painted family registers for a number of Halifax families during the 1830s.

21. Hemingway, p. 480.

22. Franklin Bowditch Dexter, *Bigraphical Sketches of the Graduates of Yale College: with Annals of the College History*, vol. 6 (New York: Henry Holt, 1885–1912) p. 705.

23. Hosea Starr Ballou, *Hosea Ballou, 2nd, D.D., First President of Tufts College: His origin, Life, and Letters* (Boston: E.P. Guild, 1896) p. 50.

24. Ibid., p. 53.

25. Castle Freeman Jr., *A Stitch in Time: Townsend, Vermont 1753–2003* (Townsend, VT: Townsend Historical Society, 2003) pp. 75, 77.

26. "Boarded around," said by Hosea Ballou 2nd, who described, as part of his early common school teaching experience in Marlboro, that he was once "given a sleeping room on the ground floor which was open to the elements underneath" and "the midwinter winds and snows rushed in through the board cracks in the floor and danced about the room."

27. HHS: Johnson.

28. Blanche Legate Sumner, West *Halifax*, monograph prepared by Ellen Hill Powers, October 1982. Sumner said that the old public schoolhouse which "set where H. D. Bowen's house now is now only a trifle nearer the brook . . . is now the ell to Ed Guild's house."

29. *Walton's Vermont Register and Farmers' Almanac for 1867* (Montpelier, VT: S.M. Walton, 1866) p. 54.

30. The deed is from the Town of Halifax to Haynes Brothers. "Westerly from the sw corner of the cemetery 320 feet to Deer Park Road, east of Deer Park and northerly of the Brattleboro Road together with the brick building thereon standing. Except reserving the bell. Signed: Lewis Sumner, Mary Burnett, Lucie Sumner. 9/15/1954."

Little Building – Long History

Probably the most recycled building in town, the structure that today serves as the Halifax Historical Society Museum has been an integral part of community life since 1843. It is the oldest building still in public use in Halifax. While not architecturally in the grand scale of the West Halifax Congregational Church built in 1844, or the two Baptist churches constructed in 1853 this little edifice has very broad shoulders, indeed. Originally, a house of worship and a schoolhouse, the building never featured a steeple or a bell tower. With extraordinary flexibility it has served as a Universalist Chapel, a select school, a high school, a district school, a theatre, a public meeting hall, a Grange hall, a firehouse, and a museum. The combination schoolhouse and chapel was the brainchild of Sanford Plumb, who was one of the largest property owners in Lot 35, the village of West Halifax, the area which for many years was referred to as "Plumb's Corners." In 1843, Mr. Plumb served as the society clerk for School District No. 15 of West Halifax and was hosted meetings of the newly founded Universalist Society at his home. Plumb, it appears, envisioned a new multipurpose building on Main Street that would serve both organizations.

HALIFAX HISTORICAL SOCIETY MUSEUM, HHS

CHRONOLOGY AND CHAIN OF OWNERSHIP

1843 – 1883: THE UNIVERSALIST SOCIETY OF HALIFAX

March 1843: The Universalist Society appoints Sanford Plumb, Nathan W. Halladay and Addison Fowler, for a committee to "locate and superintend the building of the new Chappel in connection with a new Schoolhouse about to be erected in School district No. 15."[1] October 3, 1843: the first meeting of The Universalist Society is held at the new chapel. August 1845: The Universalist Society records the "Cost of the Chappel"[2] is $346.93. Contributors listed in the society minutes "by subscription" are: Sanford Plumb, James Plumb, James Scott, Jonas Scott, Salmon Swan, Oshea Scott, William H. Stark, Willard R. Adams, Almon Ballou, Julius Clark, Benjamin Eames, Charles Fowler, Charles Goodwin, John Hamilton, Nathan W. Halladay, Timothy Larrabee, Benjamin Woodard, and Ashel Ballou. Other contributors were: Chandler Seaver, Lewis Sumner, Reuben Tucker, Ezra Thayer, James G. Worden, John Brigham, Origen Ball, Webb Cook, James Corse, Elias Fowler, Addison Fowler, Newton Gleason, Hiram Warren, Tyler Willcox, Increase Whitney, Andrew N. Jenks, Solomon Wicks, Seth M. Worden, and Joseph Fisher. Contributions of labor were made by: James Plumb and Ezra Thayer. September 1845: Fall term classes are offered at the West Halifax Select School. January 1861: Sanford Plumb deeds the land on which the building is situated to the Universalist Society. All land between C. B. Tilton's and the Universalist building to be for sole use of the society. No buildings to be erected except for sheds for the Society [HLR 12: 264] In 1873, the Universalist Society purchases the Congregational Meeting House (Community Hall) and remove seats and stovepipes from the chapel. December 18, 1880: The General Assembly of the State of Vermont approves Act No. 235 authorizing the First Universalist Society of Halifax to dispose of its chapel and its interest in the lot upon which it stands.[3] 1882: Final year West Halifax High School classes are held in this building.

1883 – 1904: LANDON H. BALLOU AND GEORGE PORTER WORDEN
June 8, 1883: First Universalist Society of Halifax Committee conveys the chapel meeting hall, to Landon H. Ballou and George P. Worden for $100.00, with "equal privileges. . . . with the School house in connection with the Chapel to repair or rebuild the building now situated thereon." [HLR 17: 250]. The lower level room still in use and maintained by local school district No. 7.

1904 – 1920: HALIFAX GUIDING STAR GRANGE NO. 163
February 8, 1904: Landon H. Ballou of Brattleboro and George P. Worden of Halifax, convey "to Guiding Star Grange No. 163 all right and title" to the premises for thirty dollars with the understanding" said Grange or their assigns shall maintain and keep in repair at all times the north side of the roof on said school house or building." [HLR 17: 262]. The town, in accordance with state law, now owns the school premises on first floor and is responsible for the south side of the roof. 1917: School directors report the upstairs to be in deteriorated condition "wind whistling through walls and open window frames." [HTC TR: 26] Recommend the building be converted to a two-room schoolhouse.

1920 – 1959: TOWN OF HALIFAX
August 10, 1920: Harry A. Learnard and Milton W. Plumb, "Agents for the Guiding Star Grange #163. . . . in consideration of the sum of Twenty-five Dollars received to our full satisfaction of the Selectmen of the Town of Halifax" convey the grange portion of the building "with the understanding that said Guilding Star Grange #163 shall not be holden for any repairs on the above described premises." [HLR 19: 276] Thirty-nine years later the town completes its new school and final classes are held in the two-level schoolhouse [HLR 20: 207].

1959 – 1978: HALIFAX FIRE COMPANY, INC.
November 25, 1959: School Directors of the Halifax Town School District and the Selectmen of the Town of Halifax, in consideration of One Dollar and other valuable Consideration, convey premises to the Halifax Fire Company, Inc. [HLR 25: 403]. Fire Department modifies the building for its use including removal of front annex. June 28, 1978: Having constructed a new building next door, Fire Department conveys the building back to the Town of Halifax [HLR 30: 342].

1979 – TO DATE: THE HALIFAX HISTORICAL SOCIETY, INC.
June 5, 1979: Lewis L. Sumner, Rodney H. Bemis, and Frederick A. Crosby II, Selectmen of The Town Halifax "in the consideration of One Dollar and other Valuable Consideration" convey the right and title to the building to the Halifax Historical Society, Inc. of Halifax in the County of Windham [HLR 30: 491].   *~ Constance Lancaster*

ENDNOTES
1 . HHS Universalist Society Record Book unpaginated.
2 Ibid.
3. Acts and Resolves of the General Assemby p. 246.

Health of Citizens

Rev. Hubbard Eastman "There have been many different physicians in the town among whom the most noted have been Drs. Williams, Miller, Johnston and Harrington. Drs. O. A. Wheeler of California, and J. M. [John Mather] Clark of North Adams, Ma. were natives of this town."[1] "The first physicians were "Drs. Hill, Ransom, Richardson, Cobb etc."[2] Eastman's overview, invites further investigation.

According to his 1805 probate record, five different doctors, including Ransom, Richardson, and Cobb, treated William Wilcox. By the end of the century, there were no resident doctors in Halifax. References to the earliest doctors are found in town and family records. Beginning in 1828, Walton's annual register lists local physicians. Only two men from the entire list, Drs. Everett and Clark, are buried in town.

RESIDENT PHYSICIANS OF HALIFAX, VERMONT

Ebenezer Parish	abt. 1771	Moses Chamberlain	1835–1841
William Hill	1773–1780	Ebenezer M. Clark	1841–1867
Peletiah Fitch	1774–1780	(Died in 1873)	
John Harrington	abt. 1783–1786	Josiah Trow	1842–1844
Jeremiah Everett	abt. 1784–1794	Sidney Brooks	1844–1845
(Died in 1831)		Ebenezer Miller	1846–1856
Luther Ransom	1794–1808	Elisha S. Plumb	1846–1850
Joseph Cobb	1796–1816	Henry Rockwood	1857–1858
Samuel Richardson	1796–1815	Hiram E. Johnson	1859–1865
Henry Williams	1808–1827	W. McGray	1866–1867
Henry Niles	1820–1830	J. L. Harrington	1867–1882
Morris Dwight	1825–1829	W. C. Whiting	1882–1885
Charles Houghton	1830–1835	B. F. Millington	1885–1889
Horace May	1833	John W. Cram	1889–1890

EARLY PATRIOT PHYSICIANS

One hears more of the political activities of Drs. William Hill [↗ 166] and Peletiah Fitch than their work as healers. Both came to Halifax before the start of the American Revolution, were leaders in town and Cumberland County politics, and both moved to Washington County, New York. Biographers of Dr. Fitch note that he practiced medicine in Norwich, Connecticut, where he also served as justice of the peace and land surveyor. He moved to Halifax, where he served as first judge of the Cumberland County Court, and moved to Salem, New York, in 1780, where he practiced medicine and kept a hotel until his death in 1803. "An ardent patriot, Fitch served during the Revolution in Webster's Regiment, N. Y. Militia and at his own expense equipped four sons for service in the Revolution."[3] Peletiah Jr. was a lieutenant in the Vermont Militia, serving in Captain John Pennell's Company in 1778. Dr. Peletiah Fitch, as chairman of the "Friends of

New York State," signed a letter recommending persons to be appointed officeholders by Governor Clinton's Council. The letter, dated July 1, 1778, specifies that Fitch was enclosing, "a Paper signed by a number of the Inhabitants of Halifax."[4] It is evident that Dr. Fitch interacted with residents of the town, yet there is no evidence that he practiced medicine while in Halifax. The house he built included a large room that Dr. Ebenezer M. Clark used some years later in his practice of Thomsonian medicine, and town records always refer to Peletiah Fitch as "doctor."

Newton Ransom moved his family from Colchester, Connecticut, to Shelburne Falls, Massachusetts, before the Revolution. Seven of his sons served in the Massachusetts Continental Line, and after the war made new homes in Vermont and eastern New York. His twin sons, Luther and Calvin, settled in Halifax about 1794. Calvin was a malt maker, who obtained a license for tavern keeping and later returned to Shelburne. Dr. Luther Ransom lived north of the Center and practiced medicine in town for more than a decade. On May 31, 1796, his father died while visiting from Shelburne. The marker for Newton Ransom, at Center Cemetery, stands alone. Luther, his wife Theodosia Bardwell, and children moved to Chazy, Clinton County, New York, where he died in 1832.

Dr. Jeremiah Everett, born in 1740 in Attleboro, Massachusetts, came to Halifax in 1784 from Westminster, Massachusetts, where he was the first practicing physician as well as a schoolmaster. In the summer of 1776, Dr. Everett was appointed surgeon of Colonel Nicholas Dike's regiment on duty at Dorchester Heights in what was virtually the coast defense of Boston.[5] Even though Hubbard Eastman did not include him on his lists of first and notable physicians, it is difficult to imagine Everett did not practice medicine in Halifax. Except for Dr. Jonathan Harrington's presence in 1784–1785, Dr. Everett was the only doctor residing in town during the decade before Drs. Cobb, Ransom and Richardson arrived. His father, Jeremiah, also served in the Revolution, died in 1798 and was buried at the Clark Farm Cemetery. Dr. Jeremiah died in 1831 and has a marked grave at Grove Cemetery.

OTHER EARLY LOCAL PHYSICIANS

Halifax had a doctor in residence by 1771. The town's earliest physician, Dr. Ebenezer Parish, appears among the customers in the Richard Ellis account book as well as on the Cumberland County census list. Parish was the first family name to be inscribed on the plat plan created at the time of the charter [↪ 149]. Originally from Plainfield Connecticut, Dr. Parish was married to Susannah Williams, sister of Joseph and Nathan Williams who were very early settlers. Nathan was the first town constable.

On his list of first physicians, Eastman mentions in addition to Hill and Ransom, Drs. Williams, Richardson, and Cobb. Dr. Joseph Cobb, born in 1767, was the son of Sylvanus of Hardwick, Massachusetts. He appears in Halifax land records by 1796 and is enumerated in the 1810 census with a family of eight. By 1817, he was living in Deerfield, Massachusetts, where several of his brothers had settled.

Dr. Samuel Richardson of Whitingham, Vermont, married Peggy Morton of Colrain, Massachusetts, in May 1791. They lived in Colrain, Whitingham, and Wilmington before settling at Halifax Center in 1796, where Samuel practiced medicine until about 1815. Three infant children and their mother, Peggy, are buried at the Center Cemetery. Dr. Richardson conveyed land in Lot 28 to the Congregational Church and original meeting house for use as part of the town common. Samuel Richardson, age eighty-three, died in 1849 at Fayetteville, Onondaga County, New York.

Dr. Henry Williams, son of Rev. Henry Williams, was born in Leverett, Massachusetts, in 1786. He became a physician and surgeon and was an assistant surgeon in a Vermont regiment in the War of 1812. Dr. Williams married Judith Corkins in 1808 and practiced medicine in Halifax for about twenty years until the fall of 1827, when he moved to New Berlin, Chenango County, New York. His service in Halifax was for some years concurrent with that of Dr. Henry Niles, son of Henry and Lucretia Minor Niles, grandson of David of Stonington, Connecticut. Dr. Niles was born in Massachusetts in 1796 during his parents' migration journey from Connecticut to Halifax. He graduated from Hanover College in 1820 and practiced medicine in town until about 1830, when he moved his family to Huron County, Ohio.[6]

PHYSICIANS LISTED IN WALTON'S REGISTERS

Dr. Morris Dwight was born about 1797, and first appears in Halifax records on September 2, 1825, when he declared his intention to marry Minerva Bryant of Williamsburg, Massachusetts, the daughter of Captain Eli. In 1829, he left Halifax and is listed in the Williamsburg 1880 census, age eighty-three, a retired physician living in the hotel of Lewis Porter.

From 1830 to 1834, Charles Houghton was physician-in-residence at Halifax Center. Born in Marlboro, Vermont, in 1804, the son of Captain Nahum, Dr. Charles married Eliza Woodman of Brattleboro, practiced medicine in Rutland, Vermont, until 1847, and moved to Bennington and then to Philadelphia. Dr. Horace May, son of Joel of Wilmington, Vermont, is listed in Walton for the year 1833. Horace and his bride, Emeline Packard, resided in Halifax for about a year and moved to Bennington. The 1860 federal census lists Horace, "a doctor of medicines", and wife, Emeline, in Brooklyn, New York.

About 1835, Moses Chamberlain, a Vermont native who had practiced medicine in Jamaica and Townshend and thus was more experienced than his predecessors, took up residence in Halifax, bought property and seemed settled for a long-term practice. He and his wife, Eliza Felton, buried a son and a daughter at Center Cemetery. By 1841, Dr. Chamberlain was ill. He died in 1842 and is buried with his widow in the Village Cemetery at Jamaica, Vermont, where she returned to live with her family and raise her children.

In 1841, the register lists, for the first of twenty-seven consecutive years, Dr. Ebenezer M. Clark, serving as a botanical physician.[7] From then on the register identifies the physicians as *allo* or *bot.*, and sometimes instead of *bot.* says *Thomp.*

WHO WAS DR. EBENEZER M. CLARK?

It is widely known that Ebenezer Meacham Clark was the son of Ebenezer Clark and his wife, Annis Meacham. He was born in Halifax on August 2, 1796. He was a physician and Thomsonian [↵ 243] practitioner, and it is widely known that he operated a sanatorium/hospital in the Clark homestead on Stark Mountain Road during the early part of the nineteenth century. It is not known where Dr. Clark received his medical training, but his patent to practice Thomsonian medicine could easily be purchased for twenty dollars, along with Samuel Thomson's *New Guide to Health, or Botanic Family Physician*, published in 1822.

Samuel Thomson, a native of New Hampshire, developed his ideas about the healing arts into a botanic system of medicine after herbalists cured his wife in 1791. After ten years of local practice, he published his book and then sent out designated agents to sell the right to use his system. The book was basically a collection of botanic recipes with key ingredients left out. Once the purchaser paid the twenty dollars, the agent filled in the blanks, swore the buyer to secrecy, and issued the patent. It is estimated that by 1840, 100,000 of these patents had been sold. Briefly, Thomson's system was based on the   elief

> that cold brought on illness and therefore restoring the body's natural heat offered the quickest remedy. This he accomplished with steam baths, cayenne pepper, and puking by means of Lobelia, a native American emetic.[1]

In a letter dated August 15, 1844, a John White of Mayville, New York, wrote to his brothers about his travels in New England:

> The last time I wrote you I was at Mass. sick not able to ride; after I got able to ride Rebecca went with me to Guilford, to visit her relatives. We first visited her grandfather Timothy Root the day we arrived there which was 28th of July, he was just 100 years old . . . I left Rebecca in Guilford & went to Rockingham, through Saxons river Village. . . . From thence I went to Halifax, staid with a Thomsonian Docter about a week: & then started for Boston called on Ashley White at Worcester, left my horse & took the Railway for Boston; staid in Boston about a week & returned to Charlemont; then started for Albany. [2]

Apparently, this ambitious traveler was cured after his weeklong stay with Dr. Clark. He continues his letter and tells about a trip from New York State to Michigan where he had purchased some land.

Joseph Smith, the Mormon prophet, had a less successful experience with the popular Thomsonian treatment. In *Brigham Young and His Mormon Empire*, Frank J. Cannon writes:

> The new religion was as catholic as it was audacious. . . . It mirrored the very health fads of the hour. "Hot drinks are not good

Continued

for the body or for the belly," declared the prophet [Joseph Smith] on one occasion—perhaps when a Thomsonian "draught was racking his internal economy;" and from that day to this, the Mormon who indulges in tea or coffee is counted a dangerous latitudinarian.[3]

A 1936 edition of the *Brattleboro Reformer* reports:

Are there many that know Halifax had at one time a hospital or sanatorium? It was operated by Dr. Ebenezer M. Clark, listed in Walton's Vermont Register as a "Thomsonian." It was in the 1840s that he had the most patients. His wife and daughters were the nurses. As the daughters married and left home, taking patients was gradually given up. Being also a general practitioner, he continued practicing until the late sixties. His good wife lived to long past 90. There are two grandchildren and great grandchildren. Some may wonder at the name "Thomsonian." Roots and herbs were used and steaming. Beside the kitchen was a small arch in which was set a small kettle closely covered. Running from that up through the ceiling was a two-inch pipe, which carried the steam to a tall box in an upper room in which the patient was seated and kept for a certain time. Then the patient was thoroughly rubbed with a crash towel . . . and put to bed where he was given a hot drink, or a cool one, of slippery elm bark steeped in cold water according to the disease. The old house, situated about two miles from the Massachusetts line, was burned about 35 years ago.[4]

The "tall box in an upper room" described in the article in the *Reformer* can easily be seen protruding from the roof line on the southern end of the house in one of several photographs taken of the Clark home on Stark Mountain Road on August 8, 1890. The photographs were taken at a gathering of the Clark family celebrating the ninety-second birthday of Ebenezer M. Clark's wife, Jerusha Bucklin Clark [*p* 92]. Ebenezer and Jerusha were married in Halifax on October 4, 1819, and were blessed with seven children: Eunice J., born in 1822 and married to Henry C. Bell; Lucy, born in 1824 and married to Mr. Babcock; Clark, born in 1828 and died in 1831; Annis P., born in 1833 and married to Alonzo Weatherhead; Susan Chloe, born in 1834 and married to Abel Gilbert Yeaw; Benjamin Ebenezer, born in 1835 and married to Lorinda Barton; and Clara, born in 1839 and died in 1840. Descendants of this family can be found in Guilford, Vermont, to this day.   ©2008 *Ray Henry*

ENDNOTES

1. John S. Haller Jr., *Medical Protestants: The Eclectics in American Medicine, 1825–1939* (Carbondale, IL: Southern Illinois University Press, 1994).
2. John White, letter dated August 15, 1844, Mayville, Chautauqua County, New York, (addressed to his brothers in Richville, New York), http://archiver.rootsweb.com/th/read/NYCHAUTA/2001-02/0982716574
3. Frank J. Cannon and George L. Knapp, *Brigham Young and His Mormon Kingdom* (New York: Fleming H. Revell Company, 1913), p. 25.
4. *Reformer*, April 12, 1936.

From 1842 through 1846, two Massachusetts doctors who were related by marriage filled the resident physician's role. A graduate of Berkshire Medical College, Dr. Josiah Trow first practiced medicine in Halifax from 1842 to 1844 moving to Sunderland, Massachusetts and eventually to Buckland. Dr. Sidney Brooks was born in August 1811 in Buckland and served together with Josiah Trow in 1844 and alone in 1845.

In 1846, Dr. Ebenezer Miller took up residence in Halifax Center and remained until 1856. Born in 1822 in Vernon, Vermont, Dr. Miller graduated from Castleton Medical College in 1843, married Lucia Whithead, and moved to town. The historian of Vernon described Dr. Miller as a "man of high intellectual attainments. His skill soon won for him an extensive practice; but the West presenting many attractions, he removed to St. Paul, Minn., Nov. 3, 1856."

From 1846 to 1850, Elisha Sanford Plumb, a Halifax native born in 1823, son of Sanford and Berilla Plumb, is listed by the register as a Halifax *bot.* physician. Later he resided and worked in Otisville, Orange County New York.

After the departure of Dr. Miller, Dr. Henry Rockwood practiced for two years, 1857–1858, served also as superintendent of schools, and returned to live in Massachusetts. He mustered into service in August 1862 with the 15th Massachusetts Volunteer Infantry Assistant Surgeon, and served until September 1863.

Dr. Hiram E. Johnson, who was born in 1835 in Vermont, became the next resident *allo* physician, and lived in the house later known as the McAllister Cottage at Halifax Center with his wife Anna and children from 1859 through 1865. The Johnson's moved west to Indian Grove, Livingston, Illinois where they appear in the 1880 federal census.

Next to arrive was a long-term resident physician, Dr. Joseph Lysander Harrington, known always as J. L., who was born in 1840 in Jamaica, Vermont. Dr. J. L. Harrington took up residence at the Center in 1867 and stayed until 1882. During his years in Halifax, he often served as town clerk or treasurer and was elected, in 1878, for one term, to the state legislature. His wife, Catherine McAllister Tenny, was born in New Hampshire, and her daughter, Flora Tenney, at times served as librarian. Zina Emery, son of Dr J. L. and Catherine Harrington, died in 1874 and is buried in the Center Cemetery with his grandparents, William and Harriett McAllister. The *Vermont Phoenix* reported in 1882, "Dr. Harrington and family left for the west last Tuesday. They intend to go to Missouri, and from there to their new home in Minnesota."[8] In the same report: "Halifax rejoices in another doctor, Dr. Whiting of Holyoke, Mass., having taken up his abode with Elijah Green."

ELIJAH GREEN   HHS

Dr. Walter C. Whiting resided in Halifax from 1882 until May 1885, served as superintendent of schools, and gave lively weekly lectures at the schoolhouse in the Center. From the *Vermont Phoenix*, May 15, 1885:

> Many are the regrets that Dr. W. C. Whiting is about to leave town. For a few years past he has faithfully served the people as a skillful physician, and as superintendent of schools, taking a deep interest in the cause of education. He goes to Brockton, Mass., and many kind wishes will go with him for success in his professional work.[9]

Two weeks later, the *Vermont Phoenix* reported: "Dr. Millington, from Pennsylvania, takes Dr. Whiting's place as the local doctor, and also occupies his old quarters at Elizabeth Green's at the Centre."[10] Serving Halifax from May 1885 until July 1889, Dr. Benjamin Franklin Millington, son of a British immigrant teamster, was born near Philadelphia and studied medicine at the University of Vermont. On December 10, 1886, the *Vermont Phoenix* reported, "Dr. Millington has returned with his bride. We tender congratulations."[11] Almost at once, the doctor was embroiled in what the *Vermont Phoenix* of December 17 called "A neighborhood sensation" regarding the "sudden death of R. P. Farnsworth." Rumors and whispers by relatives of Mr. Farnsworth, suggesting he had been poisoned, reached the ears of Watson DeWolf at the funeral. DeWolf, who was caretaker of Farnsworth in exchange for his property, demanded an investigation. A post-mortem by Drs. Millington of Halifax and Stafford of Sadawga, corroborated Dr. Millington's earlier diagnosis of a badly diseased condition of the heart.[12]

In July 1887, the post office at the Center was "removed to Dr. B. F. Millington's office,"[13] the building known also as the Fowler Cottage. Millington was appointed postmaster and served for several years until he moved his family to South Londonderry, Vermont. There he continued his medical practice until his death.

A PROSPECTIVE PHYSICIAN VISITS HALIFAX

Dr. Millington was the last resident physician of Halifax listed in Walton, but Dr. Cram, who graduated from the University of Vermont Medical College in 1888, was, in fact, the last practicing resident physician in town. Two surviving letters from Dr. John Wesley Cram to his bride, Katherine Holton, offer credence to the statement in *A History of Colrain* [14] that Dr. Cram practiced in Halifax for a year before taking over for Dr. Lamb of Colrain in 1891, where he continued to serve for forty-five years.

> July 11, 1889, South Derry, Vermont.
>
> My Dear Wife,
>   I write you a line as I am going to stay here until the noon train tomorrow. Am going with Dr. M.[illington] to aspirate a man tomorrow a.m. at Bondville. It is a job that I want to help do. Dr.

M. has not heard anything from Halifax yet, but we will go along just the same as soon as we can get ready. I am sure that I don't want to ride over there until the weather and traveling are better. John.

July 12, 1889, Halifax Vermont

My Dear May,

Well, here I am at Halifax. I reached this place about 3:30 p.m. . . . . A good day to drive, but I can tell you I have found SOME HILLS. There is one thing about it. The hill farms around here are much better looking than in Jamaica. Through Marlboro the country looks poorly most of the way but is better around here.

I shall drive over the town some tomorrow. Intend to go to Green River in the morning which will take me through the eastern part of the town, then in the P.M. go to West Halifax and perhaps to Jacksonville. I am stopping at Mr. [Elijah] Greene's, and it is a nice place. A middle aged man and his wife constitute the family. He is in rather poor health and thought he couldn't keep me, but I told him I could take care of my own team and so he said I might stay considering who I am. I like the people very much. Have met one other family by name of Leonard and have just pulled a tooth for Mr. [Charles] Leonard. I had no forceps with me, but there is a pair in the neighborhood, which he got, and I relieved him of an aching tooth. So I have done one job although I didn't charge him anything for it.

I tell you, May, the buildings on Dr. M.'s place look pretty hard to move into. It seems as if I wouldn't much more than take the gift of them. There is a good looking piece of grass that ought to be cut at once. . . .the house is just as they moved out of it in a hurry. . . . Four ladies went with me to see the house, and they say that if they had known I was coming, they would have had the loose dirt swept up. They say that if I come back, they will see that the house looks better next time.

The people think this a good chance now, considering the quality of the neighboring Drs., for a Dr. to start, and I am of the same opinion myself, and I really think I shall decide to come here.

I am glad that you didn't undertake to come today, as you would have been about dead. Hope you will sleep well tonight and have no nightmare to trouble you. I shall go to sleep thinking of you and with much love and several hugs and kisses. I am your husband,
John.[15]

First impression notwithstanding, Dr. Cram and his bride moved into the house and stayed for about a year. Emma Millington sold the property to Julia Packer in August 1889 [HLR 15:433]. She reconveyed the property to Dr. Cram, whose mortgage from her was discharged on October 1, 1890 [HLR 15: 435] presumably, the time he and his wife Katherine relocated to Colrain. Even though he no longer lived in town, Dr. Cram's patients included many from Halifax, and he was often called upon for help during outbreaks of flu.

The Fowler Cottage and McAllister place were located between the Baptist Church and the Joseph Henry homestead on Stowe Mountain Road, west

FOWLER COTTAGE   Courtesy Elinor Springer

of the general store at the Center. Beyond The Squire Henry house, also called the Charlie Learnard place, was Elijah and Annis Scott Green's large home, which became a place for physicians to board. While the record shows the turnover of physicians in town was frequent, there was one constant. Most of the ever-changing town doctors resided on properties located along the same short stretch of Stowe Mountain Road. Thus there was a period when Halifax Center featured a physicians' row.

> A paragraph in the *Eagle* a week or two since relative to aged people in Guilford, has called forth from a friend in Halifax the following facts: According to the census of 1850, there were 1133 inhabitants of that town. At the present time, there are living 71 persons over 70 years of age, 47 between 70 and 80, and 24 more than 80 years old. Of these, three males are living with their first wives—four couples have lived together about sixty years, and two have commenced on the seventieth year of their married life! —In view of these facts, it is hardly worthwhile, in our opinion, for any physician to locate in the town of Halifax unless he desires to retire from professional life.[16]

A recurring theme in the news from the town of Halifax is whether the town has or needs a resident physician. In contrast to the cavalier attitude expressed in the previous news item is the following observation published in the *Vermont Phoenix* from February 1882.

> There is quite a lot of sickness in town just at the present time. Dr. Johnson of Jacksonville is in the village nearly every day. Dr. H. D. Holton of Brattleboro was called in consultation with Dr. Johnson of Jacksonville at Henry Wheeler's. He drove from Brattleboro here in less than two hours – 19 miles. There is talk that a doctor is going to come here and locate in this village. A good place for a doctor to locate.[17]

LONGEVITY

The landscapes of eighteenth and nineteenth century cemeteries are dotted with small gravestones, decorated with carved flowers and lambs that record and memorialize the deaths of children. Among the most bitter laments incised on a childs' marker in the Center Cemetery, is one for Jonas Gillet, who died August 16, 1814 in his third year: "Blooming cheeks, Lovely charms, Lies clasped in deaths, Coald icy arms." It has been said that a child born in olden times, who survived the perils of the first five to ten years of life, had excellent prospects for reaching old age. The subject of old age and longevity, always one of great interest in the town of Halifax, is found not only on gravestones, but also in town records, newspaper stories and local legends.

DR. RICE – THE ONE-HUNDRED-AND-TWELVE-YEAR-OLD MAN

This particular longevity legend has been part of Halifax lore since the town's first written history. The gazetteers usually include a tantalizing one-liner about the man who died in 1812 who is said to have been about 112 years old. Some accounts call him Jesse Rice. Some say Jesse was a cousin of Abner Rice. Some, say Jesse Rice was 113 years of age and born in 1699. Moreover, recent editions of *The Vermont Yearbook* [18] say, "Halifax, home of Jesse Rice who is said to have been 120 years old at his death in 1812." Time to explore the 112-year-old man story with an effort to distinguish reality from myth.

A reverse chronological search to discover who first introduced the claim that a man died in Halifax at such a venerable age, and to learn precisely what the original account said, leads us back to Zadock Thompson's 1824 gazetteer and the data supplied via letter by Rev. Thomas Hough Wood [⌂ 7]. Thompson's questionnaire asked for any remarkable examples of longevity. Wood wrote: "Longevity. Mr.__Rice, commonly called Dr Rice, died about the year 1812 aged 112 years."[19] A comparison of the 1824 gazetteer printed text with the handwritten letter, reveals this to be one of only two instances in the Halifax description where Zadock Thompson did not used Wood's exact words. The gazetteer wording is, "About the year 1812, Mr. Rice died here aged 112 years."

Fifty years later, Rev. Eastman embellished the original report when he wrote for Hemenway's gazetteer, "Jesse Rice, a cousin of Abner Rice, died at the age of 113."[20] His line about Jesse Rice immediately follows his colorful, though equally undocumented story, that Abner Rice was shot for a bear while sitting under an apple tree. Yet, another hundred years later, *The Gazetteer of Vermont Heritage* for 1966, presents the longevity story as follows:

> In Halifax were born Elisa G. Otis, inventor of the first safety elevator, the steam plow and the Otis bake oven, and the founder of the Otis elevator company; Henry C. Fish, known in the Civil War as "Fighting Parson Fish"; Russell J. Waters, founder of Redlands, California; and Francis F. Browne, author, and editor of "The Dial." In 1812 in Halifax there died a man named Jesse Rice, who was said to have been born in 1699.[21]

Usually, there is a basis in truth for this type of tale. Nevertheless, vital statistics, cemetery and property records for Halifax do not mention anyone named Jesse Rice, or any other Rice who died in 1812. Nor did a thorough search of Rice genealogical material, tracking all the Jesses, and all male Rices born in 1699/1700, and all who died circa 1812 produce a match. Every uncle and cousin of Abner Rice, Halifax first settler, and of Micah Rice, Guilford's first settler was scrutinized.

The search turned to another unidentified Halifax Rice, Lt. Benjamin, whose gravestone at the Center Cemetery says he died September 12, 1804 in his eighty-second year. His wife, Rebekah, died April 26, 1817. The placement of their markers in the Pardee Dean family plot offered a clue to their identities, and a land record for property transferred from "Benjamin Rice of Gill, County of Hampshire, Massachusetts" [HLR 2: 467], to Pardee Dean of Halifax signed August 24, 1797 confirmed the connection. Further research into the Dean and Rice families showed that Pardee Dean's parents, Ithiel and Rebekah, moved their family from Connecticut to Greenfield, Massachusetts where Ithiel died in 1775. Second Lieutenant Benjamin Royce[22] born in 1723 in Wallingford, Connecticut, moved to the part of Greenfield that became Gill. Some time after the death of his wife, Anna Merriman, in 1778, Benjamin Royce/Rice married widow Rebekah Dean. They moved to Halifax, probably about 1797, to live with Rebekah's son Pardee and appear with his family in the 1800 census. Benjamin is the right age to have been the son of the 112–year-old man. Unfortunately, his father, Thomas Royce, who died in 1761, does not fit the profile, and the census records do not confirm the presence of a second elderly couple living with the Dean family in 1800.

Attempts to identify the long-lived Mr. Rice ceased when all research leads had been exhausted. There was no reason to doubt Thomas Wood, whose contributions to the Thompson gazetteer had proven to be quite reliable. Rev. Wood had moved to Halifax in 1806, and therefore must have had some first hand knowledge of the man "commonly called Dr. Rice." More about the 112-year-old man, it seemed, would never be known.

Recently, however, while checking the minutes of Halifax Town meetings from the early 1800s, I noticed in the 1808 meeting record, after highway business, the voters resolved:

> to Set up the poor of the Town to vendue and Joseph Tucker be
> vendue master and that one half the money be paid for keeping
> the poor the first of October and the other half the first of April
> after or when the time is out. Mr. Timothy Stark and his wife were
> bid off by James Clark 3rd to be kept from the 22nd day of
> current March until the first of April 1809 for fifty nine dollars.
> Old Dr. Rice and his wife were bid off by Mr. Ebenezer Clark to
> be kept one year from the first day of April next for fifty four
> dollars. [HLR 2A: 231]

In this period of annual multiple "Warnings out," the town felt an obligation to care for these particular couples, which suggests they were elderly and homeless.

The same two couples were bid at vendue over the next few years, each year each couple going to live with a different family. In the 1809 minutes, Mr. Rice is called Isachar Rice. In 1810, there is a bid for Mr. Rice but no reference to Mrs. Rice. And at the meeting of 1812, there is no reference at all to old Dr. Rice. Surely, Dr. Isachar Rice, who died before the March 1812 town meeting, was the 112–year-old man about whom Rev. Wood had written.

With an identity in hand, the search has resumed. To date, however, no confirming documentation for Isachar Rice or his wife, who likely was a younger second or third spouse, has been located. Because they do not appear in Halifax land or vital records, it would seem they did not reside in town for long. Like Benjamin Rice, they may have come to Halifax as in-laws, but in this case, his wife's family predeceased them. With no death record, obituary or gravestone for Isachar or his wife, the couple remains a mystery. The Rices of Halifax always seem to keep one guessing.

After his visit to Halifax in 1872, Oliver Norton Worden introduced the subject of Worden family longevity as part of his article for the *Athen's Gleaner*:

> These hills are favorable to longevity. The mother of Peter and
> Isaac Worden whose maiden name was Rachael Hale died in 1869,
> lacking only sixteen days of being a century old, and well to her
> last year. Isaac's father-in-law, Thomas Adams, died 1858, aged 99
> 1/2 years, and his wife, in 1854, aged 96. Sylvester Worden, 1814,
> aged 82; his relict, Rebekah, 1827, 88. Elisha Worden, Sr., 1820,
> 78; and son Elisha, Jr., 1852, 74. Sylvester Worden, 2d, nearly 90.
> Asa Worden, 1857, 92. These are specimens which fell under my
> more special attention, and are not very rare.

Among the best-known examples of longevity in Halifax is that of Jane Gault Crosier, who died in April 1850 at age one hundred and five. Her obituary, published in the *Brattleboro Semi-Weekly Eagle* May 9, 1850, emphasizes the hardships Jane endured as a young woman, suggesting, perhaps, that courage and stamina contributed to her longevity.

> Mrs. Crosier was a native of Londonderry, N.H., whence she
> removed to Halifax 86 years ago, when nearly all the territory now
> forming the State of Vermont was a wilderness. Many were the
> trying scenes she witnessed during the first years of her residence
> in the almost unbroken forest, where but few of the comforts of
> life could be obtained by any sacrifice, and trials, unusually severe
> and protracted, were endured by all who had the courage and
> fortitude to venture a settlement on the rugged hills of Vermont.

Jane is buried in the Halifax Center cemetery. Her marker says, "Jane Gaut, wife of Robert Crosier, died Apr 29 1850, ae 105-5-9."

HEALERS

Personals.

THE latest healer upon the scene is Bradley Newell, of Vermont. Unlike his recent predecessors, Schlatter and Mlle. Couédon, he bids fair to become a modern Monte Christo, for, seeing the lucrative possibilities in his calling, he has charged a sufficient fee to enable him since last January to realize $25,000 from persons he has treated. It has been computed that his income this year will be many thousand dollars larger than President Cleveland's. Moreover, the man has himself changed with his improved financial situation, for now his badly fitting clothes and long and unkempt beard have been transformed into a tailor-made suit and well-trimmed whiskers. He is over six feet high. His hair is jet black, and his face is lighted by large, lustrous black eyes. He is remarkably illiterate, and still uses the vernacular of the retired Vermont communities. Before the "call" came to him he was a village blacksmith; but success in curing his wife's headaches, and many of his neighbors' ills, capped with a description of his

BRADLEY NEWELL   HHS
at his Sprague Road blacksmith shop.
Blacksmith/healer

Courtesy Barbara Giguere
ALBERT A. LARRABEE
Butcher/healer

work by a local newspaper, all combined to herald him as the Vermont Schlatter. He left his forge and treated three thousand cases before he began to receive a regular fee. Now, however, he has a regular business manager, a gentleman from his State, formerly "connected" with several colleges. Jacksonville, Vt., the home of Newell before his fame, is not only celebrated for this healer, but has also produced no less a celebrity than Brigham Young. We may add in passing that since the fame of Newell a small horde of healers have sprung up; George Clark, of Halifax, who has been in the Vermont Legislature and there gained the title of the "great objector," is now healing; Albert Larrabee, "a bumptious youth," of the same town, and Manley Rawson, of Jamaica, another near-by town, also claim to have the art of healing at their fingers' end. In fact, the woods of Southern Vermont are getting full of them; but Newell is the only one who is becoming rich.

The Independent, 1896[23]

Brattleboro Reformer, June 5, 1896
West Halifax-
A. A. Larrabee, the healer, not the blacksmith but the "butcher healer" was in Arlington Hyde Park, West Somerville and Boston, Mass. last week where he treated a number of cases. He visited friends in Arlington, West Somerville and Hyde Park while he was gone He has had invitations to go to both New York and Massachusetts, but will remain here for the present. . . .
Our butcher, Albert Larrabee, will start his cart June 8th and will try to serve the public better than last season. . . .
–Healer A. A. Larrabee was called to Colrain Tuesday to treat several cases, where he met with good success.

Brattleboro Reformer: June 26, 1896
West Halifax.
Our butcher. A.A. Larrabee is doing a rushing business. Monday and Tuesday he sold nearly 500 pounds of meat. . . .
Several people have been here for a treatment from Healer A. A. Larrabee.

* * *

July 9, 1901
Our new stage driver, A.A. Larrabee, has commenced with new rigs and is giving us good service which is very much appreciated.

Albert A. Larrabee was the son of Timothy and Susan Stacey Larrabee.

~ Constance Lancaster

EARL EVANS, MD

Another doctor of note was Dr. Earl Evans. The following article was written by his great niece, Clara (Crosier) Barnard, detailing her mother's recollections of Dr. Evans.

Dr. Earl Evans was my great uncle. . . . Uncle Earl was born in Brookline in 1832. He was the oldest of eight children of Charles and Philena (Fuller) Evans. His sister, Sylvia, was my maternal grandmother, Mrs. Watson DeWolf. When Uncle Earl was just a small boy, his father purchased the large dairy farm in the northeast corner of Halifax and four generations of the family lived there before Charles and Philena's descendants moved to Guilford.

* * *

Uncle Earl's primary schooling . . . was received at the little red schoolhouse that was located near the top of Jimmy Hill, otherwise known as the Stafford school, not far from the Guilford town line on the Jacksonville Stage Road.

His burial lot is in Stafford cemetery, in the same part of town as his old home in Halifax. Incidentally, the old maple trees surrounding that cemetery were set out by the Evans's. It seems well to end this sketch with a touching note of interest. After Uncle Earl died, his horse "Trilby" was brought to the Evans's farm in Halifax and was cared for as long as she lived.

HOUSE CALLS WITH DR. JOHN OLSON

On October 13, 1995, Dr. Olson's daughter, Joan McQuade, was guest speaker at a Halifax Historical Society meeting. This following text is taken from a tape recording of her presentation:

In 1937, he opened his office in Colrain, and during the past twenty-five years has built up a large practice. . . .

As I recall, there was a swinging bridge below the Gorge. I think where there is a sign that says "Sand and Gravel" and every time I go by there I think about him telling me how he had to cross that bridge to deliver a baby. The bridge would swing back and forth and he just about made it across. . . . I know he had some interesting experiences at the Stone's Mill. He was always telling how he

Farm Festivals, Harper & Brothers, NY 1881

delivered a baby there (I don't know who), and a rat ran up his leg.

He had quite a time shaking his leg to get the rat out because it kept gripping on his leg. He liked to tell fish stories too. I don't know but it made for interesting listening.

I do know that he loved Halifax enough so he had to buy land there. He did buy a farm in Halifax, the Leon Shinsky farm.

My father was famous for home deliveries. . . . He had his famous bag, which was filled with you-name-it—everything he could think of. . . . Marie (LaRock) Carpenter told of his delivering her children and coming in a snowstorm.

DR. FRANK WALSH

Another doctor, who lived in Readsboro, Vermont, and who treated patients in the Halifax area, was Dr. Frank Walsh. "On September 4th, 1926, Dr. Frank A. Walsh purchased the Charles Cutler place [in Readsboro] and remodeled the house for a hospital which he soon opened as Valley Hospital. A few years later he built on a maternity ward. There are nine hospital beds and it has patients from many of the neighboring towns."[24] In a conversation in 1992 with Floyd Harris, a long-time Halifax resident, he said, "Dr Walsh maintained an office in the building where Edith Reed lived in Jacksonville."

MIDWIVES

Arlene Hubbard Fairbanks, sharing her memories with her daughter:

> I can't remember the number of midwives around as I was growing up but there were many. My grandmother, Eva Allard Hubbard, was a midwife. I was young but I do remember Clara Murdock gave birth to a son, and my grandmother was with her for a week.
>
> Mildred Sprague Hubbard, my mother, was also a midwife. She was with me when two of my daughters, Elaine and Joyce were born. She also took care of Olive LaRock when one of her children was born. Mary (Learnard) Burnett stayed at our home when her daughter Bernice (Burnett) Barnett was born. Bernice was a very tiny baby and weighed about three pounds. I know my mother fixed some whiskey and sugar water together as a weak solution for the baby. The baby's breathing was very weak but the solution was what saved her life. Mildred also assisted with the birth of one of Mary Bowen's children. Mary was the wife of Walter Bowen. At that time they lived in the Baptist parsonage, which burned a few years ago. Warren Dalrymple lives on the house spot now. I believe my mother assisted Louise Brissette during the birth of one of her children. Louise's husband was Albert Brissette.
>
> ~ Elaine Fairbanks

HEALTH CARE TODAY

Today, there are no practicing physicians in Halifax. Residents either go to the Deerfield Valley Health Center in Wilmington or doctors located in Brattleboro or Bennington, Vermont, or Greenfield, Massachusetts. The Whitingham ambulance in Jacksonville, Deerfield Valley Rescue in Wilmington, Rescue, Inc. in Brattleboro, Vermont, or Colrain ambulance in Colrain, Massachusetts, provide emergency services. Enhanced 911 is available for emergencies. Older residents of Halifax still remember the house calls made by some of doctors mentioned earlier in this article.

~ Bernice Barnett

ENDNOTES

1. Hemenway, p. 421.
2. Ibid., p. 406.
3. *History of the Fitch Family*, p. 64.
4. State of New York. Public Papers of George Clinton, Volume III, (Albany, NY: James B. Lyon, State Printer, 1900) pp. 510–512. Governor Clinton's reply to Peletiah Fitch regarding the "troubles between Vermont and New York," dated July 7, 1778, is found on pages 528–529 in the same volume. The correspondence of Fitch and Clinton offers candid views of that turbulent period in Cumberland County.
5. William Sweetzer Heywood, *History of Westminster, Massachusetts*. (Lowell, MA: Vox Populi Press, S.W. Huse, 1893) p. 160.
6. Harriet Upton Taylor, *History of the Western Reserve* (Chicago: Lewis Publishing 1910) p. 455.
7. One popular irregular medical sect, particularly in the rural areas, was the Friendly Botanical Society. Started by Samuel Thomson, a New Hampshire writer who wrote *The New Guide to Health: Botanic Family Physician*, it popularized taking herbs and drinking lots of herbal teas and wines. While Thomsonian medicine still preached the use of emetics (lobelia), it was strongly opposed to both bleedings and calomel. In some ways, the Friendly Botanical Society was like the Amway of its day as it stressed the use of door-to-door sales people to peddle its books and herbal remedies. The politically dominant system referred to as "allopathy," from the Greek allo, meaning "opposite," and pathos, meaning "suffering." This form of medicine, in general, focuses on stamping out the disease or countering the symptoms.
8. HHS: Niles, p. 3.
9. HHS: Niles, p. 38.
10. Ibid.
11. HHS: Niles, p. 48.
12. Ibid.
13. HHS: Niles, p. 66.
14. Patrie, p. 201-H.
15. Letters, via e-mail, kindness of Elinor Springer, granddaughter of Dr. John Wesley and Katherine Holton Cram. Mrs. Springer advises that there were no other references to Dr. Cram's experience in Halifax among the family papers she received.
16. *Brattleboro Eagle*, Friday April 22, 1853.
17. *Phoenix*, February 1882.
18. Published annually by The National Survey Company, Chester, Vermont.
19. Thomas H. Wood, letter to Zadock Thompson, UVM, Special Collections, Thompson Papers, (1813– 1977) Box 2 Folder 7.
20. Hemenway, p. 415.
21. David Maunsell, Lawton V. Crocker, & Dorman B. E. Kent, *Gazetteer of Vermont Heritage* (Chester, VT: The National Survey, 1966) p. 54.
22. Listed in Connecticut Soldiers of the French and Indian Wars for service in 1756 and 1758.
23. A Weekly Journal of Free Opinion, Devoted to the Consideration of Politics, Social and Economic Tendencies, History, Literature and the Arts, vol. 48, iss. 2481 (Boston: Independent Publications, June 18, 1896) p. 8
24. Frank Seth Ross, *Down Through The Years at Readsboro, Vermont, 1786–1936* (Williamstown, MA: McClelland Press, 1936).

Section Five

Halifax in the Wars

Detail from Josephus Richardson Militia Commission. VHS

Detail from Josephus Richardson Militia Commission. VHS

VERMONT MILITIA

After Vermont officially became a state, there was one militia comprising all the able bodied males between the ages of eighteen and forty-five years.[1] Militia soldiers were required to keep on hand arms and equipment needed for actual service, and by so doing would be exempt from the local poll tax. The town listers identified each militia soldier. Halifax does not have a complete set of grand lists, but those on file at the town clerk's office identify members of the militia and their cavalry horses.

The original state militia was divided into four divisions, ten brigades, and thirty-five regiments consisting of eight to twelve companies in each, with the governor considered the captain general and commander in chief. Scattered records of Halifax Militia activities and service have been found at historical societies and among the town records, and an occasional Halifax name appears in the Walton's militia lists.

The earliest state militia record on file at the Halifax Historical Society is signed by Governor Thomas Chittenden on June 5, 1792, and appoints James Tucker, "Gentleman", Ensign of the Fifth Company in the Second Regiment and First Brigade of the state militia.[2] Born in 1762 in Preston, New London County, Connecticut, Tucker migrated to Halifax before the 1790 census. He raised a family of nine children, was a deacon in the Baptist Church, and is buried with his wife, Sarah Angel, in the "Tucker Mowing" cemetery near the corner of Butterfield and Hatch School House Roads.

Josephus Richardson, tanner and shoemaker, whose tannery site is visible along the Jacksonville Stage Road, where Sperry Brook crosses, received officer militia appointments from three governors: Cornelius P. Van Ness elected him cornet in the first company of cavalry in the Second Regiment, First Brigade of the First Division, on November 15, 1827; Ezra Butler elected him lieutenant of the cavalry unit on June 5, 1827; Samuel C. Crafts elected him captain in the same unit of cavalry on December 6, 1830. In less than two months, Richardson died at the age of thirty-eight. The probate court declared him insolvent, and his properties were sold at auction, including his militia coat, cavalry cap, and red plume.[3]

A warrant to Sidney Plumb, corporal of the Halifax Company of the Second Regiment, First Brigade, First Division of the Vermont Militia from September 1827, commands him to notify a list of men to "appear at the usual place of parade near the South Meeting house . . . armed and equipped as the Law directs for military duty." The men named are Captain James Niles, William Canedy, Charles Niles, John Niles, Addison Fowler, Joshua Grant Jr., John Burrington, Dexter Gleason, Asa Wheeler, Elijah Smith, Joel W. Sumner, Elexir Smith, Owen Saunders, Samuel W. Smith, and Thomas Sumner.

In 1837, Solomon Stanclift of Halifax was appointed colonel of the artillery company of the Regiment that comprised the whole town of Brattleboro. By 1838 there were forty-eight men in the company, including musicians, one of whom, Ezra Gleason, was from Halifax.[4]

A book of Halifax, Vermont militia records was found in the possession of the New England Historic Genealogical Society. Many pages of the book were unreadable; however, several pages recount the activities of the militia during the 1830s and 1840s. Halifax was listed as the Twenty-seventh Regiment, Fourth Company. These documents recorded the election of the officers, the warning of training days, and a report on the condition of the company. Based on the number of votes cast for the officers, it may be supposed that the company numbered about twenty men. The captain of the company was William Brown. The following names appear at various times as sergeant: Russell Bascom, Jedediah Stark, Nathaniel Niles, Addison Fowler, William Wheeler, Milo Hatch, John Tyler, Elijah Kellogg, Martin Scott, and Albert Tucker.

Halifax May 22 1843

Notice of the annual review of officers noncommissioned officers Musicians and privates Belonging to and residing within the limits of the 4th company 3rd Regiment of the militia of this State, has been duly posted for their appearing on the common at the Meeting House in the center of the town of Halifax on the first Tuesday of June 1843 at 9 o'clock all fully armed uniformed and equipped as the law directs for inspection.

Elijah Kellogg, Clerk Pro Tempore

The 4th company met agreeable to notice, the roll was called the arms and equipments were inspected, delinquent noticed, and the remainder of the time spent in military exercise and appointed

Russel Bascom, Clerk
Oshea Scott
Halifax June 6th 1843[5]

The company also met at Abel Scott's Inn at Halifax Center. Orders were given to assemble at Guilford Center "for the purpose of instruction in military tactics" and "at Luther Ames dwelling house in Marlboro," suggesting that, on occasion, the nearby town militias gathered together for training. Included in these records was notice of a complaint made to Sanford Plumb, then justice of the peace in Halifax, against several men who failed to appear for "the annual review on the first Tuesday of June, 1843" and for "Lemuel Whitney for being deficient of a musket."[6]

~ Constance Lancaster and Susan Rusten

War of 1812

When war was declared in June 1812, American trade with Canada was forbidden. Given Vermont's position bordering Lake Champlain and Canada, the state's role in the war was significant. Due to Vermont's reliance upon trade with Canada, the trade embargo did not sit well. In 1813, Thomas Chittenden ran for governor of Vermont on a platform in opposition to the war. He won the election.

Vermont was ordered by the Secretary of War to supply 3,000 men for service. The first four regiments raised were in service in Plattsburgh by September 1812. Guilford historian, General J. W. Phelps, sent the following local lore to Abby Hemenway for her gazetteer:

> The war of 1812 was not very popular in New England, and it has not a few opponents in Vermont: But immediately on its declaration by our Government, June 18, 1812, a company of old men called the 'Silver Grays' was organized and drilled many of whom had been Revolutionary soldiers. They called themselves 'minute men', and with their silver locks rendered impressive by Revolutionary memories, they made an imposing appearance, forcibly to the rising generation to sustain the country in her hour of need.[7]

The men in this company of the Silver Grays included Joel Bolster, Paul Chase, Nathan Hatch, William Hines, and Samuel Shepherdson, all residents of Thomas Hill in Halifax. Their effectiveness is not easy to measure. Nevertheless, we know Dexter and Nathan Hatch Jr. both entered the war in 1812, serving in Captain Preston's Company, Colonel Jonathan Williams's Detached Militia Regiment, and later received pensions, as did another pair of nearby Halifax brothers, Stephen and Erastus Wilcox. Among other Halifax men who served under Captain Preston in Colonel Williams's regiment were David Niles, Francis Akely, William Plumb, and Samuel Crosier. Newell Adams served as private in Captain Preston's Company in Williams's Third Regiment for two months and six days in 1812. According to a family researcher,

> Newell L. Adams was the fourth son of the twelve children born to Levi and Dolly Houghton Adams. He was born on 3 Feb. 1796, on a farm in the Town of Halifax. . . . At the age of sixteen he enlisted at Halifax. . . . For this service he received a pension of $8.00 per month, commencing in 1851, and in 1853 he received forty acres of land in Montgomery County, Illinois.[8]

Halifax town meeting records dated October 13, 1812 state, "Lt. Samuel Crozier has gone into the army and left vacant the office of constable and collector of taxes" [HLR 2A: 253]. An article on the warning for that same town meeting states, "To see if the town will agree to make any additional compensation to the men who are detached agreeable to an act of Congress and have gone into actual service." Records indicate no action on this article, and no other references to the war were found in town documents.

The *Roster of Soldiers in the War of 1812–14* [9] lists those who served by name, often without reference to the town from which they were drafted or enlisted. For this reason the number and names of those who served from the Town of Halifax during 1812–1814 is not precisely known. Nearly every Halifax soldier, we identified, served in Capt. Preston's Company, Col. Jonathan Williams's Regiment of Detached Militia for 2 months and 6 days during 1812. Most include a pension file number. Among the recognizable names on the roster is that of former Halifax resident and firstborn child, William Pattison, who served as Brigade Chaplain with Brigadier General Orms of the Vermont militia. [10]

Roster of Halifax men:

Newell Adams	Nathan Hatch Jr.
Francis Akely	David Niles
William Ballou	William Plumb
John Bolster	John Thomas Jr.
Samuel Crosier	Stephen Tucker
Lucius Gillett	Erastus Wilcox
Nathan Green	Stephen Wilcox
Martin Hall	Dr. Henry Williams
Dexter Hatch	

The *Genealogical Record of Thomas Scott*, compiled by Clinton Scott in 1902, refers to members of the Scott family who may have served in the War of 1812. Abel Scott, who was born in Ashford, Connecticut, in 1774, is said to have "served as captain in the army." Joel and James are also listed as captains [HHS].

William Plumb of Halifax served in Williams's regiment and was promoted from private to sergeant. Courtesy of a descendant of Plumb, the following letter was provided, which he wrote, during his war service, to Olive Eames, whom he later married.

> Plattsburg, NY
> 20th Oct. 1812
>
> Worthy Miss
> It is with pleasure that I now sit down again to drop a few lines for the perusal of a Friend that hold most dear. It is with exquisite pleasure, joy and consolation that I can look back on the happy hours that we have passed in conversing with each other. On the other hand to think of the great distance which separates us and the length of time which probably must pass before we shall have satisfaction of seeing and conversing with each other gives me very disagreeable and unreconciled thoughts. But why should I thus complain or be uneasy at my situation for we must put our trust in Him who regulates the affairs of mortals.

We are not discharged before the first of December. I shall
endeavor to get a furlough to come home if we do not go into
Canada. We crossed the Lake last Saturday. We had a very bad
time of it on the account of contrary wind, but we arrived safe.
There was a man by the name of William Herman shot in this
place last Thursday for desertion. His boddy is now to be seen in
this place. It is the most horrible sight I ever saw. He belonged to
the regular troops. The soldiers are in general healthy and in good
spirits.

I do not like the life of a soldier any better than I expected. I do
not think I shall undertake another campaign if I can well avoid it.
It is better to dwell in the bosom of ones friends than in the tents
of sin and wickedness.

I must draw to a close as time begins to fail. This from your friend
in health whose prayers is that it may find you so and continue so
without ceasing. I should be exceeding glad to receive a letter
from under your hand for it gives me great joy to hear from my
friends.

I must subscribe myself your friend til death Miss Olive Emes.

Wm Plumb[11]

Conditions were particularly harsh after the war. With the loss of trade,
the ravages of the spotted fever epidemic and crop failures of 1816, "the year
there was no summer," many of the 1812 Halifax soldiers moved west to their
bounty lands. William Plumb returned from Plattsburg, married Olive, and raised
a family on their Reed Hill Road farm until their deaths in 1869 and 1872. William
Plumb represented the Town of Halifax in the state legislature in 1850.

~ *Constance Lancaster and Susan Rusten*

ENDNOTES

1. E. P. Walton, *Walton's Vermont Register and Farmer's Almanac for the year of our lard, 1825*, no. 8. (Montpelier,
   VT: Monpelier Bookstore, 1825) p. 121.
2. HHS, document copy donated by Jacques Tucker.
3 VHS.
4. Mary R. Cabot, *Annals of Brattleboro: 1681–1895* (Brattleboro, VT: E. L. Hildreth, 1921–1922) p. 327.
5. *Halifax Militia Record Book,* R. Stanton Avery Special Collections Dept., New England Historic
   Genealogical Society, Boston, MA.
6. Ibid.
7. Heminway, p. 58.
8. HHS, from genealogical records of O. Jean Hearn of St. Johnsville, New York.
9. Herbert T. Johnson, *Roster of Soldiers in the War of 1812–14*, State of Vermont, prepared and published
   under the direction of the Adjutant General (St. Albans, VT : The Messenger Press, 1933).
10. Ibid., p. 327.
11. HHS, from the family papers of Mary Merriam, Conway, MA.

THOMAS MINER   Courtesy Lisa Moran

CIVIL WAR

On April 6, 1861, Vermont entered the Civil War. The Vermont State Legislature authorized the formation of regiments. The First Regiment was to be raised from the existing state militia to serve for a three-month stint with Colonel J. W. Phelps. The Second Regiment was raised for three years of service and formed in the beginning of May 1861. No record exists of any person from Halifax having enlisted in the First Regiment, and it is difficult to determine to what extent a militia existed in town during that period. In general, the state militia was poorly organized and did not train regularly in most towns.

Civil War Belt Buckle

The first evidence of Halifax's entry into the war was with the enlistment of Royal Fife on May 1, 1861. The Second Vermont Regiment came together in Burlington on June 6 and set off for Washington by train on June 24. It encamped nearby in Virginia. With less than two months of training under their belts, the group saw their first action on July 21, 1861, at Bull Run. Fife, who was serving in the Second Regiment's Company C, was taken prisoner. He was one of thirty in the Second Regiment who were captured and among approximately 1,800 Union troops taken prisoner during this battle. With the news of the retreat of the Union Army at Bull Run, the governor of Vermont, Erastus Fairbanks, ordered the formation of additional regiments as soon as possible. On January 3, after nearly six months in prison, Fife was released. He continued to serve with his regiment until he was discharged, because of a disability, on April 10, 1863. He died the day following his discharge. His death is noted as follows in Halifax town records: "Royal O. Fife, April 11, 1863; age 26; cause: chronic diarrhea; occupation: farmer/soldier" [HTC: VR].

What motivated Royal Fife, a twenty-four-year-old farmer from Halifax, to enlist in the Union cause? How strong was the abolitionist sentiment in town at that time? The Vermont Anti-Slavery Society minutes reported on the activities of an abolitionist by the name of Codding, who traveled around the state lecturing on the issue of slavery and spent March 27 to March 30, 1837 speaking in Halifax.[1] Mr. Codding spent more time in Halifax than in many other towns in the area. Perhaps from this we might conclude that he had a receptive audience here. Another reference to the antislavery movement is made in a letter to James Niles of Halifax from a friend or relative who had moved from Halifax to Marietta, Ohio. The letter, dated 1838, states,

> I suppose by this time all the people in Vermont are abolitionists
> and I trust it will not be long ere this giant state Ohio speaks out
> against such a curse upon our land and liberty. I live upon the
> borders of a Slave State and witness the workings of the system

upon society both morally and politically. We see the [ ] and
misery of the captive Negro and we have seen them until our
hearts have become steeled against pity or compassion. But what
do I say! We can sympathize or at least some of us. We can lament
that things are so; but Ohio does not speak out in so loud a voice
as it will before many years. [HHS: Niles]

Following the lead of Royal Fife, there soon followed a wave of
enlistments to swell the ranks of the Fourth Regiment; however, Fife was the first
and only Halifax man to serve in the Second Vermont Regiment. One can only
assume that this young farmer had strong feelings to motivate him.

In Benedict's book, *Vermont in The Civil War*, he tells the story of an
incident which occurred when the Second Vermont Regiment stopped in New
York City, amidst much fanfare, on their way to Washington. A basket of flowers
was presented to their colonel with the following statement: "Will the Colonel of
the Second Vermont Regiment please accept for his Regiment the accompanying
basket of evergreens from a Vermont lady, who has trimmed them with the
scissors with which her mother, Meliscent Barrett, cut the papers for the first
cartridges that were used at Concord, Massachusetts and Bunker Hill in 1775."[2]
This same Meliscent Barrett came to Halifax after the Revolutionary War, where
she married Joseph Swain. She is buried in the Halifax Center Cemetery [↪ 179].

The Fourth Regiment formed on July 30, 1861 and was encamped in
Brattleboro at Camp Holbrook, where it trained until September 21 and then
boarded a train south. The conditions at Camp Holbrook were rainy, and of the
1,042 men at the camp, 300 were reported to be sick. The regiment eventually
reported to Camp Griffin in Virginia, where conditions worsened rather than
improved. The men were often wet, there were not enough blankets or warm
clothes, and disease was rampant. The governor of Vermont (then Frederick
Holbrook) was so disturbed by the reports of the poor condition of his troops
that he sent Dr. Edward Phelps from Brattleboro to investigate. Phelps informed
the governor "of the 4,939 Vermonters in camp, 1,086 were excused from duty
because of illness."[3] The predominating diseases were reported to be mumps,
whooping cough, chicken pox, diarrhea, dysentery, typhoid, and malaria. The
theories as to why the Vermonters were particularly prone to disease were that
their immune systems were weakened by homesickness, and/or their previous
isolation provided them with little immunity. Four men from Halifax died from
disease at Camp Griffin: Philip Bailey (November 17, 1862), Stephen Stratton
(January 11, 1862), William E. Goodnow (January 16, 1862), and Alonzo Niles
(February 10, 1862). It is not known how many others suffered and later
recovered; however, the following men were discharged "for disability,"
presumably related to illness: Henry Huber (December 1, 1862), William H.
Goodenough (March 3, 1862), Theodore Graves (September 8, 1862), John S.
Mannering (October 31, 1862), Fayette Niles (May 12, 1862), Henry Niles
(January 4, 1862), Sanford Stanley (May 28, 1862), Titus Stowe (October 14,
1862), Ausemus J. Warren (September 12, 1862), and Alvin L. Whitney
(December 4, 1862).

The Fourth Vermont, as part of Vermont's First Brigade, which was made up of all five regiments, fought its first battle at Lee's Mill, Virginia, in April 1862. It faced the Confederate forces across the Warwick River. The Fourth Regiment was led by Colonel Stoughton (a twenty-three-year-old graduate of West Point who came from Bellows Falls) and was ordered to cross the dam at Lee's Mill. The Vermont companies involved faced heavy fire and were eventually forced back across the river. It was during this skirmish that Stephen Brainard Niles of Halifax was "killed in action at Lee's Mills" [HLR 3A: 16].[4] He was twenty-six years[5]

Photo C. Lancaster

old, and according to family tradition was a drummer. Niles is listed in the Vermont State Roster as an infantryman, not as a musician. A drum, sent home to his family, has been passed along through the years. Members of the Lee Stone family loaned it to the Halifax Historical Museum for exhibit. Drummers and buglers were often boys (though not in this particular case). It was their job to communicate orders to their units and to keep the men together during battle. For this reason, they were usually found in the midst of the fighting and thus were the target of the enemy. Stephen Niles was one of the casualties of this battle; however, in total, forty-four were killed and 148 wounded (of these twenty-one later died of their wounds). Among the wounded in this skirmish was another Halifax man by the name of Charles Dunklee. Dunklee remained in the service and was later wounded at Wilderness on May 5, 1864. He survived this wound as well and was discharged during December 1864.

CIVIL WAR DRUM HHS

When Stephen Niles enlisted in the Army on August 27, 1861, he left his wife Clarissa with their first-born child of six months, Harvey Brainard Niles.

Letters, which were found by the Knox family in the Plumb family homestead, lend greater understanding as to the strong sentiments regarding the war and the personal conflicts and tragedy. Stephen Niles's brother, Orsemus Niles, moved out to Ohio during the late 1840s. It is through the correspondence between the Ohio branch of the family and James Niles (father to Stephen and Orsemus), that we are able to learn the full spectrum of opinion regarding the Civil War. In a letter dated July 13, 1862, addressed "Dear Father & Mother," Orsemus writes:

> Having done what I could to ascertain the facts as to the order
> forbidding the removal of the bodies of soldiers killed in Battle in
> the present war. . . . It appears that Brother Brainards [he refers to

his brother Stephen by his middle name] bones must lie where they are until all men are called to Judgement. What under the [ ] do the people of New England so clamor for the liberation and arming of the Blacks for? Why does Gen. [ ] say that it is a stretch of patriotism for his people to serve further unless the war is made one of liberation and confiscation. Such acts as New England is guilty of is prolonging this war and what is more is preparing the way for civil war in the North. I look for it and have for a half-year. The people of the North will be in arms against one another before the close of another year unless there is a change in affairs. I confess that I shall hate to see it come, not so much on my own individual account, as that of my family. Had I not them to care for, I should be where life is less uncertain than ordinary. . . . What is freedom? We have got none. We are living under a military despotism. I see no other way but for men to arm and when any dirty abolitionist dog calls men who have labored for the Union all their lives traitors, to shoot them down if you die the next minute. It matters but little when we die, for life now is good for nothing. [HHS: Niles]

Orsemus continues his letter in this bitter vein. In later letters he elaborates further on his opposition to the war and the abolitionist movement. One wonders if the death of his brother embittered him so.

In another letter to James Niles and his wife, Stephen and Lucy Tucker of Jackson, Ohio, write:

Dear Brother & Sister Niles . . . I know not what your views and would not wish to be unkind or iratable, but I believe our present administration is the most contemtable one ever administered by any yet in the histry of the world . . . I may not live to see it, but the way we are drifting our once United States will be a land governed by despots unknown in the history of civilized nations. I should like to see you and converse with you on the subject of our national difficulty but I do not know as it can be. . .The agitation of slavery by the North had been the cause of this devastation and distruction of human life. The attempt to free a few negroes makes a land desolate with mourning for the dead and maimed . . .
[HHS: Niles]

Responding to "Brother and Sister Tucker," James Niles writes:

You wrote in your letter of the death of your dear son, James. I well remember him and thought him to be a fine promising young man worthy of trust and care. His death and loss to you must be great indeed. Dear Brother & Sister we know very well how to sympathize with you. He probably was the son amidst all the others on whom your thoughts had rested as your stay in your second childhood. His loss is irreparable in the things of this life so you must sit down and mourn without hope save in matters pertaining to the spirit land. Our case is similar to yours. Four years ago this fall when we were at your home we had five living sons. Our youngest, Stephen B., was the one best fitted as we thought to be our home boy. He was truly a desireable young man—a man of sufficient powers of mind to have filled any place in society that he might have been called to act with profit to his constituents and erudite to himself. In the breaking out of this rebellion he partook largely of the spirit of freedom and national union and on the 27th of August, 1861, he gave his name as a soldier for his country's cause. In conversing with his wife on the subject, he says to her I may do my family more good to go than to stay at home. This may be prophetic. We know not what good may acrue. His death is the more aggravating it being (seemingly so unnecessary) to satisfy the foolish aspiration of a poor drunken officer, and accomplished nothing. He said to his brother when about to leave home, I may be killed and if I am to be, I hope it may be instant. In this his hope was realized. The ball passed through his head. Dear Brother, this was dreadful. It has already spread a cloud of darkness and gloom over the hopes and prospects of this generation that can never pass away until we all lay down and return to our mother dirt with our dear soldiers who have poured out their blood for their nations weal.

Now what shall we do? Shall we say we have done all we can and can do no more. If I understand your views of our national affairs from what you wrote me in your letter, it is my misfortune to think different from you. In some particulars I would ask more definitely how this rebellion could be settled short of the shedding of blood and maintain the supremacy of our national laws. The South were determined to secede. There could have been no compromise that would have been satisfactory to any northern man, yourself not excepted. They were determined on seceding or rule the roost and under southern rule you nor myself could have endured long. You say that northern men have been meddling with what was none of their business—meddling with their very precious jewel slavery. Now when I have taken a narrow and selfish view of this matter, I have thought to myself.

Now let us for a moment take a view of this thing though I am no statesman and further, this little sheet would not afford limits for a long talk. I would ask why the South is not a match for the North as they expected they were. They have every advantage in nature over us. Their territory far exceeds ours. They have the best climate. Their soil is far richer than ours. They can raise anything we can and more in abundance. Their soil and climate will produce many things that we can do nothing with. Now what makes all the difference. Do we want to be ruled by an institution that is running this down to national ruin and we go to destruction with them. My former views have not been altogether in favour of unconditional and immediate emancipation, but the older I grow and the more I see of the progress of time and its wants, my prejudices I find are relaxing. Dear Brother, let us watch the events of time with an unbiased mind and an impartial eye. [HHS: Niles]

Altogether there were thirty-two men from Halifax enrolled in the Fourth Regiment, many of them for the full three-year enlistment. The Fourth Vermont saw action in many of the major battles of the war. Among these were Antietam, Fredericksburg, Gettysburg, and Wilderness. Their final battle before being discharged home was at Petersburg, on April 2, 1865.

During the Battle at Crampton's Gap in September 1862, Francis Seaver, a sergeant in Company I of the Fourth Regiment, was wounded and taken prisoner; however, he was released about a month later and discharged from service.

Israel Stowe Jr. and John Whitney, both in Company I, were wounded at

ISRAEL STOWE JR.

the Battle of Fredericksburg on December 13, 1862. Whitney was discharged in March 1863 because of his health. Stowe continued to serve until discharged in September 1864. Israel Stowe later became a selectman. He raised French Merino sheep and had an extensive sugar lot. He and his family became the focus of tragedy when his brother Horace, in April 1897, hanged himself in the barn, which was on the former Benjamin Henry property. His brother was fifty-three years old at the time. A year later, Israel hanged himself on his sixty-fifth birthday. His obituary listed "family troubles and physical infirmities" as the cause of death. He was also credited in his obituary with taking part in twenty-seven battles during his Civil War service [HTC: VR].

Elliot Harris was wounded at Salem Heights on May 4, 1863. He was thirty years old. When the Fourth Regiment fought at Wilderness on May 5, 1864, the casualties included several men from Halifax. Lorenzo Harris, Charles Dunklee, Elliot Harris (for the second time), William E. Smith, and Timothy Larrabee were all wounded during battle.

LORENZO HARRIS

Stowe and Harris photos used with permission of Ed Italo, *The Ed Italo Collection* Vermont in the Civil War.

During the Battle of Winchester on September 19, 1864, James K. P. Crosier was wounded and died the following day. He is listed in the Halifax Town Records of the "Enrolled Militia," dated January 29, 1863, as being seventeen years old. Lewis F. Crosier of the same family enlisted at the same time and was a member of this same company.

Francis J. Hosmer was listed as "Musician" in the *Revised Roster of Vermont Volunteers During the War of the Rebellion.*[6] He enlisted in the Fourth Regiment, Company I, on September 4, 1861, and was promoted to corporal and then sergeant. He was taken prisoner on June 23, 1864 at Weldon Railroad and remained a prisoner until April 1865, when he was pardoned.

"Dad's Father's Regiment" – Frank Miner   HHS

Frank Miner, who served in Company I, Fourth Regiment, wrote home to his brother on March 20, 1864, from a camp near Brandy Station, Virginia. It is the only letter from a Halifax soldier that is in the possession of the Halifax Historical Society. It is probably a fairly typical communication of information about the weather, camp life, and inquiries about home. In the letter, Miner writes about the sale of sugar to men in his company. "Mr. Smith of our Company had a large box of sugar come in the night before last — old sugar and it was the blackest looking stuff that I ever see and he is getting 40 cents per pound." He expresses the hope that his brother has sent him the box of maple sugar and that he shall be able to sell it as well. The end of the letter shares information about other men from Halifax in his company and a hint of homesickness.

> Now Crosier has got well and so has Francis Hosmer. There is no
> one in this Company that is sick now. I should like to be home
> this spring in shugaring but I can't. I mean to next. How do the
> folks like the other call that the President has made for more men?
> They will begin to scrable. Hoyt Sumner is in the guard house yet
> and I hope that they will keep him thar a spell to.

Meanwhile, the call for additional men to swell the ranks of the Union forces led to the formation of additional Regiments—eventually seventeen altogether. Halifax men were listed in the Second, Third, Fourth, Fifth, Seventh, Eighth, Ninth, Eleventh and Sixteenth Regiments. Two men from Halifax enlisted in the Fifth Regiment in the cavalry. Nicholas Ramond and Newton Patterson enlisted on September 12, 1964; however, Ramond deserted and never joined his company.

The Seventh Regiment listed two Halifax men on its rolls for one-year enlistments. John Graham appears to be listed as "colored cook." No further mention of John Graham can be found in town records other than that he served in the Civil War. Is it possible that Graham was a freed slave? The other member of the Seventh Regiment was George Ballou. Both these men enlisted in February 1865, and were sent with the regiment to New Orleans after leaving Vermont. The regiment spent most of its service in the Deep South. It participated in the siege of Mobile, which ended the day before Lee's surrender. From Mobile, the regiment was sent to Texas, until it was sent home in April 1866.

Twelve men from Halifax were enlisted in the Eighth Regiment. Of these men, two, Patrick Bolin and Elias Prouty, were early recruits. The regiment, organized in Brattleboro during January, and in March 1861, headed by train to New York. Needless to say, their encampment in Brattleboro was miserably cold and many men were sick. In New York, the men were loaded onto ships, with their destinations of Ship Island off the coast near New Orleans. The voyage took twenty-seven days, and many suffered seasickness. Private Rufus Kinsley wrote of the passage in his diary:

> March 16. Awakened at 2 in the morning, by the howling of the tempest, and the pitching of the ship, setting me on one end, and then suddenly on the other. Moveables lashed to their places, and the sick to their berths. . . . Many were frightened out of their wits. Before noon storm abated.[7]

The Eighth Vermont Regiment spent more than a year in Louisiana in the midst of hostile citizenry on one side and malaria on the other. In July 1864, the Eighth moved north to Washington to defend the city and spent days marching in pursuit of the Confederate forces. Reports were that the heat was terrible and many men encountered difficulty—heat stroke and the like. In one forty-eight-hour period, the Vermont troops marched seventy-five miles. After this unsuccessful pursuit of Jubal Early's Confederates, Philip Sheridan was put in charge of a new army which consisted of the Sixth Corp, the Nineteenth Corps, and the remaining forces in the Shenandoah Valley, including Vermont's Second, Third, Fourth, Fifth, Sixth, Eighth, Tenth, and Eleventh Regiments. Under Sheridan's leadership, this army successfully defeated the Confederate forces at Winchester, Opequon, and Cedar Creek. At Cedar Creek, the troops were surprised by a Confederate attack in the early morning hours of October 19, 1864. While many of the forces beat a retreat, the Eighth Vermont, among others, was ordered to put up a defensive line to hold back the enemy until the rest of the army could be reorganized. From descriptions, it seemed that the Eighth Vermont saw some of the heaviest fighting. One member of the Eighth reported "men seemed more like demons than human beings, as they struck fiercely at each other with clubbed muskets and bayonets."[8] When this defensive line was forced to retreat, more than half of the regiment had been wounded, killed, or captured. The Union troops had been forced back more than four miles before Sheridan, returning after having spent the night in Winchester, reorganized the troops, ordering them to advance in the late afternoon. Under Sheridan's leadership, the ground lost was regained, and it was the Eighth Vermont, battered and much reduced in numbers, which first broke the Confederate line. In the end, the Confederates were routed, but the Vermont casualties were heavy. Among these casualties were two Halifax men, James Bigelow of the Eighth Vermont (killed in action), and Lewis Carpenter, Eleventh Vermont (wounded).

The Ninth Vermont Regiment formed in July 1862 and with very little training under their belts, was transported to the Shenandoah Valley.

Sanford Fairbanks, George Potter, and Frank Rogers from Halifax were among the first volunteers. The first action, which the Ninth encountered, was in September, when it was forced to surrender with the rest of the Union forces at Harper's Ferry. The men were prisoners for the next eight months. George Potter is listed as having deserted his company on September 16, 1862, but rejoined his company in April 1863. Sanford Fairbanks died of typhoid fever at Fort Monroe on October 31, 1864. Several months before his death, Sanford's six year-old daughter, Rosella, contracted diphtheria. It was reported in the *Vermont Phoenix* that the last words she spoke were, "I wish I could see Papa." She died March 1, 1864 [HHS: Niles].

In September of 1864, five more men from Halifax enlisted in the Ninth Regiment for one-year terms. The Ninth Vermont had not seen much action; however, in September 1864, it took part in the attack on Fort Harrison in Virginia, and later in October attacked Confederate forces in Richmond.

The Eleventh Vermont Regiment was called to man heavy artillery around Washington and did not see much action until May of 1864, when it was called upon to join the Vermont Brigade for the assault at Spotsylvania. Ten men from Halifax appear on the rolls of the Eleventh Regiment, including Frank Anson, who received the commission of First Lieutenant of Company A and Samuel B. Jones, who was promoted from private to sergeant.

Twenty-six men from Halifax served in the Sixteenth Regiment. Company F formed in Wilmington and was made up of men from Halifax, Searsburg, Dover, Whitingham, and Wilmington. This regiment was organized into the Second Vermont Brigade. One of the most significant battles faced by this regiment was at Gettysburg in July 1863. On June 23, the orders were given to the brigade to march in pursuit of Lee's forces. This march was difficult. Many men had no shoes and suffered under the heat and weight of their possessions. In a period of six days, it covered more than 120 miles. When the men arrived at Gettysburg on July 1 after the first day of fighting, 200 men of the Sixteenth were ordered to do picket duty.[9] The eyewitness descriptions of the pickets describe the horror of hearing the cries of the wounded throughout the night, but being unable to offer comfort. The following day the Sixteenth Vermont did itself proud when it broke Pickett's famous charge. By all accounts, the actions of the Second Vermont Brigade, and in particular the Sixteenth Regiment, turned the tide in the battle and with it the war. The Confederate casualties were devastating. The casualties in the Sixteenth Regiment were sixteen dead, eighty-five wounded, and thirteen missing. Among the wounded were William Barrett, Thomas Miner, and Emerson Thurber of Halifax.[10]

The earliest reference to the Civil War in the Halifax town records appears on August 21, 1862, when a town meeting was warned:

> 1st to choose a moderator 2nd to raise money to pay volunteers a
> bounty enlisting in the eleventh Vermont Regiment and those
> enlisting to fill up the old Regiments 3rd to raise money to pay a
> bounty to volunteer nine month men Fourth to transact any other
> business relating to the bounty of volunteers.

The town meeting records refer to quotas. Apparently, each town was asked to provide so many men for each regiment. As can be documented from town records, it was up to each town to determine and raise the bounty paid to volunteers and/or to collect from drafted men the amount to be paid for substitutes. Because the cost to the towns was considerable, money had to be borrowed. Town reports during this period identify the actual cost in dollars, interest on loans, and so forth. The determination of the bounty paid to volunteers was quite controversial, as documented by the town meeting records. For example, in January 1864, an article was proposed "To see if the Town will raise two hundred dollars extra, making five hundred dollars to each volunteer who may enlist before the Sixth day of January, 1864 under said call of the President for three hundred thousand men." There was a motion at the town meeting to pass over this article, and the motion passed; however, at a town meeting held on September 6, 1864, the voters authorized the town to pay the volunteers $500. Then, again, on September 10, an article was proposed by Israel Worden to pay each man $400. At a town meeting on September 14, 1864, the following minutes were recorded:

> On motion of Thomas Smith to amend said motion of Israel Worden to
> pay drafted men the sum of $400, and made it one thousand dollars, a
> division of the house was called for and on count the vote stood 51 for
> said amendment and 31 against, so the amendment carried.

The debate can be traced by following town meeting records throughout the war. One might conclude that emotions ran high regarding the issue of the paid bounty. Whether the opposition to the higher bounty was based on opposition to the war or on fiscal conservatism, we can only guess.

The bounty system offered considerable financial incentive to the volunteers. While many were likely motivated by a sense of responsibility to serve the Union cause or to an abhorrence of slavery, it is also probable that the financial rewards inspired many struggling farmers to enlist.

In Halifax land records is a listing of all the Halifax men who fought in the war along with the amount of bounty paid to each individual. Town clerk and treasurer, Charles Fowler, additionally kept records of who paid for substitutes and the total cost to the town up to December, 19, 1864 [HLR 3A: 118–120].

Total number of men furnished	109
" " paid commutation	15
Total	124

Killed in battle	3
Died in the service of disease	16
Total	19
Amount paid volunteers as bounty	$18,450.85
" " substitutes for enrolled men	$3,900.00
Total	$22,350.85
Amount paid by drafted men	$4,500.00
" " 1 drafted man	$300.00
" " enrolled man	$1,450.00
[as commutation for substitutes]	
Total	$28,600.85
Amount of expences paid for recruiting	$478.05
Total amount paid	$29,078.90

ROLL OF SOLDIERS FROM HALIFAX IN THE CIVIL WAR

Information for the following chart was drawn primarily from Halifax records [HLR 3A: 116–118], *Vermont in the Civil War* by G. G. Benedict, and *The Revised Roster of Vermont Volunteers Who Served In the War of the Rebellion.* [11]

NAME	REGIMENT/COMPANY	ENLISTED/DISCHARGED
Kendall P. Ames	16th/ F	09/03/1862 – 08/10/1863
Mandarin H. Ames	16th/ F	09/03/1862 – 12/17/1862 - died of disease
Frank Anson	11th/Several companies	01/05/1864 – 08/25/1865
Philip C. Bailey	4th/I	08/26/1861 – 11/17/1862.- died of disease
George Ballou	7th/G	02/09/1865 – 02/09/1866
William H. Barrett	16th/F	09/03/1862 – 08/10/1863
Henry Bell	8th/I	02/13/1865 – 06/28/1865
James S. Bigelow	8th/B	01/02/1864 – 10/19/1864 - killed in action
Patrick Bolin	8th/I	02/07/1862 – 06/28/1865
Joseph C. Bryant	8th/I	01/04/1864 – 09/03/1864 - died of disease
George H. Burns	16th/F	09/03/1862 – 02/19/1863
Edward E. Burrington	16th/F	09/05/1862 – 01/14/1863 - died of disease
Lewis E. Carpenter	11th/E	08/31/1864 – 08/25/1865
Charles P. Clark	16th/F	09/03/1862 – 12/11/1862 - died of disease
James K. P. Crosier	4th/I	12/09/1863 – 09/20/1864 - died, Battle of Winchester
Lewis F. Crosier	4th/I	12/09/1863 – 07/01/1865
Rufus Crosier	16th/F	09/03/1862 – 08/10/1863
Francis L. Davis	16th/F	09/03/1862 – 08/10/1863
George E. Davis	16th/F	09/04/1862 – 12/10/1863 - died of disease
Charles Dunklee	4th/I	08/31/1861 – 12/24/1864
Henry Fairbanks	16th/F	09/06/1862 – 07/31/1863 - died of disease
Sanford S. Fairbanks	9th/K	09/06/1862 – 10/31/1864 - died of disease
John M. Farnham	16th/F	09/03/1862 – 08/10/1863
Matthew Ferrin	8th/E	04/19/1864 – 06/28/1865
Royal O. Fife	2nd/C	05/01/1861 – 04/10/1863
Horace L. Fish	9th/K	09/12/1864 – 06/13/1865
Francis F. Fisher	16th/H	09/03/1862 – 08/10/1863
Sylvanus Fox	8th/I	05/21/1864 – 06/28/1865
Elisha Gates	11th/H	08/11/1862 – 12/12/1863
Peter S. Gates	11th/H	07/31/1862 – 04/26/1865
William E Goodnow	4th/I	08/26/1861 – 03/03/1862
William H. Goodnow	4th/I	08/26/1861 – 01/16/1862 - died of disease
John Graham	7th/C	02/15/1865 – 02/14/1866
Theodore Graves	4th/I	09/06/1861 – 09/08/1862

NAME	REGIMENT/COMPANY	ENLISTED/DISCHARGED
Henry Griffin	16th/F	09/03/1862 – 08/10/1863
Elliot Harris	4th/I	07/31/1862 – 04/26/1865
Emerson Harris	11th/E	08/11/1862 – 06/09/1865
Lorenzo Harris	4th/I	09/04/1861 – 09/30/1864
Francis J. Hosmer	4th/I	09/04/1861 – 05/28/1865
Henry M. Huber	4th/D	08/18/1862 – 12/1/1862
Samuel B. Jones	11th	02/26/1864 – 08/25/1865
Oliver W. Kempton	8th/E	12/29/1863 – 04/20/1864 - died of disease
Andrew J. Kenney	4th/I	08/30/1861 – 07/13/1865
Timothy Larrabee	4th/I	12/15/1863 – 07/26/1865
Henry Leet	3rd/B	02/15/1865 – 07/11/1865
Thomas Liberty	8th/B	02/22/1865 – 06/28/1865
John S. Mannering	4th/I	09/06/1861 – 10/31/1862
Henry Marcotte	8th/I	05/03/1864 – 06/28/1865
Francis T. Miner	16th/F	09/03/1862 – 08/10/1863
F. T. Miner Reenlisted	4th/I	09/10/1864 – 07/18/1865
Frank E. Miner	4th/I	12/30/1863 – 07/13/1865
Thomas Miner	16th/F	09/03/1862 – 07/03/1863 - wounded at Gettysburg
Alonzo Niles	4th/I	08/30/1861 – 02/10/1862 - died of disease
Fayette Niles	4th/I	08/30/1861 – 05/12/1862
Henry Niles	4th/I	09/02/1861 – 02/04/1862
Stephen Niles	4th/I	08/27/1861 – 04/16/1862 - killed in action
Newton C. Patterson	5th/F	09/12/1864 – 06/21/1865
Barna N. Phelps	11th/E	08/12/1862 – 06/24/1865
George H. Potter	9th/K	05/27/1862 – 02/11/1865 - died
William J. Prevere	16th/F	09/03/1862 – 08/10/1863
Elias S. Prouty	8th/I	11/12/1861 – 08/14/1864
Nicholas Ramond	5th/A	09/12/1864 – deserted, never joined company
Benjamin H. Rider	11th/E	07/31/1862 – 06/24/1865
Frank Rogers	9th/K	05/28/1862 – 05/25/1865
John R. Scears	11th/E	08/11/1862 – 06/24/1865
Francis Seaver	4th/I	08/27/1861 – 10/07/1862
William E. Smith	4th/I	08/19/1861 – 05/05/1864
Frank Snell	drafted/unassigned	02/14/1865 – 05/12/1865
Charles L. Stacy	16th/F	09/03/1862 – 08/10/1863
Josiah W. Stanclift	4th/C	09/08/1864 – 05/13/1865
Sanford E. Stanley	4th/I	09/05/1861 – 05/28/1862
Israel Stowe Jr.	4th/I	09/04/1861 – 09/20/1864
Titus Stowe	4th/I	09/04/1861 – 10/14/1862
Stephen W. Stratton	4th/I	08/27/1861 – 01/11/1862 - died of disease
Eben S. Sumner	9th/K	09/05/1864 – 06/13/1865
Hoyt Sumner	4th/I	12/13/1863 – 05/13/1865
John J. Sumner	16th/F	09/06/1862 – 08/10/1863
Thomas Sumner	16th/F	09/03/1862 – 08/10/1863
Elwin Thompson	16th/F	09/05/1862 – 08/05/1863 - died of disease
Almon E. Thurber	16th/F	09/03/1862 – 08/10/1863
Emerson H. Thurber	16th/F	09/04/1862 – 08/10/1863
Levi M. Tucker	4th/I	09/13/1862 – 01/08/1862
Charles T. Tyler	2nd U.S. Sharpshooters/H1	01/13/1861 – 10/12/1862
William H. Upton	16th/F	09/03/1862 – 08/10/1863
Ausemus J. Warren	4th/I	09/02/1861 – 09/12/1862
Frank S. Whitcomb	8th/E	09/02/1864 – 05/13/1865
Alvin Whitney	4th/I	09/05/1861 – 12/04/1862 - died 01/06/1863 of disease contracted in the service.
John D. Whitney	4th/I	09/02/1861 – 03/27/1863
Lemuel P. Whitney	16th/F	09/03/1862 – 08/10/1863
Thomas B. Whitney	16th/F	09/03/1862 – 08/10/1863
Alden C. Williams	9th/K	09/12/1864 – 06/07/1865
Otis W. Wood	9th/K	09/12/1864 – 06/13/1865
Francis L. Woodard	16th/F	09/03/1862 – 08/10/1863

Frank E. Miner

Levi M. Tucker
(Courtesy Jacques Tucker)

While the financial cost to the town was great, the human costs were immeasurable. What the statistics don't demonstrate is the number of men who survived the war with lasting scars—physical and mental. The hardships, which the enlisted men endured, were great. By all accounts, the horrors witnessed by those who served remained vivid in their memories long after the war was over. In January of 1888, the Halifax correspondent to the *Vermont Phoenix* reported:

> The old soldiers in town talk of forming a Grand Army Post in this village. Considerable has been said about it for some time but nothing definite until lately. We understand a charter is to be applied for directly and the post will soon be in working order.

Pin HHS

Postcard HHS

Later that year the Charles P. Clark, Post 103 of the G. A. R. (Grand Army of the Republic) officially established itself in Halifax. The building was torn down. Among other things, the post developed the tradition of making Memorial Day a time to recognize veterans of the Civil War and those who gave their lives. An exchange in the *Vermont Phoenix* in 1896 refers to the Memorial Day observance. Apparently the G. A. R. asked the town to contribute some funds toward the Memorial Day activities and met with some opposition. As a result, a member of the G. A. R. wrote an angry letter to the *Vermont Phoenix* denying that any town money would be squandered. He went on to say that at one time the soldiers were looked up to ". . . and worshipped by some of the stay-at-homes who were glad to get the quota filled and so be relieved from the fear of being drafted. But now the war has closed . . ." A response to this letter appears later to say, "We are all human and let us not condemn all for the utterances of a few grumblers. When Memorial Day is come you will see by the attendance and interest manifested that the old soldier occupies a very large warm corner in the affections of Halifax" [HHS: Scrapbook].   ~ *Susan Rusten*

GRAND ARMY OF THE REPUBLIC MEETING   HHS

LINES FROM A HALIFAX FARM JOURNAL DURING THE CIVIL WAR

Jane Clark, wife of James Tucker, wrote a few lines every day in a notebook that begins January 1860. Her entries include the Civil War period and continue until her death in August 1865. After her husband's death in 1862, she continued to live with their sons, Albert and George and their wives, Juliette and Cynthia, on the corner of Tucker and Stage Roads, in the house known later as the Jones/Crosby place. Another son, J. Emerson Tucker and his wife, Lucy Morrison, lived further north on Tucker Road, toward Whitneyville in the house currently owned by the Christies. The town lists Albert as a member of the Vermont Militia, and George as a selectman during the war years. Neither served in the war. The journal, in the style of most farm diaries, is reserved in emotion and offers a simple but compelling record of the details of life in Halifax during that period. Jane Tucker notes the sadness of the day when the first group of boys volunteered, describes their farewell in Brattleboro, and quietly notes her attendance at funeral after funeral.

1861	March	3	Sabbath warm as summer it has ben very pleasant all the week
		4	Some cooler President Lincoln takes his seete today
	May	3	I am going to see Maria she is not very well. They have a Miliatary meeting to the Hollow tonight to volunteer for the war.
		5	sabbath pleasant ben to meeting in the old meeting house in the forenoone
	June	4	boys gone to training to day the first in their lifetime
		8	boys plowing down south and going to training this afternoon
		15	boys to Calverts to work planting and training to the Hollow
		29	I am going to help Lucy today. Geo whitwashing Al training
	August	16	boys gone to Guilford to training, we had company all day Mrs. Niles Mrs. Henry and Mrs. Fowler.
	Sept.	1	sabbath all been to church but Father. Henry [Clay] Fish Preached.
		3	freemans meeting and Training day. it has ben a sollom day seventeen of there company have Enlisted in to the war.
		13	Ette and I ben to the sewing circle to make things for the soldiers. Geo helping Em patch his barn.
		14	very warm solgiers all gone to Brattleboro today.
		15	Sabbath quite warm and pleasant I have ben to church.
		16	boys went to Brattleboro last night and they have not got home yet there is great Excitement here, news came that the Vermont regiment was a going to start for the war 9 oclock last night and half of Halifax has gone to Brattleboro last night and to day 18 Ladies went in one waggon from the Hollow.
		17	boys got home last night, the Regament have not gone yet
		22	sabbath raind all night cleard off cold. the Reagament left Brattleboro last night for the seete of war
	Nov.	22	boys sawing loggs up in there woods, I have ben to the Hollow to the Ladies society for the benefit of the soldiers.
1862	Feb.	5	pleasant, I have ben to the funeral of Billy Goodnow [William E. 4th Regt. Co. 1]
		27	snows, all gone to the Funeral of Alonzo Niles [4th Regt. Co. 1]
	May	25	sabbath all hands ben to the Hollow to the funeral of B. [Stephen Brainard] Niles. [4th Regt. Co. 1]
	August	22	wet, lowery day Geo. out recruiting Souldiers all day.
		24	sabbath Geo. & Cynthia went to the Hollow. I went with them to Mr. [Charles W.] Emersons [Universalist] Church tonight they have all gone to the schoolhouse.
		25	Al & Ette started this after noon for Brattleboro to see the soldiers.

	Sept.	6	Extreme warm good wether to ripen of corn. Geo. gone to Brattleboro to see about the enlisting business.
		10	Pleasant Albert and Henry mowing brakes. George up in town and round seeing about soldiers, Juliette and I fussing round and going visiting.
	Dec.	28	warm and muddy all gone to the funerals of Mr. Emersons child and Charles [P.] Clark a sad day. [Sgt. 16th Regt. Co. F]
1863	Jan.	2	the selectmen met here to make out taxes. pleasant.
		8	Albert gone to the funeral of Alvin Whitiney [4th Regt. Co. 1] Geo out on the military business.
	April	6	gone to the funeral of William Eames this afternoon
		13	Pleasant sap runs well the boys Gone to the funeral of [Royal] Otis Fife [2nd Regt. Co. C. First to enlist from Halifax, May 1, 1861]
		30	National Fast Cynthia and I went to the Hollow to meeting
	May	16	The select men here all day making out the tax bills
	August	4	Nationall thanksgiveing to day.
	August	29	rainy day I am seventy years old to day
	Dec	8	a town meeting to rais monny. a housefool of Company
		10	the girls gone to Emersons Geo gone to Inlist Souldiers.
1864	Jan	1	8th day of Christmas stormed last night rains today we are expecting company Geo. out Recruiting soldiers.
		5	12 day of Christmas snos wind. N. E. Geo out this morning after Recruits Town meeting today about Bounty money.
		6	cold wind blows snow flies Geo gone to Brattleboro with mr. Howton [Selectman Houghton] to pay of the Soldiers bounty monny.
		7	very pleasant Geo. has not got home yet. Al gone to Jacksonville to mill. Cynthia spinning Ettes sewing on Al vest.
		27	the Selectmen Meete to make out the enrolment.
	Nov.	7	Lecktion day [Lincoln's second term] boys gone to town Meeting, we had company all day. Mrs. Wood from Smithfield, Penna.
	Dec,	29	Al tinkering Geo got the bleus all day Ette and I ben to the Soldier aid soc
1865	Jan	14	George gone to soldier meeting.
		18	Cold snow flies. Al and the girls gone to the Soldier aid society.
	Feb	7	baking for company. Cynthia sewing boys drawing wood.
		8	We had a hevy sno last night boys banking roads (we are having the soldier aid society here to day ther is quite a rush.
		16	Town meeting to rais monny.
	March	22	Ette gone to her Fathers to the Soldier aid Society very bad going in a wagon.
	April	5	I cam home to day snow all gone good walking. there has ben a greate work accomplished the weeke past in the war department, Richmond was taken one wake a go to day. a greate rejoicing threw the contry and fireing of canon to town.
		14	Fast day. Ette and I ben to meeting, a goodley number attended. {Lincoln shot on April 13}
		30	Sabbath I have ben to the Hollow to Church. Eld [Amherst] Lamb preached a funeral sermon on the Death of our President.
1865	Journal entry by daughter-in-law:		
	August	16	A sad and sorrowful day to us. Last night George came home with Uncle Charles & Cousin Thomas Clark and brought the sad news that Mother was dead she died Last Saturday afternoon at half past three o'clock and to day we have followed her lifeless remains to the grave.

Newspaper items, which follow, add detail to Jane Clark's journal entries.

January 23, 1862. *Vermont Phoenix*
Corporal R. O. Fife of Halifax, and Privates
Graves and Streeter of Vermont, all of
Company C, 2nd Vermont, and recently
released from confinement in the rebel prisons
at Richmond, are now at home on a brief
furlough.—

They propose to join their company in a few
days, and are very anxious for another brush
with the rebels, when they hope to wipe out
old scores.

February 1862. *Vermont Tribune*
Death at Camp Griffin, VA of typhoid fever.
ALONZO C. NILES, son of Nathaniel and
Mary S. Niles of Halifax, age 20 years, 4
months. He was a member of Company I, 4th
Vt. Regiment and his loss was much felt in the
company to which belonged.

April 24, 1862. *Vermont Phoenix*
Killed.—Among the killed at the engagement at Lee's Mills, on the 16th of April, was
Stephen B. Niles, son of James and Sarah
Niles, of Halifax, and a private in Co. I, 4th
Vermont Regiment. He was shot through the
head and died instantly. His age was [26] years;
and he leaves a wife and one child. His death is
the occasion of an address to be delivered at
West Halifax, at one o'clock in the afternoon
of the 25th inst., by the Rev. A. Lamb.

May 19, 1862. *Greenfield Gazette & Courier*
Halifax, Vt.
Of the twenty-one volunteers who went into
the Federal army from Halifax, Vt., eleven
have returned, either dead or sick unto death.

December 29, 1862. *Greenfield Gazette & Courier*
Died In Camp Vermont, Va. Dec. 11, Charles
P. Clark of Halifax, Vt., of the 16th Regiment,
aged 19 years and 9 months.

April 16, 1863. *Vermont Phoenix:*
Another soldier discharged—Royal O. Fife,
who enlisted and went to war with the 2nd
Regiment Vt. Volunteers, died at Halifax April
11. He was taken prisoner at the battle at Bull's
Run, was confined several months at
Richmond, and after being exchanged again,
joined his Regiment; was in seven days battle
on the Peninsula, also in the battles at
Antietam and Fredericksburg. After which he
was on the sick list, and was removed to
Portsmouth Grove Hospital R. I. whence he

was brought to Brattleboro, remaining a few
days at the Brattleboro house where he was
kindly cared for, and then conveyed to his home
in Halifax, where death soon discharged him
from his earthly labors and battles at the age of
26 years.

April 21, 1865. *Vermont Phoenix*
The Ladies' Soldiers' Aid Society of Halifax
Centre forwarded to the Treasurer of the
Christian Commision, on the 5th of April, the
following articles—7 bed quilts, 2 dressing
gowns, 6 shirts, 2 pair of drawers, 14 pillows—
all of the above made of new cloth; 22 pair
woolen socks, 90 yards of bandages 4 soldier
caps, 1 sheet, 11 cushions, 1 package of lint, 8
comfort bags, 3 packages of flannel, 1 package
of paper pins, 2 books, 23 towels, 5 pairs of
slippers, 26 pounds of dried apples, 2 pounds of
dried currents, 2 pounds of dried blackberries, 4
pounds of hops, 3 quarts of apple syrup, 4
gallons of pickles, 4 pounds of maple sugar, 2
quarts of maple syrup and 1 bottle of blackberry
wine.

The pastor of the Baptist church, Rev. S. A.
Blake has been absent the past six weeks
laboring for Christian Commission, and his place
supplied mostly by The Rev. Amherst Lamb of
Whitingham; who preached last Sabbath an able
and appropriate discourse from words found in
the 2nd Kings, 22 Chapter. 2nd Verse. *As Josiah
turned not to the right hand, nor to the left, but did that
which was right in the sight of the Lord.* Thus did
Abraham Lincoln the sixteenth President of the
United States.

The church was tastefully draped for the
occasion. There was also an engraving of Mr.
Lincoln hung over the pulpit trimmed with a
wreath of evergreen interspersed with white
flowers.

The Universalists also had a discourse upon
the death of Abraham Lincoln in their Chapel on
the afternoon of the same day.

May 12, 1865. *Vermont Phoenix*
West Halifax—Though we have no secret
societies to make capital by pronouncing
eulogies or passing resolutions to be published to
the country, claiming our late worthy president
to be a member of our society, yet we have
hearts that feel deeply ours and the nation's loss
in the cruel death of Abraham Lincoln. Neither
have we been without public demonstration of
our grief.

Photo of a painting by Robert Strong Woodward. HHS
House on Stage Road where Jane Clark Tucker lived when she wrote her journal, where the selectmen met
to work on the tax and militia lists, and where the Ladies Soldier Aid Society met during the Civil War.

©2008 *Constance Lancaster*

ENDNOTES
1. John Meyers, "The Major Efforts of Anti-Slavery Agents in Vermont, 1836–1838," *Vermont History*, vol. 36 (1968): 218.
2. G. G. Benedict, *Vermont in the Civil War* (Burlington, VT: Free Press Association, 1886), p. 67.
3. Howard Coffin, *Full Duty* (Woodstock, VT: The Countryman Press, 1993), p. 77.
4. The headline in the New York Daily Tribune dated April 22, 1862 was "The Battle at Lee's Mills, Virginia." Various sources including the HLR and *Vermont Phoenix* [↻ 372] used the spelling Lee's Mills. The correct spelling for the National Historic site is Lee's Mill.
5. Stephen B. Niles age when he was killed was incorrectly reported as 35 in the *Vermont Phoenix* [↻ 372]. His correct age was 26.
6. *G. G. Benedict,* The Battle of Gettysburg and the Part Taken by Vermont Troops *(Burlington, VT: Free Press Print, 1867); Jim Murphy,* The Boys War *(New York: Clarion Books, 1990); Niles Family Letters, original copies in the possession of the Ohio Historical Society, Columbus, OH. (Hereinafter cited as Benedict.)*
7. Ibid., p. 145.
8. Ibid., p. 309.
9. Picket duty involved standing guard around the camp periphery or along battle lines to watch for any enemy incursions.
10. Information gathered from a number of sources, including Benedict, Coffin, and the listing in HLR.
11. Benedict.

Later Wars

World War I

The *Roster of Vermont Men and Women in the Military and Naval Services of the United States and Allies in the World War, 1917–1919*, states that Halifax provided the following men for service:

Bowen, Pvt. David Elmer (age 22), enlisted September 5, 1918; discharged December 21, 1918
Collins, Pvt. Fred L. (age 25), enlisted November 07, 1917; killed in action September 8, 1918
Fairbanks, Pvt. Norton (age 18), enlisted October 10, 1917; discharged August 01, 1919
Hebert, Pvt. Ernest Clifford, drafted June 28, 1918; discharged January 10, 1919
Tinker, Pvt. Arthur (age 25), drafted April 30, 1918; discharged March 4, 1919
Upton, Pvt. Fred (age 23), drafted May 29, 1918; discharged May 25, 1919
May, Warren (age 21), drafted August 29, 1918; discharged December 01, 1918
Cutting, Pvt. Elmer (age 25), enlisted April 25, 1917; discharged March 31, 1919
Bowen, Frank Ellison (age 19), enlisted Navy June 17, 1918; discharged July 23, 1919
Bernard, Freddie Adolphus (age 22), drafted May 15, 1918; discharged December 11, 1918
Bovee, Pvt. Meredith (age 25), enlisted April 28, 1917; discharged July 5, 1919

Fred Collins was the only man from Halifax who was killed in action. Fred was raised on the Collins Farm, formerly owned by Kenneth and Mary Sumner, on the Collins Road. He is buried in West Halifax. His marker says "Mechanic Co A Nth Mach Gun Batt."

FRED COLLINS   HHS

World War II

As with any war roster, the list of those who served from the Town of Halifax reflects only those who lived in the town at the time they enlisted or were drafted.[1] Some of the individuals mentioned in this section were born in Halifax but did not reside in the town at the time they were enrolled, and some settled in Halifax after World War II. Following are the men whom Halifax provided for the war effort:

Poster extracted from picture of Crosier Store interior. HHS

Atherton, Leslie (b. December 10, 1919) active duty September 15, 1942–August 14, 1945, Asiatic-Pacific Theater

Bowen, Frederic A. (b. June 2, 1919) enlisted September 13, 1940; discharged June 23, 1945, South-Pacific Theater

Brissette, Earl F., enlisted August 15, 1945; discharged May 19, 1947, European theater

Brissette, Lawrence (b. April 22, 1917) enlisted November 20, 1942; discharged February 27, 1946

Burnett, Clayton A. enlisted November 4, 1942; discharged September 6, 1945

Clement, Alfred B. (b. February 1, 1920) active duty August 17, 1942–December 16, 1945, Asiatic-Pacific Theater

Clement, Elmer F. (b. April 7, 1907) active duty July 9, 1942–October 6, 1945, European Theater

Cody, Joseph F. (b. February 9, 1917) active duty September 19, 1942 – October 16, 1945

Cody, Oscar L. active duty August 17, 1942–October 13, 1942; medical discharge

Bowen, John active duty October 31, 1942–September 22, 1945, Eastern Atlantic and Mediterranean Theaters

Deane, Clifton E. (b. December 31, 1912) active duty April 15, 1942–November 3, 1945, European Theater

Hardy, Reuben (b. January 8, 1911) active duty August 17, 1942–November 13, 1945, European Theater

Fairbanks, Arland F. (b. July 3, 1909) active duty January 18, 1945–February 6, 1945, Asiatic-Pacific Theater

Hebard, Roswell G. (b. April 26, 1922) active duty February 17, 1945–November 21, 1946, Western Pacific

Mason, Stanley W. (b. July 30, 1926) active duty November 6, 1944–November 21, 1946, European Theater

Nolan, Edward C. (b. September 22, 1919) active duty October 14, 1942–January 14, 1946, China-Burma India

Porter, Harry E. (b. December 20, 1917) active duty September 15, 1942–February 24, 1946

Stone, Clayton (b. February 17, 1921) active duty February 17, 1945–August 3, 1946, Western Pacific

Stone, James W. (b. December 11, 1926) active duty March 13, 1945–October 29, 1946

Weaver, George (b. December 5, 1918) active duty July 22, 1942–October 24, 1945; medical discharge, India

Weaver, Harold J. (b. August 16, 1925) active duty October 16, 1946–March 28, 1948

Weaver, Quentin (b. November 14, 1920) active duty January 29, 1942–December 4, 1945; Asiatic-Pacific Theater

Werner, Frederick W. (b. April 30, 1927) active duty August 15, 1945–July 17, 1946

Woodard, Richard F. (b. August 4, 1926) active duty November 6, 1944–August 14, 1945; Asiatic-Pacific Theater

Both Wendall and Sherwin Collins and Floyd Canedy, who were born in Halifax, served in World War II.

A partial list of World War II veterans who settled in Halifax after the war include Alfred Corey, Edwin Whitehorne, Thomas O'Brien, William Amberg, Ferdinand Cageo, and Harry Jones.

* * *

In 1999, Clayton Burnett wrote about his "Army experience," which offers a firsthand account of his recollections during his years of service. This document was provided courtesy of his sister, Bernice Barnett.

My army experience began when I was drafted as a twenty-year-old in June 1942 and was ordered to report to Ft. Devens, near Ayer, Massachusetts, on November 4, 1942. I was discharged December 6, 1945.

Because of his prior secretarial training, Clayton was assigned stenographic duty. He describes the living conditions the first winter in Camp Pickett, Virginia as follows:

We lived in tents during the winter and encountered both snow and ice storms. Each tent had a small round soft coal burning stove in the center with a four-inch stovepipe. We would have the stoves red hot and still our backs would be cold. The soft coal would cause the stovepipes to clog up and as a result "smoke out" the occupants of the tent every so often.

He goes on to say that he qualified for the Army Specialized Training Program at Virginia Military Institute, where he studied for nine months before the need for additional troops forced the government to phase out the program. At that time, Clayton was assigned to the G-3 Section, Division Headquarters, Eighty-seventh Infantry Division and was subsequently promoted to sergeant. The Eighty-seventh Infantry Division fought in the European theater, for most of the time as part of Patton's Third Army. While stationed in France, he saw General Patton when he visited the Eighty-seventh Division headquarters.

In one of the more graphic descriptions of his war experience, Clayton refers to the carnage of war:

Photo courtesy C. Burnett
CLAYTON BURNETT

On this trip and on others we took, we were on the same roads where heavy fighting had taken place during the Battle of the Bulge and where heavy snow had fallen. As the weather warmed up and melted the snow, many bodies as well as dead animals surfaced. Also, as streams of water started running, they turned over ammunitions that were "duds." Some of these duds, when disturbed would then explode, sending spurts of water into the air.

* * *

I grew up listening to war stories recounted by my father, Edwin Whitehorne, who served in the Navy during the war. Our neighbor, Alfred Corey, was also a Navy man, and Tom O'Brien, who lived just down the road, had served in the Army in the European theater. Their war experiences left a very strong impression upon them, and that shared experience drew them together. During the war my father wrote home after a particularly frightening battle.

I have been too busy and have not had the opportunity of writing to you before, but hope this letter will get off the ship in a few days. The Navy, by special dispatch, has lifted the censorship restrictions for all those who took part in the naval battles around the Philippines, enabling us for the first time to write home about our part in an operation. I am taking advantage of it to try and let you know just what action is like and what we all feel and experience. We are not permitted to mention dates, damage, names of ships involved, etc. but nevertheless I believe you will find this interesting. From here on is my description of the action:

We arrived off Leyte Island, in the central Philippines, the morning of the day that our troops were to land. We were all at G.Q. from about 2:30 a.m. We were not in a bombardment group, but could see and hear the naval guns giving it to the Japs on the beach. Dawn brought Jap dive-bombers on the scene, and a hectic time followed, with bomb splashes all around the place and planes diving and strafing. You could see them being shot down and exploding in the water. Later on in the morning the troops went ashore, and the fighting continued on the beach. We were at G. Q. all day, repelling air attacks. The Japs were sending in a lot of planes, more than I had ever seen before. So it went for four days.

We were doing anti-submarine patrol in Leyte Gulf, and day and night we were warding off plane attacks. We got very little sleep, meals were never on time, and sometimes we did not get time to eat at all. It got so that you would go down in the chow hall and fill your tray and sit down at the table to eat a meal, maybe hours late, and just as you started the old gong went off, and over the speaker would come the call, "All Hands to General Quarters on the Double to Repel Air Attack."

Photo courtesy Susan Rusten
EDWIN WHITEHORNE

You left your tray and dashed topside, and there was another meal gone. After a while all you could hear in your ears was the noise of the gong ringing, and you imagined you heard plane motors all the time. At night it was worse, for we did not have the airfields yet, and the carrier planes could not be up at night, so the Japs had the air to themselves and they took full advantage of it. We would open up on them with all our guns, and a very lovely time was had by all.

One night about seven o'clock, after a late and hasty supper, I was standing by the lockers in my compartment, talking things over with a group of the boys. We were all dog-tired, unshaven and crummy, and I guess were a sad looking lot. All of a sudden the loudspeaker overhead blared on, "Attention, all hands; This is the Executive Officer speaking. A message has just been received that a large Jap task force is moving down on us from the North, and we expect to meet them sometime tonight. All hands are cautioned to get as much sleep as possible. We will make a short-range attack with torpedoes. The Captain sends you the following message, 'Good shooting, Good Luck and God bless you.'"

Well, sir, you should have seen all the faces. Out in the mess hall one kid stepped out of the chow line and said, "I don't feel like eating now." I know he had lots of company. "The Old Man" had never given us a "God bless you" before, so we knew it was serious.

You have to be a destroyer sailor to know what a torpedo run is, especially at short range. It means you go in against heavy ships that have you out-gunned and out-ranged all the way. They can blow you out of the water before you ever get near enough to loose your torpedoes. Very few "Cans" come out of it O.K and those that do are usually badly mauled. So nobody felt elated over the news. I went up by myself to the flying bridge, by G. Q. station, and there in the darkness I talked to God. I thought of all of you so hard that I almost had you there with me. I could plainly hear that peculiar little laugh that is typical of Dorothy, and I remember now how I grinned to myself as I imagined I could hear it. I thought of the kid, and prayed hard to be spared to get home with you all once again, then I said my Rosary and felt a lot better. I had made my peace as best I could.

I went down below, and most of the boys were in their sacks, although some were playing cards to get their minds off it, but you could see that everyone was pretty solemn. I climbed into my sack and went right off to sleep, and was awakened by the old gong going like mad. Everybody was racing for the ladder, and up we went. We donned our helmets, lifejackets, which are also some protection against shrapnel, and of course we all had our knives. Lawrence is right below me on the wing of the bridge, and I called him for the time.

It was 2:30 a.m. It was a beautiful night, warm, calm and dark and thank the Lord. Word was passed for all we topside personnel to lay down on the deck when the shooting started, for we were not going to fire our guns, as they could range us by the flashes. We were just to make a torpedo attack and retire.

We moved out in column, to the mouth of Surigao Strait, we, the flagship, leading the squadron. We were to be the first ship in—quite an honor. We cracked a few jokes with the machine gun crews over the phones and wished each other luck, and then on we went. Word had been received now that the Japs had been sighted. We are increasing speed now; everything is quiet. On we go, and they have not yet sighted us.

Now we are moving faster yet, and suddenly, without any warning, on goes a huge searchlight from one of the Jap ships only a few miles away. It plays over the tail end of the column, we all hold our breaths, but they didn't pick us up. Pitch black again, and still moving in.

Again the light goes on, and it sweeps the column and comes to a stop right on the Remey, my ship. What a feeling! as though all the worlds are saying, "There's _____." They have us now, but at the same time I hear the Captain on the bridge give the order, "Fire one, fire two, fire three," etc. And our fish go swishing over the side and on their way.

The searchlight goes out again, and now we are making a smoke screen and bagging away as fast as we can go. WHOOSH, a star shell bursts directly over us and lights us up like a Christmas tree. I hit the deck with Luca, the chief yeoman, York, the cook, and Cleverly, a soundman, all four of us hugging the deck. Shells whistle overhead, sending up big splashes. They have straddled us fore and aft on the first salvo, and that is bad; they will probably nail us next salvo.

We are zigzagging behind the smoke screen. More shells land alongside, sending water up over our decks. The star shell burns out and there in the darkness the old girl is straining herself for all she is worth, ducking those shells like a whirling dervish. WHOOSH, another star bursts over us again. They sure have the range; I feel like a fly under a microscope. Again they come, and one drops right off the fantail, far too close for comfort. That sound is the ugliest thing in the world, and makes your insides crawl. The light goes out, and the next time a star shell bursts we are away from it.

We have fooled them; they are firing now, but it is wild. By golly, it looks as if we are going to make it. There are several explosions behind us among the Japs where our fish have scored, and we are all happy about that. We retire to behind a small island, and now our battle line opens up, cruisers and wagons. We have done our part and are out of their way; the rest is up to them. We have a ringside seat now for this show.

I have never seen such a concentrated fire as our ships are putting out. We see a Jap ship blow up, her ammunition going over the sky. The sky is torn apart by the full boom of the big guns, and explosions send great red gouts of fire up into the darkness. It is all over now, the Japs have been annihilated and the Battle of Surigao Strait is history.

Well, there is nothing more to tell. I was on the first ship in and the first ship fired on. A grand thing to live through and tell about, but I want no more torpedo runs, even though they are the primary mission of a destroyer. If I have a few extra gray hairs it is quite understandable. Lawrence has written only a letter to his mother and says to give his brother the details of the action. So, Dad, you can call him up and tell him the story. I hope to hear from you soon, and love you all with all my heart. Dot, you can tell Ron the story of how Daddy's "Boat" almost went "Boom," but didn't —a good ship and a lucky one, the REMEY.

* * *

Lavern Corey assembled a World War II scrapbook, which she gave to the Halifax Historical Society. Drawing from town reports and newspaper articles, she provided a picture of what life was like on the home front.

The way it's being told today, you'd think most everyone knew we were on the brink of war with the Japanese. Nothing could be further from the truth. Things were starting to feel "normal" again to most Americans in this post Depression year of 1941. . . .

Then it happened—Pearl Harbor . . . December 7, 1941. December 8th we were at war with Japan and on December 10th with Germany and Italy. Unlike previous American wars, WORLD WAR II was a total war fought not only on distant battlefields, but also on the homefront. . . . WORLD WAR II was a war uniting us as a nation like nothing before or since.

Winning the war required sacrifices at home as well as abroad. Americans everywhere rolled up their sleeves and got to work. Some served coffee and donuts to the servicemen as they boarded ships for overseas duty. Others rolled bandages, collected scrap metal and newspapers. Women turned in silk and nylon stockings that were used to make parachutes and gun powder bags. Housewives kept fat drippings for munitions, planted victory gardens to help supplement the food supply and peeled strips of foil from gum wrappers. Children even played a role in the war effort by collecting milkweed pods. The fluffy white stuff was used in Navy life preservers. . . .

Everyone was buying war bonds. Three and a half million women reported to armament plants to help produce aircraft, naval ships, cargo ships as well as trucks. . . .

Americans had to cope with something new called rationing. First call on everything went to the Military, as well it should. There were food, shoe, tire and gas coupons. If you owned a car, you were allowed 3 gallons of gas a week. People rode to work on balloon-tired bikes to conserve precious petroleum.

* * *

The town report in 1943 included a letter from then superintendent of schools, Ethel Eddy, which made a plea for raising teachers' salaries. "Since the War began in Europe in 1939, the average weekly earnings of factory workers have increased 59%, the average annual salaries of teachers about 7%, while living expenses have increased 30%." She also called for an increase in state aid to education.

In a 1944 town report, Superintendent Eddy reported, "Unfortunately the Valley School had to be closed, owing to our inability to secure a teacher. . . . The children from this district were transported to West Halifax and Jacksonville."

The following excerpts from the *Brattleboro Reformer* articles collected by Lavern Corey also add to the picture of the home front.

o   *June [ ], 1942, West Halifax*, "Ration Boards to grant 20 lbs. of canning sugar to applicants. Those wishing sugar for canning can procure their cards by applying to Leon Parker in Jacksonville or to the rationing board office in the high school building in Wilmington."

o   *May 8, 1942, Halifax*, "At the annual meeting of the Halifax Union Society, it was voted to purchase a $500 War Savings Bond."

o   *June 12, 1942, South Halifax*, "The Valley School children have bought over $100 worth of baby bonds and war stamps. There are 14 scholars."

o   *September 4, 1942, West Halifax*, "The community each Tuesday morning is sending a box to one of the town boys who is in the U.S. Army. Anyone wishing to contribute toward these boxes is asked to leave articles or money with which articles can be purchased at the post office by Monday evening."

o   *June 2, 1942*, "Black Out Test," They blew the whistle at Stone's Mill and rang the church bell in West Halifax.

KOREAN WAR

Below is a list of Halifax individuals that appear in the *Vermont Korean War Rolls:*

Frederick Warren Bender, Jr., MR2 Navy
Kathleen Gould Grant, Cpl. Army
Alvah Jones, Navy
Bernard Leon LaRock, Cpl. Army
Amor Edward Wheeler, Cpl. Army
Reginald Willard, SR Navy
Ronald Worden, Pvt Army/SR Navy

Frank M. Stone, Cpl. Army
Carl N. Stone, SP3 Army
Kathleen Woolley, Cpl. Army
Richard T. Wright, Sgt. Army
Gerard C. Shrewsbury [Settled
   in Halifax immediately
   following the Korean War]

VIETNAM WAR

While currently there are several Vietnam vets living in Halifax, during the war four men and one woman from Halifax served in Vietnam: Gary Crosby; Leonard Derby; David Rafus, SSGT Air Force; David Ryan, SP5 Army; and Thelma Ryan, SP5 Army.

Leonard Derby (below) agreed to be interviewed during the fall of 2000 regarding his war experience. What follows summarizes his remarks.

Photo courtesy L. Derby
B-Troop, 3rd Armored Squadron, 17th Air Calvary

Leonard came from a family of men who had enlisted and served in World War II. This family tradition lead him to decide, while in his last year of high school, to serve his country in Vietnam. His initial plan was to go into the Air Force. To this end, he had to undergo several tests. The final test for this branch of the service took place in Manchester, New Hampshire. Regrettably, Leonard was unable to get to Manchester for the exam. He then enlisted in the High School Graduate Program in the U. S. Army. He was inducted into the service on February 7, 1967, flown from Manchester, New Hampshire to New York, and from New York to Fort Jackson in South Carolina, where he lived in a tent with a coal stove for heat. The Army then sent him to Fort Gordon, Georgia, for eight weeks of basic training, and then on to Fort Eustis in Virginia to be trained in helicopter repair.

In mid-September, in the middle of the night, Leonard's squadron was transported from Fort Knox, Kentucky, to San Francisco, where they boarded a troop carrier (the USS *General Walker*), which was a ship left over from World War II. It took them twenty-one days aboard ship to reach Vietnam. Leonard describes how they loaded onto landing crafts to get from ship to shore, then to an Air Force transport plane, then to buses, which convoyed them to their base at Tay Ninh near the Cambodian border. It was here that Leonard served as a helicopter mechanic and crew chief during the Tet offensive.

Many Vietnamese people worked on the base in various capacities. It was some of these same individuals who were later determined to be working for the Vietcong. Most of the action took place at night. After one such night raid, one of the Vietnamese workers in the camp was killed outside the camp perimeter when enemy fire was returned. Leonard says it was difficult to know who was the enemy and who could be trusted. The enemy could be anywhere and they were not easily recognized.

It was the job of Leonard's squadron to protect the Special Forces who were camped atop a nearby hill (Black Virgin Mountain). One of the most difficult tasks he was given was to assist in "cleaning up" the Special Forces camp after a devastating raid. They encountered the horror of having to retrieve dead soldiers, who, in some cases, were blown apart in the bombing.

A particularly positive experience for Leonard was a seven-day period of R&R in Sydney, Australia. It struck him how friendly the people were and the cleanliness and beauty of the city. He would like to return to Australia some day.

On his return to the States, Leonard encountered the hostility experienced by many Vietnam vets. He describes arriving at the airport in Seattle. Not only were they not welcomed home, but also they were told they had to remain in isolation until their next flight. The conflict at home over the Vietnam War strongly affected those who served. They were not the returning heroes of World War II.

During the bicentennial parade in Brattleboro in 1991, Leonard marched with a contingent of other Vermont Vietnam vets. This was the first time since his return from Vietnam that he felt appreciated and was allowed to experience a sense of pride in his service to his country. In 2000, Leonard helped organize a local chapter of Vietnam Veterans of America and currently serves as president of this organization. He says, "Who else can better serve the needs of Vietnam vets, than those who shared that experience?"

MEMORIAL DAY 1944   HHS

MEMORIAL DAY MEMORIES 1950S

This Memorial Day tradition continued long after the G.A.R. Post ceased to exist. I can recall Memorial Day school programs dedicated to remembering those who gave their lives in wars. As school children in the 1950s, we marched from the West Halifax School to the West Halifax Cemetery with flags to decorate the graves.

~ *Susan Rusten*

BIBLIOGRAPHY

Corey, Lavern. *World War II Scrapbook*, in collection of Halifax Historical Society.

Cushing, John, & Stone, Arthur, eds. *Vermont in the World War, 1917–1919*. Burlington, VT: Free Press Printing, 1928.

Johnson, Herbert, ed. *Roster of Vermont Men and Women in the Military & Naval Services of the United States and Allies in the World War, 1917–1919*. Rutland, VT: Tuttle, 1927.

Roster of Vermonters in Uniformed Service of the United States During the Second World War, 1941–1945. Assembled by the Vermont Adjutant General, Montpelier, VT, 1972.

Thompson, Zadock. *History of Vermont, Natural, Civil, and Statistical*. Burlington, VT: Chauncey Goodrich, 1842.

Revised Roster of Vermont Volunteers During the War of the Rebellion. Montpelier, VT: Watchman Publishing, 1892; Wilbur Siebert, *Vermont's Antislavery Record*. New York: Negro Universities Press, 1937.

ENDNOTES
1. Roster of Vermonters in Uniformed Service of the United States during the Second World War, 1941–1945, assembled by Vermont Adjutant General, Montpelier, VT, 1972.

SECTION SIX
AGRICULTURAL LIFE

SAMUEL FISH FARM, GROVE   Engraving by Van Ingen & Snyder[1]

HILLCREST FARM

Photo Porter Thayer, Postcard courtesy Charles Marchant

Situated west of Halifax Center on a hill overlooking the Stage Road, this picturesque property, known originally as "The Scoville Farm," was the residence of country lawyer Jedediah Stark and family from 1815 [HLR 5: 327] until his death in 1835. Stark's son, James Landon, who by then was living at the state line in South Halifax, sold the farm to Joseph Henry. Henry conveyed the 150-acre property to Simeon and Charles Packer of Colrain [HLR 11: 190]. On page 86 of the March 2, 1861 issue of the *Saturday Evening Post*, one finds, "There is a family at Halifax Centre, Vermont, consisting of a father 86 years of age, two sons and two daughters, all of the children being deaf, dumb, and blind, and yet they manage to carry on their farm, gaining a respectable living there from." The 1860 Halifax census lists Simeon Packer 84, Deborah 82, Deborah 56, Simeon 54, Mary 52, and Elbridge 42, with the notation, "deaf dumb and blind." Settling the estate of the Packers in 1870, Stephen Niles conveyed the farm to his nephew, H. Fayette [HLR 13: 618]. During the Niles years of ownership, games of baseball between the so-called Halifax nine and visitors from neighboring towns were held on the North Field, an exceptionally flat expanse of meadow. In 1913, Fayette and his wife, Laura, moved to West Halifax, next to the Universalist Church [HLR 19:49], and sold the farm to Rev. William R. Tinker [HLR 19: 86]. In 1918, Tinker's widow, Pluma, sold to Daniel Graton, from whom ownership passed to Paul and Margaret Crosier in 1936. Larry Crosier identified the photograph of this property as the house in which he was born in 1942. The Crosiers conveyed the property to the Burdettes, who operated an antiques gallery at the location. They conveyed the farm to Douglas Riggs. After his death in 2001, his daughters sold the farm. At present, the house serves as a residence. The sheds and barns are gone.

~ *Constance Lancaster*

FARMS AND FARM FAMILIES

From Hayward's *A Gazetteer of Vermont*:

> Halifax, Windham, County, Vermont: This township is rather
> elevated, but of good soil, finely adapted for grazing. It is a place
> of considerable trade, and of manufactures on its numerous
> streams. Its principle streams are Green river and a branch of the
> Deerfield. There are some handsome falls of water in Halifax . . .
> The productions of the town are butter, cheese, pork, sheep, and
> other cattle. The cause of education flourishes here and the people
> are generally independent cultivators of the soil.[2]

Space does not permit including the multitude of Halifax farmers. Rather, the
focus will be on a few representative farm families, organizations, events, and
stories. During early settlement times, every Halifax household was a farm family.
Pioneer settlers needed to farm in order to eat. With the 1820 federal census came
an actual tally of family members employed in four categories. The numbers for
Halifax were:

- Agriculture 453
- Commerce 3
- Manufacturing and Trades 44
- Learned Professions 5

Of 505 Halifax workers in 1820, ninety percent were engaged in agriculture.

CANEDY/FAIRBANKS FARM, STOWE MOUNTAIN ROAD   HHS

Farm economics were no less challenging in nineteenth-century Halifax than at other times. Farmers could supplement their income by working for the town as listers, school directors, or by providing room and board for teachers. They worked as surveyors, helped with road and bridge maintenance, and did carpentry. They often relied on bank notes of credit to make ends meet because of seasonal fluctuations in income. Some household members worked as milliners and made braided palm-leaf hats to trade for food or other supplies; some made shingles. Some headed west to work in mines or to cities to help support themselves and the farm back home.

FARMERS' MUTUAL FIRE INSURANCE COMPANY.

Courtesy C. Lancaster

Farming was a life full of hardships and heartbreak. Farmers lost their farms to foreclosure, fire, and premature death from accident or disease. Tom Harty, commissioner of the Vermont Department of Agriculture, commented at the opening of an art exhibit devoted to the theme of Vermont Farms, "There is a definite soul to the work of tilling the land and husbandry of animals. There exists a solitude and loneliness to the work, often not recognized even by close friends. The landscape of Vermont exists because of agriculture (and an agricultural economy) shaping it."[3] Misfortunes, nevertheless, often are alleviated by the joys of farming as a way of life and the rewards of the harvest.

When Halifax farmers produced more than needed for their own families, how did they market their products? In the early 1800s, long before the convenience of the refrigerator car, going to market involved traveling a great distance, usually to Boston. A short reminiscence of how a Halifax farm family would process and prepare dairy products for the Boston market appeared in a Brattleboro newspaper.

— Editor of the Phoenix:

Rustic asks why so many of the settlers located on top of the hills.
I asked the question many years ago of one whose forefathers

were among earlier settlers of Windham county. They were afraid of frosts in the valleys, near the streams.

As to finding time to go to Boston, it was simply a case of have to. It was the only market they had to take their butter and cheese and whatever they had to dispose of. My father and mother both told me how every fall their fathers loaded up their big wagons and started for Boston.

They didn't milk their cows all winter as now. Most of them freshened in early spring. June was considered best month for butter making. Butter was packed in firkins with clean line cloth covered with salt on top. The cover put on and set away until time came to send it to market.

First of July was time to commence making cheese. That continued until cool weather came in September, and after that butter. The usual time was from the last of October until sometime in November for going to Boston.

My grandfather owned 250 acres of land, kept from 15 to 20 cows, span of horses, yoke of oxen, sheep for wool, and raised flax. That same farm today wouldn't anywhere near keep the stock or raise the crops that it did in those early days, from 1799–1842, the time of his death.

My father's recollections were from 1822, when he was a small boy, seven or eight years old, growing to manhood.

G. W. F. Newfane, Vt., June 2, 1930.[4]

The author of this letter, Grace Worden Foster, was born in Halifax in 1856, the third and only surviving child of James G. Worden and Annis B. Lynde, who lived north of the Grove post office on the road leading to Guilford and Green River. Her brother, Milton Worden, was killed in Halifax at the age of thirty-eight "when a grain thrashing machine toppled on him on the highway moving from one job to another."[5] With his death, the three-generation family farm died. The *Vermont Phoenix* reported "the property of the late James Worden was sold at public auction" and included, "hay in lumps, a pair of steers, a part Alderney five-

Photo C. Lancaster. WCHS

year-old cow coming in milk and a farm comprising about sixty acres which sold to Alvah Cannedy of Leyden, Mass. for $325.00."[6] Grace's grandparents, who went to the Boston market, were James Worden and Naomi Clark. The exact location of their 250-acre farm is not certain, but their gravestones are in the Elisha Worden Cemetery. Grace, who in later years resided in Newfane Village until her death in 1944, donated a number of Worden artifacts to the Windham County Historical Society in Newfane, Vermont. Foremost among these items is a strikingly beautiful silhouette of her Aunt Julia (left) , who died young, created by folk artist Ruth Henshaw Bascom.[7]

In family notebooks, also housed at the Windham County Historical Society, is another example of the Halifax/Boston market connection. Of Edward Barney (1797–1873) it is said, "In his early life he was a prosperous man, buying and selling mules, dealing in country produce which he sold in Boston, and bringing back home rum and other things interesting to home people. From his profits, he was able to buy a farm near the boundaries of Halifax and Colrain."[8] Traders and drovers from Halifax may have followed the original military routes down to Palmer and picked up the old Post Road there, or could have traveled towards Keene, New Hampshire, and continued past Mount Monadnock down to Fitchburg and on to the Brighton market. It is very difficult to imagine walking or riding horseback from southern Vermont to Boston and back to do business. Vermont newspapers of the period, the *Vermont Chronicle* for one, would publish the Boston wholesale pricelist weekly for commodities such as ashes, apples, butter, cheese, flour, grain, hops, "provisions" (meat), potatoes, seed, and wool.

By the mid-nineteenth century and the advent of the railroad, a Halifax farmer could ship some products across the country. An example of this marketing method appears among the Hall papers.[9] Diary entries show that Perry Hall delivered maple sugar to the train station in North Adams to be sent for distribution out west. Hall's older brother, Israel, had moved to Davenport, Iowa, before the Civil War.[10] Found in the pages of the Justus Hall account book, is a letter from Israel to Perry, dated May 28, 1868.

> Dear Brother,
>   . . . The Suger come to hand last Thursday. The freight was 2 ¾ cents per lb. I have sold it for 17 cents per lb. Inclosed please find draft of fifty [40/100] dollars. So I have allowed you 14 cents per lb. It sold readily at that.

Driving farm products from Halifax to the train station in North Adams, Massachusetts should have been a temporary practice until the time when the trains would stop at a Halifax station. But the railroad never came to town.

From the *Gazette & Courier,* September 14, 1874:

> There are a large number of abandoned farms in the State of
> Vermont and they are chiefly confined to counties destitute of
> railroad accommodations . . . In Whittingham, during the past 5
> years, 13 farms have been abandoned, while 30 farm houses are
> now vacant. Wilmington, considered a good town, has 27 farms
> abandoned and 25 farm houses vacant. Dover, 10 vacant farm
> houses; Jamaica, 23 farms abandoned; Athens, 6 farms
> abandoned; Halifax, with 33 abandoned farm houses, and
> Marlboro, with 23 in the same condition; Newfane, the county
> seat has 16 abandoned farms, and Townsend 20 farms and farm
> houses abandoned and vacant. And so it is with the whole county,
> excepting only those towns bordering on the railroads.[11]

* * *

Announcements and commentary from the local Halifax reporter during the 1880s sound the recurring theme of farm survival. Local farmers organized both an agricultural society that planned and promoted the annual fair and a farmers' club that met in the winter and promoted discussion of farm issues. From the *Vermont Phoenix* in 1883:

> Citizens of the town met at Village hall last week for the purpose of organizing a Farmers' club. The house was called to order by C. F. Griffin. made choice of A. F. Worden for president and W.W. Stowe for secretary. They discussed the question, "How to make the farm pay." Voted to meet Jan 24 with C. F. Griffin and discuss "Winter care and management of farm stock."

The local correspondent notes the arrivals and departures of farmers, mostly departures. November 1886: "John Lambert, who moves to West Springfield, Mass., this week, leaves a good farm with a house recently remodeled—a pleasant home in view of West Halifax and also of the Centre. The soil in that locality seems to be productive. The past season the farm has produced 200 bushels of unshelled corn."[12]

Attempts to lure farmers to farm vacant rural properties gradually evolved into promotion of farms as healthy resorts for summer travelers and summer homes for urban people. By the turn of the century, "Old Home Week" had been established throughout Vermont, celebrating the traditions of farming as a way of life and inviting those who had moved elsewhere to come home to revisit their rural roots.

~ *Constance Lancaster*

ENDNOTES

1. Frontispiece *A Sketch of The Life of Henry Clay Fish, D. D. by His Children*, Delia J. Fish, Henry G. Fish, Frederick S. Fish, Wynkoop & Hallenbeck, Printers, 121 Fulton Street, New York City. 1877.
2. John Hayward. *The New England gazetteer; containing descriptions of all the states, counties and towns in New England: also descriptions of the principal mountains, rivers, lakes, capes, bays, harbors, islands, and fashionable resorts within that territory. Alphabetically arrainged By John Hayward.* 13th ed. Concord, N. H., Israel S. Boyd and William White; Boston: John Hayward. 1839. Unnumbered page.
3. "The Image of Vermont Comes to Stark House Gallery," *Bennington Banner*, March 31, 2003.
4. *Phoenix*, "Why Settlers Located on Hills," June 6, 1930, p. 6. In the 1930s, a regular column, "The Rustic View," featured nostalgic details of early rural life in Windham County.
5. HHS, Jeremy G. Freeman, *Worden Family Genealogy*, undated typescript, p. 86.
6. HHS: Niles, p. 63.
7. Ruth Henshaw Bascom (1772–1848), wife of Rev. Ezekiel Lysander Bascom, according to her diaries, began drawing the portraits using pencil and pastels, for which she became famous in about 1801.
8. Windham County Historical Society, family notebooks, volume B, typescript, no author given.
9. In November 2001 and May 2002, the curators of the Halifax Historical Society acquired a ledger, an account book kept by Justus Hall, and five diaries written by his son, Perry Hall of Halifax, Vermont (1819–1899).
10. Civil War letters from George F. Hall to his father, Israel, in Davenport, Iowa, are part of the manuscript collection at the University of Iowa.
11. The Franklin Country Publication Archive Index, posted by Barbara Stewart, http://fcpai.umassp.edu/archive
12. HHS: Niles p. 53.

Sheep Raising and Sugar Trees

Hamilton Child's 1884 business directory offered an updated record of occupations in Halifax. The data, obtained from each household, indicated who was engaged in farming and specified the numbers of acres, trees, livestock. The farmers on the following list include only those who reported having three hundred trees or more, as well as those who described their occupation as woolgrower and reported the number of sheep on their farm. In parenthesis is the postal address, the letter "r" refers to the road number on the reference map below, and the number at the end of each entry represents the acres owned or rented by the farmer. Capitalized names indicate subscribers to the publication.[1]

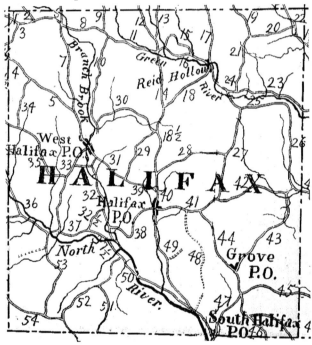

ADAMS LUTHER, (West Halifax) r 7, lister, sugar orchard 400 trees, farmer 180, and in Marlboro 230.

BELL MARY A. (South Halifax) r 46, widow of Charles, wool grower 125 sheep, apple grower 1,100 trees, farmer 380. BELL CHARLES C. works farm for his mother.

CLARK AARON L., (Jacksonville) r 54, sugar orchard 1,000 trees, farmer 180.

Clark Benjamin E., (Grove) r 47 cor 45, sugar orchard 700 trees, farmer 130.

Cook Eli S., (West Halifax) r 35, sugar orchard 400 trees, farmer 230.

CROSIER ALSON, (West Halifax) r 18, wool grower 43 sheep, sugar orchard 700 trees, farmer, 196.

Ellingwood Sumner, (Green River) off r 26, sugar orchard 400 trees, and farmer 95.

EVANS EMERY F., (Green River) off r 26, 3d selectman, wool grower 60 sheep, dairy 9 cows, and farmer 250.

Fowler Leroy J., (West Halifax) r 53, sugar orchard 500 trees, farmer 200.

FRENCH WILLIAM E., (Green River) r 43, wool grower 40 sheep, and farmer 200.

Fuller William H., (Green River) r 20, sugar orchard 750 trees, farmer 200.

GATES JESSE E., (West Brattleboro) r 16, proprietor saw-mill, dairy 8 cows, wool grower 45 sheep, farmer 330.

Green Elliot B., (Grove) r 44, sugar orchard 800 trees, farmer 160.

GRIFFIN CHARLES F., (West Halifax) r 5, president of West Halifax agricultural society, dairy 15 cows, wool grower 50 sheep, farmer 351.

Hale Orlen J., (Green River) r 22, sugar orchard 1,400 trees, farmer 300-school land.

Hall Perry, (Jacksonville) r 34, sugar orchard 900 trees, farmer 250.

Harris Seymour, (South Halifax) r 50, dairy 9 cows, sugar orchard 500 trees, farmer 370.

HATCH CHARLES M., (West Halifax) r 7, sugar orchard 550 trees, farmer 80.

Haven Charles L., (West Halifax) r 7, dairy 8 cows, sugar orchard 400 trees, farmer 235.

Hicks CHARLES H., (West Halifax) r 35, wool grower 42 sheep, sugar orchard 500 trees, farmer 230.

HIGLEY CHARLES H., (South Halifax) r 48 cor 49, wool grower 40 sheep, sugar orchard 600 trees, and farmer 272.

Hillman Anson, (West Halifax) r 5, wool grower 89 sheep, sugar orchard 400 trees, farmer 255.

HOUGHTON RUFUS H., (Halifax) r 25, wool grower 50 sheep, sugar orchard 1,100 trees, farmer 470.

Kingsley Ozias D., (West Halifax) r 33, sugar orchard 300 trees, carpenter, joiner and wheelwright, farmer 130.

Larrabee Ira, (West Halifax) r 8, sugar orchard 600 trees, farmer 130.

Legate Edwin H., (Elm Grove, Mass.) r 46, wool grower 100 sheep, sugar orchard 500 trees, home farm 200, and in Guilford 150.

Niles James M., (West Halifax) r 37, wool grower 40 sheep, sugar orchard 375 trees, farmer 225.

Niles Warren C., (West Halifax) off r 11, wool grower 50 sheep, farmer 146.

PHELPS CHARLES H.,[& NATHAN], (Green River) r 20, sugar orchard 700 trees, farmer 140, and in Marlboro 60.

PLUMB HOLLIS S. [& James N], (West Halifax) r 5, sugar orchard 500 trees, farmer 125

Powers, Milton, (Halifax) 39 cor 29, 10 head of young stock, breeder of grade Durham and Jersey cattle, sugar orchard 400 trees, farmer 160.

PRESTON ELWIN O., (Grove) r 46, sugar orchard 450 trees, farmer 142.

Prouty Almon S., (Green River) r 26, wool grower, 50 sheep, sugar orchard 600 trees, farmer 140.

PROUTY E. DEMON [& CHARLES E.] (Grove) r 44, sugar orchard 900 trees, farmer 212.

Prouty Elias, (Green River) r 20, sugar orchard 1,700 trees, farmer 201

Scott George M., (Halifax) r 49, town auditor, sugar orchard 418 trees farmer 218.

Stacy Charles L., (West Halifax) r 8, wool grower 40 sheep, sugar orchard 600 trees, farmer 180

Stark Jedediah, (South Halifax) r 50, postmaster, justice of the peace, overseer of the poor, wool grower 70 Southdown sheep, apple grower, apiarist, farmer 300.

STOWE HORACE, (South Halifax) off r 47, dairy 7 cows, sugar orchard 500 trees, farmer 250.

STOWE ISRAEL, (South Halifax) cor r 49 and 50, 2d selectman, woolgrower 200 French Merino sheep, sugar orchard 1,700 trees, farmer 400.

THURBER CHESTER O., (West Halifax) off r 15, sugar orchard 300 trees, farmer 200.

Thurber, Emerson H., (West Halifax) r 5, sugar orchard 400 trees.

Thurber Wells E., (West Halifax) r 33, sugar orchard 700 trees, breeder of grade Durham cattle, farmer 177.

Tucker David E., (West Halifax) r 29, sugar orchard 600 trees, wool grower 45 sheep, farmer 181.

WARREN, GILMAN, (West Brattleboro) r 18, manuf. cider jelly and chair stock, sugar orchard 350 trees, farmer 300.

Woodard Lemuel M., (Halifax) r 38, town treasurer, sugar orchard 600 trees, farmer 125.

WORDEN, DANIEL, S. (Grove) r 44, postmaster, sugar orchard 700 trees, farmer 230.

Worden Isaac H., (Green River) r 42, dairy 7 cows, wool grower 50 sheep, sugar orchard 600 trees, farmer 300.

~ Constance Lancaster

ENDNOTE

1. Child, p. 305. The full list appears on pp. 414–421.

SHEEP RAISING

An important asset of early settlers was the sheep they brought over from England. Even though these sheep were better for mutton than wool they were productive enough to challenge the English market. This caused England to enact the Wool Act of 1699 for the purpose of preventing the colonist from selling their wool. In spite of this, families spent the winter spinning the wool in preparation for the spring arrival of itinerant weavers from Massachusetts and Rhode Island who produced blankets and cloth for clothing [↪ 302].

NOTED SPANISH MERINO STOCK RAMS.
2003 Calendar VHS

Merino sheep were imported from Spain in 1810 by William Jarvis, American consul to Spain, to his farm in Weathersfield Bow, Vermont. He thought Vermont ideal for sheep raising and distributed sheep to local farmers to improve stock. The sheep industry thrived with the need for woolen uniforms and blankets during the War of 1812.[1]

By 1820, the industry was the most profitable in Vermont, and by 1834, more than half the residents owned sheep. In 1836, the sheep count in Halifax was 3,062, one of the most in Windham County. Later, the sheep industry declined due to competition in other parts of country.

By the late 1840s, the industry began to fall apart. The most important factor which brought about the decline

Vermont Farms For Summer Homes. Woodstock, VT: State Board of Agriculture, 1905.

Archie and the lambs at the Center   HHS

was the lowering and then the complete abolition of protective tariff rates. Factories demanded cheaper wool to provide the urban population with less expensive clothing. Consequently, the price of wool dropped. Among other factors was competition of the Western states and the introduction of Saxon sheep, which turned out to be poorly adapted to our rigorous climate. These sheep yielded far less wool than the previous varieties. Many people sold their sheep and abandoned wool growing altogether. Between 1850 and 1860, Vermont lost one quarter of its sheep population. There was a brief rise again during the Civil War due the need for wool uniforms and blankets. By 1884, Child shows very few farms with 100 or more sheep.

Presently, there is one sheep farm in Halifax owned by Andy and Linda Rice on Thomas Hill. Some residents still have a few grazing on their Halifax land.

If you were to walk the forests today, you would come across some of the old sheep fencing, which is a reminder of a time when the fields were full of sheep.   *~ Mariette Sanders,* Adapted from *Halifacts,* July 1989, no. 21, Edited by Waltraut Witte

WOOL GROWERS

Improve your Flocks!!

HAVING recently purchased a fine Flock of French and Spanish Merino SHEEP, which were formerly owned by A. V. Stockwell the subscriber would say to all interested in this branch of husbandry, that among them he has ten or a dozen fine French and Spanish.

Yearling Bucks,

(sired by an imported full blooded French Merino Buck, now on my farm, known as the Stockwell Buck,) now at GEO. H. CLARK'S in Brattleboro; for sale at prices to suit the purchaser, or to let on reasonable terms.

Farmers will do well to call and examine before purchasing.

☞ For further particulars enquire of A. V. STOCKWELL, Agent, Brattleboro, Vt.

ALMON BALLOU.

Halifax, Oct. 13, 1851.   3w19

Semi-Weekly Eagle, October 16, 1851
Courtesy Readex

A Cosset sheep is a pet lamb raised without the aid of the mother.

Mysterious Disappearance.
FIVE COSSET SHEEP

STRAYED from the subscriber, about ten days ago. The last information that can be had of them, they were in a grave yard, near Hines' brook, in the West part of Guilford. There were four Ewes, one Buck, and four Lambs. Any person who will give information where they can be found will be generously rewarded.   JOHN REID.

Green River, June 1.   86

☞ Also will be taken to pasture, from 10 to 15 Horses, horn Cattle, or Sheep in that proportion, if offered soon.

Enquire of JOHN REID, or EBENEZER TUCKER.

Semi-Weekly Eagle, June 4, 1849
Courtesy Readex

Merino crosses at the Sanders farm mid-1980s.   Photos M. Sanders

ENDNOTE
1. Nancy Dick Bogdonoff, *Handwoven Textiles of Early New England* (Harrisburg, PA: Stackpole Books, 1975).

MAPLE SUGAR

On the arrival of the early settlers, the natives taught them how to extract sap from maple trees to make syrup. From that time on, as people traveled the countryside during the months of March and April, they would see a variety of containers catching the sweet sap. Many families enjoyed the tradition of eating sugar on snow and finishing up by making maple candy. Most Halifax families enjoyed the syrup boiled down from sap on their wood stoves. A few Halifax families still enjoy this process of turning sap into maple syrup. Some larger farms turned this sugaring season into a commercial venture, which required larger and more efficient equipment.

ROLLAND HUBBARD SUGARHOUSE   HHS

MEMORIES

BURTON HILL SUGARHOUSE   HHS

Bertell (Burnett) Woods remembers one day when a child from the city noticed the containers hanging from a tree. He asked Bertell's brother, Nelson, what they were there for. Nelson explained they were getting sap from a maple tree to make maple syrup. The child responded, "What would happen if you tapped an apple tree?" Nelson replied, "Well, you'd get sweet cider."

Carrie (Burnett) Perna remembers as a child asking her grandfather, Archie Burnett, to let her drive the horses as the men gathered sap along Hubbard Hill Road. As she made the sharp turn down the lane leading to the sugarhouse, she lost control of the horses, causing them to straddle a big maple tree. The horses had to be unhitched from the

PARKER AND LEONA DEAN   HHS

sled and hitched again in order to continue to the sugarhouse. Obviously, Archie was not a happy Grampa.

SCOTT COURSER   HHS

HHS

Syrup cans, candy dishes, and tree spout. HHS   Photos C. Perna

Photo, courtesy Burnett family
NELSON, CLAYTON AND CORTIS BURNETT WITH THEIR OXEN ON HUBBARD HILL.

~ *Bernice Barnett and Carrie Perna*

TYPICAL NINETEENTH CENTURY HALIFAX FARMS

MILO HATCH FARM   HHS

ELI COOK FARM   HHS

Be It Remembered
Perry Hall Farm

Perry Hall was born in Halifax on July 10, 1819, the youngest son of Justus Hall and Nancy Pierce. Justus was a son of Joel Hall, a Revolutionary War soldier[1] who migrated to Halifax from Enfield, Connecticut, after the war. On March 21, 1850, Perry married Lois Winchester of Marlboro. They lived and farmed on the land where he was born, and Lois bore five sons and five daughters. Their sons were

LOIS AND PERRY HALL   HHS

George, Justus, Ira, Lavolette, and Israel; their daughters were Metta, Alta, Leura Ann, Marion, and Sarah. Leura Ann, born March 17, 1862, died young. Perry Hall wrote in his account book on November 1, 1863, "paid Dr. $2.00," and a few days later "paid for a coffin & box $3.50." On May 12, 1892, Perry and Lois lost two sons—Justus aged forty, and Lavolette aged thirty-two—in a grisly mining accident in California. Their bodies were brought home for a double funeral and interment at the West Halifax Cemetery. Their first son, George Winchester, taught school in West Halifax and ventured out west. "Geo. Hall has returned to town from a three years sojourn

SONS, JUSTUS AND LAVOLETTE   HHS

in the gold mines of Arizona and Mexico."[2] He married and raised his children in California. Metta married Henry Whitney of Marlboro and lived at the Zenas Whitney farm on Higley Hill Road. After his marriage, Ira lived next to his sister in Marlboro. Alta married Matthew Barber of Colrain. Marion and Sarah moved to Boston. Israel married Clara, daughter of Albert J. Tucker. They lived on the family farm, raised eleven children, and cared for his parents. Lois died on February 5, 1899; Perry died the following day.

THE DIARIES

In 2002, the Halifax Historical Society acquired Perry Hall's line-a-day diaries for the years 1876, 1882, 1883, 1887, and 1895 and a small leather ledger entitled, "Perry Hall's Book," containing his receipts and payments from January 1, 1861 through December 1863. In addition to daily comments, which always begin with the weather, Perry used the backs of some of the diaries as cash journals. He received payments for services as a Halifax lister and as a selectman. He recorded his payments of town tax, school tax, minister tax, and road tax.

Perry Hall's diaries offer a sense of the rhythm of farm life. In his 1883 diary beginning in January, Perry noted, ". . . drawed 14 logs to E. E. Putnam's mill to saw into boards & plank." Many other entries for January and February reported cutting wood for the two sugarhouses, "drawing" loads of wood to various family members, working on the woodpile, and plowing out the roads. Israel, youngest son of Lois and Perry, worked training his steers. His teams of oxen won prizes at local fairs.

On March 26, Perry wrote that Ira began tapping trees and "the sap run some." Most of the March and April notes were related to work associated with sugaring (tapping trees, gathering sap, boiling, and cutting more wood for the sugar houses). On April 16, the first of the lambs were born. An entry for April 19 stated, "Boys trimmed apple trees." Pruning the various orchards occupied "the boys" periodically throughout the remainder of April. On May 4, Perry noted, "Finished washing sap tubs and storage." In May, the boys fixed fences and on May 9 they began plowing and spreading manure. There were occasional notations about breeding cows and the births of calves. They began planting potatoes on May 16 and corn beginning May 19. In his 1887 diary, Perry wrote about getting the livestock out to pasture. The sheep numbered seventy-five that spring, and he delivered sixteen cattle to one pasture and thirty-one to another. On June 11th, "Boys peeled bark in east wood." Another of the moneymaking measures was selling bark to the local tannery. There were several entries that reported working on the roads. This was an activity for which they were paid by either Halifax or Whitingham. Toward the end of June, they began mowing the many hayfields and recorded the number of loads of hay. Mowing continued into July. Hoeing and various other garden chores continued throughout the summer, as did work on the wood supply for the sugarhouses. They also were occupied with clearing pastures — picking stones and cutting brush. Perry worked repairing farm buildings. Toward the end of August, they began cutting oats and more hay.

The growing season ended early in 1883. On September 4, Perry wrote, "A frost this morning cut the vines." The next day they began harvesting the potatoes — "15 bu [bushels] of potatoes — good ones" and 20 bushels were dug the following day. A few weeks later they began cutting the corn. The remainder of the month of September was taken up with harvesting, and this continued into October. An entry for October 19 stated, "finished the carrots one hundred bu — dug 30 bu of turnips." October was also the time for picking apples from the many orchards. With the arrival of November, they returned to cutting wood. On November 25, Perry wrote, "Dogs got after our sheep in the evening." The following day Perry reported, "found 10 sheep killed and 2 more bit." Two days later Perry found another dead sheep. He calculated his loss totaled twenty-eight dollars. On December 11, the Halls' killed their hogs.

The accounts kept in the back of the diaries bring to light the economy of the farm. Income was recorded for selling boxes of butter, cheese, eggs, and maple sugar. The garden and orchard produced income. Perry sold steers, hogs, and sheep. He sold the wool from the sheep. He reported income from selling wood, bark, and hides to A. J. Tucker. In addition to this, he was paid for his work on the town roads. During the period covered by these diaries, it would seem that Israel and various hired men did most of the farm work. Frequent mention is also made of the comings and goings of his many children and of his sons Ira and George helping with chores.

Among the expenses listed by Perry were the fees associated with educating his youngest children. Sarah and Israel attended high school in Brattleboro and boarded there during school sessions. They had to be transported back home on weekends, which also involved considerable time and expense. One can assume that education was important to the Hall family. At times, Perry noted in his diary that Ira took a book from the library. He was personally involved with School District No. 8, built on land he donated, and served as clerk for more than forty years. Perry and his sons used to mow the school grounds and supply the firewood for the schoolhouse. The record book of minutes for Hall district school, spanning the years 1830–1877, is archived at the Historical Museum in Halifax. William Plumb and Solomon Bascom recorded the minutes for the earliest years, and beginning in 1844, every set of minutes is in the clear careful writing of Perry Hall.

> The District met according to the foregoing warning & Chose Charles F. Griffin moderator Chose Perry Hall District Clerk and pruden tial committee and Treasuor Chose William Guild collector of taxes Voted to have two months school the coming summer or fall left discresionary with the comm ittee voted to pass over the article of getting wood voted to pay the expences of the school out of the public money if it is sufficient if they have one Voted to dissolve the meeting.
>
> Halifax March 22th 1859
> Perry Hall District Clerk

HHS

Perry subscribed regularly to the *New York Times* or the *New York Tribune* and to the *Vermont Phoenix* newspapers. Trading was also widely practiced. One entry in his accounts mentions trading four bushels of potatoes for a subscription to the *Vermont Phoenix*. In another entry, Perry "drawed 3 cords of stove wood to Mr. Baker to pay for painting our sleigh."

The conclusion drawn from the farm accounts is that it was a tough business from a financial point of view. The income during several months seems considerably less than the expenses. In July of 1883, the only income Perry reported was "Sarah let me have $10.00." On the other hand, the month of May was a profitable one, with income from sales of eggs, butter, maple sugar, steers, sheep, and sheep pelts, totaling $224. Expenses for the same month added up to $47.46. Hall family agricultural accomplishments were noted in the local papers. In the account of the 1882 "Halifax Fair," at which the show of cattle was better than usual, "Perry Hall led the rest by an entry of seven yoke of oxen and steers."[3] At the fair in 1886, his son Israel "showed a pair of two years old steers that weighed 2780. They were trained to follow the motion of the whip like soldiers at drill, and were fine looking steers. We understand that they were sold during the day but were unable to learn the price."[4] His maple sugar was considered some of the highest quality in the county. "Some of the whitest specimens of maple sugar that has been produced in southern Vermont were made in this town, and we are proud and happy to say that granulated sugar and glucose did not enter into its composition . . . if you need proof. Just examine the sugar made by Perry Hall or Warren Niles."[5]

THE FARM

PERRY HALL FARM   Courtesy Jane Luschen
In later years, Israel and family resided in the main house. Parents Perry and Lois lived in the ell.

According to Rev. Eastman, five brothers who were sons of John Hall and Hannah Guild, came from East Enfield, Connecticut to Halifax, Vermont, between 1776 and 1780.[6] Their immigrant ancestor was Edward, of Henbourough, Gloucestershire, England, who died in 1670 in Rehoboth, Massachusetts. John, son of Samuel, was said to have learned the ironworks trade at Taunton, Massachusetts, and moved to Enfield, Connecticut, where he set up a foundry. According to Eastman, John, Joel, Azariah, Levi, and Hiram, settled in the northwest part of Halifax and raised large families.[7]

Uncle Israel Guild, who was on the scene in Halifax before the Revolution, may have influenced the Hall brothers' choice of location in Vermont. The Guild family of Hatfield, Massachusetts, most likely knew Oliver Partridge an original proprietor. Israel acquired his Halifax Lot 49 property from Partridge in exchange for clearing and settling. A loyal Vermonter, Guild was the sixth person to sign the freeman's list and was chosen to serve as a selectman during the first four years of recorded town government. His brother-in-law, William Frazier, received property in Lot 41 also from Partridge for settling duty, [HLR 1A: 41] and his nephew, John Hall, acquired property in Lot 50 under the same terms. Lot 41 is where the original Hall Road, Hall Schoolhouse, and the Perry Hall farm are located. Cousin Jesse Guild built a house and set up his blacksmith shop at the corner of Hall and Reed Hill Roads.

In May 1777, Perry's grandfather, Joel, purchased fifty acres in Lot 58 from Preserved Gardner of Halifax, blacksmith [HLR: 1A 199]. From that time forward, Joel Hall and his brothers make frequent appearances in the land and vital records as well as town meeting records of Halifax. Hiram died in the War of 1812. The 1784 list of families by school district places in School District No. 5: Jasper Hunt, Joel Hall, Joshua Rich, Joshua Lamb, Jethaniel Rich, John Hall, Levi Hall, Zerah Brooks, Daniel Delano, Jonathan Rich, Joseph McClure, Jonathan Wells, Jonathan Kellogg, Benjamin Lyman, Benjamin Tilden, James P. Frazier, and Azariah Hall. The census of 1791 lists four Hall heads of family: John, Joel, Azariah and Widow. District 5 was in the Northeast part of town. Hall properties were located on Tony Hanson, Hatch School and Hall Roads. Burials took place in the Hatch, Bascom and West Halifax Cemeteries.

Joel Hall lived to the age of ninety-six and is buried at the cemetery on Hatch School Road. His son Lotan lived on the original Joel Hall property. His son Justus, father of Israel and Perry, purchased property from Sarah Frazier, Jessie Guild, and Jeremiah Kinsbury in Lots 33 and 41. His account book details farm economics during the 1820s. Hall worked as a carpenter. Many of his entries are for making "lights and sashes" (windows) and for building coffins. During the summer and autumn of 1799, the Whitingham meeting house was framed and raised by Levi Conant of Halifax and finished off later by Justus Hall of Halifax. In Jeremiah Kingsbury's account book, Justus Hall was paid for drawing timber, planking, and framing.[8] It seems likely that Justus built the house and barns of the farm on Hall Road, where his youngest son, Perry and wife, Lois, resided and where their youngest son, Israel and his wife, Clara, also lived.

FAMILY RECOLLECTIONS

The youngest of Israel and Clara's eleven children, Charlotte, was born April 10, 1911 on what she described to her children as "a cattle and maple sugar farm."[9]

> The winter after Charlotte's eighth birthday, the farmhouse and barn burned to the ground. Nothing was saved but the family Bible and the cattle. Corinne [the oldest daughter] was teaching in Danbury, Connecticut, and the remaining older children were sent to live with relatives while Charlotte and her parents moved into a cramped one-bedroom home in West Halifax. Having no insurance, Israel was forced to sell the cattle and oxen and seek work on nearby farms that spring. Disaster struck again in May of 1921, when Charlotte's mother, Clara, died.[10]

Courtesy Jane Luschen
ISRAEL AND SARAH HALL
in front of school

After Clara's death, Charlotte went to live with her Aunt Sarah in Newton, Massachusetts. Israel moved back to the farm property and took up residence in the only building that survived the fire. This was the old Hall Schoolhouse. Israel called it "The Byegone Inn." Towards the end of his life, he was cared for by his sister's Whitney family on Higley Hill, where he died in 1940.

A letter from Israel and Clara's son, Robert, sent in 1975 from Vancouver, Washington, to the Halifax Historical Society describes the whereabouts of his many brothers and sisters. He mentions that a new campus building at Framingham State College in Framingham, Massachusetts was named "Corinne E. Hall Towers" for his sister, who taught there for many years. His brother Justus was killed in a logging accident at the Will Warren Mill. His brother Stephen, who lives in Kansas City, Missouri, has a picture of the old Hall farmhouse and buildings that burned.

Charlotte's daughter, Jane Luschen, visited Halifax with her mother on one of her annual trips back to Halifax. They brought Stephen's ashes to bury in the Hall family burial ground in West Halifax. Charlotte was always amazed that the 10-gallon apple tree, so called because its apples were huge, was still thriving on the old farm property. On her last visit, the tree was no longer there.

The old Hall farm is gone, and the special apple tree, but the schoolhouse still stands and is used as a private home. The school records and diary entries written by Perry, as well as the stories and recollections written by his children, endure.

Today, one can observe the unique design of the stone walls that mark the boundaries of the Hall farm. Placed in the wall every few yards is an upright slab of stone (below) with a carved-out u-shape at the top for holding a wooden rail for the purpose of raising the height of the fence. Not only is this an unusual design, but also the walls are so well constructed that many of them are still very much intact, despite the passage of years and the growth of the forest that threatens them. In some cases, the placement of the stone appears whimsical — as if placed by an artist for visual affect. An example of this can be seen bordering sections of Hall Road. It is not certain who built these walls, but Sarah Hall wrote in her family account that Perry had hauled the stones for the walls that fenced off the lands into pastures, fields, and orchards.[11]

~ Constance Lancaster and Susan Rusten

VIEW OF THE U-SHAPED CARVED STONES   Photos S. Rusten

ENDNOTES

1. He served in Captain John Couch's Company, Colonel Bradley's Regiment, and was imprisoned during the Revolutionary War.
2. HHS: Niles, p. 38.
3. Ibid., p. 18.
4. Ibid., p. 60.
5. Ibid., p. 38.
6. Hemenway, vol. 5, p. 417.
7. Ibid.
8. HHS, Justus Hall's account, Jeremiah Kingsbury of Halifax, 1807–1815, p. 3.
9. Life Story: Charlotte Kleinheksel. http://www.lifestorynet.com/print_lifestory.php?obitid=1632 (accessed 6/12/07).
10. Ibid.
11. Ibid.

A THANK YOU NOTE TO DR. NILES – à la Halifax

Sarah Hall Cone, the youngest daughter of Perry and Lois, found herself a widow living in a seventeen-room house in Newton, Massachusetts, with two young children to raise. She supported the family by taking in boarders. After the death of Israel's wife Clara (Tucker), their daughter, Charlotte, went to live with her Aunt Sarah. Dr. James P. Niles, who formerly was her neighbor in Halifax, was now her neighbor in Newton, where he practiced dentistry.   ~ *Constance Lancaster*

SARAH HALL CONE   HHS

16 Linden Ter.
Newton, Mass.

Dear Dr. Niles:—

I want to thank you for doing such good work for Charlotte, and I believe she will save her teeth because of your good judgment — à la Halifax.

I am enclosing a bit of Niles' Transcript genealogy as it sounded much like the Wordens and Meeks that Father once knew. Esther Chase Thompson has died, after a long illness, she went to her old home on the Hill with her sister Amy Tenney and a Vt. letter says she has gone – a real nice cook and person and I shall miss her cheery ways.

"One by one the shadows fall but the old Halifax hills will stand forever."

I hope to go up there Aug 7 or 8th — for a month —

Appreciating Dr. Niles' help in my toothless stage I am coming back for a new set later —

Hastily,
Sarah Hall Cone

Courtesy Niles Prouty

NATHANIEL NILES FARM
TILL DEATH US DO PART

Little is known of the boyhood of Nathaniel N. Niles, the fourth and youngest son of Oliver Niles and Lydia Plumb. The house where he was born in 1812 and the nearby district No. 2 schoolhouse where his early learning took place, no longer exist. Both were located in Original Lot 18, near the North River, Route 112, and Larrabee Road. His father was a farmer and carpenter and operated a sawmill. Many years hence, Nathaniel's son James Philand said of him, "Father was brought up to farming, which he chose for his life occupation. A man of large heart and broad intellect, he was well qualified by nature to fill a wider sphere than that in which he found himself placed." [1]

Like most members of the Niles families, Nathaniel was introduced to the local Baptist Church, and there he met the preacher's daughter, Mary Survier Fish. On December 4, 1833, they were married. In 1834, he purchased fifty acres from Chipman and his mother, Meliscent Barrett Swain. The deed describes the property as parts of Original Lots 26, 27, 34, and 35 [HLR 7: 527–528]. On today's map, that would include land on all four sides of the intersection of Sprague Road and Reed Hill Road. Blanche Legate Sumner recalls the original Swain dwelling, located about twenty rods east of the Niles house, which once served as an early school, and Leon LaRock, who owned the farm from 1926 to 1966, built his sugarhouse on the old school foundation. [2]

Courtesy Niles Prouty
NATHANIAL AND MARY FISH NILES
WEDDING PHOTO

Nathaniel built a Greek Revival style house at the top of Sprague Road, facing east. He completed the structure in time for the birth of their first child in 1836. Today, the massive weathered barns are gone, but the house still stands, overlooking a broad meadow and the village of West Halifax in the valley below. The short section of Reed Hill Road leading from Sprague Road down to the West Halifax Bridge was surveyed and laid out as a public road in 1856, two decades after Niles had built his farmhouse and barns. The Reed Hill Road runs behind the house. Current owners, Bruce and Joyce Doing, not only, have restored the homestead, but also have restored the name of its original owner. Once again, the property is known as the Nathaniel Niles homestead.

The Doings welcomed me to visit my great-grandfather's [3] birthplace. We met in the kitchen, where the original paneling of horizontal wide boards, now darkened with age, evokes the nineteenth century. Before visiting, I read what Olive LaRock had written about the house for the Halifax Historical Society.

When we lived there, off the kitchen was a milk room where in
olden times people used to set their milk on racks in shallow pans,
then later skim the cream off to make butter. The remaining milk
was then used to make Dutch cheese (now called Cottage cheese);
after that the residue was given to the animals, pigs for instance . .
. the milk room or buttery as they called it then, [was] made [into]
the kitchenette. There was a fireplace off the dining room and a
large chimney closet. Alternate "white maple" and cherry wood
were used for flooring.[4]

I was shown a videotape of the "before" condition of the house with all
its challenges, and sensed Bruce's appreciation of the building and pride in its
careful restoration and rescue. As he guided me through the parlor towards the
narrow staircase, my host commented with a knowing smile, "The person who
built this house was no carpenter!" The attic is not readily accessible, but it was
worth the climb to view the rafters, halved tree trunks, and the year 1836 carved
above an attic window. No doubt, this was the date Nathaniel Niles, with the help
of family and friends raised the rafters of his new home.

Over time, as his family grew to nine members, Nathaniel's property grew
from fifty to one hundred and forty acres through purchases from Asa, Edmund,
Seth, and Delight Worden, as well as the "Bennet Lot" from his brother Oliver
Jr., and the Elizabeth Sumner Woodlot from the widow of Joel Sumner. From
June 1838 through June 1843, Nathaniel trained with the Halifax local militia. His
name appears as 2nd Lieutenant on the roll and return of the 4th Battalion
Company, 27th Regiment of the militia of the state of Vermont.[5] Grand lists for
the period indicate that Nathaniel was a prosperous, successful farmer. His son
Edward, described his father as a farmer who was "conspicuous in church
affairs."[6] In fact, Nathaniel was, for most of his adult years, a deacon of the
Halifax Baptist Church and at times served as its clerk. At the time of the
rancorous split of the Baptist Society in 1852–1853, he, together with his brother,
James M., voted in favor of building the new church in West Halifax, [7]and they
both joined that church. Their brother, Stephen, chose to stay with the Baptist
Church at the Center. Not only did Nathaniel split with his brother, but also with
his wife's father, Elder Samuel Fish, who served as pastor of the new Center
Church. Those must have been difficult choices. However, the steep three-mile
climb by horse and buggy to the Center, no doubt played a role in the decision to
support a church in nearby "Plumb Hollow."

Mary Niles bore four sons and three daughters in the homestead on the
hill in West Halifax. First to leave was the eldest daughter, Survier Louisa, who
married Dr. John Mather Clark, son of Nicholas and Clarissa Hall Clark . They
moved to North Adams, Massachusetts, where Dr. Clark set up his practice at 10
Main Street. Judson, the eldest son, studied dentistry and set up a practice in
Bennington. On the August 30, 1861, their son, Alonzo Charles, was part of the
first group of Halifax youths to enlist in the army. He mustered in as a private on
September 21, 1861, at Brattleboro, in Captain Stearns's Company I, Fourth
Regiment of Vermont Volunteers.

He died at Camp Griffin, in Virginia, near the Chain Bridge, on the Potomac, above Washington, February 10, 1862. Visiting the camp while lying there, we saw and conversed with the patient sufferer, then sick, and learned how eagerly he and the rest of the "Vermont boys" were looking forward to active service. To him it was denied. He fell a prey to disease, but not less bravely or worthily than if by the sword. His remains were brought home, and now rest in the quiet burial ground near where his ancestors have long resided.[8]

In 1869, at the age of fifty-six, Nathaniel wrote his last will and testament, bequeathing his estate to his "beloved wife" Mary S. The witnesses were L. M. Tucker, Stephen Niles, and Eunice Niles. Within a few weeks, the *Vermont Phoenix* published his obituary, written by a Halifax correspondent:

The most important event, which has recently occurred here, has been the death of our beloved friend, Deacon Nathaniel Niles. He fell asleep on the morning of February 20th, after having calmly prepared for the great change, which awaits us all. His disease was consumption. We saw him fading, but were in a degree unprepared to part with him. The church and community deeply mourn because, "He is not." and we ask, on whom may we expect his mantle to fall? His labors were varied and extensive; he filled well the several offices of sexton, clerk and deacon, and was also a member of the choir from many years. Surely his bereaved family can have to comfort them this beautiful thought, that he is their pioneer to a better country.[9]

Later that year, a letter from Mary to her son, James, at Shelburne Falls Academy reveals how the family was faring.

Monday Sept 27th 1869 Good morning Dear Philan
Mother was glad to hear from you hope you are getting along well in your studdys. I think you never was from our home so long before. Judson Alexander said you went with the Excurtion on Saturday to the [Hoosac] tunnel thinks you had a good time . . . We hear from Adora think she is some homesick. Judson is going to Greenfield tomorrow Edie is cutting corn has cut the tobacco it made him vomit all night after it. Have the old oxen yet. If you see a man that wants to buy tell him to come up. . . . It is very lonely at home only three of us in this great house to sleep and eat. Be a good boy and come home sometime. Mother

Written on the side of the letter,

> Philan I often think how much your dear Father would think about you if he was alive. You know he always felt so anxious when we were away" [10]

The 1870 Halifax census listed for the N. Niles household: Mary, 54 (keeping house); Judson 32, (dentist); Delia, 25 (Milliner); Adora, 22 (Teacher); Philand, 20 (farmer); and Edward,, 17 (farm laborer). Within a few months, Mary, Delia, and Judson would die, having contracted consumption from Nathaniel. Notices of the deaths of Adelia on September 29, and Mary on October 9, 1870, appeared together in the *Vermont Phoenix*. Judson died about a month later. The Niles farm was advertised for auction in January of 1871, per order of the administrator of the probate court, "in the best interest of the children," and in two weeks was purchased by Prescott Eames, one of the appraisers of the estate.[11]

With the decimation of their family, followed immediately by the sale of the farm by the estate administrator, the three surviving Niles children were forced to find new places to live and work. Despite the trauma of losing so many family members and their home within the same year, Adora, James, and Edward, went on to lead successful and productive lives.

* * *

ADORA LYDIA married Sabin Tillotson Goodell in October 1871, and they went as missionaries to India. He died of fever in 1877 in Rangoon, Burma, as did their two children: Judson Niles Goodell, born February 7, 1875, and Addie Niles Goodell, born October 12, 1876. Upon returning to the United States, Adora lived in Boston, where she met poet and performer, Will Carleton. Like Adora, he had spent his childhood on a farm. Carleton, who was a handsome charismatic figure, had developed a following, in part through public readings from collections of his poetry, which included such titles as, *Farm Ballads, Farm Legends and Farm Festivals*. They married in 1882. Carleton dedicated his next book of poems, published in 1885, "To ADORA: Friend, Comrade, Lover, Wife." Whenever Adora and her husband visited Halifax, the

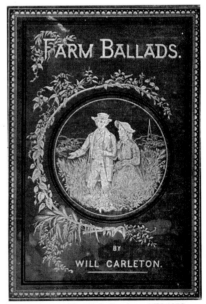

Harper & Brothers, NY 1873

locals referred to him as Will Carleton, the famous poet. Adora died on November 9, 1904 in Brooklyn, New York, where Carleton ran a publishing business.

DR. JAMES PHILAND, following in the footsteps of his brother, Judson, entered the field of dentistry.

> [He] took a course of study at Shelburne Falls, Massachusetts, and after a year's study at North Adams, Massachusetts, studied at the Philadelphia Dental College. He entered the practice of his profession in Albany, New York where he remained for five years, located for eight years in Ballston Spa New York, and then set up practice in Watertown Massachusetts. He married Catherine Frances Doncaster in Albany. Dr. Niles held minor political offices in New York, and was elected a State senator from the Second Middlesex District of Massachusetts for the terms 1895 and 1896. He was appointed chairperson of the State House Committee. "An able and convincing speaker, he always held the close attention of his colleagues."[12]

DR. EDWARD SAMUEL, the youngest child of Nathaniel, and Mary, studied medicine with his brother-in-law in North Adams, and began study of dentistry in the office of Dr. W. H. Jones, in Northampton, Massachusetts. He entered Harvard Medical School, and graduated in 1879 with the degree of D. M. D. In 1880, he married Elizabeth Pomeroy Wright, of Northampton, Massachusetts. Dr. Niles established a dental practice at Copley Square in Boston. He "made a special study of what is known in dentistry as the chemistry of decay, was the first to demonstrate the presence of the phosphoric acid in dental cavities and explain the uses and manufacture of phosphate fillings."[13] His writings were published in numerous medical and dental journals. An avid student of Hebrew languages and religion, Dr. Niles became fluent in Hebrew, published several books concerning his avocation.

The local newspaper correspondent for West Halifax reported in July 1880:

> The remaining members of the Nathaniel Niles family met here on Tuesday, and visited the old homestead, now owned by Welles E Thurber. The sons, Philand and Edward S. have chosen the dentist profession and are located, the former at Ballston Spa, N.Y., and the latter at Boston, Mass. The younger daughter, Mrs. Adora Gooddell, intends soon to return to India, where she has spent several years as a missionary.[14]

* * *

Fifteen years after the death of Nathaniel Niles, his surviving children made their first move to reclaim their family ties to Halifax. In 1885, Samuel Judson Niles of Halifax conveyed to his cousins Adora N. Carleton, James Philand Niles, and Edward S. Niles of Brooklyn, Ballston Spa, New York and Massachusetts "a piece of land being the burial lot for the Niles Cemetery so called occupied by the family of the late Nathaniel Niles" [HLR 15: 239].

Ten years later, in 1895, they purchased, as joint-owners, the estate of Ruby A. Fish, widow of James P. Fish. On the 1869 Beers map, this property is identified in Halifax Center as that of Elias Fowler. It is the property that eventually would become the summer hotel called "Maplehurst." In 1897, James Philand conveyed his interest in that property to Edward Samuel. In 1906, Edward S. purchased his boyhood home, the original Nathaniel Niles farm, from which he had been evicted by the probate court when he was seventeen years old. He bought the property from Wells E. Thurber, a farmer who raised beef and sugared there for about thirty-two years. James Philand purchased an eighty-five acre Halifax property from Diantha Whitney. The *Vermont Phoenix* reports in August 1910, "Philand Niles of Boston is in town working up the slate quarry which he recently bought of Zora Whitney."

Dr. James P. Niles had a dental office in Newton, but at times he also shared the Boylston Street office with Edward. After the death of her husband, their sister, Surviah Clark, lived in Boston as well. By then, one imagines the brothers often traveled with their families from Boston to spend time in Halifax. The Center Baptist Church and Library records include Edward, his wife, Elizabeth, and their children, Nathaniel, David, Helen and Eliot as active members at the turn of century. Halifax land records show that for some of the nine years Edward owned the Nathaniel Niles farm, he leased it furnished and equipped for farming and sugaring. "The lessee to have use of furniture that is now on the property. . . . In the matter of the sugar tools, it is understood that at the close of the sugaring season of 1912 all of the buckets shall be thoroughly washed and scalded and put away in proper condition for the coming season" [HLR 15: 23]. In 1914, Edward sold the Nathaniel Niles farm to Elbert Roberts. One imagines he must have been preoccupied with the demands and expenses of operating "Maplehurst," his "memorial to the intrepid first settlers of Halifax."

Edward and Elizabeth's children and grandchildren were frequent visitors to the family resort. In her journal, my grandmother, Helen Adora Niles MacDougall, recalls fondly her summers in Halifax. She photographed her children, Florence Wright and Nathaniel Niles MacDougall, smiling from perches in the apple trees by the hotel porch. Another photo shows Helen (in full-length white dress) with tennis racquet in hand. By then her brother, Nathaniel, who had learned to play tennis at Maplehurst, was winning major tournaments. A versatile athlete, he went on to become an accomplished Olympic figure skater, and to this day holds numerous records both in the world of tennis and figure skating.[15] His

Courtesy C. Lancaster
HELEN ADORA, Dr. Niles's daughter
at the Maplehurst piano, 1911

brother, David Sands, was a longtime chairperson of the national tournament for the U. S. Lawn Tennis Association as well as a Davis Cup umpire.

In 1922, Dr. Niles's hotel closed. By 1927, he had sold the property and all its contents to pay off his creditors. A copy of the fourteen-page-long bill of sale for the furnishings of Maplehurst Lodge and Cottage, dated July 2, 1927, exists at the office of the Halifax town clerk. The extensive inventory of every room, shed, and garage ranges from a Ford automobile, to cookie cutters, garden tools, and teacups, and includes one piano, two tennis nets, and nine golf balls. Edward's grandson, Robert Niles, attributes the loss of Maplehurst to a combination of factors. "Grandfather's hotel project was way ahead of its time. He had to rely on others to run it which caused some problems; perhaps he was simply not a very good business man" [HLR 15: 372]. Certainly, another major factor would have been the economic and social consequences of World War I. Dr. Niles had challenged the state legislature and lost the battle to bring the railroad to Halifax.[16] The closest railroad station for hotel guests was Shelburne Falls. Wartime restrictions made it virtually impossible for guests to reach the hotel except by private automobile.

In 1905, Edward had purchased two acres connected to the Niles Cemetery, from the Mitchells [HLR 17: 562]. He wished to be buried in his hometown, on the knoll near the knoll where his parents and siblings were buried.[17] In failing health from diabetes, during his latter years, Edward nevertheless, kept a sense of humor. His granddaughter remembers him rapping his cane on his wooden leg to amuse her. "Bet you can't do that," he would say. She recalls being told that her grandfather had told his wife, Elizabeth, "where to put him after he died." And she did; right on the second knoll.[18] However, when the town cemetery commission decided to flatten the knoll, Edward's body was exhumed and relocated to the center portion of the newer flat part of the Niles burial ground. Robert Niles said, "Grandfather would have been disappointed as hell." According to Robert, Edward and an uncle had given the knoll property to the cemetery group. In 1970, another grandson Richard Morgan Thompson Jr., donated to the Town of Halifax, two acres on Route 112 adjoining the Niles Cemetery to the west. A newspaper report announced the "gift of two acres of land by the grandson of late Dr. Edward Niles, former resident of Halifax. Dr. Niles donated the land for the cemetery named in his honor."[19]

Photo C. Lancaster

Dr. Niles's marker is somewhat unusual in that it includes his Niles lineage. Perhaps this was the idea of Elizabeth's father, William King Wright, whose genealogical research was published by the New England Historical and Genealogical Society. Edward's marker also tells the visitor that his wife is buried in Northampton, Massachusetts. Elizabeth's grave, together with that of her infant daughter, Mary Fish Niles, is at the Bridge Street Cemetery in the Wright family plot.

BRINGING THE FARM BACK TO LIFE

A few years before the deaths of Edward and James, their father's farm property had a change in ownership and a change in fortune. From 1914 to 1926, there had been three owners and a steady decline in the building and the land. According to Marie LaRock Carpenter and Bernie LaRock., the place was rotting away. The third owner, a Mr. Barnes, who was aging and realizing that his son would never take an interest in farming, worked out a friendly price and friendly terms to win over Leon and Olive LaRock. He knew they knew how to work and to farm and could bring the property back to life. His confidence was not misplaced. The LaRocks became the new owners in 1926 and stayed for forty years. Marie Carpenter, who was six years old at the time, took her first step into their new home and slid all the way across the kitchen pantry on the green moss-covered floor. Sixteen feet of green slime! She recalls that the windows were knocked out, and from the three large maple trees in front of the house down to the raspberry patch, the pasture was totally overgrown with brush and alder. It took weeks of cutting with hand tools to tame the front meadow. Leon added onto the barn across Sprague Road and began to develop a dairy herd. He also built a new sugarhouse.

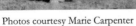

Photos courtesy Marie Carpenter

Top left and above: The horse barn was attached to the house. Bernard with horse "Buddy," who was honored for his sure-footed assistance, helping to lay the electric cable in Halifax.

Bottom left: Leon and Harry LaRock. The cow barn was across Sprague Road, and there was a sheep barn beyond that.

Marie's brother, Bernard Sr., was born in the west room of the big house. Marie, who was ten years older, says that she needed to be her father's son when it came to farm chores until her brother grew to working age and they could share the workload. She attended school in West Halifax, when all eight grades were on one floor, but there came a time when four grades were upstairs. They closed the school every spring for "mud season," which in reality was sugar season; the children were needed to work at home during those weeks. Their sugar orchard was on a hillside, and Marie drove the horses to help with the gathering. In peak years, they had more than 2,000 taps. Also, they had forty head of cattle and as many as seventy or eighty at times. Bernie remembers that the milk would be picked up and taken to Springfield, Massachusetts, to be processed by Mallory's, a company later taken over by H. P. Hood and Sons. He notes that they were getting thirteen dollars per hundred pounds of milk, but it went as low as eleven dollars, which is what the price is today. "The farmer is always on the bottom, you know." Both Bernie and Marie recall how hard the work was and how much they enjoyed their lives on the farm. "When dad was working down at the mill, they needed someone to cut hair, and he did the best job, so I guess they elected him." Pretty soon the LaRocks had a barber chair in their kitchen. "There were always folks coming and going—it was always a pretty full house," Marie commented. "It was a wonderful place to be."

Bernie was surprised to learn the connection between their farm, the Niles family, and Maplehurst. When he was about ten years old, he remembers getting to explore inside the old hotel. It was unlocked, and a person could walk through the whole place. He recalls that it was totally empty but very clean, and all the windows were still in place. There was beautiful wood everywhere. The rooms had heavy wooden doors and paneling, and there was a magnificent maple and cherry staircase. Not too many years later, Bernie had a construction job at the first place on the Deer Park Road. When he drove through the Center, he saw the empty field with the stone chimney, where the hotel had formerly stood. It made him terribly sad that such a beautiful building had been torn down.

After the LaRocks sold the Niles farm in 1966, Leon's barn, which had, "through his agreement with the Lord," continued to stand well beyond its appointed time, finally gave in to gravity.[20] The property changed hands several more times and went into yet another decline. In 1992, Bruce and Joyce Doing saw an ad for the house in the *New York Times* and accepted the challenge. They poured in time, work, and care; once again, the future of the Nathaniel Niles homestead is bright. Chances are this will never again be a working farm, as it was during the LaRock period of ownership.

The homestead might serve from time to time as a bed and breakfast; most likely, it will serve as a country home where a family can enjoy the comfort and care of an early Vermont house that has undergone and survived a fair amount of "character building." And always there is the possibility on an autumn afternoon, one can drive up Sprague Road, round the bend and happen upon a scene reminiscent of days of old— a herd of Jersey cows[21] quietly grazing in the sunlit meadow in front of Nathaniel Niles' house.   ©2008 *Constance Lancaster*

NATHANIEL NILES HOUSE   Photo Malcolm Sumner

ENDNOTES
1. Citizens of Middlesex County, Massachusetts (Boston: Biographical Review Publishing, 1898) p. 555.
2. HHS, Blanche E. Legate Sumner, *"West Halifax"* undated typescript. Could this have been the original West Halifax district school?
3. Edward Samuel, born 1853, youngest son of Nathaniel.
4. HHS, Housebook.
5. NEHGS, R. Stanton Avery Special Collections Dept. Roll and Return, kept in back of Russel Bascom Diary.
6. Jacob G. Ullery, *Men of Vermont : Biographical History of Vermonters and Sons of* Vermont (Brattleboro, VT: Transcript Publishing, 1894). (Hereinafter cited as Ullery).
7. HTC, Halifax Baptist Church Records, Book Two, p. 72.
8. Henry Clay Fish, *The Golden Wedding of Rev. Samuel and Mrs. Bersheba P. Fish* (New York: Wynkoop & Hallenbeck, 1867) p. 67.
9. *Phoenix,* March 5, 1869.
10. Letter courtesy of Niles and Bonnie Prouty of Bradford, Vermont, from family papers of James P. Niles.
11. Marlboro Probate Court File no. 2468, vols. 25 & 26.The estate was distributed to the four surviving children. Survier received $480.33 and Adora, Philand, and Edward, $680.33 each.
12. Middlesex County, p. 556.
13. Ullery.
14. *Gazette & Courier,* Greenfield, Massachusetts, July 26, 1880.
15. Nathaniel William [Nat] Niles practiced and played tennis on the courts at his father's hotel in Halifax Center. While a student at Harvard, he was NCAA doubles champion in 1907 and singles champion in 1908. He competed in USTA tournaments from 1904 to 1926 and was posthumously inducted into the USTA Hall of Fame. His even greater accomplishments, as a figure skater from 1914 to 1932, include three USA singles titles and nine consecutive pairs titles with partner Theresa Weld Blanchard, who became America's first ladies' figure-skating champion in 1914. Niles and Blanchard won five USA ice dancing gold medals and represented the United States in the Olympic games of 1920, 1924, and 1928. They founded Skating magazine. Nat Niles died in 1932 at age 45.
16. VHS, Lou A. Foster, *Life Sketch prepared by himself,* p. 1.
17. Interview with Richard Morgan Thompson, May 2002.
18. Interview with Elizabeth Dodge, May, 2002.
19. *Brattleboro Reformer.* Thursday, October 29, 1970, p. 18, courtesy of Molly Stone.
20. A heartfelt thank you to Marie (Sally) LaRock Carpenter and Bernard LaRock Sr. for sharing memories of their years at the Niles farm.
21. Malcolm Sumner, neighbor and one of the only remaining Halifax farmers, rotates pasture for his dairy herd.

Wheeler Farm Families

Three distinct Wheeler families from Stonington, Connecticut, enhanced their prospects by relocating in Halifax in the late 1700s and early 1800s. The first Wheeler documented in Halifax was Miner Wheeler, a sixth-generation American born in Stonington in 1771.[1] He brought his first wife, Taca, also known as Tacy, with him from Stonington, and in 1795, their first child, David, was born in Halifax. After Tacy died in 1803, he married Hulda Thurber from Guilford in 1805 in Halifax. Tacy's burial card notes her final resting place is "In field on Niles farm," or the so-called Niles Farm Cemetery.[2] All seven of David's children were born in Halifax.

This branch of the family located in School District No. 2, which would be known in the 1800s as the Niles District, and in the 1900s as Valley. The 1856 McClellan map shows A. M. Wheeler—likely Asa Miner (1807–1864), son of Miner and Huldah Wheeler—located at the top of Larrabee Road where it intersects with Jacksonville Stage Road, not far up the hill from the Nathaniel Niles place.

Jesse, first cousin once-removed of Miner and a seventh-generation American, with his wife Prudence, settled in the southeastern section of town known as Grove. Jesse was born in Stonington, Connecticut, in 1792 and died in Halifax in 1869. He came to Halifax about 1814. "He served a short time in the War of 1812, receiving a government land warrant in acknowledgement of his services."[3] He married Prudence Denison Green in 1815 in Halifax. She was born in Stonington in 1792 and died in Halifax in 1843. The 1856 McClellan map shows a Wheeler farm on the east side off Amidon Road, near neighbors of the Worden family. This is presumably the original homestead passed on to his son William (1813–1897), who married Jane Parmelia Wheeler of Guilford.[4] The Beers atlas of 1869 shows W. Wheeler on this farm.[5] His son, William Edward, born in 1865, along with his wife, Marion Lois Ward Wheeler, also farmed that area until his death in 1916. Marion Wheeler (1870–1963) lived for many years with her daughter, Eleanor, in West Halifax and became known to everyone in town as "Grandma Wheeler." Also shown on the McClellan map is the Wheeler farm on Larrabee Road, located where Craig Stone, in recent years, built his house on the original cellar hole. The Beers atlas of 1869[6] shows this as the Mrs. H. E. Wheeler farm (Mrs. Harriet E.). The 1870 census shows Harriet, sixty-three, and Henry, twenty-two. They were the wife and son of Asa. Asa and Asher were the sons of Miner and Huldah.

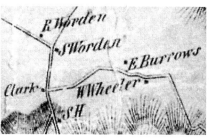

Detail McClellan

Charles Edward (1833–1904), the son of Silas, owned the farm near the William Niles place that was later owned by Floyd Stone.[7] Silas (1792–1869), brother of Jesse, married Salome Green (1767–1801), sister of Prudence. Their oldest child, Salome Surviah (1824–1905), who changed her name to Surviah or Survier S., married James Merrill Niles, who lived across the valley. It seems Surviah and James inherited or bought the farm of C. E. Wheeler at some point. In October 1884, Merrill Niles sold the former C. E. Wheeler farm to his son, Add C.[8] Add C. and his new bride, Mary Perry, lived there a short time before she died, after which Add rented it to his father-in-law, John Perry.

The death of Salome Green Wheeler, mother of Salome Surviah Wheeler Niles, Silas Whitman (1827–1906), and Charles E. Wheeler, was noted in this newspaper clipping of July 1867:

> Mrs. Salome Wheeler, widow of Silas Wheeler, late of Halifax, Vt., was found drowned in Wm. Mowrey's mill pond in Halifax on the morning of the 13th. She had been living the past winter and spring with her daughter in Wilmington, Vt., who has been sick, and came to Halifax and Colraine to visit her children and to rest and recruit her health, and was stopping with her son, Charles E. Wheeler, at the time of the sad affair. She went to bed in her usual spirits, although not feeling as well as usual. She complained to the little girl who slept with her, after retiring, of feeling very tired, bones and head aching bad, &c. After the family were all asleep, she arose and threw herself into the pond, it is supposed. No cause can be assigned for the fatal deed. She was in independent circumstances and a person greatly beloved by all who knew her. The supposition is that she was taken with the brain fever in the night, which caused her to take the final step. It is a sad and heart rending blow to her affectionate children and friends. She was 66 years old.[9]

It was the tradition in the Niles family to keep a diary of daily activities, and one written by Surviah and J. Merrill in 1877 has survived. Three persons, as evidenced by different handwriting and different points of view, wrote in the diary. It can be deduced that most of the writing was that of Salome (Surviah) and Merrill, but one entry was that of one of their sons, Eddie (Edward Houghton, 1866–1934) in which he wrote, "farther was sick today." Addie (Addison Charles, 1856–1904), their other son, at twenty-one years of age, was away at work on the Clark farm in town, where he met and married, in 1877, Clara Esther Clark.

The diary shows us that Niles men were farmers who raised horses, beef and dairy cattle, sheep, pigs, geese, and chickens, in addition to garden vegetables that included a large-scale planting of potatoes, corn for fodder, rye, and oats. In addition to farming and work as a blacksmith, Merrill hired out as a day laborer for $1.25 per day. He frequently worked on the roads in town or with neighboring farmers.

He and his neighbors and relatives often shared work and equipment, Merrill using his horse and a pair of oxen. One entry said the men worked at

"Sam's place," plowing with Sam's horse and Merrill's oxen, then at Merrill's or Charles's fields. Charles Edward Wheeler, Surviah's brother, worked several days each week at Merrill's farm. At one job, "on the upper lot, the oxen ran away with the cart." Eddie, at eleven years old, often worked with his father. Several persons often borrowed Merrill's horse or oxen, including Elias Stone (who is frequently mentioned), Charles Wheeler, and Sam Niles. Merrill likewise worked at their farms. It was the only way to take advantage of the weather and to keep up with the hustle and bustle of haying and planting during those short seasons when there was an enormous amount of work to be completed within a very limited period of time.

Once the season of work started, they worked at that job for seven days a week for a month or two. They were fortunate if there was bad weather because it forced a little respite between the intense hard work of snow shoveling; butchering; sugaring; plowing the fields; hoeing the corn and potatoes; haying; cutting fodder corn; harvesting and threshing the oats; picking apples; digging, drying, and storing potatoes in the cellar; planting rye in November; and logging, or "drawing wood." Then they started all over again. Somewhere in this mix of huge seasonal jobs was the everyday chores, like feeding, breeding, and raising horses and beef and dairy cattle (that have to be milked twice each day); training oxen and colts; shoeing horses; raising pigs, sheep, chickens, and geese; washing the sheep for shearing; cutting and hauling logs out of the woods to the sawmill, or sawing the wood into smaller pieces then chopping it into firewood; and repairing and maintaining buildings.

Inside the house, there was nearly nonstop baking and cooking for three to six or seven hard-working men with super-size appetites, not to mention visitors—up to five or seven per visit—several times each week. In March, a list of pies shows Surviah made twenty-nine pies in batches of one to nine at a time, and on February 10, she made ten pies. She baked several days each week. The only relief, it seems, was when the men were all working on one of the other farms or when leftovers would suffice. Sandwiched into Surviah's day was spinning fleece into yarn; knitting socks, sweaters, hats, and mittens; sewing all the family's clothes; making soap (a two-day project); washing clothes; cleaning the house or cellar; or dipping candles. On April 26, she "dipt 33 dozen candles." Since there is only one such entry, one wonders whether that was enough to supply the family for a year. Likely she used the tallow from two hogs and a beef cow that Merrill, with Sam's help, had butchered earlier in January for their own consumption, as well as for sale to others. It took him two days to butcher and then cut up a beef cow. An account in the back of the diary shows he sold pork to Cousin Samuel.

On January 10, Surviah was busy salting meat. Some meat might have been frozen in the springhouse or the smokehouse during the frigid winter. Smoking hams or salting or storing cuts in brine in the cool cellar were the preferred methods used to preserve meats for a longer period and to make meat available in the warmer months. In addition, in the warmer months they ate chickens and geese they had raised. It is clear their diet consisted mainly of meat and potatoes.

Merrill spent several days in February "drawing wood." The long logs were sold to Stone Brothers, while the tops and limbs were used for firewood for the chunk stove, which provided heat for the house, and for the cook stove used by Surviah in the kitchen.

All entries include a weather report. The weather usually drove the activities of the day. When it was "unpleasant" one day in January, Merrill "did the harness." One can imagine blustery winter days and evenings when the only outside activities were morning and afternoon chores of feeding and watering the animals and milking the cows. After the chores were done, the family gathered around the wood stove or fireplace. Merrill oiled and mended the harness while Surviah spun stocking yarn or knitted stockings for the family. One day she cut out seven shirts, while another day she finished "two shirts for Eddie and a pair of overhalls for Addie." A good deal of work was undoubtedly done while they "rested." Likely, much work had to be done during daylight hours, as 516 candles did not allow even frugal farmers much more than one candle each night, and the amount of light would be insufficient for the fine handiwork of sewing quilts or clothing. There was also a great deal of mending, since hand-sewn seams, even with sturdy cotton thread, would not stand up to the abuse of active, hardworking farmers. It is certain they lived by that frugal Yankee adage, "Use it up, wear it out, make due, or do without."

In spite of the long days and hard work demanded by a thriving farm, it is surprising to see that they had time to visit, welcome visitors, or to travel, nearly every day of every week, weather permitting. Their only mode of transportation was by horseback, horse and carriage, wagon, or "shank's mare" (walking). In the course of that year they went to nine funerals in Halifax or Guilford, including that of Mrs. Thurber in Guilford on October 21, when Merrill was one of the pallbearers. Mrs. Thurber was Barnabus Thurber's wife, Arsena[10] Smith Thurber, daughter of Rowe and Diantha Smith, all of Halifax. Several references to "Em" Thurber indicate they were also friends of Emerson Thurber. The other funerals they attended were for: Edd (Surviah's spelling) Roberts (January 14); Rufus Smith (February 25); Mr. Scott (April 28); Mrs. Barber (June 10); Mrs. Follett, who died on June 13 (the funeral was likely three days later); Mr. Stetson (June 17); Frederick Munson Stark, infant, who died November 19; Mr. Tucker (November 10).

When the men worked at another farm, there was time for Surviah to "call on" neighbors and friends all over town. On Sunday, February 25, they "went to West Halifax to Rufus Smith's funeral, tipt over coming home." There had been a snowstorm the day before, when Merrill had worked to "open roads." No matter which road they took into West Halifax (Larrabee Road to Jacksonville Stage Road, Hubbard Hill, or down Route 112 and along Branch Road), they would have had to negotiate steep hills and sharp curves, tricky with a horse and carriage or sleigh on icy, snow-packed roads. In one entry, Merrill went to Colrain to get 186 pounds of feed, 50 pounds of rye, one barrel of flour, and other items.

In an interesting and puzzling entry in July, Merrill went to West Halifax to "watch them train." On August 13, he went "to see the company start for

Bennington." The Civil War was over for twelve years; for what was this company training?

Several times in 1877, family members "went to Greenfield, took the cars to Worcester." In two entries, Merrill listed all the stops the train made: Montegue, Grout's Corner, "Urvin" (Erving), "Windal" (Wendall), Orange, Athol, Royalston, Baldwinsville, Templeton, "Prinston" (Princeton), Jefferson, Holden, and Worcester. On January 24, they "arrived at Cousin Houghton's[11] about four o'clock." The next day they went to a concert and "S." and Marsy went to Cousin Niles in the afternoon. S. would have been Surviah.[12] They went to a doctor, apparently in Worcester, then to another doctor in Boston about Eddie's eye. On February 1, "Eddie had his eye operated on today at Cousin Houghton's." Eddie was born with some unidentified problem with his left eye. Though there may have been other problems, it can be seen in pictures that a good deal of his eyelid is missing. This trait makes him easy to locate in early family photographs. They returned home after eleven days. It seems that Fayette (also known as Horace Fayette) and Laura Niles looked after the farm while they were away. The next entry says they returned home (presumably, to West Halifax).

It is exhausting just reading about their daily activities, because we know they had neither electricity nor any of the tools and conveniences we have today. We can only guess how fatiguing their jobs would have been given the primitive tools of 1877: for example, mowing fields of hay with a scythe, then raking it by hand and pitching it all onto wagons to be pitched into the hay mow in the barn; or plowing acres of fields behind a horse or oxen; or baking ten pies in one day, only after stoking the wood stove to achieve exactly the right oven temperature. Cleanup would only be possible after heating gallons of water on top of the cook stove, then carrying it to the sink to wash dishes by hand, using your own homemade soap. The same routine would have been used to do the laundry—scrubbing the heavily soiled work clothes of three farmers on a washboard that likely resulted in constantly bruised knuckles.

These were not the only Wheelers in Halifax. Miner's cousin Nathaniel (1766–1821), with wife Prudence Breed (1766–1837) Wheeler of Stonington, were the parents of Jesse and Silas. They died in Halifax and are buried in the Bell Cemetery in the Grove section of town, as are all of Jesse's family members. Silas's family is buried in the Niles Cemetery. Since their children were born in Stonington and lived there to adulthood, it is unclear how long Nathaniel and Prudence lived in Halifax.

The immigrant ancestor of all these Wheelers is Thomas,[13] who immigrated to Lynn, Massachusetts, in 1635, where he is first noted in public record upon his election as constable.* He became the owner of large tracts of land and a gristmill and sawmill. Richard Anson Wheeler's[14] family history and genealogy says it is uncertain why he sold all his holdings and businesses to move to Stonington in 1667. Thomas was made a freeman in Connecticut in 1669. He held many important offices in Lynn and Stonington at the local and the state levels. Wheeler descendants still living in Halifax in 2003 are from the Jesse

---

* A constable in those days was like a minor governor rather than a policeman.

Wheeler line. They are Thomas D. Rafus, second great-grandson, and Vivian Wheeler Smith, third great-granddaughter. Tom is the son of the late Eleanor Wheeler Rafus Guyette, and Vivian is the daughter of the late Edward Wheeler and granddaughter of Ralph "Joe" Wheeler, brother of Eleanor. Vivian is also descended from Silas Wheeler through her grandmother, Mary Niles Wheeler (1900– 1965).

An interesting member of the Wheeler family is Dr. Orswell Asher Wheeler, son of Asher and Eunice, according to the 1860 Halifax census, when he was nineteen years old. The 1880 census for Bernardston, Massachusetts, shows Orswell A. Wheeler, age forty, physician, with wife Emily N., thirty-four, son Lawrence, ten, and daughter, Eva N., aged one; but Eastman says in 1891, Dr. O. A. Wheeler was in California. He understood the problems of farmers and laborers. In 1884, he was the keynote speaker at the annual Halifax fair. The following is the speech, as it appeared in a September 26, 1884 newspaper article written by Add Niles.

Detail *Farm Festivals,* Harper & Brothers, NY, 1881.

The address was given by Dr. O. A. Wheeler of Bernardston who was born and brought up in Halifax. It was a vigorous and valuable piece of work because, instead of threshing over old straw, which agricultural orators have threshed since the year one, it took hold of the subject, which was quasi-political to be sure, but which directly interested farmers, and which they ought to go to thinking about. He treated the tariff, not only in its relation to the farmers, but as a principle of government taxation. There never was a time, he said, when agriculture was at such a disadvantage, when it was so nearly impossible for farmers to get along and politics are responsible for it, simply because the tariff is such a ceaseless drain upon them and brings almost nothing back to them. The tariff is simply a tax which is not based upon any principle of taxation, like that of the state, for the protection of life and property, but simply upon what a man eats, wears, or consumes. If you were a millionaire you would like it, because it would cost you no more, if you choose to live as economically, than if you were worth $1000. But how does the poor man like it? And a protective tax is still worse for it is impossible not to yield revenues to the government but to individuals. Take woolens for example. Suppose 9–10 of them to be manufactured in this country and 1–10 imported. The government gets its tax on that 1–10, but the people have to pay it, or a part of it on the other 9–10 just the same though it goes to the manufacturer. If every product of the country could be protected alike, there would be no inequality and obviously it would amount to nothing. All there is to "protection" is its own inequality and injustice—the taxation of a whole people for the benefit of a part. There are some articles which cannot be protected because we export them. Agricultural products cannot be protected because their prices are fixed in Liverpool and in countries in Europe. It is the farmers then who are competing with the "pauper labor of Europe" and are contributing besides to swell the profits of corporate monopolies. With a few blows of fact, the speaker then demolished the humbling pretense that the tariff increases the price of labor. It isn't so in the Hocking Valley, Ohio, where the companies won't even pay their miners as much as the duty that protects them. It isn't so in France or Germany or any of the high tariff countries of the world which pay lower wages than even free trade England. The truth is that we have free trade in labor, the manufacturer imports it from Europe whenever he finds it necessary to screw down prices, and the result is that wages which have been kept up by the fact that this is a new country, are steadily going down. The tariff benefits do not reach beyond the corporations and manufacturers to the laborer.[15]

His speech shows the problems inherent in a system with a large gap between the "haves and the have-nots," as well as the pinch of price controls and tariffs put upon the farmers. Does this all not sound familiar? What is new in 2007? Only the names and placement of the price controls put upon the farmers are different 123 years after Dr. Wheeler's speech. Today, with the worst recession in over forty years, farmers are in dire need of more income. It seems nothing has changed much.

~ Molly Stone

ENDNOTES

1. Church of Jesus Christ of Latter-day Saints, "Family Search," www.familysearch.org (hereafter cited as Family Search).
2. The Farm Cemetery is the very old family burial ground located up the hill along Larrabee Road in the woods near Keith Stone's house. The Niles Cemetery is located on Route 112.
3. Child, p. 222.
4. Jane Parmelia Wheeler, daughter of Sylvanus and Eunice Torry Anderson Wheeler, was born in Guilford. She was descended from John, who was born in 1589 in England and died in 1670 in Newbury, Massachusetts. No connection is known, at this time, between John and Thomas, the two immigrant ancestors of Jane and William.
5. Beers, p. 37.
6. Ibid.
7. HHS: Niles, Beers Atlas.
8. HHS: Niles, p. 31.
9. Ibid., p. 33.
10. Family Search. Arsena is also spelled "Arcena."
11. Edward Houghton Stark (1829-1900), son of Jedediah Hyde and Lydia Stark. Lydia was daughter of Oliver and Lydia Plumb Niles and grandmother of James Merril.
12. Marsey is probably Mary, daughter of Edward Houghton Stark, while cousin Niles is Oliver Niles Stark, brother of Edward Houghton. The two men were in business together in Worcester, Massachusetts.
13. A complete family genealogy is on file at the Halifax Historical Society Museum in West Halifax.
14. Richard Anson Wheeler, *History of the Town of Stonington, County of New London, Connecticut, From its First Settlement in 1649 to 1900, With a Genealogical Register of Stonington Families* (New London, CT: Press of The Day Publishing, 1900).
15. HHS: Niles, p. 29.

CARE OF DEPENDENT CHILDREN

Vermont law relating to the poor was modeled along the lines of English poor laws. In 1797, the Vermont legislature created and defined the powers of the overseer of the poor. The overseer was the town officer responsible for those individuals who resided in the town who were incapable of supporting themselves or their families. The law afforded the overseer tremendous latitude in how to address the problems of the indigent, and several common practices evolved. Some of the larger towns established poor houses (sometimes referred to as the work house or alms house) to provide for individuals and families who could not fend for themselves.

The first line of defense was to "warn out" newcomers to town whom the selectmen feared might become dependent on the town for support. The law allowed the town one year in which to notify these individuals that they needed to leave town. If the selectmen failed to do this, the so-called transients would become the town's financial liability. Halifax town records indicate that this custom was applied to many people who eventually became respectable members of the community. Whether or not warned individuals were actually physically removed from Halifax by the constable is not clear.

When a family or individual did become dependent on the town for support, the overseer could provide for them in a number of ways. The practice of auctioning off the poor to the lowest bidder was one of the methods employed. It was not uncommon for another struggling family to take on the responsibility of the town's paupers in return for cash. The town reports listed many of these arrangements.

Care of dependent children also fell to the overseer of the poor. In the event that a parent or guardian was unable to care for a child, an agreement was often made to "bind out" the child to someone willing to provide for the child in return for his or her labor. Essentially this was a written agreement between the parent and the appointed guardian arranged by the overseer, which bound the child to the guardian for a specific period of time in return for their care. For girls, the typical period of time was until the age of eighteen. For boys, the age was twenty-one. Binding out was also referred to as indenture or apprenticeship.

The sad case of Margaret "Peggy" Deland is an example of how the law dealt with child abandonment. Several references to this case can be found in the early town records. An order from the county court stated, "Daniel Deland of Westfield, in the State of New York Father of Margaret Deland of said Halifax — a person naturally wanting in understanding so as to be incapable of providing for herself and chargeable to the said Town of Halifax, should pay to the Selectmen of said Halifax at and after the rate of two shillings per week towards the support of said Margaret during her life. . ." [HLR 1A: 357]. The selectmen in this same order were granted the authority to seize Deland's property and to deliver him to the county jail in Westminster until he paid his debt to the town. Thereafter there are numerous references to the confiscation and sale of Daniel Deland's holdings in Halifax to pay for his daughter's care. At a town meeting in 1786, it was voted "that Peggy Deland be putt to Dr. Bernard upon Tryal" and further, "that Daniel Deland's land be looked after for the support of Peggy Deland by the selectmen" [HLR 1A: 434]. At a town meeting in 1787, the town voted "to set Peggy Deland up at vandew to the lowest bidder till she arrives at the age of 18 years" [HLR 1A: 437].

On April 2, 1849, Alvin S. Whitney was placed by the overseer of the poor as an apprentice to Luther Tisdale. Alvin was nine years old, and he was "to dwell and serve from the day of the date of these presents until said Alvin S. Whitney shall attain the age of fifteen years." Luther Tisdale was to "instruct or cause to be instructed the said Alvin S. Whitney in the occupation of farming" and the boy was "to be instructed to read, write and cypher." Luther Tisdale signed in the presence of Rufus K. Henry and John Fowler. Newton Gleason signed as overseer of the poor.

The papers for the indenture of John D. Whitney were made out on April 13, 1852. John, the son of Able Whitney, was eight years old at the time. The papers stated that John was "to dwell and serve from the day of the date of these present until the said apprentice shall attain the age of nineteen years." He was apprenticed to Newton Gleason, and the papers further stated that he was to "demean and behave himself towards his said master during the said term." The indenture also stated, "that the said Newton Gleason shall and will instruct the said John D. Whitney the said apprentice in the art or trade of a farmer in all its various branches." John was "to be instructed in the English branches of a common school education." Upon completion of his term, Newton Gleason was to "make, allow and provide and deliver unto the said apprentice good, suitable, and proper clothing proper for one of his age and acquirements in comparison with young men of his age in the vicinity." Newton Gleason and the overseer of the poor, Oshea Scott, signed the papers.

The youngest to be placed was the infant girl, "not named," of Willard Sumner. The child was born February 16, 1852. On April 29, 1852, the baby was apprenticed to E. P. Hitchcock "until the said apprentice shall attain the age of eighteen years." The baby was to be instructed "in the art of sewing, knitting and house work." The indenture stated that such things as doctoring and nursing and sufficient food would be provided for her. E. P. Hitchcock signed in the presence of W. J. Hitchcock and Oshea Scott, overseer of the poor.

Martin Sumner was apprenticed to Prentice Fowler at the age of three. He was to serve from April 25, 1852 until he was twenty-one. His papers stated, "The said apprentice shall faithfully serve his Master." Washing, mending and lodging were often specified in the indenture. Martin's indenture was signed by Oshea Scott, overseer of the poor, and by Prentice Fowler.

On May 5, 1864, Charles Huber was apprenticed to Luther Adams at the age of six. The indenture stated that he was to stay until he was twenty-one and was also to learn farming. H. N. Houghton, Chas. F. Griffin and Jedediah Stark signed as overseers of the poor with Luther Adams.

William Huber, five years old, was placed as an apprentice on August 12, 1864, to Thomas Sumner. William was to be an apprentice until the age of twenty-one in the occupation of farming. William's papers were signed as follows.

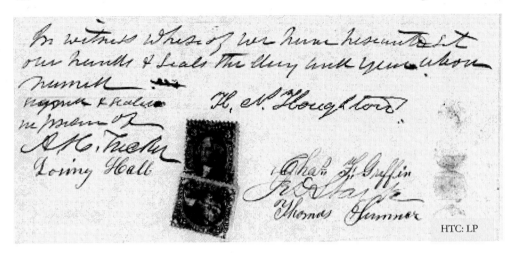

HTC: LP

Imprisonment for debt was another common practice. Many cases are found in the Halifax Land Records of orders to the town constable from the county court to order payment of a debt or to convey the individual "to the gaol in Westminster until the sums are paid" [HLR 1A: 357]. Land was often confiscated and sold off by the town justices of the peace if the debtor could not be located.

While many of these practices seem harsh, it must be remembered that the citizens of Halifax (and of the state as a whole) were struggling to seek a living from the land. One poor year of harvest or the death of a father or mother could plunge a family into the depths of poverty. Life was hard for people, and the town did not want to take on added financial responsibilities that would fall on the backs of the people. Until the responsibility of the poor was taken over by the State Department of Public Welfare, the overseer of the poor had the daunting task of holding starvation and homelessness at bay.

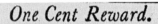

One Cent Reward.

RUNAWAY from the subscriber on the 6th inst. an indented boy, by the name of Thomas Downing. All persons are forbid harboring or trusting said boy on my account, as I will pay no debts of his contracting.
GEORGE BOARDMAN.
Halifax, (Vt.) Feb. 8, 1813.   7*

The Reporter, vol. X, issue 499, p. 4, courtesy Readex.

RAN AWAY,
On the 7th inst. and inden-tured Boy by the name JOSEPH CAR-PENTER, about 15 years of age—All persons are forbid harboring or trusting him on my account—and one cent reward to have him returned, no charges paid.
SAML STAFFORD, Jun.
Halifax, Dec. 8.

Federal Galaxy, vol. II, issue 85, p. 4, courtesy Readex.

~ *Elaine Fairbanks and Susan Rusten*

BIBLIOGRAPHY
    D'Agostino, Lorenzo, Ph.D. *The History of Public Welfare in Vermont.* Winooski, VT: St. Michael's College
    Press, 1948.
    HTC: LP.

AGRICULTURAL FAIRS

The Halifax Town Charter stated that when the population grew to fifty families, the townspeople would hold two annual fairs — one in April and the other in September. No documentation was found to indicate that any fairs were formally organized until the 1880s, when articles about the Halifax Fair began to appear in local newspapers. Given the importance of farming in this community, it is very likely that there were agricultural fairs held much earlier in the 1800s.

Based on information gleaned from the *Vermont Phoenix*, the first Halifax fair of this period took place in 1880 and continued in some form into the early 1900s. The fair was organized by the Halifax Agricultural Society and was held in late September or early October. The fair featured livestock exhibitions and competitions of all sorts, with small cash prizes. On Wednesday, September 27, 1882, the *Vermont Phoenix* boasted that there were "as many as 60 yoke of oxen on the grounds." The livestock competitions included horses, oxen, dairy cows, steers, sheep, swine and poultry. Competitors came from all

Courtsey Barbara Giguere
ROY THURBER

the neighboring towns and as far away as Boston. Local produce was also displayed and prizes awarded for the finest apples, pears, quinces, grapes, beans, pumpkins, rutabagas, potatoes, and corn. Grain and grass offered another category for competition. Butter and cheese, jams and jellies, maple syrup and honey, floral displays, and fancy work of all sorts were displayed in "the hall." One of the exhibits was entitled "Antiquarian Relics and Natural Curiosities." This was an odd assortment of articles — anything from live raccoons to one-hundred-year-old corsets.

Courtsey Jane Luschen
ISRAEL F. HALL

Various instrumental groups entertained farmers and their families over the years. These included the Jacksonville cornet band and the Readsboro band, which boasted "nineteen pieces." A speaker of some note addressed the crowd in the afternoon. The topic of the presentation related to agriculture. Footraces were held for the men and boys. Dances were sometimes featured at the end of the day.

The location of the fair was on the present Brook Road, between the road and the brook opposite the old town garage. One of the newspaper articles stated that the fair would be held in "the west village." The Community Hall was probably "the hall" where the fancy work, and so on, was displayed.

Weather played havoc with fair plans on September 23, 1885. The *Vermont Phoenix* reported, "A good show for a September day of rain, hail and snow." The 1884 fair had also been plagued with bad weather. There were "fewer exhibitors, but good quality" and reportedly, fifteen hundred people attended. In 1886, the *Vermont Phoenix* reported:

> Almost always when the date is set for the fair, fate, or something
> else equally potent, brings it upon a rainy day. Wind, rain, and
> even snow, have played an important part in the society's history,
> and it has become a standing joke that the only thing needful to
> wreck a dry spell, even of long standing, is to hold a cattle show at
> West Halifax, and the thing is done. Yet with true New England
> hardihood, this has made no difference with our farmers, for they
> rally to the meetings each year just as enthusiastically as ever,
> seemingly determined to make the next exhibition the best of all,
> bad weather to the contrary notwithstanding.[1]

ARRIVING AT THE FAIR   Postcard courtesy C. Lancaster

A fine image is created for our imaginations in the description of the beginning of the fair day in 1882:

> The day appointed for the third annual fair of the Halifax
> Agricultural Society (Wednesday, Sept. 27) dawned auspiciously,
> and at an early hour vehicles of all sizes and descriptions
> commenced to wend their way towards the village, laden with
> their human occupants, while turnips, beets and squashes, with an
> occasional fat calf or sheep and a belated oyster peddler or two
> served to give variety to the procession.[2]

The newspapers carried no notice of fairs in Halifax for a number of years. During this period, the Valley Fair in Brattleboro received top billing. In the *Vermont Phoenix* issue of October 5, 1900 the Halifax column stated, "Halifax was in luck at the Valley Fair, W[alter] Hubbard taking first money in one class of the drawing contest and I. Hall first in heavy cattle, while others took premiums in other departments." The drawing contest referred to is the horse drawing which continues at local fairs today.

BEN LEARNARD'S AWARD-WINNING PIGS   HHS

In the early 1900s, the Grange took over responsibility for the fairs. The *Windham County Reformer* reported that the Victory, North River, and Guiding Star Granges worked together on this endeavor. The fair then rotated in location between the three towns. As the farm population dwindled, the agricultural fairs survived in the larger towns and became more regional affairs. Some Halifax farmers took part in the Deerfield Valley Farmers' Day in Wilmington and in the Guilford Fair. The fair in Wilmington maintains some features of the earlier agricultural fairs, and Halifax people compete in many of the contests for farm products; however, the livestock exhibition is minimal and reflects the demise of farming in this region. Andy Rice, a sheep farmer from Halifax, continues to bring sheep and demonstrate shearing at the fair in Wilmington.

~ *Susan Rusten*

FAIR DISPLAYS

Curiosities such as 140 year old cane, ancient spoon mould, an Indian axe of stone, Indian spear heads, a metal relic of the Chicago fire, Indian pine clay, petrified insect tracks, three live raccoons.

Live stock of all ages and sizes: Stallions, speed horses, saddle horses, carriage horses, brood mares and sucking colts. Bulls, oxen, steers, dairy cows, sheep, swine, and poultry.

Roots and Garden Vegetables; Beans, Turnip, Wild Goose, Beets, Coffee, Large Oranges, Onions, Melons, Peppers, Curled Dandelion.

Butter, cheese, maple sugar and honey.
Grains and Grasses.

Fine Arts: Wax fruit, wax wreaths, varieties of plants and flower arrangements.

Fancy articles: Air Castle, Lamp Mats, Hair Receiver, Brush Receiver, Card Receiver, Match Safe, Pin Cushions, Cigar Holder, Wall Scrapbag, Spectacle Case, Paper Flower Wreath, Design Silk Bed quilt, Ladies underwear, embroidery work, homemade worsted fox and geese mittens.

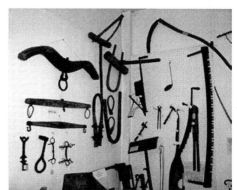

Photo C. Perna HHS wall display

Information taken from various pages of HH: Niles

FAIR NEWS

Was again unfortunate in a lowering, drizzly day, which induced people at a distance to believe that it would be postponed. But for the weather there is reason to believe that it would have been the most successful exhibition of the society's history. As it was there were fully 1500 people in attendance, and the show though necessarily small in all departments, was generally of very good quality.

* * *

The fancy articles were all worth the time spent in examining, and it would be hard to tell which was "the best and the prettiest." A darned toilet set, pillow shams and tidy made by Mrs. D. Tucker were delicate and beautiful pieces of needlework, and attracted much attention, as did also two collars of feather edge braid made by Mrs. Albert Thurber.

HHS: Niles, Sept. 26, 1884
West Halifax, Vt.

The Halifax Agricultural society held their picnic at Worden grove as per appointment, but met with its usual fate, as rain began to fall in a few minutes. They adjourned to village hall, where, after the usual time spent in eating dinner, the meeting was called to order by the president Luther Adams. Geo. P. Worden, Geo. L. Clark and Geo. M. Scott were appointed committee on music, L. H. Ballou and F. T. Miner committee on amusements and Frank Worden and A. A. Hill, weighing committee .It was voted to meet the Saturday before the date set for the fair, or if stormy the next pleasant day, to prepare the grounds. It is hoped that there will be a good attendance, as a quantity of stalls must be built for the better display of our large horse exhibit, which has completely out-grown its present quarters. After the business meeting closed, music and singing were in order…. after which croquet and ball playing amused many.

Gazette and Courier August 18, 1888
West Halifax, Vt.

~ Carrie Perna

ENDNOTES
1. *Phoenix*, 1886, articles from a Halifax Scrap Book (#372), HHS.
2. Ibid., 1882.

DOWN THE OLD ORCHARD ROAD

Take a right off the Jacksonville Stage Road onto Amidon Road, and continue past the former Grove Schoolhouse. Proceed with care down the dark, narrow, winding, densely wooded dirt road that leads to a panoramic view at the crest of a hill. In the valley below, you'll see a house, shed, large barn, cemetery, pastures, and the remnants of what once was one of the largest orchards in Vermont. Before the peak apple years under the stewardship of the Amidons and the Bishops, several generations of the Bell and Fish families worked the land as both apple growers and sheep ranchers. Currently, the property, owned by the Trillium Land Trust, includes a small orchard, a horse stable, and riding trails.

You can wander through the little cemetery, enclosed by its original stone wall, and read the stones marking the graves of the first families who cleared this land, built homes and barns, farmed and raised their families here: Samuel Fish, Jesse Wheeler, John Green, Jeremiah Everett, and John Bell. The earliest recorded burial dated April 1813 marks the death of an infant child of Samuel and Mary Packer Fish.

Farm Festivals, Harper & Brothers, NY, 1881

Land records for properties in this vicinity of Grove refer to Lot 8, the southern portion of Lot 16, and the eastern portion of Lot 7. The orchard land is on a south-facing slope in the southeast corner of Halifax, bounded by Guilford, Vermont, and Colrain, Massachusetts. A brief chronology of ownership follows.

By 1820, the area included two large farmhouses built by Samuel Fish Sr. and his son, the Rev. Samuel. The cemetery was located on their property. North was the Wheeler Farm and the farm of Solymon and John Bell. South was the Green Farm, and to the west, was the colonial style home of Dr. Jeremiah Everett. By 1840, the Samuel Fish farm, orchard, and cemetery property had been conveyed to Jeremiah's son, Jacob W. Everett. However, Samuel Fish Jr. , who moved to the Center, reserved all apples raised or grown on twenty-five apple trees in the orchard during his residence in the town of Halifax [HLR 9: 24]. By 1860, the Fish/Everett orchard property, with cemetery, had sold to Charles Bell. His new neighbor to the west, in the former Jeremiah Everett home, was Benjamin Barber. South of Bell was a smaller farm owned by George and Elwin Preston. The Wheeler Farm had not changed.

MA BELL'S RANCH

Until 1907, the Bells farmed the property for several generations. Gerry Bell, of Maine, a descendant and an active participant in the Bell Cemetery Association, and his late father, George, contributed to the chronology. In their family, "The Ranch" is often used when speaking of early farm years. They explained that it goes back to when sheep raising was the focus of the Bell family farm. After the Civil War, "some of the brothers wanted to go into apples." Gerry's great-great-grandfather, Charles Bell (1820–1873) ran "The Ranch" with the help of his wife, Mary A., affectionately referred to by her descendants as "Ma Bell." Mary outlived Charles, and in 1884, Child's business directory lists Mary as owner of 380 acres, 125 sheep, and 1,100 apple trees. The directory says, "Charles C. works the farm for his mother."[1] The family enjoys the notion that Mary "ran the ranch for twenty two years like a hill town version of Tugboat Annie."[2]

After the death of Charles C. Bell, (1863–1900) his widow, Etta Canedy Bell, daughter of Israel and Lucy Sanders Canedy, managed the farm for a few more years before selling. The matter of getting the harvest to markets in Colrain and Greenfield was always a challenge; a round trip to Greenfield by wagon was an all-day event. Gramma Etta Bell needed help from teamsters to deliver barrels of apples to the railroad. She succeeded in recruiting that help by paying five dollars per barrel, which was about double the going rate. This caused a furor among the other farmers in Halifax. "Imagine the widow Bell disrupting the economic structure of this small Vermont town."[3] Eventually, however, she sold the farm to Otis Amidon and moved to South Deerfield where her son, George, set up his own business.

AMIDON'S FRUIT FARM

According to Anna Marie Amidon, wife of Aubrey, Otis Amidon bought the farm from Etta Bell in 1907. He enlarged the property by buying the adjacent Barber and Wheeler farms. A 1927 list of "Large Orchards in the State of Vermont" includes O. Amidon of Halifax — 1000 trees.[4] The obituary for Otis W. Amidon, who died in 1940 at age sixty-nine, tells us he had been a resident of the town of Halifax for thirty-five years and its representative in three legislatures. At the time of his death, "he was the owner of three farms in Halifax which he had developed into orchard properties and had long been extensively engaged in fruit raising" [HTC, LP]. In February 1945, Aubrey O. Amidon Jr. and Averill A. Amidon registered a Vermont business under the name Amidon Fruit Farm before the town clerk and justice of the peace, H. E. Goodnough [HTC: Misc.]. The stated activities of the business were fruit growing, lumbering, and general farming. In January 1948, the business became Halifax Fruit Farm, under owners Aubrey O. Amidon Jr. and Anna Marie Amidon. They grew, graded, and sold apples and other fruit and made and sold maple syrup, maple sugar, and other maple products.

* * *

Anna Maria Amidon, now over eighty years old, shared some of her memories of life at the fruit farm with her daughter, Bonnie Lee Nugent of Charlemont, Massachusetts, who e-mailed her notes to us.

o   Whenever Otis bought a new car, he always went off the road between Elm Grove and the farm. He said that the car went too fast. [Note: Even today, this is a very narrow, steep, twisty road.]

o   Sometime in the early forties, the snow was so deep and packed from Clark Mountain Road to Gates, that dynamite was needed to help open the road. Aubrey had to ski from the top of the hill to Route 112 in order to go to town. In 1945 there was a snowstorm on Mother's Day. It froze so many buds that only 2,000 bushel of apples were picked that year.

o   During harvest time, neighbors, such as, Dick Winston, Lee Barber, Charlie Hepburn, Win Amidon, the Hebbard girls and Rozzie, the Purringtons, The Grants, Myron Fish, Bill Petrie, teachers and students from Marlboro College all came to pick apples. So many people came to work, I fear I may have missed quite a few names. Everyone needed money and so everyone came. Many people came after supper to work till dark for extra money. They brought their families and all worked together.

o   At that time we grew about twenty-nine different varieties of apples, plus peaches, plums, crabapples and quince trees. All during the forties, three thousand five hundred buckets were set for sugaring. Aubrey Jr. made a power driven screw to tap the maple trees. Aubrey Jr. was the first farmer to put syrup in small containers and apples in plastic bags. In '48, '49 and '50 Jr. made it into the Massachusetts Red Apple Club. That was because 85% of his apples were considered perfect. (Part of the farm was in Massachusetts.) Experimental sprays were applied to the orchard on the recommendation of both MA and VT State Universities.

$7.50, Ingenuity and 3 Men Set 1,500 Buckets in Day

Three men on the farm of Aubrey Amidon in Halifax tapped for and hung 1,500 sap buckets in a single day recently, a feat accomplished by good, old-fashioned Vermont ingenuity.

Amidon hunted around until he found a right-hand starter motor off an old car. This took some time, because modern starters are of left-hand rotation. He fitted a chuck on the old motor and the tapping bit was inserted. Then, with a 15-foot cable connected with the electrical system of his tractor, he was all set.

One man drove the tractor, one man tapped, and a third hung the buckets. Although Amidon has hung 3,500 buckets, the tractor would reach only enough trees to hang 1,500. He figures that the gadget cost him about $7.50. So far, he has produced 170 gallons of syrup, all fancy.

Phoenix, March 28, 1947

o   In 1947 the eight-foot deer fences were put around the orchards. It was the only way to keep the deer from destroying the apple trees. When the deer would eat the ends off the limbs of the apple trees they were eating three years of apples. There were many, and they ate a lot of limb tips. At some places where the fences followed the land, the deer were able to jump over the fences. The apple trees were still eaten.

Bonnie Nugent added the following:

When Anna Marie was the lady of the house between 1946 and 1953, the salesmen would always arrive at the house at 11:30 in order to be invited for the main dinner meal. They all knew what a great cook she was and never missed the opportunity to partake of her cooking.

Corn husking parties were held in the barn in late fall. One of my memories was when I was about five years old. Charlie Hepburn was working for us that year. The corn had been picked and lay in a long high row down the center of the barn. Stools and benches were lined up along the row of corn. The deal was as people husked the corn, they looked for a red ear, which meant that they could kiss anyone they wanted to. Well now, you can understand why all the single men on the farm wanted to get a head start on finding a red ear. Charlie found four red ears that day. He made a deal with me to hide the ears upstairs in my hide-a-way and sneak them to him one at a time during the party. I thought that was just a great thing to do, so as the party went along, I watched for his signal to bring him each ear. We laughed so much that night.

Aubrey lost both the Halifax and Haydenville, Massachusetts farms after the hurricanes of '53 and '54. The orchards were devastated, and there was no money to keep them going. The banks took the property in the fall of '55. Arthur Bishop of Shelburne Falls, Massachusetts purchased the farm shortly there after. He ran it beautifully as an orchard. He sold it to just two years ago. It is now a horse farm.

The original houses on the orchard properties have either burned or fallen in. Before the most recent transfer of ownership, three quarters of the 150 acres of orchard trees were cut down. Currently, there are about five acres of orchard, plus fruits and berries in organic production for home use. Under new ownership, the unheated building, said to have been a camp where the migrant workers stayed, has been converted into a year-round home. One old barn is still in use, and there is a newly constructed barn for horses.[5] Future uses of this property are under consideration. Meanwhile, there is considerable interest in trail riding.

~ Constance Lancaster

ENDNOTES
1. Child, p. 414.
2. Gerry Bell, telephone interview, June 2003.
3. George Bell, telephone interview, June 2003.
4. Stone, vol. II p. 493
5. Penfield Chester, telephone interview, September 2004.

Reluctant Farmer

From the *Pickaway Quarterly,* Pickaway County Historical Society, Circleville, Ohio, March 1963.[1]

A Personal History of Orsamus Elliott Niles From His Own Pen

I was born on the 13th of April 1826, in the town of Halifax, Windham County, Vermont. This town borders on the Massachusetts line, and is about twenty-eight miles west of the Connecticut River. My father, James Niles and my mother, Sarah Tucker Niles, settled on a farm which my grandfather had given them in 1818, known as the Pennel farm. The place was known as Pennel Hill. It was certainly a hill if not a mountain. The eastern approach to it from the north river was a mile and a half climb— so steep that a horse could no more than pull a buggy and one person up the slope without frequently stopping to get wind. The top of the hill was comparatively smooth, but the surface was covered with small stones or pebbles and occasionally ledges of rock.

Farming upon the land was a task, which brought poor returns for hard labor. However, some potatoes, flint corn, oats occasionally, a little spring wheat, or barley, and some peas and buckwheat were annually grown. Two good orchards of seedling apples for that day produced fruit for the family use, and quite a quantity, which was made into cider. This cider was stored to be drank in the wintertime or taken to the still to be made into cider brandy. These crops together with the produce of a good sugar camp comprised the resources of the farm.

On this farm was where my early boyhood days were spent. I never had any particular love for this kind of farming. I had to pick, and shovel too many stone heaps, which often wore my fingers until they would bleed. Besides, I had a great fondness for catching young squirrels, crows, robins, chipmunks and rabbits, and making pets of them. Not only that, it was a great pleasure for me to steal away to the trout brook to catch a string of fish.

My father had a strong suspicion that I would never make a farmer, so when I became fifteen years of age he secured for me a place to learn the printing business with a Mr. Ryther who published the *Vermont Phoenix* at Brattleboro, Vermont. While learning the "art and mystery of printing" I was to have each year three months' schooling at the town school.

* * *

From this introduction, Mr. Niles continues his narrative by telling that his apprenticeship was cut short due to an injury sustained while skating on the Connecticut River at the noon hour. He spent a year recuperating, studied with a Yale senior at the academy in town, then spent a term at school in Marlboro, and that was the end of Vermont for him.

He became a salesman, part of a group of ten young men "engaged to sell Grammatical Correctors, Gazetteers, Charts, and some other papers published by Jeremiah Greenleaf of Guilford, Vermont," who had mapped out their routes of travel. He traveled from place to place wearing a silk hat and kid gloves and keeping his temper when folks refused to buy his wares. His method and modes of travel and the places he visited are included in the account, followed by his life experience in Ohio. His detailed narrative illustrates the type of migration made by young unmarried males, who would wander from place to place until the combination of location and employment seemed right. Niles settled, finally, in Circleville, Ohio, where he published newspapers, married, and held public office.

In a letter dated on July 23, 1848, addressed to Mr. and Mrs. James Niles "from your prodigal son," he comments on the abundance of wheat crop in Ohio saying,

> The West is a fertile country. Those Eastern barrens where
> crows carry knapsacks for fear of starvation where you have to
> hold a sheep by the tail with head down between the rocks to get a
> nip at one spear of grass is no place . . . to live.

Ironically, Orsamus Niles tells how he became a farmer after all. "In 1850 while publishing the *Democratic Watchman*, I bought land in Jackson Township and engaged in farming with my brother Horace as a tenant. We farmed Indian corn and wheat up

Office of

O. E. NILES,

GROWER AND DEALER IN

BROOM-CORN.

HHS

to 1866. In 1867 I commenced the growing of broom corn. . . . This I did with general good success up to 1890, when the business, becoming no longer profitable, I sold out." From time to time Orsamus visited his family back in Vermont and over years of correspondence, continued to urge them to leave the hills of Halifax for the flat fertile fields of Ohio. Today his boyhood home on "Pennel Mountain" is surrounded by fenced pasture land full of grazing Belted Galloways who look well fed and content.

~ *Constance Lancaster*

ENDNOTES
1. Used with permission

Today there are only a few working farms. Nevertheless it is not uncommon for folks in town to keep a few laying hens, a heifer or two, or a pig. There are many who cultivate a vegetable garden or small orchard to put up food for their families. There are even a few vineyards being established. Perhaps the grape will be in the future of Halifax.

~ *Susan Rusten*

HHS

Citations and Awards Presented at the 87th Annual Meeting
of the
National Grange, November 10-19, 1953,
in
Burlington, Vermont

CENTURY FARMS

Initiated by the Vermont Historical Society in cooperation with the State Grange and State Farm Bureau, this program seeks to identify and recognize "farm people of Vermont who for over one hundred years have maintained the home farm in the family."[1] At the awards program on October 19, 1953, Arthur Packard, president of the Vermont State Farm Bureau, said:

> I consider it a high honor to any farm family who has lived on a Vermont farm and kept it in the family name for over 100 years. These families have done much to make Vermont a great state. Over these years, they have seen progress and have faced disaster. They have lived in periods of comparative prosperity and probably more years of depressed prices. They have been stalwart leaders in the promotion of better schools, better roads, better churches. . . . Most of them have carried on because of their love of the land . . . and the opportunity which it gave their children to grow up in one of the best environments known to man. . . . [T]hese Vermont farm families who have weathered the storm, who have been an example of progress to their fellow citizens. . . have probably done more than their share towards making Vermont a great state.[2]

Printed on the back of the 1953 program is a list of designated Century Farms in Windham County. On the list are three Halifax farms, one of which, fifty years later, is still active.

ARCHIE D. AND MARY E. LEARNARD BURNETT

HHS

This family farm, located on Hubbard Hill, dates from 1781, when Moses Learnard purchased the land. He transferred the property to son Nathan in 1844. The farm passed to Horace Learnard (b. 1853) and from Horace to daughter, Mary (b. 1896) and husband Archie Burnett. During its existence, the farm grew to 160 acres, and activities included sheep raising, dairying, a horse riding stable and sugaring. The Burnetts were active in town and school government, the Grange, and the Baptist Church.

HENRY MERTON SCOTT

HHS

Henry Merton (Mertie) Scott, born in 1874, spent his life on the farm that had been in his family since 1785 when Thomas Scott bought the land at Halifax Center. The farm, located on Stow Mountain Road, passed from Thomas to son Abel in 1802. Abel's son,

Martin (b. 1815) was succeeded by his son, George (b. 1845) who was the father of Henry Merton. The farm began small and grew to about 300 acres. The Scotts raised livestock and won awards for many varieties of apples and grains. Mertie had no children, and after his death in 1956, the farm contents were auctioned and the property was sold to Anne DeWitt.

LEWIS A. AND MARY D. WORDEN SUMNER

HHS

The Sumner Century Farm, located on Branch Road, dates from circa 1791, when Joel Sumner purchased the property. Lewis (b. 1803), son of Daniel and Elizabeth (Betsy Snow) Sumner, acquired the property from his Uncle Joel's widow, Elizabeth in 1833. After Lewis's death in 1870, his only son, Lewis Worden Sumner, continued the family farm. In 1921, his son, Lewis Asa Sumner, took over the farm. In 1956, the farm passed to Lewis Asa's son, Homer Malcolm. In 1979, Homer and Lucie Peterson Sumner were among the guests of honor at the 108th Annual Meeting of the Vermont State Grange. Featured speakers included: Sen. Patrick Leahy, Sen. Robert Stafford, and Vermont Farm Bureau president, Rupert Chamberlain, who presented the Sumner's with a plaque. Their farm "consists of 75 acres, with a dairy herd of 55 animals. For many years, the family operated a sawmill and gristmill. The Sumners have been active in grange, church, town and community affairs."[3] Currently, the Sumner Century Farm is owned and operated by Homer's son, Malcolm and family, the fifth and sixth generations at this location.

~ *Constance Lancaster*

ENDNOTES
1. Gov. Lee E. Emerson, *Century Farms of Vermont 1953, Citations and Awards Presented at the 87th Annual Meeting of the National Grange, Nov. 10–19, 1953, in Burlington, Vermont* (Montpelier, VT: Vermont Historical Society, 1953) p. 3.
2. Ibid., p. 5.
3. Deacy Ford Leonard, *Century Farms of Vermont* (Montpelier, VT: Vermont Historical Society, 1986) p. 48.

HANSON HOME

THE HANSON SIBLINGS, Maria with her brothers Hans Olaf, known as "Jack" (in scout-master's uniform), and Anton Christian, who resided full-time at the old saltbox house. None of them married. Their graves are at the Hatch School Road Cemetery in Halifax.

Photos courtesy John and Jean Jenkins

TONY HANSON with his horse and wagon. He never owned a car.

A Letter From Breidablik Farm

Breidablik Farm, Vt.
Easter Sunday Eve. April 16, 1933
Dear Marie and Olaf:

You must have read something in the New York papers about the enormous snowfall that struck this section last Wednesday night didn't you? – which delayed my last letter two days for the Phoenix said it was one of the most damaging storms that has struck Brattleboro for many years. But that statement must be taken with a grain of salt, for "many years" ago Brattleboro was not so dependent upon electrical service as it is to-day and the damage that this snow did was entirely confined to the electric wire system except that it did break down many branches from trees right across in our orchard its weight bore down one big branch from one of the old apple trees. All this damage was due to the fact that there was no wind to accompany the "storm", so the snow clung and piled in to everything including electric wires until they snapped and all electric service in Brattleboro was put out of commission lights and power wires as well as telegraph and telephone. And according to the Phoenix it caused much hardship for a day or two to the inhabitants as they had to do without radios, telephones, refrigeration, etc and had to fall back on old-fashioned ways of toasting their bread and percolating their coffee. Shades of the old New England Fathers! Could they but read that copy of the Phoenix![1]

With these words, Anton Christian Hanson of Halifax began a letter to his brother and sister in Elmhurst, New York. At the time, Tony was about fifty-four years old and had lived for ten years at the old saltbox farmhouse on the road that now bears his name. Born in Denmark, Hansen, who immigrated to the United States with his sister Marie and brother Olaf, had worked as a machinist in New York City until his union called a strike that did not reach a settlement. Given his almost total deafness, Tony despaired of finding another job and bought a property in Halifax with his siblings as co-owners [HLR 21: 170–171]. On this farm, which he called "Breidablik" (broad splendor) after the home of Baldur in Norse mythology, Tony Hanson resided until his death in 1961.

His letter continues:

> The mailman did not come either Thursday or Friday but
> yesterday he came with a horse and a two wheeled gig and I got
> your letter all right and the little package with the trick rule. . . . It
> is a marvelous invention and very handy and useful. . . . I also read
> the three clippings you sent with great amusement . . . the one
> about the maple sugaring seems to make liars out of us farmers. If
> you see it in The Sun, it is so, hey? Well that article must be one of
> those sun-spots, it is <u>not</u> so. Everybody up here will agree with me
> that all the main statements in it as to this year's season are
> absolutely at variance with the truth. That article is simply a stock
> article that they pull out of a cabinet-file to use for any year. The
> conditions have <u>not</u> been ideal for sugar-making, the prospects are
> <u>not</u> for a good crop, good weather has <u>not</u> prevailed since the
> season opened, the season has been full of interruptions from bad
> weather, and the season was <u>not</u> earlier than usual but
> considerably later than usual. So there! Hatch has made 166
> gallons, I haven't heard from Plumb's. They don't expect to make
> much more now. I haven't had a chance to boil any more, just
> when I figure on collecting the sap rain or snow comes and fills
> the cans as they are not covered. Much rainwater has been boiled
> in the big evaporators this year, believe me.

Tony's ironic sense of humor is evident in this letter as well as his interest in farming and gadgets. He was a voluminous correspondent who wrote for more than an hour every day, both in his journal and in his daily letters to his family. Special Collections at the University of Vermont has seven boxes called "The Anton Hansen Collection 1902–1956." The library lists the "Scope and Content" as follows: "Correspondence from (1923–1935), Diaries 1902–1905, 1924–1956, and miscellaneous clippings, photos, papers. . . . Letters and diaries give good descriptions of rural life in early 20th century Vermont. Some of the subjects include farming, philosophy and religion, early airplane trips, a Long Island Boy Scout troop's excursions on the farm, the 18th Amendment, the Green Mountain Parkway, unemployment and overpopulation, mathematical problems and puzzles."[2]

Dwindling hay supply is mentioned in this letter and in an earlier one dated April 13, written just after more than two feet of snow had fallen.

> I was congratulating myself when I finally dug my way over to the
> barn in the morning that I had enough hay to last me another
> good week or so, for I would have been in a terrible predicament
> if I had been short of it now. And then about 10:30 along came
> Cannon and Norman with the same old tale of woe—they were
> entirely out of hay and it was impossible for them to go to
> Person's barn today for some more of what they have bought
> there. They came with the single bob-sled and two horses and had

had an awful time getting over here, it had taken them an hour
and a half to get through and the horses were tired out completely.
I had to give them enough for two feedings, of course, on their
promise to return it as soon as they can. As it is I've got the barn
filled to the roof-beams with promises which I can't get on my
pitch-fork and if I could I would hate to offer them to the
animals, but I think there is still enough hay left for a whole
week."[3]

However, his April 16 Easter letter reports a promise kept:

Cannon drove to Person's and out of the load he got he dutifully
gave me back just as much as I had loaned him. I am not stuck for
hay yet, it holds out well and now I can soon drive over myself
and get what is left at Emily's. . . . I killed another rooster and
roasted it for my Easter dinner and gave Cannon's one for theirs,
so now there are only 3 left and last night I put those three back
into their earthly paradise after having sped all their companions
to an unearthly one. The hens are now speeding up production, it
seems, I got 10 eggs yesterday and 8 to-day. I have over 50 eggs
on hand so I may send you the big box even if I only put 4 or 5
dozen in instead of 6.

Hanson's wide range of interests included music and musical instruments. Susan
Rusten notes that Tony had a machine shop on his property where he did odd
jobs for people. One such project was helping a local teacher fashion parts for his
homemade banjo. Tony's Easter letter continues:

Every now and then Georgie has brought over to me music books
belonging to Louise for me to try on the mandolin and I have
made a music stand to hold the sheets in correct line of vision. . . .
I get much pleasure out of it. To-day I went over to visit them.
Norman having asked me to come over because he had taken
their "Aolian" organ all apart to make a writing desk out of it, and
he wanted my advice and wanted to show me all the curious
mechanisms it contained. . . . [A]t the same time I looked over all
of Louise's music and I was astonished at the wonderful collection
of piano music she had accumulated in her younger days.

Tony's brother Olaf led a Boy Scout troop on Long Island, and some
summers brought his scouts to "Big Pine Camp" on the Hanson Halifax
property. In 1937, while Tony and Olaf were burning brush in a field, the fire got
out of control; Olaf rushed to town to report the fire, rushed back, and in his
agitated state suffered a fatal heart attack. He was buried at the Hatch Cemetery in
the Christian Dreyer lot. The Hansons and Dreyers were related. Donald Dreyer
Cael's mother, Helen, was also a Dreyer.

A UVM student[4] who wrote a paper about Anton Christian Hanson interviewed several local people by phone in 1990. She said, "People recall that he always walked or drove a horse and wagon; he never had a car. He kept his house cold and always wore a wool jacket indoors and outdoors in the winter."[5] Mary Sumner, a neighbor, told the story of the time she saw Tony walking through the deep snow to the post office. It was two miles to town, and she realized that he would be late for the last mail pickup. It was Friday, the day he always mailed his order to the Grand Union, which delivered to him the following week. She found a way to retrieve his letter, opened it, and phoned in his order. He never knew.[6]

Courtesy Helen McDaniel
TONY HANSON

His neighbors considered Tony something of a recluse and a loner. Described as a very bright and self-educated man, he regretted not having gone to college. Perhaps his deafness made college impossible. "He seemed compelled to leave a legacy of his life and times with his writing."[7] In a letter written in 1930 to a friend in the city, Tony considers the question of whether it was wise or prudent to "settle down for the evening of my life" in the country. "I do believe that when a man has labored at a trade for 27 years and is still in vigorous health and has prospects of a small steady income for the rest of his life . . . then it is wise for him to retire to a farm provided he really enjoys such a life in preference to city life."[8] Anton Hanson died in Brattleboro Hospital on June 30, 1961. He was eighty-two years old. The Breidablik saltbox still stands on Tony Hanson Road.

~ *Constance Lancaster*

ENDNOTES
1. UVM, Anton Hansen Collection 1902–1956, Special Collections Bailey/Howe Library, carton 3, folder 8, letters 1933.
2. http://bailey.uvm.edu:6336/dynaweb/findingaids/hansen
3. Ibid.
4. UVM, Elizabeth F. Pritchett, *The Life and Times of Anton Christian Hanson*, spiral bound, December 4, 1990.
5. Ibid., p. 19.
6. Ibid., p. 23.
7. Ibid., p. 23.
8. Ibid., pp. 19–20.

Sumner Family Farms

Homer and Kenneth, sons of Lewis Asa and Blanche Sumner, were born in Halifax and spent their entire lives engaged in farming. They built up a dairy herd on their parent's farm and ran the family saw mill as well. Homer's son Malcolm went into partnership with his father in 1978 until Homer's death in 1989 and has been working on the family farm ever since. The farm has been in the Sumner family for more than 200 years and was distinguished as a "Bicentennial Farm" by the State of Vermont. He and his wife Monica live across the road from the farm in the home, which they completed in 1988 where they raised four daughters, April, Kimberly, Maria and Lauren. Malcolm maintains a dairy herd of about seventy head of cattle including forty milkers. Continuing the family tradition, he has mostly Jersey cows. In addition to the dairy, Malcolm does maple sugaring, some logging, and sells hay. He was the first farmer in Halifax to purchase the new hay baler that makes bales wrapped in white plastic that resemble giant marshmallows.

When Kenneth Sumner married Mary Wrisley in 1941, they spent the first few years of their married life living with his parents at the old homestead on Branch Road. Ken and Mary bought the Collins farm on Collins Road where in addition to their dairy operation, they raised laying chickens. Ken delivered eggs to Greenfield and Turner's Falls, Massachusetts for more than thirty years. One of my childhood memories from the 1950's was the familiar sight of Homer and Ken's cows trotting past the school yard in West Halifax as they were herded to pasture after milking. I loved watching the beautiful Jersey cows pass by with their soft brown eyes and jingling collars.

All of Ken and Mary's children remained in Halifax. Sons Lewis and Homer "Chum" and daughter Laura went into farming.

In 1973, Lewis along with his wife, Laura began their own dairy herd at his parents homestead on Collins Road. At one time, they had as many as sixty-five head of cattle - mostly Jerseys. In 1988, they gave up dairy farming; however, their daughters Marylee and Holly grew up helping on the farm.

Laura and husband Barry Gerdes live on Reed Hill Road and operated a dairy farm until 1985. They now run Gerdes Transportation - providing school buses for area towns. Their two children, Wendy and Tim no longer live in Halifax.

Homer "Chum" Sumner and his wife Deborah bought their farm on Collins Road in 1973. Before this Chum farmed with his father as well as working on the Ranney Farm in Dummerston. Chum developed his herd of Jerseys to number about seventy-five milkers and had in total as many as one hundred and fifteen head of cattle. He also raised Fjord horses. In addition to the dairy farming, Chum used his horses as part of a logging business. In 1996 Chum sold off his herd. Chum and Deborah raised their four children on the farm - Lori, Krista, Andrea and Daniel. I recall many summer evenings seeing the entire family out in the hayfields gathering in the hay before nightfall.

~Susan Rusten

Hayed Until the Stars Shone

The title of this story is a quote from a diary of the Halbert Eames family, showing that haying in the summertime was sometimes an all-night affair. This family owned property both in Halifax and Jacksonville, Vermont. Their home was located at about the town line. Their everyday routine touched the lives of people they worked with or people who were their friends, relatives, and neighbors. The diaries also recorded events in surrounding neighborhoods, thus providing dates that are important for town histories. We have tried to include some of the more interesting events and dates recorded. The title of this article reflects the hard work necessary to keep a family farm going. The Eames family is remembered for their self-sufficiency and hard work.

Excerpts from the diaries begin in 1874. April 7: "We went to Mr. Winchester's in a sleigh and came home on bare ground" (apparently, that same day, the snowed thawed so quickly that it left the road bare). Before the invention of the automobile, huge rollers, which were heavy and wide, rolled winter roads so the snow could be compacted. On a least one occasion, a diary indicated that they tried to roll the road but "it did not work" so they drove through with horses and sleds.

In the very early days, mail delivery was accomplished with horse-drawn vehicles until 1923, when the diary notes; "The mail carrier had an automobile for the first time." Road conditions in the summertime must have brought earlier delivery for everyone, and for these people who welcomed a friendly face and a little diversion from work, we're sure his brief visit was welcomed.

Another notation in 1923 indicated that the roads started thawing early in March, and when "Mr. Wolf went to visit the home of Mr. Wloch on horseback, he tied his horse to a tree and went on a foot."

Two auctions caught the attention of the family that year. Mr. Wloch sold out at auction in August, and Will Warren also sold out by auction. Warren owned a sawmill in the eastern part of Halifax. From that auction, the diary mentioned "buying a feather bed, organ and a pair of horse collars."

Between 1900 and 1926, there were six more auctions. The attending of auctions also meant saying good-bye to neighbors and friends. Notations revealed they went to the following auctions: Sam Niles, Mr. Hicks, Ed Larrabee, Mrs. Ball, Wilson Pike, and Royal Collins.

* * *

Well, at least the year 1923 started with a bright spot in the neighboring town of Jacksonville. On January 27, "the people in Jacksonville turned on their electric lights tonight."

This was a time of inventions, and we are sure that no one enjoyed these happenings more than the people who lived out in the country or in more unpopulated areas. To have electricity in the barn was a great asset, and therefore lanterns were not needed as much, thus eliminating a potential fire hazard.

While the family mentioned the invention of the "graph-o-phone," it was during the 1920s that they were intrigued by two new inventions. April 1925: "I heard their radio—it was fine—the first one I ever heard." Seventeen years later, the radio was mentioned again. The water pipes froze in December and they finally got the water running at three o'clock, a sound "better than the radio." Another notable event was "the first moving picture in the Knight of Honor Hall—the films got on fire, so the people rushed out."

At least one happy occasion was recorded for July 10, 1925: "Reception tonight in the North River Hall for Wesley Stone and bride."

Neighbors relied on neighbors in time of need. One such time was noted in 1926 when Mr. Hatch came to get their help and use their telephone because his horse had broken through the barn floor. Telephones were not widely available and so often times neighbors used the Eames family phone.

It wasn't until 1929 that a diary entry spoke of the family buying a new car, an Essex, for $925. A diary entry mentioned a trip they took in their new car. "We went to Brattleboro today, the road was rough, Ed had a sick headache, Pa was cross and I was tired."

Various jobs spoken of in the diaries related to the "hard work" emphasized earlier. When we were first introduced to this family, wood was being cut in the woods and was the main source of heat for the family home. Also, "sugar wood" had to be cut for the fires for the boiling of maple sap in the early spring. Snow season kept the family busy. A team of horses pulling a two-runner sled through the sugar bush broke sugar roads. Later the road was used to gather the sap. Sap buckets were also scattered at the trees, ready for the trees to be tapped and the expected sap run. Cold nights and warm days during the month of March produced a good sap run. In the time period in which these diaries were written, the sap was gathered by hand in buckets and poured in a gathering tub drawn by horses or oxen. There were times when not even a pair of snowshoes held you up while carrying buckets of sap. From the gathering tub, sap was piped into a storage tub at the sugarhouse. From there, gravity feed took over and the sap ran into the evaporator and was controlled by a faucet. Once in the evaporator, sap was boiled at 219 degrees to evaporate the water. The boiling of the sap at the sugarhouse filled the air with a sweet aroma. It takes about forty gallons of sap to make a gallon of syrup. The bigger the evaporator, the faster the water evaporates. For instance, with a 4' x 12' evaporator, about four gallons of syrup can be made in an hour. A hydrometer is used to measure the density of the liquid so those state standards can be met. When the sap becomes syrup, it is piped into a filter tank that strains and purifies it. The hot syrup is then poured into containers and sealed, ready to be enjoyed on sugar-on-snow, hot pancakes, or in general cooking. It is a coincidence that while interviewing Malcolm Sumner for the above description of boiling syrup, we learned that he purchased, along with his father, his first sugaring equipment from the Eames family. The family filled a lot of syrup orders by shipping in crates that they made. In 1913, a gallon of syrup made by them sold for 75 cents. The price in 1944 was $3.25. Today's prices range between forty and fifty dollars a gallon.

Soon after the snow and frost left the ground, the ground had to be readied for the planting of corn and potatoes. The family raised a few sheep that had to be sheared, and in order to put the livestock out to pastures, fences had to be mended. These were all chores that couldn't be done in the winter.

* * *

With the warmer weather, gardens had to be planted, and by the end of June, silos were being filled with green fodder. Later, in July and August, they "hayed until the stars shone." Many times neighbors were hired to help with the workload, both in and out of the house.

Harvest time meant preserving food for winter months. This was done by canning and drying. Apples were picked and stored in bins in the cellar, along with potatoes. Cider was made from the apples and stored in kegs. Butchering was done in late fall. On one occasion, "the men cut up half the pig and made twenty-five pounds of sausage with Old Plantation seasoning."

During the winter, ice was cut with a special saw on nearby ponds, one of which was Roberts Pond in Jacksonville, now called Laurel Lake. Some of the customers who purchased ice were W. P. Gates, J. Corkins, and Norton Thurber. E. C. Larrabee ordered 325 cakes of ice, which the Eames family delivered in thirteen trips. They received eight dollars for drawing [delivering] and four dollars for cutting. Each load consisted of twenty-four cakes of ice.

Each day was devoted to the farm, which supplied a good percentage of their food, while the sale of eggs, apples, syrup, potatoes, and ice provided them with cash for property taxes and other necessities. When possible, the men worked for the town shoveling snow or whatever jobs were available.

One of the daily chores of Ed, the Eames' son, was to check the traps he had set. As noted in the diary in 1920, four foxes, fourteen rats, and one mink all sold for $127.50. However, four years later, neither trapping nor hunting were allowed because of dry weather conditions at that time. Twenty years later, "around nine in the morning, Cleon Upton dropped dead in the river near Harry Morse's in Medburyville* off Route 9 on the way to Bennington. He had a pack of traps on his back. His wife and mother-in-law were watching him from the road. The funeral was held in West Dover, Vermont.

At night, after milking was done, the cattle were fed and bedded down, their day's work was finished, only to start again the next morning.

Interspersed in the diaries were notations of Mrs. Eames' chores. She was always busy preparing meals—washing, ironing, cleaning, papering, and all the other jobs that were required in the house.

Even though the farm required a lot of their time, they still enjoyed going to a movie, paying the neighbors a visit, and also sharing their evening meal with

---

* A very small community within the town of Wilmington

friends who dropped by. Now and then there were anniversary or birthday parties to attend. One entry mentioned, "attending the 17th birthday party of Mabel Canedy. About sixty attended the party and had a fine time."

* * *

In those days dentists also visited the house, which is how Dr. Richie "who pulled Joe's tooth for four dollars" came to be mentioned in the diaries.

Of course for general aches there were people like Watson Hicks, who sold Watkins extracts and medicine. A family member had their eyes tested and was charged two dollars; the eyeglasses cost fourteen dollars. Another diary entry told of a neighbor who suffered from "milk leg," which is "a painful swelling of the leg at childbirth caused by inflammation and clotting in the veins," according to Webster's Dictionary.

Dr. Hopkins, a local veterinarian, checked and tested the cattle for tuberculosis. The State of Vermont required these tests at no charge.

Tragic accidents also happened. "Floyd Stone got badly cut with a saw. The cut was 14 inches long and took 60 stitches." And "Oscar Gates was killed in the Harrisville Mill. The belt broke and a piece of steel flew and hit him. It lodged in his heart."

There were three paragraphs relating to the 1938 flood. On Wednesday, September 21: "Rained hard all the morning. Then the storm began about two-thirty. Rained, hailed and the wind blew a hurricane until dark. They said nine inches of rain fell. The men went out after dark and got 'Ruby,' the heifer, and then stayed up until eleven o'clock. The next day was pleasant." The morning after the disaster, "No roads, no telephone, no radio. Just water everywhere—could not get to Jacksonville. Moody came home at three o'clock a foot. They worked until midnight to save the village from going. The men went and fixed the fence on the Gallup pasture. The next day was pleasant." The dam referred to is in Jacksonville, the next town over. On the third day, "They fixed the school flat so Moody came home with the car at noon. Marion was over and told the news. It took the cylinder from Hager's Dam, Roberts Grist Mill, Cement bridge back of Floyd Reed's and the Clyde Reed's store, and moved Mrs. Stowe's barn, part of Leon Williams' house, and the three bridges by Hager's."

During World War II, the diaries did not escape Mrs. Eames' pen. Notations said, "Edward paid for two defense bonds $15.00 and one for Pa $7.50." Gas was rationed and the family, "got gas coupons for the 3rd quarter in 1944 and turned in six coupons, which bought 30 gallons of gas." In January 1946, she wrote, "no butter—in the stores anywhere." On November 4, 1950 she noted, "we come down 57 years ago. It was colder and the road was not as good."

The diaries leave us with the elder "Pa" having died, leaving the mother and her son to carry on the farm. Poor health and age were noted by Mrs. Eames, who wrote of being lonesome and missing "Pa."

~ *Elaine Fairbanks*

HAYING THE WAY IT WAS

Cutting the tall grass was done with scythes and later with mowing machines.

Farm Festivals
Harper & Brothers, NY 1881

Farm Festivals
Harper & Brothers, NY 1881

Horace Learnard   HHS

Many times women or children operated the raking machine.

Unidentified

After the hay dried, it was raked into long rows. The rows were then rolled with pitchforks into piles and loaded onto the wagons.

Halifax Center   Photo courtesy Gregg Orifici

Whitneyville

The person on top of the wagon usually drove the horses and packed the hay down as each new batch was thrown on. This was a family affair with everyone helping out. Children would also ride on top of the hay and help with packing it down. Lastly the hay was tossed with pitchforks into the barn.

Left on his doodlebug, Rolland Pearl Hubbard

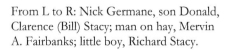

Above photos HHS

From L to R: Nick Germane, son Donald, Clarence (Bill) Stacy; man on hay, Mervin A. Fairbanks; little boy, Richard Stacy.

Photo courtesy Barbara Stacey Brooks
~ *Carrie Perna*

SECTION SEVEN
COMMERCIAL LIFE

WEST HALIFAX GENERAL STORE – 1908

Halifax Business Directory.

Collins R., Jr..General Dealer in Dry Goods, Groceries,
    Boots, Shoes, &c., West Halifax
Harris, E..Manufacturer and Dealer in Chair Stock,
    District No 10
Harrington J. L., M.D..Residence Halifax Center
Scott M., 2d..Residence West Halifax
Stark J..Proprietor Hotel, South Halifax, District No 3
Stone E..Manufacturer and Dealer in Chair Stock,
    District No 2
Tucker A. J..Proprietor Tannery, West Halifax
Worden G. P..Residence West Halifax
Warren, G..Manufacturer and Dealer in Chair Stock,
    also all kinds of Lumber, District No 11

WEST HALIFAX

Town of Halifax
Scale 30 Rods to the Inch

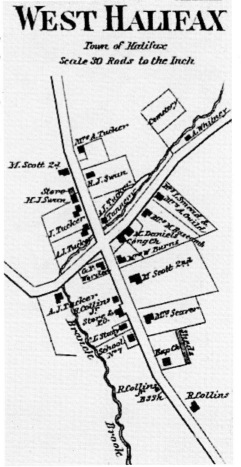

Detail Beers Map

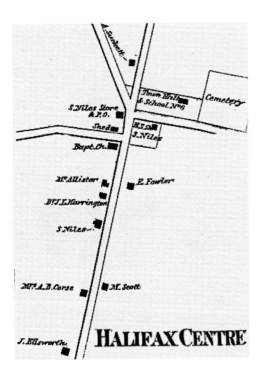

HALIFAX CENTRE

Previous page: Proprietor, George Lyman Clark (1845–1912), wife, Sarah Jennie Follett (1850–1910) and daughter, Clara, who married storekeeper George Chase.

Note the campaign posters of William H. Taft and his running mate James Sherman who were elected in 1908. Also note the lower left pane of glass, which was replaced with a letter delivery box.

INDUSTRIES

FRONTIER HARVEST POTASH

The first cash crop for Halifax settlers was potash. This "dirty unromantic substance"[1] was the by-product resulting from clearing densely forested land, using felled trees to build log houses, and burning the leftover tree parts. As early as 1764, the account book kept by Richard Ellis at his store and ashery in Colrain lists payments to Halifax settlers for bushels of ashes delivered to the store and traded for commodities such as nails, sugar, rum, and tea.

Another early record of the commercial value of potash dates from about 1774. When asked to underwrite the cost of a petition to the king requesting confirmation of their New Hampshire grants, several Halifax settlers donated money, but most donated products and labor. More than any other commodity, "Salts" appeared on the list of donations shown here. These may have been black salts of pearl ash, a purified form of potash. Potash was used to make soap, glass, printing ink, and gun powder.

> Subscriptions raised to send a petition to the King, to con-firm our lands to us, who settled them under New Hampshire charters.
>
> From Draper, and Halifax
>
> Sam'l Murdock, in work, 1 dollar.   Benj'n Henry, 1 dollar.
> John Rugg, 1 dollar, in salts.   Phineas Smith, 1 dollar in salts.
> Simeon Smith, 1 dollar in pails. Israel Guild, 1 dollar, in salts.
> Sam'l. Brown, s3, in salts. Capt. Nathan Williams, 1 dollar, salts
> Elisha Pratt, s3, in salts.   Simeon Smith Jr s3, in salts.
> James Woodward, 1 dollar, in salts.   Joseph Stewart, 1 dollar.
> Sam'l Woodward, 1 dollar, salts.   John Stewart, s3, in salts.
> Tho's Williams, 1 dollar, in boards. Jacob Shepherd, half a dollar
> Edw'd Harris, 1 dollar, in smith work.   Elijah Clark, 1 dollar.
> Tho's Clark, s4, in butter.   Sam'l Thomas, s7, Lawful Money.
> Peleg Thomas, s6, L. Money.   John Thomas, s6, L. Money.
> Sam'l Baker, s6, in salts.   Asa Haven, one dollar.

VHS, Phelps Collection, undated loose paper, courtesy library staff

Potash kilns, though not mapped, apparently were widely distributed throughout the town. References appear in property descriptions, surveys, and meeting records. For example, at a meeting in October of 1786, it was "Voted that the Surveyors be directed not to obstruct Jonathan Lamb in Building a potash on the highway near his Tanyard in Halifax" [HLR 1A: 435]. Lamb's property was in Lot 41 on Hall Road. A 1790 deed between Amos Muzzy and Isaac Orr describes "a certain tract of land . . . where Muzzy has dug and turned the waters out of the brook to accommodate a pearlash" [HLR 2: 57]. The Orr/Muzzy property was in Lot 21 on Stow Mountain Road. Moses Jackson conveyed to Dudley Fish and Benjamin Henry Jr., a piece of land "with the potash Stand Standing thereon and three potash kettles and three fireboil kettles with all the other tools belonging to said Potash" [HLR 2: 406]. Fish & Henry's ashery was in Lot 6 on Route 112 on the state line. In 1829, the selectmen laid out a new road beginning "about 3 rods west of the Potash now in the occupancy of Simeon Fish, [Dudley's brother] on the south line of Halifax and on the north line of Massachusetts."[2]

FIRST ESSENTIAL INDUSTRY MILLS

A major attraction for pioneer settlers who chose Halifax was the abundance of waterpower. The North and Green Rivers offered multiple sites suitable for industrial use. Therefore, it is not surprising one of the first published maps of the town featured mills and owners. Even though ownership changed frequently, and buildings and dams succumbed to fire and floods, mills were rebuilt, and the same sites continued in use well into the twentieth century. Mills saved manpower. A water wheel used to rotate millstones to grind grain replaced the labor-intensive hand-plumping process. Water-powered saws cut boards to build frame houses that replaced log dwellings. Mills were an essential contribution to the growth and prosperity of the town.

This 1796 Vermont map (right), published by C. E. Bohn, locates the families of David Allen and Samuel Thomas on the Green River, Joseph Tucker at Halifax Center, Joseph McClure in West Halifax, and Daniel Sumner and Philemon Stacy on the North River. Stacy's mill was located at the Gorge. Sumner's mill may have been on Route 112, or on Pennell Hill where he first settled. The symbols for gristmills are displayed as circles with spokes. A sawmill was located on McClure's land. The meeting house symbol (building with cross) represents the original Congregational and town meeting house at the Center.

Halifax detail Sotzmann 1796
David Rumsey Map Collection
www.davidrumsey.com

A great boon to women was the introduction of carding machines, which saved long tedious hours of preparing the wool for spinning and weaving, and fulling machines, which saved laborious hand washing and finishing the woven cloth. These processes were offered at several locations, as shown by classified ads published in both *The Reporter* of Brattleboro and the *Gazette & Courier* of Greenfield.

Take Notice.
The subscriber wishes to in-
form his friends and the public that his
Carding Machines
in Halifax, about 50 rods weft of Mr. Knight's Mills, are now in compłete repair, where he will brake and roll wool for fix cents per lb. and for rolling only, four cents. Moft kinds of country produce will be received in the feafon of them, and all favers duly acknowledged by the public's humble fervant.
SYLVESTER TINKER.
Halifax, September 17th, 1806.

The Reporter, September 1806

The Subscriber informs his friends and customers that he continues to carry on the clothiers business on Green River, this season near Israel Jones's mills in Halifax and is determined in future to work as reasonable as any clothier in the neighborhood —he flatters himself that he can do his work in the neatest despatch in workman-like—those who are pleased to favor him with their custom may depend upon the strictest attention. Wanted, to hire a JOURNEY-MAN CLOTHIER, this season to whom good wages will be given, also, an APPRENTICE to the above business.
TILLINGHAST POTTER.
Halifax, July 13, 1810.

The Reporter, August 1810

The 1810 Halifax census details the impressive productivity of cloth-making machinery. David Fisher on the North River is said to "card by machine, yearly 6,000 lbs. of wool, and his fulling mill dresses yearly 3,000 yards of cloth" Tillinghast Potter's fulling mill on the Green River "dresses yearly 1,500 yards of Cloth."[3]

Although we think of the North River in terms of mill power, it is evident there were significant, though brief, efforts to establish a retail store in the area. In 1794, William Forbes, whose family operated a store in Greenfield, established a branch store on the former Stacy property. Forbes sold to James and Robert Henry. The ad placed by the Henry brothers (below) clearly indicates their interest in creating a "Country Store." Soon they transferred ownership to James Mullet,

**JAMES HENRY,
& ROBERT HENRY,**

HAVE again entered into Copartnership, under the name and firm of JAMES & ROBERT HENRY.

All persons indebted to JAMES HENRY, or to ROBERT HENRY, must make payment to the present firm of JAMES & ROBERT HENRY, by the 20th day of November next; as they are determined to close their former accounts, and other demands, by that time—any *law, usage or custom, to the contrary notwithstanding.*
JAMES HENRY,
ROBERT HENRY.

Halifax, Oct. 20, 1804.
N. B. They have as handsome an assortment of ENGLISH & WEST INDIA GOODS, on hand, as is generally found in a Country Store, and expect their Fall Supply, as usual.

Gazette & Courier, October 1804

who, after a year or so, married Lucy Henry and headed west. Other early North River mill owners were: John Kirkley; James Knight; Ashbel Mason; Timothy, Samuel and Art Woodard; David Fisher; and David Stowe. The earliest Green River sawmill land record is for Hazael Shepard for Lot 59 in 1782 [HLR 1A: 76]. In the eighteenth century, mills along the Green River also underwent a rapid succession of owners—James Barney, Nathan Hatch, Thomas Scott, Edward Harris and Israel Jones. In 1823, historian Rev. Thomas Wood reported three gristmills, eight sawmills, and four fulling mills [↺ 7, ↻ 459].

SECOND ESSENTIAL INDUSTRY BLACKSMITHING

Early settlers depended on local blacksmiths for a variety of essential commodities. Pots, kettles, fireplace cranes, hinges, and nails, as well as hardware for wheels, wagons, whiffletrees, and bridles were forged out of iron by the local smith. In a horse-drawn community, horseshoes were a mainstay of the smith's trade. In1774, Edward Harris contributed smith work to support the petition to the king. His properties included a trading store at the Center and a mill on Green River. Both were appropriate locations for a blacksmith shop. The need for smiths was widespread. Jonas Shepard [↺ 132] had been active in the Halifax community for several decades in 1792 when he placed this classified ad (right). He conveyed property to his son, Abel, near Stacey's mill. In 1823, according to historian Thomas Wood, there were six blacksmiths in Halifax [↺ 7, ↻ 467]. Three of these tradesmen arrived in Halifax after the Revolution: Thomas

WANTED,

A Journeyman Blacksmith one who is master of the trade. Constant employ and good wages will be given.

An apprentice to the above trade, about 14 years of age, is likewise wanted. Inquire of
JONAS SHEPARD, jun.
Halifax, November 7th, 1792.

Greenfield Gazette, November 15, 1792

Farnsworth, at the Center; Jesse Guild, at the corner of Hall and Jacksonville Stage Roads; and Joseph Swain, in West Halifax, on Sprague Road, then part of Stage Road. During part of his service in the Revolution, Swain, as an artificer, cared for officer's horses in General Gates's regiment on expedition from Crown

Point to Canada and back to Ticonderoga. Blacksmithing tools, such as an anvil, tongs, bellows, harnesses, and vises are itemized in his pension file.

The dependence on horses for work and travel created a commercial demand for quality stock. Horse breeding was big business in Colonial Halifax and surrounding towns. Most eighteenth century newspapers include advertisements for sires from the finest bloodlines with charismatic names such as Roebuck, King Herod, Republican and Jolly Robbin to be made available for breeding at the local inn or tavern. John Green advertised his mule.

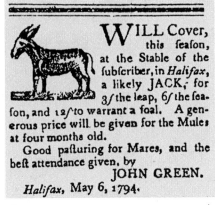

Will stand for covering, at the stable of the subscriber, in Halifax, the famous

Young HERO,

Or *CULVER HORSE*,

At 2 dolls. and 50 cents the leap, 4 dolls. the season, and 6 dolls. to insure a foal.

He is, perhaps, equal to

any horse in the state of Vermont, for a sire, and is so well known, in this and the adjacent towns, that any further description or recommendation is tho't needless. Constant attendance, and every favour gratefully acknowledged, by

CALVIN RANSOM.

Halifax, April 20, 1797.

Federal Galaxy, April 21, 1797. Courtesy Readex

WILL Cover, this season, at the Stable of the subscriber, in *Halifax*, a likely JACK, for 3/ the leap, 6/ the season, and 12/ to warrant a foal. A generous price will be given for the Mule at four months old.

Good pasturing for Mares, and the best attendance given, by

JOHN GREEN.

Halifax, May 6, 1794.

Greenfield Gazette, May 7, 1794

EARLY TANNING TRADE

At the earliest town meetings, the freemen chose, annually, a person to serve as Sealer of Leather. William Scott was the first known to hold that office [↪ 103]. Samuel Fish, cordwainer (shoemaker) and veteran of the Revolution who settled in town by 1779, served a number of terms as leather sealer. He set up a tanning operation that was carried on by his son, Nathan. His production of $1,000 worth of leather was cited in the census of 1810. Other known early tanners were Israel Bemis, Pardee Dean, Joseph Bell, Jonathan Lamb, Lucius Gillett, Stephen Gates, and Josephus Richardson. In 1797, a fully described tanning operation was advertised for sale to settle the estate of Jareb Crosby. His tannery included a bark mill. Tannic acid found in oak and hemlock bark was used to preserve leather hides. The hides would be laid in shallow clay pits and soaked in water and

TO be sold at public vendue, on Monday, the 23d day of April next, at 2 o'clock P. M. at the dwelling house of Calvin Ransom, innholder in Halifax—the Real Estate of Jareb Crosby, deceased, containing Forty Acres of LAND, with a dwelling house, tan yard, bark house, and bark mill ; lying about half a mile from the meeting house, on the road from Halifax to Colrain. The pay can be made easy. For particulars, inquire of the subscriber, in Somerset, or of Calvin Ransom, in Halifax, Vermont.

SILAS CROSBY, *Administrator*.

March 12, 1798.

Federal Galaxy, March 13, 1798. Courtesy Readex

bark to cure. Thus tannery sites required a water source and a sizeable area of flat ground. The demand for shoes, boots, saddles, bridles, harnesses, especially during the time of rapid population growth after the Revolution, suggests there was sufficient business for multiple tanners in diverse locations [↪ 465].

~ *Constance Lancaster*

MILLS

By the middle of the 1800s, another industry came into vogue. As the log homes decayed or were outgrown by families, and with the invention of the up and down saw, Vermonters set their hand to making framed houses. They took advantage of the many rivers and brooks, using the water from them to power the many, many sawmills that sprung up. Some towns would have as many as three or four sawmills.

These early sawmills sported wooden water wheels. Perhaps the most popular of these wheels were the overshot wheel. This type of wheel was turned by the weight of the water falling from above. It required a dam, the water being delivered by a channel called a millrace. The paddles of the wheels were formed into buckets. A ten-foot wheel had about twenty-four buckets, and a twenty-foot wheel had about fifty-six buckets. The overshot wheel was preferred because of its efficiency, which reached up to seventy-five percent.

As sawmills were needed, some talented men made their living by designing and building them. The miller, millward, or millwright was a special man. He was accomplished in many areas. He was a carpenter, engineer, basic mechanic, and had knowledge of hydraulics. While some may have had formal training as millwrights, some Yankee carpenters learned the trade by visiting existing mills and studying them.

* * *

In many instances the sawmill was a gathering place for locals to catch up on gossip or news of the outside world. However, the most important function of the mill was to provide the service of sawing lumber for the people who abandoned their log cabins and built the beautiful frame houses and barns, many of which still stand today.

Sawmills provided many jobs for people of that era. Some mills employed as many as thirty men. The men not only worked in the mill itself, but they were choppers, haulers of the logs, and pilers of the sawed lumber in the lumber yard.

By the early 1900s, the circular saw had been invented and the wooden water wheel became obsolete with the invention of the steam powered engine. The steam provided more power, and less consideration was needed regarding the water level of the river or brook. These steam mills, however, required a boiler. Some of these boilers used the sawdust and shavings from the mill as fuel.

One long ago scene was that of logs floating on a river on their way to a sawmill. The logs were put into the river near the site where they were cut, and then they floated down to the mill. The river provided a much faster way to transport many logs to the mill than by horse and wagon.

A long ago sound was that of a whistle that was blown at certain times of the day by the firemen of the steam sawmills. Many people waited for the noon day whistle, especially if they were working in the fields or in their gardens.

While the sawmills provided a necessary service and created jobs, there were certain dangers that lurked in these old mills. Some of the safety features of today had not made their debut and men lost life and limb, either from getting too close to the saw, or by logs rolling on them. Also many a miller lost his life as he was tending the primitive water wheel mills. He would slip into the wheel and be crushed to death.[4]

~ Bernice Barnett

According to land records, Philemon Stacy purchased from Ezekiel Bundy and Asa Starkweather a sawmill that was built before 1780. It was located on the North River at the foot of the hill below the Gorge [HLR 1A: 29]. Stacy's will, dated 1786, also mentions a corn mill that was deeded to his son, Philemon. The sawmill was then deeded to his son, Joseph. The sawmill had several owners, including Fred May Sr., who owned it in the early 1900s and passed it down to his son, Fred Jr. They produced chair stock.

"Elias Stone's saw-mill and chair stock . . . is operated by an excellent water-privilege. The mill was formerly used as a grist and carding-mill and cloth dressing factory, and was converted into its present use by Mr. Stone in 1845. He turns out about $6,000.00 worth of chair stock per annum."[56] By 1888, Elias and his son-in-law Charles F. Clark had added to their business that of turning hubs and handles for children's carriages. They bought a hardwood timber lot and shipped a large amount of ash lumber from their mills [HLR 15: 373]. Their chair stock "was sold to . . . plants in Gardner, Wakefield, and Baldswinville; while tennis rackets were sold in Chicopee, Massachusetts, and Pawtucket, Rhode Island."[7] In the early 1920s, Frank H. Stone purchased the buildings, machinery, tools, and the mill, which he operated until the early 1950s [HLR 19: 362–363].

During its lifespan, many families and individuals worked at Stone's sawmill. Philip G. Hardgrove worked at the mill in the 1940s. He remembers "the mill was operated by a steam engine and a fireman named Shelley kept the boiler going all night during the winter until the 7 or 8 o'clock workers arrived. Shelley also stacked lumber and drove a team of horses. He lived in the mill yard area where other employees lived. The space in his cabin or 'shanty' was approximately 8 foot by 6 foot. Another worker,

STONE'S SAWMILL   Photo Porter Thayer, Postcard HHS

'Frenchie,' also worked with Shelley cutting trees. They never used a power saw; only a crosscut saw. The wheels on the mill's engine were six feet high. When the governor stuck, the whole mill vibrated. And everyone ran except one person, who had to run back and shut off the steam valve."[8] Phil remembered others who worked at the mill, among them Rolland W. "Hap" Hubbard, Walter Dean, Fred Pollard, Norman McKinnon, Herman Drost, John Bezanson, Raymond Wrisley, and Clint Pease. Small cabins lined the immediate area along Route 112 in the vicinity of Frank's large two-story home (next page), which was located across Route 112 away from the mill. Josephine Costello cooked and served meals for those who boarded at the house and worked at the mill. The rooms in the house were large, with several bedrooms upstairs and a small first-floor apartment at the rear of the house.

The part of Hubbard Hill that joins Route 112 has been rerouted. It used to curve sharply near the woodshed area of the home of F. H. Stone. This home, purchased by Herman and Thelma Drost, burned in 1969. John and Thelma Bezanson and family lived in the area. Raymond and Ellen Wrisley and family lived in a cabin in the area, also. Across Hubbard Hill from the woodshed stood a

Painting donated by Brenda Drost Kempton. HHS
MILL WORKERS LODGING

square run-down house with a large chimney, which was probably occupied in the 1930s. Harry Murdock Sr. and his wife, and Robert Green and his wife, Lottie, were among the last to live in the house. Harry Murdock and Robert Green went over the bank near the May mill with F. H. Stone's Mack truck loaded with lumber.[9] Neither was hurt, and the truck made its regular trip Friday.

"Frank B. Stone [no relation to Frank H. Stone] came to this valley in 1882 and ran a sawmill for a Mr. Mowry of Readsboro."[10] After running the mill for two years he bought it and a sawmill has been in the family ever since. About 1912 it burned and was rebuilt. It was then operated with a steam engine and sported one of the first circular saws in Halifax. This mill later had wood lathes for the turning of hardwood chair stock. In 1976, James and Virginia Stone's son, Craig, started the only sawmill business in town. It is located on the former James Niles property adjacent to the former Valley School property, which is now the home of James and Virginia Stone. "Now, the sawing is done on a Lane handset circular saw, powered by a diesel engine. People come from all over to get a bottom sawed for a boat or the runners for a sled."[11]

OTHER MILLS

Another early mill on the North River was located on a small brook that empties into the North River near the present Butler home. James Stone, a lifelong resident of Halifax until his death in 2005 believed that this mill was a gristmill owned by Captain James Roberts, who later moved to Jacksonville [HTC: GL, 1851–1946]. This mill may still have been in operation in 1892 under the ownership of James Roberts and Chester Guild.

John Reid bought property on the Green River from Holbrook and Fessenden in 1829 [HLR 6: 455]. Reid and later owners used this site as a gristmill, sawmill, and cider mill. Chair stock was turned there, wagons manufactured, and during the fall, cider jelly was produced. The mill burned and was rebuilt in 1900. It remained in the Warren family until the middle 1920s. It fell into disrepair about 1940. A wooden flume brought water to the mill site. A worker of the mill went to the Marlboro Pond (South Pond) area to open the gate and later it was necessary to close it at the end of the day."[12]

Detail McClellan
Key:
BS – blacksmith
SM – sawmill.

Jesse Gates owned and operated a lumber and jelly mill in 1885, which was about one tenth of a mile west of the Warren mill. "J. E. Gates is making preparation to start his jelly mill early in November."[13]

HHS   HHS

Left to right—Gilman, William, and Mable Warren; Clara, Addie Warren, and Mary (wife of Wm.). Hired man holding Spot, the family dog. Horses with teamsters. Warren house and mill, which could be seen from the house before the trees grew up.

Two early mills were in operation in Harrisville. Elisha Otis, the man of elevator fame, built a mill in 1838.[14] This mill engaged in the manufacture of wagons and carriages. It is not quite clear when the other mill was established; however, Joshua Harris Jr. owned a mill in 1853 [HLR 11: 8]. "Harris Brothers have bought the saw mill and chair shop with house attached of their father, J. R. Harris and will commence to run it immediately."[15] According to information gleaned from *Vermont Phoenix* articles, some time after 1853, Lorenzo Harris came into possession of the mill. In 1865, he filed for bankruptcy, after which there were several more owners. Eventually, it was owned by Albert Thurber and lastly by George Hill. Raymond Miller, who owned a fish farm and designed and built a small hydroelectric power plant near the site, which has remained in the family since his death in 2007 [HLR 11: 8].

Other early sawmills in West Halifax Village, according to Blanche Legate Sumner, were as follows: "A sawmill stood by the bridge, which leads to Mr. Sprague's. Seth Worden built this soon after the first houses. A. F. Worden built a chair shop on the same site about 1850. Lewis Sumner built another sawmill about a quarter of a mile below this one more than eighty years ago. This burned on Christmas day in 1857 and was rebuilt the following spring. This was torn down and the present mill built 1880."[16] It was also a grist, cider, and shingle mill. In 1928, the mill was moved across the road and converted to use a diesel-powered engine.[17]

Detail McClellan

The Denison sawmill was in existence in 1850 in the eastern part of town.[18] He said Peter Worden Jr. formerly owned it [HTC: GL 1833]. A Halifax grand list book lists a Peter Worden Mill in 1833. According to Freeman, it was in operation until sometime in the 1890s and also was a chair-stock factory.

~ Bernice Barnett and Elaine Fairbanks

FAR CORNERS MILLS

Several less central and therefore less familiar milling operations appear on maps and in other printed sources. The McClellan and Beers maps show a sawmill in the northeast corner of Halifax near the Phelps and Fessenden properties. The *Vermont Phoenix* of September 24, 1869 reported, "Nathan Phelps of Halifax is repairing his saw-mill, putting in a new wheel and making other improvements, to be ready for fall business." Perhaps because of its location, this mill dam has withstood the ravages of floods; the stone foundation is clearly visible from Hale Road just beyond the turn onto Thomas Hill Road.

The Hagar Mill (right) was located in the southwest corner of Halifax off McMillan Road. Maps place the family home in Halifax, with the sawmill located across the line in Whitingham. Child's gazetteer lists Albert M. V. Hager's sawmill and chair-stock factory in Halifax.[19] In the business directory, Mr. Hagar is described as, "justice of the peace, proprietor of saw-mill and chair-stock factory, farmer" owning 126 acres on road 54 and employing his sons, Freeman and John M.[20] His mill is listed again in the Whitingham business directory.

HAGER MILL   HHS

In this same area, Norris Shepherdson, an owner of the Deacon John Pennell house, is thought to have set up a mill on Fowler Brook. September 1882: "A. E. Day has sold about 15 acres of his 'Miller' lot lying near 'Fowler Brook' to N. H. Shepardson who intends to erect a wood mill thereon"[21] and the foundation of a crib mill is visible in the brook that runs behind the house.

LOGGING THE WAY IT WAS   HHS

Postcard back

"Dear Hen,
Will write
just a line to
let you know I
am pretty well
and will send you
a picture that you probably
will not know.
Uncle Geo"

Postcard from Uncle George to Mr. Henry Porter, not mailed, undated.

UNPRECEDENTED FLOOD

The *Vermont Phoenix* describes the ravages of the storm on October 3–4, 1869. A calm sunny day was followed by thirty-six hours of unrelenting rain. The flood report and details of destruction to Brattleboro and many surrounding towns appeared in the October 8 issue. The following week's issue included additional reports, and from the Halifax correspondent we learn:

> Halifax – The flood in this town, as in others in the neighborhood, was very destructive to property, but fortunately, no lives were lost. On the North River, a branch of the Deerfield, which runs for the distance of about seven miles through the southwesterly part of town, all the bridges but one were swept away. Wm. Mowrey's sawmill and broom handle factory, with their entire contents and the dam, were washed away. Elias Stone's chair factory was severely damaged, and two dams carried away. The road along this river was badly damaged in many places, and it will take weeks to repair it. On the stream that rises in Marlboro and runs through West Halifax, the bridges for two miles are all washed away and the road rendered impassable. Tucker's[,] Worden's and Sumner's dams are all carried away. The damage to Tucker's tannery besides the dam is $200. All the bridges but two on Green River in Halifax are gone, and the road badly cut up and impassable for the present. Throughout the town generally all the roads along the streams are badly washed and gullied and the bridges destroyed. Many individuals have sustained greater or less damage to their property, but it is impossible to estimate the exact amount of their loss.[22]

STONE AND CLARK MILL   VHS

~ Constance Lancaster

TANNERIES

During the 1800s, tanning was an up-and-coming business. The 1810 census documents two separate tanneries owned by Pardee Dean and Nathan Fish. Also listed in the Halifax grand lists book were four other tanneries: the Daniel Dean Tannery (1834); the Warren White Tannery (1834); the Goodwin Tannery (1845), which was transferred to Caleb Corkins; and the Nicholas Clark Tannery (1847), which was transferred to S. Plumb with a reference to ninety-five acres [HTC, GL, 1834, 1845, 1847].

Albert J. Tucker's tannery at West Halifax, was established by Nathan W. Halladay about 1836. By 1860, it had been rebuilt five times. Hamilton Child's gazetteer lists Albert Tucker as owner of the tannery in 1884.[23] The *Vermont Phoenix* noted he had bought the tannery in 1860 and that "He employs fourteen men and tans 400 sides of leather per week, manufacturing upper leather extensively. The establishment is operated by both steam power using 500 to 600 cords of bark per annum."[24] The tannery was located near Branch Brook on land that is now owned by Roger and Betty Dann. According to Mary Reynolds's genealogy records, the James Plumb tannery was in existence in West Halifax from 1852 to 1859, and the owner moved from Halifax to Wisconsin.[25]

FIRE IN WEST HALIFAX, VT.—The Tannery in West Halifax, owned by Nicholas Clark, Esq., and occupied by Messrs. C. S. & M. S. Stearns, was destroyed by fire about 3 o'clock on Thursday morning last. The loss is estimated at $3,000, about half of which is covered by insurance.

Semi-Weekly Eagle, May 5, 1849

HHS

TWO VIEWS OF THE COLLINS ROAD BRIDGE

Fire.
The tannery owned by A. H. Tucker & Co., at West Halifax, VT. was burned on Saturday morning, the 28th. Loss estimated at $8,000. The property was insured for $4,000 in Home Insurance Co. of New York.   *Phoenix*, May 1, 1866

* * *

A. H. Tucker & Co. of West Halifax are rebuilding their tannery that was lately burned. Have got the frame up and partly covered, will start business again soon.
Phoenix, May 29, 1866

Photo Porter Thayer, HHS

Maude Hebard mentioned a tannery on Pennell Hill.[26] It is believed that the Burrington family once owned it. Another very early tannery was located on the Sperry Brook on Stage Road, leading from Halifax Center to West Halifax. The closest residents at that time were C. M. Rice and J. Tucker. Records indicate that James Tucker and Jonas Scott owned a tannery there [HLR 12: 427].

Detail McClellan

SHOEMAKING

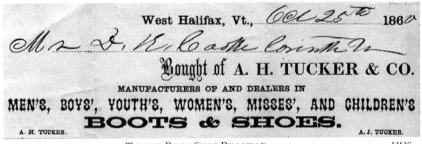

West Halifax, Vt., *Oct 25th* 186*2*

Mr. D. K. Castle Corinth Vt.

Bought of A. H. TUCKER & CO.

MANUFACTURERS OF AND DEALERS IN

MEN'S, BOYS', YOUTH'S, WOMEN'S, MISSES', AND CHILDREN'S

BOOTS & SHOES.

A. H. TUCKER.   A. J. TUCKER.

TUCKER BOOT SHOP BILLHEAD   HHS

Boot shop on Collins Rd. HHS

Photo C. Perna

In the village of West Halifax, just up the hill from the bridge on Collins Road, there was a boot shop, which, it is believed Samuel A. Clark owned and then sold to a Harvey J. Swan. In 1869, Swan sold his store and shop to Jesse M. Niles [HLR 13: 566], who conveyed the shop to the G. A. R in 1896 [HLR 16: 319].

The *Vermont Phoenix* newspaper, dated 1888, stated, "Clark and Ballou were making preparations to double their moccasin and mitten business for the season. They cut their boots that year after an entirely new pattern invented by Mr. Clark. His pattern did away with the back seam, which was so troublesome to sheepskin boot manufacturers."

Blanche Legate Sumner said, A "house owned by Frank Hill was built by Samuel Clark: The lower part of the house being used as a shoe store and the upstairs for the custom manufacture of boots and shoes. The main part of the house next to the schoolhouse [which] was formerly a shed to the lower store, burned some years ago. The upper part of it being used at one time for a tailor's shop."[27]

BLACKSMITHS

Several residents engaged in the art of blacksmithing near the Scott homestead in the Center. Among these were Luther Farnsworth, S. P. Worden, Jack Scott, James Sackett, and Alva A. Fairbanks. Land records indicate that John Alverson was a blacksmith [HLR 1A: 169, 4: 322]. His business was located in Lot 54, which would place it somewhere in Reid Hollow. In West Halifax, Francis T. Miner operated a blacksmith shop in 1868 and the shop was still in business in 1920.[28]

W. E. CLARK,
BLACKSMITH,
WEST HALIFAX, – VT.

Having purchased the Shop and Tools of F. T. Miner, I am prepared to do all kinds of work in my line in a thorough and workmanlike manner.

I have engaged Mr. F. E. Leman, an experienced and first-class workman, to work for me, and I guarantee all my work to give satisfaction in both quality and price.

Hoping to receive and merit your patronage I can be found at the old stand near the Baptist Church.

HHS   Annual Report February 10, 1885 HHS

BLACKSMITH SHOP RE-OPENED!

HAVING LEASED THE BLACKSMITH SHOP

AT PLUMB HOLLOW,

In Halifax,

AND FITTED IT UP WITH

NEW TOOLS,

I am prepared, with the aid of first class workmen, to do *all kinds* of

SHOEING AND BLACKSMITH WORK.

We buy and use only the best kinds of iron and are determined all our work shall be of the first quality and give satisfaction.

By doing work promptly and in an efficient manner we trust we may receive a portion of your patronage.

F. T. MINER.

West Halifax, May 5, 1868.

HHS

HHS

Top left: Shop once owned by J. Swain, later by W. Upton, B. Newell: located on Sprague Road. Top right: Shop once owned by F. T. Miner, later by W. E. Clark, Zina Learnard, Emery Whitney, located next to the West Halifax Baptist Church.

According to a taped interview with Archie Whitney, "The blacksmith shop located by the West Halifax Community [Baptist] Church was a two-story building. A woodworking shop occupied the second floor. I remember helping to put linseed oil on the sleds made in that shop. The first floor had two forges and two anvils. So this enabled two blacksmiths to work shoeing horses at the same time. A building across the road was used to store and dry the lumber."[29] This building was destroyed by fire in 1920.[30] It was never rebuilt. In more recent years, Henry Wonsey conducted a horseshoeing business across the road on property where Joan and Wayne Courser now live.

OTHER INDUSTRIES

Daniel Bixby of Halifax won an award at the Windham County Agricultural Fair at Newfane, Vermont, for the best "cheese sample."[31] Floyd Canedy talked about a Mr. Harry Thompson, who had a "tin cart" business and canvassed the area. Canedy said that on Mr. Thompson's travels he met another peddler and exchanged business talk. They discovered that they had each taken some hard cheese in trade and decided to test its strength by rolling each chunk of hard cheese down the hill. "When the cheese hit the trees at the bottom of the hill, it bounced like rubber tires in the air. Each one examined the cheese and it didn't even show a dent. They figured they had gotten their money's worth."[32]

SLATE QUARRY

Courtesy C. Lancaster
PYRITE/FOOLS GOLD

Halifax had a small slate quarry. It is believed the slate was used in the manufacture of piano sounding boards. It did not prove successful and was abandoned within a few years. The opening of the quarry probably was in 1923; however, the ownership of it is not known. Only one mention of it appeared in the *Vermont Phoenix*. "John Dennis is boarding at D. E. Harris's and works at Whitneyville where he will open the quarry to show the grades of slate obtainable there."[33] A Halifax grand list book indicates that the land on which the quarry was located at one time belonged to Diantha Whitney [HTC: GL, 1903–1906] [ↄ 412]. For about three years, it was recorded as a "gold mine." Following this period of time, it was listed as just a quarry. By then, someone must have realized it was only "fools gold."

HALIFAX HAD A SKI AREA

It was started by Joseph Darrow Jr., and his wife Thelma, who moved to Vermont from New London, Connecticut, in 1948 and leased part of the former Loren Dean farm for the purpose of starting a ski-tow business. Funding was needed, so a corporation was organized, and ten people worked to get the business started. The president of the corporation was Kenneth W. Suhl, the treasurer was Stanley J. Powers, and the name was North River Ski Area, Inc. [HLR 24: 29]. Frank Stone said his family "took timber and removed the stubs." The tow was set up on the mountain behind the Niles Cemetery on Route 112. It was not successful, and in 1951 the ski area surrendered its lease to the Arthur Purrington family, who were original owners of the land. The Darrow family, whose children attended Valley School, moved away from the area. Their son, Jeff later enlisted in the armed services. From the Purringtons the property was sold to Richard Heyward and the original house divided. The ell was moved to the side hill on the same side of the road. The main part of the house was moved across the road to the field. It later burned, but was rebuilt.[34] ~ *Bernice Barnett and Elaine Fairbanks*

Cottage Industry Braiding Palm

Russell Bascom (1819–1864), a second-generation Halifax farmer, lived and worked on Collins Road north of the Hall Road intersection. The family farm included land that became a neighborhood cemetery for the Hall, Bascom, and other families. The foundation of the Solomon Bascom place is in a wooded area on the former property of Bob and Sue Rusten. Sue transplanted some of the old varieties of rose and peony bushes from the original home site.

A ledger-sized diary,[35] kept by Russell Bascom from 1838 to 1864, was donated to the New England Historic and Genealogical Society in Boston. His journal entries include details that his family supplemented their farm income by braiding palm-leaf hats. In his entries for 1858, Bascom mentions days his family worked on hats, how many they completed, and when they sold them. He mentions purchases of palm leaf from local stores and from Mr. Austin Hunt. He refers to his wife, Sally Maria Plumb (Maria), and her mother, Olive (wife of William Plumb). Others in the household include his children: George, age fourteen; Ellen, age twelve; and William, age ten; his mother, Rhoda Hall; and his brother, Luther. To create a slice of their family life and activities, not every diary entry that follows refers specifically to hat making, which seemed to occur most often on stormy days when outside activities would have been curtailed and schools were closed.

January 22 ^{d}, 1858.
>   Pleasant Drawed 4 loads of Wood I went to lyceum in the evening and carried the Schoolteacher and George and Ellen. Question for discussion: Resolved that early marriage is advisable.

23 ^{d} Pleasant Drawed 5 loads of wood I went down to the Post Office Luther went to singing School at Jacksonville and carried C. F. Griffin

February 1, 1858
>   Cold. Pleasant. Nobody went to meeting from here.

February 2 ^{d} 1858
>   Pleasant I went to Jacksonville and got 100 lb. of meal for $185. Mr. Austin Hunt came here & got 99 palm leaf hats of Maria & 101 of Mother & Olive and left 11 lbs of leaf for Maria & 20 for mother & Olive.

February 10
>   Windy. Our folks finished five Palm leaf Hats. Ellen did not go to School.

11th Cold and windy Ellen did not go to School, finished 4 hats.

12   Cold Pleasant. Luther broke out the roads Ellen did not go to School.

13   Pleasant. Father & mother Plumb was here visiting. Our folks finished thirty eight hats this week.

23   Pleasant Drawed Six Maple logs to Sumners Mill
      Mr. Washington Putnam paid me $1.00 for pig & $1.00 for making frocking
      coat. Hunt here the 22nd and got 32 hats & 20 of Mother and left 12 pounds
      of leaf for each.

24   Snowed & rained in the morning, pleasant afternoon. Paid A.K. Davis $2,
      08 for chopping. I went to the Holler, bought a cap for George & paid
      $1.02.

25 th Cloudy Maria and I went to Father Plumbs. School closed C. F. Griffin &
      Volney Clark here in the evening George and I down to red school House
      to Spelling School.

26 th Snowed about Six inches, finished threshing & cleaned up ten bushels of
      wheat. A daughter born to C. F. & Alma Griffin.

28   Very Windy. We braded palm leaf.
      March 1st, Windy

2 d   Broke out the roads I went to Mill

7   Pleasant Elder Bucklin here & I went to the hollow with him.

8   Rainy We braded palm leaf. Pleasant I carried Henry to Colerain Maria went
      to her Fathers & Perry Halls. Stopped at C. F. Griffins in the evening.

11   Pleasant Chopped in the dooryard. Dr. Streeter here & pulled two teeth for
      Maria

12 th Rainy Braded palm leaf

15   Rained hard all day. We began twenty palm leaf hats. We went to Melinda's
      wedding in the evening.

May 14, 1858:

      Pleasant Drawed stones and ploughed greensward east of the house
      Drawed three loads of manure down to the new piece and began to plant it.
      Dodge worked here. Maria & Ellen finished their palm leaf and have 214
      hats.

May 22 d

      Cloudy Luther and Olive went to Shelburne Falls and got two new axes and
      left four shovels to be repaired. I went to Jacksonville and got 9 $^{1/2}$ lbs. of
      Palm leaf for our folks and 10$^{1/4}$ for Olive.

The economics of braiding palm are not evident in this record. Bascom does not
say what they paid for the raw materials and how much they earned per hat. It is
evident a considerable amount of braiding took place in this Halifax home.

* * *

PALM-LEAF HATS MADE IN HALIFAX, VERMONT   Courtesy C. Lancaster

A three-hundred-page account book,[36] kept from 1872–1874 by Levi Murray Tucker, storekeeper of West Halifax, includes frequent references to the hat trade. During this period, about one in three families doing business with Mr. Tucker purchased raw palm leaf and traded back completed hats. The customary credit given was nine cents per hat. There is no mention of cash exchanges for hats. By comparison, Mr. Tucker credited twenty-nine cents a pound for butter and eighteen cents per dozen eggs. Groceries and general merchandise were purchased using hat credits. In his journal (right), L. M. Tucker notes receipt of men's, boys', misses' and speckled or "spec" hats. He sold palm-leaf or "leaf" for about eighteen cents a pound. Several transactions in his ledger reference the "Baptist Sewing Society." While women and children did most hat weaving or braiding in private homes, apparently the church held braiding bees as a combined social event and fund-raiser. There is no record in the ledger of what Levi Tucker did with the finished hats. West

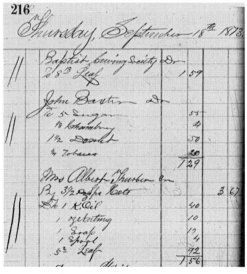

L. M. TUCKER LEDGER   Courtesy C. Lancaster

Townshend and Jacksonville were locations in Windham County, Vermont known to promote the hat business.[37] "Daniel Howard of West Townshend and Levi Howard of Jacksonville were palm-leaf hat dealers in the 1870s and 1880s."[38] During the latter part of the nineteenth century, thousands of pounds of palm leaf were converted into thousands of pounds of finished hats. The demand for palm hats was significant, as were the financial benefits to all concerned. Braiding palm was a thriving cottage industry in Halifax.

~ *Constance Lancaster*

Chapter taken from *Green Mountain Reflections*, B. B. Woods & Bernice Barnett, Halifax, VT. 1995. Used with permission.

CHAPTER 18

HOME INDUSTRIES OF YESTERYEAR

One of the stories my mother used to tell had to do with the making of palm leaf hats in the home. She used to work with her parents in this endeavor. I became so interested in the subject of home industries before the turn of the century that I did some research and would like to share it with our readers.

One such industry, now a lost art, was braiding ladies' fancy bonnets made out of palm leaves. This art is as old as history itself, the skill having been perpetuated by word of mouth from mother to daughter. In many households in Vermont, women and children made these hats.

While there are different varieties of palm leaves, it was quite likely that the cabbage palm or palmetto was used. The leaves are fan-shaped and have a shiny deep green color. They reach a maximum length of five to eight feet and are somewhat wider. For braiding, the leaves were divided into strands, two inches wide.

Recently, I spoke with mom's brother, Harold Learnard of Indiana, age 94, who remembered as a child, helping his mother trim the excess palm from the hats after they were made. He said that the palm strips were picked up at local stores where the storekeeper acted as a shipping agent. An 1846 edition of the Boston Almanac listed five firms which supplied the palm leaves.

The hats were made in several different patterns, the names of which reflect a primitive, rustic flavor such as closecurl, fishtail, gooseye, and fishpot, which

Continued

was patterned after the weave used to make fish traps. According to author Nell Kull's "History of Dover," (VT), where the hats also were made, "few hats were made in the summer months, but by early October they were brought into the local stores in considerable numbers. By January the industry was in full swing."

The hats had to be carefully braided. Reportedly, one lady made two dozen hats, but because the rim of one was a little broken, six cents was deducted from the price. She received only $1.94 for the 24 hats. On another day three ladies each received $1 for one dozen perfectly-made hats.

One of the markets for the completed hats was L. M. Mills & Sons in Amherst, MA. A notation regarding one shipment of hats reads: 380 doz. #2 hats at $.09 plus; 96 doz. #3 hats at $.08 plus; 84 doz. #2 hats at $.07 plus. From this it can be estimated that on an average the women were paid just under 10 cents per hat, but even that little bit of money went a long way in those days.

Sometimes women made baskets from the palm leaf. The market for these baskets was the Arts and Crafts Society of Boston, MA.

Making the palm hats continued into the 1920s. Finally, this home industry was forced into extinction because it became impossible to obtain the palm leaf already separated into the strips. Most Vermonters were unfamiliar with this procedure and the industry faded out of practice.

Today, making the palm leaf hats is done as a craft in the southern states, where the coconut palm is used. Anyone interested in trying their hand at this old art may obtain information by writing to Box 58, West Halifax, VT, 05358.

As the years slipped into the '30s and the Great

Continued

Depression hit with its economic hard times.
Vermonters looked to yet another source of extra
income which was not done just by the women but
enjoyed by the whole family. This industry entailed
going into the surrounding woods and picking ferns.
In those years, a few local residents called packers,
who acted as agents, shipped the ferns to the
greenhouses in larger New England cities, where they
were used in floral arrangements for weddings,
funerals, and the like.

For the families who needed extra income, picking
ferns was a convenient home industry. No babysitters
were needed. Just a basket of food and perhaps some
extra outer garments in case one of the children
accidentally fell into a brook on their way to the
woods.

The ferns were picked in the fall of the year. The
fancy fern was the one most often picked. Sometimes
the so-called dagger fern was picked, but these were
harder to find. However, the price paid for these was
a little higher.

Our family used to pick ferns. On a typical day
we'd hitch the horse to the buggy and head for the
woods. After a short ride, the horse was tied to a tree
and the family would walk farther into the deep
woods. Once a good bed of ferns was located, our
parents would designate a spot as home base. The
children were always cautioned to stay around that
area so we would never be out of hearing range from
our parents. The older kids who were taught how to
pick the ferns were promised a few pennies for their
labor, but the for most part they spent their time
playing and climbing trees. Then mom would
announce that the picnic lunch was ready. This was
usually grape jelly sandwiches made with home-baked

Continued

bread and, of course, there was always apple pie.

After lunch we'd pick more ferns and then pack them in baskets or on fern racks and head for home. On the way we children would plan how to spend the money we had earned. It was just a few pennies but the options were varied. Ice cream cones were five cents, and several trips of picking ferns would provide enough money to attend the county fair, where balloons or rides on the merry-go-round were ten cents each.

When the family got home there was still more work to be done. The ferns had to be sorted, and any that had red spots on the underside of the leaf were discarded. They also had to be at least a foot long, then tied 25 to a bunch. Then they were taken to the packers, who packed the bunches into wooden crates lined with newspapers. They would pack 200 to 250 bunches in a crate with a layer of peat moss and a couple of hemlock boughs on top to keep everything firm before the crates were nailed shut with wooden slats.

For all their labor the fern pickers got paid one cent and a half for a bunch. By the end of the season the price usually went up a quarter of a cent more. Ferning lasted into the '60s when the price per bunch had increased to four cents.

Home industries are still being pursued as a means to supplement family incomes, but today they're measured in dollars instead of pennies.

BERNICE BURNETT AND ANNETTE WOODS   HHS   Photo M. Sanders

ROADS AND TRANSPORTATION

FIRST TWO ROADS

The first mode of transportation was oxen, or horse and buggy in the summer and horse and sleigh in the winter. Before the town's government was organized in 1778, Halifax had a road known as a scout's trail. Even though there was only about a mile of this famous road that traversed Halifax, it became a very important road to the area. It was part of a military road that extended from Fort Massachusetts to Fort Dummer. Built during the French and Indians War, the mile in Halifax begins on the road in back of Gates Pond in Whitingham, joining the present-day Gates Pond Road. Following Gates Pond Road, it turns left and follows the present-day Winchester Road to the Marlboro town line.[39]

Another very early road in Halifax is the County Road, which extended from the Phillips Hill Road at the Massachusetts border, crossed the North River over a bridge below the Gorge where the Fisher Mill stood, and joined and followed the present-day Stowe Mountain Road into Halifax Center. From Halifax Center, it is called Old County Road. This road continued down through Whitneyville and crossed the Green River in Harrisville to connect with the Moss Hollow Road. It then continued through Marlboro and on to the county seat in Newfane. Parts of the Old County Road are not travelable by automobile today, but some of it can be hiked.

In 1786, the town voted that "Esq. Henry" confer with the selectmen of Colrain in regards to building a new bridge "over the North River at the ford way" [HLR 1A: 432]. Three years later, Henry Henderson of Halifax was hired by Colrain to build the bridge below his home on the present-day Route 112 [ₚ 114].

~ Bernice Barnett

RAILROAD PROSPECTS

Halifax might be very different today if the railroad had been routed through our town. What follows are articles that appeared in the Brattleboro newspapers in the late 1800s.

1882 Yesterday's Railroad Meeting – Discussion of Bonding
Halifax held an enthusiastic railroad meeting yesterday despite the storm, which prevented the attendance of those from the adjoining towns, same two zealous Wilmington citizens. The meeting organized with Warden Sumner in the chair and Millard Weeks as secretary. Upwards of 100 of the old, sturdy Halifax farmers were in attendance, and speeches were made favoring the project.

The article lists comments made by several in attendance. After these speeches, an informal vote was taken as to whether Halifax would bond or not, and nearly all of those present were favorable to bonding, provided the road came through that town. The following resolution was adopted:

Resolved, that the canvassing committee for the respective towns be invited to employ engineers and assistants and proceed at once to cause the preliminary survey to be made over the respective route between Brattleboro and Wilmington; and that this committee be authorized to call a meeting of the citizens at such times and places as in their judgment will most conduce to the advancement of the railroad interests.

February 1883

A railroad meeting will be held in the village, March 1st at 10 o'clock. . . . A town meeting will be held at the center on March 3rd at 1 o'clock, "To see if the town will vote to aid the Brattleboro and Bennington railroad in its construction; and if such aid is granted, to vote how much aid is granted, to what amount, and in what form the money shall be raised and how paid by the town.

March 27, 1885:

Halifax: Other towns are speaking of their industries, fine scenery, expectations, etc. And Halifax although she expects no railroad, and has in the past been considered free plunder for those that live by their wits, yet she wishes to let the outside world know that her pulse still beats.

January 4, 1886

This town is situated in the southern tier of towns in Windham county, bordering on the Massachusetts State line. Shelburne Falls, Mass., eleven miles to the south, Readsboro, VT., twelve miles to the west, and Brattleboro, Vt., fourteen miles to the east are her nearest railroad stations. She has had several railroad excitements; the most recent being the "Green Mountain Railroad," running north from Shelburne Falls, Mass., up North River, which soon died a natural and easy death. The last agitation was the "Brattleboro and Bennington Railroad," running westerly across the hills. This, at one time, bid fair to be a success; enthusiastic meetings were frequently held all along the line, this town bonding for $10,000, the vote standing 111 to 69. "But of all the sad words of tongue or pen, the saddest are these: it might have been." Marlboro and Whitingham, adjacent townships, refused to bond, and the enthusiasm of Halifax and the other public-spirited towns came to naught.

~ *Susan Rusten*

TRANSPORTING GOODS FROM MAKER TO MARKET

Goods were carried by wagon to the train in Shelburne Falls to be delivered to destinations where they could be sold. This was an important way for makers of chair stock to reach manufactures in Gardner, Massachusetts. Makers of palm hats, cider jelly, bundled ferns, and other farm produce were carried by trolley from the Stark's Tavern to Colrain, Massachusetts, or the stage line by South Halifax to Shelburne Falls, Massachusetts, the northern route by stage to North Adams, Massachusetts.

Some are earnestly wishing the trolley road would extend certainly as far as the Starks place, for often it is wheeling below it and sleighing this side. A short time ago several loads of apples were drawn as far as the Starks place on runners then transferred to wheels then to the electrics, making changes on an average of every five miles.

Gazette & Courier, January 12, 1901

GENERAL STORES

There were stores in town as follows: one in District 1, one in District 3, one in District 6, six different places in District 7, one in District 10, two in District 11.[40] These would be the school districts as delineated on the Beers map of 1869.

HALIFAX CENTER District 6

Colrain History says that for a few years Clark Chandler of Colrain, Massachusetts, was interested in a store in Halifax with Joseph Henry as partner and manager.[41] In 1819, a record in the Vermont secretary of state's office shows that Joseph Henry applied for a retailer's license [⌀ 239].

CROSIER STORE. Lilla and children   HHS

There may have been a trading store as early as 1770 where the former Crosier family store was located in Halifax Center. This would have been the logical place for the first store in Halifax since it was located at the intersection of two main roads, old County Road and Stage Road. This was the business center of the town. A newspaper article dated May 1882, states, "The store at Center came very near being destroyed by fire last week. Rufus Crosier was passing by and discovered a fire on the roof of the piazza, but immediately gave the alarm and it was subdued, after having burned quite a hole in the roof. Had the store burned it would have destroyed one of the old landmarks of the town, for the building has been devoted to public use for nearly or quite seventy years, being first used as a hotel and store, and in late years as store and post office."[42] In the 1885 Halifax town report, an ad appeared in the inside cover showing that C. H. Learnard was a dealer in "Choice Family Grocers" in Halifax Center [HTC: TR, 1885]. In 1889, Watson DeWolf owned this store.[43]

From Clara Crosier Barnard.

The ancient wood arm chairs which were always in the store, and the grain gig used to wheel out heavy bags of feed were essential properties of the old structure as was of course the wood stove in winter. . . . Some other special characteristics of the old store were the scales, the roll of wrapping paper, the tobacco cupboard. . . . The scales were always on the counter near the corner where the passageway behind the counter made a sharp turn to go into the Post Office area in the Northeast corner. . . . Below the shelves were nutmegs, cinnamon bark, cloves, alum, salt petre, etc. were kept in the built in drawers. There would be kegs of nails on the floor. The barrels for crackers, sugar and flour were kept under the counter space.   HHS

INTERIOR OF CROSIER STORE Circa 1942   HHS

PERLEY E. CROSIER

Dealer in General Merchandise
And Pure Maple Products

HALIFAX, VERMONT

L. DALRYMPLE

HAS taken this opportunity to inform the inhabitants of Halifax and vicinity, that he has began his TAILORING BUSINESS in the centre of Halifax, where he will accommodate all that will favor him with a call.

☞ Cutting warranted.

Halifax, July 2, 1845.   *46

Phoenix, July 31, 1845

C. H. LEARNARD,

DEALER IN

CHOICE FAMILY GROCERIES,

MEDICINES, TEA, COFFEE, SPICES,
FLOUR, SALT FISH, PORK,
CHINA & GLASS WARE, KEROSENE OIL,
LAMPS, FIELD & GARDEN SEEDS, &c.

Customers will find my stock complete
and all sold at moderate prices.

HALIFAX CENTRE, - - VT.

Town of Halifax Annual Report, 1885, HHS

JOSEPH HENRY

Has just received from Boston a fresh supply of

Spring Goods;

A FEW OF WHICH ARE

1000 YDS brown sheeting, 1000 yds shirting, 100 pieces PRINTS, printed lawns, muslin de laines, broadcloths, cassimeres, satinetts, drilling, ticking, a full assortment of blk and col'd French and Italian Silks, blk alpine, a good assortment of Shawls and Fancy Hdkfs., black Italian Cravats; flag, bandanna and pongee Hdkfs.; straw and florence BONNETS; a good assortment of ribbons and bonnet Trimmings; ladies kid Slips; 1 box brush Hats; Fur do.; also a general assortment of

Crockery, Glass and Hard-Ware,
W. I. Goods and Groceries,

Oil, Paints, Nails, Glass, &c. &c. &c.

All which will be sold as low as at any other Store in the County.

Produce of all kinds taken in exchange.

Halifax, May 20, 1840.   38*

Phoenix, May 22, 1840

NOTE THE VARIETY OF GOODS AND SERVICES ONCE AVAILABLE IN HALIFAX CENTER.

PENNELL HILL DISTRICT 1

According to Charles McCune, who has lived on Pennell Hill since the 1930s, a store was located at the foot of State Line Hill and was owned by C. G. Burrington. He bought this property from Samuel Goodnow, who applied and received a retailer's license in 1819. McCune related to Bernice Barnett that Leon Shensky, who lived in the area in the 1920s, showed him where the store was located [HLR 6: 195]. The cellar hole still exists. Maude Hebard stated in the *History of Halifax* that, "A Mrs. Barnes had a confectionary store" in the Pennell Hill area.[44] Also, in an interview with Fred Bernard, about the Pennell Hill, he said, "Barnes ran a little store. It was located this side of Dr. Olson's home."[45] Mary Davis recalls hiking up the hill with her sisters to buy candy from Mrs. Barnes, who kept the store merchandise in a locked drawer so her husband could not get at the tobacco.[46]

FISHER/STOWE DISTRICT 3

In reference to the District 3 store, (across the road from the former swinging bridge on Route 112, known as the Higley house), a newspaper article from 1884 states, "D. D. Barnes is making the old store into a comfortable building. It is lighted by thirteen large windows and one side shines with white paint."[47]

HARRISVILLE DISTRICT 10

Because the Grange had purchased the W. C. Niles home in the Harrisville area, it is reasonable to believe that this is where the store was located. This home was once owned by Burton and Grace E. Hill. According to Ellen (Hill) Powers, the Grange started their sale of goods in 1877, and by the end of 1888 phased it out.

WEST HALIFAX DISTRICT 7

Semi-Weekly Eagle, April 2, 1849. Courtesy Readex

Courtesy C. Lancaster

NOAH BALL IN FRONT OF HIS WEST HALIFAX STORE   HHS

In 1834, Sanford Plumb advertised his new store and new goods in this building. Martin Scott 2nd opened a store and hotel at this location in 1869. Later owners were Oscar Howe, Noah Ball, George L. Clark, and George Chase.

DALRYMPLE STORE   HHS

Fred Robinson on wagon, Fletcher Dalrymple and Carrie Chase Dalrymple, daughter of George and Clara Clark Chase. Both stores burned within a few years of each other by 1923.

According to Eastman's article, there were stores in West Halifax as follows: George Lyman Clark and Oscar Howe, each ran a "general assortment" store; Jesse M. Niles sold boots and shoes; and Lewis W. Sumner sold flour, feed, and oats. Other storeowners in West Halifax Village were: Clarence Clark, George and Clara Chase, Edward and Dorothy Melius, Harold and Vivi Weaver, and Fred

Bowen. For a short time in the mid-1950s, William and Rachel Eddy kept a small store opposite the Halifax Historical Society building. Leon and Olive LaRock operated a store from 1963 to the early 1980s, presently the second house on the left on Collins Road after the bridge. For a short time, Ronald and Richard Gouin had a store at the present post office location on Reed Hill Road. This was the last store in Halifax.

~ Bernice Barnett and Elaine Fairbanks

ENDNOTES

1. Bernice Barnett, "Early Vermont Industries from potash to sugaring," *The Cracker Barrel*, Spring-Summer, 1991, Wilmington, VT, p. 4 (hereinafter referenced as Barnett).
2. Windham County Courthouse, Newfane, VT, *Record of the Proceedings of The Road Commissioners for the County of Windham, 1828 & 1829,* unpaginated.
3. HTC, census 1810.
4. Barnett.
5. Child, p. 217–218.
6. *Phoenix,* April 8, 1864.
7. G. Moxon, John Pynchon, John Endicott, Increase Nowell, et al., eds. *Western Massachusetts: A History: 1636–1925* (New York: Lewis Historical Publishing, 1926) p. 581.
8. Conversations with Phil Hardgrove, Halifax, VT, 1980s.
9. Ibid., January 25, 1924.
10. Ellen Sullivan, ed., *A Vermont Scrapbook*, (Huntsville, AL: Honey Suckle Imprint, 1991) p. 249.
11. Interview with James Stone, a descendant of Frank B. Stone, Halifax, VT, 1990s.
12. HHS, Beatrice Warren, *Audio Autobiography*, vol. 13, March 30, 1993.
13. *Phoenix,* October 30, 1885.
14. *National Cyclopaedia of American Biography* (New York: James T. White, 1956) p. 119–120.
15. *Phoenix*, December 1864.
16. HHS, Blanche Legate Sumner, West Halifax, VT, typescript, p. 3.
17. Conversations with Mary Sumner, Halifax, VT, 1980s.
18. HHS, Jeremy Freeman Jr., *Jacksonville Stage Road, Halifacts*, no. 24,.
19. Child, p. 218.
20. Ibid., p. 416.
21. HHS: Niles, p. 15
22. *Phoenix,* October 15, 1869.
23. Child, p. 419.
24. Child, p. 217.
25. HHS, Mary Reynolds, genealogy records of the Plumb family, family files.
26. HHS, Mrs. Emory B. Heberd, *History of the Town of Halifax Vermont, 1750–1961* (Halifax, VT: 1961).
27. HHS, Blanche Legate Sumner, West Halifax Vermont, typescript.
28. *Phoenix,* June 18, 1920.
29. HHS, Archie Whitney, *Audio Autobiography*, vol. 7. August 10, 1977.
30. *Phoenix,* June 18, 1920.
31. *Phoenix* of October 9, 1845
32. HHS, Floyd Canedy, *Audio Autobiography*, vol. 5, October 14, 1976.
33. *Phoenix,* October 5, 1923.
34. Interview with Frank B. Stone, Halifax, VT, 1980s.
35. *Farm Diary of Russel Bascom*, R. Stanton Avery Manuscript Collection. NEHGS, Boston, MA.
36. This book of accounts was purchased at auction by the author.
37. John Helyar, "Vermont Was in the Hat Business," *Vermont History*, vol. XXII, no.2, Burlington, VT: April 1954, p. 134.
38. Ibid., p. 135.
39. B. B. Woods & Bernice Barnett, *Roads In The Wilderness* (Halifax, VT: self-published, 1993).
40. Hemenway, p. 421.
41. Patrie, p. 127-H.
42. HHS: Niles, p. 13.
43. Hemenway, p. 421.
44. Heberd.
45. HHS, Fred Bernard, *Audio Autobiography*, vol. 16. September 14, 1979.
46. HHS, Miss Mary Davis, *Audio Autobiography*, vol. 7. Feb. 1, 1974.
47. HHS: Niles, p. 32.

Postal History
Driving the Stage Road

In 1900, five Halifax post offices served a population of 662 residents. Mail was distributed from three private homes and two general stores, which served also as dwellings. At the crossroads in Halifax Center, Watson DeWolf handled incoming and out-going mail at his old country store, as did postmaster, George Lyman Clark, at his "Ready Pay Store" on Main Street in West Halifax. Residents of South Halifax could drop off and pick up mail on Route 112, at the home of postmaster Charles H. Higley, a woolgrower whose Merino sheep grazed on the hillside. "Valley" folks could accomplish their postal transactions by walking through the front door of Frank B. Stone's house, and turning right into his multipurpose office where Hattie Clark served as postmaster. At Grove, postmaster Daniel Sumner Worden managed the mail from his stately hip-roofed abode. His spacious barns provided the perfect place for postal route carriers to exchange their tired horses for fresh ones.

Not every resident patronized a designated Halifax post office. The Green River post office, located in the general store of postmaster Henry Stowe, served residents of northeastern Halifax, who could send and receive mail while shopping for goods and supplies. Residents near Pennell Hill in Halifax and Christian Hill in Colrain shared a Franklin County post office called Line that operated at the Massachusetts/Vermont border on Phillips Hill Road.

Today, the turn-of-the century post office structures at Halifax, South Halifax, and Valley are private homes. Clark's combined store, home, and post office building in West Halifax was destroyed by fire in 1923. Currently, a row of mailboxes is found at the crossroads in Halifax Center across from the discontinued Halifax Post Office. The house containing the discontinued Grove

Photos C. Perna

Mail delivery at Halifax Center 2005 pictured with former Halifax Post Office on right.

Post Office was torn down in the 1930s. A similar a row of boxes along the edge of the Stage Road, where the Worden home and post office once stood, serves as a mail drop off and pick up place for families in Grove and South Halifax. Today's mail carriers continue to travel the route called Jacksonville Stage, or more commonly, Stage Road.

FROM WILDERNESS TO POST ROADS

Mail communication during the frontier days of Halifax was painfully slow. Settlers depended on the kindness of travelers to convey their letters to friends and relatives back in Connecticut, Massachusetts, and Rhode Island. A letter would be passed from person to person, depending on which direction they were traveling, and might take months to reach its destination.

In 1775, the Continental Congress appointed Benjamin Franklin Post Master General for the thirteen American colonies. Franklin, for several decades, had helped set up post roads and a postal system on behalf of the British Crown; but in 1774, he was dismissed for "actions sympathetic to the cause of the colonies."[1] The systems he designed became the basis for the American postal service, as it is known today.

Franklin's original network of post roads, needless to say, did not extend into early New Hampshire grant settlements. After 1777, and creation of the Republic of Vermont, the General Assembly needed to communicate its rulings to the inhabitants of the state. This resulted in Vermont's first printing presses, newspapers and post riders to carry the news from town to town. Anthony Haswell of Bennington started publishing *The Vermont Gazette*, in June 1783. In November of that year, he notified the public that post office business would be transacted at his printing office "under the same regulations as in the United States."[2] In February 1784 at Bennington, the Vermont General Assembly passed an act establishing five post offices within the state to be located at Bennington, Rutland, "Brattleborough," Windsor, and Newbury, "under such regulations as are established for the government of the post-offices in the United States."[3]

> The post-rider between Bennington and Brattleboro was allowed for travel three pence per mile, while riders on other routes were allowed only two pence, the additional rate being on account of the extremely mountainous country between Bennington and Brattleboro. These post-riders were allowed the exclusive privilege of carrying letters, papers and packages on their respective routes, and any person who infringed upon their rights was subject to a fine of ten pounds.[4]

The act also awarded Governor Chittenden, and persons authorized by the legislature, free mailing rights. On March 5, 1784, the governor's council appointed newspaper publisher Anthony Haswell of Bennington, Postmaster General for the State of Vermont. Legislators considered the establishment of post offices and post roads essential for spreading information that would connect and unite people throughout the state.

Innkeeper John Arms was appointed the first postmaster of Brattleboro in 1784. On the day the post-rider was due, people would gather at the Arms Tavern to await the unpacking of the saddlebags and distribution of the mail.[5] One can only guess how letters addressed to Halifax were claimed and carried from Brattleboro during the years before 1816, when Halifax first had its own post office. When Brattleboro began printing newspapers, such as *The Federal Galaxy*, established in 1797 and *The Reporter*, in 1803, a regular feature was the lists, by town, of letters remaining in the Brattleboro post office.

James Crosier, Post-Rider, To Halifax,

Wishes to inform his customers, That he shall discontinue riding on his route after three weeks more ; having then engaged a trusty person to succeed him—Those who have become indebted to him for newspapers, are now earnestly requested to make payment by that time. The money may be left where their papers have been—and he hopes for it as punctually.

Halifax, October 3d, 1806.

The Reporter, October 18, 1806

The earliest known newspaper post rider for Halifax was James Crosier, who delivered *The Reporter* from an unknown date until October 1806, as documented by his announcement of plans to discontinue his route. In 1806, James, son of Arthur Crosier, was about twenty-three years old.

Continued efforts to connect Halifax to points north, south, east and west via post roads appear in resolutions from the journals of the House of Representatives of the United States.

1804–1807 On motion of Mr. Taggart, and seconded, Resolved, That the Committee on Post Office and Post Roads be directed to inquire into the expediency of establishing a post road from Greenfield, in Massachusetts, to Wilmington, in Vermont, to pass through the town of Colrain and part of Shelburne, in Massachusetts, and Halifax and part of Whitingham, in Vermont, until it shall intersect the route already established from Brattleborough to Bennington, in Vermont; and that the committee have leave to report by bill, or otherwise.

1821–1822 On motion of Mr. White, Resolved, That the Committee on the Post Office and Post Roads be instructed to inquire into the expediency of discontinuing the present post route, from Colerain, in the state of Massachusetts, through the towns of Halifax, and Whittingham, to the town of Wilmington, in Vermont; and of establishing a post route from the village of Brattleboro, state of Vermont, through the towns of Guilford, Halifax, Whittingham, and Wilmington, to the town of Dover, in said state.

From the *Annals of Brattleboro* we learn that a stage house tavern, open both day and night, served as a distributing post office from 1811 to 1841 under Mr. Asa Green's administration. At one period, it was the "post office for Guilford, Dummerston, Halifax, Vernon, Whitingham, Newfane, Weybridge,

Marlboro, [Vermont] Hinsdale and Chesterfield New Hampshire, and Gill, Bernardston and Leyden, Massachusetts."[6]

Details of an early mail carrier's life appear in an agreement, made on May 27, 1829, between Paul Chase, landlord of the Stage-House of Brattleboro, and Amos Tucker, driver of the stage for Halifax. Tucker's arrangement with Mr. Chase included supper, lodging, and breakfast for himself and "good hay" for his horse and "horse-keeping" whenever he should "tarry over night" in Brattleboro. Per the agreement, he was to pay thirty-five cents each time. The agreement specified that "In taking those meals, if he [Amos] is present with us at mealtime, he is to have an equal chance with the family, or those present, with a warm meal; Other wise he is to take such victuals as is already Cooked. or such as can be obtained without the extra trouble of cooking particularly for him."[7]

Halifax Post Offices

Halifax

Records from the National Archives[8] indicate that on December 2, 1816, the first post office in Halifax was established at the Center with the appointment of Rev. Thomas Hough Wood. He served until his death in December 1843—a tenure of twenty-seven years! His entire term in office predated postage stamps, which were introduced in 1847. His cancellations most likely were handwritten. Precisely where these stampless mail exchanges took place is not known; however, Squire Joseph Henry contributed the required $300 bond on behalf of Rev. Wood, which suggests that the postal operation may have taken place at Henry's store at the Center. This building, one of the oldest in Halifax, later housed the post office of Stephen Niles and son Albert, as well as of Watson DeWolf, his son-in-law, Perley Eugene Crosier, followed by his son, Paul DeWolf Crosier.

Two postmasters: Perley and Paul Crosier   Photo (1919) HHS
with Lilla, Bertha and Clara in their Studebaker

West Halifax

Postcard HHS

Originally the Sanford Plumb store, which housed the West Halifax Post Office under numerous postmasters for many years until it was destroyed by fire in 1923.

The second official mail distribution center of Halifax, and the only one still in operation, commenced with the appointment of James Plumb, postmaster, on December 1, 1834. His successor, Salmon Swan, appointed in 1841, continued in office through the initial period of postage stamp usage. Prepaid letters set the stage for affordable letters, which inaugurated a major period of growth and expansion of the postal system. Located at Plumb's Corner's, the West Halifax Post Office was housed at a number of different residences and stores. It moved back and forth and up and down Main Street and even for a brief period, in 1923, operated from the Universalist Church after the devastating fire at the George and Clara (Clark) Chase store.

POSTOFFICE IN VERMONT BURNS WITH $10,000 LOSS

BRATTLEBORO, Vt, May 25—Property valued at $10,000 was burned in West Halifax this morning and included a two-story house and other buildings owned by Mrs George A. Chase and a two-story house owned by Mrs Will Fish of Providence. The Chase house contained a general store and the Postoffice, but the mail and Postoffice documents and articles of value were saved. The fire was caused by a chimney burning out.

Scrapbook of newspaper clippings
Courtesy Vera Crosier

South Halifax

Jedediah Stark, proprietor of the State Line Tavern, was appointed postmaster of the newly established South Halifax Post Office on December 4, 1840 and served until his death in September 1888. During the era of the James Landon and Jed Stark ownership of the tavern, the post office was part of a complex that included a law office, hotel, farm, orchard, apiary, and popular stagecoach stop. A few month's after the death of Jed Stark, the office moved up the road to the Charles H. Higley sheep farm. Higley continued as postmaster until the South Halifax office was discontinued in 1909. The Hartmanns, recent owners of the Higley farm, unearthed an old postal scale at this site, which they believe must have been used when their home served as a post office.

GROVE

Postcard HHS

On February 2, 1884, Grove Post Office was established. The original handwritten application submitted by Daniel Worden, reveals that he intended to name his post office "Maple Grove," perhaps in keeping with the Elm Grove Post Office further south in Colrain, but he crossed out the word maple. Directions on the form asked the applicant to choose a short name. Grove post office was located, in a large elegant home at the junction of Amidon and the Jacksonville Stage Road. It was always managed by Worden family members and was discontinued on October 21, 1919.

First Assistant Postmaster General.

To Mr. *Daniel S. Worden*

care of the Postmaster of *Halifax*, who will please forward to him.

STATEMENT.

The proposed office to be called ~~Maple~~ *Grove*

☞ Select a short name for the proposed office, which, when written, will ☜
not resemble the name of any other post office in the United States.

NARA

VALLEY

Valley Post Office was established May 5, 1899, at the home of Frank B. Stone; however, Frank Stone, himself, was declared "ineligible" to serve. The office was run by a succession of women postmasters and was discontinued on July 25, 1921. Philatelic enthusiasts report that "Valley" is an exceptionally rare and collectible postmark in use for only twenty-two years.

Postmark HHS

Postcard courtesy Charles Marchant

LINE

Equally rare is the postmark from a Franklin County, Massachusetts post office that operated from July 30, 1890 to February 28, 1914 in Colrain or in Vermont, depending on who was postmaster. The *Vermont Phoenix* reported, "Residents of Pannell Hill in this town and Christian Hill in Colraine have united and secured a new post office. . . . It will be located about halfway between the two schoolhouses and will be known as Line."[9] Maude Hebard credits Norris Shepardson's "ability to cope with the U.S.

LINE POST BOXES   Photo E. Fairbanks

Government"[10] for the establishment of the Line Post office. Shepardson lived in the Deacon John Pennell home. Ellsworth Kemp recollected that Shepardson crafted the post boxes used to hold the mail, and painted them red, white and blue.[11] At some point, the boxes were located at the Phillips house, then occupied by the Uptons. The foundation of the George Phillips house literally straddles the borderline. Eventually, the house was moved entirely into Vermont, getting stuck in the mud and blocking the road for several months in the process, and it burned to the ground in 1980. The family of Arland F. Fairbanks of Halifax donated a section of the oak mailboxes as shown above from the original Line Post Office to the Colrain Historical Society. Arland's grandparents, Frank and Addie Upton, were postmasters.

PHILLIPS HOUSE FOUNDATION   Photo E. Stamas

HORSE AND BUGGY DAYS

News reports of seasonal mail delays along the Stage Road include axle-breaking ruts, merciless mud and six-foot high snowdrifts that would prevent passage of even the most rugged team of horses. During fair weather days, however, prompt service was expected. The following barb from the local correspondent to the *Vermont Phoenix* in 1882 is gentler than most: "A letter was received at the West Halifax post office, Nov. 28th, that was mailed at Hinsdale, N. H., July 31. Where has it been all this time? Perhaps it walked."[12]

CHANGING HORSES AT GREEN RIVER   Photo courtesy Jeremy Freeman

In addition to mail distribution, the mail stage provided an important mode of transportation for local residents. A Stagecoach ran from Jacksonville to Brattleboro, picking up and leaving passengers at Halifax Center and other post offices en route, so some offices needed to furnish fresh horses and to provide wagon and equipment repairs. Stage drivers returning from Brattleboro to Jacksonville often changed horses at Green River because of the long steep climb to Grove.

STAR MAIL ROUTES AND STAGE LINES.
No Stages Run on Sunday.

BRATTLEBORO BY GUILFORD, GUILFORD CENTER, GREEN RIVER, GROVE, HALIFAX, JACKSONVILLE, WHITINGHAM, READSBORO, &c. TO NORTH ADAMS, MASS., 17¾ miles and back daily. Leave Brattleboro at 1 P. M., arrive at Jacksonville by 7 P. M ; leave Jacksonville in the morning, and arrive at North Adams by noon; leave North Adams after noon, arrive at Jacksonville in the evening; leave Jacksonville in the morning, and arrive at Brattleboro by 10 A. M. H.G. Davis is mail carrier between Jacksonville and North Adams, and M. F. Perry between Brattleboro and Jacksonville. Two horse coach. Fare from Brattleboro to Guilford 25 cents; Guilford Center, 50 cents; Green River 75 cents; Halifax $1.00; West Halifax, $1.25; Jacksonville, $1.50; North Adams, $3.00. Express and telegrams should be sent via North Adams or Brattleboro.

* * * *

JACKSONVILLE BY SOUTH HALIFAX, ELM GROVE. MASS., COLERAINE, GRISWOLDVILLE AND SHATTUCKVILLE to SHELBURNE FALLS, 18 miles and back, daily. Leave Jacksonville at 6:30 a. m.; arrive at Shelburne Falls by 10 a. m., or in time to connect with mail train; leave Shelburne Falls at 1 p. m., arrive in Jacksonville by 5:30 p. m. J. A. Alexander, mail carrier; two-horse stage. Fare through $1.25. Express and telegrams via Shelburne Falls.

Child, p. 14

In her description of the early, "Store and Post Office at Halifax Center," Clara Crosier Barnard wrote:

> The Star Route, mail route stage was very much like the old
> English stages, because it would accommodate passengers aboard
> and also do errands for people along the way. I remember winter
> nights when the snow was blowing and the roads were practically
> obliterated we would wonder when the mail carrier could get to
> us. We might telephone to Grove to find out if the driver had left
> there.[13]

More details on this mode of transportation appear in *Epitaphs from Halifax, Vermont* by Elaine Fairbanks and Regina Carr Hardgrove:

> Two horse coaches and sleighs were used in the early days. The
> round trip fare from Halifax to Brattleboro, Vermont was one
> dollar and from West Halifax it was a dollar and twenty-five cents.
> The fare for passengers by mail truck today [1973] has not

changed much. Round trip from Halifax to Brattleboro...is about $1.00. It might be noted here that the comfort of vehicles has not raised the price[14]

For most of his boyhood, Malcolm Burnett was a frequent passenger on the mail stage. His daughter, Carrie Perna, asked him about his memories.

> My dad recalls traveling by horse and buggy in warm weather, and by sleigh in winter, on "the stage" from West Halifax up to Halifax Center and over Jacksonville Stage Road, en route to the Austine School in Brattleboro, Vermont. He remembers helping with the delivery of mail along the way. He said this trip would take a whole day. He shared that in winter, they would have to stop at homes along the route in order to get warmed up.[15]

Marie Learnard Taylor spoke of "running to catch the sleigh" with her cousin, Malcolm Burnett, on their way back to school from February vacation. Only two passengers could ride with the driver, but it was a "good wide seat." Asked if it was a chilly ride, she replied, "We had muskrat rugs around us, so we were comfortable." The mail carrier would leave the horses in Green River, and "we'd all get into a car for the rest of the drive to Brattleboro." She then took the train to Greenfield where she lived with her aunts in order to attend high school.

Marie recalled how hard the winter roads were on the horses. "I know that Mr. [Fred] Bowen that lived in the house on the corner, he used to drive the stage an awful lot, and he had quite a time with his horses. Once he got up to the center all right but he couldn't get from there over to Guilford because he lost his horse—it was a deep snow . . . it was too much for the horse [he died]."[16]

Driving the mail stage was not a job for the meek or mild mannered. The work attracted colorful characters, of great physical strength and stamina. Vera Crosier tells the story told to her by one such mail carrier who met his match at Halifax Center.

> Pappy Haskins began driving the mail in horse and buggy days and drove the stage route for years. Springtime was horrible because he would get stuck in deep mud and ruts took a toll of his horses and wagons. One day he arrived at the post office stop in the Center feeling decidedly ill. Grandma Crosier [Lilla] cooked up a brew with herbs and said, "Now I want you to drink this." Wanting nothing to do with her concoction, he replied, "You must be kidding!" In her most commanding voice, she told him, "You must drink this or you'll get lots sicker." He choked down the terrible tasting stuff. By the time he got to his next stop, he recalls, he felt quite a lot better and never got sick at all.

Pappy was still driving and telling stories in his eighties.

DRIVING A HIGHWAY CONTRACT ROUTE

In 1971 Star Routes were changed to Highway Contract Routes. HCR drivers for the post office were paid by the government and supplied their own vehicles. They were paid by the mile and by the number of delivery stops. They delivered wood stoves and library books to shut-ins. In addition, they were responsible for dropping off and picking up all the mail for distribution out of the West Halifax Post Office.

Bob Bowen and later Fred Bowen had the contract that included Halifax. One of Fred's drivers was Floyd Canedy who drove the stage route for years in a cut-down car he used like a pick-up truck. Vera Crosier took over Ray and Susie Putnam's contract route in 1977 and delivered mail along the Stage Road in her jeep until 1989. When Vera was unable to drive, her husband, Larry was authorized to drive in her place. They never missed a day. The contract required the carrier to arrive in Jacksonville at 8:00 AM to sort all the mail for delivery on the route: Jacksonville Hill, West Halifax, Halifax Center, Grove, Green River, Guilford Center, and on to Brattleboro. There the carrier would wait for afternoon mail to arrive, sort the mail, and do the trip in reverse, arriving back in Jacksonville at about 5:30 PM.

From horses and saddlebags, to mail delivery by jeep, the route along the Jacksonville Stage Road has changed little over time.[17] The landscape now includes fewer original homes, and the picturesque Halifax post offices exist only in memory or as black and white images on real photo post cards.

THE MAILBOX painted by Stanley Woodward, appeared in *Yankee Magazine*, as the centerfold picture of the month in February 1967. It was so popular; Yankee used it again as the cover for their 1971 recipe calendar. Joseph Crosby,[18] owner of the house in 1980, when he spoke to the HHS, said when Mrs. Sherman Harris owned the house, it was the subject of many paintings by Robert Strong Woodward, a Buckland, Massachusetts artist, and brother of Stanley. Originally, the James Tucker farm, later owned by the Milton Powers family and for many years it was the home of town clerk, Ansel Jones.

POSTMASTERS

The following list is from NARA M1131, *A Record of Appointment of Postmasters, Oct. 1789–1832* and NARA M841, *A Record of Appointment of Postmasters 1832–Sept. 30, 1971.* Information covering 1971 to 2005 is from the list prepared by Lucille Cook found at the West Halifax Post Office. (Note: these lists do not include substitutes, assistants or any of the many other people who may have worked in the local postal system.)

HALIFAX

Name of Postmaster	*Date of Appointment*
Thomas H. Wood	December 2, 1816
Stephen Niles	February 16, 1843
Charles Fowler	November 2, 1846 (declined)
Francis Henry	November 23, 1846
Stephen Niles	May 3, 1849
Albert S. Niles	October 15, 1855
Calvin L. Stockwell	February 17, 1858
Henry Ames	December 20, 1859
William B. Holmes	September 12, 1860
Albert S. Niles	November 14, 1861
F.C. Beck	October 10, 1881
Alpheus F. Stone	October 9, 1882
Benjamin F. Millington	January 6, 1888
Watson DeWolfe	November 7, 1890
Perley E. Crosier	October 28, 1903
Paul D. Crosier	October 01, 1937

Discontinued March 5, 1954. Mail to West Halifax

Courtesy Bill Lizotte
Manuscript postmark on a stampless letter, 1830 handwritten by Thomas Wood.

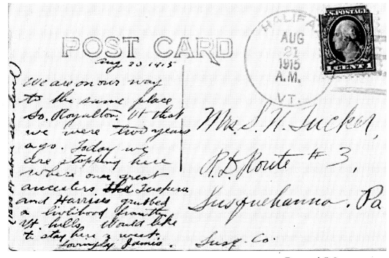

Postcard C. Lancaster
Written by James C. Tucker, great, grandson of Stephen and Lucy Harris Tucker.

WEST HALIFAX

Name of Postmaster	*Date of Appointment*
James Plumb	December 1, 1834
Salmon Swan	November 10, 1841
Hollis S. Plumb	February 28, 1854
Albert Richardson	February 8, 1858
Francis E. Plumb	October 6, 1858
Chauncey B. Tilton	January 28, 1863
Harvey J. Swan	September 18, 1865
Titus Stowe	September 30, 1867
William C. Plumb	June 8, 1868
Robert Collins, Jr.	April 12, 1869
Martin Scott, 2nd	February 2, 1870
Levi M. Tucker	November 3, 1875
Albert J. Tucker	January 21, 1878 (declined)
Lemuel B. Hall	January 29, 1878
Oscar Howe	July 7, 1886
Merton W. Plumb	October 18, 1894 (declined)
William H. Hancock	December 15, 1894
Millard Weeks	June 24, 1897
George L. Clark	February 20, 1899
Clara C. Chase	August 17, 1912
Gertrude H. Clark	January 29, 1924
Edward E. Melius	February 12, 1932
Mrs. Vivi W. Weaver	March 11, 1938
Eleanor W. Rafus	January 11, 1954

(Name changed by marriage to Guyette, July 27, 1957)

Lucille Cook	February 1, 1975
Rodney Crawford	May 14, 1994

Courtesy Rodney
Crawford, Postmaster

WEST HALIFAX PO 2007

Manuscript
postmark and
hand cancel
by Francis
Plumb, 1860

Envelope
C. Lancaster

Before 1845, the year adhesive postage stamps were first issued for optional use in the United States, stampless covers, such as folded letters and envelopes, displayed the town and rate marks usually in manuscript. [Examples: Halifax - Wood and South Halifax - Stark] Most stampless mail was sent collect. In 1855, Congress enacted mandatory prepayment of postage through use of adhesive postage stamps. From 1847–1890, postmasters had to provide their own stamp cancellation devices, made of cork, rubber, wood, metal or other material. In the absence of a hand or machine-made device to obliterate stamps, a postmaster was permitted to apply a pen-cancellation by an X or other ink mark on the face of the stamp. See above.

SOUTH HALIFAX

Name of Postmaster	Date of Appointment
James L. Stark	November 12, 1840
Jedediah Stark	December 4, 1840
Discontinued	May 29, 1854
Reestablished	June 9, 1854
Jedediah Stark	June 9, 1854
James L. Stark	November 26, 1858
Jedediah Stark	December 17, 1858
Mary E. Hall	September 20, 1888
Charles H. Higley	December 17, 1888
A. C. Jones	August 17, 1895 (Order Rescinded)

Discontinued August 14, 1904, Mail to Elmgrove, Massachusetts

Courtesy Bill Lizotte
Manuscript postmark on a
stampless letter, Feb. 3, 1849
by Jedediah Stark.

GROVE

Name of Postmaster	Date of Appointment
Daniel S. Worden	February 2, 1884
Sumner B. Worden	April 24, 1908

Discontinued October 18, 1919. Mail to Halifax

Postcard HHS

VALLEY

Name of Postmaster	Date of Appointment
Frank B. Stone (was ineligible)	November 18, 1898
Hattie E. Clark	May 5, 1899
Alice L. Stone	February 27, 1907
Nellie M. Bolton	July 8, 1908
Susie L. Stone	May 1, 1909
Nellie M. Bolton	July 8, 1909
Helen M. Livermore	October 25, 1919 (declined)
Harry R. Osgood	November 23, 1920

Discontinued July 25, 1921. Mail to Colrain, Massachusetts

Postmark HHS

LINE

Name of Postmaster	Date of Appointment
Frank L. Upton	July 30, 1890
Frederick M. Thompson	June 11, 1897
Rachel Taylor	August, 1, 1901
Addie A. Upton	April 28, 1911

Discontinued February 28, 1914. Mail to Adamsville, Massachusetts

Mr. A. Deane Hillman.
Line.
, Mass.

Postcard courtesy
Judith Sullivan,
Colrain Town Clerk

Currently one post office, located in West Halifax, serves the town. The postmaster cancels and postmarks local mail, "West Halifax, Vermont." Other mail travels the Stage Road, with the contract driver to Brattleboro. Trucks carry it to the distribution center at White River Junction, Vermont where it is postmarked, cancelled, sorted and sent out to various destinations.

OTHER PRIVATE HOMES THAT ONCE HOUSED POST OFFICES

STARK SOUTH HALIFAX

HIGLEY SOUTH HALIFAX

STONE VALLEY

MELIUS WEST HALIFAX

CLARK WEST HALIFAX

RAFUS/GUYETTE WEST HALIFAX

WEAVER WEST HALIFAX   Private home/ post office photos HHS

©2008 *Constance Lancaster and Carrie Perna*

ENDNOTES
1. *History of the United States Postal Service 1775–1993,* www.usps.com/history/his1_5.htm
2. George C. Slawson, Arthur W. Bingham, & Sprague W. Drenan, *The Postal History of Vermont* (New York: Collectors Club, 1969) p. 3.
3. William Slade, Jr., *Vermont State Papers* (Middlebury, VT: J. W. Copeland, printer, 1823) p. 399.
4. Lyman S. Hayes, *The Connecticut River Valley in Southern Vermont and New Hampshire Historical Sketches* (Rutland, VT: Tuttle, 1929) p. 114.
5. Mary R. Cabot, *Annals of Brattleboro: 1681–1895* (Brattleboro, VT: E.L. Hildreth, 1921–1922) p. 171.
6. Ibid., p. 184.
7. HHS, copy of original on file courtesy of Jacques Tucker.
8. NARA, Record of Appointment of Postmasters, October 1789–1832. Windham County, Vermont, microfilm ID M1131, Record Group RG028.
9. Phoenix, August 15, 1890.
10. Mrs. Emory B. [Maude] Hebard. *History of the Town of Halifax, Vermont 1750-1961.* Typescript. p. 9.
11. HHS, Ellsworth Kemp Christian Hill, Colerain, MA. An Audio Autobiography, Volume #18, 1976.
12. HHS: Niles, p. 9.
13. HHS, Clara Crosier Barnard, handwritten loose pages, 1975.
14. Regina Carr Hardgrove, Elaine Claire Fairbanks, *Epitaphs from Halifax,* (Brattleboro, VT: John B. Fowler, printer, 1973).
15. Carrie Burnett Perna, interview with Malcolm Burnett, September 2004.
16. Marie (Learnard) Taylor talk in 1997 at HHS meeting. *An audio Autobiography Volume #9.*
17. In 1919, the town voted to discontinue "that part known as old Stage road leading . . . past the Edmund Worden place to the road that leads to the cemetery on said stage road." [HTC: TR: 31]
18. HHS, Joseph Crosby *Description of the Crosby House,* An Audio Autobiography Volume #16, 1980.

APPENDIX

CONTENTS

PETITION TO GOVERNOR SHUTE

We whose names are underwritten, Inhabitants of ye North of Ireland, Doe in our own names, and in the names of many others, our Neighbors, Gentlemen, Ministers, Farmers, and Tradesmen, Commissionate and appoint our trusty and well beloved friend, the Reverend Mr. William Boyd, of Macasky, to His Excellency, the Right Honorable Collonel Samuel Suitte, Governour of New England, and to assure His Excellency of our sincere and hearty Inclination to Transport ourselves to that very excellant and renowned Plantation upon our obtaining from His Excellency suitable incouragement. Given under our hands this 26th day of March, Anno Dom. 1718. www.eastdonegalulsterscots.com/history.html

This petition, signed by 319 Ulster Scotch-Presbyterians from the counties of Londonderry and Antrim, Ireland, is displayed at the New Hampshire Historical Society in Concord. The list of signers includes the names of many families who were pioneer settlers of Colrain, Massachusetts, and Halifax, Vermont.

CHARTER OF HALIFAX 1750

HALIFAX.

*Province of New Hampshire   *1-63

Halifax

P: S-

George the Second by the Grace of God of Great Brittain France & Ireland King Defender of the Faith &c[a]—

To all Persons to whom these Presents Shall come Greeting—

Know ye that we of our Especial Grace Certain Knowledge and mere motion for the Due Encouragem[t] of Settling A New Plantation within our Said Province by & with the advice of our Trusty & Well beloved Benning Wentworth Esq our Governour & Coma'nder in Chieff of our Said Province of New Hampshire in America & of Our Council of the Said Province Have upon the Conditions & reservations hereinafter made Given & Granted & by these Presents for us our hiers & Successors Do Give & Grant in Equal Shares unto our Loveing Subjects Inhabitants of our Said Province of New Hampshire & his Maj[tys] other Governments and to their hiers and Assignes for ever whose names Are Entred on this Grant to be Divided to and Amoungst them into Sixty four Equall Shares all that Tract or Parcell of Land Scituate Lying & being within our Said Province of New Hampshire Containing by Admeasurement Twenty three thousend & forty Acres which Tract is to Contain Six Miles Square & no more out of which an Allowence is to be made for highways and unimprovable Lands by Rocks Mountains Ponds & Rivers One thousend & forty Acres free According to A Plan thereof made & Presented By our Said Governours Order and hereunto Annexed Butted & Bounded as follows (Viz) Begining at A Marked Tree Standing half a Mile West of Green River in the boundary line between the Government of the Massachusets Bay & New Hampshire and from thence Due West on Said Boundary line Six miles & at the End of Said Six miles to turn off at a Right Angle and run Due North Six miles & at the End of Said Six Miles to Turn of At A Right Angle & run Due East Six miles, and at the End of Said Six Miles to turn A Right Angle & run Due South Six Miles to the Tree first mentioned And that the Same be & here is Incorporated into A Township By the name of HALIFAX and that the Inhabitants that do or Shall hereafter Inhabit the Said Township are hereby Declared to be Enfranchized with and Intituled to all & Every the Previledges and Imunities that Other Towns within our S[d] Province by Law Exercize & Enjoy and further that the Said Town as Soon as there Shall be fifty families

resident & Settled thereon Shall have the Liberty of Holding
Two fairs One of which Shall be held on the Last monday
*1–64   in the Month of * April and the other in the Last monday
of the month of September Annually which Fairs are not to
Continue and be held Longer than the respective Saturdays following
the said Mondays And As Soon as the Said Town Shall Consist of
Fifty Families A Market Shall be opned and kept one or more Days
in Each Week as may be tho^t most Advantagious to the Inhabitants
also that the first Meeting for the Choice of Town Officers Agreable
to the Laws of our Said Province Shall be held on the first
Wednesday in August next which meeting Shall be notifyed by
Oliver Partridge Esq who is hereby Also Appointed the Moderator
of the Said first Meeting which he is to notify & Govern Agreeable to
the Law & Custom of Our Said Province and that the Annual meeting
for ever hereafter for the Choice of Such officers for the Said Town
Shall be on the Last Wednesday of March Annually To HAVE & TO
HOLD the Said Tract of Land as above Expressed togeather with All
the Previledges & Appurtenances to them And thier respective heirs
and Assignes for ever upon the following Conditions—Viz—

Imprimis That every Grantee his heirs or assignes Shall Plant or
Cultivate five Acres of Land within the Term of five years for every
fifty Acres Contained in his or thier Share or Proportion of Land in
Said Town Ship and Continue to Improve & Settle the Same by
Aditional Cultivations on Penalty of the forfeiture of his grant or
Share in the Said Township and its reverting to his Majesty his heirs
& Successors to be by him or them regranted to Such of his Subjects
as Shall effectually Settle & Cultivate the Same—

Secundo—That all white & other Pine Trees within the Said
Township fit for Masting our Royal Navy be Carefully Preserved for
that use & none to be Cut or felld without his Maj^{tys} Especial
Lycence for So Doing first had & Obtained upon the Penalty of the
forfeiture of the right of Such Grantee his heirs or assigns to us our
heirs or Successors as well as being Subject to the Penalty of Any
Act or Acts of Parliament that now are or hereafter Shall be Enacted

Tertio—That before any Divission of the Said Land be made to and
Among the Grantees a Tract of Land as near the Center of the Said
Township as the Land will Admit of Shall be reserved & Marked out
for Town Lotts one of which Shall be allotted to Each Grantee of the
Contents of one Acre—

Quarto—Yielding & paying therefor to us our heirs & Successors
for the Space of Ten Years to be Computed from the Date hereof the
rent of One Ear of Indian Corn only on the Twenty fifth
*1–65   Day of December *Annually if Lawfully Demanded the

first payment to be made on the Twenty fifth Day of December next Insueing the Date hereof—

Quinto—Every Proprietor Settler or Inhabitant Shall Yield & pay unto us our heirs and Successors Yearly & Every year for ever from and after the Expiration of Ten Years from the Date hereof Namly on the Twenty fifth Day of December which will be in the year of our Lord one thousand Seven hundred & Sixty & one one Shilling Proclamation money for every hundred Acres he So owns Settles or Possesses & So In Proportion for a greater or Lesser Tract of the Said Land which money Shall be paid by the respective Persons above Said their heirs or Assigns in our Council Chamber in Portsm° or to Such officer or officers as Shall be Appointed to recieve the Same & this to be in Lieu of All other Rents or Services whatsoever

In Testimony Whereof we have Caused the Seal of our Said Province to be hereunto affixed Wittness Benning Wentworth Esq our Governour & Com'ander in Chieff of Our Said Province the Eleventh Day of May in the year of our Lord Christ One thousand Seven hundred & fifty & in the Twenty third year of our reign

B Wentworth

By his Excelencys Com'and
with Advice of Council

Theodore Atkinson Se^ry

Entred & recorded According to the Original under the Province Seal this 11th Day of May 1750—

℗ Theodore Atkinson Se^ry

Names of the Grantees Viz—

Oliver Partridge Esq	Ebenezer Barnard	Joseph Barnard
Abner Barnard	Selah Barnard	Tim° Woodbridge
Charles Couts	David Hoit	Jesse Heath
Eleaz^r Hawks	John Hawks	Benj^a Man
Seth Catlen	John Catlen	George Howland
John Taylor	Jon^a Ashley	Sam^ll Partridge jun^r
Tim° Childs Junr	Gad Corse	Sam^ll Brown
Abraham Bass	Peter Bover	Willm Bull
Edward Partridge	Aaron Denieur	Nathan Frary
Benj^a Sheldon	David ffield	Elnathan Graves
Seth Graves	Perez Graves	Silas Graves
Ephraim Allen	Sam^ll Bodman	Joseph Bodman
Israel Graves	Oliver Graves	Zech^r Billing
David Billing	Seth Dwight	Seth Dwight jun^r
Daniel White	Dan^ll White Junr	Salmon White
Elihu White	Obediah Dickinson	Elij^a Dickinson

XIV

Ebenez^r Bardwell   Ebenez^r Bardwell jun^r Benning Wentworth Esq
     Bennigh Wentworth Esq Theodore Atkinson Esq
*1–66   Richd Wibird Esq *Samuel Smith Esq Samuel Solley Esq
     Sampson Sheaffe Esq First Minister School Meshech Wear
Esq Joseph Newmarch Esq John Wentworth Esq Ebenez^r Wentworth
Esq John Wentworth jun^r Esq

Entred and recorded According to the Original this 11th Day of
May 1750
                                                    ⅌ Theodore Atkinson Sec^{ry}

A Plan of the Township of Halifax Granted by his Excelency
Benning Wentworth Esq Governour &c^a an the Honble his Majesties
Council of New Hampshire in America Unto Oliver Partridge Esq
& Others May 11th 1750 as it is to be Plotted by A Surveyer & Chain
men upon Oath unto Each Proprietor or Grantee in Equal Shares be
their Lotts better or worse (Excepting the four Lotts next the Town
Plot or Scite which Are Sixteen Acres Less measure than the Other
Lotts) as they were Drawn by the Agents for the Proprietors in
Portsmouth May the 11th 1750 and were Entred by the Secretary of
Said Province upon this Plan each man takeing His Chance whose
name Stands in the Schedule annexed to the Grant of Said Township—

Mem^o A Plott Agreable to the within order was made by Mathew
Clesson Survey^r & Aron Denieu & John Morrison Chain men under
Oath was filed in the Sec^{ry} office the 2^d of April 1751—
                                          Attest^r Theodore Atkinson Se^{ry}

Names of grantees with lot numbers as inscribed on the original lotting plan follows.

1. Charles Coats	23. David Hoyt	44. Benning Wentworth Esq
2. Selah Barnard	24. William Bull	45. David Field
3. Theodore Atkinson Esq	25. John Taylor	46. Jesse Heath
4. Seth Graves	26. Joseph Barnard	47. Eleazer Hawks
5. Ebenezer Bardwell	27. Samual Partridge Jr.	48. Seth Dwight Jr.
6. John Catlin	28. First Minister	49. Daniel White Jr.
7. Gad Corse	29. Samuel Bodman	50. Daniel White
8. John Wentworth Esq	30. Silas Graves	51. Elnathan Graves
9. Nathan Frary	31. Perez Graves	52. Zechariah Billing
10. John Wentworth Jr. Esq	32. Salmon White	53. Abraham Bass
11. Edward Partridge	33. Ebenezer Bardwell Jr.	54. Obediah Dickinson
12. Ephraim Allen	34. Richard Wibird Esq	55. Benjamin Munn
13. Seth Catlin	35. David Billing	56. Meshach Weare
14. Joseph Newmarch Esq	36. Benning Wentworth Esq	57. John Hawks
15. Seth Dwight	37. Timothy Childs Jr.	58. Samuel Brown
16. Sampson Sheaffe Esq	38. Timothy Woodbridge	59. Aaron Denio
17. Joseph Bodman	39. George Howland	60. Benjamin Sheldon
18. Elijah Dickinson	40. Samuel Solley Esq	61. Peter Bovee
19. Ebenezer Wentworth Esq	41. Ebenezer Barnard	62. Oliver Graves
20. Oliver Partridge	42. Jonathan Ashley	63. Elihu White
21. Samuel Smith	43. Israel Graves	64. School
22. Abner Barnard	44. Benning Wentworth Esq	

* * *

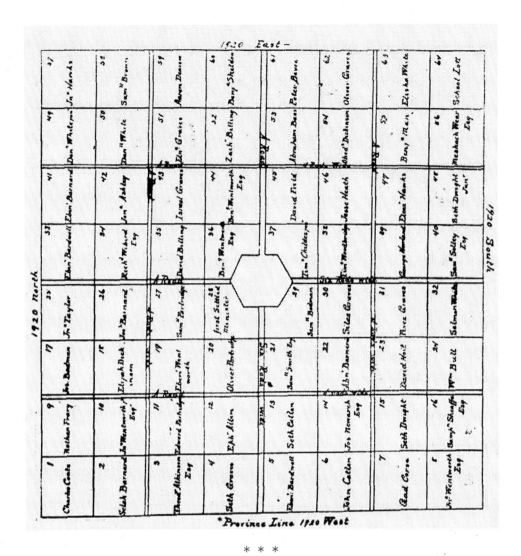

* * *

Theodore Atkinson ⎫ Agents for
John Wentworth   ⎬ the Grantees
Olr Partridge   ⎭

Entred & Recorded May the 11 1750 According to yᵉ Original
on file—

℣ Theodore Atkinson Secʳʸ

Albert Stillman Batchellor, ed.. *The New Hampshire Grants: Being Transcripts of the Charters of Townships and Minor Grants of Lands Made by the Provincial Government of New Hampshire, Within the Present Boundaries of the State of Vermont, from 1749 to 1764*, vol. 26 of the New Hampshire State Papers series, vol. 3 of *Town Charters* within that series (Concord, NH: Edward N. Pearson, 1895) pp. 207–211.

*   The term Province Line refers to the border between New Hampshire and Massachusetts during the
    colonial period prior to statehood. The directions North, East, South and West are incorrect on this plan
    and should read as follows: North – top and South –bottom.

PETITION FOR A HIGHWAY TO HALIFAX – 1762

Partridge Esq.
Petition

The Petition of Oliver Partridge in behalf of Himself and others Proprietors of the Township of Hallifax Vz which lies north of and adjoining to Colrain humbly showeth. That there are several Townships laid out northerly of Colrain particularly the Township of Hallifax where are some families settled and a number of Men at Work on the Lands in said Township and the Situation of the Land in sd Township is such it is quite necessary that there be a Communication between them and the County of Hampshire by the Way of Colrain which will be of public Service to this County as well as those people. And altho there be a County Road already laid out as far as Colrain Meeting House which is about four miles from the Line of said Township of Hallifax After repeated Applications to the Select Men of Colrain to lay out a Town Road from their meeting House to their North line they wholly neglect and refuse to lay out a road there. I would therefore humbly pray your Honors to appoint a Committee to lay a road from Colrain Meeting house to the north line of said Town so as best to accommodate the public. And as in Duty bound shall every pray Oliver Partridge.

Order Thereon

Read and Ordered that Elijah Williams Esq. John Hawks Esq. David Field gent. Joseph Barnard gent. and Seth Catlin gent. all of Deerfield in said County be a Committee to view and lay out the HighWay prayed for Which said Committee are to give Reasonable Notice to all persons interested of the Time and place of their Meeting for this purpose and Shall be under Oath to perform the said Service according to their best Skill and Judgment with most Convenience to the Public and least Prejudice or Damage to private Property and shall also ascertain the place and Course of said Road in the best Way and Manner they can Which having done the said Committee or the Major part of them shall make Return thereof to the next Court of General Sessions of the Peace to be held in said County after the said Service is performed under their Hands and Seals. And if any person be damaged in his or her property by the laying out said Way the said Committee are empowered and required under Oath to Estimate the Same and make Return thereof as aforesaid and it is also ordered that the said Committee be served with a Copy hereof—

Copy & Warrant made Oct. 6th 1762—

Court of Sessions, Hampshire County Courthouse,
Northampton, MA. Book 7, p. 47

REPORT OF THE HIGHWAY SURVEY COMMITTEE

Highway from
Colrain
Meetinghouse
to Halifax

Whereas We the Subscribers were appointed by the Court of General of the peace at their Term in august last to lay out a HighWay from Ye Meeting House in Colrain to the north Line of the Town afores'd after having been sworn before Thomas Williams Esq as by his Certificate Returned ...of Court will appear. Pursuant to s'd Order after giving reasonable notice to all Persons interested by sending a Notification to the Selectmen of Colrain that we would meet at the house of Mr. John Workman Innkeeper in order to proceed on s'd business on the 4th of November. We met at the place accordingly and having heard the persons present we proceeded to the meeting house in s'd Colrain from whence we have laid the Road as follows— Beginning at the West Door of s'd Meeting house went from there N 35° W 10 rods to a birch Tree, then N 55° W 24 rods to a beach Straddle, then N 44° W 30 rods to the North Side of Deacon Cochran's house then WS° 22 Rods to a Chestnut Stump then N 52° W 20 rods to a hemlock tree then N 25° W 44 rods to a birch Tree then N 15° W 44 rods to a beach Tree then N 24 rods to a birch Tree then N 15°°W 10 rods across North River N 16°E 46 rods to John Clarks farm east of s'd Clark's house then N 48° 32 rods to a bass tree N 60° E 46 rods to a beach Tree N 25° E 30 rods to a birch tree N 24° W 30 rods to a birch Tree N 11° E 30 rods to a hemlock Tree then N 20° E   rods to a birch Tree then N 30° E 12 rods to a maple Tree then 60 rods to John Morrisons East Door still on same Course 60 rods passing by s'd East End of Capt. Morrisons house still ye same Course 124 rods to a maple straddle then N 36° W 42 rods to a hemlock tree then N 15° W 92 rods to a birch them N 96 rods to a birch N 38°W 28 rods against the East End of Hugh Boltons Jun'rs house then N 9 East 70 rods across north River then N 20° W 100 rods to a Birch Tree then N 18°° W 104 to a hemlock tree then N 40° W 36 rods to a Tree then N 50° W 124 rods to a Beach Tree standing in the Province Line one mile and three quarters and four rods to the W of the Southeast Corner of Hallifax. Sd Beach Tree standing against the Lot No 6 in Hallifax said Beach Tree in marked COMTee EW JH DF JB SC MB

Width Ø of the said Road is four Rods in Width from the meeting house aforesaid to North River before it comes to John Clark's house from thence to the Province Line the Road is two rods and a half in Width . The Line We run to be ye Center of the Road Test our Hands & Seals at Deerfield Nov. 8th 1762.

The foregoing Return of the Doing of Sd Committee was now made And this Court having read and Considered the Said Return do allow & accept the same--& it is ordered that the s'd Return be put upon ye Records of this Court & that ye Way therein described be hereafter known as a HighWay.

{ *JosephBarnard & Seal Elijah Williams & Seal*
{ *Seth Catlin & Seal Jahn Hawks & Seal*
{ *David Field & Seal*

Court of Sessions, Hampshire County Courthouse, Northampton, MA, Book 7, p. 69
Transcribed by C. Lancaster

MAP OF THE HIGHWAY

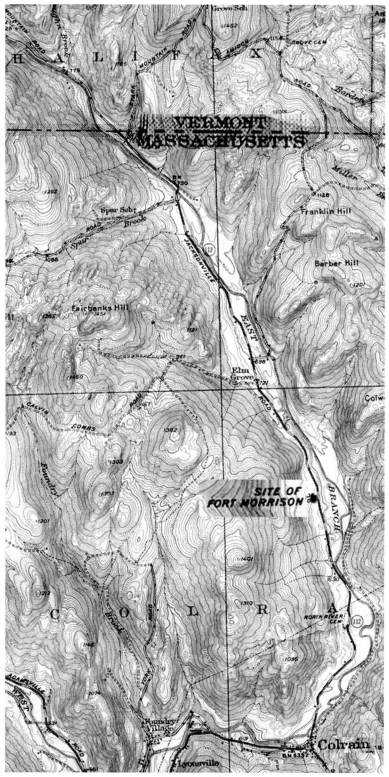

Adapted from U.S. Geological Survey map, Colrain, MASS –VT, 1946

PETITION — YORKER REBELLION

FOR ADVICE AND AID IN BRINGING RIOTERS TO JUSTICE
xvii, 9

State of Vermont {   Hallifax September ye 26: 1778

Cumberland County {

To His Exelency the Governor To his Honour the Lieut Governor to the Honourable Council and House of Representatives Greeting —
The Complaint of William Hill Most Humbly sheweth that your Complainant Did on the 24th Day of Instant September receive a Warrant from Hubbel Wells Esq to arrest the Bodys of John Kirkley and Hannah his Wife of the Town and County afore Said for asault and Battery parpetrated in the Highway on the body of David Williams in Hallifax afore s^d: I therefore took the Said John and Hannah persuant to the orders and Brought them Before Said Athority without any abuse. the Warrant was returned the partys Called and the Cort Opened — then there Came Thomas Clark Thomas Baker Isaac Orr Henrey Henderson Alexander Stewart Jonathan Safford Elijah Edwards Peletiah Fitch with about Sixteen Others of Said Town armed with Clubs to attempt to Resque the prisoners or to set the Court aside and in a Tumultuous Manner Rushed into the House Drew their Clubs and Shok them over the Justises Head and Swore he Should not try the Case Called him a Scoundral and that [he ?] to Shew himself Such was forgery Which he Should Answer for and Bid Defience to the State and all its authority with Many more Insults and abuses Which Stagnated the free Course of Justice. in that way overpowered the athority and Stopt the Court — all Which is against the peace of the Community Subversive of the athority of the State against the peace and Dignity of the Same your Complainant prays for your advice and assistance in this Matter that Some Method may be taken Whereby the above Said Offenders may be Brought to Justice for Such acts of Contempt of athority and for Such atrotious acts of out rage. —
this Granted and Your Complainant as in Duty Bound Shall Ever pray
William Hill {
{ Constable

State Papers of Vermont, Volume Eight, General Petitions 1778–1787, p. 6. Edward A. Hoyt, Ed. Howard E. Armstrong, Secretary of State, Montpelier, VT, 1952. Burlington, VT: Lane Press.

PETITION OF THE SELECT MEN

FOR A TAX ON LAND TO BUILD ROADS
xvii, 285

To the Honourable Assembly of the State of Vermont to be Holden at Benington [Bennington] the third thursday of February Instant

The petition of the Select Men of the Town of Halifax Humbly Sheweth —

That Whereas said Town has Several Large Streams that Run through the Town over Which it is Necessary that Bridges should be Built and Maintained for the Benefit of the publick and the Land in S^d Town Naturally Very wet & Springey so that Notwithstanding all the Work by way of a Highway Rate agreable to the Law as it Now Stands is insoficient to Make the Roads Comfortable and Safe to pass in & Several of S^d Rivers over Which Roads are Laid have no Bridges to this Day —

And Whereas there is about five Thousand Acres of Non Residents land in the Town Who have Never bin Called upon by way of a Tax to assist the Town in Mending their Roads or other publick Uses the Town has Built a Meeting House and Settled a Minister Besides Working on the Roads Near twenty years all Which has Greatly Increased the Real Value of all the Lands in S^d Town

and Whereas the people are so publick spirit^d as to be willing Still to Do more on the high ways accordingly have Voted to Request a land Tax of one penny on the acre of all the land in S^d Town publick Rights Excepted for the Sole Use of Mending the Highways in S^d Town   These are therefore Humbly to Request your Honours to Take there Case into Your Wise Consideration and Grant the Contents of this petition as your petitioner in Duty Bound Shall Ever pray

Halifax February ye 17th 1787

Hubbel Wells	
Benjamin Henry	Select
Nathan Fish	Men

— ⚭ —

Petition of the Select-men of Hallifax
Fil^d Feb^r 20. 1787
. . .*

— ⚭ —

A. J.: *Read and granted, 20 Feb. '87, S. P. of Vt., III (III), 276; leave given to bring in a bill accordingly, 20 Feb. '87, Ibid, III (III), 276; bill read and accepted and sent to Council, 10 March '87, Ibid, III (III), 330; bill, having been concurred in by Council, passed into law, 10 March '87, Ibid, III (III), 330.[1] C. J.: Act read and concurred in, 10 March '87, G. and C., III, 142.

State Papers of Vermont, Volume Eight, General Petitions 1778–1787, p. 328. Edward A. Hoyt, Ed. Howard E. Armstrong, Secretary of State, Montpelier, VT, 1952. Burlington, VT: Lane Press..

PETITION OF AMOS MUZZY

FOR AN ACT OF INSOLVENCY
xix, 121

To the Honorable Legislature of the State of Vermont in General Court Assembled at Rutland on the second Thursday of October Annoque Domini 1794 —

The Petition of Amos Muzzy of Halifax in the County of Windham — Humbly Sheweth —

That your Petitioner served some years in the late Continental Army — that in the year 1787 he came into this State where he has ever since lived and Conducted himself as a good Citizen to the State of Vermont by whom he has been honourd with Four Inferior [*commissions?*] and a Commission of Lieutenant Colonel in its Melitia in which office he hopes he has gained the Approbation of both Officers and Soldiers — That he supported himself by Farming and Trade but being unfortunately engaged in the latter with another person it has with other Misadventures unhappely proved his ruin — That in consequence of his partners failing to pay for a large Invoice of goods (of which your Petitioner had little or no avails) your Petitioner was obliged to Deed his Farm in Halifax and a special Writ being soon after sued out against him he was thrown into the Goal in New Fane where he lay for upwards of Seven months and untile he was released by his taking the Poor Mans Oath Ever since which your Petitioner has worked in said Halifax as a Common Day Labourer to endeavour to support his Wife and Six small Children —

Your Petitioner would humbly Suggest that his Creditors living entirely in the State of Massachusets and in the neighbourhood of Boston he has caused a Notification of his Intention to prefer this petition and Citation to his Creditors to appear before the Honorable Assembly and shew cause if any they have why the prayer of the same should not be granted to be inserted in a Boston Newspaper

which has a general Circulation on the 9th of last September and so on Until the sitting of the Honorable General Court —

Wherefore Your Petitioner humbly Prays for the Interference of the Honorable Assembly and that an Act of Insolvency may be passed in his Favour or such other relief granted as his present necessitous Circumstances in the opinion of the Honorable Legislature may require

And your Petitioner as in Duty bound Shall ever Pray —

Halifax October 3 — 1794 —   Amos Muzzy

— & —

To the Honorable Legislature of the State of Vermont in General Court Assembled at Rutland the Second Thursday of October Anno Domini 1794 —

We the Subscribers Inhabtants of the Town of Halifax & County of Windham —

Having long known Colonel Muzzy Signer of the Annexd Petition & having read the same and believing the Material Facts stated therein to be True Do humbly join our prayers to the Petitioners that the relief prayed for therein may be granted —

We are Induced to do this — From the Uniform good Conduct of said Muzzy as our Fellow Townsman for nigh 7 years —

From the propriety of his behavour as a Town officer From the advantage he has been to the Melitia in this quarter —

From his Conduct since his misfortunes which has been patient and very Industrious —

And from the Regard we have for his Wife & Children who will be much necessitated if some Relief by the Honorable Legislature is not Speedily granted —

Wherefore the Subscribers as aforesaid Humbly pray that the Prayer of Amos Muzzy in his Petition annexd may be granted —

And the Subscribers as in Duty bound shall ever pray —

Henry Henderson	Josiah Crain	Joseph Willcock
James Pennel	Cyrus Wells	Alexander Little
Isaac Ord	Silas Clark	Thomas Little
Benj. Barber	Aaron Sanders	Bariah Hall
Nathan Fish	Thomas Fowler	Jonathan Kellogg
Thomas Taggart	Thomas Scott	Edmund Fish
John Taggart	Elihu Hotchkiss	William Dalrymple
Hubbel Wells	Jarib Crosby	Amos Conant
Joel Hall	Hubbel Wells 2ᵈ	Aart Woodard
David Goodall	Edward Dalrymple	John Hall
John Pennel	Timothy Woodard	Samˡ Wood
James Henry	Samuel Henry	Jonathan Allen
Seth Johnson	Charles Hunt	Artʳ Crozer
Daniel Sumner	Jonathan Wells 2ᵈ	Willard Lesuer
Abel Shepard	John Kirkland	Daniel Sumner Junʳ
Samᵉˡ Clark	John Crozer	Thomas Woodley
Jonathan Wells	Jonas Shepard Junʳ	Israel Bemiss
Gerthom Orvis	William Garet Juner	Titus Woodard
Thomas Clark	Ebenezer Sabin Juʳ	Pardee Dean
Joseph Cluer Junʳ	Ebenezer Sabin	James Woodard
	Abel Haynes	David Alverson

* * *

Amos Muzzy's Petition with the Petition of Sundry Inhabitants of Halifax — Filed Octʳ 15th 1794 —

Ros. Hopkins Secy.

In General Assembly Octʳ 15th 1794

Read & referred to messʳˢ <J. Robinson> Woodbridge Harrington & J. Robinson — State facts & make report. Att. R Whitney Clk

— ⁊ —

A. J. 1794: *committee report read, not accepted, and leave given to withdraw petition, 124-5.

State Papers of Vermont, Volume Ten, General Petitions, 1793–1796. pp. 134–136. Allen Soule Ed., Howard E. Armstrong, Secretary of State, Montpelier, VT 1958. Burlington, VT: Lane Press.

PETITION OF EBENEZER CLARK FOR A NEW TRIAL
Filed October 19, 1809

To the Honorable – Legislature of the State of Vermont to be convened at MountPelier on the second Thursday of October anno Domini One thousand Eight Hundred and Nine. The Petition of Ebenezer Clark of Halifax in the County of Windham and State of Vermont.

Humbly Showeth—

That at a session of the Superior Court of Indictment and court of Chancery begun and Held at Newfane within and for the County of Windham and State of Vermont on the first Tuesday of August Anno domini one thousand Eight Hundred and eight, your Petitioner was indicted by the Grand Jurors serving before said Court for ploughing up and disturbing a certain burial ground so called in the town of Halifax aforementioned and defacing the monuments therein in the word & figures following viz—

"State of Vermont

Windham at a Superior Court holden at Newfane in and for the County of Windham on the first Tuesday of August Anno domini One thousand Eight Hundred and Eight— The Grand Jurors from the body of the County of Windham Superior Court sworn upon their oath present that the burying ground or graveyard in Halifax in said County, being three quarters of an acre of land lying in Lot No. fifteen in said Halifax situate west of the road leading from Colerain to Guilford is a public burial ground and for more than thirty years past has been used by the good citizens of said Halifax as a place wherein to bury their Dead peaceably, quietly and after the manner of their forefathers, And the jurors aforementioned do further lament that Ebenezer Clark, late of said Halifax being an evil disposed person and regardless of the laws and good and wholesome institutions of the State and also desirous to wound and injure the feelings of the good citizens of the Town of Halifax and others. The same burial ground and graves therein being, wherein the bodies of the Dead persons even deposited, did at said Halifax on the first day of October last passed with force and arms? furiously with his Plow in ploughing turn up and deface and with horses Oxen and sheep in and upon the same did trample and the Graves Stones and monuments then and there standing did throw Down and destroy, and the good people of said Halifax from burying their Dead in said burial ground did then and there forbid hinder and prevent to the great injury and affliction of many of the good people of the State. To the evil example of others and likewise offending and against the good and wholesome laws of the State and against the peace and dignity of the State.

Newfane August 6th 1808."

Your Petitioner further humbly shows that the above indictment came in for trial at a session of the superior Court being held at Newfane within and for the County of Windham on the first Tuesday of August Anno Domini One thousand eight Hundred & Nine—

When your Petitioner was found guilty by a petit Jury and sentenced by said court to pay a fine of Twenty Dollars and cost of prosecution and stand committed till sentence complied with. That since the said trial your Petitioner has discovered New and important evidence which was totally unknown to your Petitioner at the time of said Trial, which said Evidence, if your Petitioner had known and had at said Trial, Your Petitioner verily believes would clearly and fully establish his Innocence relating to the offence complained of in said indictment. That Your Petitioner even has been and still is desirous to maintain inviolate the good customs and manners of his ancestors, and punctiously tender of and unwilling to afflict the good citizens of this State, And that without intention no crime can be committed, and that the intention to constitute the guilt must be either manifest or naturally informed from the commission of the crime. That your Petitioner verily believes that at a new Trial of said Indictment Your Petitioner would be adamantly able to show his innocence and the punctilious regard he has even had to the laws, customs and feeling of the fellow citizens, in regard to the crime alleged in said Indictment—

Your Petitioner, therefore humbly prays that this honorably assembly would take his case into their wise consideration and under such terms and regulations as to your wisdom shall deem ____, shall Grant your Petitioner a New Trial on said Indictment and enable him to again retrieve the loss of character (Dearer to your petitioner than life) sustained by a conviction had on ____ and against him.—Your Petitioner further humbly prays that (security having been given for the fine and cost aforementioned) the Attorney for the County of Windham might be directed to stay proceedings in collecting said fine and cost until a new trial may be had on said indictment—To the wisdom of this Honorable Assembly, your Petitioner submits his deplorable case in hope
And in duty bound shall ever pray.
Halifax 5th Oct. 1809   Ebenezer Clark

MsVtSP, Vol. 47, p. 147. Courtesy VSS

BAPTIST LIST

From 1785 to 1806, residents, listed below, registered with the Halifax Town Clerk as Baptist or "not of the opinion of the majority" and therefore were not taxed to support the South Meeting House and Congregational or Presbyterian ministers.

Allen	Dea. David	1789		Esterbrook	Robert	1805
	David Jr.	1789		Fessenden	Solomon	1792
	David 2nd	1792			Benjamin	1800
	Jonathan	1789		Fish	Samuel	1792
Alverson	David	1789		Foster	John	1705
	David Jr.	1800		Fowler	Curtis	1792
	Widow Hannah	1789		Frink	Tristram	1800
	William	1792		Gay	Jonathan	1795
	Jonathan	1800		Gore	Elijah	1792
	James	1800			Ezekiel	1792
Baldwin	Daniel	1800			Amos	1799
	Peter	1801		Green	John	1795
Ballou	Asahel	1801			John Jr.	1804
Barney	John	1800			Caleb	1801
	James	1800		Hamilton	John	1800
	James Jr.	1800		Hatch	Nathan	1800
	Martain	1800		Harrington	Job	1800
Bell	Joseph	1792			Elisha	1789
	Joseph Jr.	1801			Daniel	1795
	James	1800		Hewes	William	1800
Bemis	Rev. Abner	1799		Houghton	Philemon	1792
Bolster	Joel	1800		Hunt	Jonathan	1796
Breed	Capt. Oliver	1801			Salmon	1800
Brooks	Lemuel	1791		Jackson	Ebenezer	1801
Bullock	Asa	1789		Jenks	Benjamin	1789
	Darius	1789		Joiner	John	1790
Burdick	Henry	1806		Jones	Israel	1792
Calef	Stephen	1792			Eliakim	1792
Canedy	Hugh	1790		Kemp	James	1800
	Alexander	1795		Kingsbury	Jared	1803
Carpenter	Asaph	1795			John Jr.	1803
Chase	Asaph	1800		Kirkley	John	1804
	Allen	1800		Lamb	David	1791
Clark	Ebenezer	1792		Lamphere	Jlatham	1800
	Asa	1800		Little	Alexander	1802
	Thomas	1802		Littlefield	Jesse	1795
	Josiah	1802			Josiah	1795
	Abner	1802			Elisha	1795
	Alpheus	1804		Marble	Jonathan	1800
Cook	Stephen	1800		Marsh	Osborne`	1800
Crandal	Paul	1805		Matthews	Benjamin	1789
Cutler	Joel	1800		McAllister	Benjamin	1800
Dalrymple	William	1804		Miner	Adam	1800
Darling	Peter	1792		Mullet	James	1796
Denison	Adam	1804		Nichols	Samuel	1801
Dunikin	Andrew	1790		Niles	Henry	1799

Niles	Jesse	1799		Thomas	Capt. John	1789
	Samuel	1799			Peleg Eaton	1789
	Oliver	1799			Benjamin 2nd	1800
Orr	Isaac	1802		Thomson	Daniel	1796
Orvis	Josephus	1805		Treadway	Benjamin	1792
Owen	Caleb	1785		Tucker	Joseph	1800
Pennell	Widow Jane	1795		Underwood	Samuel	1792
	Lt. Andrew	1795		Woodley	Thomas	1800
	James	1795		Waters	Oliver	1789
Pearce	Nathaniel	1800		Weeks	Benjamin	1789
Pierce	Reuben	1792			Benjamin Jr.	1800
	Allen	1792			Thomas	1800
	Joseph	1789		Wells	Jonathan	1791
	James	1800		Wesson	Thomas	1800
Perry	Joseph	1794		Wheeler	Miner	1799
	Simeon	1800			Denison	1800
	Benjamin	1800		Whitcomb	Samuel	1800
Phelps	Francis	1795		Wilcox	Benjamin	1789
	Dana	1800			William	1789
Philips	Ezekiel	1789			Stephen	1789
Pike	David	1800			Wicks	1800
Raymond	Paul	1792			Taber	1800
Read	George	1800			Joseph	1800
Roberts	Isaac	1800			William Jr.	1800
Sanders	Aaron	1795			William 3d	1800
	Jonas	1795		Winslow	Kenelm	1800
Shepard	Jonas	1785			John	1800
Shepardson	Jared	1800		Wolly	Thomas	1792
	Alfred	1802		Wood	Samuel	1800
Slade	Aaron	1792		Woodard	Samuel	1785
Scott	Thomas	1794			Samuel Jr.	1792
Smith	Hezekiah	1790			Timothy	1793
	Isaiah	1800			Jedediah	1795
	Capt. Joel	1800		Works	William	1800
Stacy	John Richardson	1800		Worden	Sylvester	1788
Stafford	Samuel	1800			Joseph	1789
Stanclift	Solomon	1792			Elisha	1791
	Eldah	1800			Peter	1792
Stowell	David	1790			Asa	1792
Streeter	Nathaniel	1789			Elisha Jr.	1800
Sumner	Jotham	1800			Ichabod	1800
Thomas	William	1789			Amos	1800
	Benjamin	1789				

Compiled from Halifax Land Records by Ruby Bruffee Austin

PETITION OF SUNDRY INHABITANTS OF HALIFAX
AGAINST THE DISTILLING OF ARDENT SPIRITS IN THIS STATE

To the Honourable the Senate and house of Representatives of the State of Vermont to be convened in October 1837 ~

We the Undersigned Inhabitants of the town of Halifax in the County of Windham Pray your Honourable body to Pass an act laying a duty on domestic distilled spirits manufactured in this State, so as entirely to prohibit the manufacture of that articles from Grain in this State and as in duty bound will every Pray ~

John Reid	Nathaniel Niles	Ruth Winchester
Green Nichols	Asher M. Wheeler	Gratia Hall
Jonathan Allen	Eunice Wheeler	Lovisa Kingsbury
Stephen Otis	Samuel Tyler	Almira Kingsbury
Elisha G. Otis	Thomas Miner	Huldah Hall
Bartlet Whitney	Sally M. Plumb	Clarissa Clark
Rowe Smith	William Plumb	Sabra L. Halladay
Amos Tucker	Calvin Guild	Caroline S. Halladay
James Tucker	Asa Guild	Berilla S. Plumb
Israel Jones	Spencer Guild	Dorothy F. Coleman
Amos H. Tucker	Jesse Guild	Bersheba P. Fish
Sanford Standclift	Jonas Brown	Jane Tucker
Ezra Hatch	Joshua Grant	Lucy N. Tucker
Willard Wilcox	Stephen Gates	Lucinda Allen
James C. Smith	Nehemiah Blanchard	Nancy Niles
Origen Ball	Silas O. Fife	Patty Smith
John Kingsbury	William Burns	D. M. Whitney
Lyman Kingsbury	Laura Smith	Delight S. Worden
Nicholas Clark	John Robertson	Survier F. Niles
Chandler Seaver	Samuel H. Miner	Eunice B. Niles
Nathan W. Halladay	Luther Edwards	Betsey B. Bullock
Henry Halladay	Ephraim L. Pierce	Patience Bucklin
Sanford Plumb	Ezra Gleason	Clara Bullock
Jedidiah H. Stark	Laura Hall	Meliscent B. Wood
Samuel Fish Jr.	Ann Reid	Hannah N. Niles
Benjamin Bucklin	Eunice M. Cole	Lydia A. Allen
Stephen Niles	Eunice Wilcox	Lucy Tucker
Thomas H. Wood	Ephemia Stanclift	Betsey Smith
Thomas Scott	Eunice Allen	Temperance Fife
Caroline G. Scott	Kezia Nichols	Olive W. Smith
Eunice N. Scott	Cintha Allen	Elizabeth Smith
Jonas Scott	Lydia Allen	Elizabeth A. Brown
James Tucker 2nd	Nancy Harris	Lucinda Dammon
Samuel Niles Jr.	Diantha Smith	Mary F. Gleason
Moses Chamberlin	Sarah Tucker	Polly Crosier
John Brown	Sarah Tucker 2nd	Lavina Crosier
Chandler Brown	Abigail Jones	Diadamia Coats
Joseph Brown	Eunice Carleton	Nancy Tyler
Dexter Gleason	Mary Bullock	Olive Plumb
William L. Crosier	Cynthia Tucker	Mary Ann Plumb
Asa Whitney	Esther Stanclift	Julia Guild
John Smith	Lucy Hatch	Olive Bascom
Samuel H. Smith	Mary Ball	Mary E. Edwards
Oliver A. Coats	Sarah Putnam	Betsey P. Edwards
S. M. Worden	Lucinda Hall	

MsVtSP, Vol. 65, pp. 78-80. Courtesy VSS

TOWN CLERKS

1770–1773	Samuel Woodard	1797–1833	Darius Bullock
1774–1777	Peletiah Fitch	1834–1852	Rufus King Henry
1778	James Gray	1852–1853	Whitney J. Hitchcock
1779	Hubbel Wells	1854–1866	Charles Fowler
	Amos Peabody	1867–1881	Joseph L. Harrington
1780	James Gray	1882–1898	Millard Wicks [Weeks]
	Hubbel Wells	1899–1915	Ansel C. Jones
1781–1786	Hubbel Wells	1916–1952	Harry E. Goodnough
1787	Nathan Fish	1953–1967	Margaret Hill Crosier
1788–1792	Hubbel Wells	1967–	Laura Sumner
1793–1796	Nathan Fish		

SELECTMEN

1778	Capt. Hubbel Wells		Thomas Scott
	Dr. William Hill		Lt. Thomas Clark
	Thomas McClure	1785	Hubbel Wells
	Elias Parsons		Benjamin Henry
1779	Capt. Hubbel Wells		Thomas Taggart
	Dr. Wm. Hill		David Allen
	Israel Guild		Capt. James Pennell
	Capt. John Thomas	1786	Hubbel Wells
	Edward Harris, Esq.		Benjamin Henry
1780	Hubbel Wells		Thomas Taggart
	Edward Harris		James Pennell
	James Gray		Nathan Fish
	Dr. Wm. Hill	1787	Judge Hubbel Wells
	John Sawtell		Nathan Fish
	Israel Guild		Joel Hall
1781	Hubbel Wells		Thomas Farnsworth
	Benjamin Henry		Thomas Scott
	Dea. John Pennell	1788	Hubbel Wells
	John Sawtelle		Nathan Fish
	Joseph Tucker		Benjamin Henry
1782	Lt. Thomas Taggart	1789	Hubbel Wells
	Lt. James Clark		Nathan Fish
	Capt. Robert Pattison		Benjamin Henry
1783	Edward Harris	1790	Benjamin Henry, Esq.
	Lt. Henry Henderson		Darius Bullock
	Daniel Isham		Capt. James Pennell
	Jonathan Wells	1791	Benjamin Henry, Esq.
	Samuel Woodard		Nathan Fish
1784	Hubbel Wells		Thomas Taggart, Esq.
	Benjamin Henry	1792	Benjamin Henry, Esq.
	Lt. Joseph Tucker		Lt. Darius Bullock

	Joel Hall		George Boardman
1793	Benjamin Henry, Esq.		Asahel Ballou
	Nathan Fish	1820	Darius Bullock
	Darius Bullock		Asahel Ballou
1794	Benjamin Henry, Esq.		Israel Worden
	Lt. Darius Bullock	1821	Darius Bullock
	Capt. James Pennell		Benjamin Henry Jr.
1795	Names not recorded		George Boardman
1796	Benjamin Henry, Esq.	1822	Darius Bullock
	Darius Bullock		Benjamin Henry Jr.
	Capt. James Pennell		Abel Scott
1797	Benjamin Henry, Esq.	1823	Darius Bullock
	Darius Bullock		Benjamin Henry Jr.
	Capt. Thomas Farnsworth		Thomas Little
1798–1799	Benjamin Henry	1824	Darius Bullock
	Darius Bullock, Esq.		Benjamin Henry Jr.
	Capt. James Pennell		George Boardman
1800–1801	Benjamin Henry, Esq	1825–1826	Darius Bullock
	Darius Bullock		George Boardman
	Capt. Thomas Farnsworth		James L.Stark
1802–1803	Benjamin Henry, Esq	1827	James L. Stark
	Darius Bullock		Azariah Hall Jr.
	John Taggart		John Farnum
1804–1806	Darius Bullock	1828–1829	James L. Stark
	Joel Hall		Azariah Hall Jr.
	Samuel Wood		Robert Collins
1807–1811	Darius Bullock	1830	William Plumb
	Joseph Henry		Elisha Hager
	John Taggart		Azariah Hall Jr.
1812	Darius Bullock	1831	Darius Bullock
	Asahel Ballou		Azariah Hall Jr.
	Ebenezer Clark		Park Williams
1813	Darius Bullock	1832	Joseph Henry
	Joseph Henry		Isaac Worden
	Jeremiah Kingsbury		Park Williams
1814	Joseph Henry	1833	Sanford Plumb
	Jeremiah Kingsbury		Benjamin Woodard
	Hubbel Wells Jr.		Park Williams
1815	Joseph Henry	1834	Sanford Plumb
	Darius Bullock		Elisha Hagan
	Thomas Little		Timothy Larrabee
1816	Darius Bullock	1835	Sanford Plumb
	Thomas Little		Elisha Hagan
	Benjamin Henry Jr.		Timothy Larrabee
1817–1818	Darius Bullock	1836	Sanford Plumb
	George Boardman		Benjamin Woodard Jr.
	Erastus Hall		James L. Stark
1819	Darius Bullock	1837	Sanford Plumb

	Benjamin Woodard Jr.		Luther R. Farnsworth
	James L. Stark	1861	Daniel Bixby
1839–1840	James L. Stark		Perry Hall
	Isaac Worden		H. N. Houghton
	Timothy Larrabee	1862–1863	H. N. Houghton
1841–1842	James L. Stark		Perry Hall
	Timothy Larrabee		George C. Tucker
	Newton Gleason	1864	H. N. Houghton
1843	Isaac Worden		Jed Stark
	Timothy Larrabee		Charles F. Griffin
	Newton Gleason	1865–1866	Stephen Niles
1844–1846	Benjamin Woodard Jr.	1865	Albert J. Tucker
	Timothy Larrabee	1865–1866	William E. French
	Newton Gleason	1866	Perry Hall
1847	Timothy Larrabee	1867	Martin Scott, 2nd
	Newton Gleason	1867	Prescott S. Eames
	Isaac Worden	1867	Israel Canedy
1848	Timothy Larrabee	1868	Lorenzo Harris
	Chester Nelson	1868	Lewis W. Sumner
	John Fowler	1869–1870	Gilman Warren
1849	Timothy Larrabee	1871–1874	Charles H. Higley
	Samuel Smith	1871	Martin Scott, 2nd
	Chester Nelson	1871–1872	Stephen Niles
1850	Timothy Larrabee	1872–1877	Prescott S. Eames
	Jonas Scott	1872–1877	Israel Canedy
	Chester Nelson	1873–1874	Martin Scott, 2nd
1851	Timothy Larrabee	1875–1876	Albert J. Tucker
	Jonas Scott	1875–1878	Gilman Warren
	Daniel Bixby	1893–1896	Lewis W. Sumner
1852	Benjamin Eames	1869–1870	Alcander Preston
	E. Seymour Worden	1875–1878	Gilman Warren
	Calvin Buckland	1877–1878	Luther Adams
1853	Benjamin Eames	1878	Charles H. Higley
	E. Seymour Worden	1879–1888	Lewis W. Sumner
	Almon Ballou	1879–1882	B. F. Roberts
1854	Benjamin Eames	1879–1882	Fosdick P. Prouty
	Newton Gleason	1883–1884	Israel Stowe
	Daniel Bixby	1883–1884	Emory F. Evans
1855	Alpheus Stone	1885–1887	Luther Adams
	Lemuel M. Woodard	1885–1888	Orlen J. Hale
	Asher M. Wheeler	1885–1891	Elijah B. Green
1856	Alpheus Stone	1892	Warner W. Stowe
	Daniel Bixby	1892	Fosdick P. Prouty
	Asher M. Wheeler	1889–1891	Emory F. Evans
1857–1859	Daniel Bixby	1889–1892	Luther Adams
	Asher M. Wheeler	1893	William. E. French
	Luther R. Farnsworth		
1860	Asher M. Wheeler		
	Daniel Bixby		

1893–1896	Charles H. Higley
1894–1896	Elijah B. Green
1897	Orlen J. Hale
1897–1900	Frank B. Stone
1897–1900	Watson DeWolf
1898	William B. Warren
1899–1901	William E. Higley
1901	Lewis W. Sumner
1901	Elijah B. Green
1902–1904	William B. Warren
1902–1904	Norton E. Thurber
1902–1904	Charles F. Cook
1905	William E. Wheeler
1905–1907	Orlen J. Hale
1905–1907	Frank B. Stone
1906–1907	Lewis A. Sumner
1908	William E. Higley
1908	Sumner B. Worden
1908	Charles E. Thurber
1909–1910	Otis W. Amidon
1909–1910	James Niles Plumb
1911–1912	Benjamin G. Worden
1911–1916	William B. Warren
1912–1914	Otis W. Amidon
1913–1916	Newton G. Stone
1915–1917	Charles H. Learnard
1917–1922	Zina A. Learnard
1917–1918	Otis W. Amidon
1918–1920	Merrick C. Harris
1919–1921	J. S. Koshinsky
1921–1925	Frank H. stone
1922	James Niles Plumb
1923–1925	Mervin A. Fairbanks
1923	Milton A. Bickford
1924	A. R. Allen
1925–1927	Bryan E. Warren
1926	Merrick C. Harris
1926–1930	J. S. Koshinsky
1927–1930	Frank B. Stone
1928–1930	Paul D. Crosier
1931, 1967	Emory B. Hebard
1931–1933	Otis W. Amidon
1931–1932	Zina A. Learnard

1932–1934	Floyd N. Stone
1933–1935	Lewis A. Sumner
1934–1936	Paul D. Crosier
1935–1940	Zina A. Learnard
1936–1938	Otis W. Amidon
1937–1939	Floyd C. Harris
1939–1941	Fred A. May
1940–1948	Scott E. Courser
1941–1945	Sebastian Visser
1942–1947	Zina A. Learnard
1946–1956	Wesley A. Stone
1948–1949	Aubrey Amidon
1949–1956	Burton C. Hill
1950–1956	Floyd C. Harris
1956	Eugene V. Gates
1957–1963	Kenneth Sumner
1957–1962	Archie Burnett
1957–1964	Paul D. Crosier
1963–1965	Barry Gerdes
1964–1966	Cleon Kingsley
1965–1968	Floyd N. Stone
1966–2002	Lewis L. Sumner
1968	Raymond E. Putnam
1969	Carl N. Stone
1969–1977	Eugene V. Gates
1970–1977	W. Harold Gregory
1978–1983	Frederick Crosby II
1978–1983	Rodney Bemis
1983–1988	Thomas D. Rafus
1985–1990	Luther A. Ray
1989–1991	Richard Holschuch Jr.
1991–2002	Frank Maltese
1992–1994	Murray Ellison
1995–2000	Allan C. Dacey
2000–2003	Frank Maltese
2001–2004	Raymond White
2002–2005	Harold Smith
2003–2006	Carl Barmen
2004–	Mitchell Green
2005–	Lewis L. Sumner
2006–	John LaFlamme Jr.

TOWN REPRESENTATIVES TO THE GENERAL ASSEMBLY

1778–1783	Edward Harris		1882	Lemuel M. Woodard
1778–1779	Hubbel Wells		1884	George L. Clark
1780	Hazael Sheperd		1886	Lemuel M. Woodard
1781	Benjamin Henry		1888	Luther Adams
1783	Joseph Tucker		1890–1892	George L. Clark
1784–1788	Hubbel Wells		1894	Emery F. Evans
1789–1798	Benjamin Henry		1896	Hollis S. Plumb
1798	Darius Bullock		1898	Lewis W. Sumner
1799–1802	Benjamin Henry		1900	Samuel J. Smith
1802–1808	Darius Bullock		1902	Ansel C. Jones
1808–1811	Stephen Otis		1904	Francis T. Miner
1812–1817	Darius Bullock		1906	Fayette H. Niles
1818	Russell Avery		1908	Charles E. Thurber
1819	Darius Bullock		1910	James N. Plumb
1820–1821	Benjamin Henry		1912	Frank B. Stone
1822	George Boardman		1915	Charles E. Thurber
1823–1828	James L. Stark		1917	Otis W. Amidon
1829–1830	Sanford Plumb		1919	Lewis A. Sumner
1831	Darius Bullock		1921	William B. Warren
1832	Sanford Plumb		1923	Otis W. Amidon
1833	Benjamin Woodard		1925	Otis W. Amidon
1834	James L. Stark		1927	Fred A. May
1835-1836	Benjamin Woodard		1929	John S. Koshinsky
1837-1838	Isaac Worden		1931	Mervin A. Fairbanks
1839	James L. Stark		1933	Lewis A. Sumner
1810-1811	Rufus K. Henry		1935	Lewis A. Sumner
1842	William H. Stark		1937	Fred F. Pratt
1843	Benjamin Woodard		1938	Fred A. May
1844	Nicholas Clark		1941	Emory B. Hebard
1845	William Plumb		1943	Fred A. May
1846	Stephen Niles		1945	Fred A. May
1847–1848	Jonas Scott		1947	Fred A. May
1849	Joseph Henry		1949	Fred A. May
1850	Amos Tucker		1951	Raymond H. Ouellette
1851	Jonas Scott		1953	Raymond H. Ouellette
1852	Elisha Hager		1955	Raymond H. Ouellette
1853	Isaac Worden		1957	Raymond H. Ouellette
1854	Martin Scott, 2d,		1959	Fred A. May
1855–1856	Alpheus H. Stone		1961	Raymond H. Ouellette
1857	Amos H. Tucker		1963	Roger L. MacBride
1858–1859	Stephen Niles		1965	Floyd N. Stone
1860	Martin Scott. 2d			
1861–1862	Charles Fowler		In 1965, the State of Vermont	
1863–1864	Amos H. Tucker		reapportioned the legislative body.	
1865–1866	Albert J. Tucker		One representative represents Halifax	
1867–1868	Almon Ballou		with three other towns.	
1869–1870	Alpheus H. Stone		1967–1969	Erma Puffer
Biennial sessions			1971–1976	Ralph Bullock
1872	Charles F. Griffin		1977–1982	Stuart W. Hunt Sr.
1874	Alpheus H. Stone		1983–1986	Michael Kimack
1876	Albert M. V. Hager		1987–1996	David Larsen
1878	Joseph L. Harrington		1997–2006	Robert Rusten
1880	Lewis W. Sumner		2007–	Ann Manwaring

INDEX OF MAPS

Fold out maps that follow:
Lot map
McClellan, 1856
Beers, 1869

THE NATIONAL SURVEY, CHESTER, VT.

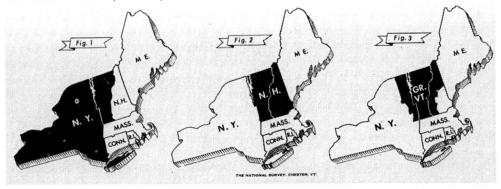

Edmund Fuller, *A History of the Green Mountain State.* Published by the VT State Board of Education, Montpelier, VT (Brattleboro VT: Vermont Printing, 1952).

Fig. 1 New England if New York had had its way
Fig. 2 New England if New Hampshire had had its way
Fig. 3 if Greater Vermont had become permanent [↝ 189].

Afterword

Photo C. Lancaster, 2007

Schoolmates, Elaine Fairbanks and Bernice Barnett, at the former
Plumb Schoolhouse, now the Halifax Historical Society Museum.

Elaine Fairbanks and Bernice Barnett have long been recognized as Halifax town historians. Both are founding members of the historical society. Both helped to launch the town history project and have been involved throughout the more than decade-long process. As reporter, feature writer, and book author, Bernice's story-telling abilities are well known and widely enjoyed, as are Elaine's efforts to rescue and promote town history, especially through her energetic involvement in the historical society. Diminutive in stature, both are local history giants.

While working on the town history, book committee members enjoyed knowing in our midst was a direct descendant of Sally Pratt from the popular story, whose mother Lucy, according to tradition, tied her apron around a tree to deter a bear and defend her children. They were en route to Captain Pennell's to obtain a knot of fire; Captain Pennell escorted them to the treed bear and shot it with his "trusty flintlock."

Research for this work revealed that even though people named Pennell are no longer in town, Pennell descendents remain. Much to our surprise, we learned that Elaine is one of them. It was her ancestor, Deacon John Pennell, who shot the bear that menaced Bernice's ancestor, Lucy Fletcher Pratt, many generations ago in the dark forest.

We revere the Pratts and the Pennells for their hard work and courage and applaud their roles as featured actors in the greatest bear story ever told in this town. Most especially, we honor their descendents, Bernice and Elaine, for promoting interest and enthusiasm for the history and stories of Halifax, Vermont.   ~ *Constance Lancaster*

History Committee

Bernice Barnett
Taken from Green Mountain Reflections
Bernice has remained in Halifax, where she was born and raised, and where she was married to Carleton Barnett (she insists that she didn't choose her husband based on the fact that she would only have to change one letter in her last name!). Bernice has been a reporter for the *Brattleboro Reformer, The Green Mountain Courier,* and for the *Deerfield Valley News*. Bernice, along with her sister, Bertell Burnett "B. B." Woods, began contributing articles for the *Cracker Barrel* in 1985. The sisters' first book, *Roads In The Wilderness,* an account of old roads in southern Vermont, was published in 1993, with a second edition printed the following year. Their book, *Green Mountain Reflections* was published in 1995. Bernice has been involved very early on with the making of this publication and has watched it go to print.

Elaine C. Fairbanks
Elaine C. Fairbanks was born in her grandparents' home in Halifax, Vermont in 1934 and still has family remaining in town. She attended one Massachusetts school for a brief period and the rest of her formal education was in Vermont. Her elementary education was in Halifax and her high school education was at Whitingham High School in Jacksonville. She has been involved in cemetery restoration. Elaine and Regina Hardgrove co-authored *Epitaphs from Halifax, Vermont*. Her other interests are reading and sewing. She was present at the first meeting of the *Halifax History* book committee in 1991. She has put countless hours into preserving the history of Halifax, including her work at the Halifax Historical Museum. She has contributed greatly to this history. She has been the driving force and motivator behind the book writing committee.

Constance Lancaster
Like her Halifax ancestors, Samuel Fish, Oliver Niles, and Lydia Plumb, Constance Lancaster chose Vermont to live, work, and bring up her children. Raised in Springfield, Massachusetts, she graduated from Smith College, and held teaching positions in Darien, Connecticut, and New York City before moving to Marlboro in 1967, where her daughter was born. She joined the English faculty at Leland & Gray in Townshend, moved to Saxtons River, and since 1981, and the birth of her son, has operated a family business with her husband, Alan. Connie's enthusiasm for research and family history pointed her toward Halifax when the history book project was first announced in 1991. She enjoys roaming through early records and newspapers, exploring and photographing old cemeteries, and her activities as a member of The Halifax Historical Society, which have included serving on the board of directors, holding various offices, and serving as genealogy curator. While researching and writing for the book project, Connie was surprised and delighted to discover another Halifax connection. She descends from Col. Oliver Partridge, the man who chartered the town in 1750.

Carrie Perna
Carrie is a seventh-generation descendant of the Elisha Pratt family who settled in Halifax circa 1762 and a sixth-generation descendant of Moses Learnard. She was raised in Halifax, attended local schools, married Don Perna and together they raised their four children who have given them thirteen grandchildren. Don and Carrie continue to live on the only portion of the Moses and Sally Pratt Learnard homestead remaining in the family. Carrie worked along side her husband in his Office Products business for over twenty years, owned and operated North River Graphics, a printing company, and currently is the proprietor of Itty-bitty Publishing, the company responsible for the publication of this work. She has published various small booklets, newsletters, and recent issues of the *Halifacts*. She has held positions in the accounting field, is a certified Christian Counselor, and is self-taught in the building and maintaining of computers. She and her husband, the Rev. Don Perna currently serve as missionaries with Campsite Evangelism, Inc. during the winter months in Florida. She considers it a privilege to have worked alongside the other committee members on the production of this work.

Susan Rusten
Susan Whitehorne Rusten grew up in Halifax in the Harrisville section of town, where she spent much of her childhood exploring old roads and trails in the woods and imagining what life was like when homes existed on the sinking stone cellar holes that remain as a sign of former times. This fascination with history was fed by many of the "old-timers" in town whom she sought out over the years for their reminiscences. She is a graduate of Marlboro College where she studied history and religion. After several lengthy absences from Vermont to experience the world beyond, she returned to Halifax in the late 1980s with her husband Bob to raise their two sons, Lucas and Peter. Sue has been an active member of the Halifax Historical Society since 1988 and served as curator of the museum for several years. She has recently moved to Wilmington.

MARIETTE SANDERS

Mariette Sanders is an artist who fell in love with Vermont in the 1960s. She came with her husband, Steve, for the beauty in the summer and fall, and skiing in the winter. They ended up staying, raising four children and sheep here in Halifax. She had a career spanning thirty years as an artist-etcher and was twice awarded the Medal of Honor for printmaking from the National Association of Women Artists in New York. She taught art in the New York City area in the early 1970s. After the family permanently moved to Halifax, she started an art program in the Halifax Elementary School. A founding member of Windham Art Gallery in Brattleboro, and of the Halifax Historical Society, Mariette was a past president and curator for several years. She started the Halifax Hat Company with Gretchen Becker to make felt hats with the wool from their own sheep.

STEPHEN SANDERS

In 1967, Steve and his wife Mariette purchased a run-down house in a beautiful remote location. Unbeknownst to them at the time, it was the first settled property in Halifax (1761). They have been restoring this house and the grounds to its former glory for the past thirty-five years. Originally trained as a mechanical engineer, Steve pursued a lifelong dream by changing careers midlife to become an archaeologist and architectural historian. In 1984, he completed an architectural and historic survey of the Brattleboro Retreat, resulting in its listing on the National Register of Historic Places. Similar projects in Windham County have followed. A founding member of the Halifax Historical Society, Steve has been a trustee for many years. A photographer for over fifty years, Steve has recorded many beautiful places, especially in his home state of Vermont.

MOLLY STONE

Marion "Molly" Eddy Stone was born and raised in West Halifax where she attended school through eighth grade, before graduating from Whitingham High School in 1957. She married Forrest Stone and had two sons, Glen and Michael, who provided five grandchildren. Throughout the 1960s she was a fourth-generation newspaper correspondent for the *Brattleboro Reformer*, following the tradition of her grandmother and great-grandfather, Mary Niles Wheeler and Add C. Niles. Molly has served on several town committees and offices in Vermont and Florida, currently (2007–2008) on the board of directors of the Holiday Park Homeowners Association. She graduated from Massachusetts College of Liberal Arts, earning a Bachelor of Science Degree in 1976 and Masters Degree in 1982, both with honors. Elected in 1984 to Delta Kappa Gamma Society International, which recognizes key women educators, she held numerous offices at the local and Vermont State level. For several years she was a consultant for the Vermont Department of Education, sharing expertise with other Vermont teachers of writing and thinking across the curriculum. She served on the committee that wrote and tested the fourth grade Vermont Writing Portf olio Assessment rubric, the first such standardized writing assessment in the nation. In 2000, Molly retired from active teaching after twenty-four years in Arlington, Vermont, yet she considers herself a lifelong learner. She is descended from the Niles, Plumb, Green, Atherton, and Wheeler families and married into the Stone family. Molly is the current holder of a rather massive collection of Niles and Wheeler family papers and diaries dating back to the 1700s, preserved and passed along by her aunt, Eve Wheeler Weaver.

SUMMARY

As members came together over the past fifteen plus years, many decisions needed to be made concerning the overwhelming amount of material submitted. Over two years ago a smaller group of three, Carrie Perna, Constance Lancaster, and Mariette Sanders were appointed to make final decisions on arranging content, design and layout for the publication as it appears in this printing. The work involving research, writing, design, and layout has been a long, tedious, but rewarding process.

COMMITTEE AT WORK   Photo Laura Sumner
From left: Stephen Sanders, Mariette Sanders, Carrie Perna, Molly Stone, Susan Rusten, Constance Lancaster, Bernice Barnett and Elaine Fairbanks.

INDEX